CW01667789

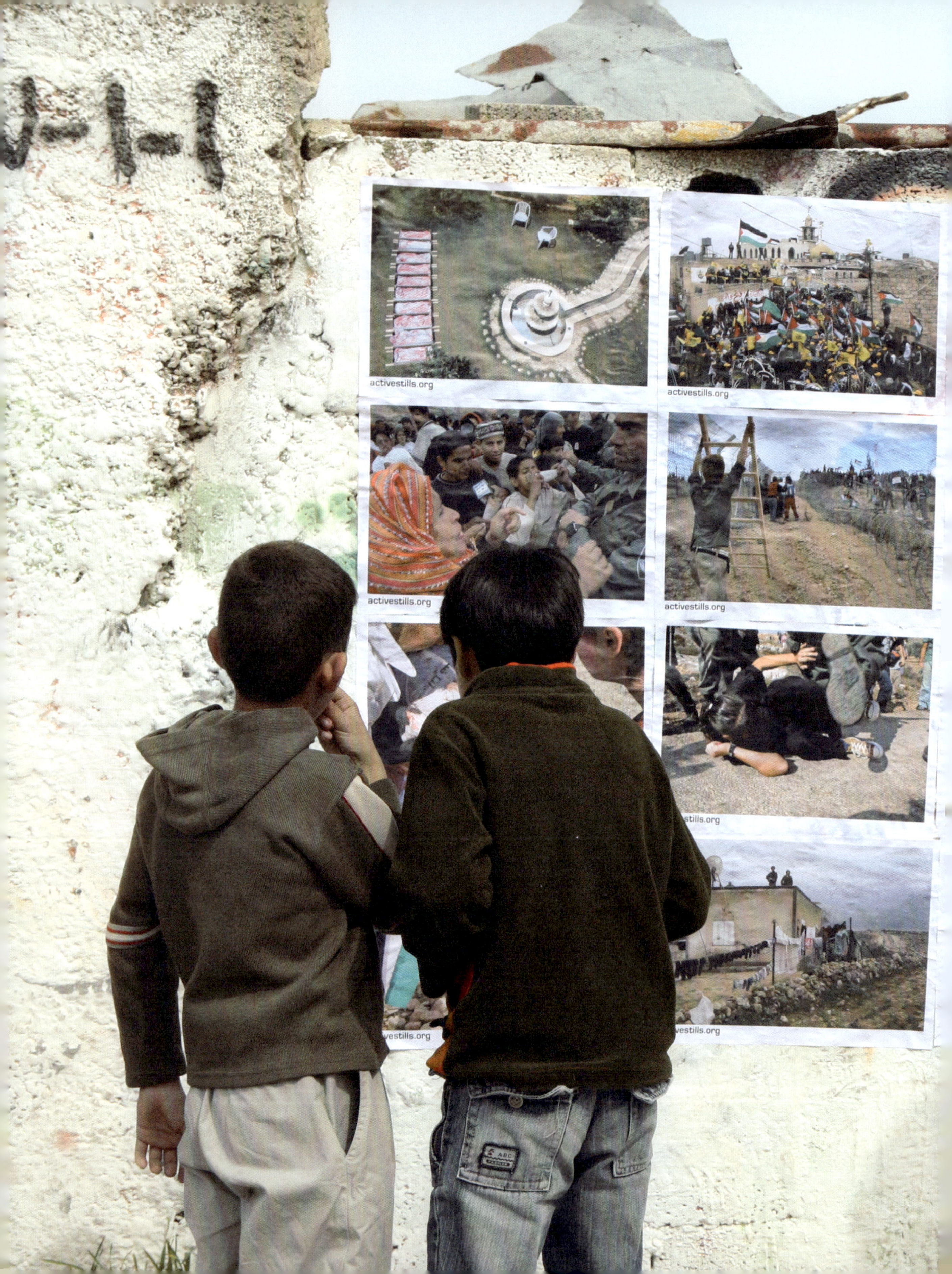
activestills.org
activestills.org
activestills.org
activestills.org

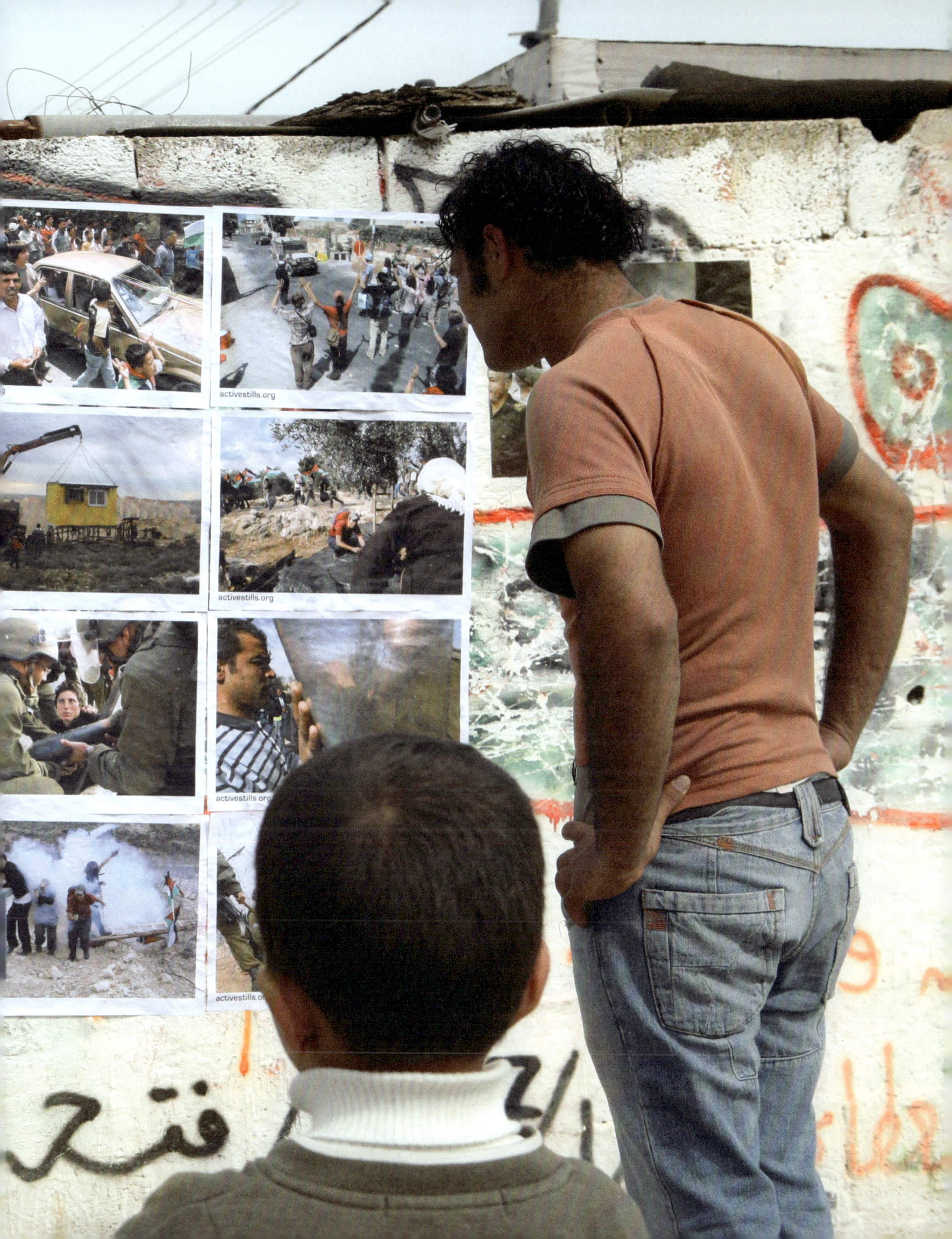
activestills.org
activestills.org
activestills.org
فتح

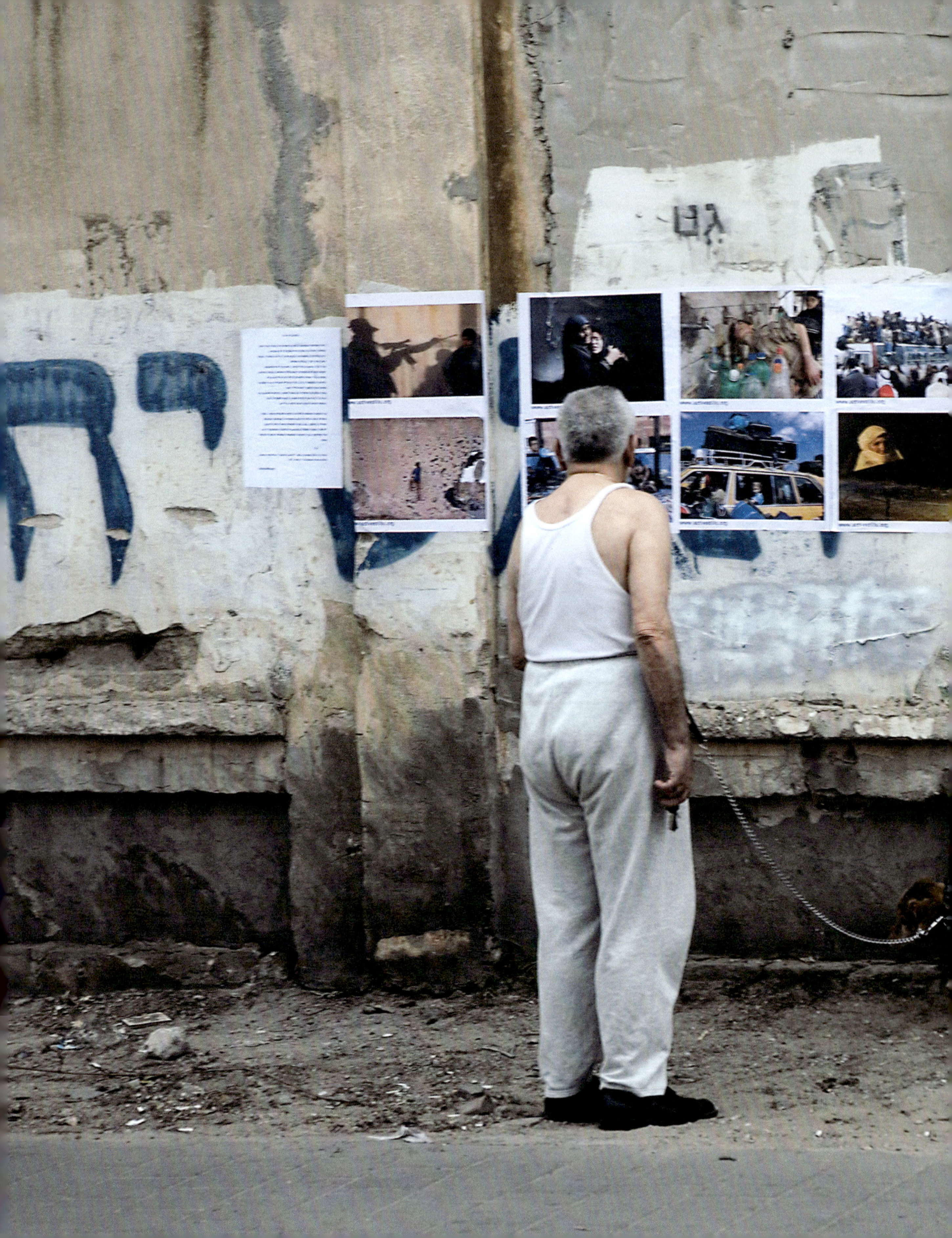

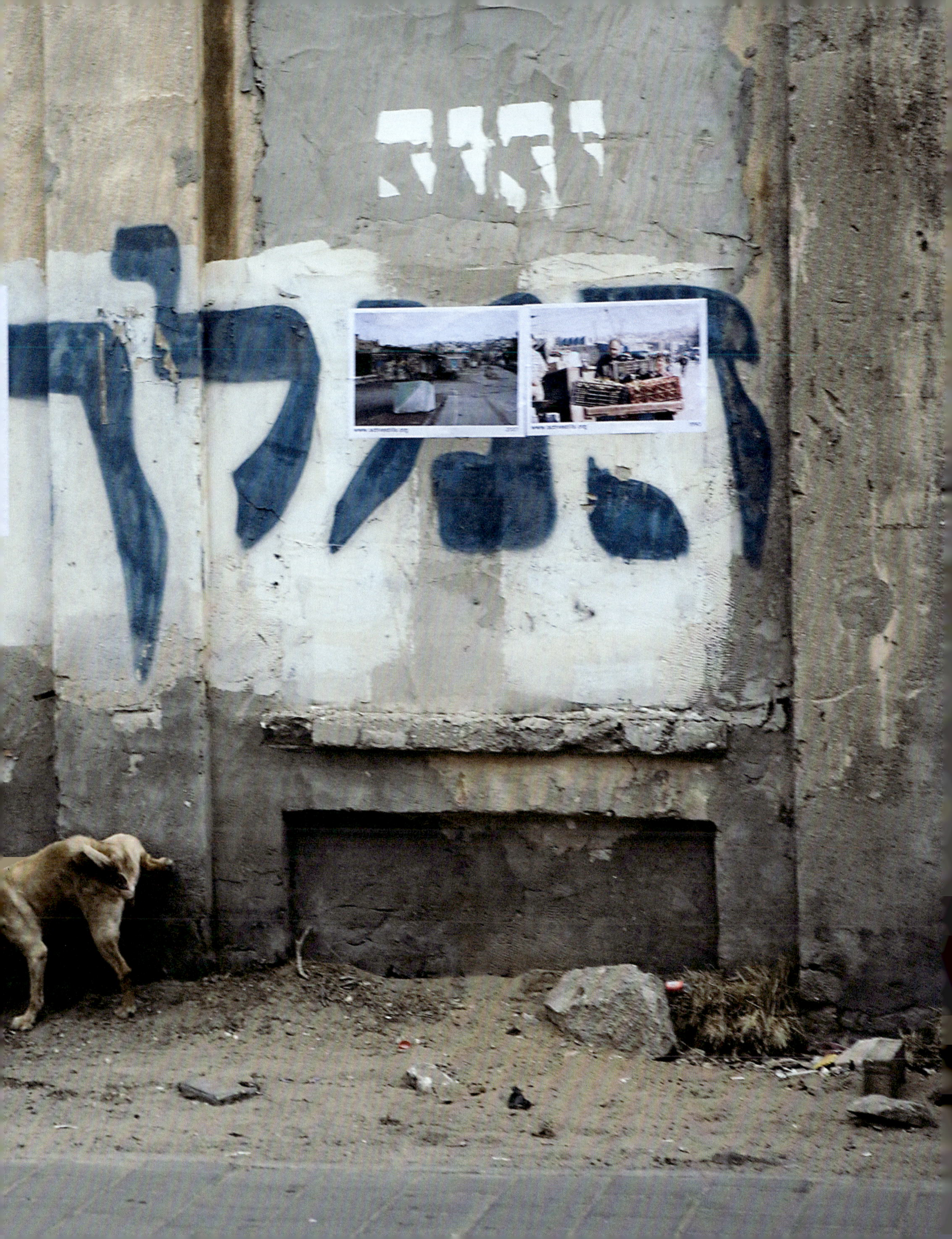

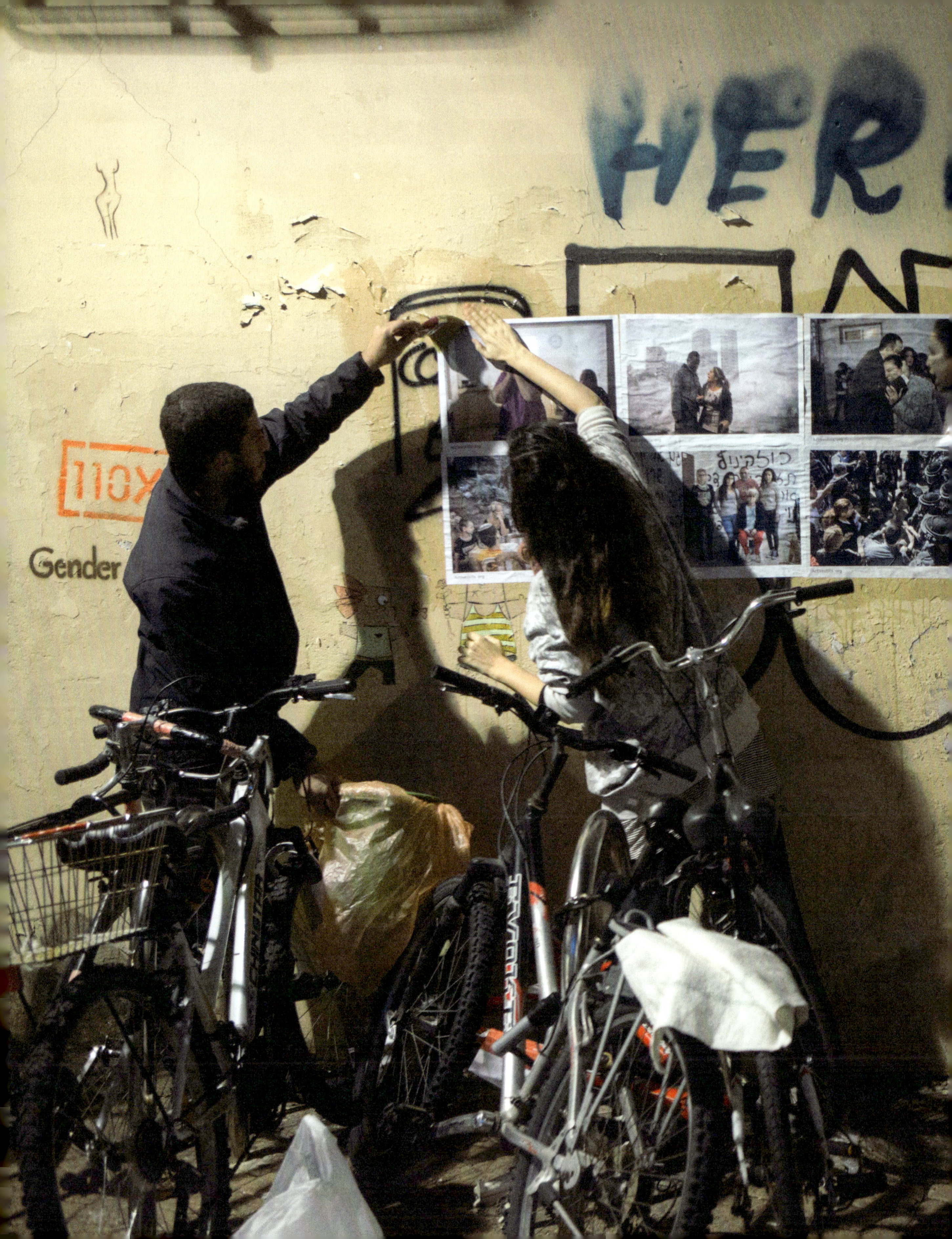
HER
Gender

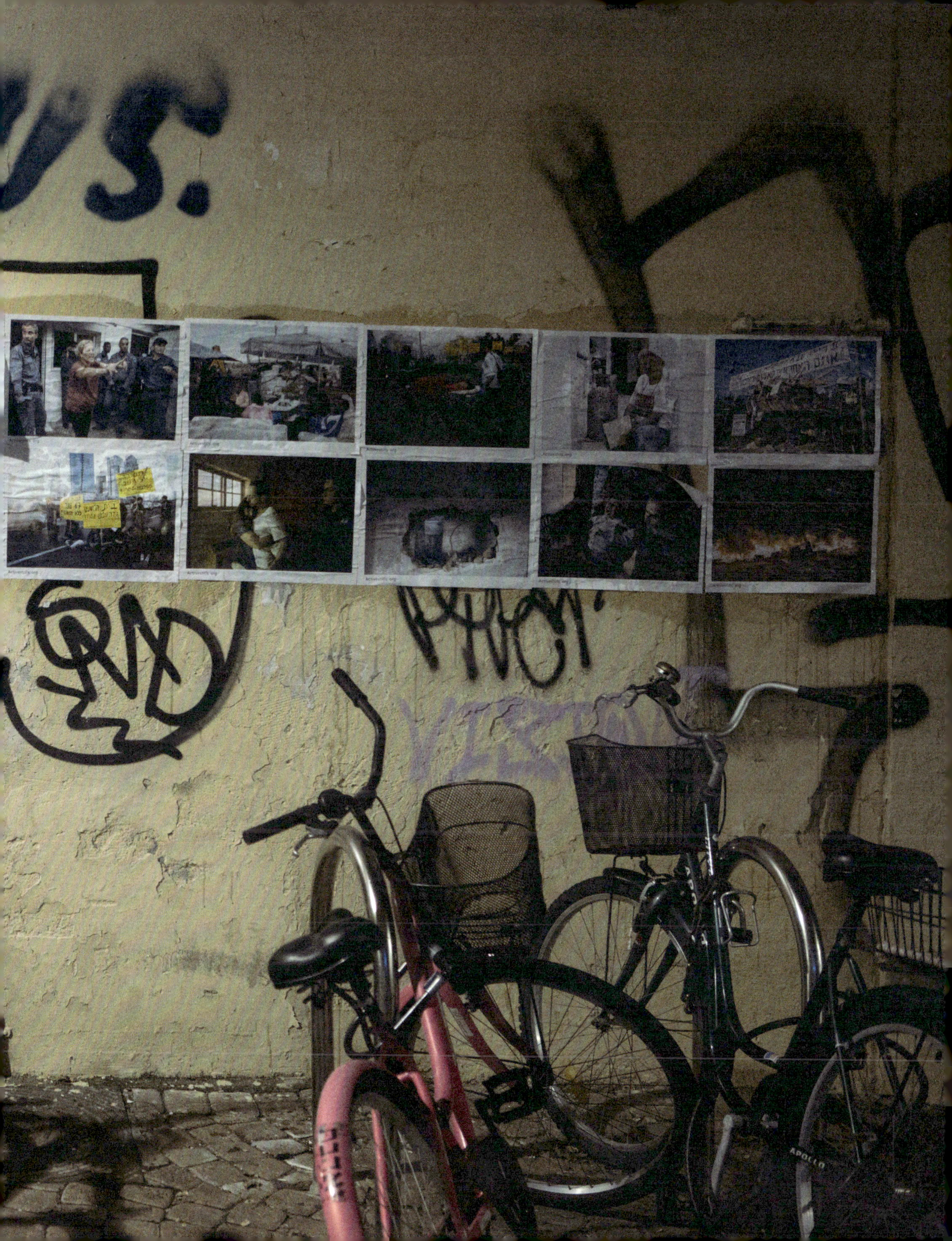

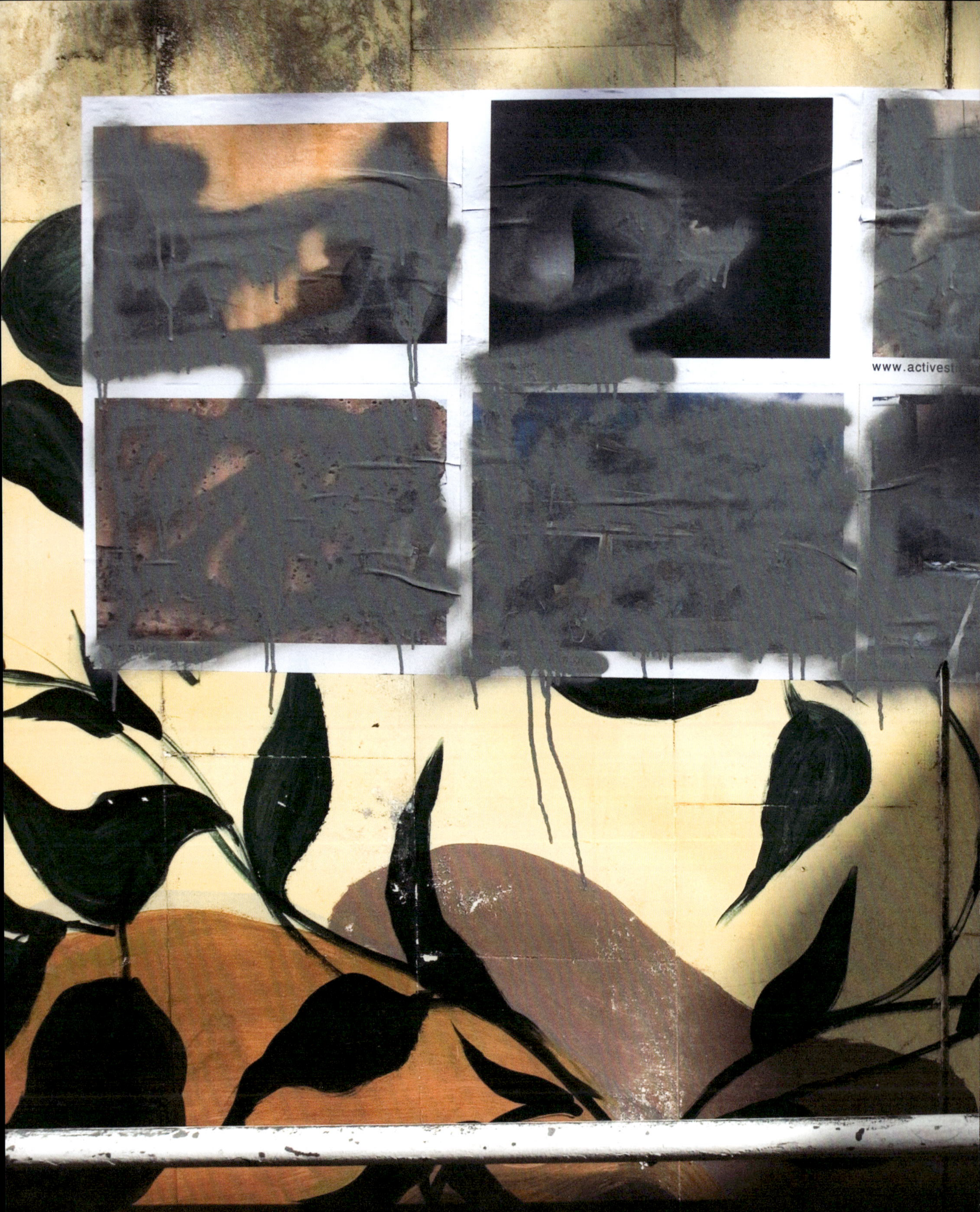
www.activest

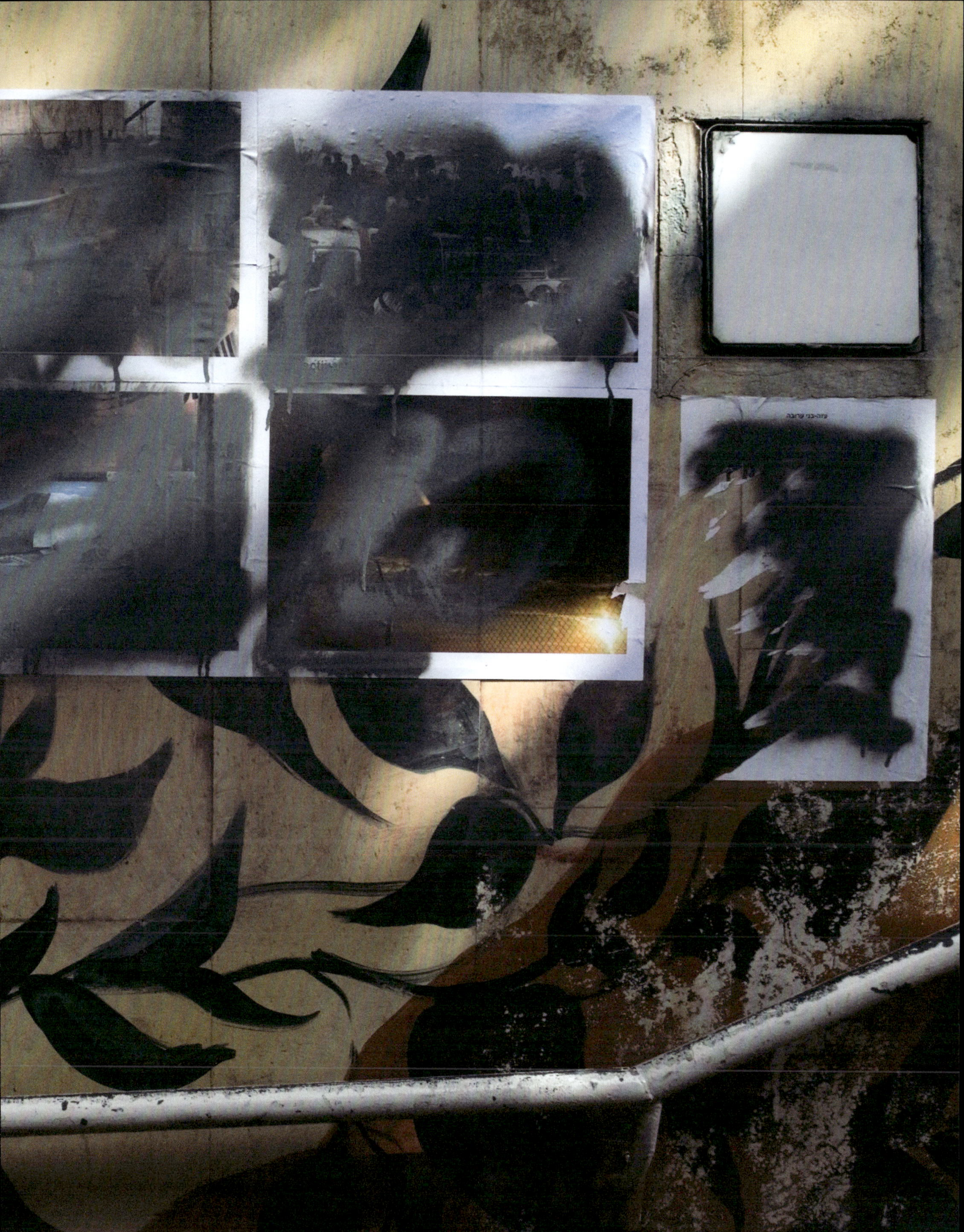

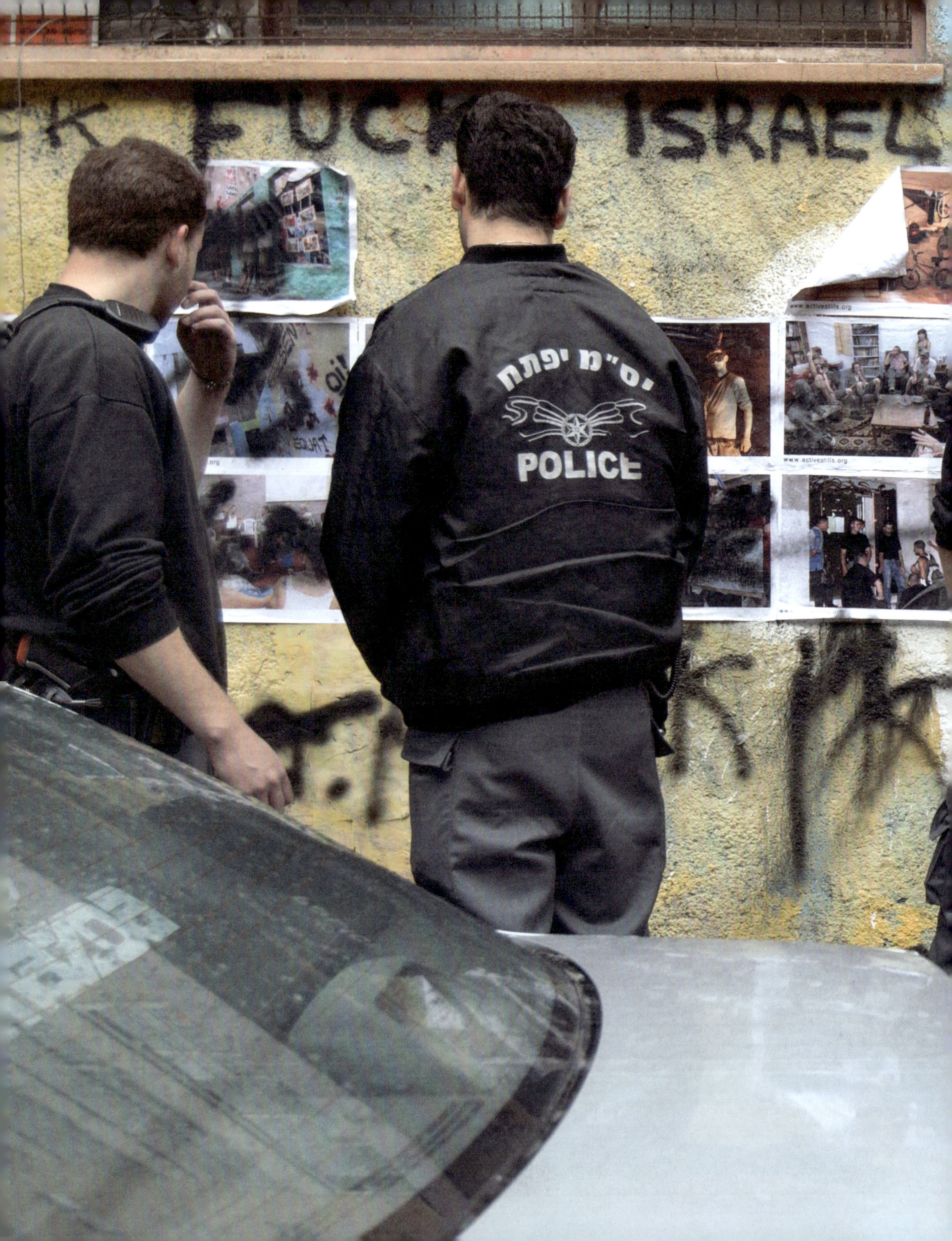
FUCK ISRAEL
יס"מ יפתח
POLICE
www.activestills.org

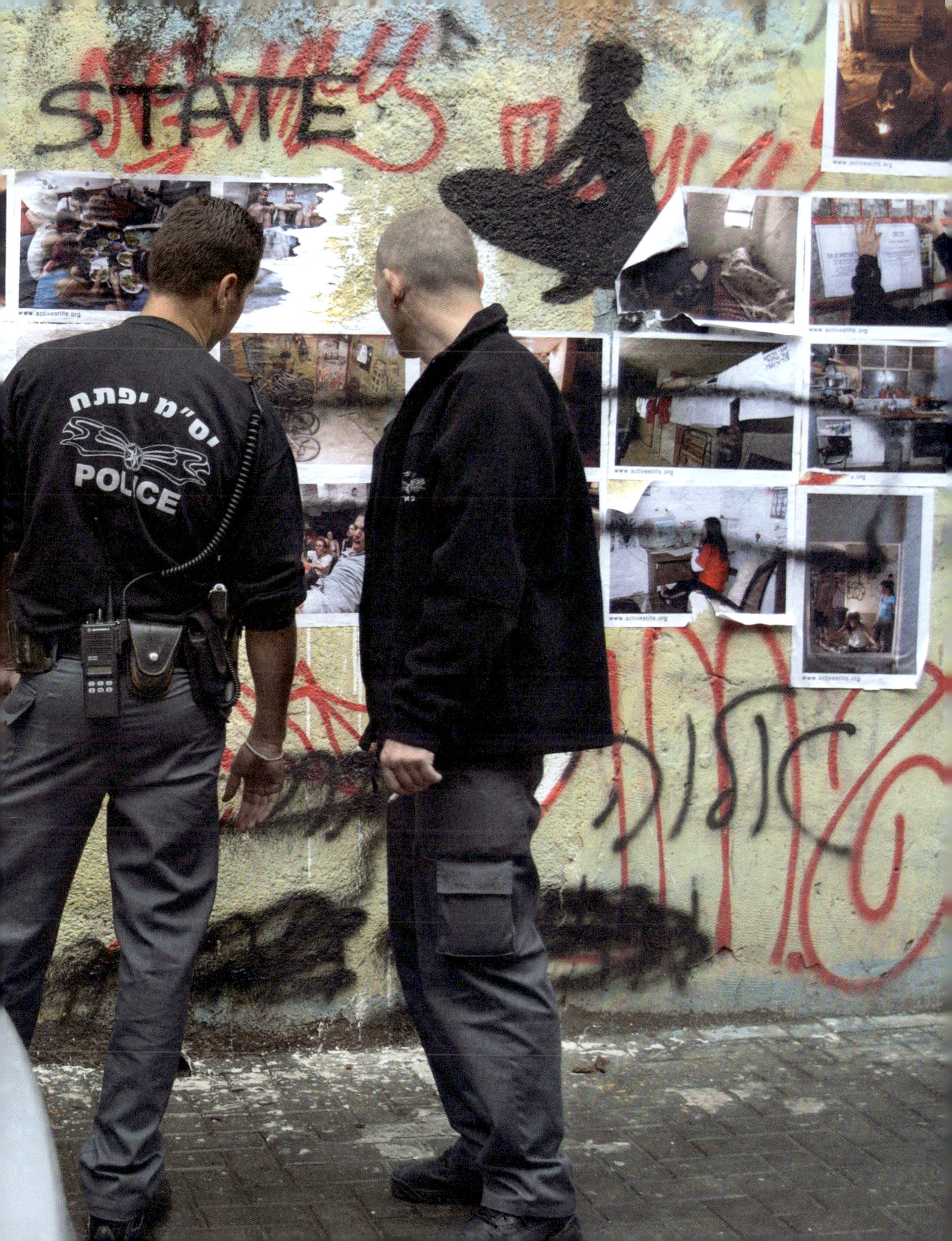
STATE
יס"מ יפתח
POLICE

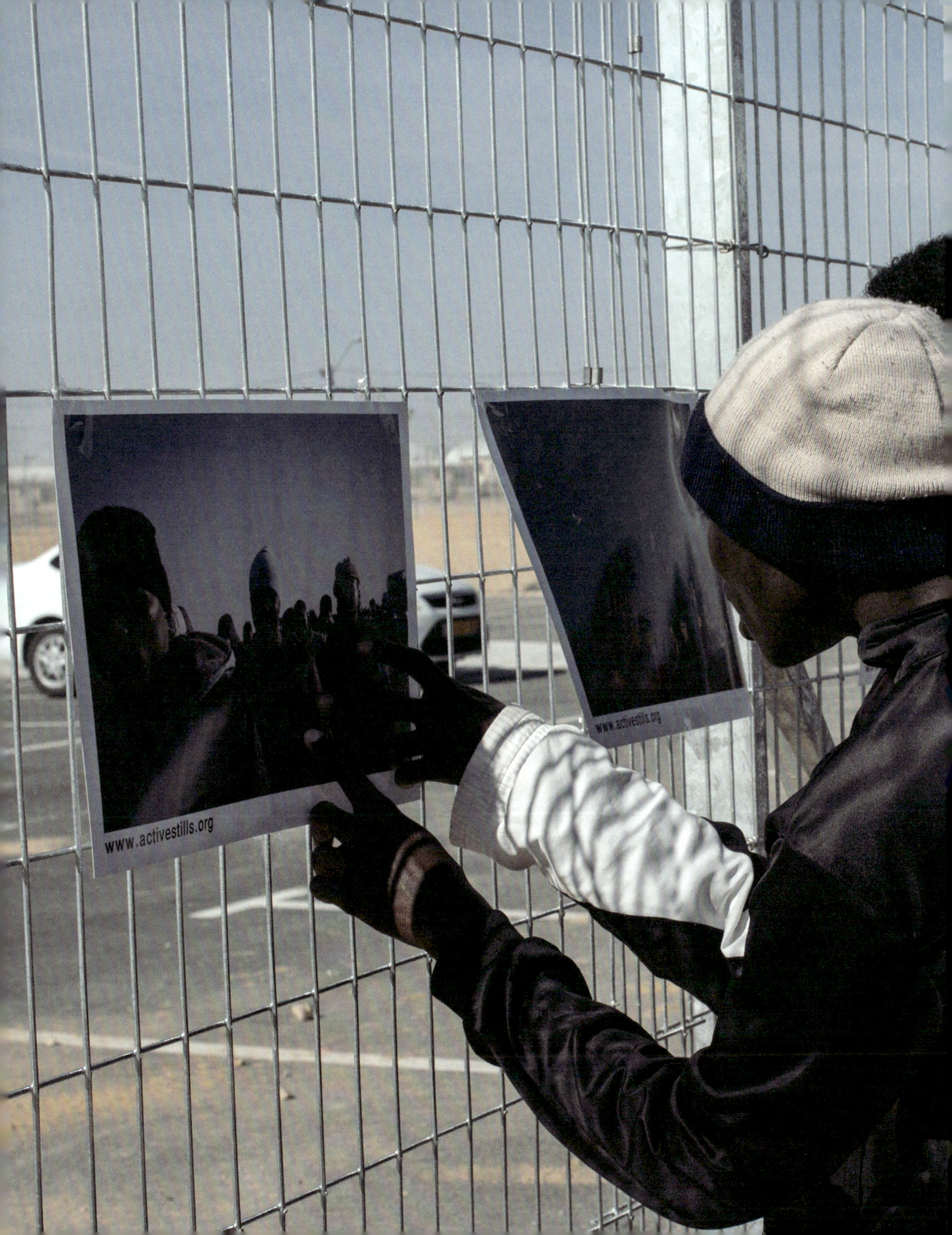
www.activestills.org
www.activestills.org

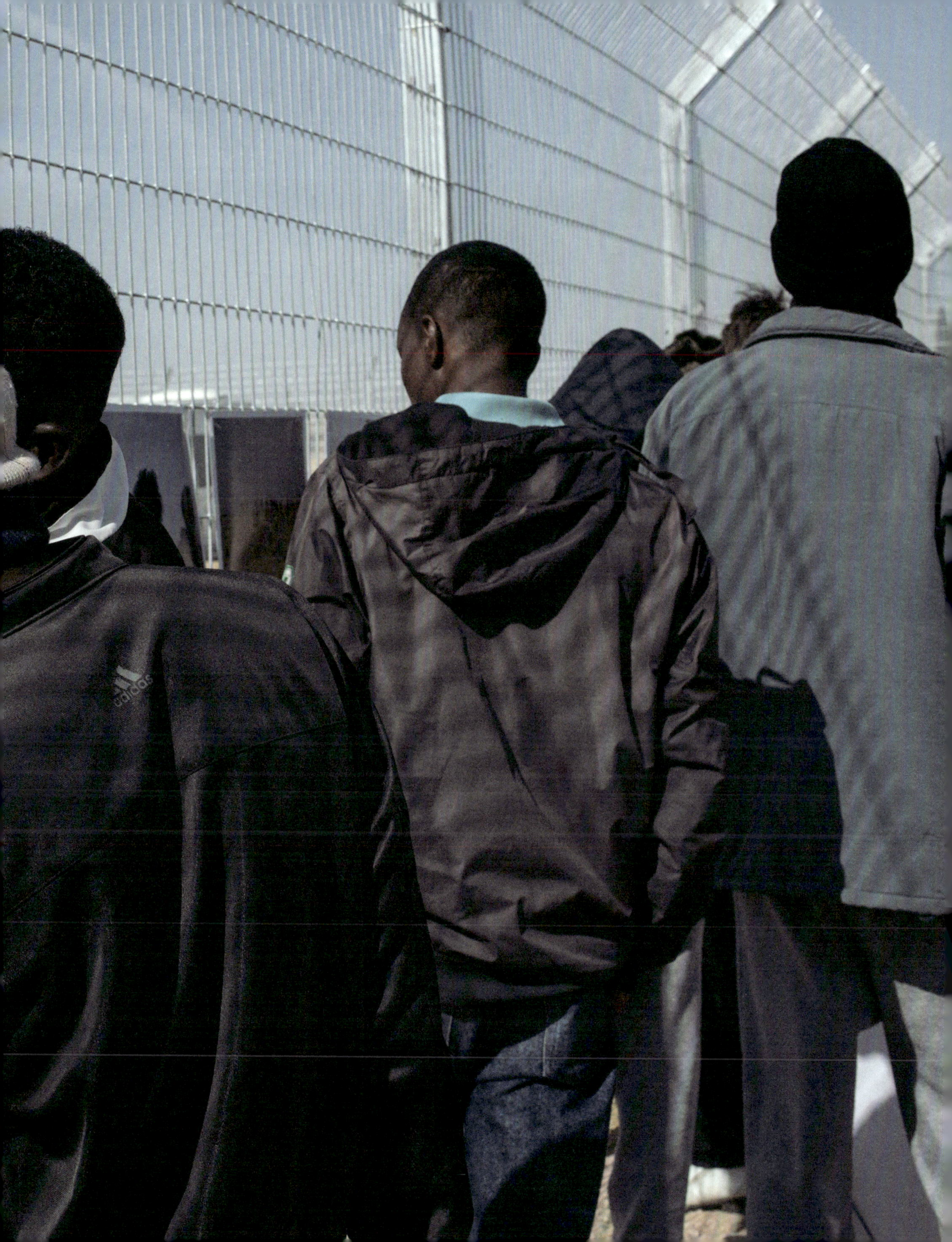

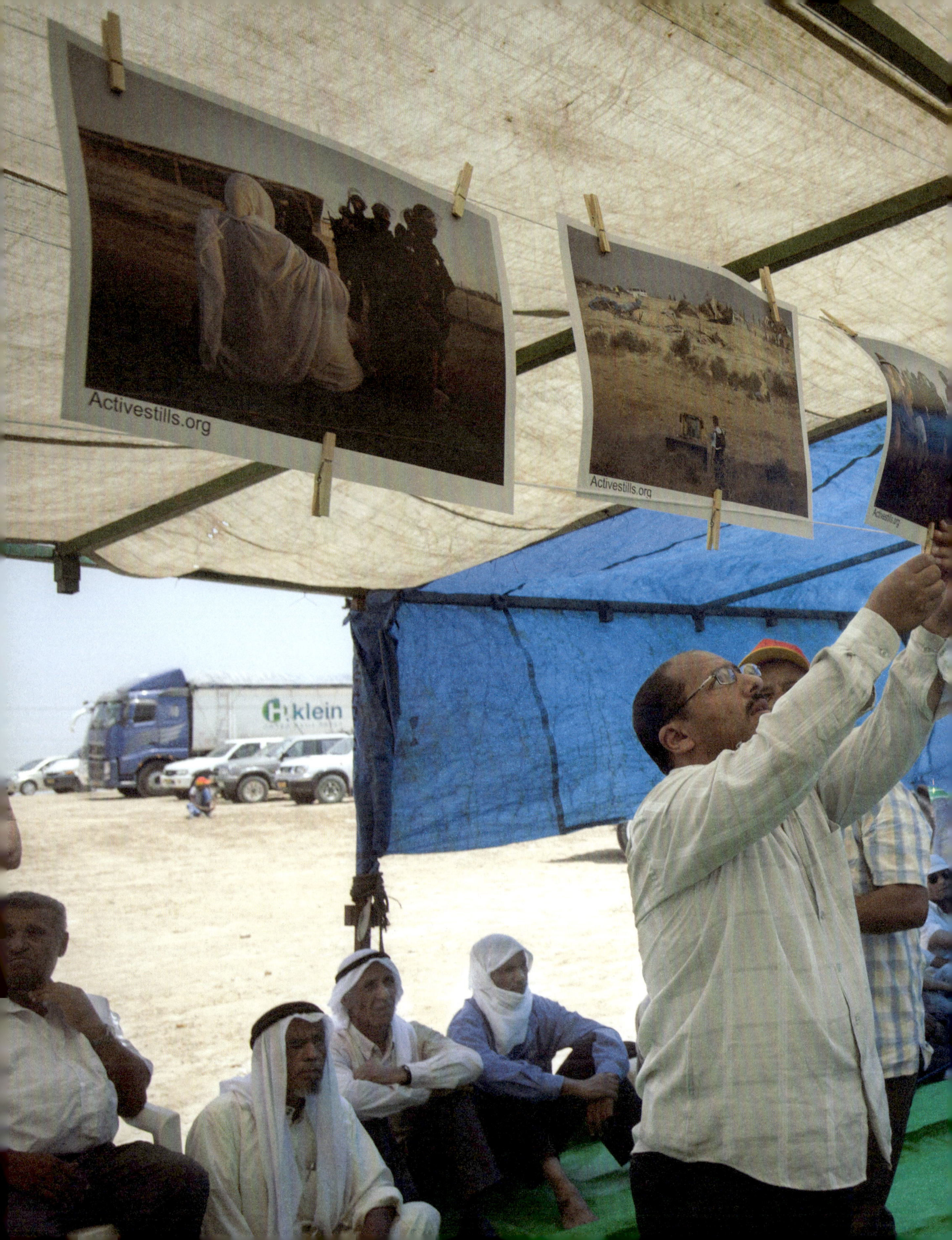
Activestills.org
Activestills.org
Activestills.org
klein

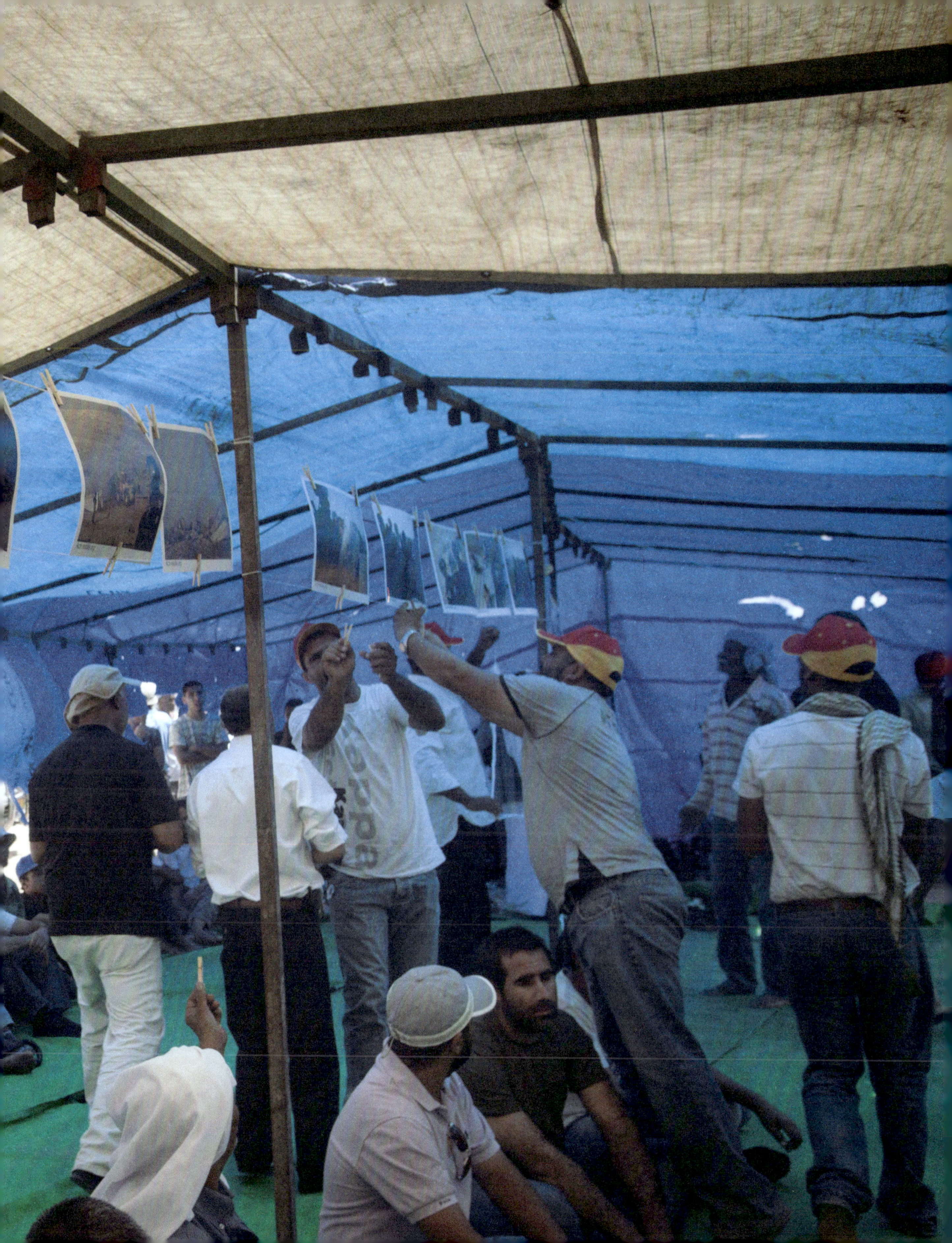

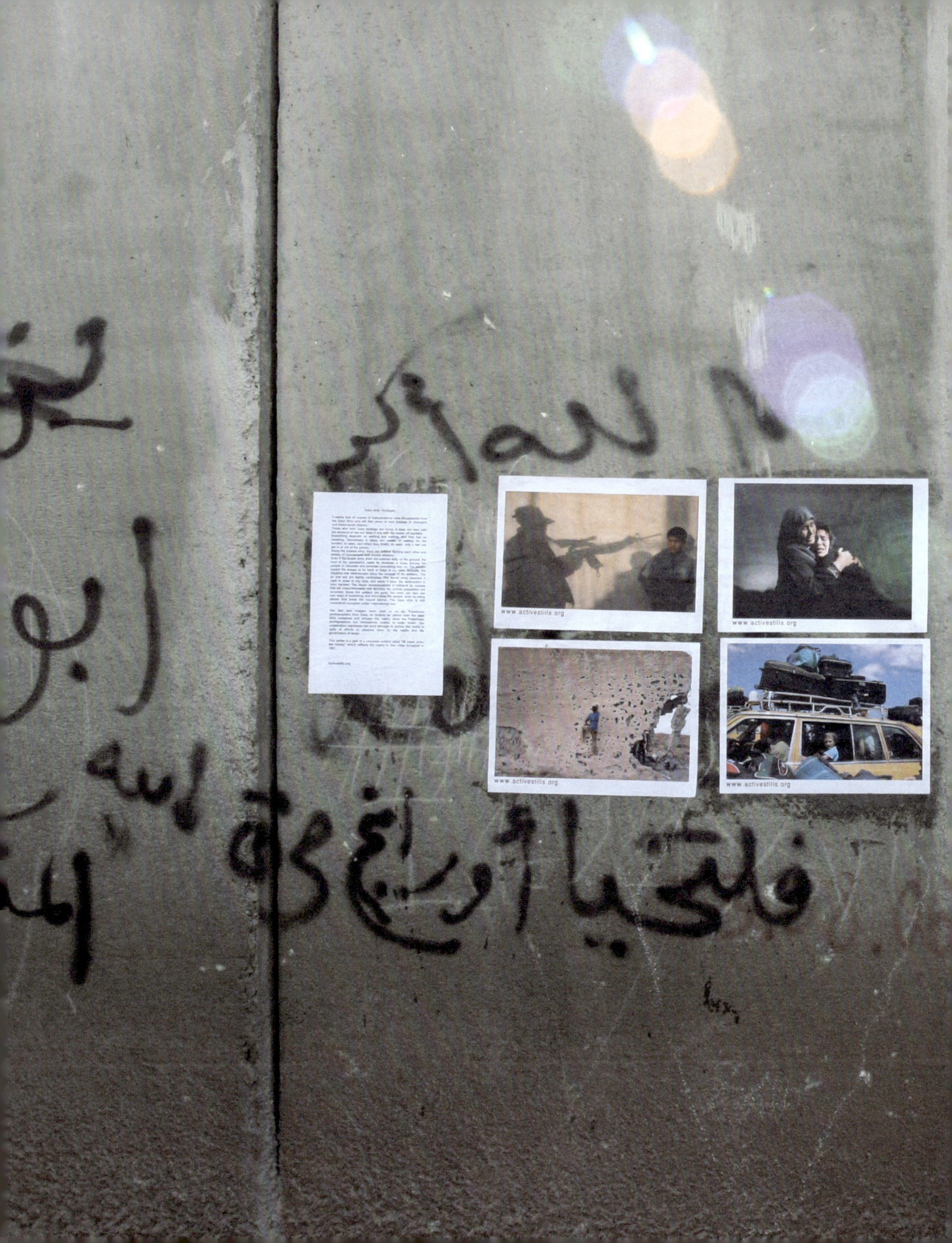
www.activestills.org
www.activestills.org
www.activestills.org
www.activestills.org

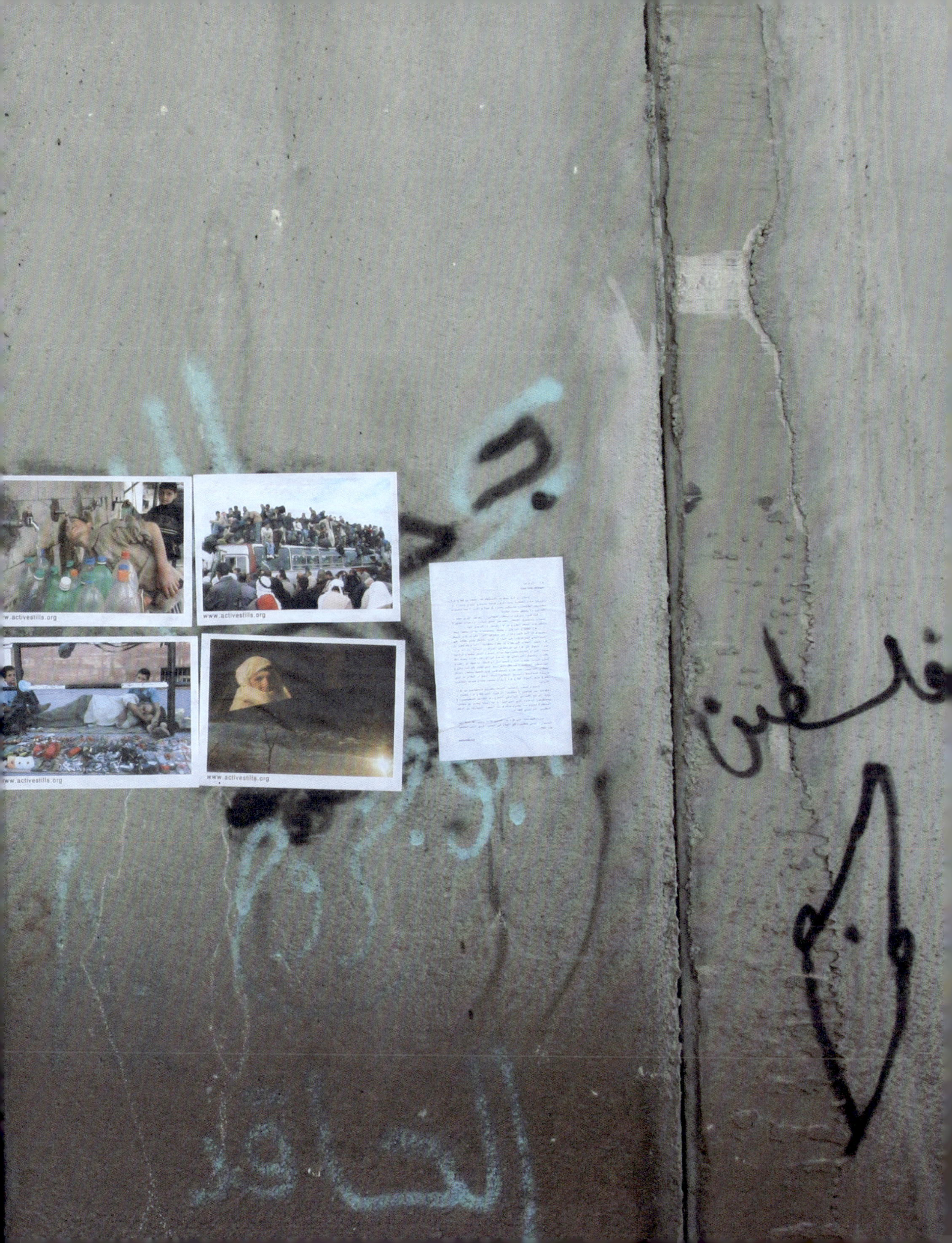
www.activestills.org
www.activestills.org
www.activestills.org
www.activestills.org

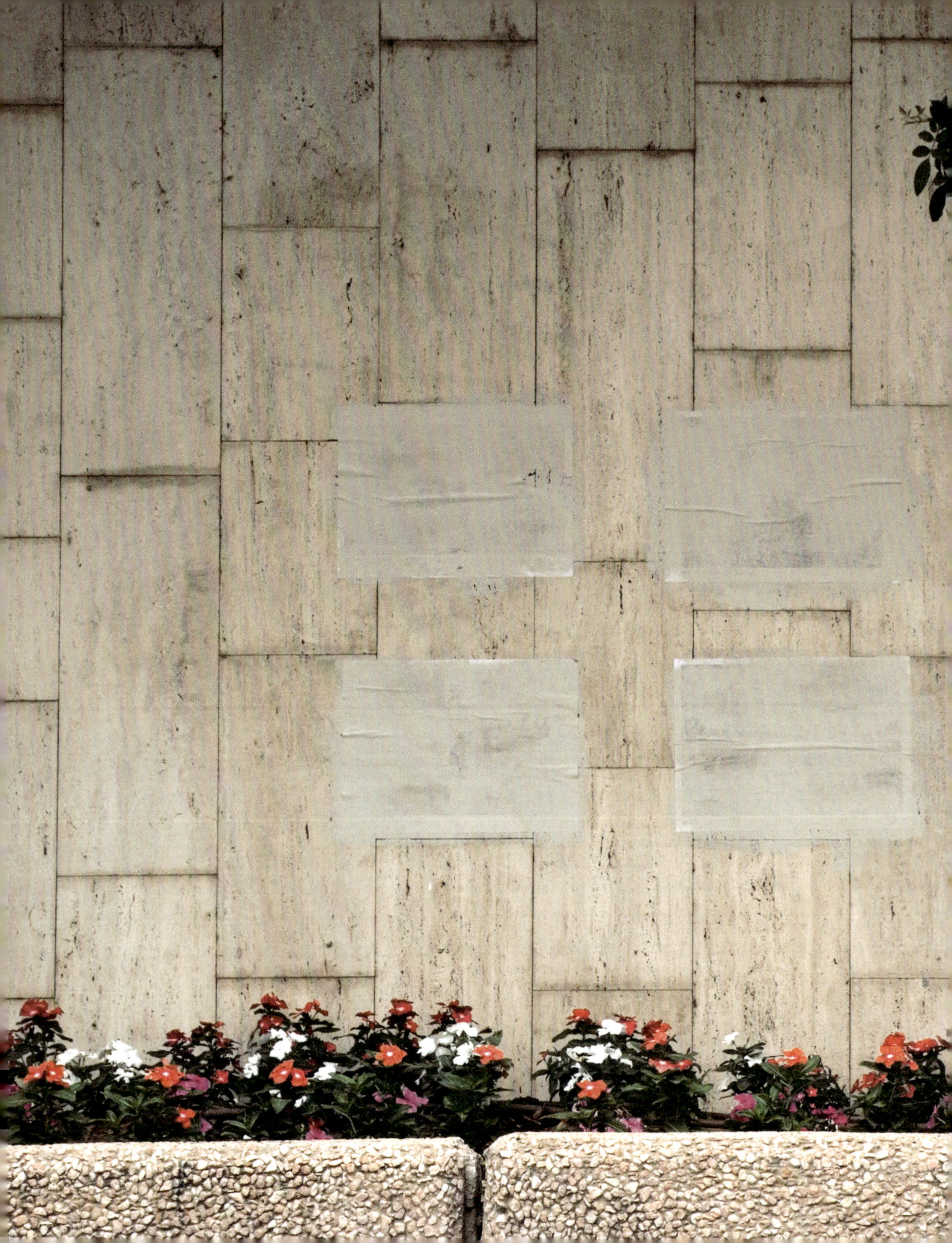

זורע

Activestills
Photography as Protest in Palestine/Israel
Editors: Vered Maimon and Shiraz Grinbaum

Graphic editing and design: Studio Gimel2
Translations from Hebrew and text editing: Sharon Assaf
Translations from Arabic: Deema Darawshy

Cover photo: A protest marking Nakba day ("Day of Catastrophe"), outside the Ofer military prison, West Bank, 15.5.2012 (detail)

Pluto Press Team
Copy-editing: Jeanne Brady
Proofreading and index: Susan Curran
Production and management: Kerrie Barlow and Robert Webb

First published 2016 by Pluto Press
345 Archway Road, London N6 5AA

www.plutobooks.com

Copyright © Vered Maimon and Shiraz Grinbaum 2016

The right of the individual contributors to be identified as the authors of this work has been asserted by them in accordance with the Copyright, Designs and Patents Act 1988.

British Library Cataloguing in Publication Data
A catalogue record for this book is available from the British Library

ISBN 978 0 7453 3669 5 Paperback
ISBN 978 1 7868 0010 7 PDF eBook

Front images, Activestills street exhibitions:
1. Bil'in, West Bank, 23.2.2007 / 2. Tel Aviv, 10.5.2007 / 3. Tel Aviv, 5.1.2015 / 4. Haifa, Israel, 13.5.2007 / 5. Tel Aviv, 21.11.2007 / 6. Negev Desert, Israel, 25.1.2014 / 7. Negev Desert, Israel, 30.7.2010 / 8. Anata, East Jerusalem, 5.6.2007 / 9. Tel Aviv, 11.5.2007

Activestills

Photography as Protest in Palestine/Israel

Edited by
Vered Maimon and Shiraz Grinbaum

PlutoPress
www.plutobooks.com

All the photographs in this book are signed collectively by Activestills members.

This book is dedicated to all the
communities, groups, and activists
that invited us to take part
in their struggle.

Contents

Foreword

Miki Kratsman

When I started teaching photojournalism at the Geographic Photography College in Tel Aviv back in 1997, the local news field was in the middle of a crisis. It was only five years since *Hadashot*, the groundbreaking newspaper that had set a new standard for the profession and had been a key player in the articulation of Israeli photojournalism, had closed its doors. *Hadashot* drew on the photographic tradition of the local newspapers in Israel, such as Tel Aviv's *Ha'ir* and Jerusalem's *Kol Ha'ir*, which were characterized by photography that was not committed to or dependent upon text. It also succeeded in establishing a dedicated group of photojournalists who viewed their work in the light of social and political responsibility. Although this approach was not spelled out explicitly, and did not necessarily hold true for all of the group's members, it was the dominant attitude of the newspaper's core photojournalists.

As a lecturer at the Geographic Photography College at that time, I needed to help my students who had dreamed about working in something bigger than a local newspaper come to terms with the hard truths of working in a dwindling photojournalism market. In 2005, my eighth year of teaching, a new photographic practice began to make its way into the classroom: a group of third-year students started bringing photos to class that they had taken at the weekly Friday protests against the Israeli separation wall, which were being staged in the West Bank village of Bil'in. While it was understandable that the students would travel together to the occupied Palestinian territories rather than go separately, there was something new in their photos that had begun to coalesce over time. Over the course of that year, the students—Oren Ziv, Yotam Ronen, and Keren Manor—together with the Argentinean photographer Eduardo Soteras, created a photography collective under the name "Activestills."

In the photographs, I could see a relationship forming between my students and the demonstrators, Palestinians and Israelis from the Anarchists Against the Wall group. Such relationships are rare in conventional photojournalism. Furthermore, the students became part of the protest and, in that position, it became appropriate for them to photograph other photographers who were also present at the same event. The act of reexamining the position of the photojournalist in an event was both interesting and challenging, especially when viewed in light of the recent Iraq War, during which the very institution of journalism had been put to the test and failed. The Iraq War was not the first time photojournalists were forced to examine the power relations between themselves and the establishment and question who had the right to determine the boundaries of the freedom of information. In contrast to journalistic writing, photojournalism requires a constant repositioning of oneself in the field, in real time, as well as examining the political forces that allow one to be a photographer in a particular place and position, which leads to questions such as: Which side should I stand on? What are the political structures that make my presence in a specific territory possible? Activestills photographers decided to stand with the protesters in Bil'in and position themselves in the field within the boundaries that the protesters determined. The choice to stand with the protesters rather than behind the soldiers neutralized any control the ruling power may have had on their photographic act. It was important for me to understand that this was an ideological position that preceded the journalistic position, and that it would engage every aspect of their work.

Photojournalism has traditionally relied on the circulation of its product through news agencies and related media outlets. In the 1940s, freelance photographers would dash from the scene of an event to news desks in a bid to be the first to sell their wares. Later, agency-affiliated photojournalists from agencies such as Associated Press and Reuters could rely on wide circulation through the teleprinters that were installed in newspaper headquarters. This new technology displaced the intimate familiarity that photojournalists had once shared with newspaper editorial boards. In a certain sense, digital circulation methods continue to maintain the same "disconnection" between the photojournalist and media outlets. Activestills photographers have made the ideological and ethical choice to disseminate their materials through media with which they identify politically, such as *Local Call* and *+972 Magazine*, or through nongovernmental organizations. Though they do publish and sell their photographs to local and foreign media, they refuse to be dependent on newspapers for their livelihood. They are truly bringing the term "freelance," or "free-lens," back to its original meaning.

In another challenge to traditional photojournalism practice, they choose to present their materials in the same communal public spaces where they photographed. This is an exceptional strategy, since the people being photographed for newspapers often do not have access to the media outlets that cover them. This strategy also has an aesthetic aspect. While most photographers envision their work printed in large scale, on quality paper, framed behind glass, and exhibited in some contemporary photography gallery, the Activestills photojournalists continue to imagine their photos in a size not exceeding A3, unframed, and glued, pinned, or taped on to a wall. Activestills photographers thought of their work from the beginning as a tool for social and political change. The collective's drive and idiosyncratic practices anticipated the rise of the smartphone and digital photography as mobilizing tools on social media.

Activestills have not just survived, they have grown in a decade that has witnessed the switch from negative film to Twitter and seen cooperation between Israelis and Palestinians reach an all-time low. This has been possible only because of the commitment of all the members to work jointly—the occupier and the occupied—based on a clear political stance against the Israeli occupation, to observe and photograph the act of occupation itself.

After following the collective's work for a decade, in 2015 I joined Activestills. For over three decades as a press photographer, I was lucky to be able to choose my own subjects. Now I have the chance to act and witness from within, and never before did I feel as close to those I photographed as I have over these last years.

Activestills members maintain an ongoing relationship with the communities they photograph and their struggles. This creates a kind of partnership and intimacy that goes beyond journalistic coverage. Every so often, it is not the photographers who are initiating the coverage; rather they are invited by the communities to join their actions as photographers. Activestills realized in practice, before the support and also the disruption that technology would bring, the affinity between the producers, subjects, distributors, and recipients of information, which for me is the base and the power of photojournalism in the future.

Bil'in, West Bank 19.11.2005

Israeli soldiers arrest a protester during a demonstration against the construction of the Israeli separation wall.

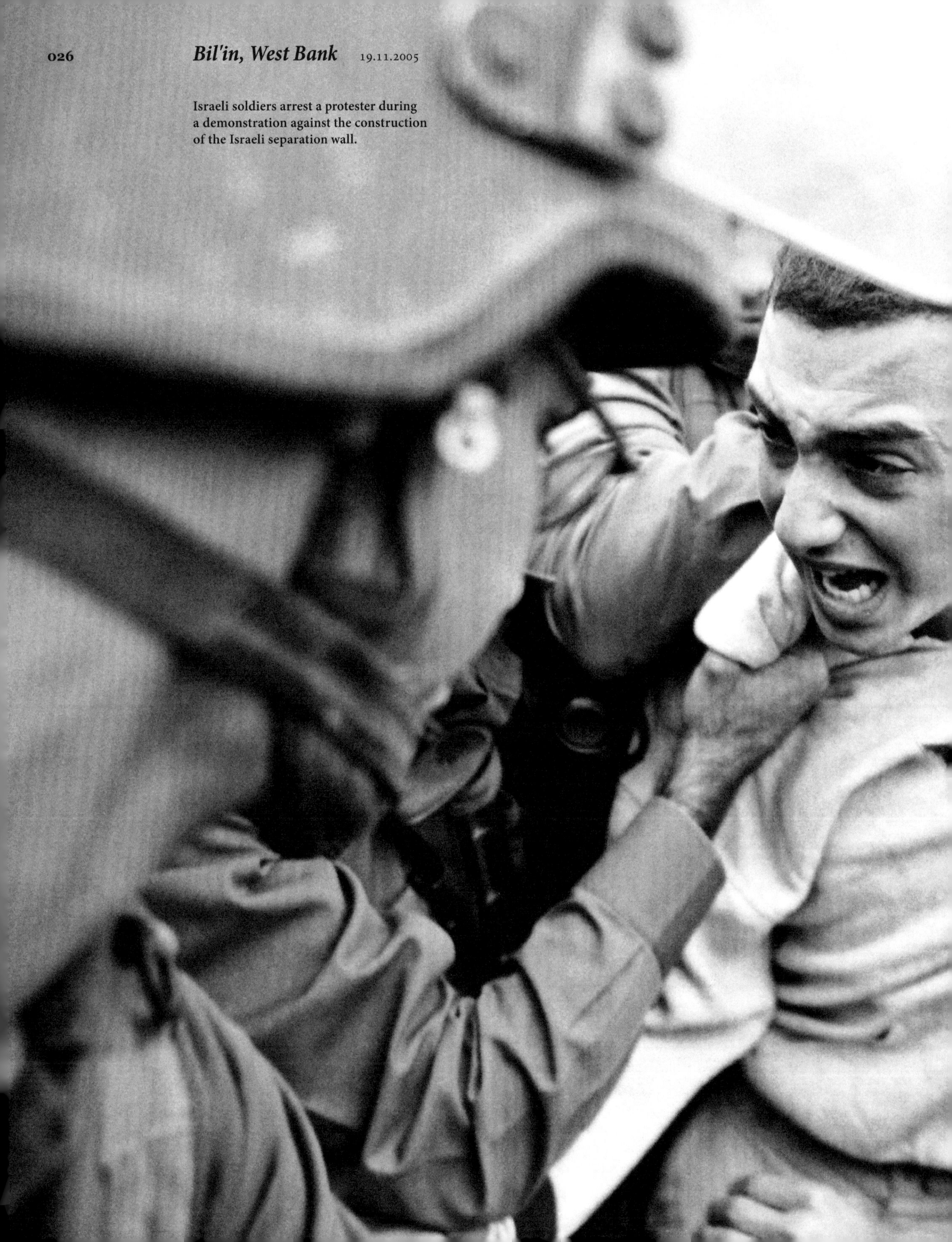

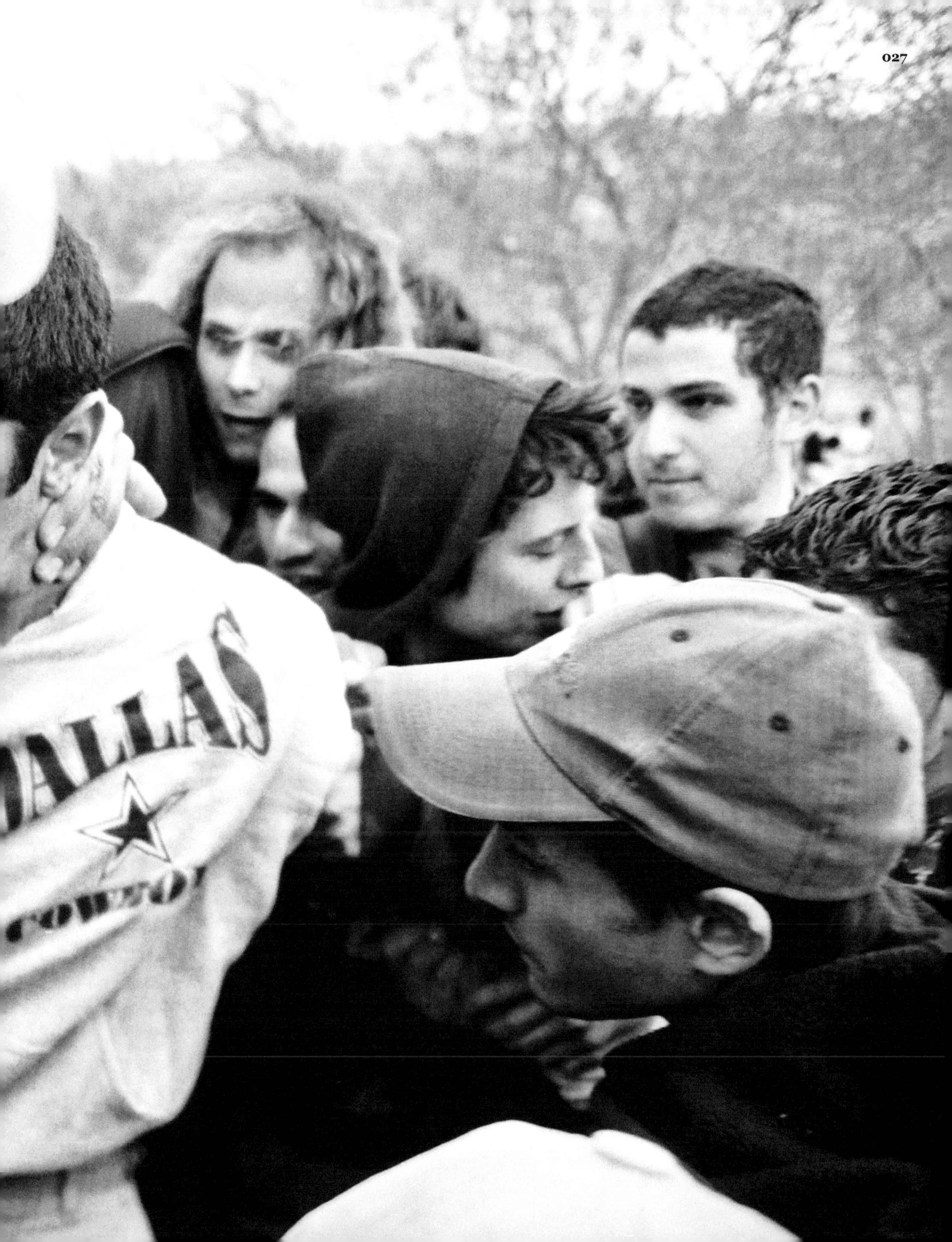

Introduction

Vered Maimon and Shiraz Grinbaum

> The photograph therefore does not only look backward … but it also opens onto a future: it is in fact displaced toward the future.[1]

This book is a joint contemplation about the body of work produced by the Activestills photography collective from its inception in 2005 up to the current moment. It includes the perspectives of activists, journalists, historians and theoreticians of photography, and the collective's members themselves, in an effort to articulate the distinctive position that Activestills embody within the fields of photojournalism and documentary photography as well as within the realm of political engagement. With this collaborative project, we wish to place the collective's now decade-long involvement with political struggles in Palestine/Israel as a milestone of *activist photography*.

Our examination is directed at both the past and the future. By looking back at the collective's political and photographic forms of intervention in specific historical and geographical milieus, we aim not only to point to photography's changing status and role within contemporary global visual culture, but also to outline the possibilities and potentialities for a critical practice and theory of photography in the future. We conceived this project as opening a shared space for thought *and* action, photographs *and* texts; a dialogic sphere between viewers, photographers, and subjects photographed, marking Activestills' long-term commitment to cooperation and joint communal struggles. In this regard, this book is configured not as a catalogue documenting or summarizing the work of the collective, but as an effort to continue and expand its political, material, and perceptual modes of mediation, intervention, and action.

Looking Back—Stepping In Action

The Activestills collective was formed in response to the Israeli media's highly restricted and biased coverage of the Palestinian unarmed popular struggle against the Israeli military occupation of the West Bank and Gaza. In 2005, co-founders of the collective—Oren Ziv, Keren Manor, Yotam Ronen, and Eduardo Soteras, then emerging documentary photographers—met in the West Bank village of Bil'in, joining the protests as activists with the Anarchists Against the Wall (AAtW) group.[2] At the time, villagers from Bil'in started staging weekly protests against the confiscation of the village's agricultural lands for the construction of the Israeli separation wall and the nearby Israeli settlement of Mod'in Illit.[3] Following other protesting villages, Bil'in residents wished to raise international and Israeli left-wing support for their struggle, while also turning to Israel's High Court of Justice in order to stop the construction.[4] Wishing to expose the villagers' struggle, the group met to discuss methods of reaching out to the Israeli public.

Up until the first intifada (1987), most media coverage of the Israeli military occupation was done by local Israeli media and international wire agencies that employed both Israeli and foreign photojournalists. This situation changed when international and local media began hiring Palestinian photographers, with Reuters news agency distributing cameras to Palestinians, paving the way for their training and incorporation by international wires. Within the Israeli media, coverage of the Israeli military occupation changed in 1984 with the launching of *Hadashot* newspaper, which had a declared left-wing agenda and prioritized graphic and visual content. The newspaper was responsible for creating a new visual iconography of the Israeli occupation, sometimes publishing photographs that violated the restrictions of the Israeli Army's censorship.[5] Yet it closed unexpectedly in 1993 with the beginning of the print media's decline.

The formation of Activestills marks a response not only to the prevalent mode of reporting or lack of it on the Palestinian popular struggle in Israeli media, but also to the global crisis of photojournalism following recent institutional, technological, and economic changes in the global media arena. The introduction of new digital media and the rise of the Internet, as Roger Hallas has recently argued, led in the last few decades to shrinking advertising revenues for print media, and consequently, photo editors are "commissioning fewer and fewer photojournalist assignments and paying far less for the completed work than in previous decades." Photographic reporting is thus outsourced to commercial photo agencies "which have also dwindled in number as the industry moves closer and closer toward a duopoly of Getty Images and Corbis."[6] Almost concurrently, media outlets began incorporating citizen journalism, amateur imagery, and NGOs' visual advocacy information as equally important producers of visual knowledge.[7] This "new media ecology," as Hallas terms this new condition, challenged the traditional function of photojournalism and called for a reexamination of its ethical paradigms, as well as giving rise to independent journalism which questioned mainstream corporate media narratives and the latter's increasing concern with commercial interests.

The need to challenge the Israeli media's official narratives motivated different activist groups to initiate independent advocacy projects which are based on records and testimonies of human rights violations in the occupied Palestinian territories. Israeli NGOs such as Physicians for Human Rights (1988), B'Tselem [The Israeli Information Center for Human Rights in the Occupied Territories] (1989), and Machsom Watch (2001), began to produce and disseminate visual documentation of Palestinian life under occupation as early as the beginning of the 1990s.[8] This process culminated with the "Shooting Back" project (2007) initiated by B'Tselem's video trainers, who handed out cameras to Palestinians living in highly conflictual areas where settlers and army violence were especially acute. The project's main goal was to overcome the "hostility wall that was blocking the gaze of Israeli addressees, preventing them from *recognizing* an assault on Palestinians as an assault."[9] The wish to overcome this "active non-seeing mechanism" was shared by many human rights NGOs and activist groups, as well as by Activestills members to a certain degree.[10] In retrospect, B'Tselem's project worked to constitute Palestinian "camera-holders" as sources of visual testimony.[11]

During that time, independent online news websites started reporting on Palestine/Israel in English, at first addressing international audiences of activists, journalists, and diplomats, but soon engaging the Israeli audience as well. Websites such as that belonging to the joint Palestinian-Israeli Alternative Information Center (an organization established in 1984), *Electronic Intifada* (in 2000), *+972 Magazine* (in 2009) and its Hebrew counterpart *Local Call* (in 2014), were focusing on topics related to the Israeli occupation and the Palestinian popular struggle against the construction of the Israeli separation wall, while gaining ongoing credit for their bottom-up reporting and analysis.[12] These outlets often report on human rights violations in Palestine/Israel in order to connect journalism with an activist agenda while expanding the range and scope of political discourse regarding the Israeli occupation.[13]

Activestills came into being within these structural changes in media and activism. From the beginning, its co-founders viewed themselves as activists *and* professional photojournalists, thus shaping a unique position that went beyond "citizen photography," by combining ethical responsibility with aesthetic skillfulness and long-term commitment to joint documentation and reporting. Viewing their photographic act as tantamount to the act of protest itself and *not* simply as a form of witnessing, the group emphasis was not on "representation" of the "suffering of the other," or on victimhood, but on the *enactment* of political agency and the demand for rights—to mobility, livelihood, and protection from violence. Shortly, the group formulated its shared political stance in a collective statement [**p. 31**].

Configuring their work as interventionist, the collective were not eager to incorporate their images in the Israeli media or to present their photographs in galleries or museums. They soon decided to create street exhibitions to be posted in dozens of different locations on the walls of abandoned buildings and empty billboards, in order to reach different sections of the Israeli public. The first action that took place in 2006 in Tel Aviv bore the name of the collective—Activestills—and embodied its members' wish to amplify the pubic visibility of the struggle in Bil'in through photographs. The exhibition consisted of 16 photographs placed in a grid form with an accompanying text that informed passers-by about the Palestinian popular struggle and urged them to join the weekly protests. The new chosen name for the group derived from the decision to refrain from personal emphasis by signing all images by the name Activestills.[14] This act harnessed the individual author to a collective statement, one that was articulated explicitly as political in nature, agreed upon, and promoted by all the members.

Concurrently, the collective began to consolidate their modes of action and put up a website, *activestills.org*, where members posted their images, creating a joint archive where the copyrights of all the images are shared. Simultaneously, they created a Flickr account which updated daily. Their photo-stream soon became a source for activist communities, both Israeli and Palestinian, for imagery and news about different direct actions and protests in Palestine/Israel.

The collective's political stance and independent, non-profit agenda soon became the threshold for newcomers. New photographers who saw eye to eye with the small emerging group joined: French photographer Anne Paq joined in 2006; Israeli photographers Tess Scheflan, Shachaf Polakow, and Silan Dallal joined during 2007–08; Palestinian photographer Ahmad Al-Bazz, American photographer Ryan Rodrick Beiler, and Israeli photographer Shiraz Grinbaum in 2012, and Palestinian photographers Basel Alyazouri and Faiz Abu Rmeleh joined in 2014.

The expansion of the collective deepened both its photographic work and its political insight. Quite early on, the group's meetings relocated from Tel Aviv to the West Bank where all members of the collective could have access. This kind of cooperation—between Israelis, Palestinians, and international activists—is even rarer today than in 2005. By collectively documenting the struggle against the Israeli occupation and its implications for the struggling communities, the group wished to actively resist the occupation's prescribed political positions of occupier and occupied. As Maxine Kaufman-Lacusta observes in her *Refusing to be Enemies—Palestinian and Israeli Non-Violent Resistance to the Israeli Occupation*, "Ironically, perhaps, the hated security barrier (aka apartheid wall) has been a catalyst in forging a new brand of joint activism."[15] Looking back at this promising constitutive moment in the collective's history, it is clear that this ground of alliance was made possible by intense decision-making processes through which all aspects of the group's work—ideological, terminological, economic, technical, and visual—are decided together.

This political stance also helped to set and prioritize future subjects of coverage. The collective's field of documentation soon extended to other political and social causes: demonstrations supporting Palestinian prisoners, state appropriation of Bedouin lands, everyday life in the Palestinian refugee camps, Palestinian economic struggle under the occupation, the Israeli siege and military assaults on Gaza, as well as social issues in Israel such as the struggles for public housing, women's and LGBTQ rights, the lives of asylum seekers and foreign workers, animal rights, and incarcerations of military conscientious objectors.[16]

Seeing themselves as part of these struggles necessitated an ongoing coverage on a repetitive basis,

Activestills Collective Statement

Activestills collective was established in 2005 by a group of documentary photographers out of a strong conviction that photography is a vehicle for social and political change. We believe in the power of images to shape public attitudes and raise awareness on issues that are generally absent from public discourse. We view ourselves as part of the struggle against all forms of oppression, racism, and violations of the basic right to freedom.

The collective, whose members include Israeli, Palestinian, and international photographers, operates in Palestine/Israel and focuses on social and political documentation, publications, and exhibitions. We work on various topics, including the Palestinian popular struggle against the Israeli occupation, rights of women, LGTBQ, migrants and asylum-seekers, public housing rights, and the struggle against economic oppression.

Israeli public opinion is shaped first and foremost by the mainstream media that are becoming more racist and inciting. The impact of this process is evident in increased public support for violent military operations, racist legislation, and discriminatory policies. We wish to challenge this state of affairs by producing work that exposes inequality and conveys messages that contest oppression and brings the voices and images of those who are invisible and unheard into the public discourse.

Our collective is based upon the belief that mutual work serves each photographer's personal expression, and that joint projects create powerful shared statements. We believe that the photos we take belong to those whose struggles are documented, and so we share our archive with different activist groups. Our photos are often exhibited by local communities at events, conferences, demonstrations, and court hearings. Our images are frequently published in alternative and leading media as well as by human rights, development, and advocacy agencies.

In solidarity with the Palestinian people's struggle for their inalienable rights, Activestills call for:

+ The end of Israel's ongoing illegal occupation and colonization of Palestinian and Syrian territory, and the removal of the Israeli separation wall;
+ The end of institutionalized discrimination against non-Jewish citizens of Israel, and respect for the human rights of all, regardless of ethnicity;
+ Recognition and implementation of the rights of Palestinian refugees according to UN Resolution 194, including the right of return, and
+ Prosecution of those responsible for war crimes.

which led to a strengthened relationship with the communities photographed and to the notion that the images belonged to them.[17] As early as 2006, the collective supplied its images to the struggling communities to be used in press releases, advocacy campaigns, and signs held at demonstrations. Subsequently, Activestills' imagery spread to international groups, various media outlets, and social media networks.[18]

An Image-Event: Activists, Journalists, Witnesses

By defining their photographic work as a form of protest, Activestills share a common position with the South African collective Afrapix, a joint activist group made up of black and white photographers who worked under apartheid during the 1980s. Afrapix termed their political and photographic work as "resistance," or "struggle photography" whose "intention, beyond the aesthetic, is to document the conflicts between oppressors and their victims so as to alert, persuade, and elicit support for the oppressed. The reality captured by the photograph is from the vantage point of the subjugated person."[19] Their collective statement emphasized their distinct position:

> [We] strive not only to advance social documentary photography but also to help in a small way redress the grossly inequitable distribution of skills and unequal access to information … [T]o overcome the blind spots resulting from an internalized apartheid ideology. To see what had not hitherto been seen; to make visible what had been invisible; to find ways of articulating … a reality obscured by government propaganda and mass media.[20]

Although unfamiliar with the work of Afrapix during their early years of operation, a quarter of a century later, Activestills' collective statement echoes a surprisingly similar message: "We believe in the power of images to shape public attitudes and raise awareness on issues that are generally absent from public discourse. We view ourselves as part of the struggle against all forms of oppression, racism, and violations of the basic right to freedom." This motivation turns the photojournalist from an "impartial" and external witness into a participant in the struggle who takes the side of the oppressed.[21] In the case of Activestills, this political framework had practical implications: members consistently accompanied the protests from the activists' side, marching with them and joining them in direct actions, sometimes being the only professional photographers present. This activist position of coverage also extended their documentation to the aftermath of the events, to arrests, house raids, court hearings, visits to injured activists in hospitals, and so forth. Activestills' photo-stream was soon filled with a wide range of images relating to the lives of the struggling communities, bringing forth social and political issues that were not covered or addressed in mainstream media, either for lack of interest due to ratings considerations or as a result of sheer intentional disregard.

In directing their audience's attention also to the "margins" of the events, Activestills' work displaces the photojournalist "decisive-moment" paradigm and challenges the logic and economy of news consumption. This act of constituting the "non-newsworthy-event" as an event reflected the collective's political perspective, as well as their effort to address and make both visible and intelligible the enabling conditions and relations that make a (political) event possible. Working independently, Activestills photographers took care to stay clear of external editorial and commercial pressures, a position which allowed them to remain loyal to a "spectacle-less" aesthetic by giving equal visual and political weight to scenes of hard clashes attended by hundreds and to small static solidarity vigils. Activestills' work can thus be considered as part of the shift, described by Hallas, from "photojournalism to visual activism," and from the documentation of victimhood and destitution to the visualization of the social relationships and networks that underlie the activities of struggling and protesting communities.[22]

The collective's public exhibitions display method in photographic grids functions as an aesthetic and formal embodiment of their political and ethical positions and as a rethinking of the classic journalistic photo-essay. The grid format challenges the viewer to reflect on his/her own engagement with the images, posing questions of narrative and duration, bringing the act of observing closer to a montage-like viewing experience. Refusing to lay the burden of mediation on one iconic frame also echoes the notion of *being part* instead of aiming to "represent" the event or summarizing it for fast utilization. By the same token, one can consider the collective's photo-stream as depicting political struggle as an ongoing, if not never-ending, *event*.

In many ways "struggle photography," and the forms of visual activism that emerged from it, can be seen as offering an apt response to the radical critique that was directed in the 1980s at documentary photography by critics such as Martha Rosler and Allan Sekula.[23] Rosler in particular emphasized the way documentary photography, by focusing on victimhood, empathy, and compassion, was complicit with liberal politics and completely divorced from any program of social reform or revolutionary politics. She argued that by focusing on the one hand on the "brave photographer," and on the other on the feelings of the spectator, but not on the subject of the photograph, traditional documentary photography produced a passive viewer and perpetuated existing power relations in which information about a group of powerless people was addressed to the socially powerful.[24] In this way, documentary photography failed to point out and address the economic, social, and political structures and conditions that enabled inequality in the first place. Rosler thus called for a "real documentary" that will not transcend or substitute "social activism" but will take part in it.[25]

Struggle or activist photography is intrinsically bounded within the structures that it works to expose, depicting its subjects not as "victims," but as struggling political agents within specific historical, geographic, and economic environments. Activestills' work is meant to address the community first—its visual and material needs—while also working to emphasize the specific conditions of life under Israeli occupation and segregation policies. This position is constituted by depicting endless "mundane" photographs of the construction of the Israeli separation wall, military checkpoints and illegal settlements, house demolitions, infinite lines of Palestinians waiting for hours at Israeli checkpoints and so forth. By focusing on the everyday and the "non-event," Activestills aims to expose the material conditions of the occupation and the actions of the communities struggling against it.

Activestills' work demonstrates that within visual activism, the emphasis is not simply on the joint production of images as means of representation, but on their status as tokens of exchange, circulation, and dissemination within specific "visual economies."[26] Thus the images produced by the collective are meant to undermine and disturb existing power relations, while the photographers take an ongoing obligation to look for ways to both generate and propagate resistance against inequality. As Kari Andén-Papadopoulos points out, the "idea of a 'visual economy' signals a shift from an understanding of visual images as illustrations and carriers of information to an appreciation of their power to enact and perform in the social field."[27] She argues that the current global visual economy of digital cameras and smartphones is "turning us all into witnesses of sort," but what fundamentally differentiates the act of seeing from the act of witnessing is "the commitment to an ethics of responsibility."[28] Furthermore, when participating as *citizens* in "camera-witnessing," we are engaged in a corporal-performative act of *being-there*, which is also an "intensely subjective experience," often blurring the lines between the act of witnessing and political action.[29] In this regard, by turning their photographic witnessing *into* political action, Activestills' practices of intervention offer to consider "the photographed" and "the photographer" as positioned along an axis that hosts them both as *ethically response-able* partners in the struggle for political change.

Complementary to that, Ariella Azoulay's critical model of "visual citizenship" also brings the viewer into the frame, suggesting that via the act of "ethical spectatorship," the three—the producer of the image, its subject, and the spectator—share an egalitarian "civil contract of photography."[30] With this term, Azoulay emphasizes that photographs are acts and not exclusively owned objects and, as such, they constitute a shared civil field through which they are constantly reinterpreted and repurposed. Thus photographs can become a space in, and upon which, different kinds of citizenship—not just those that are dispensed or privileged by sovereign state power—can be exposed, contested, and imagined.

There is no doubt that within the "new media ecology," the proliferation of photography via the Internet has complicated matters even further: placing, or rather displacing, the question of political engagement and responsibility to the realm of network spectatorship.

But, at the same time, it also served to create effective advocacy and awareness-building campaigns that were not possible when photographs of injustice and atrocity were circulated only through printed media and TV.

Yet, some scholars have criticized the prevalent belief underlying the practice of human rights organizations that the exposure of violence, atrocity, and injustice will lead to public action against oppression. Thomas Keenan, for example, points out that human rights advocates' tendency to attribute to images the power to "mobilize shame" is based on an Enlightenment ideal regarding the powers of reason and forms of public judgment, what he calls the "If-Then" paradigm: "The lockstep logic of if-then, in which knowledge generates action (reaction) seems to suggest a wishful fusion of an Enlightenment faith in the power of reason and knowledge with the realistic pessimism that retreats to the shame appropriated to the unenlightened."[31]

Keenan argues that this paradigm became untenable in the current moment not only due to overexposure of atrocity images or "compassion fatigue," but because of the fact that in the age of "photo-opportunity," violent acts are not concealed or remain hidden but are performed in front of the camera or for it.[32] By analyzing a "simple gesture"—Serbian looters waving their hands toward the television cameras following an ethnic cleansing operation in the village of Mijalic—Keenan uncovers a historical borderline crossed almost absentmindedly: the exposure of violence is no longer feared by its perpetrators. Hence, the ethical premises of both photojournalists and human rights advocates are in need of serious reconsideration because

> … images, information, and knowledge will never guarantee any outcome, nor will they force or drive any action … Because images are so important, we cannot count on their obviousness, [or] fall for the conceit that information leads ineluctably to actions adequate to the compulsion of the image. *There is no compulsion, only interpretation and reinscription.*[33]

What becomes clear in the midst of this ethical breakdown is that there is no one universal ethical response that can be anticipated. In other words, Keenan's analysis points to an irreducible gap between *if* and *then*: the political responses and effects triggered by powerful images of war, injustice, and human struggle cannot be predetermined in advance because there is no collective *we* that is the ultimate addressee of images.

In many ways, the disposition of Activestills, working under conditions of continuous occupation, encompasses the abovementioned "gap"—its primary scene being one of a crisis of *mutual response-ability*. Not only that different audiences' identification and solidarity cannot be taken for granted, but also that the violations of human rights and atrocities are carried out in broad daylight and for decades. What could it mean then "to strike on behalf of justice" under prolonged conditions of oppression and its ongoing traumatic effects? What is actually being seen, witnessed, and exposed in the work of Activestills? And what possibilities of reinscription and circulation are opened by the collective's political and photographic forms of intervention and collaboration? Answering these questions is what underlies the premises of this book.

Archive and Book

This book was created by inviting contributors to engage with and explore Activestills' online archive, which currently contains over 35,000 photographs from over 200 locations in Palestine/Israel. In histories and theories of photography, the term "archive" is often employed in relation to historical and institutional collections of documents and to issues of testimony and memory. In the 1980s, the term was used by scholars such as Rosalind Krauss, Allan Sekula, and John Tagg to challenge modernist histories of photography with their emphasis on notions of authorship, authenticity, and originality.[34] By focusing on the use of photographs within disciplinary archives as well as public institutions, these writers have demonstrated that the meanings of photographs hinge on historically specific sets of regulatory epistemological conditions. In this sense, the term "archive" was used either to identify a specific institution that stores and preserves documents, or to point to the more general and conceptual system through which knowledge is produced, classified, annotated, and validated.

Yet, what defines Activestills' archive is not its fixed status or regulatory functions, but its openness to perpetual updating and rewriting as an online live streaming archive.[35] It thus functions as an archive of the *present*, vibrating with political potency and urgency as it constantly displays, circulates, and reframes the precariousness of its subjects and their images of relentless protest. It is an *archive of struggles* that in its intentionally non-hierarchical order offers the possibility to align and connect different struggles and at the same time to emphasize their specificity and difference. In this regard, Activestills' archive is *operative* and not simply contemplative; it invites *use* and action, rather than regulated procedures of classification, signification, and memorization. Like Activestills' street exhibitions, it invites its users to join struggles and to *become* a public of egalitarian subjects—it is directed toward the *future*.

In compiling the texts and images for this book, we tried to expose the richness and scale of the work of Activestills and their archive, and at the same time, to underline its operative nature by inviting dialog and collaboration. The book is divided into two parts: the first is titled "Active" and the second "Stills."

The first part includes essays that analyze the collective's practices of intervention and visualization of different struggles in Palestine/Israel and contextualize its work within recent shifts and developments in Middle East media. Ariella Azoulay's photo-essay focuses on the Israeli separation wall and Activestills' role in visualizing and documenting its presence and violent, devastating effects on Palestinians and Israelis, as well as the creative demonstrations against it. Haggai Matar's essay explores the collective's practice of connecting, perceptually and visually, different social and political struggles, and its unique modes of distribution within Israeli alternative media. Ramzy Baroud's essay examines the recent transformations in Arab media in light of the emergence of new media technologies. He contextualizes Activestills' work within these changing conditions and links it to the independent citizen journalism that developed in recent years in the Middle East. Simon Faulkner's essay explores the collective's street exhibitions displayed over the course of the last decade. It analyzes the exhibitions' compositions and forms of display, and the varied responses to them by different publics. This part is followed by conversations between Activestills members and activists regarding the role of photography within specific political struggles. It concludes with short responses of various activists to photographs they selected from the collective's archive.

The second part of the book consists of essays that consider the critical implications of Activestills' work within the history and theory of photography. Vered Maimon's essay focuses on the circulation of the collective's images and on their performative role in the enactment of political forms of agency and solidarity within the context of the Palestinian popular struggle in Bil'in. It shows how within conditions of precariousness, the survival of images, their active and fluctuating modes of reinscription and transformation become inseparable from strategies of survival. Meir Wigoder's essay addresses the reflective aspect of the collective's work, which includes records not only of their public exhibitions, but also of displays within the actual sites of struggle. His essay analyzes images where the photographs' subjects become the spectators of their own struggle and points to the way acts of viewing contribute to the creation of "communities of touch." Sharon Sliwinski's essay focuses on two series of photographic portraits initiated by Activestills: one of asylum seekers in Holot detention center, and one of the Women in Black activists. The effort to make the illegally detained subjects visible, the essay argues, not only serves to illuminate the political disregard toward them by denying them basic human rights, but also becomes an act that questions the authority of discriminatory laws. Ruthie Ginsburg's essay examines the collective's insistence on continuous presence, "being there," in protests, and on the close connections with the photographed communities in relation to photographic indexicality. Her essay reconsiders the notion of indexicality through an examination of the dual and sometimes conflicting roles of Activestills members as both activists and photographers. This section of the book ends with reflections about their work by Activestills members.

We hope that with the images and essays featured in this book, Activestills' *archive of struggles* will reach more publics and contribute to the continuous regeneration of imaginative strategies for the visualization of the political sphere, while pointing to new possibilities for the enactment of collective forms of agency.

1. Eduardo Cadava and Paola Cortes-Rocca, "Notes on Love and Photography," *October* 116 (spring 2006): 16.

2. Anarchists Against the Wall (AAtW) participation in the Palestinian popular struggle protests in the West Bank started in the village of Mas'ha in 2003 and then spread to other villages. For an excellent account of the joint unarmed struggle in Palestine see Maxine Kaufman-Lacusta, *Refusing to be Enemies — Palestinian and Israeli Nonviolent Resistance to the Israeli Occupation* (Reading, UK: Ithaca Press, 2011). For an account on the influence of AAtW on Israeli public opinion and media see http://972mag.com/anarchists-the-most-important-activists-on-the-jewish-israeli-left/50269/, accessed 27.1.2016. For a critical account of the Palestinian-Israeli joint struggle, see Judith Butler, "Palestine, State Politics and the Anarchist Impasse," in *The Anarchist Turn*, eds. Jacob Blumenfeld, Chiara Bottici, and Simon Critchley (London: Pluto Press, 2013), 203-23.

3. As with most aspects of Israel's systematic oppression of Palestinians, the words used to describe the Israeli separation wall matter. Supporters frequently call it the "security fence" to promote the myth that it protects Israeli lives and to diminish connotations of a physically imposing structure. But the wall can claim no credit as a security measure for the simple fact that it was never completed. It is easily circumvented by thousands of Palestinians who enter present-day Israel on a routine basis as unauthorized workers. Supporters of the wall once claimed it stopped attacks on Israelis. Since such attacks once again increased in the fall of 2015, those claims have been replaced with calls to complete the wall. Critics use a variety of terms including "apartheid wall," "segregation wall," or "annexation wall." Both of these latter terms are more accurate in that they describe how the wall actually functions—enforcing discriminatory policies and confiscating land. Some eighty-five percent of its route was built inside the West Bank, not on the internationally recognized border or Green Line, which is why the International Court of Justice declared it illegal in 2004. In this book, we prefer the term "Israeli separation wall" for several reasons. First and foremost, it is a structure imposed by Israeli forces. It is important to note, however, that while it does often separate Palestinians from Israelis, it also separates Palestinians from other Palestinians and from their own land.

4. In 2005, the local council of Bil'in hired Israeli human rights lawyer Michael Sfard to represent the village in a petition to the Israeli High Court of Justice. On 4 September 2007, the Court ordered the government to change the route of the Israeli separation wall near Bil'in. The Israeli Defense Ministry said it would respect the ruling and in 2011 began dismantling a section of the barrier in order to relocate it along an alternative route.

5. The most famous example was the "Bus 300" affair, in which four Palestinian militants hijacked an Israeli bus and its passengers, intending to negotiate for the release of Palestinian prisoners. *Hadashot* newspaper was the only media outlet to disobey the Israeli military censor in publishing Alex Levac's photograph of one of the Palestinian hijackers, who was arrested during the Israeli police and Shin-Bet forces takeover operation and, soon after, beaten to death in a nearby desolate area. Levac's photo proved that the Israeli authorities had lied to the public, trying to hide the fact that two of the militants were executed by the Israeli forces without trial.

6. Roger Hallas, "Photojournalism, NGOs, and the New Media Ecology," in *Sensible Politics: The Visual Culture of Nongovernmental Activism*, eds. Meg McLagan and Yates McKee (New York: Zone Books, 2012), 99. The important photo agencies covering the Middle East are Getty Images, Reuters, Associated Press, AFP, and EPA.

7. Julian Stallabrass stresses that the proliferation of citizen journalism and amateur imagery added an economic blow to trained photojournalists: "Economically pressed news organisations often prefer to provide cameras (but little training) to willing locals rather than fly out professionals to a scene": Julian Stallabrass, "The Power and Impotence of Images," in *Memory of Fire: Images of War and the War of Images*, ed. Julian Stallabrass (Brighton, UK: Photoworks, 2013), 43.

8. For an extensive research and visual analysis of the work of these organizations, see Ruthie Ginsburg, *And You Will Serve as Eyes to Us: Israeli Human Rights Organizations as Seen through the Camera's Eye* (Tel Aviv: Resling Press, 2014) [Hebrew]. There were, of course, Palestinian and international organizations working at the same time. To mention just a few major ones: Palestine Monitor (Exposing Life Under Occupation), Al-Haq (Defending Human Rights in Palestine since 1979), Human Rights Watch, Amnesty International.

9. Ibid., 78 (translated from the Hebrew by Shiraz Grinbaum, emphasis added).

10. The term "active non-seeing mechanism" was coined by Ruchama Marton and Dalit Baum; see Ruchama Marton and Dalit Baum, "Transparent Wall, Opaque Gates," in *Against the Wall: Israel's Barrier to Peace*, ed. Michael Solkin (New York and London: The New Press, 2005), 214.

11. We view Activestills' work as formulating a different position than the one of "participatory photography." The latter assumes that giving underprivileged subjects cameras as a means of self-representation yields a direct or "authentic" witnessing position. Yet, as recent discussions have shown, "participatory photography" carries its own ethical risks, among them, the replication of prescribed political, discursive, and perceptual binary positions through which excluded "non-subjects" are defined solely as victims rather than as active political subjects. See, for example, Sam Gregory, "Cameras Everywhere: Ubiquitous Video Documentation of Human Rights, New Forms of Video Advocacy, and Considerations of Safety, Security, Dignity and Consent," *Journal of Human Rights* 2:2 (2010): 191–207. See also his "The Participatory Panopticon and Human Rights: Witness's Experience Supporting Video Advocacy and Future Possibilities," in McLagan and McKee (eds.), *Sensible Politics*, 517–49; Margaret Olin, "Looking through Their Eyes," in her *Touching Photographs* (Chicago, IL and London: University of Chicago Press, 2012), 131–58.

12. The Alternative Information Center (AIC) is a joint Palestinian-Israeli organization reporting about human rights violations and promoting responsible cooperation between Palestinians and Israelis in order to challenge the prevailing notions and practices of separation between the two communities, see http://www.alternativenews.org. *Electronic Intifada* is an independent online news publication and educational resource focusing on Palestine, see https://electronicintifada.net. *+972 Magazine* is a blog-based web magazine that is jointly owned by a group of journalists, bloggers, and photographers whose goal is to provide fresh, original, on-the-ground reporting and analysis of events in Palestine/Israel, see http://972mag.com. In 2014, the group initiated a similar Hebrew language website, see http://mekomit.co.il/.

13. It is also important to note that during the first few months of protests in Bil'in, the local popular committee in the village set up a website in which activists reported weekly about the protests. Other villages and protesting groups, such as the International Solidarity Movement, have created similar information databases online. See http://palsolidarity.org/, https://nilin.wordpress.com/.

14. This collective signature is still used to this day in Activestills' exhibitions and street displays where each image is marked with the collective's graphic watermark.

15. Kaufman-Lacusta, *Refusing to be Enemies*, 202.

16. Activestills' first book *"We Never Finished 48": The Continuing Campaign of Internal Displacement in Israel/Palestine* (2011), focused on displacement of Palestinian communities in different villages and cities within the Green Line, and in the West Bank and Gaza. The book was done in collaboration with the Israeli Committee Against House Demolitions (ICAHD). Download link: https://athens.indymedia.org/media/old/activestills_displacement.pdf.

17. Activestills' ongoing coverage extended to protests in the West Bank villages of Bil'in, Ni'lin, Nabi Saleh, Al-Ma'asara, Kafr Qaddum, Silwad, Al-Walaja, and many more.

18. As of 2015, the collective's diverse archive has been used by dozens of human rights organizations in Palestine/Israel and abroad as well as by independent and mainstream media, educational institutions, and countless activist communities (to which the collective has consistently allowed free access to its images). To name just a few of these bodies and communities: Popular Struggle Coordination Committee, Al-Araqib village, B'Tselem—The Israeli Information Center for Human Rights in the Occupied Territories, Physicians for Human Rights-Israel, Adalah—The Legal Center for Arab Minority Rights in Israel, Amnesty International, The Association for Civil Rights in Israel, Coalition of Women for Peace, Public Housing Forum, Worker's Hotline, Hotline for Refugees and Migrants, Rabbis for Human Rights, Negev Coexistence Forum for Civil Equality, Breaking the Silence, Public Committee Against Torture in Israel, Yesh-Din, and activist groups such as the international network in support of the BDS (Boycott, Divestment and Sanctions), AAtW, Tarabut—Arab-Jewish Movement for Social and Political Change, Ta'ayush, the Refuser Solidarity Movement, Women in Black and 269Life for Veganism in Israel. Hundreds if not thousands of independent bloggers, researchers, artists, and filmmakers have also made use of this archive. Activestills started using social media in 2010 and currently have over 16,000 followers on Facebook and 12,000 Twitter followers.

19. David L. Krantz, "Politics and Photography in Apartheid South Africa," *History of Photography* 32:4 (winter 2008): 290.

20. Ibid., 293–4.

21. For more examples of political photography collectives, see: SUB photography cooperative funded in Buenos Aires in 2004, http://www.sub.coop; NAR Photos, a collective based in Turkey established in 2003, http://www.narphotos.net/AnaSayfa; and Ruido photo collective based in Spain established in 2005, http://www.ruidophoto.com/photo/?p=434. All these collectives share a non-profit approach to their work with a self-articulated political agenda supported by all the members.

22. Hallas, "Photojournalism, NGOs and the New Media Ecology," 101.

23. See Martha Rosler, "In, Around, and Afterthoughts (On Documentary Photography)," in *Decoys and Disruptions: Selected Writings*, 1975–2001 (Cambridge, MA: MIT Press, 2004), 152–206; Allan Sekula, "Dismantling Modernism, Reinventing Documentary (Notes on the Politics of Representation)," *The Massachusetts Review* 19:4 (winter 1978): 859–83. For a recent excellent reconsideration of this critique, see Sharon Sliwinski, *Human Rights in Camera* (Chicago, IL and London: University of Chicago Press, 2011).

24. Rosler, "In, Around, and Afterthoughts (On Documentary Photography)," 179.

25. Ibid., 196.

26. The term "visual economy" was elaborated in Deborah Poole, *Vision, Race, and Modernity: A Visual Economy of the Andean Image World* (Princeton, NJ: Princeton University Press, 1997).

27. Kari Andén-Papadopoulos, "Citizen Camera-Witnessing: Embodied Political Dissent in the Age of 'Mediated Mass Self-Communication'," *New Media Society* 16 (2014): 755.

28. Ibid., 756.

29. Ibid., 766.

30. Ariella Azoulay, *The Civil Contract of Photography*, trans. Rela Mazali and Ruvik Danieli (New York: Zone Books, 2012).

31. Thomas Keenan, "Mobilizing Shame," *The South Atlantic Quarterly* 103:2/3 (spring/summer 2004): 437.

32. Ibid., 438–9.

33. Thomas Keenan, "Publicity and Indifference (Sarajevo on Television)," *PMLA* 117:1 (Jan. 2002): 114 (emphasis added).

34. See Rosalind Krauss, "Photography's Discursive Spaces," in *The Originality of the Avant-Garde and Other Modernist Myths* (Cambridge, MA: MIT Press, 1986), 131–50; Allan Sekula, "The Body and the Archive," *October* 39 (winter 1986): 3–64; John Tagg, *The Burden of Representation* (London: Macmillan Press, 1988).

35. On the difference between classical archives and digital ones, see Wolfgang Ernst, *Digital Memory and the Archive* (Minneapolis and London: University of Minnesota Press, 2013).

{Opposite page}
A Palestinian youth waves the Palestinian flag during a protest against the Israeli separation wall in Beit Sira, West Bank, 16.3.2006

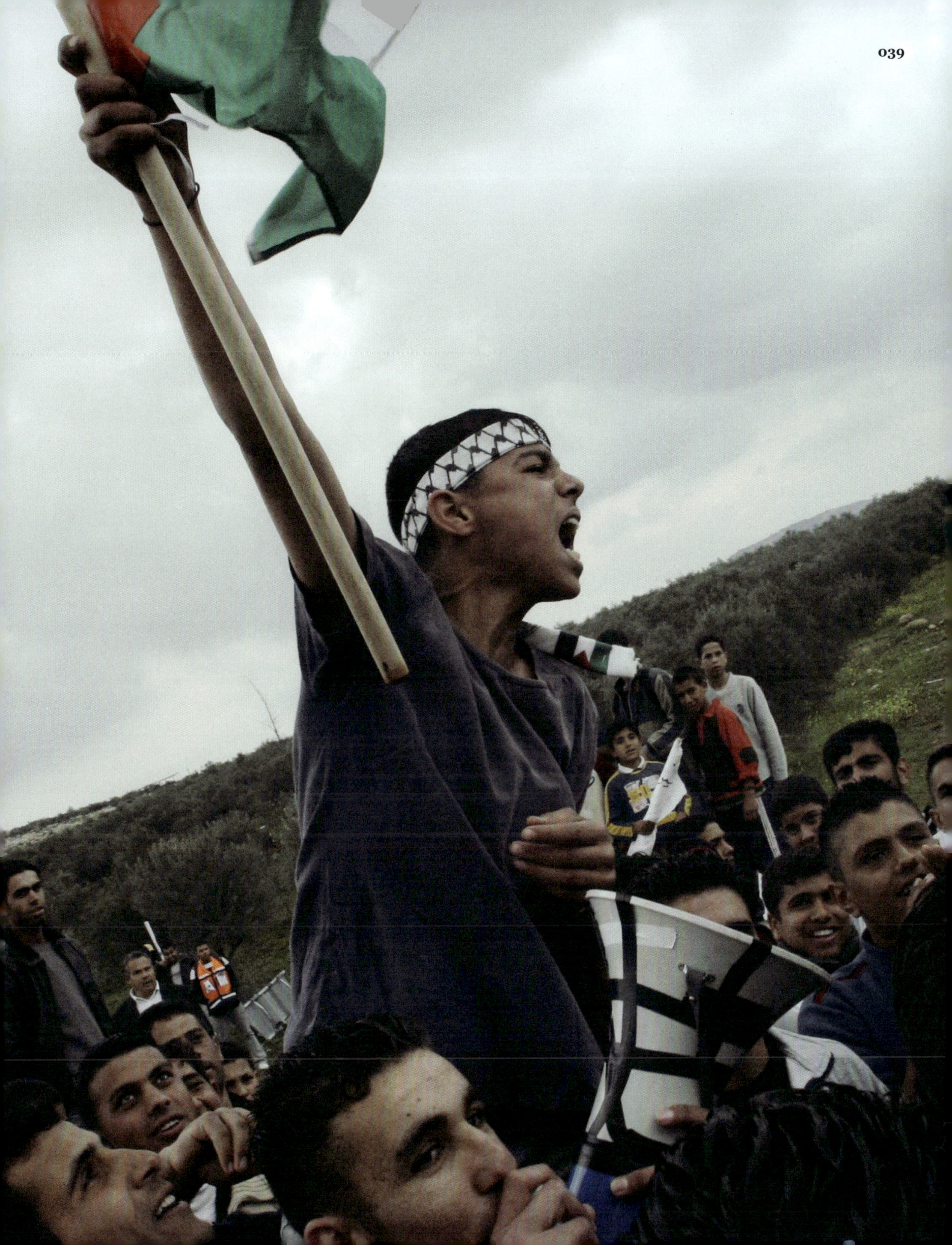

Active

The Visual Rhetoric of Dissent: Practices of Intervention, Political Agency, and Sites of Struggle

Bil'in, West Bank 22.2.2008

Palestinian, Israeli, and international protesters run from tear gas shot at them by the Israeli Army during the weekly demonstration against the Israeli separation wall.

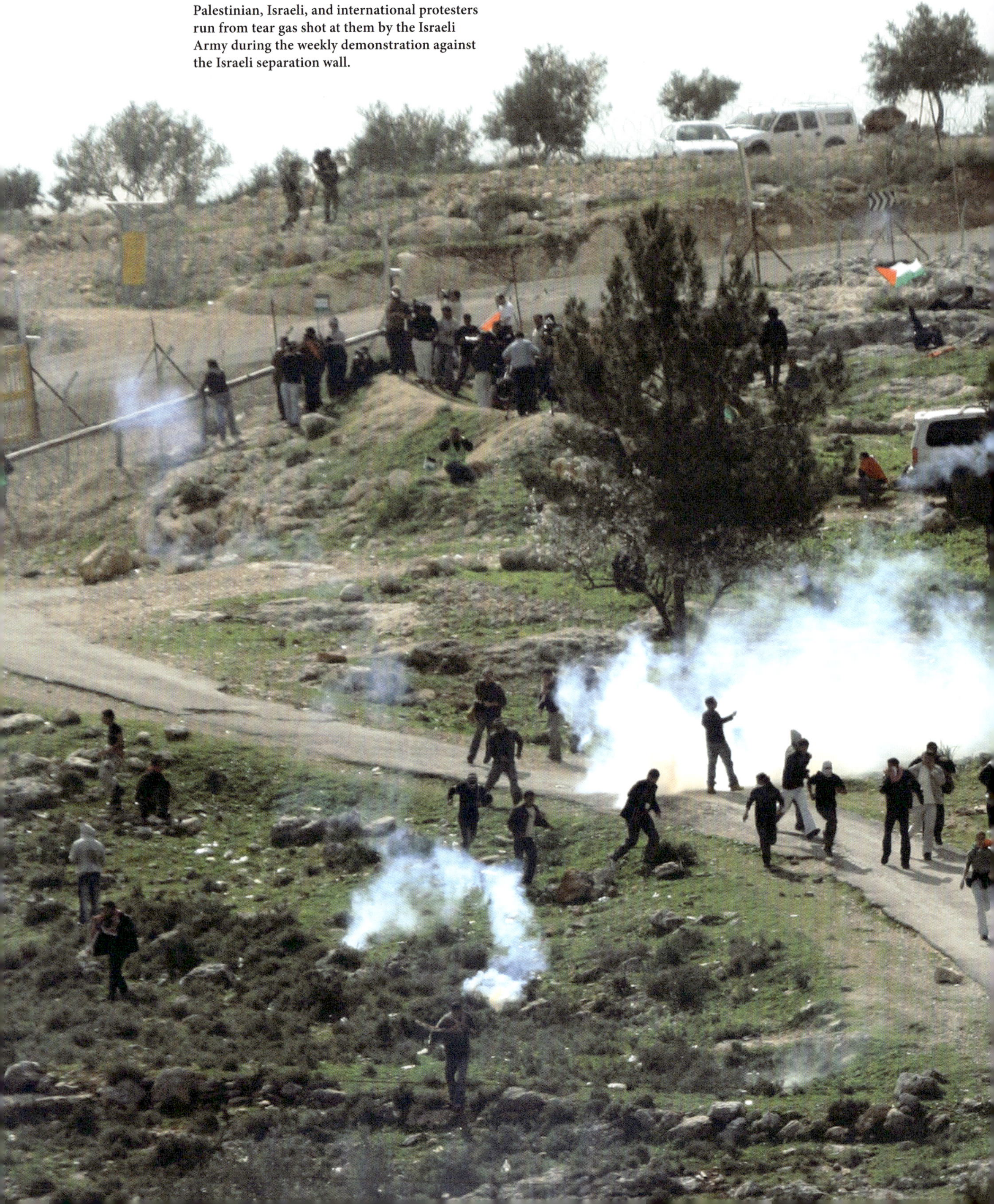

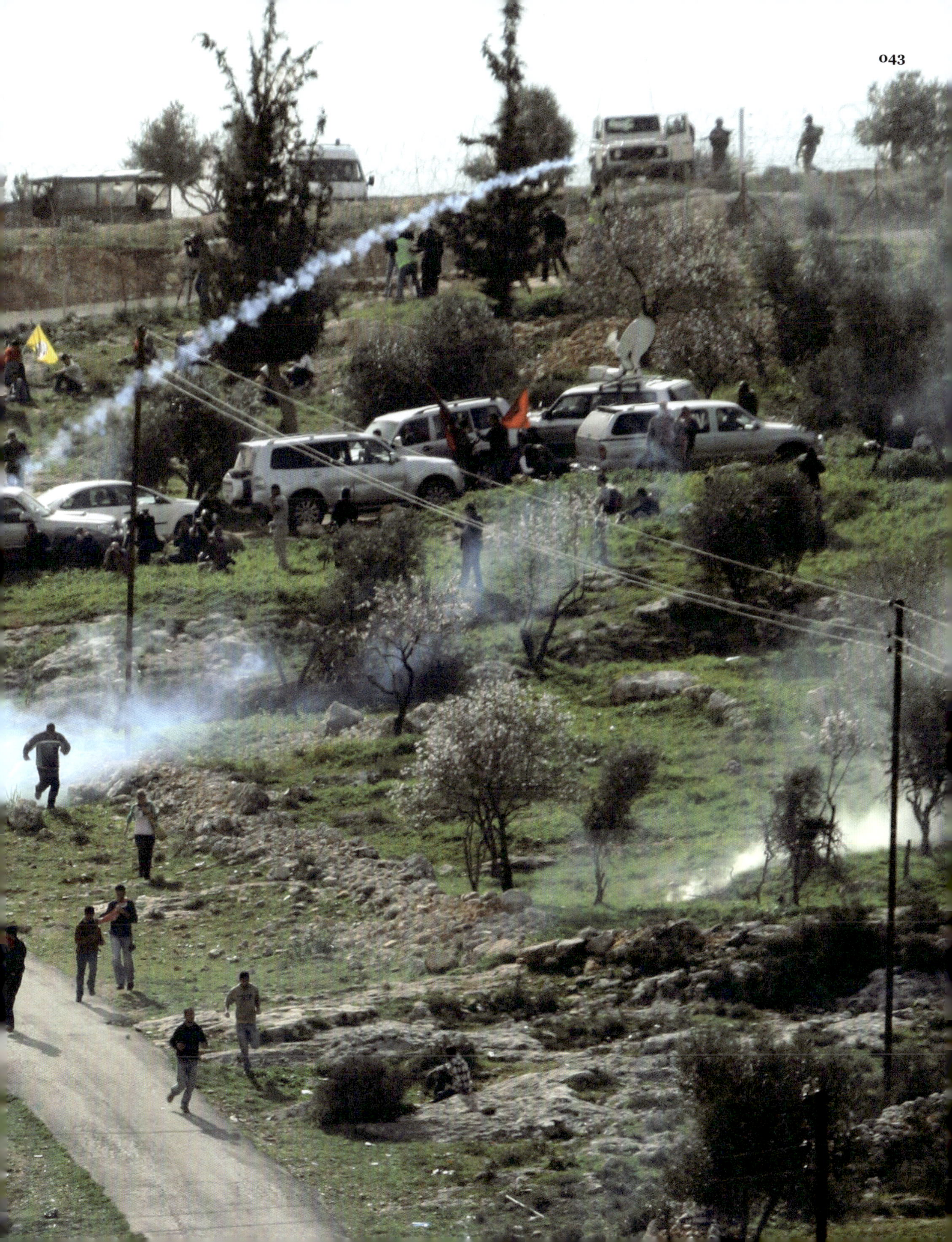

Activestills' Photographic Archive: A Common Treasure

Ariella Azoulay

The cemented violence known as the Israeli separation wall is not the monster; it is merely its tail.[1] However, it is quite big for a tail, big enough not to slip out of people's sight. And even though it stands still in broad daylight, many people pass by it without shouting "monster!" Monster is the word used to describe an unusual creature whose appearance, mode of being, and acting deviate from the accepted norms. Calling something a monster is sometimes a way to awaken it. The monster should be roused, not because it doesn't bite when it seems to be sleeping but because there are too many people who behave as if it does not bite and, with the many norms established by the Israeli regime of occupation from which it does not deviate, it is no wonder that people have become inured to it and can barely recognize its monstrosity. Awakening it is a way of forcing it to stop passing for something else and make it appear, not only in the eyes of the victims it explicitly targets who never, not even for a second, confused it with something else in all its monstrosity, as part of larger state apparatuses for which it functions merely as the tail. The monster, of which the wall is a part (whatever it is exactly and regardless of its size), continues to pass for many other things that are casually discussed and debated in common languages, in national and international forums, and by people in official positions of authority. We must say what it is, clearly and simply: the Israeli separation wall is part of a monster that not only deprives Palestinians of their right to move freely, to access their workplaces, lands, institutions, and facilities, but it is part of a larger apparatus that consolidates the continuous expulsion of Palestinians from their homeland and the differential inclusion of those of them who remained in Palestine or were added to the body politic of its governed as non-citizens in 1967, when more areas of what was Palestine were colonized. In this sense, qualifying the wall as a "separation" wall dismisses the very political principle on which the Israeli regime is built—Palestinians are included in the body politic of the governed, but they are governed differentially. The imaginary separation imposed and nurtured by the Israeli state propaganda apparatuses is so strong that Jewish citizens could refer to separation as a reality rather than as the devastating project that they are engaged in implementing against people with whom they are governed, i.e., Palestinians. The photographic archive produced by members of Activestills over one decade is an unprecedented opportunity to study the tensions between the reality in which people live, act, and interact with each other, and the devastating political project of separation whose implementation requires more and more violence.

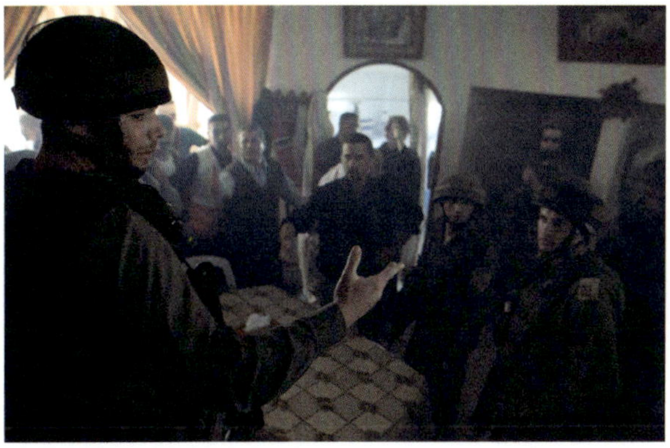

Fig. 1. Jayyous, West Bank, 13.2.2009

A look inside a Palestinian home makes it less abstract [**Fig. 1**]. *But, is this a home or a military post? The army needed an outpost, and this house was in just the right place to serve this "military" need. Its height and proximity to the wall turned it into a strategic point for snipers who could hit anyone in the crowd taking part in the weekly demonstration against the wall. The photograph was taken a few minutes after the soldiers had entered the house and a few minutes before they clashed with its residents and ransacked their living space. In the photo, one can see how Palestinians, together with international activists and Israelis (some of them members of Activestills), insist on not letting the soldiers' invasion of a private space be dominated by military logic, in other words, carried out behind closed doors without anyone else able to see. If this home is no longer a private space, at least they are there to make sure that this event will be made public. They refuse to be deprived further of their right and ability to accurately frame the act of this invasion for what it is: violence, with them as the target, not because of something they did, but, simply, because of who they are.*

The wall does not separate two communities living on either side. Rather, it differentiates between them. Most, if not all, Palestinian declarations and actions are treated as suspect and as a kind of terror. This is not surprising since, by definition, any claim to abolish differential rule actually means the abolition of Jewish supremacy. The monstrosity of the wall is not only because of what it does to Palestinians, but also because of what it does to Jewish Israelis: it naturalizes their privilege and diminishes their encounters with those who are its direct victims, and thereby damages their ability to recognize their role as the perpetrators of its despicable effect. If people were struck by the monstrosity of the wall, less paperwork—and fewer photographs—would have been necessary in order to persuade different persons in the chain of command to either forbid its presence altogether, or at the very least, to change its location in order that it be able to impose only the tiniest bit of its tail.

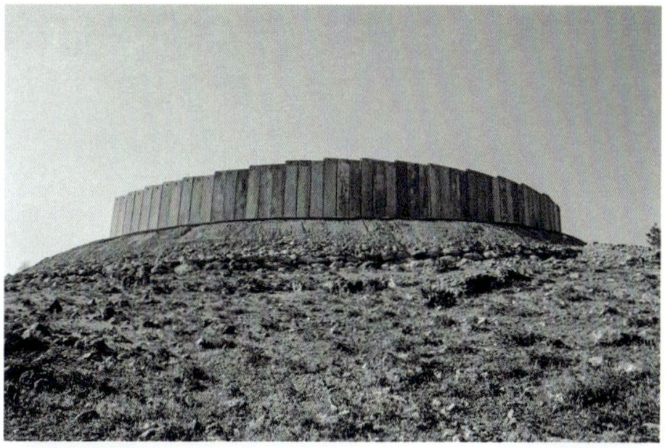

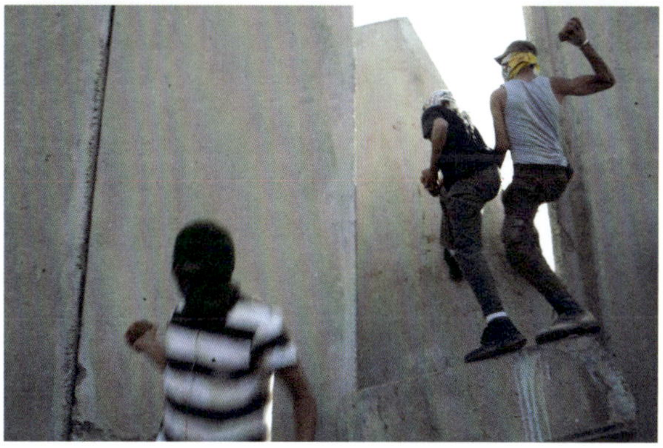

Fig. 2. Abu Dis, near Al-Quds University, West Bank, 2004 / **Fig. 3.** Ni'lin, West Bank, 6.11.2009

In this photograph, the wall appears curled up in a sleeping position that makes it hard to imagine the bully it really is [**Fig. 2**]. *Poised ceremoniously like a crown atop a head, it reveals little about the nature of its* *cruelty, or about how it functions, or what its mission or role is. This photograph is hard to comprehend at first since it does not convey an existing situation but rather, it presents a psychic image of some of the desires and expectations involved in the wall's construction and euphemistic name, "the separation fence." Palestinians are absent from the photo, assumed to be contained within its circular shape, kept obedient behind it, subservient to its authority. But as other photographs often reveal, instead of absent, the Palestinians are present, refusing to obey the set of commands the wall represents: "Do not approach," "Do not climb," "Do not pass through," "Do not infiltrate," "Do not damage," "Do not touch"* [**Fig. 3**]. *Moreover, since they recognize it for the monster that it is, they challenge it, and take joy in seeing how they can make it betray its role. Rather than a firm and solid wall that can stop them, they find ways to go through it, to transform it into a platform for the performance of their refusal to be confined by its violent presence, and disregard of its illegitimate authority. Regardless of whether photographers or spectators are present, or the time of the day, Palestinians act individually or in groups against its violence, making concrete gains such as farming their fields, or more abstract ones such as being with their peers and realizing together their ideas of freedom and sharing.*

No matter how many times its violence is made visible, whether by infographics, photographs, or actions, an individual image can never provide the ultimate and decisive proof that this is indeed a monster, or even the tail of one. The Israeli separation wall does not consist solely of cement panels and blocks. It consists of piles and piles of archival documents written in the evil language of the law. The brutality of the wall engenders the imperial archive, its very essence, if it would not produce that excessive amount of paper to nurture it. This is what makes it an imperial monster. The species of imperial monster is known for never having to be pulled out of a drawer, not because it excels in hiding, but because it never existed in a drawer hidden from people's inspection. It has always lain out in the open, growing bigger and bigger with every new document that feeds it. Hence, it cannot suddenly appear and surprise people with its peculiar form. It is the people who will suddenly realize that they were the ones who had ignored the monster that was always out in the open, not because it was sometimes unveiled and other times cloaked, but because even though some recognized it, they did not. Using the term "monster" to speak about imperial creatures is an effort perhaps as futile as others that preceded it to convey in images or in words on paper, the abnormality of a monster that is not different from the conditions that created it, conditions that affect the capacity to recognize it since its contours are blurred. An imperial monster cannot be either visible or not visible; moreover, visibility cannot be assumed to be its quality. The use of the term "monster" is not intended metaphorically, but rather as a denotation: Here is an imperial creature, present, manifest, *demonstrable*, when called by its name. Under the imperial condition, monsters are far from extraordinary. Their existence should be noted and their forms drawn and redrawn until others can recognize not only the monsters themselves, but those who serve as their spokespersons and interlocutors.

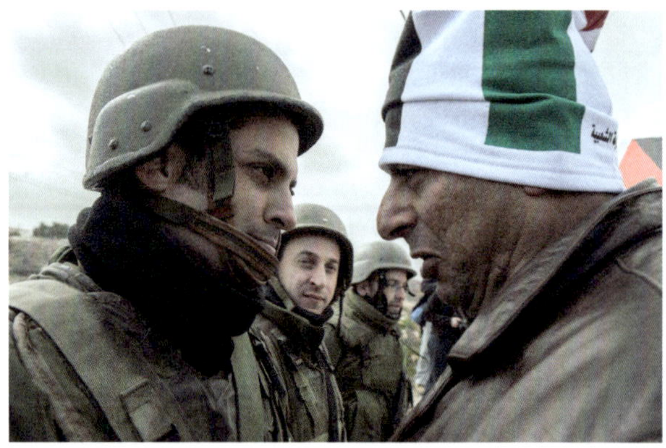

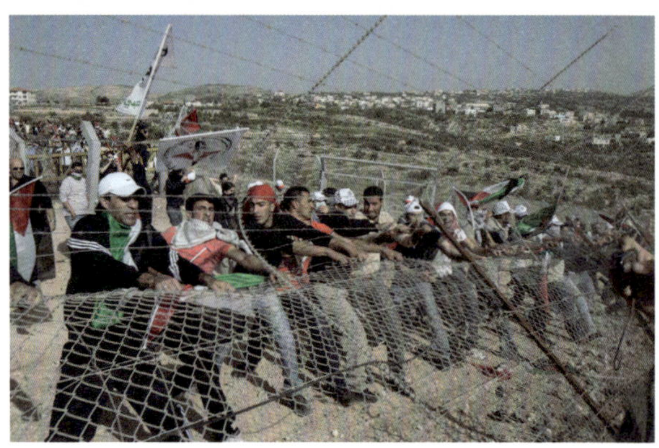

Fig. 4. Al-Ma'asara, West Bank, 27.1.2012 / **Fig. 5.** Bil'in, West Bank, 19.2.2010

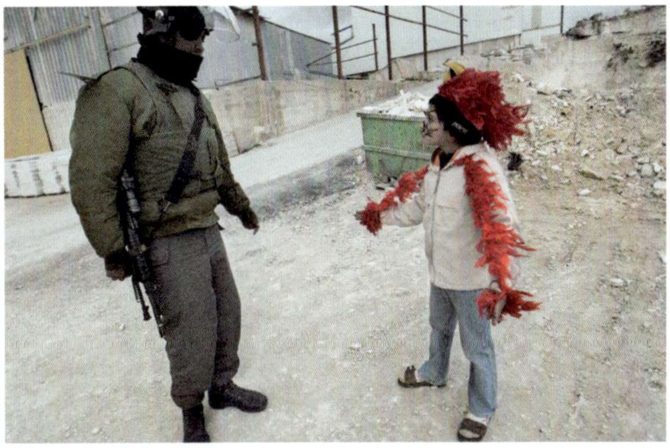

Fig. 6. Al-Ma'asara, West Bank, 27.1.2012

This photo captures a face-to-face encounter between a soldier, one among many in the line, and a Palestinian [**Fig. 4**]. *While a still photograph deprives us from hearing the actual words the two may have exchanged, we can assume that they did not see things eye to eye. We can even speculate that it was all about the monster: the soldier denying its essence and existence and the Palestinian denying it and the soldier's authority. The Palestinian refuses to be stopped by the monster's presence embodied in the soldier and moves closer. The Palestinian is unarmed; approaching the soldier can endanger his life. The soldier is armed and he also has the support of the other armed soldiers next to him. Once the Palestinian succeeds in standing close to the soldier, a certain balance of power is installed and their assigned roles are somewhat disturbed. Though they are so near to each other, there is an unbridgeable gap that separates them, but also compels them to keep their emotions in check as they stare each other down. And while such face-to-face confrontations do occur from time to time, they are never ordinary. The soldier refrains from physical violence; the Palestinian refrains from responding violently to the violence that is constantly being perpetrated against him even when a particular soldier refrains from adding more. Despite their physical proximity, the soldier does not seem to grasp what the Palestinian is trying to explain to him either through his words or by his presence. The Palestinian's clearly visible frustration stems not only from the fact that he and other Palestinians are being blocked from moving freely and that they are being deprived of their rights, but also from the fact that this basic fact is not clear to others. In another photo, a few dozen Palestinians are seen holding a bit of the fence in their hands and in their frustration and rage are moving it back and forth, as if, at some point, through their orchestrated movements, it will be uprooted* [**Fig. 5**]. *They are aware that dismantling part of the fence will be met with punishment, but their action is not a matter of reasonable weighing of pros and cons; it is a performance of freedom to publicly state that this is a monster and they are not afraid of it. And if what they are saying is not understood, they are not afraid of showing that it is a monster. Once they run through the breach in the fence, like birds freed from a cage, they expect others, though perhaps not the soldiers themselves, to see the soldiers as the keepers not of the law but of the prison from which they are fleeing. Dressed up as a bird, the child may be more confident as he provokes the soldier, asking him: "Don't you see what I see? Can't you feel what I feel?"* [**Fig. 6**].

In the thousands of demonstrations against the Israeli separation wall, it is never just about the wall; it is also about the monstrosity it represents, and its imperial particularity for not being immediately discernible as such. Rather than asking what are the conditions necessary for the wall to be seen as an imperial monster—as if dealing with an imperial monster were some kind of abstract situation—we should ask, what are the imperial conditions that enable such monsters to lie in the sun, to flourish, expand, and remain acceptable, within the accepted norms? To answer this, however, would require one to dwell on the transformation of imperial norms into "accepted norms" and the role of liberal citizens in maintaining them.

Palestinians and those who join them in their struggle know that the monster's tail is just one element in the imperial apparatus of differentiation that is constantly pushing them to the other side of not just the physical wall, but the cognitive wall at which they are left practically alone in recognizing its monstrosity. When, from time to time, a window of opportunity opens, they appeal to international law, but they are not unaware of the role of international law in the imperial

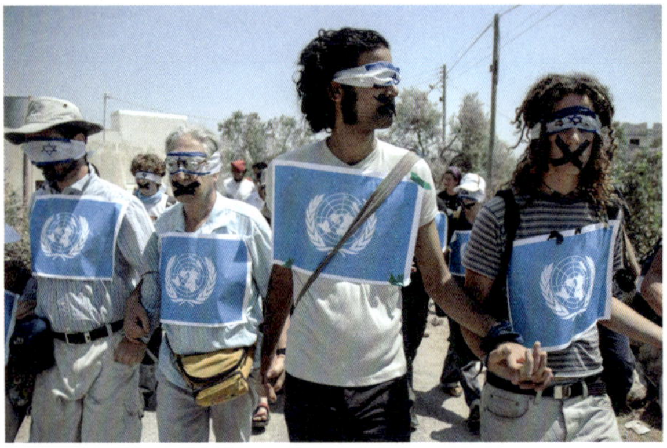

Fig. 7. Bil'in, West Bank, 26.8.2005

conditions that render such visible monsters invisible. Not only were Palestinians already betrayed by international law and the international community in 1949 when the Jewish state, believed to be peace-loving, was admitted as a member to the United Nations, after already expelling the majority of the Palestinians from their lands, but now they know that their absurd situation of being "stateless" while being governed by a state—Israel—is part of the logic of international law, and this logic is part of the imperial legacy against which they struggled previously during the British occupation.[2] *In this photo* [Fig. 7], *the activists' mouths are covered with black tape, signifying the value of their claims, which are dismissed as if never uttered; their eyes are covered by the flag of the Israeli nation-state, signifying the power of the Israeli state to provide the lens through which Palestinians would be perceived—always as a threat from the outside, even though it is the state that expels them and has positioned them there; on their bodies the symbol of the United Nations, whose resolutions, even when in their favor, work against them.*

Imperial monsters are not distinct creatures but the embodiments of their condition of possibility. If and when they are discernible, it is often only briefly and partially; first, because they are often experienced as part of given conditions, and second, because those who recognize them and protest against their presence, are incriminated for committing "ideological crimes" and organizing and participating in "illegal demonstrations," and are dispersed, arrested, and exposed to violence. Even when these monsters first emerge, as in the form of the Israeli separation wall, they lack the traits of inconceivable creatures whose presence surprises and scares, since in so many ways they, or their body parts, have always been there, assimilated into accepted norms or tools. Not only was the State of Israel constituted through expulsion followed by a fencing project, but even prior to that, Palestine itself was a product of imperial partitions, delineated from other areas that were divided and shared among different imperial powers. The imperial principles upon which an international organization like the United Nations is constituted has prevented the acts and crimes of nation-states from being dealt with as they should—subject to disruption and sanctions by the international community—and instead, has enabled them to be recognized as legitimate actions and the policies conducted by a sovereign state as a mode of self-defense.

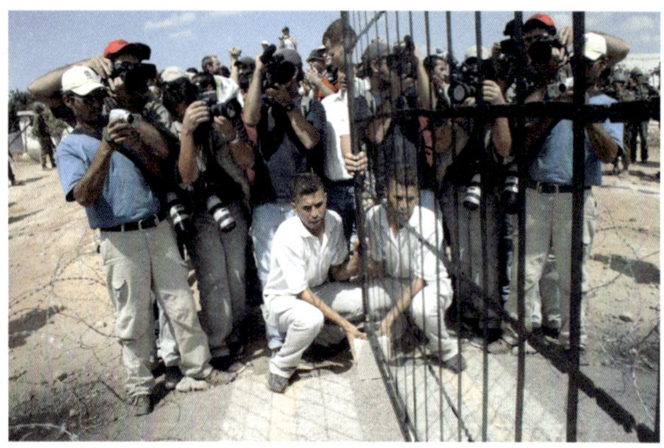

Fig. 8. Bil'in, West Bank, 12.9.2005

The imperial language that prioritizes sovereign state rights is the language through which citizens in these states acquire their civil skills. From time to time, Palestinians expect these citizens, whom they often meet in their role as soldiers, to look at themselves from the outside, to be horrified by their own image as they submit themselves to imperial logic and are made indifferent to their complicity in depriving others of what should be basic rights of citizenship and of acting and interacting as co-citizens with each other. In this photo, taken in July 2005, Mohammed Khatib, one of the leaders of Bil'in's weekly protests, holds a large mirror in front of Israeli soldiers [**Fig. 8**]. *The mirror is meant to show what Jewish Israelis fail to see when they face the Palestinians they oppress: seeing themselves as oppressors. The mirror is held up to the face of the Israeli soldiers, forcing them to recognize their own role in the imperial order. It is a mode of address that expects the soldiers, who do not share their language, to be engaged in the conversation. Nevertheless, it is part of a language that I call the civil language of revolution, which Palestinians elaborate among themselves and others, for whom their claims resonate with meaning.*

The different moments when this language is used are not epoch-making events. They are rather like opportunities for this language to be enriched by local dialects and shared with more people involved in the conversation. This language consists of statements, practices, gestures, rules, and civil grammar that contest their differential inclusion. The Activestills photographic archive is a treasure for studying this language—for ten years, its members have insisted on consistently being there with their cameras, alongside those for whom there was never a doubt regarding the monstrosity of the imperial state apparatus and the necessity to claim its withdrawal and aspire for its reversibility so as to enable the renewal of other options it had eliminated. The photographers join the conversation by participating in practicing this language in public, by rehearsing the possibilities to see the world together from a non-imperial perspective. This civil language emerged centuries ago, with the beginning of imperialism and the imposition of a differential body politic. Since photography's invention, photographs have been used as the "written" or durable support of these dialects. These dialects form a political alternative to the violent language of the nation-state, and when enough people are engaged in using them, sooner or later, they are violently dispersed by the sovereign power of the state in such a way that agents of the law and the press treat them as the violators or rioters. With the invention of photography, this language has flourished, its speakers benefiting from more and more occasions to speak it, to conduct conversations about different aspects of these imperial apparatuses, without reiterating the imperial point of view that intimidates them and may sow doubt in their conviction that what is called "democracy" today is a form of organized violence.

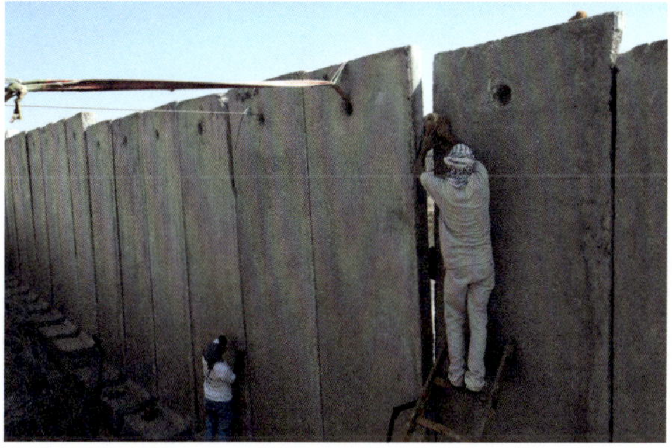

Fig. 9. Ni'lin, West Bank, 23.10.2009

Only two Palestinians are visible in the frame, but from what is visible in the upper part of the photo, we can infer that what we see is a complex homemade engineering mechanism for dismantling the wall that requires the involvement of many hands [**Fig. 9**]. *Reiterated here is the same gesture of which we have visual documentation from as far back as the eighteenth century, a gesture that enabled the many to come together and invent ways to use ropes in order to topple the sculptures of kings whose power they contested. The photo conveys, at once, the power of those performing the act and the finitude of power of those who claim their rule to be absolute.*

My argument that the civil language is contemporary to the implementation of imperial language is not a historical argument but an ontological one.[3] It is based on the assumption that people, though they may have been belittled by imperial agents, have always resisted being oppressed, even if it was only by refusing to think in the way the imperial language interpellated them. With the help of photographic archives such as the one created by Activestills, this argument can be historically proven by negation. Had Activestills been present in 1948 in the way they are today, we would have been able to "hear" this civil language spoken by many Palestinians who were deprived of their lands, rights, and goods, as well as by some Jews who, at the time, could have easily recognized the violence being perpetrated in order that they could become lords of the land.

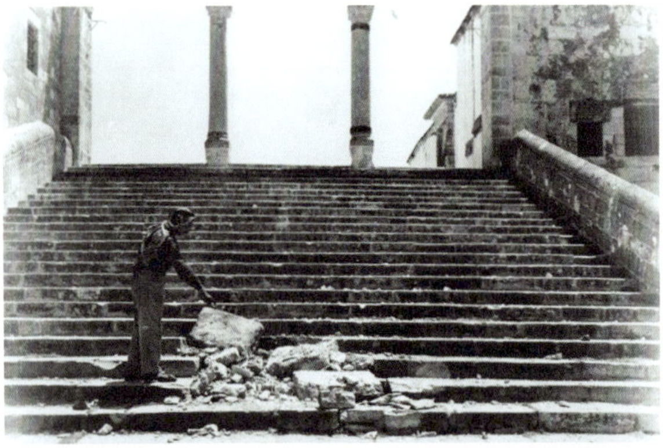

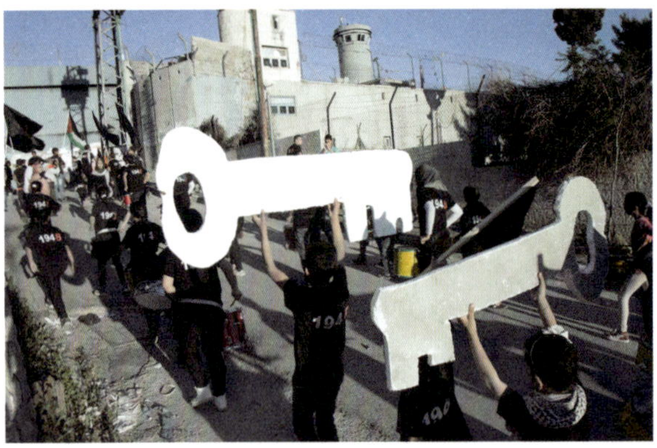

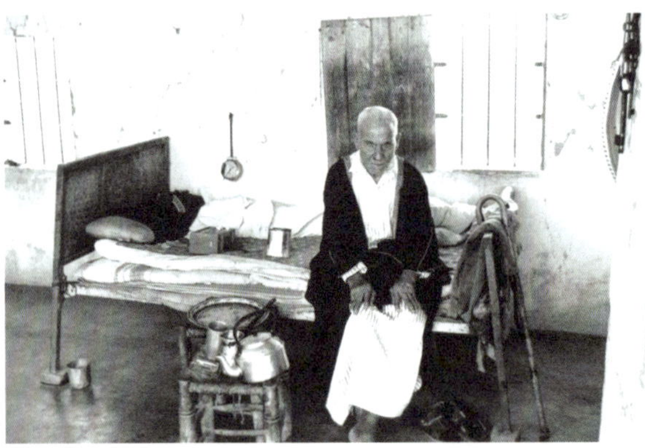

Fig. 10. Al-Aqsa Compound, Jerusalem's Old City, 1948 [Courtesy of Ali Zaarour family] / **Fig. 11.** Aida refugee camp, West Bank, 14.5.2014 / **Fig. 12.** The Aqabat Jaber refugee camp, near Jericho, West Bank, 1977 [Courtesy of Shuka Glotman]

In a photograph taken in 1948 on the steps leading to al-Haram al-Sharif (Dome of the Rock) by the Palestinian photographer Ali Zaarour, we see a man stretching his arm and pointing with his finger to three very large limestone tiles that probably collapsed in an explosion [**Fig. 10**]. *Compared with the destruction elsewhere in Palestine at the time, including holy places, the damage here was minor and could be repaired. However, this is one of the rare photos from 1948 that I was able to find where a Palestinian is shown expressing a corporeal gesture of grievance.*[4] *It is not his pointing gesture but rather the encounter between this lone Palestinian who, in the midst of the catastrophe, refuses to accept the harm done to him, to his people, to Palestine, and who advocates his right to frame the damage as a harm and to call others to recognize it, and the photographer who, passing by with his camera, recognizes the man's gesture and interacts with it. The rarity of photographs in which a common gesture of grievance is recorded in a catastrophe of such scale as the ruination of Palestine is by no means an indication that Palestinians were not engaged in direct, vigorous actions of opposition to their fate. Rather, it was because there were not more photographers who spoke the same civil language and sought to interact with Palestinians' gestures of resistance.*[5] *With the concept of "potential history" that I developed in relation to the civil revolutionary language, I argue that under the imperial condition, civil statements uttered in public nowadays necessarily have previous manifestations, even if these were not recorded or did not find their way to archives. After all, this is what makes these statements part of a language as a generative system whose elements are constantly composed and recomposed. In this photograph taken in Aida refugee camp on Nakba (Arabic for "Catastrophe") commemoration day in 2014* [**Fig. 11**], *children are seen walking with big paper cut-outs in the shape of old keys. The earliest photo I was able to find featuring a key as a statement is from 1975 from Jericho refugee camp, taken by Shuka Glotman* [**Fig. 12**]. *Keys hang from a rope on the wall close to the bed, like a cherished object from which its owner will not be separated. Almost thirty years had passed, and the man continued to display the same keys that he carried with him when he was expelled from his home in 1948. The keys helped him to feel more confident* *to say, "This is my home," even though for decades, others have been allowed to live in it. Where are all the photos that should have been taken from 1948 and after of the hundreds of thousands of Palestinians who took their keys with them when they were expelled?!*

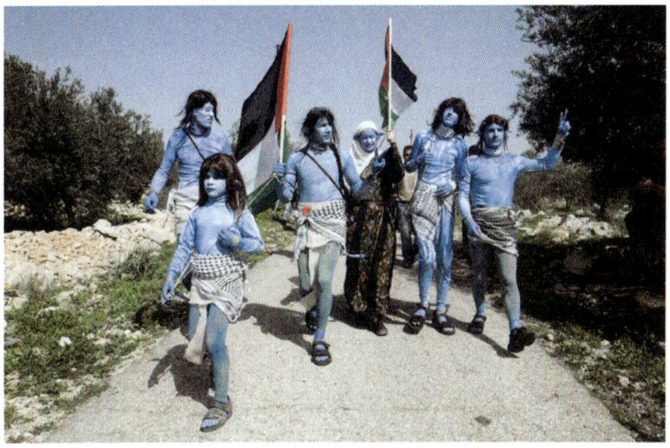

Fig. 13. Bil'in, West Bank, 12.2.2010

When the spoken language is civil, imperial monsters cease to live in peace, camouflaged by the conditions of their acceptability. The use of a civil language, by itself, is an act of resistance, a counter-movement, whose goal should be understood as going beyond its explicit demands and claims. It is an effort to rewind the course of history, to insist on the possibility and the duty to undo these monsters along with the conditions that make them acceptable. Thus, for example, dismantling a segment of the wall is not only an opportunity to move beyond the wall, but a call to dismantle the wall and the entire political apparatus that enabled it. This means not relating to the achievements of the imperial enterprise as what determines the terms of the future, but calling for a reversal of the terms and recognizing Palestinians as not only participants in any conversation about the future of this place, but also their position as natives, whose rights should be unconditionally recognized, including all the reparations and compensations that this entails. Here, in this photo, they are dressed in the Na'vi's garments [**Fig. 13**].

Once we understand Palestinians' actions as language, we can relate to props like the mirror not as an attempt to offer the ultimate statement to be valued for its success or failure to stop the occupation, but as a syllable, a rhyme, an element in a continuous communal effort to make their language resonate with meaning among others and to preserve the conditions for practicing this civil language that is constantly endangered under the imperial condition. It is endangered not only because its speakers are oppressed and dispersed, but because of the ubiquity of the imperial language that turns many of the civil statements into provocations and aberrations, and depicts their speakers as violators of law, as rioters, and conspirators. As a language, it is not just descriptive but performative. Not only is the world seen differently but so are its speakers. This is why its statements often are not just about abuses and unjust laws, but about who its subjects are, its legislators, for whom and against whom its statements are made. Thus, shortly after the film Avatar *came out and was embraced by the Jewish-Israeli public, Palestinians challenged the Jewish-Israeli audience who, as is often the case, identified with the freedom fighters, and adopted the position of the indigenous in revolt against an imperial power. They dressed up in blue to embody the Na'vi, the indigenous people fighting imperialism, thereby turning the film into an allegory of Palestinian existence. They thus challenged the Jewish-Israeli soldiers who continued to persecute them, as if to say "Not supporting our just struggle against the regime means that you are playing a dubious role in the plot." This challenge may have been greater, since in addition to Palestinians, the group also included some Jewish Israelis, with all of them together refusing to occupy the positions assigned them by the political regime meant to keep them apart.*

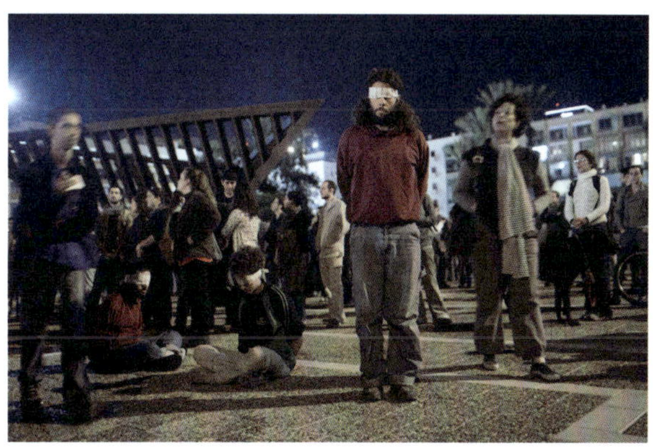

Fig. 14. Tel Aviv, Israel, 12.11.2011

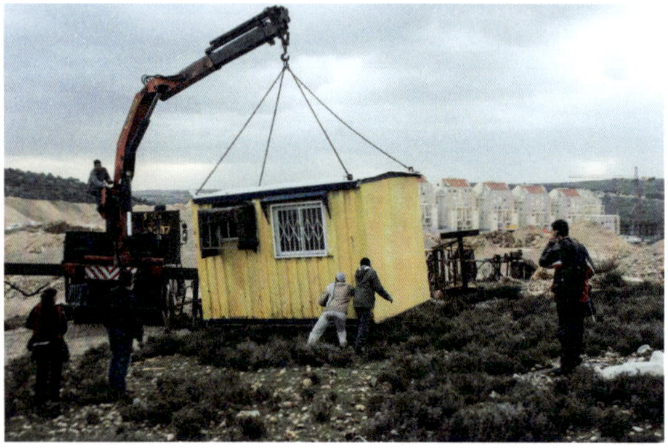

Fig. 15. Bil'in, West Bank, 25.12.2005

Photographs are not representations of those moments but one type of this language's components. Disseminated along with other elements—verbal or spatial—used by this language, they are easily recognized by those who are familiar with it. Among those who speak it, utterances that to the uninitiated might sound "unheard of," make quite a bit of sense. They are understood, adopted, reiterated, altered, and extended. A language emerges from the many who speak it and its variations are endless.

Often the civil language is spoken with reiteration of imperial statements. When reiterated, they are devoid of the violence they exercise on others who are deprived of their rights and compelled to embody the political category imposed on them [Fig. 14]. *Thus, for example, when a group of Jewish Israelis are blindfolded the way Palestinians are often treated, the expectation is that the gesture itself, detached from the body with which it is associated, will be perceived for what it is: violence. Reiteration is a common mode to expose what would otherwise pass for non-violence, but it is also used in the perspective of restoring plunder, of asserting one's right to land or property, even though its appropriation by another was carried out a long time ago and everything has been done to erase its legal owners* [Fig. 15]. *The caravan is placed on Bil'in land, near the illegal Jewish settlement of Modi'in Illit. Deprived of half of their lands, the Palestinians assert their right to these lands through the implementation of a temporary housing unit—a caravan. By placing the caravan on their confiscated lands, they not only seek recognition for the legitimacy of their act, but also the recognition of the Jewish settlement as the illegal enterprise.*

One day, from the civil claims treasured in these photos, the clauses of a new civil contract will be formulated. It will not lead to a new beginning but rather to a movement of rewind that will be a joint movement that will dismantle all the mechanics of violence and of differential rule, and will offer compensation and reparations, until a complete redistribution of wealth is achieved. Not the concrete demands voiced in one document or another, but the foundations they lay down—not for the constitution of another imperial sovereignty, but for a common effort to rewind the existing one, enabling a new form of partnership to emerge out of the abolition of the principle of differentiality on which Israeli democracy is built.

1. When the Israeli separation wall was first being built, Adi Ophir and I called it "The Monster Tail," in Michael Sorkin, ed., *Against The Wall: Israel's Barrier to Peace* (New York: The New Press, 2005), 2-27.

2. Even the United Nations resolutions denouncing Israeli violence or asserting the Palestinian right of return were not respected. The "International Day of Solidarity with the Palestinian People," held annually on 29 November, often takes place in "nearly empty rooms," as Edward Said wrote of the 1983 event, as depicted in one of John Mohr's photos. See Edward Said, *After the Last Sky - Palestinian Lives* (London: Vintage, 1993), 122-23.

3. See my "Actions, Non-Actions, Interactions, and So On and So Forth" in a special issue on "Visual Activism," *Journal of Visual Culture* 15:1 (April 2016): 5-23.

4. Something about the man's gesture made this photograph stand out as a rare image in the archives I consulted while working on *From Palestine to Israel: A Photographic Record of Destruction and State Formation, 1947-1950* (London: Pluto Press, 2011), 241.

5. I propose five other reasons in my above cited essay, "Actions, Non-Actions, Interactions."

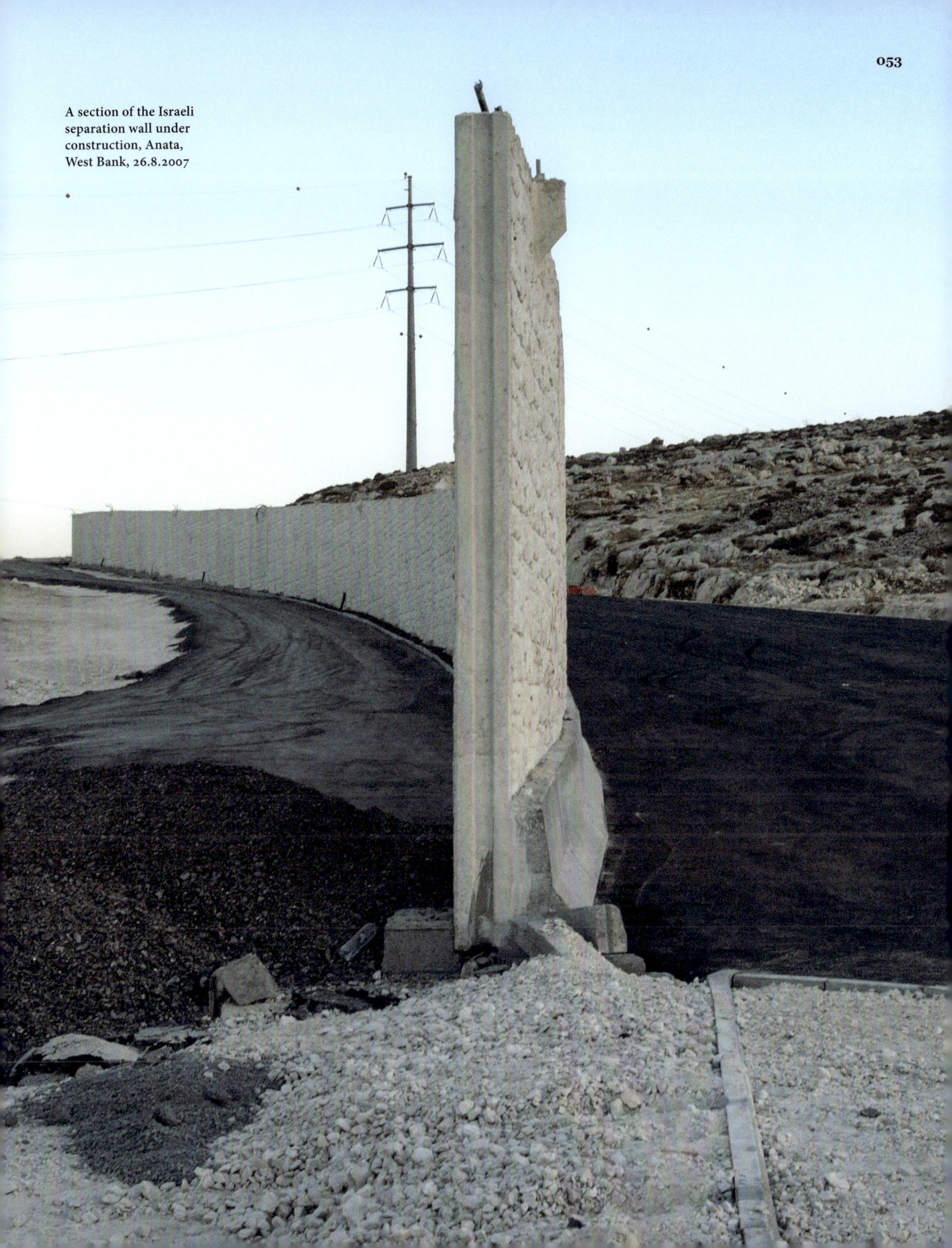

A section of the Israeli separation wall under construction, Anata, West Bank, 26.8.2007

Bil'in, West Bank 18.11.2005

Residents of Bil'in sit atop their olive trees that were cut down to make room for the route of the Israeli separation wall, and look at the new buildings under contructions in the settlement of Modi'in Illit.

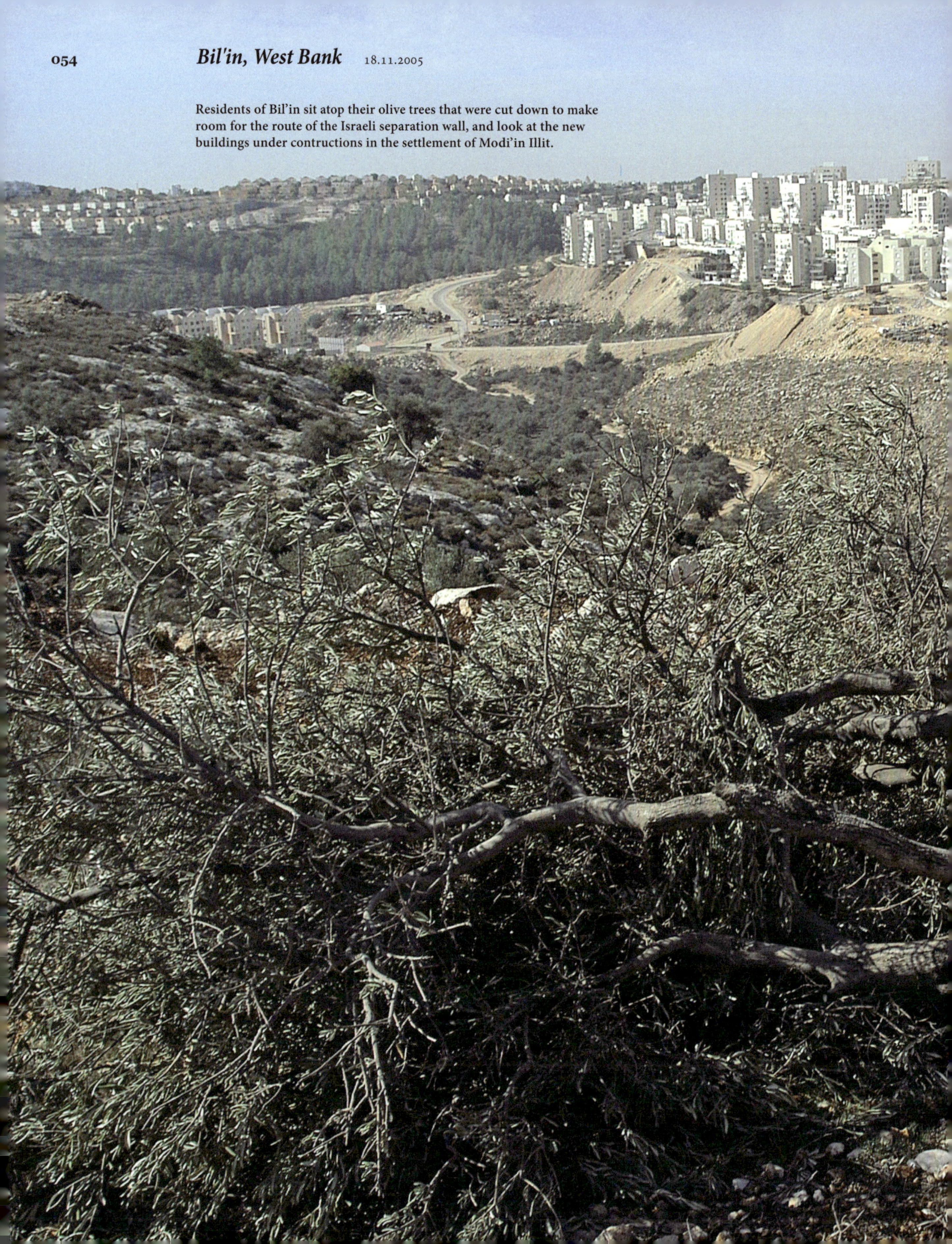

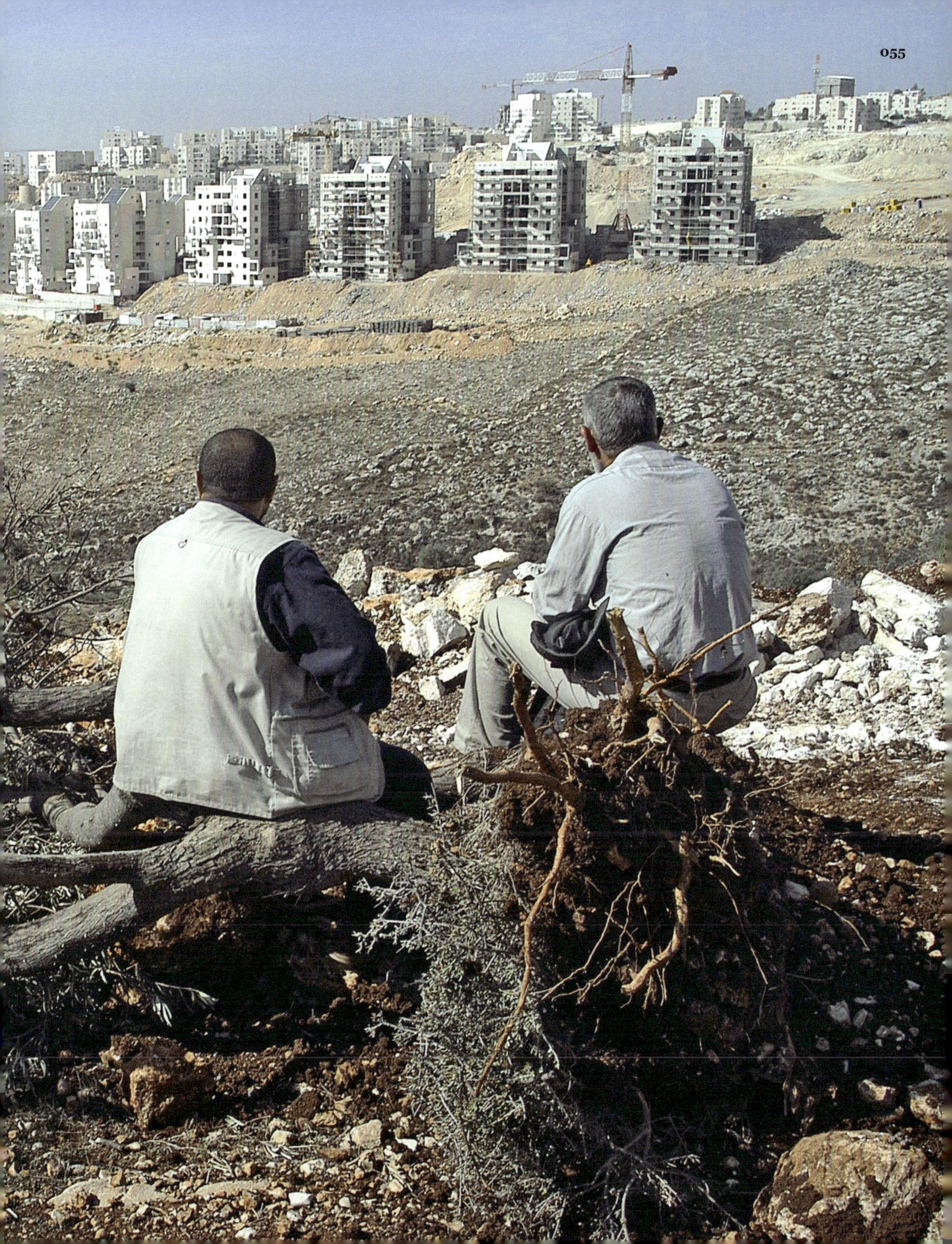

Biram, Israel 29.12.2012

Palestinian residents of the Upper Galilee village of Biram, expelled in 1949, were not allowed to return even after the Israeli High Court of Justice upheld their right. The village is now part of a national park. UNRWA estimates over 5 million Palestinian refugees are denied the right to return to their homes in contravention of international law.

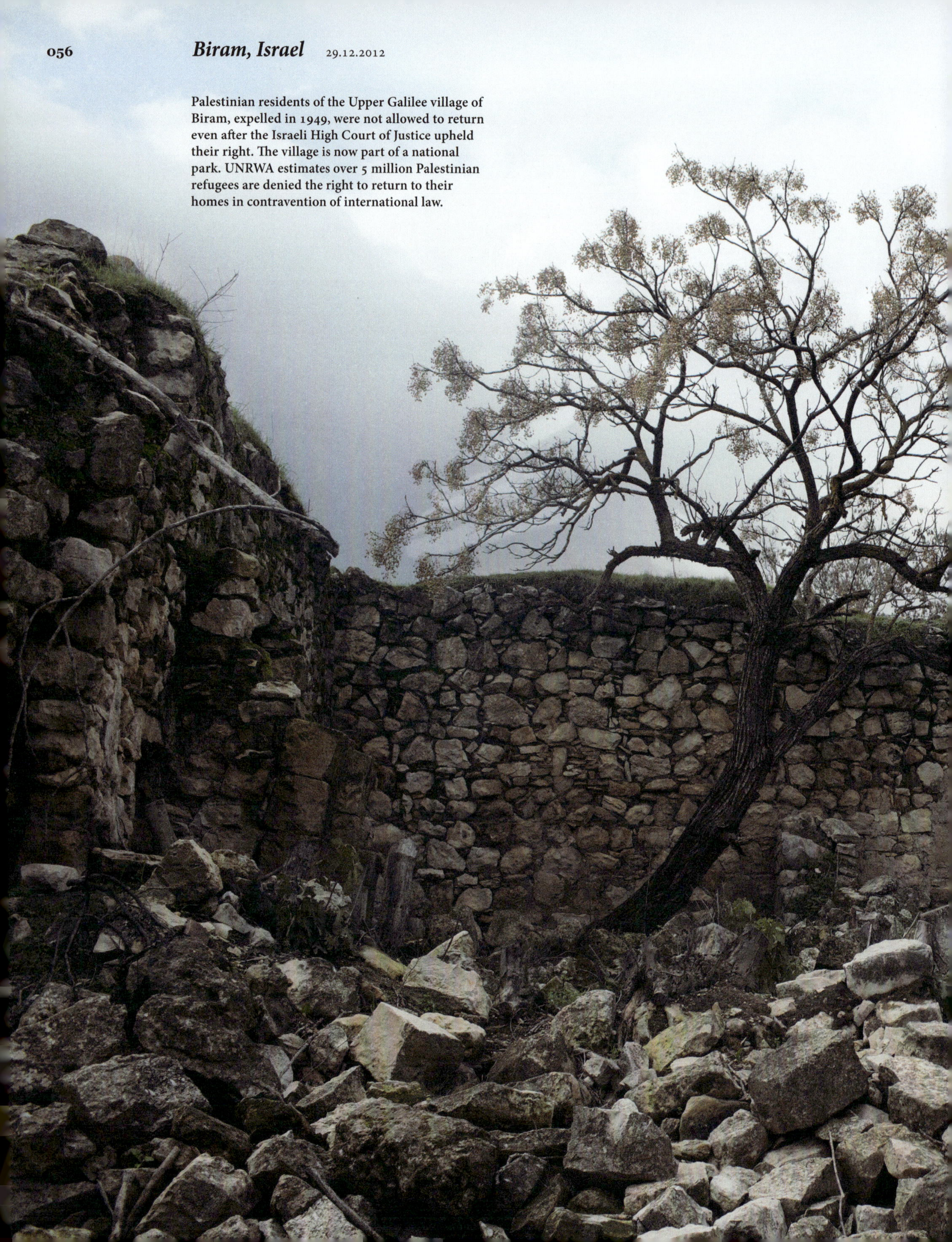

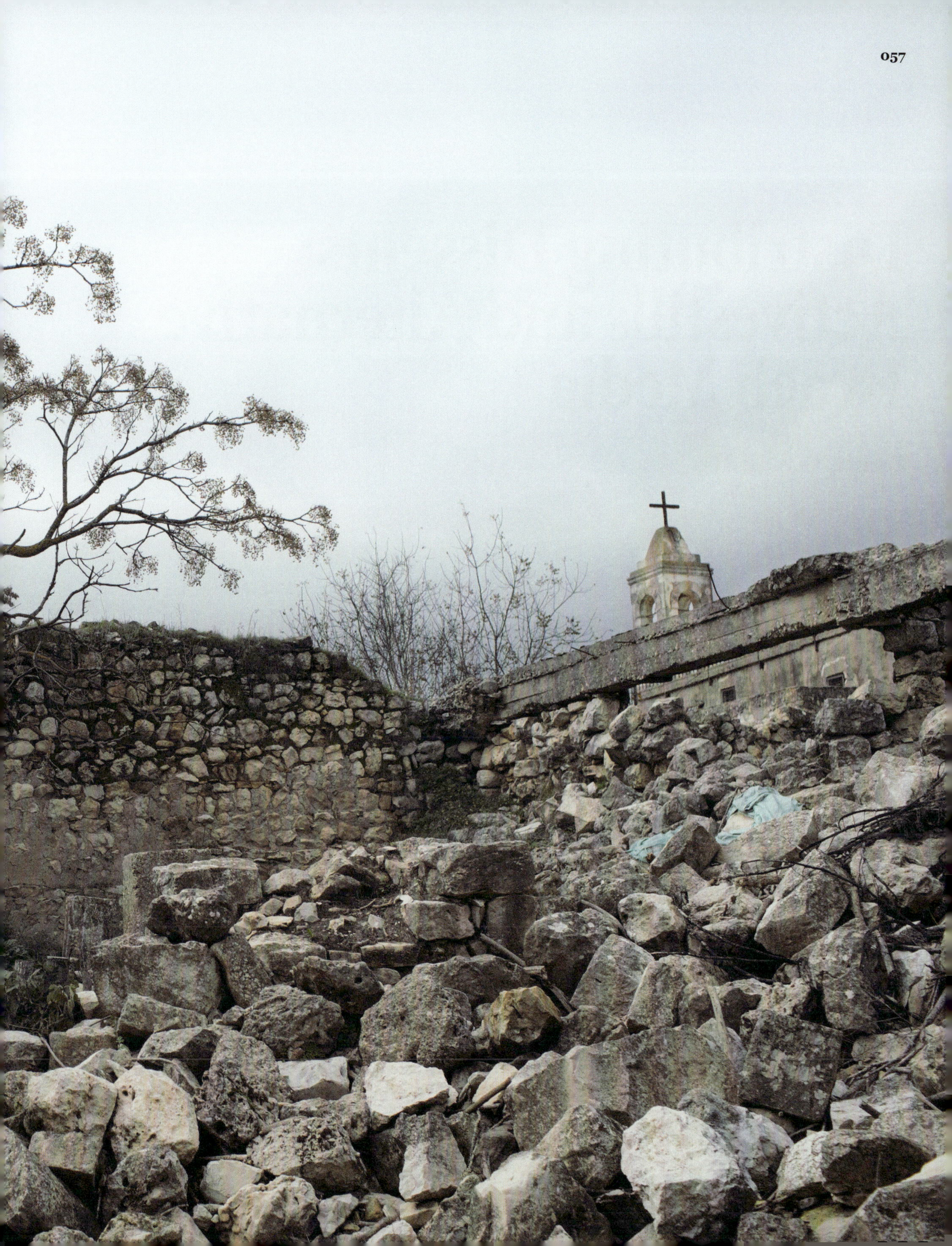

Distributing Dissents: Activestills and Alternative Israeli Media

Haggai Matar

In this photograph we see a family in what clearly is an unusual situation, or rather, in what is a completely usual situation, but extremely troubling circumstances [**Fig. 1**]. The family is gathered for an early dinner. There is not much food on the table, but the three different pots suggest that someone obviously took the time and trouble to prepare it. They are seated around the table, their faces and gestures expressing a wide range of emotions: amusement, calm, distress, even grief.

The background tells us why: all around them is the visual evidence of destruction—probably fairly recent—of what we might assume was this family's home and neighborhood. A felled tree, flattened earth, debris from a house that was destroyed, another house half standing, a pile of dirt—all this wreckage corresponds to the dinner table standing in the open air and the deep concern transmitted by some of the family members.

This picture was taken by an Activestills photographer in September 2014. Had it not been for the *kippot* (skullcaps) on the older men's heads (and the upside-down *kippah*-like disposable bowl on the head of the child in the center), one might have thought that, based on the date, the location is a devastated neighborhood in post-war Gaza. Similar images were being distributed by photographers in Gaza at exactly the same time.

But this is actually Tel Aviv; the people are a Jewish Mizrahi family (that is, descended from immigrants from an Arab or Muslim country), and the destruction is not the result of war, but of an ongoing campaign led by Israeli capitalists and the Tel Aviv municipality to displace poor residents from their homes in areas where real-estate prices are soaring in order to make room for luxury high-rise apartment buildings (like the one visible in the distant background on the right). Welcome to the neighborhood of Giv'at Amal.

Dissent

Much as Israeli politics, media, civil society, and culture as a whole are often examined outside of Israel solely through the lens of "the conflict," or the Israeli occupation of Palestinian territories, so the work of Activestills is at risk of being viewed as a one-dimensional project devoted to documenting the occupation and resistance to it. While the occupation does play a pivotal role in their work (and rightly so), as other contributors to this book show, Activestills from the beginning have been about much

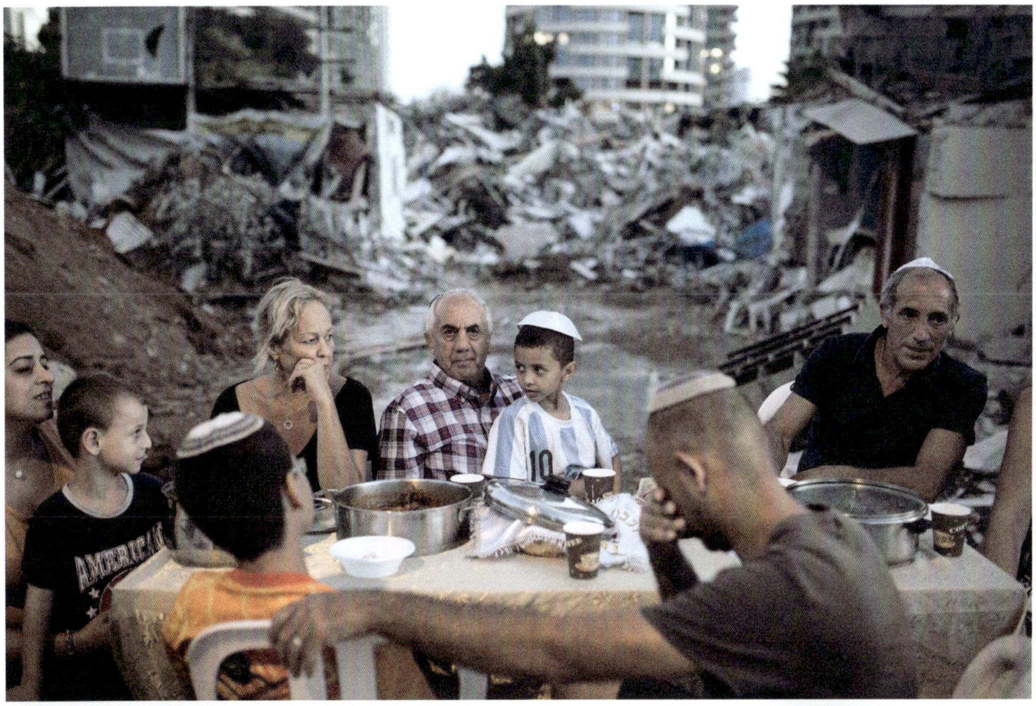

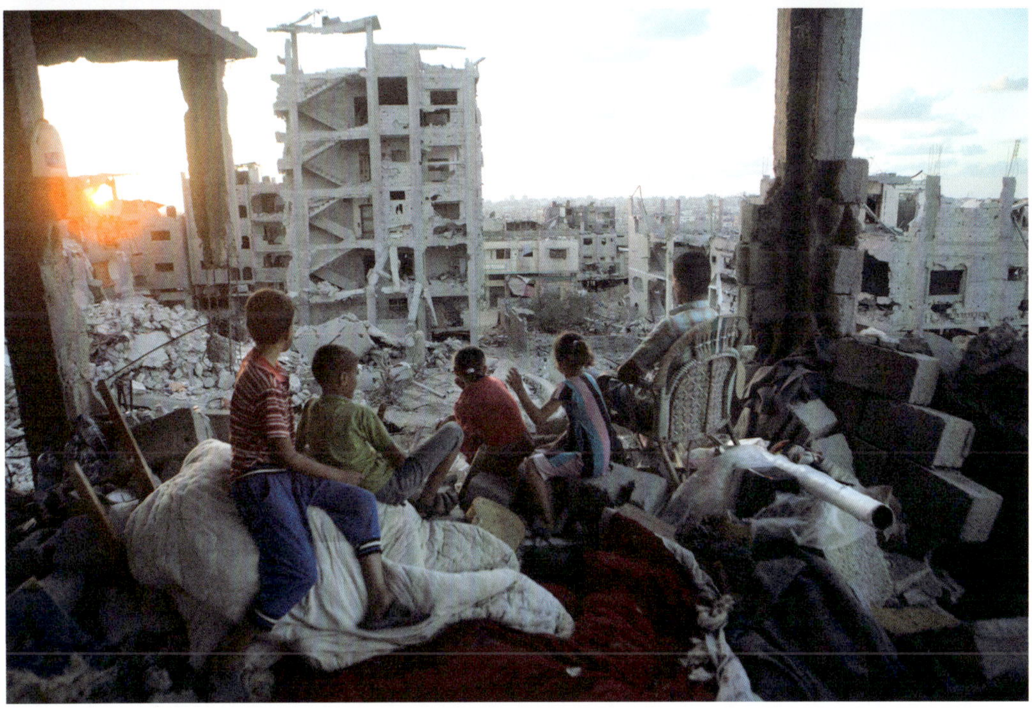

Fig 1. The Kadoori, Hamias, and Ashram families sit around an improvised Sabbath table near their demolished homes in the Giv'at Amal neighborhood, Tel Aviv, 19.9. 2014 / **Fig 2.** A Palestinian family in the ruins of their home in the Al-Tufah district of Gaza City, which was heavily bombed during the Israeli military offensive, Gaza Strip, 21.9.2014

more than that. They have always directed their lenses and activism at a vast, but not unlimited, array of topics and struggles within Israel (inside the Green Line) itself.

Although they cover news and explore in-depth stories throughout Palestine/Israel, the collective are not a regular journalistic photography agency engaged in supplying news editors in the mainstream media with images to correspond to tomorrow's (or the next hour's) headlines. Activestills photographers choose the subjects of their stories carefully, and the result of their selection has its own internal logic and significance. It is the choice and its rationale that I wish to examine below. (It is worth noting that due to limitations on Palestinians' freedom of movement, the Palestinian photographers in the collective cannot enter Israel, that is, inside the Green Line, while Israeli photographers may move freely throughout the most of the West Bank. Thus, in discussing Activestills' work within Israel, I am forced to address only the work of the Israeli members of the group—a limitation I lament, but crucial to my point.)

What are the topics Activestills have chosen to address through a decade of photography, aside from the Israeli occupation and Palestinian resistance in the West Bank and Gaza? There is the issue of Arab citizens of Israel, commonly known as "48 Palestinians," for having remained within Israel's borders following the 1948 war. Often framed in Israel as an issue of an ethnic minority within a "Jewish democracy," and by Palestinians as part of the larger question of Palestinian rights in this land, this community suffers from continuous discrimination in legislation, municipal zoning and planning, state budgets, house demolitions, land expropriation, political representation, and more. These issues, along with the struggles against them, are some of the main issues Activestills are concerned with inside Israel.

A topic of international concern is that of migration and asylum seekers. The photographers have long been covering the arrival in Israel of migrant workers and asylum seekers, documenting their daily lives and hardships, work or lack of it, detention, deportation and, at times, protests and victories.

Documentation of social struggles within the Jewish society, from housing rights to organized labor, the demand for better welfare, the resistance against privatization of natural resources, is also the focus of Activestills photographers. Women's groups combating sexual violence, the ultra-Orthodox community's resistance to compulsory military enlistment, the Mizrahi struggle against Ashkenazi (European Jews') cultural and economic hegemony, LGBTQ campaigns for equality, Ethiopian Jews' protests against police brutality, animal rights—Activestills are present at these fronts as well.

Yet, by categorizing in words the specific struggles that Activestills train their lenses on, we miss something essential about this political and journalistic project, which can only be understood by looking at the images themselves which, through their visual language, suggest links between the struggles that cannot be reduced to a single essence, issue, or category.

Consider again the picture of Giv'at Amal in Tel Aviv. As I noted above, without the *kippot*, this photograph could have been taken in Gaza. If we compare it with a photograph also from the Activestills archive taken in the Al-Tufah neighborhood in Gaza just two days after the Tel Aviv photo **[Fig. 2]**, it is possible that they could be mistaken as two related scenes in a single neighborhood, the Mizrahi family sitting around their table on the next street over from these Palestinian children. Both of these compelling images could be viewed as two parts of a single tragedy. This unspoken, elusive link between Gaza and Tel Aviv is imparted to the viewer almost instinctively through the visual language that has come to be recognized with the Activestills project.

An entire book would be required to replicate in words the fragile, fleeting sentiment summoned by these images, individually and in correspondence. By simply starting to tell the stories behind the two pictures, linguistic barriers spring up that divide them; the human condition of forced homelessness split into different categories of speech and thought. Notice how naturally this happened when I described the various fields in which Activestills operate: the political sphere of national conflict and oppression, the international dilemma of migration, the social struggles within Israeli society. Words encourage us to group things in unrelated categories (and all too often as a result to compare levels of pain and suffering in order to prioritize political agendas). How naturally we pull them apart by assigning names to them.

I would argue that this is precisely what Activestills refuse to do. In using photography as their medium and carefully choosing the subjects and establishing a constant visual language throughout their coverage that is faithful to their political beliefs, they challenge the commonsense and "natural" distinctions that usually help us to determine friend from foe, and separate the important from the trivial, the mainstream from the subversive.

This visual language builds its story upon the individual person. The picture is not about the house that was demolished; it is about the person whose house it was. A photograph of a demonstration is not about the protest march; it is about the person taking part in it—a specific human being in the center, with his or her own special story. Yet, at the same time, if we review the entire Activestills project, the picture is also a part of something greater happening in the world and that "something" does not necessarily fit in with the regular categories we have constructed. More often than not, it dissolves them.

What remains after relieving the viewer of previously held beliefs and categorizations is a humane and resolute look at *oppression* and the *resistance* it arouses. When, for example, in an International Women's Day exhibition of photographs, the camera lens is always focused on the individuals in scenes of women evicted from public housing, women asylum seekers protesting against incarceration, Bedouin women amid the ruins of their demolished homes, women in post-war Gaza refugee camps, and women at a rally in support of rape victims, we understand that the intent of the photographers was to erase the boundaries that separate these stories so that they may be seen as part of one inclusive story of oppression.

Connections

Before discussing how the Activestills collective transmit their challenging political message to the broad Israeli public, it is worth mentioning, in brief, two immediate consequences of their use of a universal language of oppression and resistance, which has led to new, albeit hard to achieve, political alliances.

The first is the creation of a dialog between Activestills and the Israeli left, the latter ranging from the radical, non-Zionist, joint Arab-Jewish left, having socialist (or anarchist) affiliations, to the more social-democrat Zionist left. Across this spectrum, there is often a tendency (that is not unaffected by the foreign perspective that comes with foreign funding for NGOs) to isolate the issue of the ongoing occupation of Palestinian territories as the single focus of the left. This matter has come to be used in public political discourse as the litmus test for the "left," to the exclusion of other traditional leftist concerns like class divisions, attitudes toward organized labor, redistribution of wealth, social equality, and so forth.

The left-wing Israeli citizen is trapped by the colonial-like situation that is the result of the continuing occupation: on the one hand, Israelis are currently benefitting from maintaining the occupation and the status quo more than they probably would from the possibility of peace, liberty and equality for Palestinians; protesting against the siege on Gaza and military rule over millions of Palestinians in the West Bank runs the risk of alienating potential left-wing supporters in Israel. On the other hand, by accepting the situation and focusing instead on "internal affairs," those on the left run the risk of becoming complicit with the current colonial system.

Activestills—a joint Israeli-Palestinian-international collective whose unquestionable commitment to documenting and resisting the occupation derives from a profound refusal to accept any manifestation of oppression—offer the Israeli left another option through their humane and empathic presentation of the struggle of both Palestinians and Israelis, whose different circumstances but shared human experience is portrayed in their imagery. The left is repeatedly challenged to simultaneously adopt and promote both sides of the different fronts, even if at times they might feel conflicted.

The second consequence involves the effect of Activestills on the very people who are engaged in struggle. According to the collective's statement, Activestills photographers view themselves "as part of the struggle against all forms of oppression, racism, and violations of the basic right to freedom." This is a crucial point, for not only do the photographers document, publish news, and offer a theoretical framework for linking struggles with their pictures, they are themselves activists. This fact has an immediate impact on whoever they choose to join in struggle and the wider campaign against oppression in Palestine/Israel. Their presence for the last ten years on many different fronts has made them carriers, as well as transmitters, of valuable knowledge.

On many occasions, Activestills photographers have been known to put down their cameras at the end of a protest rally and offer basic yet crucial tools to the untrained activists, from the phone number of a lawyer who could help demonstrators who have been arrested or of an NGO or political activist with experience on the rally's specific issue, to information about how to deal with tear gas or police brutality, or how to chain yourself to a building threatened by demolition so that it would be virtually impossible for security forces to pull you away. Activestills might show victims of the Israeli public housing system pictures of Palestinians fighting against house demolitions or connect striking workers with others who have been through similar hardships. The members also offer basic photography lessons as tools of empowerment for communities to document and publicize their stories.

Activestills succeed in dismantling the conceptual borders between different struggles through their visual language as well as the real borders between the subjects of their photographs through their actions on the ground. In this sense, their *activism* is at one with the totality of their *stills*.

This is how the group has become a focal point, connecting different communities and the Israeli left and offering all of these players some basic tools to talk with each other.

Distribution

Activestills' audience is not limited to their own political circles and communities in struggle. In their capacity as both journalists and political activists, they aim to reach the Israeli public as a whole and expose it to stories not shown in the mainstream media.

The Israeli media have always been very loyal to government policies on the Palestinian issue, especially in times of war and uprising. Also, in recent years, as a growing portion of the media has come under private ownership, it has become less of a forceful defender of the underprivileged.

The rise of online news has dealt a heavy blow to the field of print journalism worldwide. For an Israeli newspaper with a small Hebrew readership, trying to sustain an online presence is challenging due to low revenues from online ads and competition with free content available on the Web. But local print journalism has recently also had to deal with another, exceptional, threat: in 2007, the American multi-billionaire and hard-right Republican Sheldon Adelson launched the national newspaper *Israel Hayom* (Israel Today), dedicated to promoting Benjamin Netanyahu's political ideology and personal interests. Subsidized by his international casino empire, the paper could afford to be distributed for free throughout the country, sell advertising space for below market rates, not turn a profit, and still, within four years, become the most widely read newspaper in Israel.

Israel Hayom has replaced the liberal newspaper *Ha'aretz* in the list of papers that gain public-funded government ads and it has also contributed to the collapse of the one-time newspaper giant *Ma'ariv*. By setting a new standard of "patriotic" journalism—which means keeping criticism of the government to a minimum—it has led to a growing right-wing, national chauvinist, and militarist trend among local print and online journalism.

The effects of these dramatic changes have also been felt in Israeli radio and television journalism. In recent years, the government has tried to increase its influence on the public Israel Broadcasting Authority and the two privately owned channels, 2 and 10. This campaign has been led by Prime Minister Netanyahu himself, who, following the 2015 elections, appointed himself Minister of Communications and specifically instructed all members of his coalition to vote on media-related bills following his orders. The two private channels, and especially the larger Channel 2, have been conforming to the change as a result.

This, in brief, is the background against which Activestills attempt to disseminate their images and message to the Israeli public. Yet, despite the gloomy picture presented here, the photographers insist on working with—and often within—the mainstream media, such as with the left-oriented *Ha'aretz*, and the popular news website *Walla!*, among others, where they continue to offer their unique view on publicly debated news items and try to introduce into newspapers and online sites with a broad readership the stories that generally are not given news coverage.

At the same time, the members of the collective, aware of the limitations of the mainstream media, must keep looking for alternatives to it. These limitations are not only financial, legal, structural, and political in nature, but include also basic linguistic limitations that are the very same ones the media use to differentiate between and prioritize matters deemed important or trivial, internal affairs or foreign affairs (the latter of which includes the Palestinian society under occupation, but not the Jewish settlers and the Israeli Army within the same Palestinian territories, whom the media cover as part of the former), or that separate issues of "security," "society" and "politics" as described above.

Consequently, Activestills have endeavored to create their own tools of distribution. The best-known examples are the collective's street exhibitions, described in depth elsewhere in this book. In addition, Activestills challenge the common notion of copyright by declaring in their mission statement that their pictures belong to "those whose struggles are documented," and are "often exhibited by local communities in events, conferences, demonstrations and court hearings." They distribute their images through alliances with independent media, and by offering free use of their archive to left-wing publications that cannot afford to pay for photography, such as the local version of *Indymedia*, which was a central stage for alternative news in the early 2000s. They have also collaborated with *Haokets*, *MySay*, *+972 Magazine*, and others.

In early 2014, Activestills became a founding member of a new, independent, collectively run news site called *Local Call* (or *Sikha Mekomit*, in Hebrew), together with *+972 Magazine* and *JustVision*. The basic mission of *Local Call*, of which I am one of the editors, corresponds closely to that of Activestills'. It offers grassroots, bottom-up reporting from communities in struggle and volunteer leftist activists from varied backgrounds, and like the photographers' collective, aims to dismantle hierarchies and remove the separations commonly seen in media coverage. In so doing, *Local Call* tries to challenge the Israeli left and promote the connection between different struggles. At the same time, it challenges mainstream media with stories that are overlooked and voices that are unheard, and though the general direction of media coverage is still shifting to the right, more and more *Local Call* news stories are being picked up by other publications, which is having an effect on the way journalists and the public experience and understand local politics. *Local Call* and Activestills offer their continuously growing readership a perspective on the links and similarities between the family in Giv'at Amal and the family in Gaza.

Illustration

There is another point about Giv'at Amal worth mentioning. Up until 1948, Giv'at Amal was a Palestinian village. The current Jewish inhabitants were sent there by the newborn state to keep Palestinians from returning to it. The descendants of those original inhabitants are probably living in refugee camps somewhere to this day. The uprooting of the latter residents echoes that of the former, and in a sense, Israel's current political and economic situation is a derivative of that as well.

Thus, we see that offering a perspective that unites the human stories of Tel Aviv and Gaza, and that attempts to delete the boundaries separating them, not only exposes an interesting humanitarian perspective, but is also grounded in real politics.

However, this kind of politics undermines the entire premise of this essay, which has attempted to distance the discussion from "the occupation"—the subject of many of the other essays in this book—and look only at Activestills' coverage of the society "within Israel," a term I have used several times throughout this essay. As the ongoing story of Giv'at Amal tells us, even drawing this line of "within" and "without," of "Israel" versus the "occupied territories," is a tricky business. What better than the pictures of Activestills to illustrate that?

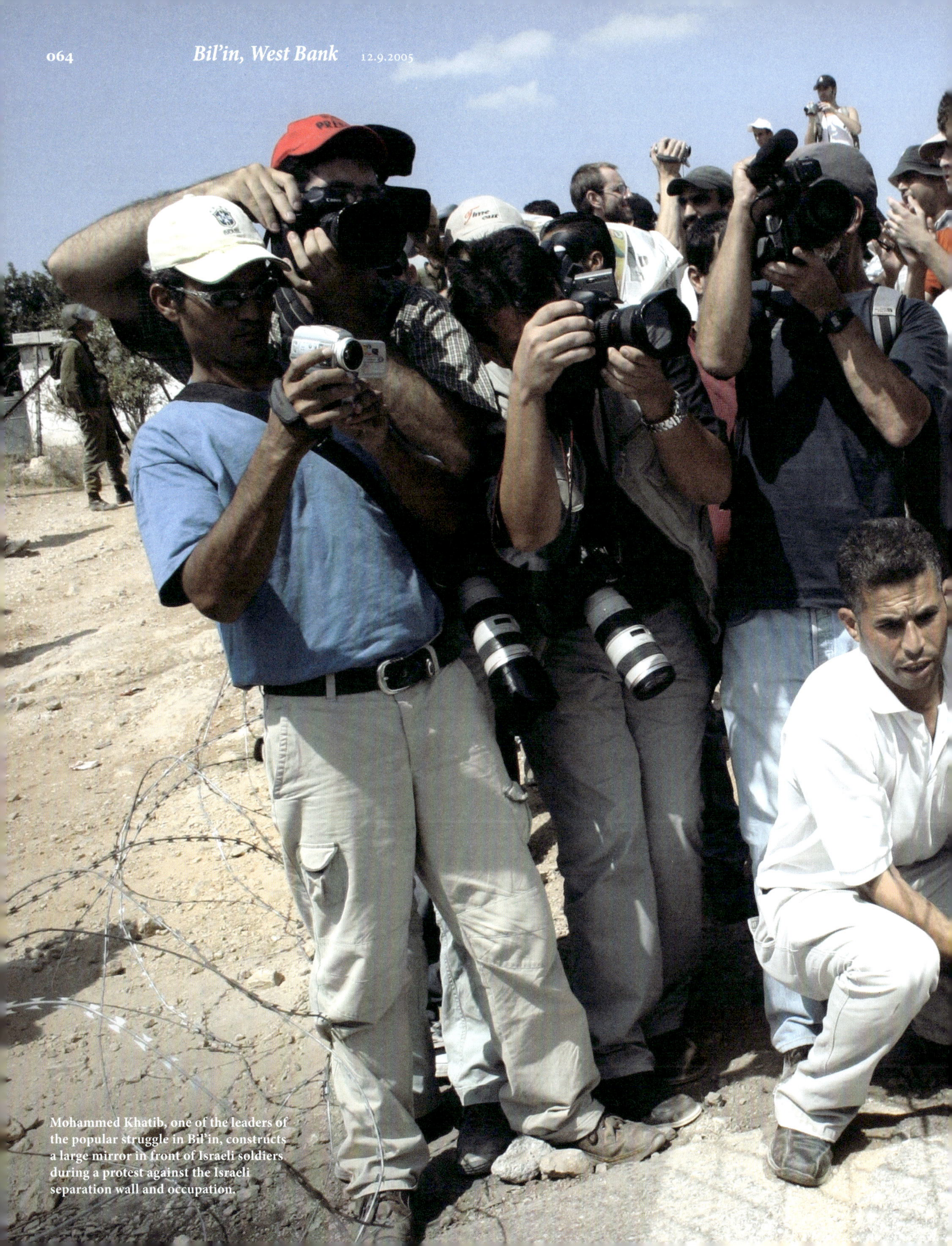

Mohammed Khatib, one of the leaders of the popular struggle in Bil'in, constructs a large mirror in front of Israeli soldiers during a protest against the Israeli separation wall and occupation.

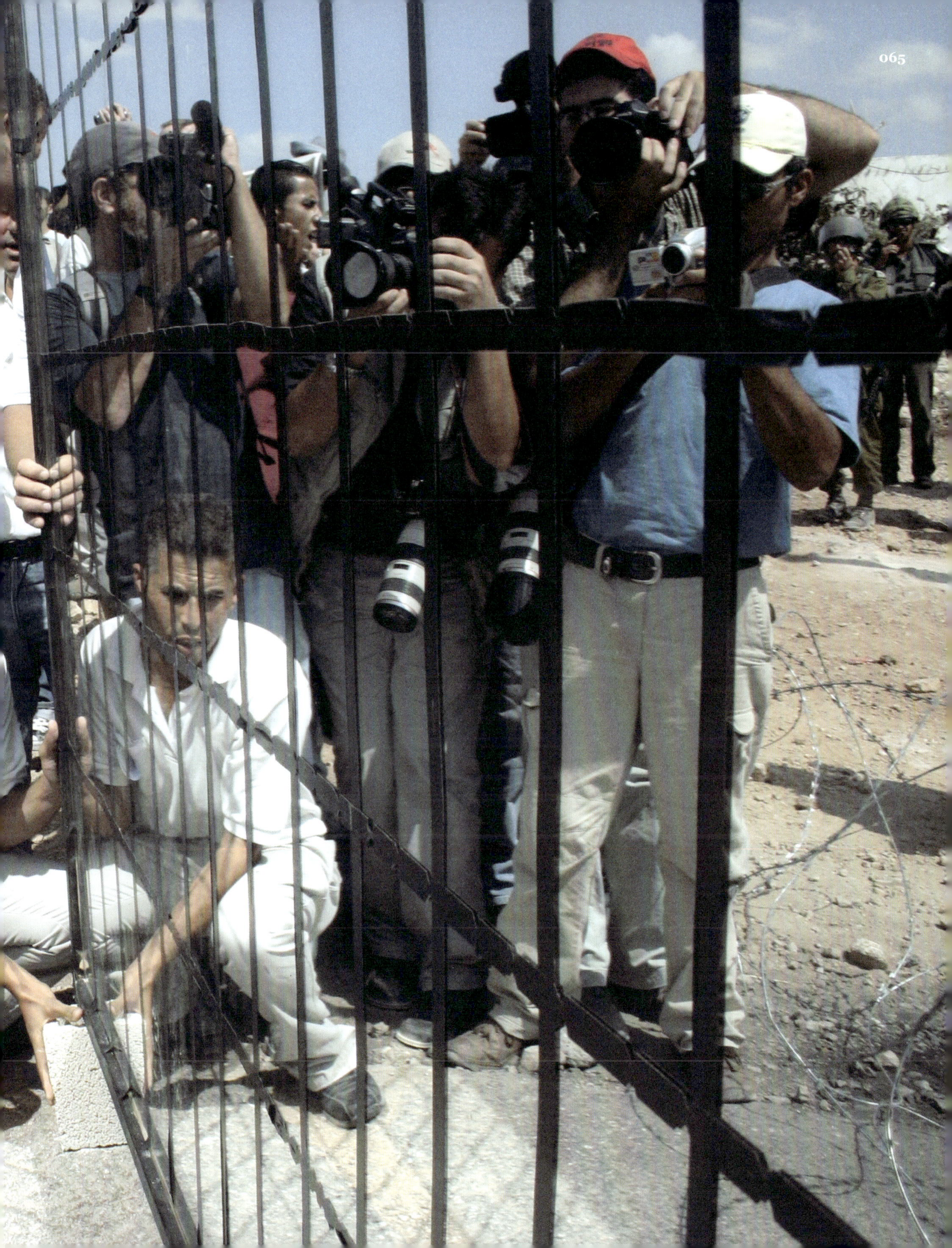

The Middle East and New Media: The Challenge and the Opportunity

Ramzy Baroud

The current state of Middle Eastern media in general, and Arab media in particular, is one of adversity but also opportunity. The adversity stems from the near-total hegemony of self-serving governments and empowered elites over nearly all media discourses. The opportunity, on the other hand, is a result of various Internet technologies and social media platforms that are available to a growing number of people across the region.

The accessibility and openness of this new technologically based media have ushered in the rise of citizen journalism—a new media content producer which is able to counter, and at times overtake, dominant traditional media narratives. However, as with all forms of media, it too comes with its own challenges. The agendas of many media platforms are generally controlled by the well-funded few. Hence, one challenge faced by independent citizen journalists is the lack of independent media platforms that could offer them a free and neutral stage and space for their work without being coerced into tailoring their content to fit existing media agendas. The current state of Arab media is in particular need of such alternative platforms, for it remains hostage to ruling parties, dictators, and their wealthy benefactors.

Owning the Media and the "Arab Spring"

Paul Cochrane argues that the Iraqi invasion of Kuwait in 1991 was a breaking point between attempts at manipulating and intimidating media and owning it.[1] The regional breakups that resulted from that war were so severe that they effectively ended the Arab Cooperation Council (ACC), an alliance that had united Iraq, Jordan, Egypt, and North Yemen, and further strengthened the Gulf Cooperation Council (GCC). The latter had wealth and thus, media access. The post-war period brought about a buying frenzy during which some rich Arab countries and wealthy businessmen attempted to consolidate their control over Arab public opinion by using newly founded satellite television stations, and by uniting various Arab societies around cheap entertainment.

When Al Jazeera was launched in 1996, despite being funded by Qatar, a country that is not an icon of freedom of expression, a new type of competition arose between rival Arab countries. Other media that were also funded by rich Arab states and staffed mostly by Arab intellectuals and journalists from poorer countries also emerged soon enough. Within this new realm of media, "freedom of expression" existed so long as views were offered that matched the political agendas of the funders. However, it should also be mentioned that despite the apparent media rivalry, independent journalists and intellectuals still managed to navigate space for themselves, and by doing so, pushed the boundaries of debate like never before.

Then came the Arab Spring: its decisive collective agenda was that of regime change, and this left no room for political bargaining or compromise. It further muddled regional agendas, creating new alliances and, once more, emphasized the power of the media to harness and sway public opinions. Even pan-Arab news networks, which held some level of credibility, were soon tainted in their rush to influence the public discourse. The media split; their differences based on geopolitical allegiances as each camp had its own funders and multiple propaganda arms.

In contrast, social media were harder to control, for they remained a relatively free space. However, since they compel a degree of anonymity to their users, they opened up a completely new challenge in attempting to authenticate information through the endless stream of content, and to distinguish genuine voices from those of government and other forms of propaganda.

As was the case of the interruption of the democratic experience in Egypt, any attempt at an equitable media platform in many Arab countries was quelled. Numerous voices, however small, continued to fight for space and raise their own cry against the brazen attempts to silence anyone who did not agree. Once more, truly independent Arab intellectuals found themselves having to navigate an impossible media terrain.

However, the failure to allow an authentic and just media presence is not specific to Arab countries. Western mainstream and corporate media have done a dreadful job at presenting an accurate picture of the reality in the Middle East. The core of this failure was exemplified in the coverage of the Palestinian-Israeli conflict, during which Israel was repeatedly presented as the victim and Palestinians as the aggressors—this misrepresentation being itself a transgression against facts, common sense, and the need to report "real" situations experienced in very real situations of aggression.

The Arab Spring complicated an already difficult and convoluted media scene. While physical maps remained largely intact, the geopolitical map of the region was in a state of constant flux. Following and reporting about these constant changes without a deep and compassionate understanding of the region achieved little but predictable and lackluster content that offered only recycled ideas and stereotypes.

While official Arab media venues sang the praises of the ruling elites, Western coverage of the region was predicated on unmistakable economic and political interests. In fact, during the decade-long blockade that followed the US-led war on Iraq (1990–91), and the further war and invasion (2003), the Middle East was back at the center of neocolonial activities, Western economic interests, and strategic and political maneuvering. This renewed interest introduced a huge list of terminology that was rarely ever questioned by those who promoted US/Western interests. Terms such as extremist, radical, moderate, terrorist, pro-Western, liberal, socialist, Islamist, anti-Islamist, secularist, and so on, became commonplace and all too often accepted at face value without further attempts to understand or examine their meaning or context. Their use was often political as opposed to a direct reference to an ideological or political position.

Ultimately, there was a mix of media agendas: Arabs dedicated their platforms to hailing the dictator and demonizing his enemies; Iranian media pushed a government line whether right or wrong; Israeli media grew more blatant and rightwing; Turkish media fought a political war between the ruling party and the opposition, and Western media remained true to form, promoting whatever war was deemed necessary, and insisting on seeing the Middle East and its conflicts wearing the very same biased spectacles of the ever-present past. In the midst of it all, the majority of the region's people were neglected, misrepresented, stereotyped, criminalized and, at times, entirely overlooked.

Arundhati Roy once wrote: "There's really no such thing as the 'voiceless.' There are only the deliberately silenced, or the preferably unheard."[2] It rarely dawns on many journalists to position their reporting on the Middle East from the grass roots, beginning with people who are mostly disgruntled by whatever story is being reported: the victims, their families, and the community as a whole. While such voices are often neglected or used as content fillers, they are seldom the center of any serious reporting from the region, especially when it comes to portraying the Israeli occupation.

Palestine—The Opportunity

But it is not all doom and gloom. Things began to change in recent years, especially following the massive shift that the Internet, independent, and social media has brought about. When the Internet was first introduced, it quickly started to make its way toward greater participation from people around the globe, hence challenging the traditional media and their hegemony over the Middle East, as well as similar discourses across the world.

Of course, the Internet has not fully closed the inequality gap, democratized society, or put an end to the dominance of traditional and mainstream media. It has, however, launched a process that has revitalized society sufficiently to seek its own alternative in any area pertaining to information, which various segments of society felt was deceitfully imparted or tightly controlled.

Currently, the Middle East is rife with citizen journalists: bloggers who express the ordinary person's view regarding the political failure of Egyptian dictator Abdul Fatah al-Sisi; Moroccan journalists who take on the task of recording the spoken lyrics of their countrymen; Palestinian videographers who daringly record the killing of Palestinians in the West Bank at the hands of Israeli troops or armed settlers, or Activestills photographers who keep the world abreast of the social inequality, political upheaval, and the immorality of the Israeli military occupation. While the likes of Activestills would have existed in one form or another before the advent of the Internet, this platform gave them the ability to distribute their content, engage civil societies around the world, and connect with other like-minded activists and journalists.

There is still a long distance to go before mainstream, corporate, and self-serving media are fully challenged, if not sidelined. But the unmistakable trend has already been unleashed, ushering in a new kind of thinking and information that was once either wholly unavailable or inaccessible. The media conflict is likely to continue for years to come, but the battle lines have been drawn and are in a process of change and expansion. They favor the new media platforms, empowered by a new generation whose priorities reflect those of the majority of peoples, not just the privileged few. The outcome of this conflict will define our relationship with information altogether and thereby shape not only our awareness as societies, but our actions and mobilization for generations.

1. Paul Cochrane, "Saudi Arabia's Media Influence," *Arab Media and Society* 3 (2007), accessed 10.1.2016, http://www.arabmediasociety.com/?article=421.

2. Arundhati Roy, "The 2004 Sydney Peace Prize Lecture," University of Sydney (2004), accessed 10.1.2016, http://sydney.edu.au/news/84.html?newsstoryid=279.

{Opposite page}
1. A Palestinian activist streams live video during the weekly demonstration in Kafr Qaddum, West Bank, 30.12.2011. Kafr Qaddum started to organize regular demonstrations in July 2011 in protest against the blocking of the main road east of the village that used to link it to Nablus / **2.** Palestinian activists live blog from the Palestinian tent camp "Bab al-Shams" (Gateway to the Sun), constructed by the Popular Struggle Coordination Committee in protest at Israel's plans to annex the "E1" area, West Bank, 11.1.2013

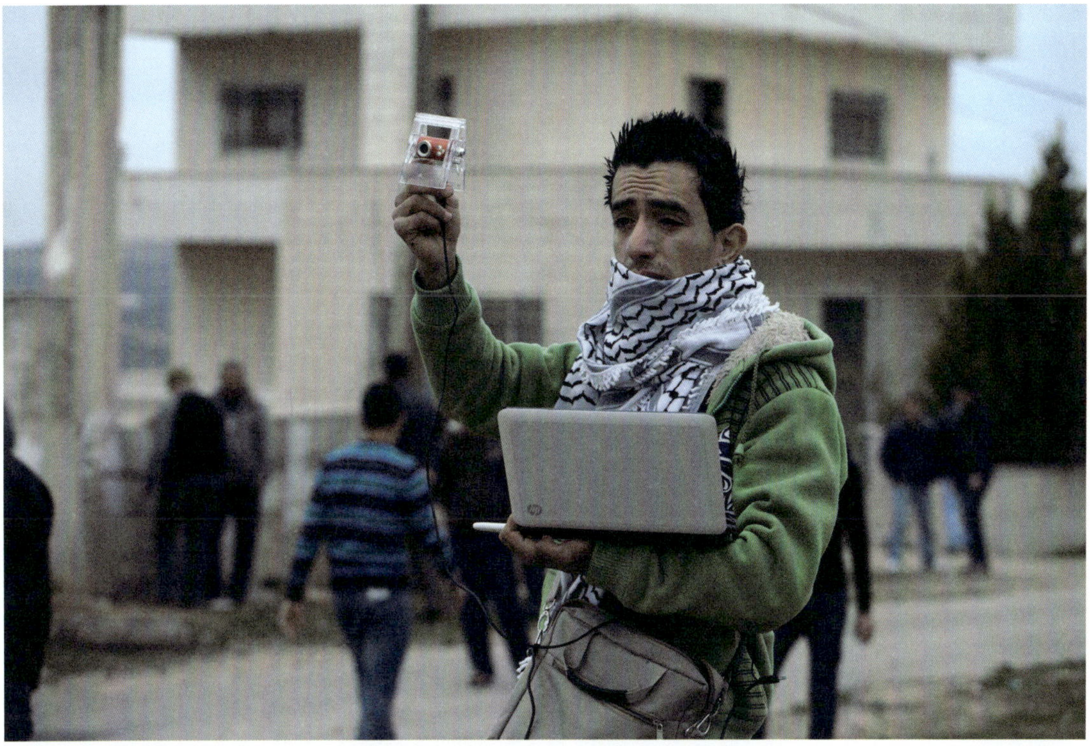

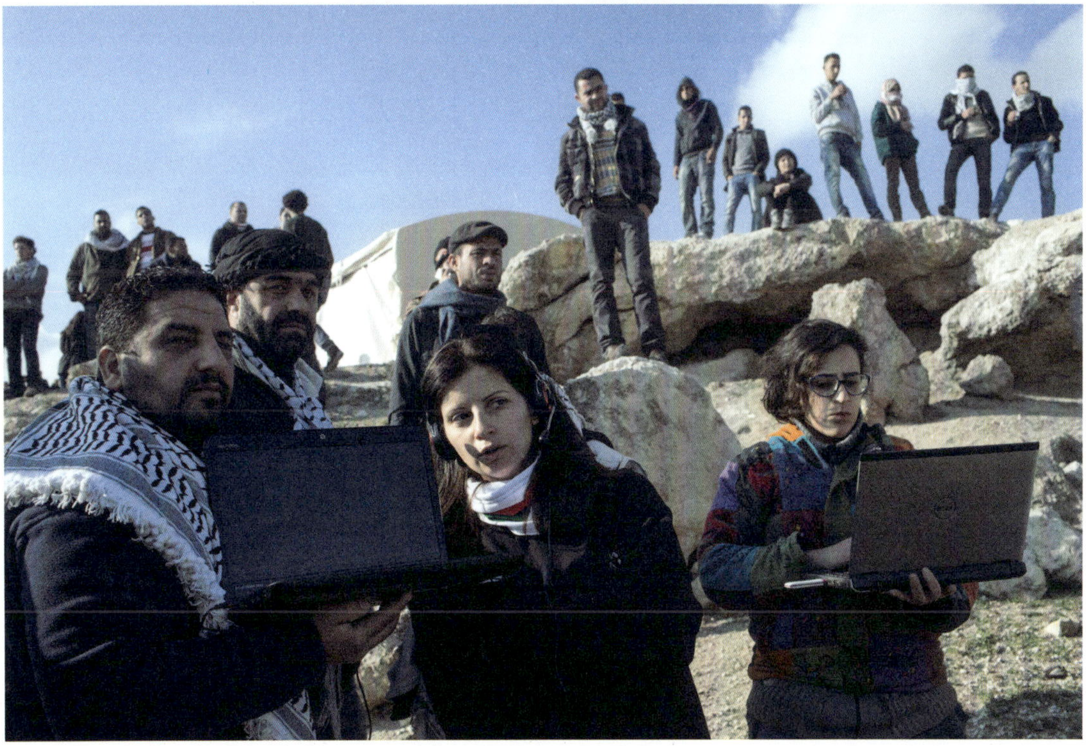

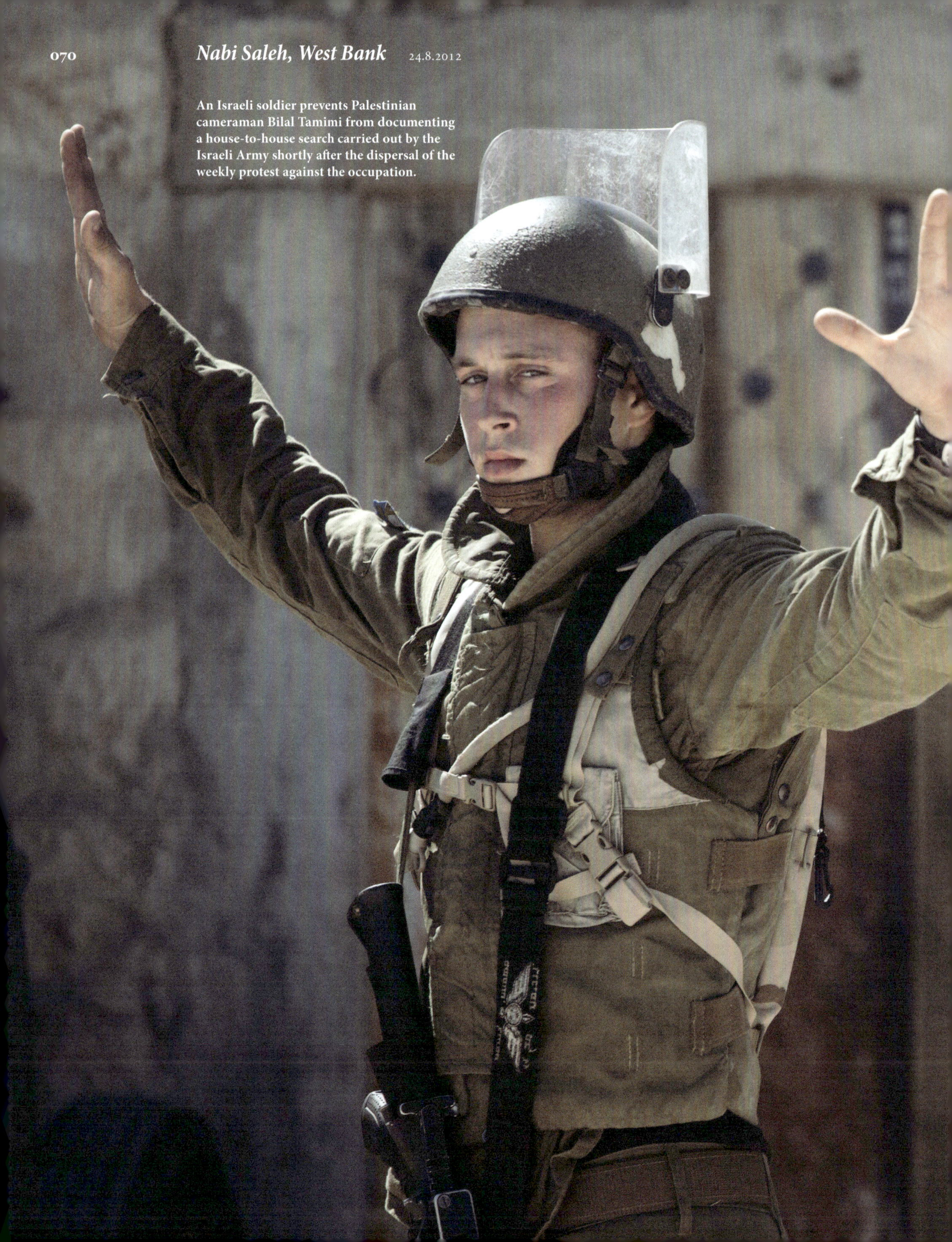

Nabi Saleh, West Bank 24.8.2012

An Israeli soldier prevents Palestinian cameraman Bilal Tamimi from documenting a house-to-house search carried out by the Israeli Army shortly after the dispersal of the weekly protest against the occupation.

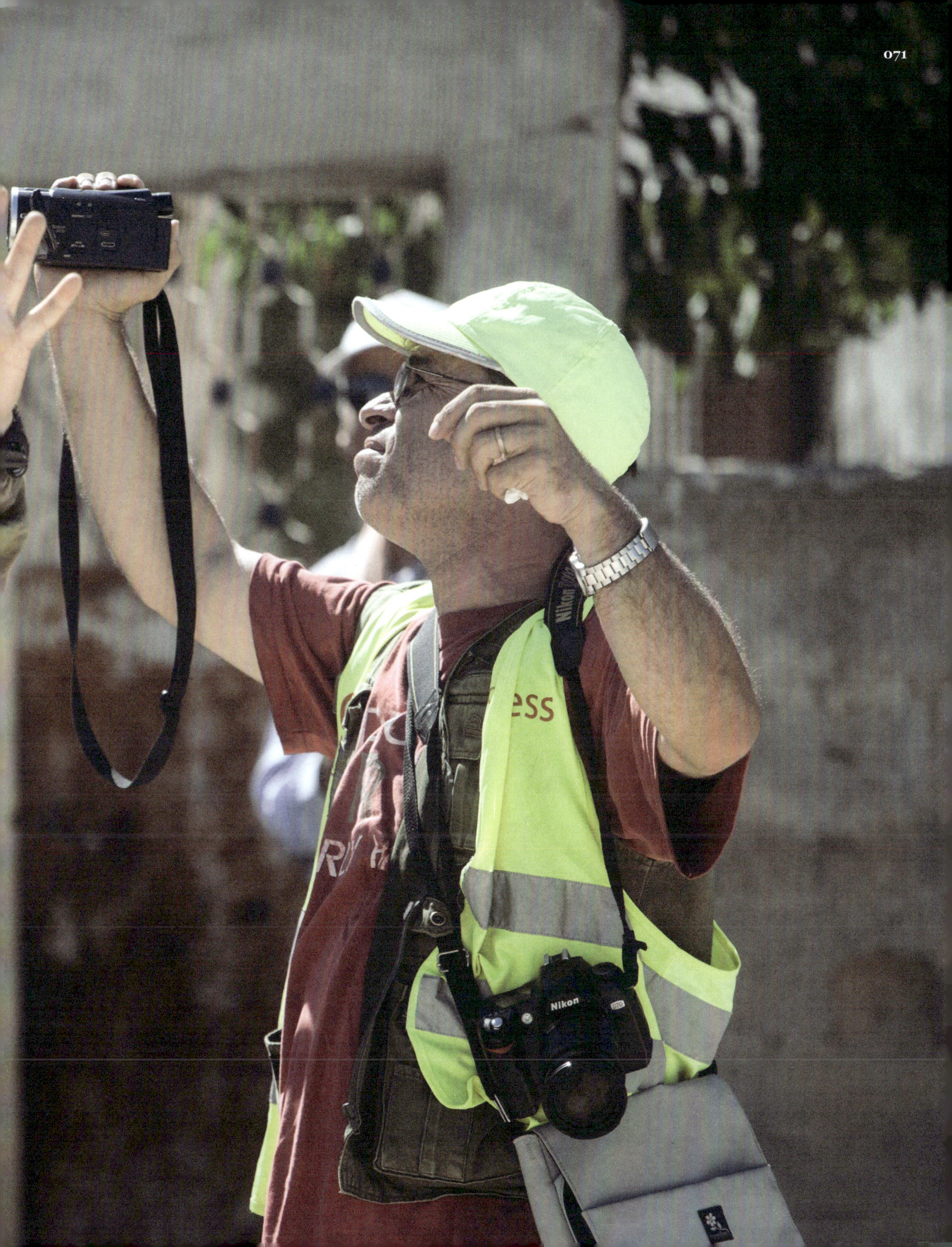
Nikon

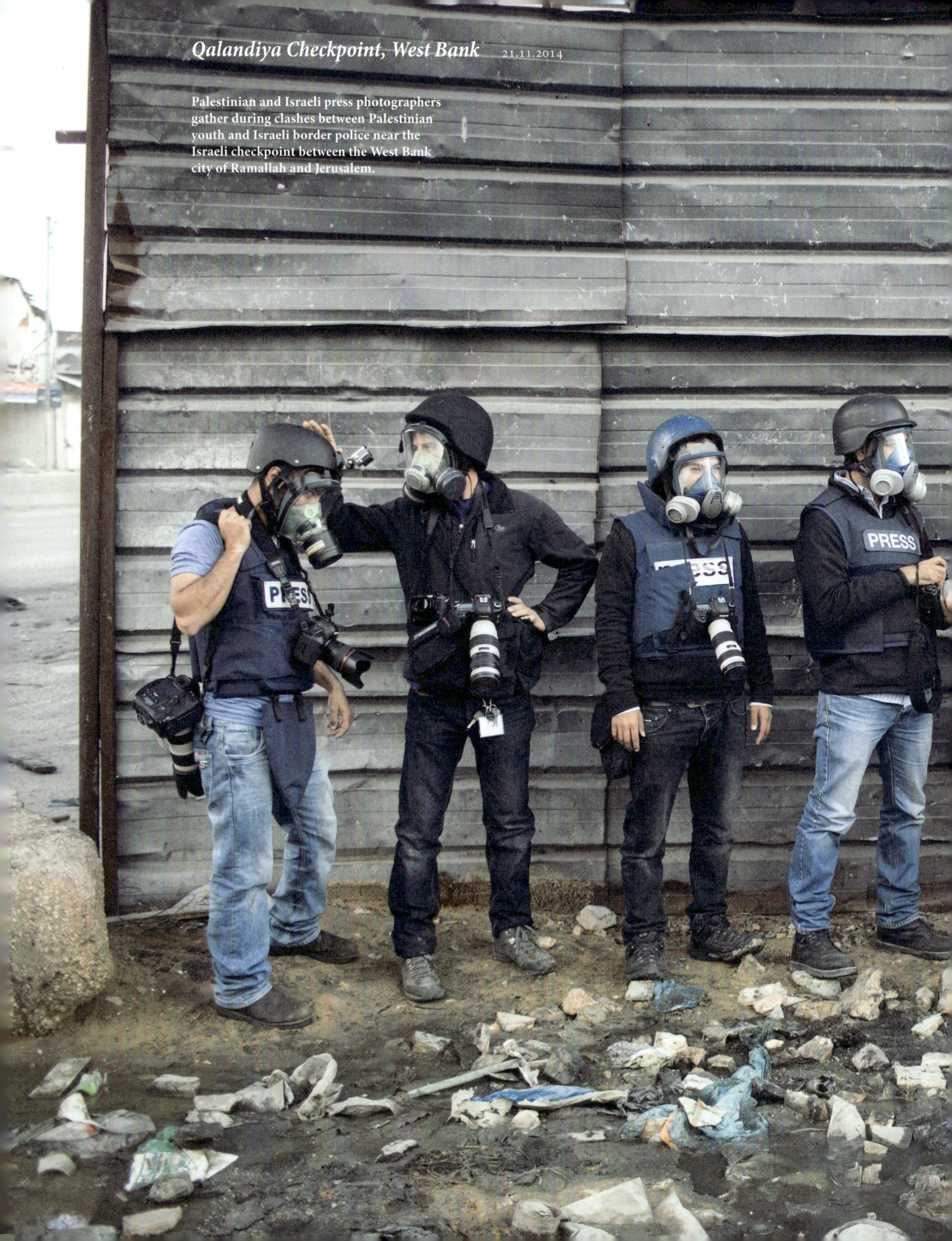

Qalandiya Checkpoint, West Bank 21.11.2014

Palestinian and Israeli press photographers gather during clashes between Palestinian youth and Israeli border police near the Israeli checkpoint between the West Bank city of Ramallah and Jerusalem.

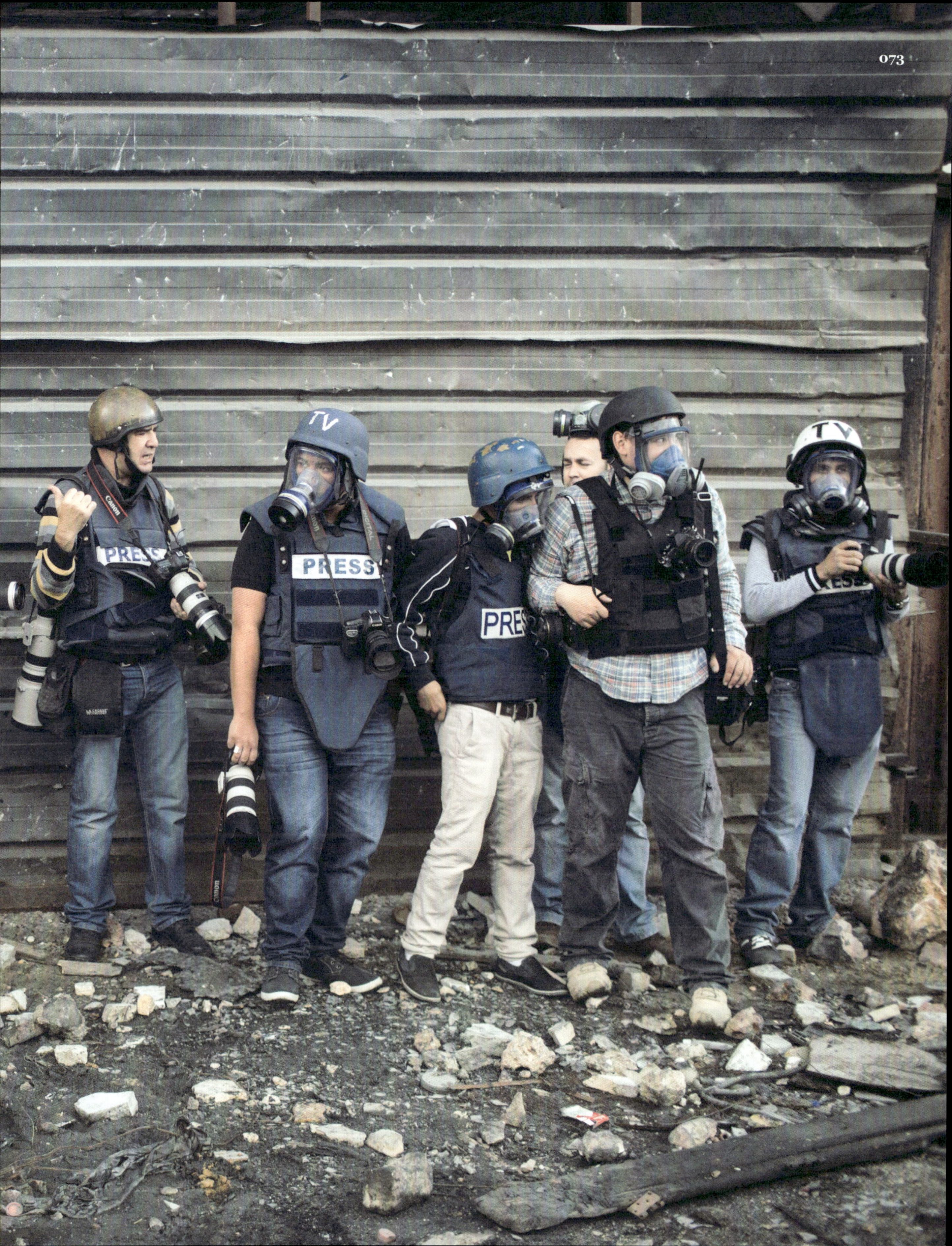
TV
PRESS
PRESS
PRES
TV
PRESS

Contentious Displays: Activestills' Street Exhibitions

Simon Faulkner

The organization of photographic exhibitions in the street and other public places has been an important aspect of the work of Activestills since the formation of the collective in 2005. The street has been viewed by members of the collective as a relatively unregulated space for communication. Exhibitions in this context have been envisaged as both a means to avoid the limitations of the mainstream news media and as a way to address the public directly, as opposed to through institutions. The significance and effect of these exhibitions has varied, depending on their content and context and on the audience that this context provides. This essay addresses street exhibitions produced by Activestills between 2006 and the present by dividing them into two categories. The first category involves exhibitions displayed within the internationally recognized borders of Israel as defined by the Green Line (the 1949 ceasefire line). These exhibitions were generally presented in Israeli cities to Jewish-Israeli spectators. These spectators were, on the whole, distanced—both spatially and ideologically—from the situations and struggles that were depicted in the images shown in the exhibitions. The second category involves exhibitions presented in close proximity to particular struggles, in both Israel and the West Bank. These exhibitions were integrated to differing degrees with these struggles and often involved presenting images of participants back to them. In general, the spectators of these exhibitions could be described as being proximate to the situations and struggles depicted in the images on display.

In what follows, these two categories of exhibition will be explored in relation to specific examples, with a concern to understand the different dynamics of spectatorship involved in each case. Key to this discussion is the consideration of the spatial and temporal relations that defined this spectatorship. Also of concern here is the way that the different kinds of Activestills exhibitions under discussion can be thought about in terms of the differentiated field of vision relating to the complex historical and political situation in Palestine/Israel.[1] As Gil Hochberg has recently argued, when it comes to visual mediation, what is generally called the Israeli-Palestinian conflict does not always appear in the same way.[2] This is partly because different kinds of spectators are exposed to different images of the conflict, but also because even when these different spectators view the same images,

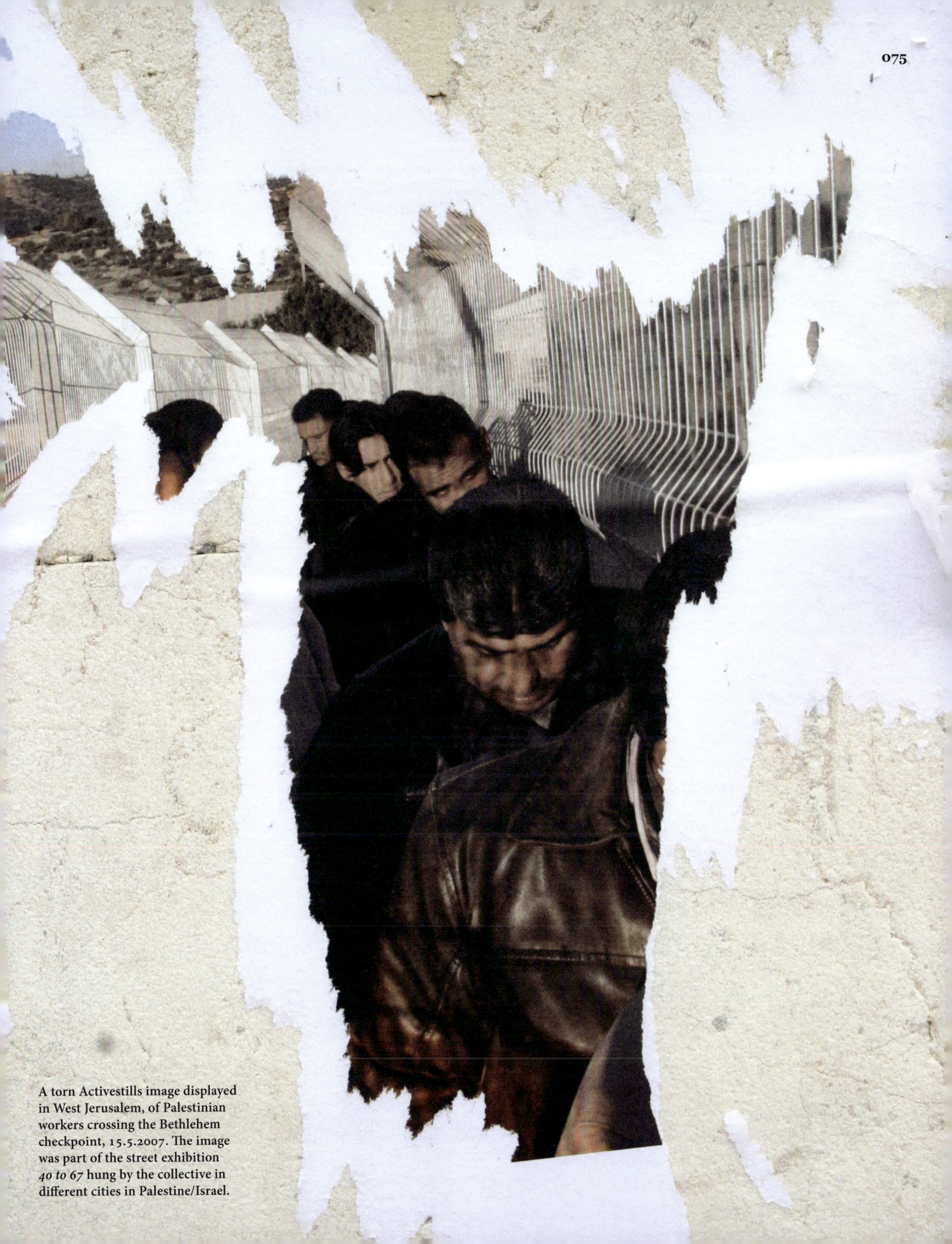

A torn Activestills image displayed in West Jerusalem, of Palestinian workers crossing the Bethlehem checkpoint, 15.5.2007. The image was part of the street exhibition *40 to 67* hung by the collective in different cities in Palestine/Israel.

they do not necessarily see them in the same way. Indeed, as Hochberg suggests, it is likely that different kinds of spectators will see things in radically different and countervailing ways depending on how their outlook is shaped by their national and political context. This is not just a matter of images, but also of the material reality within which people live their everyday lives. For Israelis living as citizens under the protection of a sovereign state, the violence of the post-1967 occupation of Gaza and the West Bank is kept at a distance and usually out of sight. For Palestinians, their condition as a displaced and occupied community of people without citizenship means that the occupation is an all-too-visible living reality. Similar points could be made about the distance between the realities of most Israelis and those of Bedouin and refugee communities in Israel, who have also been exposed to state repression. In general, the exhibitions organized by Activestills have, by necessity, worked within and in response to the divided reality of Palestine/Israel and in relation to a contested field of vision. But these exhibitions have also constituted interventions into, and transgressions of, the differentiated space and actively policed boundaries of this physical and perceptual terrain.

The Occupation on Display

The first Activestills exhibition, presented in multiple locations in Tel Aviv in late January 2006, was organized to mark the first anniversary of struggle against the construction of a fenced section of the Israeli separation wall in the West Bank on the land of the Palestinian village of Bil'in, near Ramallah. The exhibition was also the first coordinated action by the collective, for which the name "Activestills" was invented as a means of maintaining the anonymity of those involved. The exhibition lasted for only one week but had to be repeatedly repaired because of vandalism inflicted upon the displays in different locations. The collective sent press releases for the exhibition to the press and alternative websites. They also created a flyer identifying the locations of the exhibition and left copies in cafes and bars around Tel Aviv **[Fig. 1]**.[3] Each display was accompanied by an A3-size text, which stated at the bottom that "This exhibit is the fruit of the labor of four photographers who have documented Bil'in's struggle in the last year." The images themselves depicted different scenes relating to the struggle in Bil'in, showing the Israeli separation wall's construction site, confrontations between demonstrators and soldiers, army invasions of the village, villagers looking at the construction of the neighborhood Matityahu East (part of the Modi'in Illit settlement) on the village land, and acts of communal solidarity. The images were not organized to establish a timeline or narrative about the struggle in Bil'in. Rather, the images provided pictorial impressions of the intensity of the struggle and the way that the Israeli occupation was impacting upon village life. The images could also be understood to function symbolically. For example, one image presented a close profile portrait of a male soldier with a group of village women in the background. Consequently, the image could be read as one that presented a gendered opposition between the masculinity of the military invader and the femininity of the domestic space of the village.

In spatial terms, the function of the images and the exhibition was to transport appearances derived from a reality that was generally invisible to people living

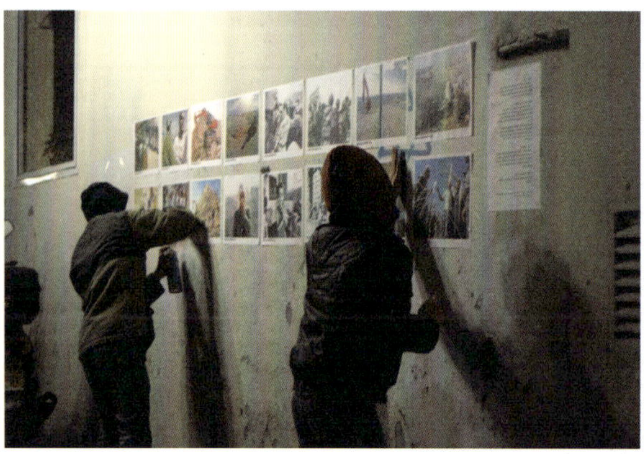

Fig. 1. Members of Activestills hang the collective's first street exhibition in Tel Aviv, 24.1.2006

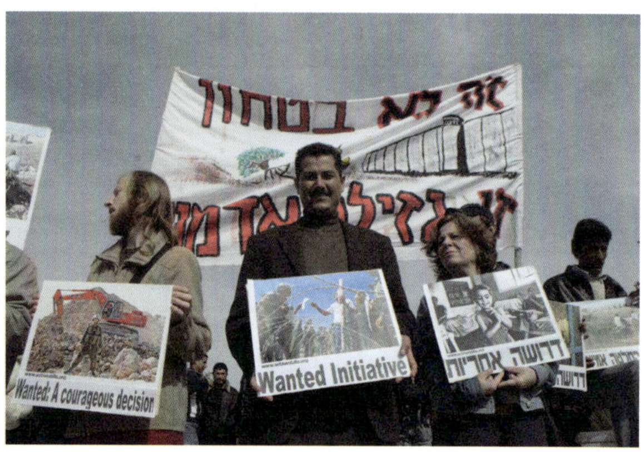

Fig. 2. Activists protest outside the Israeli High Court of Justice, West Jerusalem, 1.2.2006

in Tel Aviv.[4] This is why Keren Manor has observed of this exhibition, that Activestills "wanted to bring this reality to Israeli cities—to present these views of the occupation to people who are mentally living at a great distance, despite their geographical proximity."[5] In this sense, the images were intended to bridge the seemingly inviolable divide between the realities of the occupied West Bank and the civil space of Tel Aviv. As such, the exhibition constituted a visual transgression, of not only the physical boundaries between Israeli civil life and the occupation, but also the mental and ideological borders between the *here* of life within the Green Line and the *there* of the occupied West Bank.

Thought about in temporal terms, the photographic images in this exhibition were literally of the past but, at the same time, were meant to attest to a current political struggle and condition.[6] In this sense, the images were not intended to have a historical or merely photojournalistic purpose in the sense of reporting on something that had happened. Instead, the exhibition was intended to work in two temporal directions, one marking the past year of struggle in Bil'in and the other looking to the present and ongoing struggle against the Israeli separation wall and settlement construction on village land. The accompanying text affirmed an overriding present/future temporal orientation to the exhibition, in that it drew attention to the petition against the construction of the wall on village land currently going through the Israeli High Court in Jerusalem. This part of the text was laid out like a wanted ad, involving four paragraphs, each with a heading prefixed with the word: "Wanted." These headings were: "Wanted: Initiative"; "Wanted: Open-mindedness"; "Wanted: Responsibility"; "Wanted: A Courageous Decision" [**Fig. 2**]. These "wanted" characteristics were rhetorically aimed at the High Court and its deliberations, calling for a just solution to an unresolved situation. When combined with this text, the images functioned as evidence of an injustice that required a solution. More directly, the images and the accompanying statement were aimed at viewers who might themselves be moved to think more about, and even act in response to, what was happening in Bil'in.

In June 2007, Activestills mounted another exhibition, under the general title *40 to 67*. The exhibition entailed four different displays relating to Gaza, Bethlehem, Hebron, and East Jerusalem that were displayed in different locations in Tel Aviv and also elsewhere within the Green Line in Haifa, Jerusalem, Be'er Sheva, and Ashdod.[7] Like the Bil'in exhibition, these displays involved photographic images printed in color on A3 paper and were accompanied by a text; however, they were not uniform in the number of images they involved. The displays were sometimes presented together and sometimes separately. Each involved an attempt to represent something of the contemporary occupation as it affected different places. The display about Gaza, entitled "Gaza Strip—Hostages," was meant to show how the residents of this densely populated area had been enclosed and effectively held "hostage" by the Israeli state after the so-called "disengagement" in 2005 [**Fig. 3**]. The display dealing with Hebron, entitled "Hebron—Absentees," addressed the division of the city into the "H1" area, under Palestinian administration and where the majority of the Palestinian population lived, and the "H2" area where a smaller Palestinian population lived under a situation of Israeli

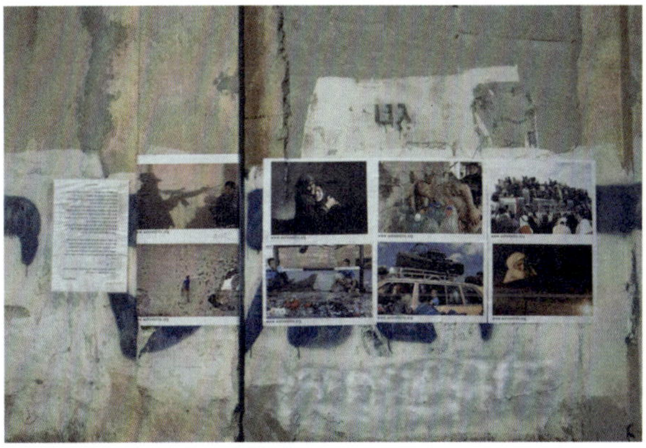

Fig. 3. *40 to 67* exhibition [Gaza grid], Tel Aviv, 10.5.2007

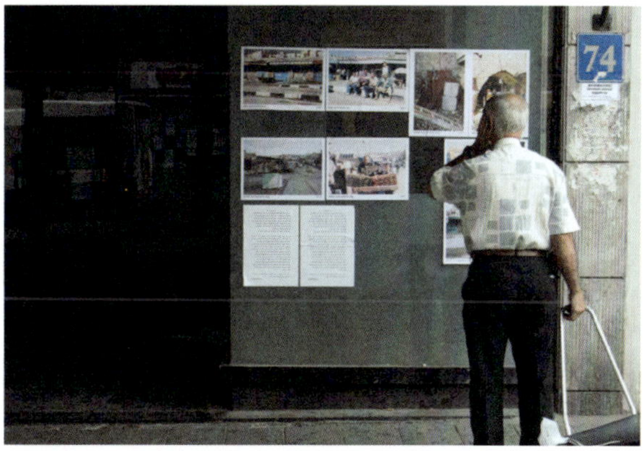

Fig. 4. *40 to 67* exhibition [Hebron grid], Tel Aviv, 10.5.2007

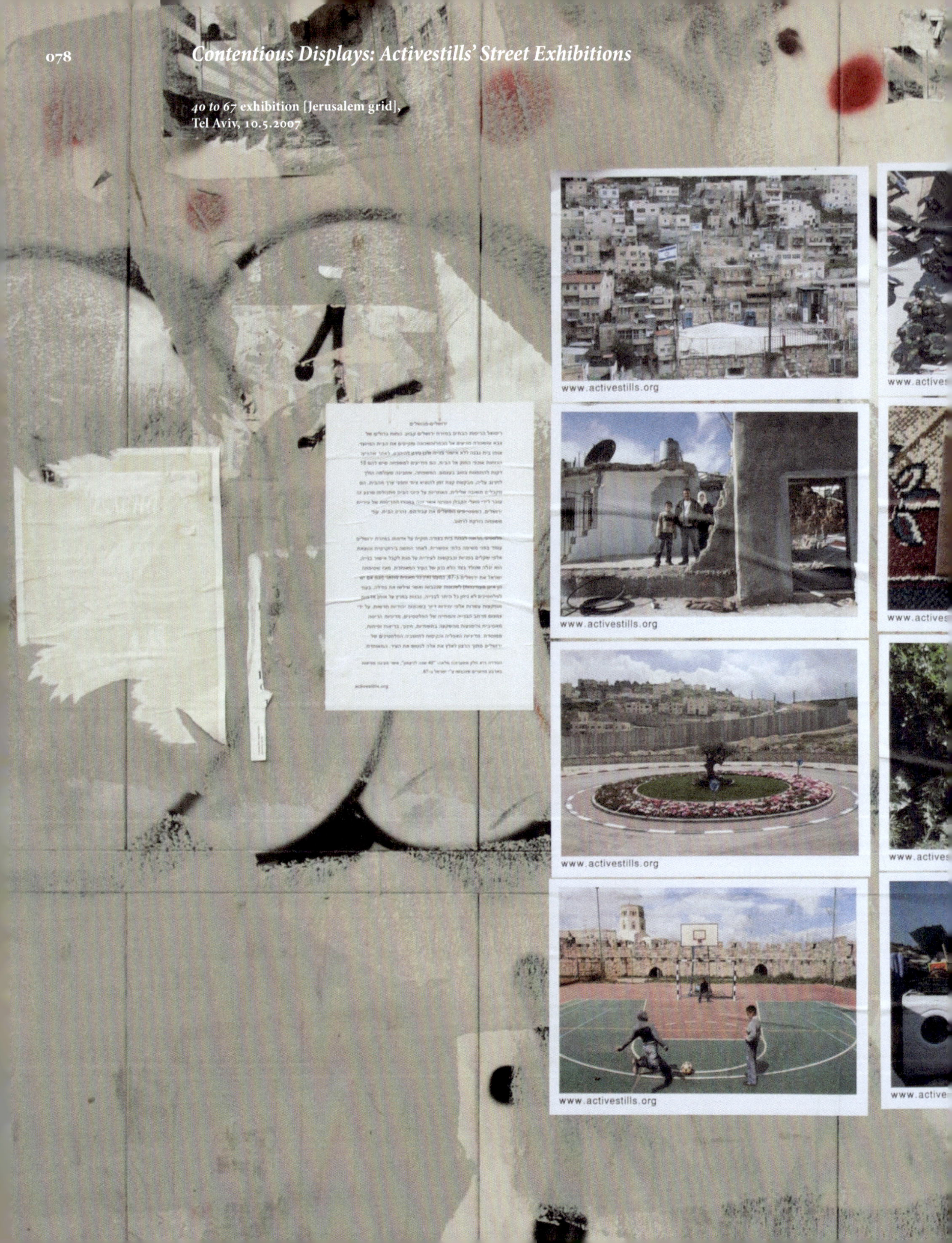

40 to 67 exhibition [Jerusalem grid],
Tel Aviv, 10.5.2007

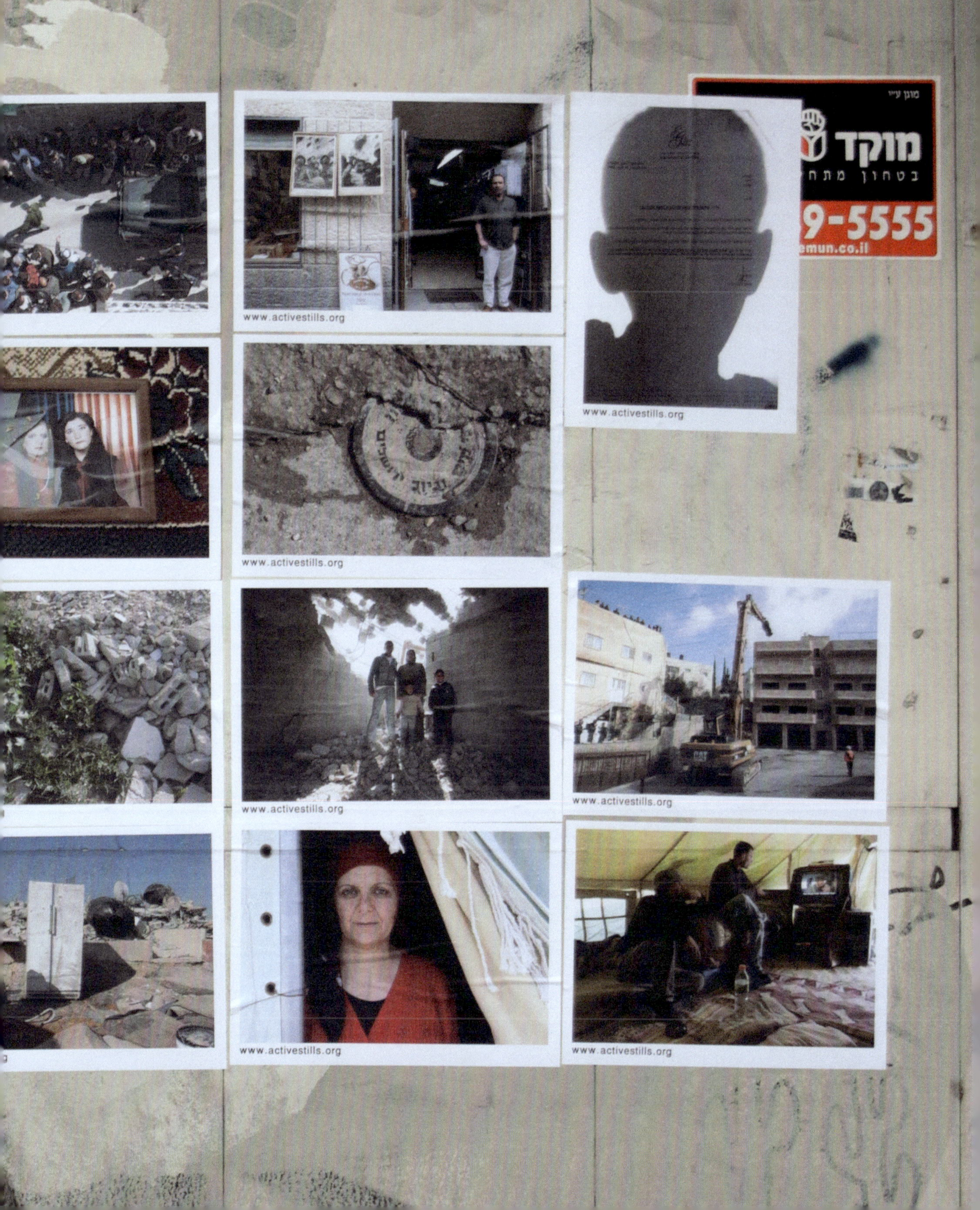
www.activestills.org
www.activestills.org
www.activestills.org
www.activestills.org
www.activestills.org
www.activestills.org
www.activestills.org
מוגן ע״י
מוקד
בטחון מתח
9-5555
emun.co.il

military control that enabled the continuing presence of small settler groups in the city. The images for this display were divided equally between those picturing scenes in "H1" and "H2," the former showing bustling city life and the latter depicting Shuhada Street, a main shopping street, that was now empty as a result of the occupation [**Fig. 4**]. The display about Bethlehem, entitled "Bethlehem—Trapped," focused on the effects of the building of concrete sections of the Israeli separation wall on Palestinian life, especially around the Aida refugee camp and upon the difficulties of Palestinian workers crossing through the wall to work in Jerusalem [**p. 75**]. The larger Jerusalem display, entitled "Jerusalem—Expelled," addressed situations in East Jerusalem and, in the main, presented images dealing with the displacement of Palestinians by settlers in the Old City and the village of Silwan, as well as house demolitions and their effects elsewhere [**pp. 78–79**]. The photographs for the four displays of the exhibition were taken by the regular membership of the collective, now expanded to six photographers, and also by Palestinian photographers from Gaza (Mohammed Abed and Wissam Nasser)[8] and Hebron (Nayef Hashlamoun), who were invited to contribute.

As with the Bil'in exhibition, *40 to 67* was primarily concerned with transporting appearances relating to the contemporary occupation to Israeli public spaces where such sights were generally absent. The exhibition was also organized to mark the fortieth anniversary of the beginning of the occupation. As such, the exhibition was also intended as an intervention into the public remembrance of the June war of 1967 that was generally presented as a great victory for Israel. Consequently, the accompanying text for the displays stated that the "show will relate to the 'victory' of the 1967 Arab-Israeli War as it is perceived by the Israeli public." The concern of the collective was to question the nature of this "victory" by revealing something of the conditions of those people who were paying the price for Israeli military hegemony. Despite this relationship to the collective remembrance of June 1967, *40 to 67* was patently not a historical exhibition. As such, the Activestills exhibition can be contrasted with Ariella Azoulay's contemporaneous exhibition *Act of State* at the Minshar Gallery in Tel Aviv, that presented a timeline of photographs by multiple photographers relating to the development of the occupation of Gaza and the West Bank from June 1967 to 2007.[9] This comparison is not made to

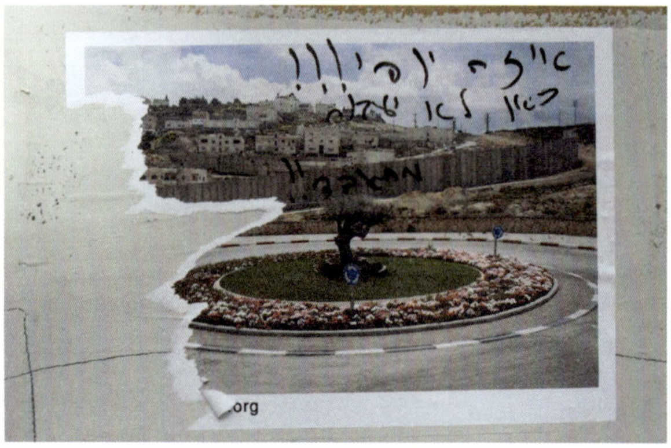

Fig. 5. *40 to 67* exhibition [Jerusalem, detail], Tel Aviv, 9.6.2007

suggest that Azoulay's exhibition was not concerned with how the history of the occupation related to the present. The purpose of *Act of State* was, in fact, to set the past in dialog with the present and to understand the occupation as a system that was continuing to emerge. However, the difference is that *40 to 67* functioned exclusively in terms of establishing a relationship between images taken in the very recent past and the ongoing conditions of the immediate present. Both the Activestills exhibition and *Act of State* were meant to function as photography-based counters to dominant and official narratives of the "greatness and heroism of the state." Yet, the Activestills exhibitions can, in part, be seen as an attempt to exploit as well as intervene into the public commemorations around the fortieth anniversary of the June 1967 Arab-Israeli War.

It is also significant in relation to the temporal orientation of *40 to 67* that there was less emphasis upon action and events in the images constituting the four displays in comparison with the 2006 Bil'in-related exhibition. The images in the display relating to Bethlehem focused predominantly on architectural structures, especially the Israeli separation wall in the West Bank, while half the images of Hebron depicted streets devoid of people. The other displays were also less dramatic in content in comparison with the images in the exhibition on Bil'in and thus seemed to be more about the everyday hardships and low-key structural or "withheld" violence of the occupation, than about "eruptive" violence and obvious struggle.[10] These displays presented an impression, not so much of past events, but of the ongoing material order of the occupation. The images of the concrete wall in

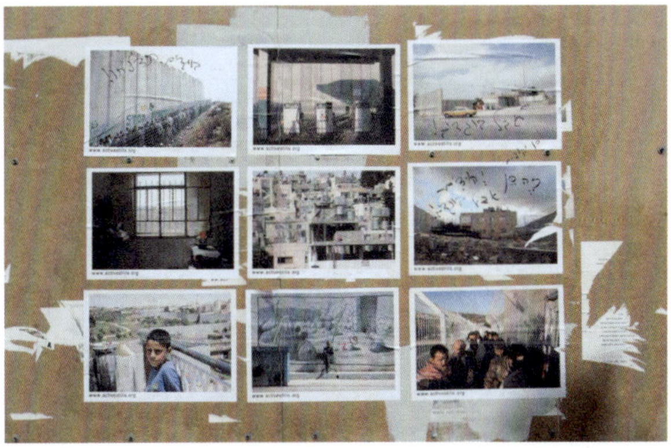

Fig. 6. *40 to 67* exhibition [Bethlehem grid], Tel Aviv, 9.6.2007

particular appeared to attest more to something that continued to be, rather than working in terms of Roland Barthes' definition of photography in general, something that asserts "that-has-been."[11]

Refusing to See

The problem faced by Activestills in their attempts to make the continuing reality of the occupation visible in contexts where it was generally invisible, was that much of the evidence of responses to these exhibitions indicates that Israeli spectators were strongly opposed to the intentions of the collective. Photographs taken by members of Activestills of both the 2006 Bil'in exhibition and the June 2007 displays show Israelis looking at or, apparently, ignoring the images. However, some of these photographs also document damage inflicted on the exhibitions. At its most extreme, this damage involved the total removal or erasure of the displays. In less extreme instances, respondents merely defaced or wrote onto the images and accompanying texts. These acts appear to have been generated by opposition to what the images showed and to the political objectives of the collective. Both seem to have been perceived as offensive and unacceptable. These responses can also be understood as attempts by ordinary citizens to police aberrations within the Israeli field of vision and, at the same time, to secure the boundaries of Jewish-Israeli identity. In particular, the writing of graffiti over the displays was intended to verbally reframe the images and, in some instances, to comment on Activestills themselves. For example, in response to an image that depicted a concrete section of the Israeli separation wall dividing the Shuafat refugee camp from the settlement of Pisgat Ze'ev, one spectator wrote: "How lovely! Here a suicide bomber will not pass" [**Fig.** 5].[12] This statement seems to have been intended as a redefinition of the image's significance in terms of dominant Israeli discourses on security, by recasting the wall as a legitimate means of Israeli self-defense as opposed to an oppressive and divisive architectural form.

The same spectator also wrote "Traitors Good Luck" on another image depicting Palestinian men waiting in line to pass through a checkpoint in the wall near Bethlehem [**Fig. 6**]. This statement indicates that it was not only the content of the image, but also the very act of making and displaying an image of Palestinian life under occupation, that was unacceptable to the respondent. From this point of view, displaying an image that encouraged sympathy for the Palestinians was viewed as a betrayal of the Jewish-Israeli community defined in strict national terms. It is significant in this respect that another respondent wrote on the same image: "You're not Jews." Such statements not only exclude the Jewish members of Activestills from what Amalia Ziv terms the "Jewish Israeli discursive community," but also constitute attempts to silence the collective by situating them "in a location from which it is impossible to speak legitimately."[13]

Similar responses were also generated by an exhibition of 70 images from the Activestills archive that was staged in April 2014 as part of a conference entitled "Visual Culture Between Obedience and Resistance" at the Shenkar College of Engineering and Design in Ramat Gan, near Tel Aviv. These images were varied in their subject matter, some depicting struggles against the occupation in places like Bil'in, while other images depicted demonstrations involving Jewish Israelis, such as the social protests in 2011 and ultra-Orthodox Jewish opposition to the military draft in 2014. Consequently, the exhibition covered a range of issues and struggles inside and outside the Green Line that members of Activestills had photographed in recent years. Nevertheless, for some right-wing students, such an exhibition in what they defined as public space was completely unacceptable.[14] Their first response was to tear the exhibition down and throw it in the garbage. When the images were remounted in their original position on a display case in the main entrance hall to the college, these students then demonstrated in front of the exhibition, calling for its removal. The students also added to the display by attaching two Israeli flags and taping images of weeping Israeli soldiers and Israeli Army medics treating injured child victims of suicide attacks to the display [**Fig. 7**]. These images were meant to function as counters to what these students described as "Palestinian propaganda."[15] It might be suggested that these additions to the Activestills exhibition were meant to "balance" the display in the eyes of the right-wing students, by adding another side to the visual argument. However, it should be remembered that the students had originally attempted to remove the exhibition altogether, indicating that what they really wanted was for the images to disappear altogether. Adding the counter-images was a secondary response on the second day of the conference, but one that affirmed their basic opposition to the exhibition. It was not simply the case that the protesting students thought that other students at the college should be shown images of injured Israelis alongside images of Palestinian suffering, but also that the Activestills exhibition was itself a kind of attack that was somehow equivalent to the violence toward Israelis shown in the images they had added to the display. In this sense, the latter images were illustrative of the potential consequences of Israelis breaking ranks with the national collective. The students also added a notice to the exhibition that implied something along these lines, which read: "Freedom of speech does not mean freedom of consequence." Although this statement is somewhat ambiguous, it seems to suggest that the students thought that freedom of speech should not be prioritized over the security of Israeli Jews who might be endangered as a consequence. How exactly the Activestills exhibition constituted a danger to Israelis was not made clear, but it seems that a conceptual linkage existed for the students between images that were attempts to show injustices inflicted upon non-Jews and the betrayal and endangerment of Israeli Jews. Consequently, for them, it was a necessity that the images be removed from view.

As with the responses to the earlier street exhibitions, these responses to the Shenkar exhibition indicated a strong refusal to see Activestills images as anything but national betrayal. Though in relation to the Shenkar exhibition, it should also be added that other students defended the exhibition, either because they felt it should remain on the grounds of freedom of speech, or because they were sympathetic to what the collective was trying to do. This suggests other possibilities of viewing and response to the images besides those performed by the right-wing students. Perhaps there is something revealing about this, in that the latter students felt strongly that they had to remove the images and subsequently be visible and vocal in their opposition to the exhibition precisely because other students might not feel the same way as them.[16] Such responses indicate a confidence on the part of the right-wing students about being able to act within and police the Israeli public sphere, but at the same time they suggest a degree of defensiveness concerning the commitments of other Israelis to Zionist beliefs about what it is to be a Jewish Israeli.

Displaying Struggle

The Activestills exhibitions discussed in the preceding section of the essay involved the presentation of photographic images depicting situations in the West Bank and Gaza to Israeli spectators who would not normally see such things. In contrast to this, the following section addresses exhibitions that involved displaying images in the actual locations where the political struggles depicted in them were occurring, or in locations that were in some way related to these struggles. These exhibitions often involved an emphasis upon the transportation of appearances across time rather than space. As such, they involved the re-presentation of struggles back to their participants, allowing them to re-view what they had

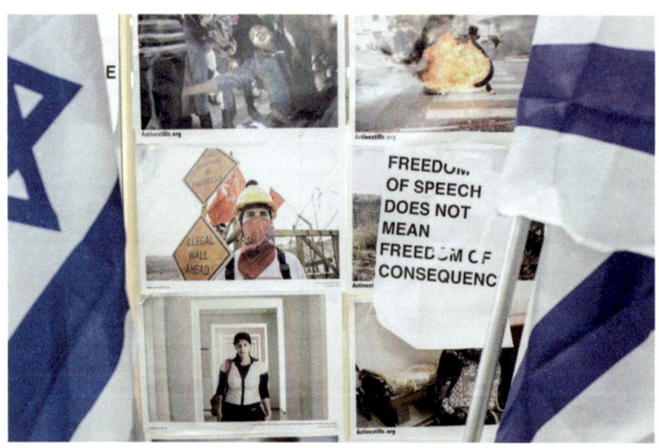

Fig. 7. Activestills photos between two Israeli flags placed by students in Shenkar College, Ramat Gan, Israel, 31.3.2014

achieved.[17] The value of this practice has been summarized by Keren Manor when she observes that in her experience, "people like to see their struggles."[18] Yotam Ronen has also suggested that presenting people's actions back to them through photographic images affirms the significance of these struggles by demonstrating that such actions are "important enough" to be photographed.[19]

As an example of this practice, we can return to the relationship between Activestills and the struggle in Bil'in. As already discussed, the collective formed in response to this struggle, and they developed their first exhibition in an attempt to publicize to Israeli spectators what was happening in the village. In addition to this, members of the collective saw themselves as participants in this struggle acting in solidarity with the villagers. This solidarity primarily took the form of a sustained documentation of the demonstrati ons, but it also involved sharing the resulting images with the village community as a resource for their struggle. The latter practice included the sharing of images through public exhibitions, the first of which involved the re-showing of the exhibition presented in Tel Aviv in January 2006 in the community center in Bil'in.[20] This was followed, in February 2007, with the presentation of a second exhibition exclusively in Bil'in on the same day as a large demonstration organized to mark the second anniversary of the struggle against the Israeli separation wall. Like the 2006 exhibition, this display involved images of the demonstrations and confrontations between demonstrators and the army, but it also included a number of images documenting the creative activism for which the struggle in Bil'in had become well known.[21] Photographs of the exhibition and the demonstration show people from the village and demonstrators looking and pointing at the images. Activestills also mounted a similar exhibition in Bil'in in February 2015 as a contribution to the tenth anniversary of the struggle in the village. Again, members of the collective took photographs of people interacting with the images. This time the photographs explicitly showed people pointing at themselves in the images on display. For example, one image showed Mohammad Khatib, a member of the Popular Struggle Coordination Committee in Bil'in, pointing at an image showing him arguing with soldiers ten years previously in 2005.[22] In this context, the images in the exhibition worked in terms of familiarity and recognition as opposed to unfamiliarity, distance, and rejection, as was often the case when Activestills images were presented within Israel.

Comparable interactions with Activestills images also occurred in 2010 in the "unrecognized" Bedouin village of Al-Araqib in the Negev Desert, which was demolished by Israeli authorities in July that year in the first of a protracted series of demolitions. Members of Activestills had photographed the village prior to and during the demolition in July 2010. In particular, Oren Ziv developed a working relationship with the villagers, providing images to be carried in a demonstration in Tel Aviv against the proposed destruction of the village in May 2010 and returning to the village with further images in the immediate aftermath of the July demolition. Some of these images were selected and displayed in a protest tent set up by the villagers. These images placed an emphasis upon showing what the village had been like before the demolition. What this suggests is that the images functioned for the villagers as mementos of the past existence of the village as well as a means of remembering what had happened to their homes.[23] When used in demonstrations before and after the main demolition, these images also functioned as a means of showing this destruction to others. The printed images were visual artifacts that were both viewed and shown by the villagers as part of a political struggle over the future existence of the village that was simultaneously a struggle to remember what the village had once been.

A related example can also be identified in relation to the involvement of Activestills with actions taken by Sudanese refugees held in the Holot "open" detention center in the Negev. Holot was opened in December 2013 as a site to hold refugees who had previously been detained by Israeli authorities in the nearby closed prisons of Keziot and Saharonim. Israel currently hosts a population of African refugees, predominantly from Eritrea and Sudan, who number in the tens of thousands. This population is denied basic rights and access to services as well as being pressurized to leave Israel through indefinite and arbitrary detention and the refusal of asylum claims. Since 2008, African refugees have also been subject to the "Prevention of Infiltration Law" that was created in the 1950s to stop Palestinian refugees returning to their homes after the establishment of the State of Israel (within the Green Line) in 1948. This law was amended in 2011 to formally include African refugees.[24] On 15 December 2013, 150 detainees began a march from Holot to Jerusalem to protest against their detention without trial and the failure of the Israeli government to respond to their asylum claims. On the first day of the demonstration, the marchers walked to Be'er Sheva where they slept in the main bus station. On the second day, they walked to Kibbutz Nachshon in central Israel, where they stayed a second night, before traveling on to Jerusalem and the Knesset, where they were beaten and arrested by the police. The marchers were then held in secure prison sites for a number of weeks, before being sent back to Holot. Members of Activestills followed and photographed the march, which was reported by them on social media using the hashtag *#MarchForFreedom*. On 25 January 2014, Israeli activists organized a "Solidarity Visit" to Holot. As part of this event, Activestills displayed about 40 images on one of the fences of the site. People involved in the march came out of the prison to look at the images. From the perspective of the collective, what was important about the exhibition was that it enabled the marchers to see images of their action that they could not have seen while being held in closed detention sites. As Ziv has observed in relation to this, "people do their action ... and then don't get to see the result."[25] In this sense, the images fulfilled a similar mnemonic role to those exhibited in Bil'in and Al-Araqib. The images of an action in the past were fed back into a struggle, enabling the participants to see themselves as resisters through the photographs, perhaps affirming their sense of self as political subjects and agents.

Something different can be observed about the staging of a street exhibition in the Old City in Nablus on 29 October 2012. This exhibition was organized by Ahmad Al-Bazz and presented images taken earlier in 2012 by different members of Activestills of demonstrations in the West Bank and Israel in support of hunger-striking Palestinian prisoners held in Israeli prisons. The exhibition was staged in an alleyway that led to the house of Hassan Safadi, a Palestinian prisoner who had engaged in two long periods of hunger strike, but was released on the same day as the exhibition [**Fig. 8**]. The aim of the exhibition was partly to display popular responses to the hunger strike to the members of the Palestinian media who would inevitably visit Safadi's home after his release. The demonstrations depicted in the images included one in Jaffa that involved Israelis protesting in support of the Palestinian prisoners, something that surprised some spectators. The exhibition also showed Safadi images of events that he could not possibly have seen while being held by the Israelis under administrative detention. Al-Bazz wanted to show Safadi that "the street" had supported his struggle while in prison. This latter intention appears to have been welcomed by Safadi and his family, who later took the images from the exhibition as mementos of the popular support he had received while on hunger strike.[26] Unlike the other examples discussed in this section, the exhibition relating to the Palestinian prisoners on hunger strike involved the collection of images depicting events in multiple places. Although some of the images pictured demonstrations in Nablus itself, many depicted things that had happened elsewhere. Consequently, the exhibition involved the transportation of appearances across spatial distances as was the case with the exhibitions within the Green Line discussed in the last section. However, unlike the exhibitions in Israeli cities, the subject matter addressed by the Nablus exhibition was one that was politically and socially proximate to its spectators. It is significant in this light that one of Al-Bazz's photographs of the exhibition shows that the Activestills images were presented alongside images presented by other people, including a framed portrait of Safadi and political posters that included portrait images of Safadi and other hunger strikers.

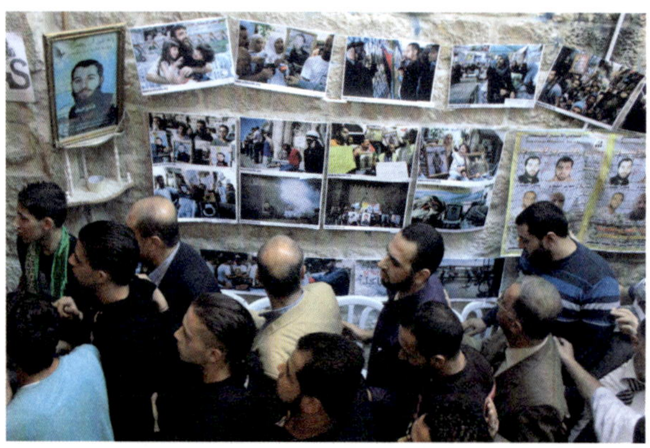

Fig. 8. An Activestills exhibition displayed near the house of the Palestinian hunger-striker Hassan Safadi, in tribute to his release from Israeli prison, Nablus, West Bank, 29.10.2012

Conclusion

The significance of Activestills exhibitions staged in different places was subject to discussion at a meeting of members of the collective in Ramallah in mid-August 2015.[27] The key concern addressed in this discussion was the relative value of exhibitions in Israeli cities as opposed to exhibitions presented in contexts where the struggles pictured in the images on display were actually occurring. On this subject, Ahmad Al-Bazz expressed the opinion that it was better for Activestills to organize exhibitions for spectators who were not familiar with the situations and events depicted in the images. In line with this, he stated, "I don't like the exhibitions in Palestinian places." He affirmed this point by observing that he is "very attracted to exhibitions outside," where "we are presenting something that is new to people." One might understand these points in relation to the long-standing idea that documentary photography has a primarily revelatory role. It is meant to show that which has not been seen to those who have not seen it. At the same time, this approach could also be related to a more general concern among Palestinian communities living under occupation to find ways to show "the world" their situation and, through this, give voice to their political plight.[28] Framed in terms of this imperative to show unseen things to others, exhibitions in the West Bank, for example, might be viewed as acts that show people what they already know. Yet, in response to this, we might recall that the 2012 exhibition in Nablus did, in a sense, show spectators images of a familiar struggle but, at the same time, brought together images of demonstrations in different places that many observers could not have seen in such a combination if not for the exhibition.

Other members of the collective expressed less faith in the ability of the exhibitions to affect spectators distanced from the struggles depicted in their images. For some of them, the exhibitions in Jewish-Israeli cities, in particular, had come to have a "symbolic," rather than practical value.[29] Such symbolic, but perhaps impractical, gestures within Israeli public space were contrasted with the different kind of symbolism involved with the presentation of exhibitions in solidarity with communities engaging in struggles. Some members of the collective articulated this contrast in terms of a sense that they had learned through experience that presenting images of struggles back to their participants was more worthwhile than staging exhibitions for a general Israeli audience that is on the whole disconnected from and indifferent or hostile to these struggles. Consequently, Oren Ziv observed, with reference to the organization of exhibitions, that "today, many times, personally for me, it's in solidarity with people." This point of view requires contextualization not only in relation to the developing experience of the collective but also in relation to the further hardening of Israeli public opinion toward the Palestinians in recent years. Currently, there seems to be even less space for dissent within Israel, when it comes to relationships between Israelis and Palestinians, than there was in 2006. This situation potentially makes exhibitions within the Green Line simultaneously less effective and more symbolically significant. Also raised during the group discussion as an important consideration in relation to the relative merits of Activestills exhibitions in different places, were changes in the surrounding media landscape. When Activestills began organizing exhibitions in 2006, the Internet and social media were much less significant as an alternative means of distributing information and images between the West Bank, Gaza, and Israel. This meant that exhibitions in public places had a potentially significant role as a means of showing images of things happening in one place to people located elsewhere under conditions of limited access to information about these events. Social media have transformed this situation to a large degree, providing immediate online sources for images rarely found in the mainstream news media. This has meant that, to some extent, Activestills have had to reframe the purpose and meaning of their exhibitions, either by focusing more on the idea of using exhibitions to directly support struggles or by focusing on exhibitions within the Green Line as symbolic intrusions into a more or less homogeneous political and related visual field.[30]

Given the changing conditions under which Activestills have developed their collective project, it is difficult to identify what kind of exhibition in what context is the most politically useful or where the collective might develop this practice in future. What is clearer is the significance of the group's different exhibitionary practices for their own development and for the development of visual activism within Palestine/Israel over the past decade. As Andrea Brighenti has observed, "Visibility lies at the intersection of the domains of aesthetics (relations of *perception*) and politics (relations of *power*)."[31] Visibility is coterminous with power in that it is both the product and a means of power. Where the power of the state and of the primary media institutions are set against you, making things visible that are not in the general interests of power can be very difficult. Under such conditions, as is the case for Activestills, interventions into the field of the visible take on larger significance.

1. I use this phrase to designate the territorial space of former Mandate Palestine in terms of its current geographical organization and in terms of the unresolved historical relationship between Israel and what was and might be Palestine.
2. See Gil Z. Hochberg, *Visual Occupations: Violence and Visibility in a Conflict Zone* (Durham, NC and London: Duke University Press, 2015). I also address the subject of appearance and visibility in Palestine/Israel in my essay "On Israel/Palestine and the Politics of Visibility," in Katarzyna Marciniak and Imogen Tyler, eds., *Immigrant Protest: Politics, Aesthetics, and Everyday Dissent* (Albany: State University of New York Press, 2014), 147–67.
3. Shiraz Grinbaum and Oren Ziv, interviewed by author, Tel Aviv, 1.6.2014.
4. Here, I am thinking about John Berger's definition of cameras as "boxes for transporting appearances": John Berger and Jean Mohr, *Another Way of Telling* (London: Writers and Readers Publishing, 1982), 92.
5. Quoted in Ben Ronen, "I Am a Camera," *Programma* 3 (fall 2010): 95.
6. Ariella Azoulay has suggested a similar way of regarding photographs as evidence of ongoing conditions: Ariella Azoulay, *The Civil Contract of Photography* (New York: Zone Books, 2008), 16.
7. Displays were also presented on a concrete section of the Israeli separation wall in Anata in East Jerusalem and in Bethlehem.
8. Basel Alyazouri, another photographer from Gaza, later joined Activestills in 2014.
9. See my article, "The Black Box of the Occupation Revisited: Photography, Responsibility, and the Israeli Occupation," *Afterimage* 35:3 (November/December 2007): 13–16.
10. Here, I am using Ariella Azoulay and Adi Ophir's distinction between "withheld" and "eruptive" violence that they articulate in relation to the occupation. See Ariella Azoulay and Adi Ophir, "The Order of Violence," in Adi Ophir, Michal Givoni, and Sari Hanafi, eds., *The Power of Inclusive Exclusion: Anatomy of Israeli Rule in the Occupied Palestinian Territories* (New York: Zone Books, 2009), 99–140. See also Hochberg, Visual Occupations, 13.
11. Roland Barthes, *Camera Lucida: Reflections on Photography* (London: Vintage, 1993).
12. The author took photographs of the graffiti on Activestills displays discussed in this section in central Tel Aviv in June 2007.
13. Amalia Ziv, "Performative Politics in Israeli Queer Anti-Occupation Activism," *GLQ* 16:4 (2010): 544.
14. Shiraz Grinbaum, who witnessed and documented student protests against the exhibition at Shenkar, has identified the students as members of the right-wing Zionist organization Im Tirtzu ("If you will it"). Discussion between David Reeb, Oren Ziv, and Shiraz Grinbaum, and the author, Tel Aviv, 2.6.2014.
15. Shiraz Grinbaum, "Out of Sight, Out of Mind: Right-wing Students Tear Down ActiveStills Photo Exhibit," *+972 Magazine*, 2.4.2014, accessed 3.4.2014, http://972mag.com/out-of-sight-out-of-mind-right-wing-students-vandalize-activestills-exhibit/89212/.
16. It is also worth noting that Palestinian students with Israeli citizenship attending Shenkar College were intimidated by the actions of the right-wing students and as a consequence felt unable to speak up.
17. Another example of this practice is presented in the documentary film *5 Broken Cameras*, when one of the makers of the film, Emad Burnat, is shown screening his own video footage of the preceding five years of

resistance in Bil'in to other people from the village: Emad Burnat and Guy Davidi, *5 Broken Cameras*, 94 min., New Wave Films, 2011.

18. Statement made during Activestills group meeting, Ramallah, 14.8.2015. Present at this meeting were Ahmad Al-Bazz, Faiz Abu-Rmeleh, Mirela Gallardo Avellan, Shiraz Grinbaum, Keren Manor, Yotam Ronen, Oren Ziv, and the author.

19. Ibid.

20. Oren Ziv and Shiraz Grinbaum, interviewed by author, Tel Aviv, 1.6.2014.

21. See Maia Carter Hallward, "Creative Responses to Separation: Israeli and Palestinian Joint Activism in Bil'in," *Journal of Peace Research* 46:4 (2006): 541–58; Rania Jawad, "Staging Violence in Bil'in: The Performance of Violence in a Palestinian Village," *TDR: The Drama Review* 55:4 (winter 2011): 128–43.

22. Haggai Matar, "PHOTOS: Pepper Spray and Arrests as Bil'in Marks Decade of Struggle," *+972 Magazine*, 28.2.2015, accessed 19.9.2015, http://972mag.com/photos-pepper-spray-and-arrests-as-bilin-marks-decade-of-struggle/103430/.

23. Oren Ziv, interviewed by author, Tel Aviv, 17.8.2015.

24. See the website for the African Refugee Development Center in Tel Aviv, accessed 12.12.2015, http://ardc-israel.org/en/content/refugees-israel.

25. Oren Ziv, interviewed by author, Tel Aviv, 17.8.2015.

26. Ahmad Al-Bazz made these points about the Nablus exhibition during the Activestills group meeting in Ramallah, 14.8.2015.

27. See above, n. 4.

28. See Lori A. Allen, "Martyr Bodies in the Media: Human Rights, Aesthetics, and the Politics of Immediation in the Palestinian Intifada," *American Ethnologist* 36:1 (2009): 161–80. See also Amahl A. Bishara, *Back Stories: U.S. News Production and Palestinian Politics* (Stanford, CA: Stanford University Press, 2013), and Faulkner, "On Israel/Palestine and the Politics of Visibility."

29. Yotam Ronen, in particular, expressed this view.

30. Shiraz Grinbaum used the term "intrusion" to describe Activestills exhibitions in Israel during the group discussion.

31. Andrea Brighenti, "Visibility: A Category for the Social Sciences," *Current Sociology* 55:3 (2007): 324; emphasis in the original.

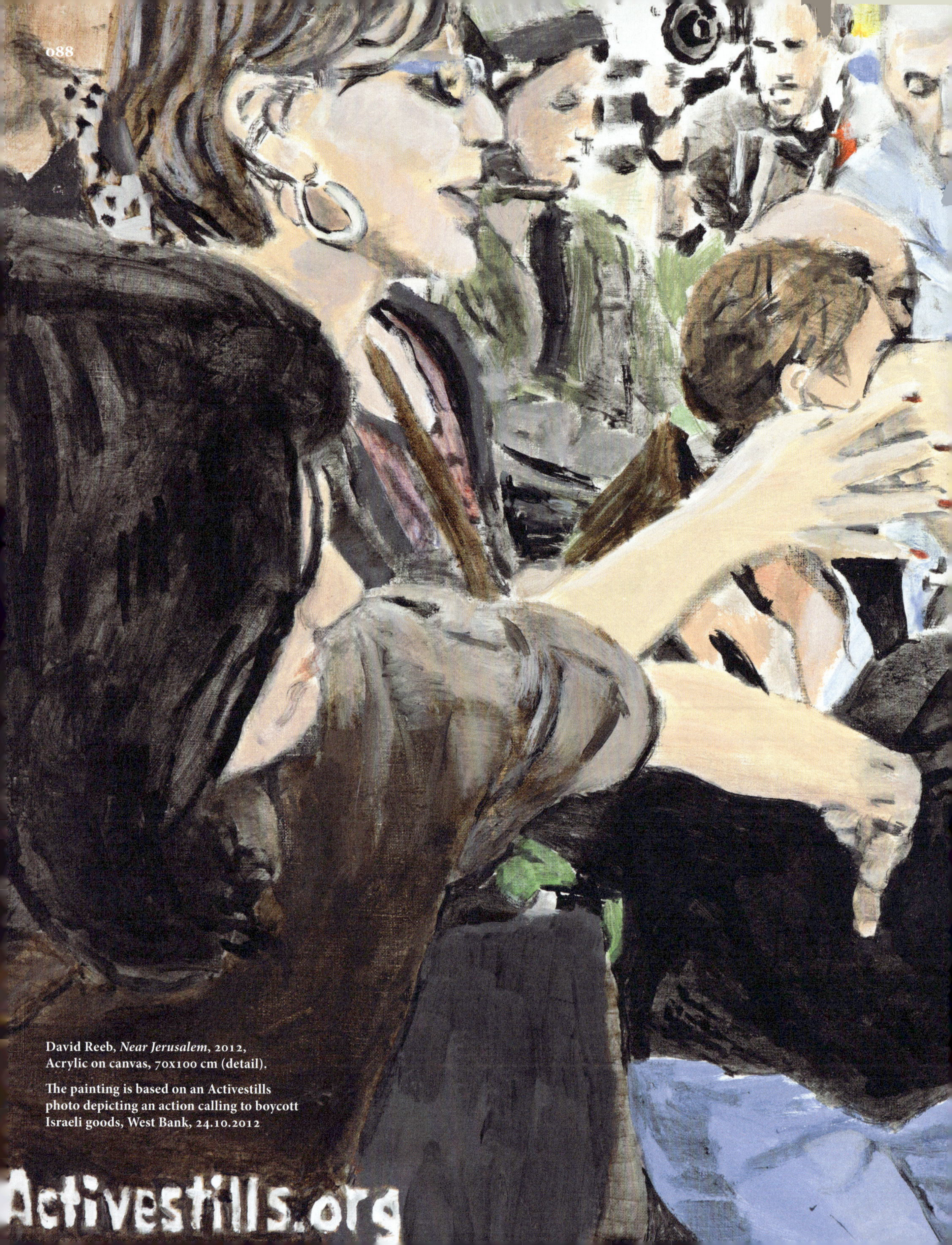

David Reeb, *Near Jerusalem*, 2012,
Acrylic on canvas, 70x100 cm (detail).

The painting is based on an Activestills photo depicting an action calling to boycott Israeli goods, West Bank, 24.10.2012

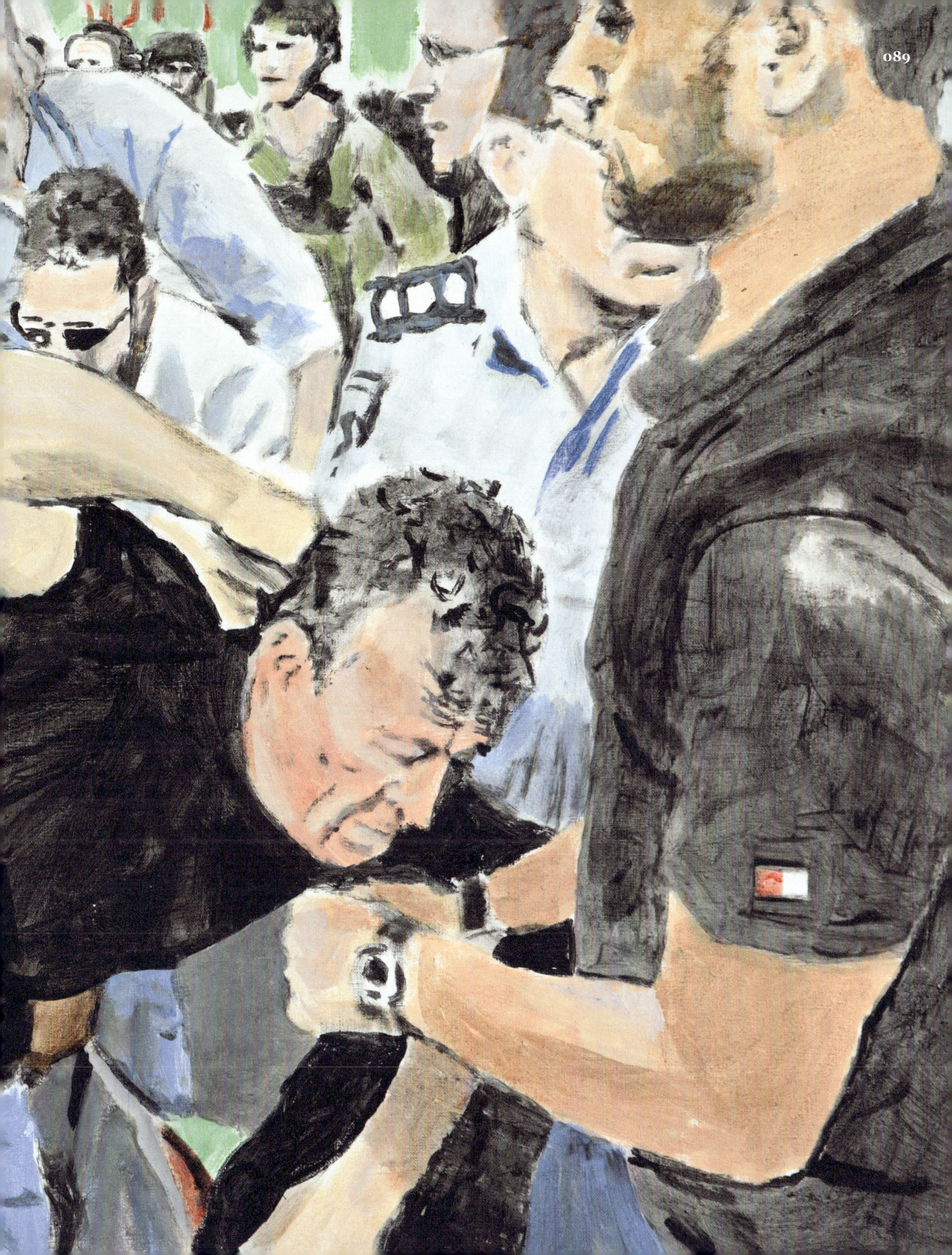

Conversation with
Zehava Greenfeld

Zehava Greenfeld is active in a group that is fighting for public housing in Israel. She also has been participating in demonstrations against the Israeli occupation in the village of Nabi Saleh in the West Bank since 2011.

Oren Ziv: You are one of the few people involved both in the struggle of Nabi Saleh and the struggle for public housing. How do you see the connection between the two depicted in these photographs?

Zehava Greenfeld: This demonstration in Nabi Saleh was very emotional. Men and women rise up from the midst of grief and loss and join hands and walk together to protest. This is a strength that I have never seen anywhere else. On the poster that we are holding is a picture of the soldier who supposedly killed Mustafa [Tamimi].[1] Halla, the woman to my right, who doesn't go so much to protests ever since she was nearly arrested, said to me, "You hold this poster and I will hold that one and we will walk together." And this was very moving for me. This is a picture within a picture. It carries a lot of pain in it. And that is one of the more beautiful things about Nabi Saleh—when someone dies, it's not that it doesn't hurt, but from that pain, the women go out and grieve almost with joy. And this is something that I wasn't familiar with and that I learned there. I call it Palestinian psychology—you take the place that breaks your heart the most and that throws you into the deepest despair, and from there you grow.

OZ: Because you are actually smiling in the photograph and this is a terrible picture.

ZG: This is because we managed to break the wall between us for a moment. For me, this ties in to the struggle for public housing, because I come to Nabi Saleh and I hold out my hand as if for an infusion of strength, for my life, for the other struggles that I am engaged in.

OZ: Maybe tell us a bit about what we don't see in the picture; something that a person who looks at it doesn't know, besides that you are holding a poster and the two of you are marching in the protest.

ZG: I have been going to Nabi Saleh for about four years. The first time I went they burned the Israeli flag and I was shocked. And then I decided that I wanted to get to know these women. It wasn't easy at that moment. But the decision to stay, in retrospect, gave me many gifts that I am grateful for every day. And one of the things that you don't see in this photo is mainly the strength of the women and the heavy price they pay for the struggle; their decisions in their roles as mothers; their children, who instead of them being more and more scared and afraid, they [the mothers] move them forward. What you don't see are the injuries and all the arrests, the children taken to jail.

OZ: What is it like for you to reach the occupied Palestinian territories, because not many women engaged in the public housing struggle go to protests there and not many Israelis in general?

ZG: Among those of us fighting for public housing there is a kind of identification and empathy about all those [who are] oppressed whoever they are. Some of us are still bound up in the lies that Zionism has taught us. I have asked myself many times, can someone who is oppressed really see someone else who is oppressed? This is a question that I can't yet answer. Once I was with Nariman Tamimi at her home during a protest and she was baking pita bread and at the same time we were being shot at from all sides of the balcony, there were explosions, and she kept on with the pita bread until she had finished baking. I left full of emotion and wrote a post about this, titled "How to Bake Pita in Nabi Saleh." A friend from the public housing struggle read it to her entire family at lunch on Shabbat [Saturday]. So I think that if there is only oppression in most cases it puts you in a cave. But if there is also struggle, it opens your eyes to see others and to understand that my cry will be louder only when it includes many voices.

For example, take the picture of the eviction of Rachel from her home. This was the first time that I witnessed an eviction. I was alone fighting against the policies of the government and the public housing companies for years. Every day I would run home from work in a panic hoping we had not been evicted from our home. And then suddenly, I was present at the eviction of Rachel. At the beginning of the formation of a united front in the public housing struggle we were just three women: Samira from Jaffa, Rachel from Yavne, and myself. We looked for other women and this was a sort of magical unity. So the question is: am I ready to be in a place where there is a major emotional shift, and on the other hand understand that in the political realm, in the field, I don't see something drastically changing across the board. I'm split. And it is harder for me now than ever, because the struggle in Nabi Saleh separates me from my friends in the public housing struggle, because let's say that they managed to get a housing solution from the state, they will send their kids to the army to kill the children in Nabi Saleh. So then I have a problem. And I don't know how to solve it. I know that there is a theory that says you don't solve anything, you just go to support people where they need you, because that's who you are. But it's a bit tough on me.

OZ: What's going on in the second photo?

ZG: Here, at six o'clock in the morning, Rachel called me saying she is being evicted from her home owned by a public housing company. I and some other activists and friends quickly drove there. Here you can see that we thought that if we stood in a line then the evictors wouldn't be able to pass us. But it was so fast, and they had already started with the eviction. There are tougher pictures, where we take cement blocks and try to stop them. But Rachel, after struggling longer than any other human being I know, began to give up. That same day she had no strength. She said, "Enough, just go." This was the first time I saw an eviction and you don't forget a thing like that. Every time I see this photo my heart skips a beat, because I know that on that day we lost. As opposed to Nabi Saleh, here I'm not sure we know from where to take strength. Somehow in Nabi Saleh, maybe because they are oppressed to the core, then they find the strength to fight back.

OZ: Maybe it's connected to [the fact] that Nabi Saleh has an entire community, families.

ZG: Yes. It's hard to create solidarity. I think that if you know that they can shoot and kill your child, your resistance grows even greater, it is a physical instinct. In the public housing struggle, the different affiliations are somehow too mixed up. You see, many of the women struggling for public housing love their country, and they won't reject the government altogether. And this dissonance is hard for me. I want a war. I want them to throw stones in the streets, make a magnificent civil intifada. And I don't see this happening. The more you fight, the more your consciousness is built. Here we are kicking with the cement blocks that they were starting to seal the house with. After the eviction, we tore the seal open and went inside and drew on the walls, in order to let out our frustration.

OZ: Both in the public housing struggle and in Nabi Saleh there is great importance to photography and documentation. Not only Activestills, many other independent photographers are also documenting the village. How do you see photography's role in these struggles?

ZG: Photography has a huge importance, to the level of saving lives. For example, in documenting illegal arrests, or shooting at demonstrators, also children. In addition, I think that the photographs capture moments that would disappear otherwise. I think that even though Nabi Saleh is a very well-documented place, there are still millions of things that have not been photographed there. First of all, because this struggle is unique and so is the public housing struggle. It's not usual that a woman steps out of her house and says "I am fighting for my home." And in fact, this is the way of solidarity—here we see you, here you are seen. And I saw people in the public housing struggle who would see their picture online and something would happen to them. There was a woman, who came from a very prominent family, and she didn't want to disclose her name in public, and she was engaged in a struggle over her home. And she came with us to a demonstration and we made a video clip for ourselves, and she said to me afterwards, "See what I said there. Did you see how they heard me?" Suddenly she was present. And specifically these kinds of women who are practically invisible, and have no solidarity net that keeps them together, the photo says to them: here, you are present, which is the most basic thing you can say to someone, "I see you." It's like "to be or not to be." I will never in my life forget that moment. And this picture that you [OZ] took with Halla moves me so much. Every time anew. So it's true, I experienced the moment and I remember it, but there is something in the photograph that makes it actually exist in reality.

OZ: As a photographer, I admire the ability of the protesters to come every week and to march, when it's clear that you are going to be shot at and will need to run away. Do you, as an Israeli protester marching and facing the soldiers, feel that photography succeeds in transferring something of the experience of protesting in the occupied territories?

GZ: I think that I can say about Activestills as a group that you see in the photographs that you are there with all your souls. And because of that, the pictures come out that way. And they would not come out like they do if it were from a photographer who was a bit more detached. But there is something in what you are photographing that [shows] your heart is there. And I can see and begin to identify the signs of each one of you in the pictures. There is something very personal in this. I don't think of photography as a tool. It's much more. Through these photographs I can see, and I know that you know. And that changes everything.

1. Mustafa Tamimi was hit by a tear-gas canister shot at him by an Israeli soldier from very close range on 9 December 2011, during a protest in the West Bank village of Nabi Saleh. He was critically injured and died the next day at Beilinson Hospital in Israel. On 5 December 2013, the Israeli Military Advocate General closed the investigation in his case, stating that the canister that killed Tamimi was fired "according to the relevant rules and regulations and did not involve any illegality."

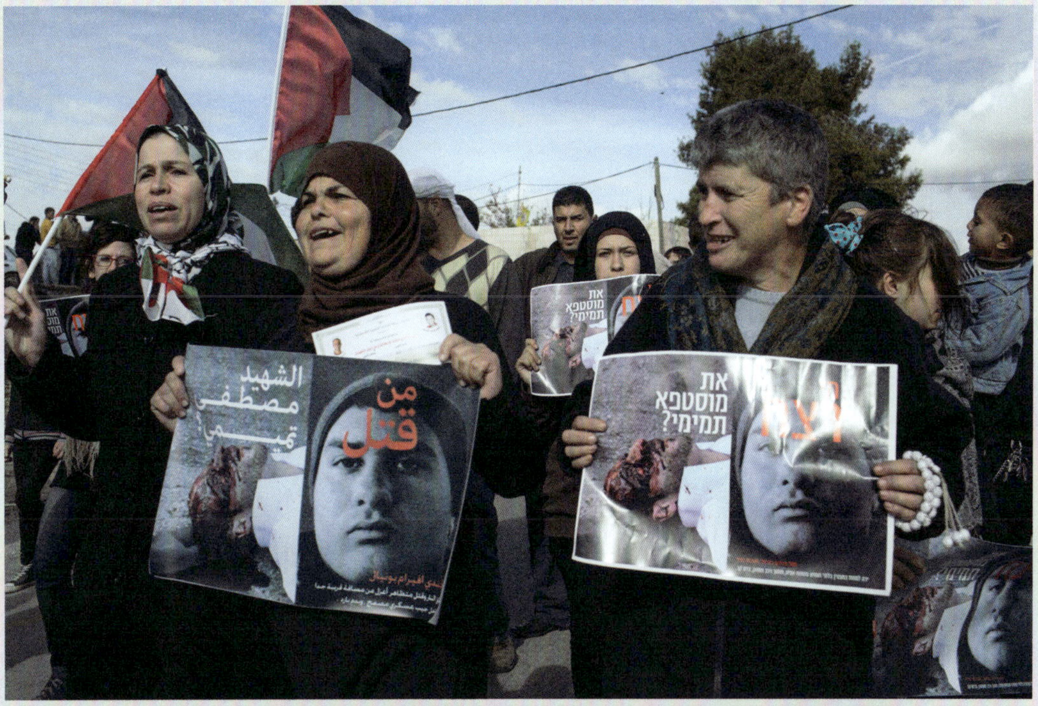

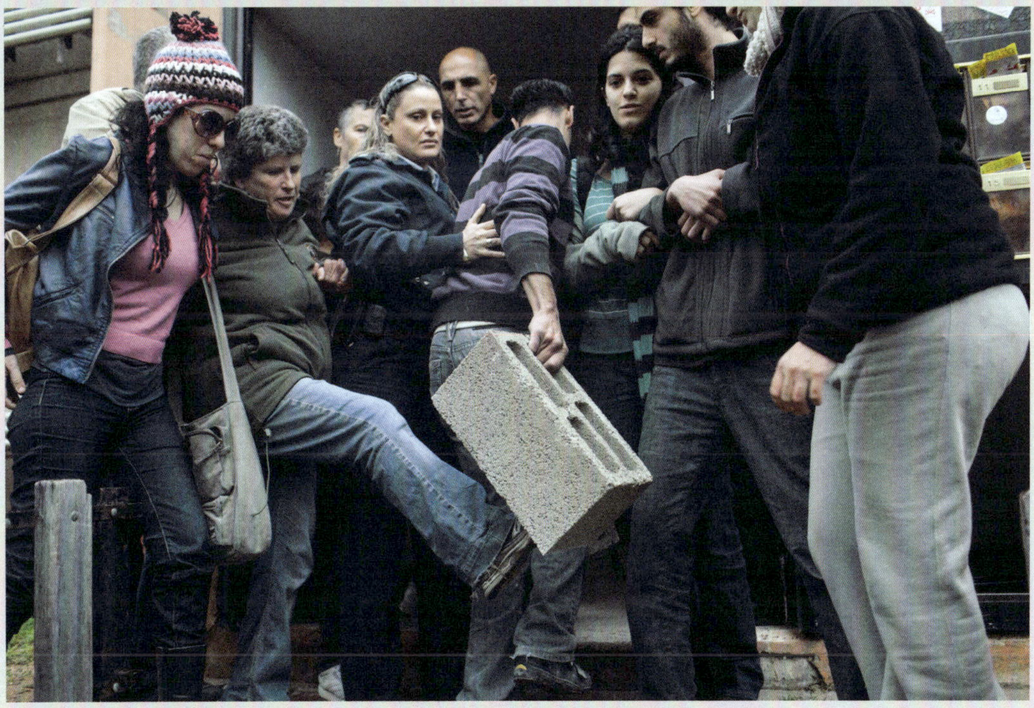

1. Palestinian and Israeli protesters hold posters with the words: "Who Killed Mustafa Tamimi?" at the weekly protest against the occupation in Nabi Saleh, West Bank, 7.12.2012 / **2.** Public housing rights activists try to prevent the Israeli police from evicting Rachel Levi-Davida, a single mother, and her daughter from their public housing apartment, Yavne, Israel, 23.1.2012

Nabi Saleh, West Bank 28.8.2015

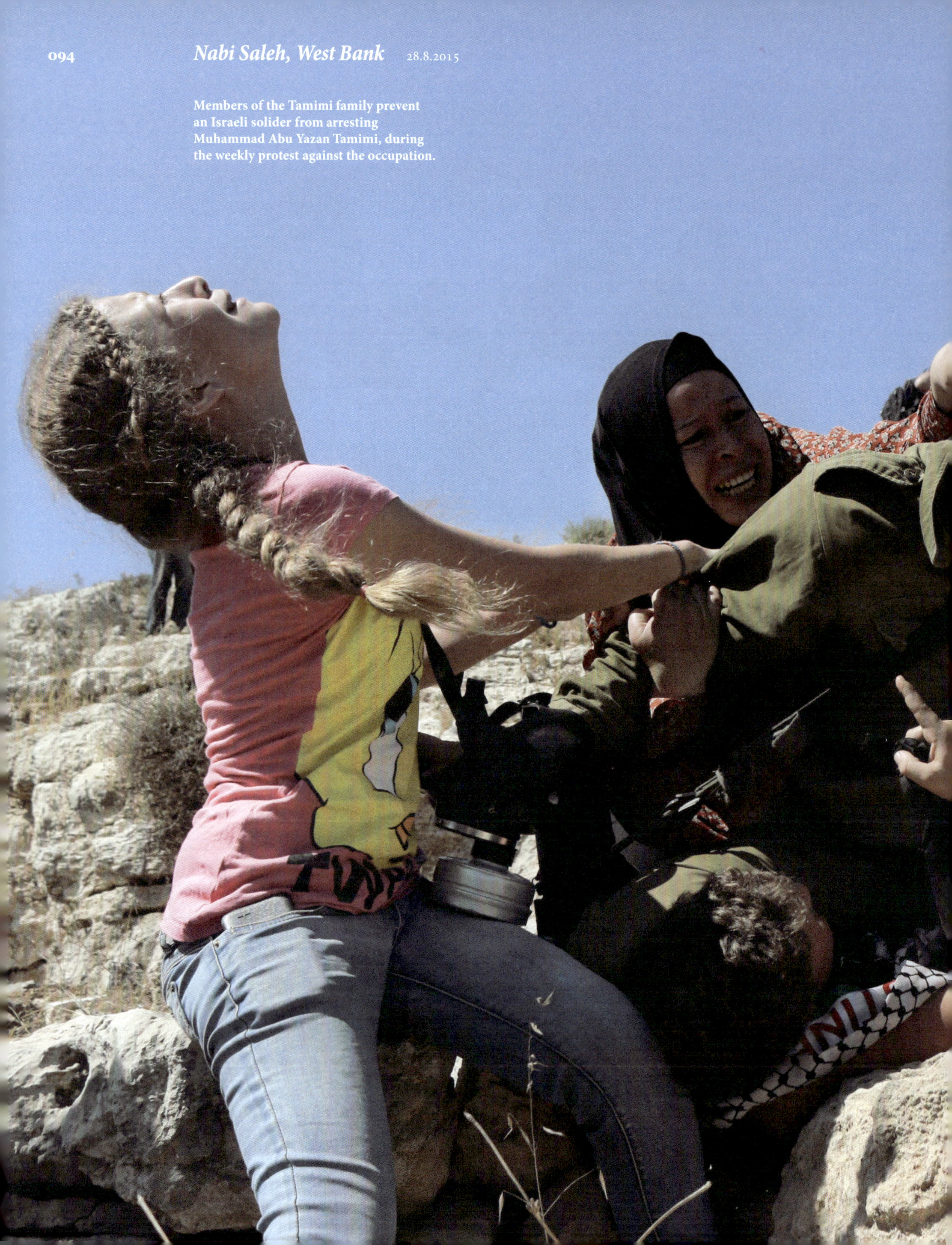

Members of the Tamimi family prevent an Israeli solider from arresting Muhammad Abu Yazan Tamimi, during the weekly protest against the occupation.

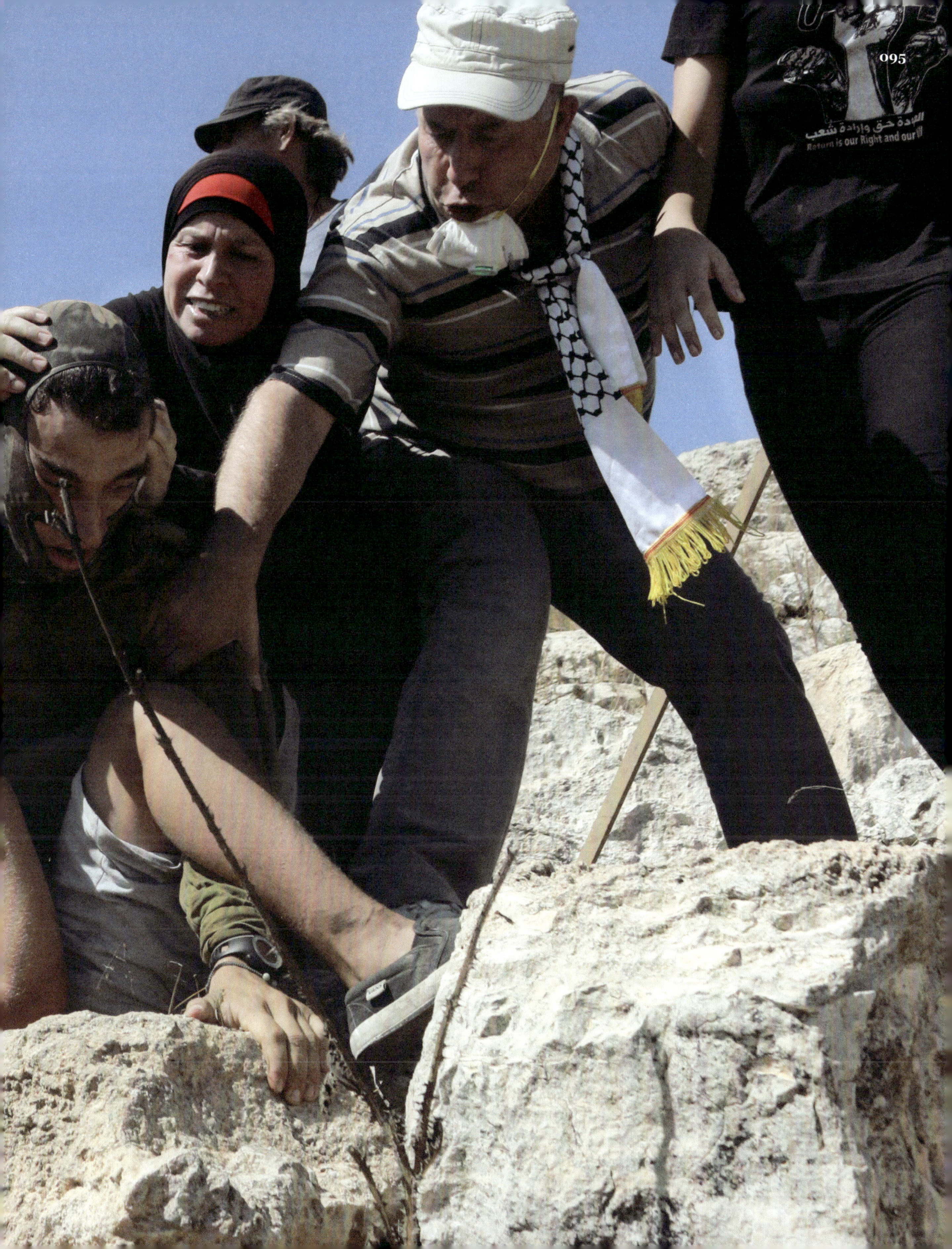
حق وإرادة شعب
Return is our Right and our

Conversation with **Nariman Tamimi**

Nariman Tamimi is among the leaders of the struggle against the occupation in the West Bank village of Nabi Saleh.

Keren Manor: For me, the most important thing is to ask you about all the years when you were taking part in the struggle in the village and also documenting it. How did it begin, how is it today, and what do you think about the role of the camera in the story of Nabi Saleh?

Nariman Tamimi: The role of the camera was important in many things. For example, there were instances when Palestinians were accused by the army of striking soldiers, and that was a lie, and they were released after five or six days in prison because of the documentation. Also international and Israeli activists, after being falsely accused by the Israelis, were helped through our photographs. I think that it will be possible to benefit from these photographs in claims to the International Criminal Court in The Hague about human rights violations that took place here.

Oren Ziv: Are there people who come to the village after they see the photographs and say, we saw the documentation on TV or the Internet and have come to see it in person?

NT: Yes. There were many video clips that we posted, and afterwards many Israelis and foreigners came. They came in order to show solidarity with us and also took away what they saw and published it, because the popular struggle is very important to the Palestinian cause against the occupation.

KM: For me, at the demonstrations you are a superwoman—you photograph, you get arrested, you give first aid. In all the years using your camera, do you recall a particular event when you had to choose whether to photograph something or not, an event when you had to decide if you were going to continue to take pictures or stop?

NT: My connection to the camera is very significant; I think of the camera as a kind of weapon because with the camera and the photographs I take, I talk with the other, so that he/she will change his/her mind, because I see the vast majority of Israelis as victims of the occupation, just like the Palestinians are victims. With my weapon, the camera, I show them the truth about the occupation that

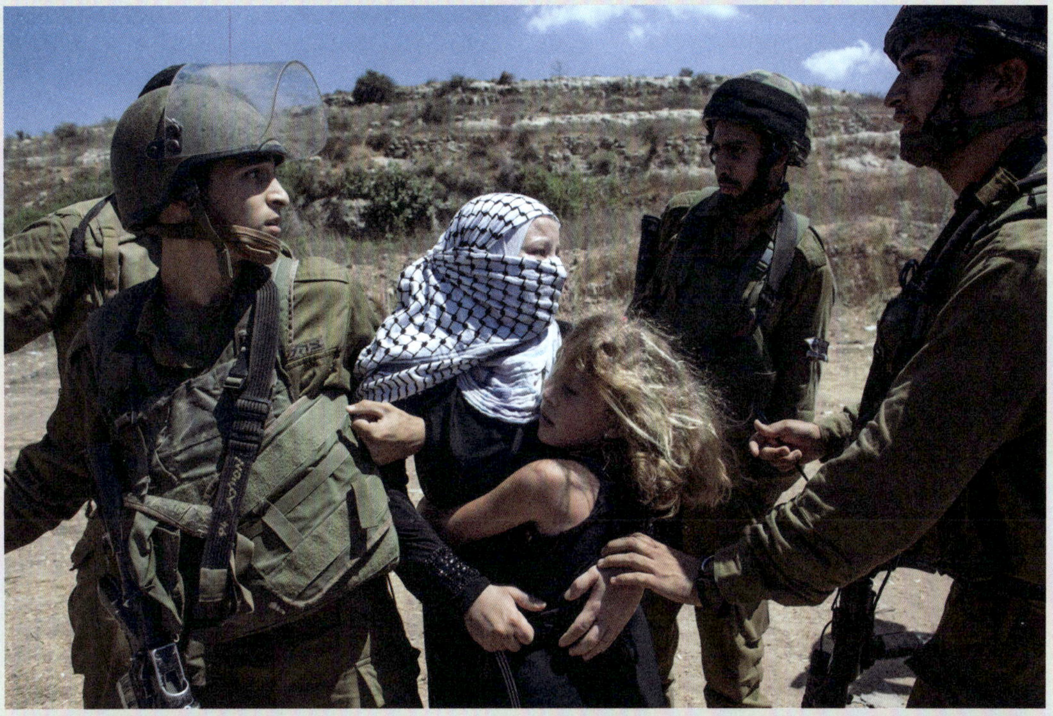

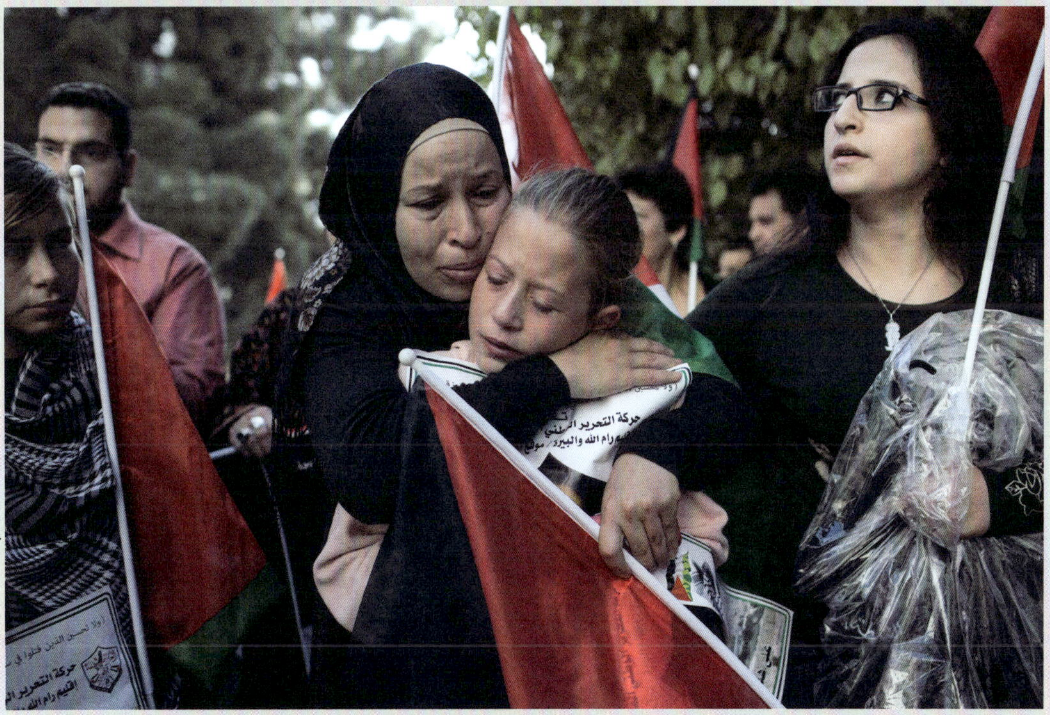

1. Israeli soldiers arrest Nariman Tamimi as her 8-year-old daughter, Ahed, tries to free her during a protest against the occupation, Nabi Saleh, West Bank, 24.8.2012 / **2.** Nariman at the funeral of her brother, Rushdi Tamimi, Ramallah, West Bank, 20.11.2012

the Israeli government is trying to hide from them. I try to revive the humanity in the other.

As for the second part of the question—whether to photograph or not, that's very difficult, because I am not a journalist and sometimes my presence is more important than my photography. But all this is opposed to what I did when I documented the killing of my brother [Rushdi Tamimi].[1] I don't know how at that moment I was able to continue to hold the camera. I sensed how much the soldiers were afraid of my camera and how important it was that I was documenting this event. Somehow in the big events I am able to keep photographing. That's what happened at the event with Rushdi. But there are moments when I feel helpless, and can't continue to document. Today I mainly photograph with a smartphone, because I still am not able to hold the same camera I used to record Rushdi's death. I feel guilty, because my brother should have been in my arms, and not the camera.

KM: You take pictures also when soldiers enter your home, right?

NT: Yes, and also outside the village. I try to document everything I can, even when I was shot by a soldier and broke my leg, I tried to photograph things with the zoom function on my smartphone. My faith in the camera is very great, so much so that we, my husband Bassem and I, have taught our children how to photograph. I gave my camera to every child so that they will learn how to document because at any moment the camera can fall out of my hand and they will need to continue to document. Every time soldiers are in the area, the children have learned to pull out the camera, because my belief in the camera has passed on to them. For us, this is a tool to expose the abuses of the military.

KM: In situations when the army comes to your home, do you feel more safe or less with the camera? Or in other situations?

NT: Not always. It depends more on the soldier's mood. If the soldier is weak, then he is likely to be afraid of the camera and won't try to do anything, but if he is strong, and has come on purpose to carry out something, then nothing will matter to him. On the contrary, there were times when I was injured and also arrested while I was photographing, and sometimes the camera gives soldiers an excuse to attack you in order to move you away from the place.

KM: There are also pictures of the killing of Mustafa Tamimi,[2] and in the end no one paid a price. Visual evidence does not necessarily promise justice in the framework of occupation.

OZ: I would like to show you a few pictures.

NT: This picture, of me and Ahed, was taken when the children came to the spring and I was far from the demonstration and the army separated the little ones from the rest.[3] I was able to reach the children, and there was an argument between myself and the commander and he told me to take the children and move them away because it was a closed military zone. The children would not agree to go, because why are the children of the settlers allowed to remain and not them? And if this is a closed military zone, then it has to be closed to everyone. There were arguments and it was very tough because I saw how they were pushing Ahed, Marah, and Wiaam, and beating them in front of me.

OZ: Many people who see these pictures comment about what children are doing at these demonstrations; that the children should be at home. What do you think?

NT: The children really should be at home, but soldiers also come to our homes. You know, the army descended on our house more than 150 times over the last six years. At first the children really did not come to the protests, but when the army started entering the homes, during the day and at night, breaking windows, then the children said they wanted to join. In a normal situation, when a child deals with violence, he will be afraid or weak. But this does not happen in Nabi Saleh. The children are stronger, healthier, more responsible, and they have more belief in themselves. They too want to tell the soldiers "no" to occupation.

KM: I have a question about the photograph taken by Muhannad Sallem Darabee. This was published in many places, even the Israeli right used this photo and claimed,

"See what the Palestinians are doing to our soldiers." Everyone, on both sides, used this photo. What is your opinion?

NT: When you look at this picture, the viewer wonders to himself what are those girls doing to the soldier. One doesn't always understand the whole event from stills. But when you see the video you understand more. I didn't see what was happening. I was far away. I heard journalists yelling to me to come, but I didn't see what was happening, I thought someone was hurt. When I came over they started to yell that they were going to arrest Muhammad Abu Yazan, my son. I came quickly and saw Ahed and Noor talking with a soldier and trying to free him. I didn't see Abu Yazan because I was behind him. I am pushing the soldier and hitting him and don't see the face of Abu Yazan underneath him. And then when I saw the video, I saw the scared look of the child, and I think that if I would have seen this first (like in the video) then I don't know what I would have done to the soldier. I was far away and didn't see the pain in his eyes, and this video was very hard for me to watch. This video shows that we are human because it shows that our only goal was to move the soldier away from Abu Yazan because his arm was broken. Our purpose was not to harm the soldier, even though inside of us there is great pain about the deaths of Rushdi and Mustafa. When I see this video I know how far we have come to our own inner peace, and this is important.

OZ: Do you think it helps to understand the situation outside of Nabi Saleh? This is perhaps the best best-known photograph from here. What was the effect of this photo?

NT: From my point of view, the attempt of the Israeli right to appropriate the picture for their own needs shows their fear of it. I would like to say something. I think that my, Nariman's message, with or without the camera, is that I am a human being who loves all human beings. I do not have a problem with anyone, because you are Keren, my friend and you are an Israeli, Oren is my friend. Jonathan Pollak is my brother. My brother Rushdi was killed, and he is in the place of Rushdi for me. Any person who consciously rejects the occupation, for me, that person is a brother or sister and a loved one. Even the soldier who killed my brother, if he were to come here now and you were to give me a gun with which to shoot him, I would not shoot him. Inside of me there is a pain I live with every second and I see it in my mother's eyes, I felt it in the voice of Bassem when Rushdi was killed because it reminded him of the death of his sister. With all of that, I will not kill the soldier, because I would not want his family to experience my pain. I hope that the soldier who killed Rushdi will return to his humanity because the most important thing is the human being, more important than the land.

KM: There are men in Nabi Saleh who are very brave, women who are very brave, and this is unique for me. This is very powerful and has also taught me a lot. And thank you for speaking with us.

NT: I feel that you are partners with me in my struggle; you are not distant people. You don't have to thank me, because you and I are in the same bunker and in the same place. This is very important. Do you understand?

KM: I understand. I do.

1. Rushdi Tamimi was critically injured by live ammunition fired by an Israeli soldier during a demonstration in the village of Nabi Saleh. He died two days later, on 19 November 2012, at the hospital in Ramallah. The Israeli Military Advocate General closed the case in May 2014. No soldier was prosecuted.

2. See note on p. 92.

3. Nabi Saleh's residents have organized weekly demonstrations to protest against the confiscation of the village's lands and the takeover of their spring located at the outskirts of the village near the Israeli settlement of Halamish. Since 2009, the Israeli Army has declared the spring a closed military zone, and access to it is forbidden to Palestinians. Israeli settlers often use it while escorted by Israeli soldiers.

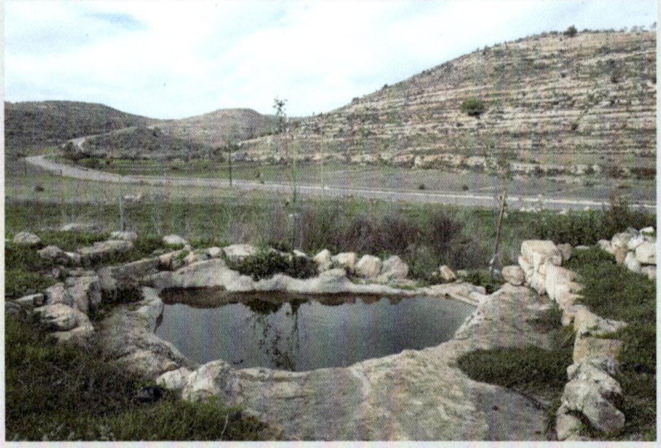

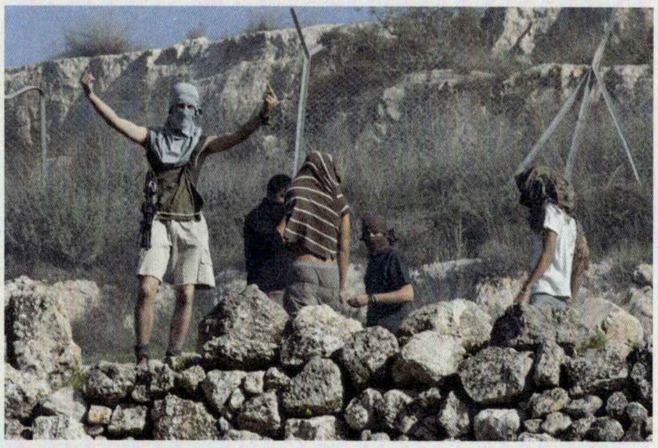

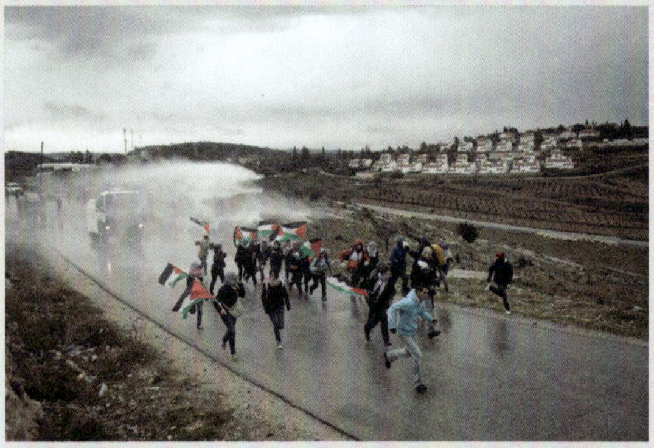

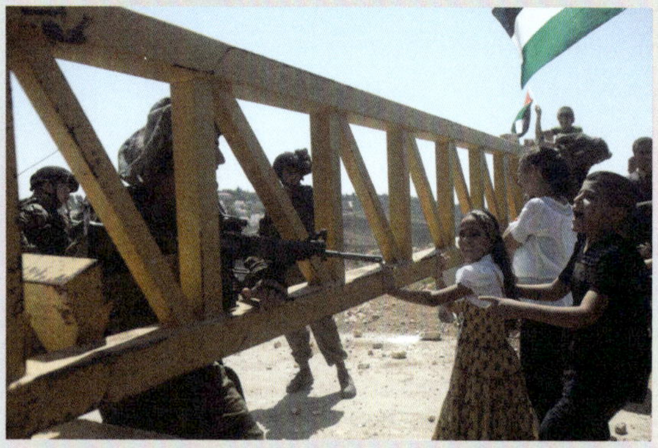

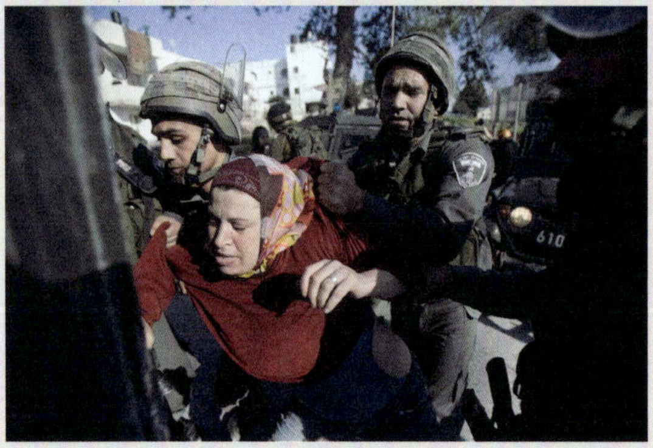

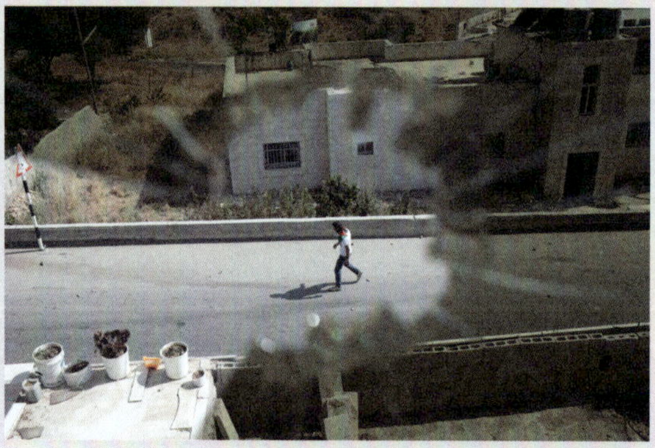

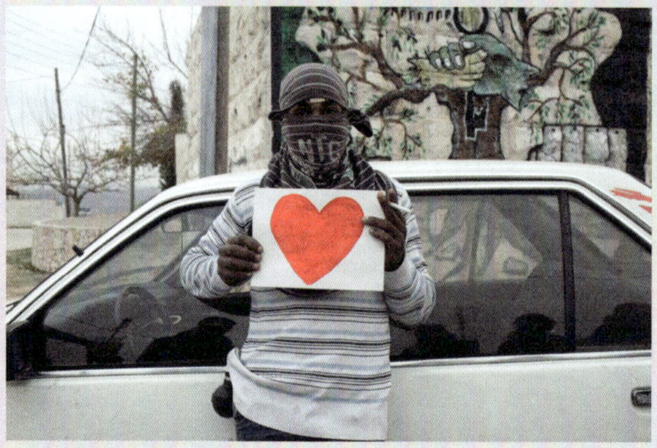

{Top left to right}
1. Nabi Saleh spring, 15.12.2009 / **2.** Armed settlers gesture at protesters, 8.1.2010 / **3.** Protesters run from army truck spraying "Skunk" water, 13.1.2012 / **4.** Protesters reach an army gate, 10.9.2010 / **5.** Arrest of Manal Tamimi, 22.1.2010 / **6.** Palestinian youth seen through a broken window, after the Israeli Army shot 15 rubber-coated bullets into a home during the weekly protest, 18.5.2012 / **7.** A Palestinian youth holds a sign before the beginning of the weekly protest, 30.12.2011

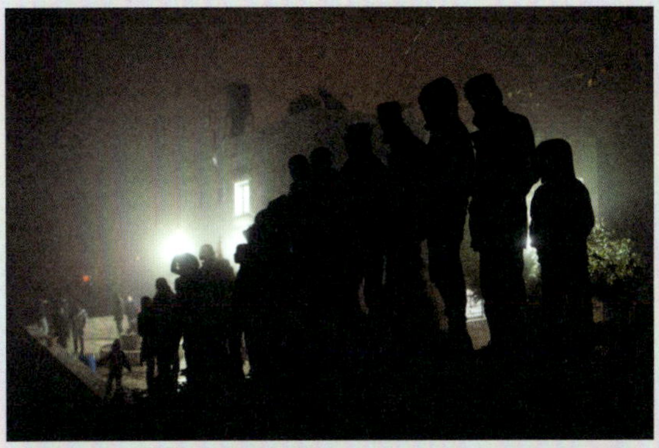

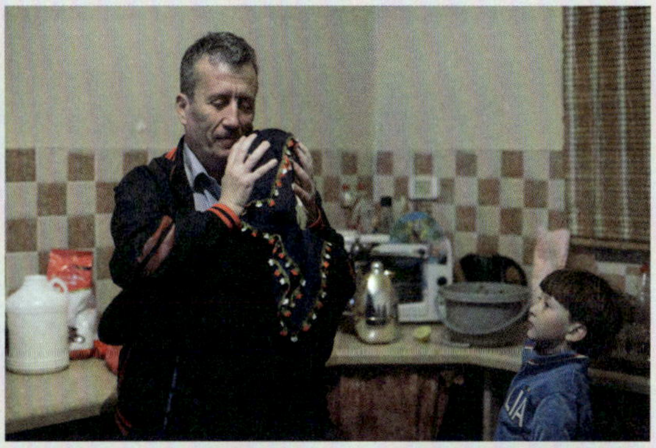

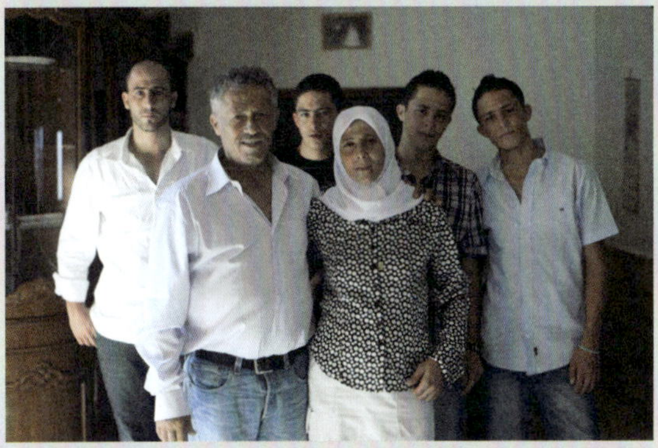

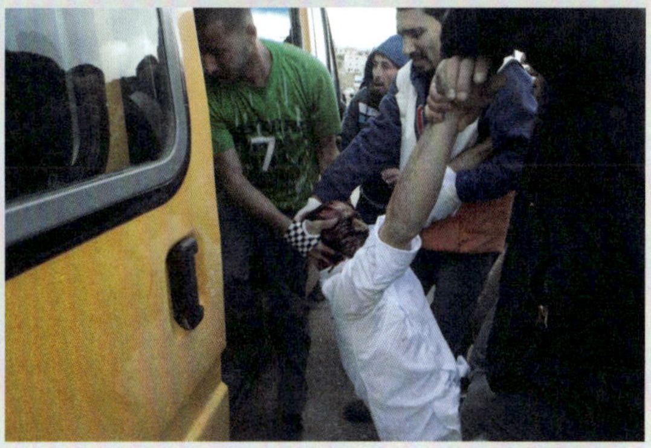

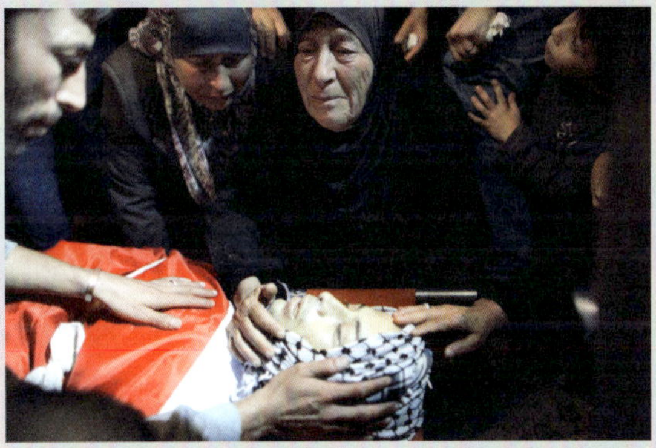

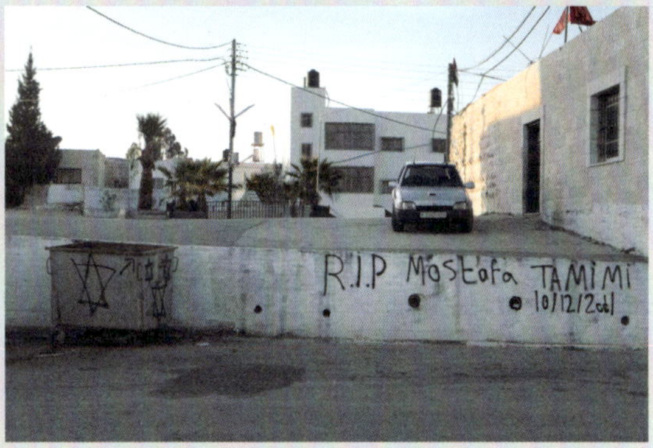

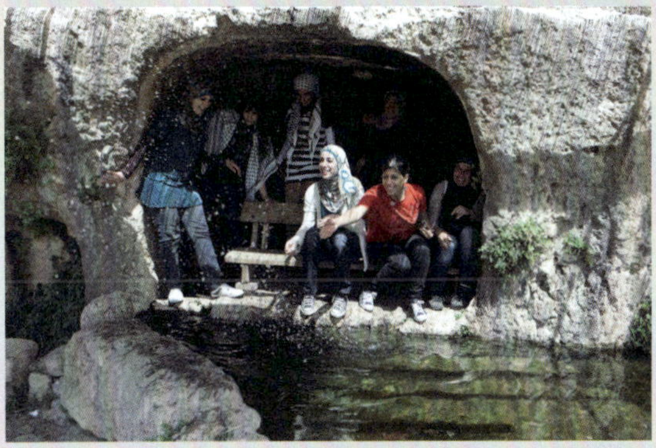

{Top left to right}
1. Palestinians await the arrival of Naji Tamimi released from Israeli prison, 1.3.2012 / **2.** Bassem Tamimi hugs his wife after his release from Israeli prison, 10.2.2013 / **3.** The Tamimi family, 10.9.2010 / **4.** Mustafa Tamimi evacuated to the hospital in critical condition, 9.12.2011 / **5.** Relatives of Rushdi Tamimi lean over his body, 20.11.2012 / **6.** Graffiti, 6.1.2012 / **7.** Activists reach the spring of Nabi Saleh during a women's action, 22.4.2012

Nabi Saleh, West Bank 8.1.2010

Palestinian protester opposite an Israeli soldier during the weekly demonstration against the occupation.

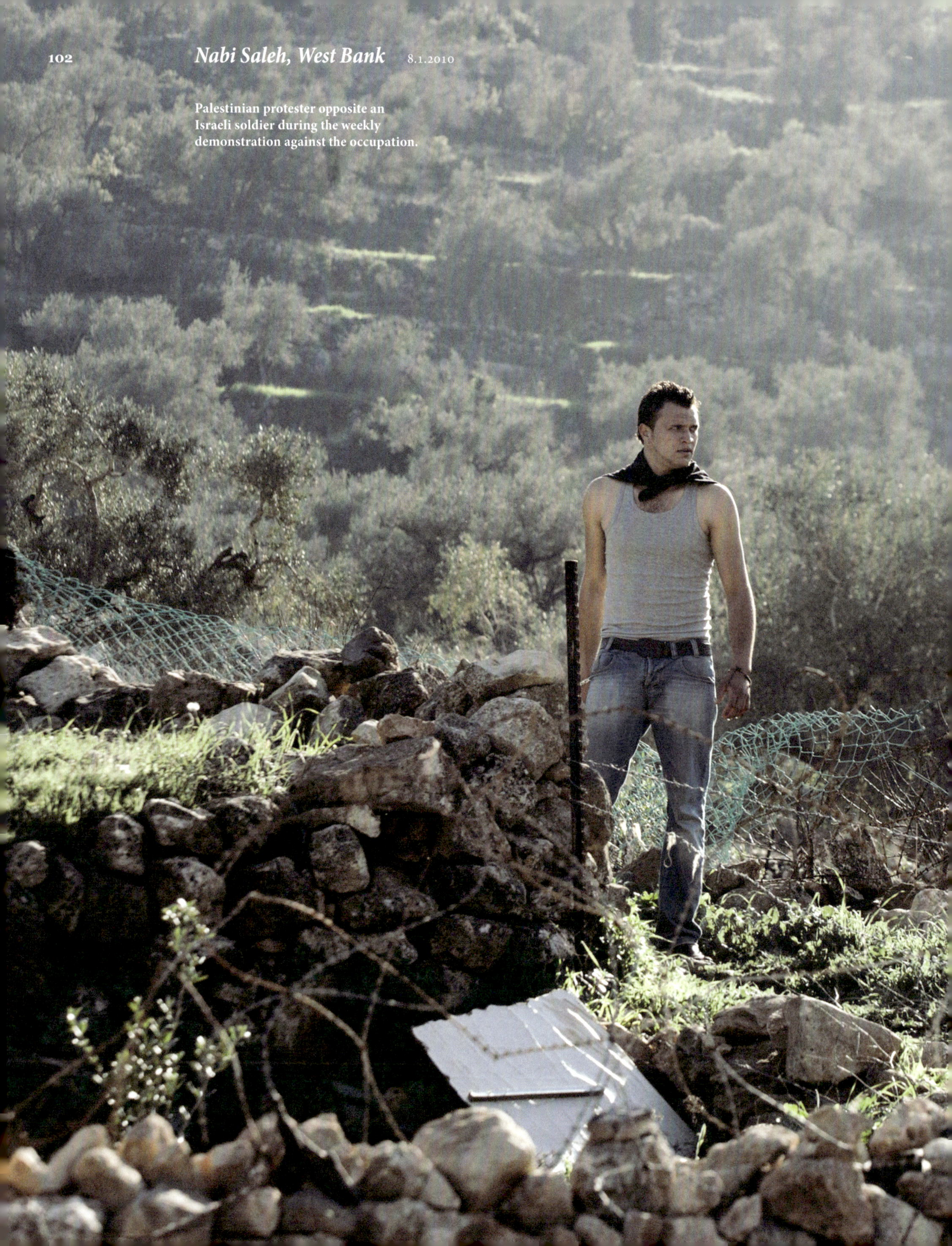

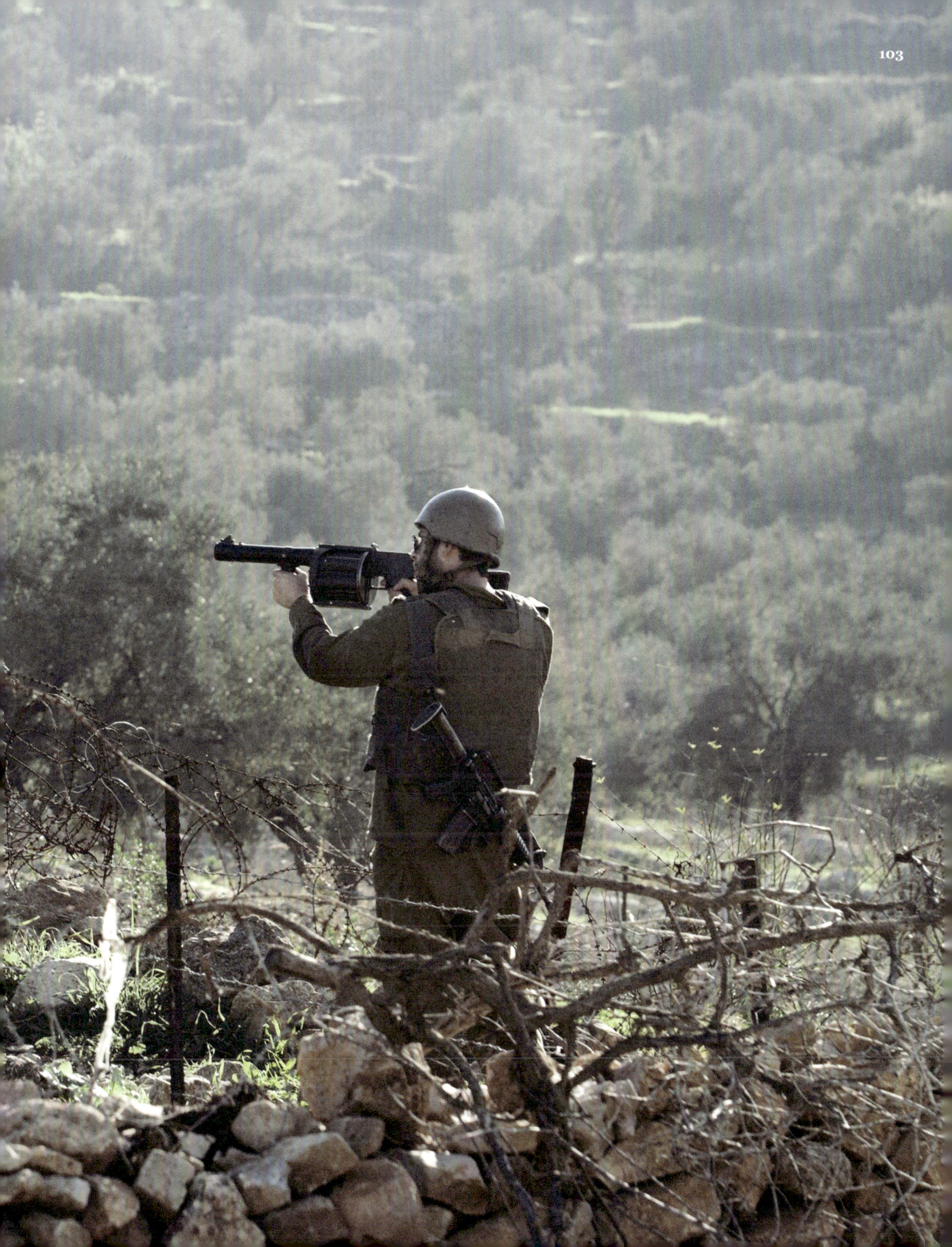

Conversation with
Ḥakmih Abu Mdīġim and Salim Abu Mdīġim

Ḥakmih Abu Mdīgim and Salim Abu Mdīgim are residents of Al-Araqib and owners of this area's land along with other families from the Aturi tribe. They have six children. Even after their village has been demolished more than 100 times, they are still fighting for their rights to their land and are living in makeshift shelters and vehicles.

Ḥakmih Abu Mdīġim: These photographs are not easy for me. It was when we were sitting by the graves of our fathers. The children were crying a lot and hiding behind the graves. Of all the demolitions in Al-Araqib until then, the destruction in 2014 was the hardest for me. I didn't care any more about the house, only about the cemetery.

Oren Ziv: Did you think they would really take the cemetery?

Salim Abu Mdīġim: Yes, they threatened us with this in the Israeli court, and said they considered closing the cemetery the same day.

HAM: I sat at my father's grave, which is the first one before the tent we put up after the last demolition. I thought that if they want and are able to destroy the tent—so be it, but they will never touch my father's grave.

OZ: For you, this grave is also proof that this is your land, that this is your house from time immemorial.

HAM: Yes. I was fasting that day and from fear I began to throw up. I said to myself, let them come in, yallah, they have nothing more to do, just the tent and the cemetery. I sat and spoke with the police, but I was shaking inside. It was like taking a huge gamble—either they enter the cemetery or they don't.

OZ: Up to that day, the cemetery was a protected place.

SAM: At the last hearing the police said to the judge, "We pushed them back from that hill to the cemetery." They admit it!

OZ: Do you use photographs much to show what is going on in Al-Araqib?

HAM: Yes. We show people who visit here, [we] show the destruction, what there was before. We try to show everything we have that's on the computer.

OZ: Does it help people to understand?

HAM: Yes, it makes them understand how we live here.

SAM: They get a shock. They can't believe that this is how we live and this is what we suffer at the hands of the authorities. They come in order to learn and then they tell other people. This is very important.

OZ: On the day of the demolition, there were a lot of photographers. Does this make you feel more secure that the police won't do something?

HAM: The police don't care at all about the photographers. I couldn't calm down until they had left the place.

SAM: It's impossible to really know what the police's original decision was when they came, or whether the presence of the media helped or not.

OZ: Even today, when I tell people about Al-Araqib, I say that this is the only place in the world where they chase people away and then plant trees instead. All over the world, trees are cut down in order to make room for human beings, in order to build a city or a village, and here, the JNF [Jewish National Fund], which serves the civil municipality, cooperates with the attempt to drive you out and after the fact to plant a "forest" on your lands in place of the village. And this is the only place that I know of in the world where people need to hide in the cemetery for protection.

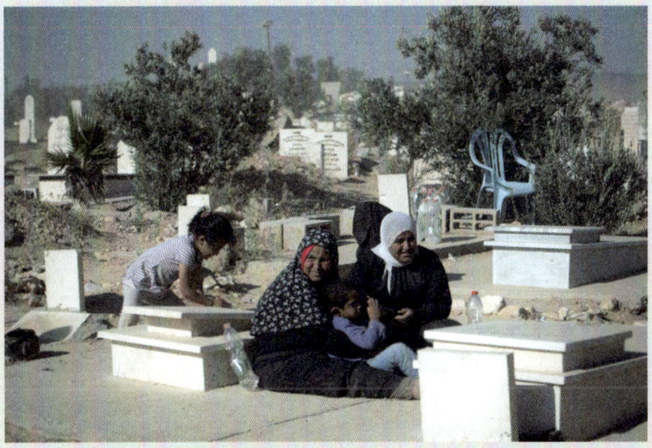

Ḥakmih Abu Mdīġim [center] sits with fellow villagers on graves in the cemetery of Al-Araqib during the demolition of the village, Negev Desert, Israel, 12.6.2014

HAM: After the first demolition in 2010, I would wake up at night inside the tent and think that I am still inside the house. This was how it was for a long time. And Salim would calm me down, because when I would wake up all confused, he would tell me "everything is OK, they already knocked down everything." If there is something that makes me want to destroy this country, it's about the border of the cemetery. If they would say to me—we want to go in with a tractor and take your house, this would somehow still be OK as far as I'm concerned. I wouldn't get excited because I'm already used to it from all of the demolitions. The children now sleep in the car—six children in one car.

OZ: And now, in fact, there is no place that is safe during a demolition, there is no place to hide like there was in 2014. And there is also no safe place for your belongings.

HAM: Now I am less afraid because on the same day that they destroyed our lives they also broke everything outside. After it was all over I said to the police "Thank you very much for not destroying the cemetery."

OZ: They surely didn't understand at all what you said.

HAM: Yes. They did not understand what this meant for me or the joke.

OZ: What is it like for you to see these pictures today?

HAM: I want to cry over these pictures. On that day I cried a lot. There are also videos from the same day, but I am not ready to watch them. It's hard for me to hear my own voice. I would be happy to erase that awful day from my memory.

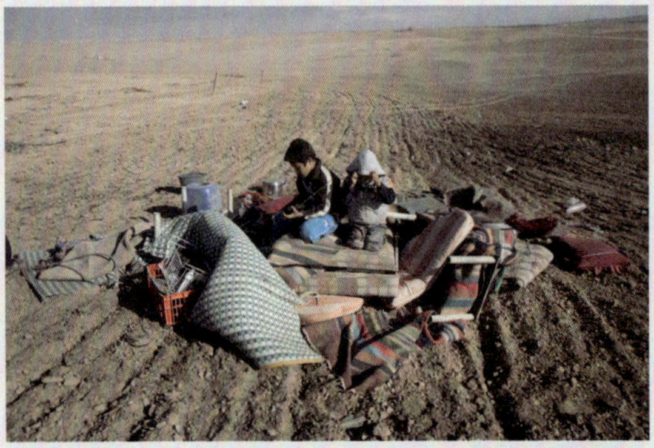

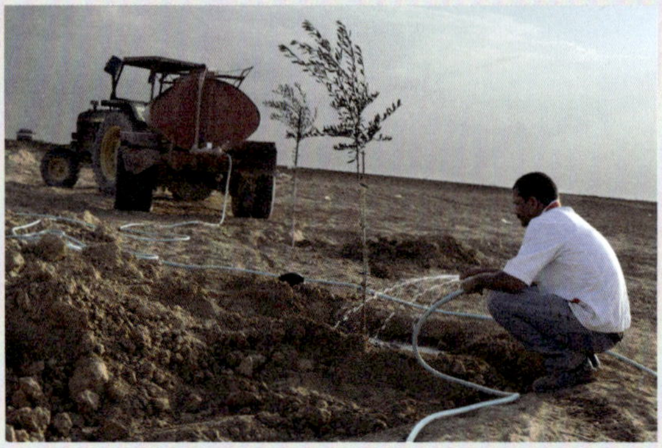

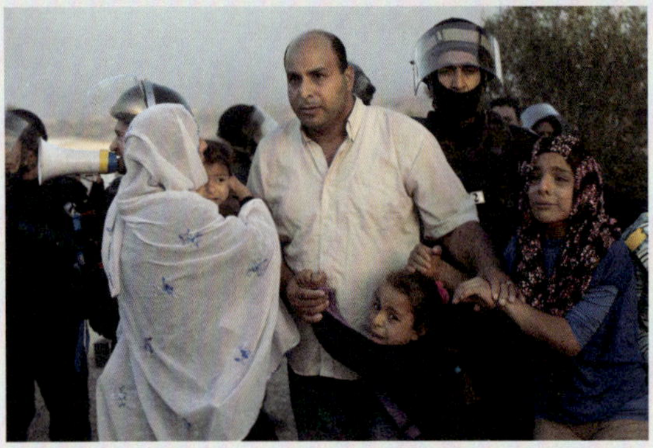

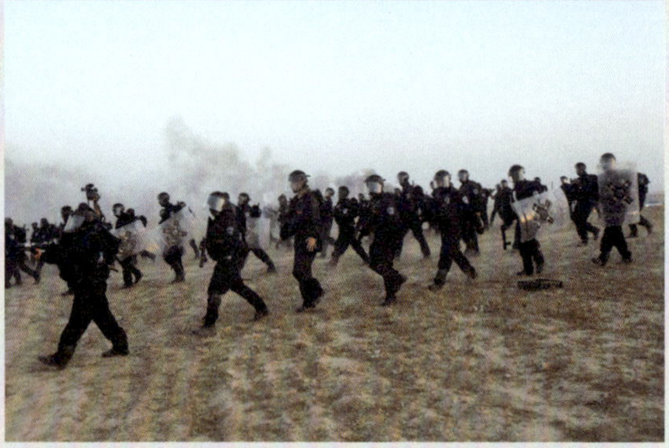

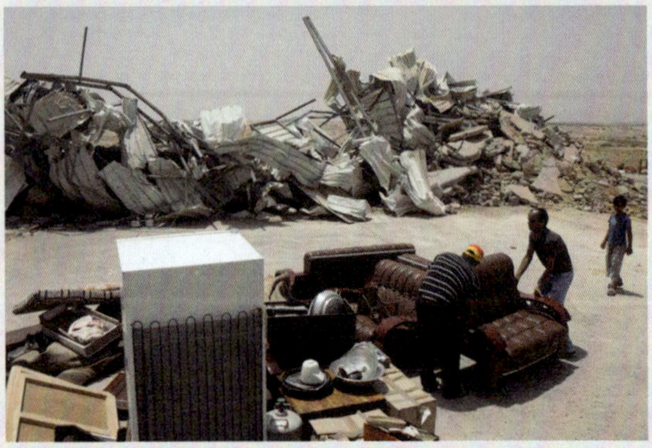

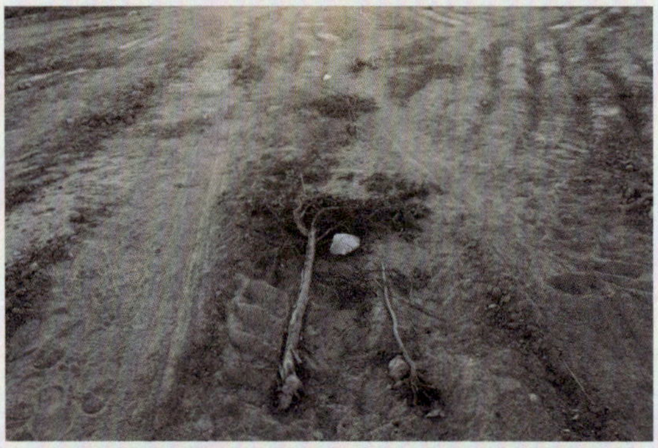

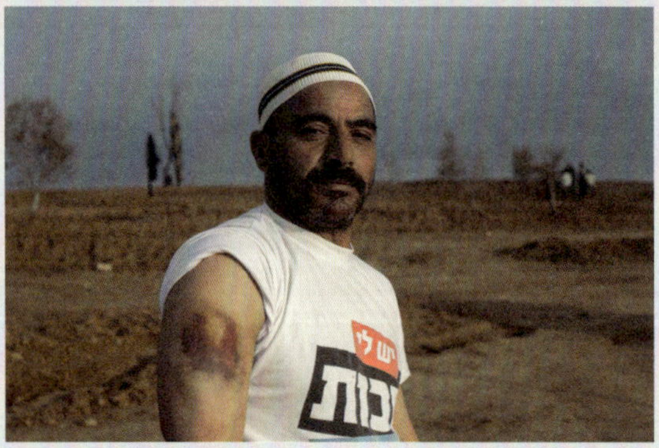

{Top left to right}
1. Children amidst their belongings after a demolition in the village, 30.10.2009 / **2.** A resident waters newly planted trees, 29.10.2009 / **3.** Residents react to the demolition of their village, 27.7.2010 / **4.** Police storm the village, 27.7.2010 / **5.** Residents work among demolished structures, 30.7.2010 / **6.** An uprooted olive tree left after the demolition of the entire village, 28.7.2010 / **7.** A villager posing after being shot with a sponge bullet by the Israeli police while trying to rebuild his home, 13.2.2011

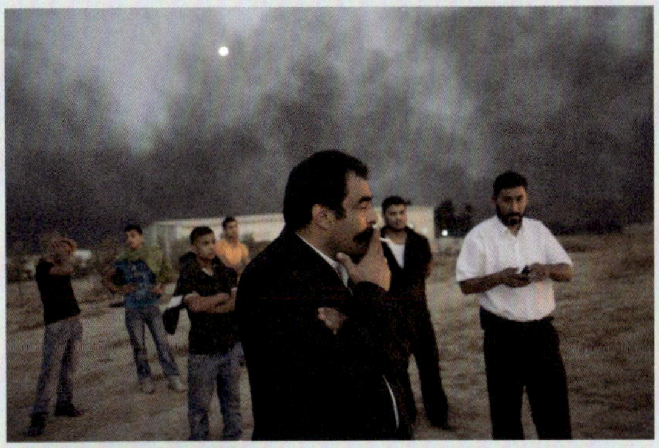

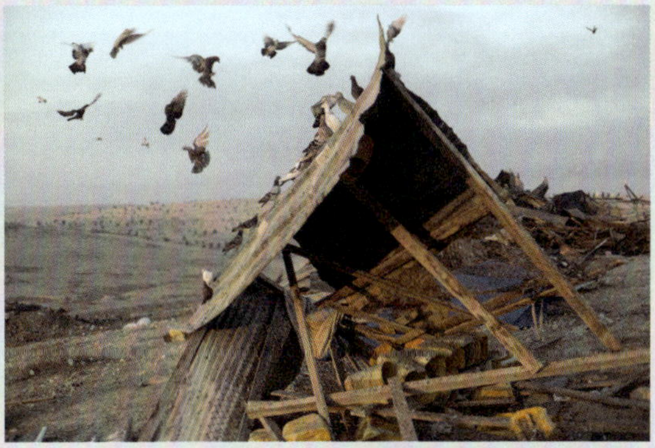

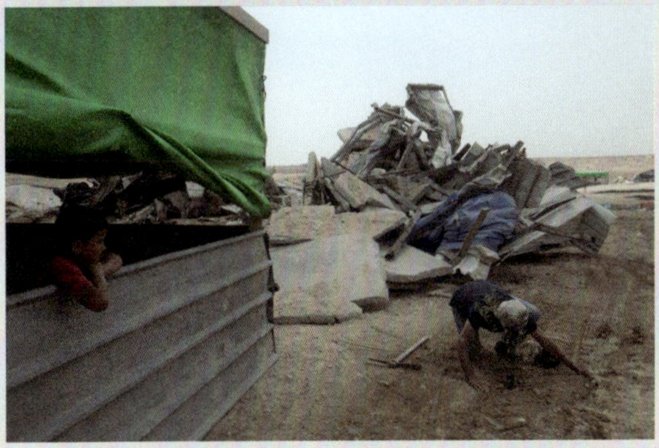

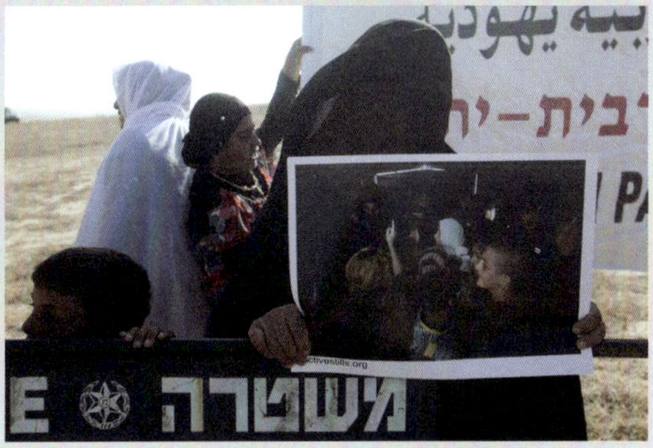

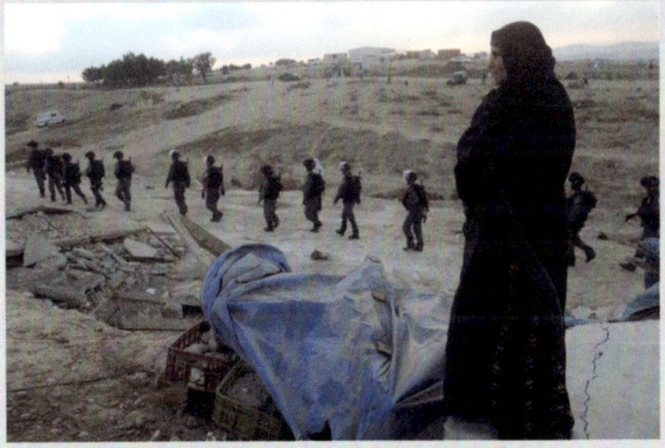

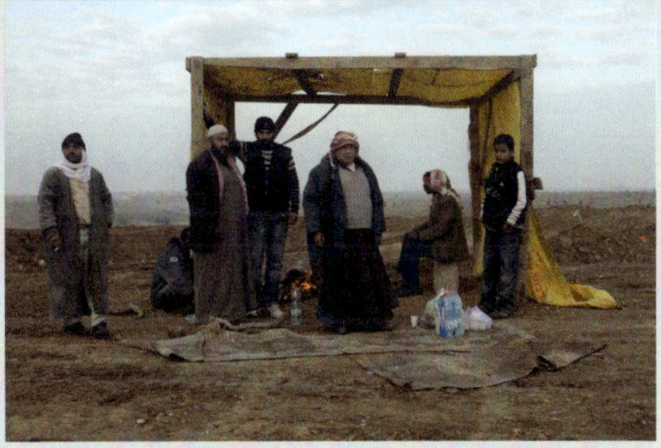

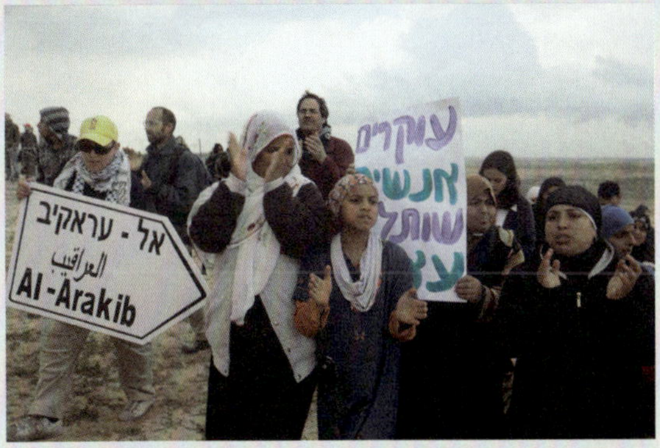

{Top left to right}
1. Residents await the police before an upcoming demolition, 27.7.2010 / **2.** Doves hover next to a demolished dovecote, 9.9.2010 / **3.** A resident plants an olive tree, 31.7.2010 / **4.** Residents protest against the displacement of the Bedouin community, Lehavim Junction, Israel, 9.8.2010 / **5.** A resident watches police arrive at her village, 12.9.2010 / **6.** Residents stand next to a tent reconstructed on the village's lands, 9.2.2011 / **7.** Residents and left-wing activists protest against JNF (Jewish National Fund) plans to plant a national forest on the village's lands, 12.3.2011

Al-Araqib, Negev Desert, Israel 16.1.2011

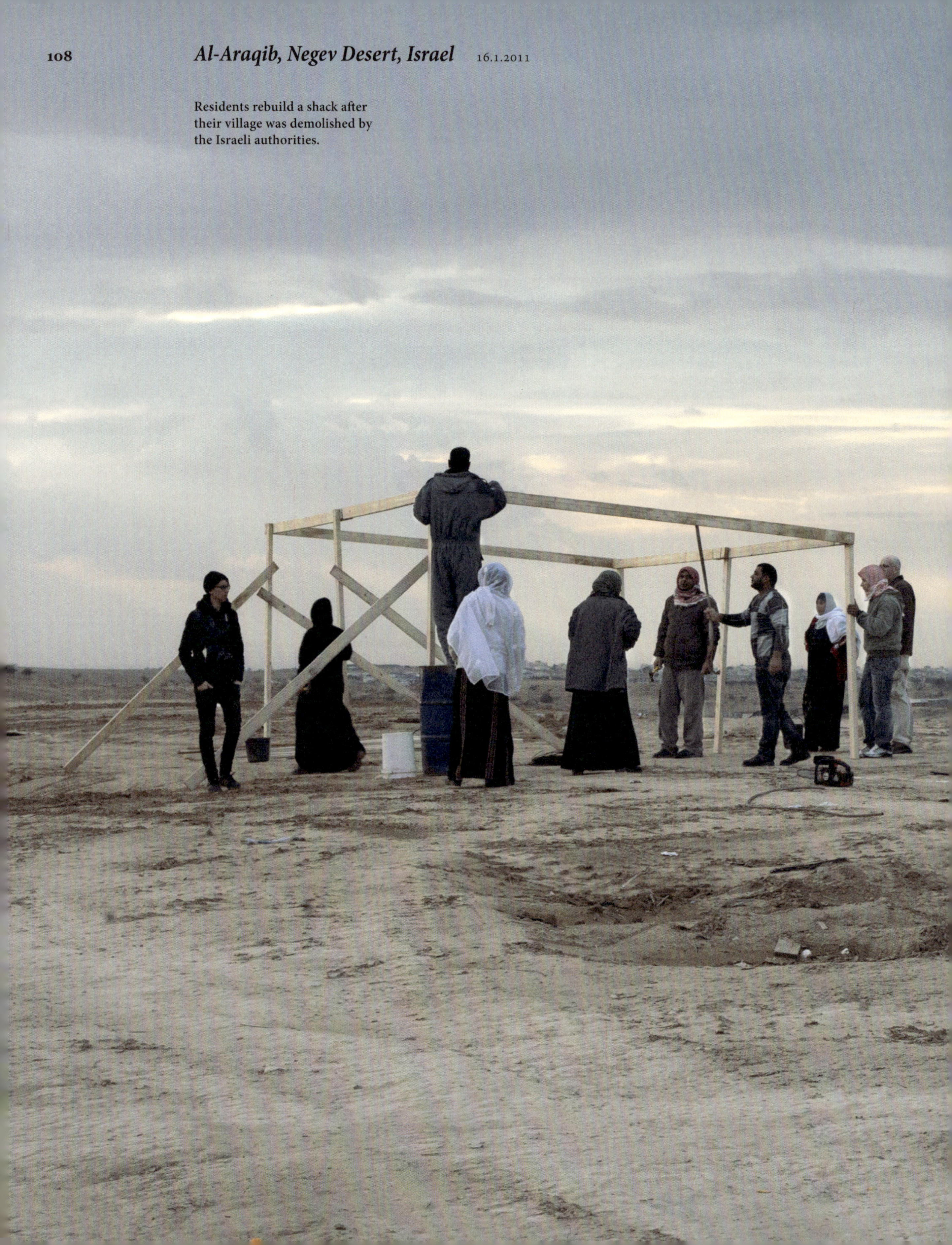

Residents rebuild a shack after their village was demolished by the Israeli authorities.

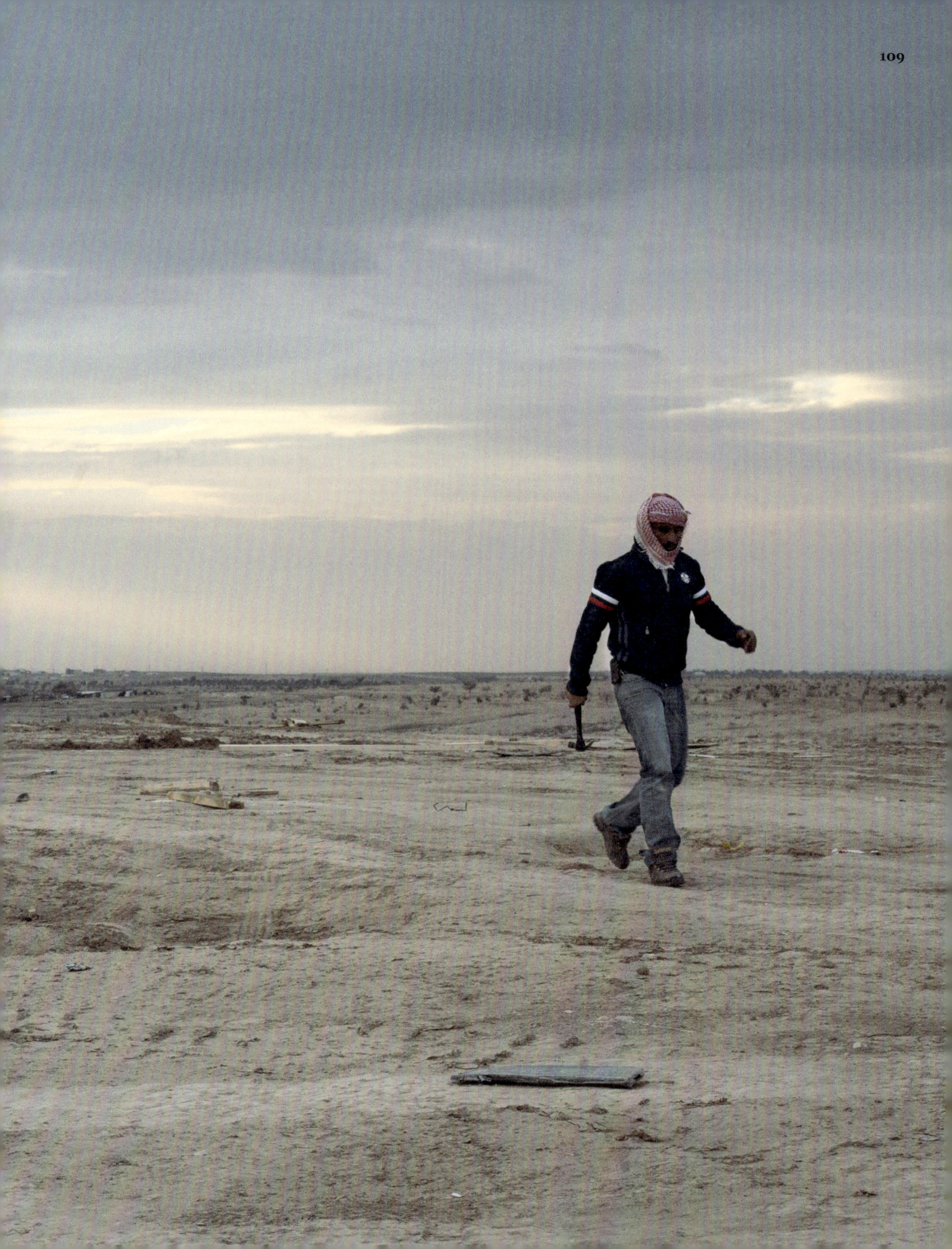

Conversation with
Issa Amaro

Issa Amaro is a prominent human rights activist from the West Bank city of Hebron. In 2009, he won the One World media award for his involvement in B'Tselem's "Shooting Back" project, which provides media training and distributes cameras to Palestinians to document settler and military abuses. He established the Youth Against Settlements organization whose center was closed in 2015 by the Israeli Army. Issa has been arrested countless times by the Israeli Army for his work against the occupation.

Oren Ziv: Do you feel photography gives power to the Palestinians who have been living under oppression for so many years?

Issa Amaro: We had two intifadas, the first one was non-violent. The weakness of the first intifada was that we did not use photography to support our activism and the Palestinian cause. These days the cameras are showing the real images of the occupation. Now, the Palestinians can tell about their lives directly, not mediated through the press. They can tell about their oppressors and their suffering. Whoever owns the media, owns the battle. That's it. That is why the army also targets Palestinian journalists and photographers.

OZ: So the action depicted in this photo was when US President Barack Obama arrived in Palestine in 2013. What was the idea of this action?

IA: We were trying to tell Obama that he should come here to see the real apartheid, and to remind him of the legacy of the civil disobedience that was part of the civil rights movement of the '60s—the movement that enabled him to become president of the United States decades later. We wanted him to understand that not only Palestinians are protesting, but also Israelis who are against the occupation. That he should work to end the occupation by putting pressure on the Israeli government, which refuses to give the Palestinian people their rights. And we tried to draw attention [to Hebron] as a symbol of apartheid.

OZ: You wore masks of Barack Obama and Martin Luther King, Jr. and the idea wasn't only to do it in front of the soldiers, but that these images will spread widely.

IA: Yes. We wanted to tell the Americans that the Palestinians are using the methods of Martin Luther King, Jr., the same methods of every people claiming their rights throughout history. We ask to be protected according to international law and also to declare that we are against racism and apartheid of any kind.

OZ: The action worked!

IA: When we were planning the action, we were afraid that it would not get the media attention we wanted. My freind asked me, "You think the soldiers will let the protesters wearing the masks reach Shuhada Street?" I assured him, "the occupation usually gives us the image we want." The moment we got to Shuhada Street we were all arrested.

OZ: So was it successful from this perspective?

IA: We wanted the Israeli Army to arrest Obama and Martin Luther King, Jr., and to show the world that this is how they treat non-violent protesters. And I know Obama saw this on the same day.

OZ: Usually in protests the settlers try to break your camera or your sign. Here they were going for the mask directly.

IA: Yes, they were very angry. And following this action they started an incitement campaign against me, writing letters in English, trying to make the army put me in administrative detention. I have the letter; they wanted to get rid of me, and they still do.

OZ: I remember a small child, maybe 10 or 11 years old, a settler's child who tried to take off your mask. The mask was more annoying to the settlers than the Palestinian flag.

IA: Yes. They knew this image would be effective and that they will get less support. With these images, we are saying to the international community: if you want to help Israel, first make it end the occupation. This is why we are trying to reach as many publics as possible. Israel has many allies and support, so we are trying to win the international community. The T-shirt with the quote "I have a dream," also drove the settlers wild because what it meant was that "We, Palestinians, have a dream." We tapped into that moment from the past, from the collective memory when everyone recognized that something was wrong, and we asked them to make that comparison, to make everyone understand that the occupation must come to an end.

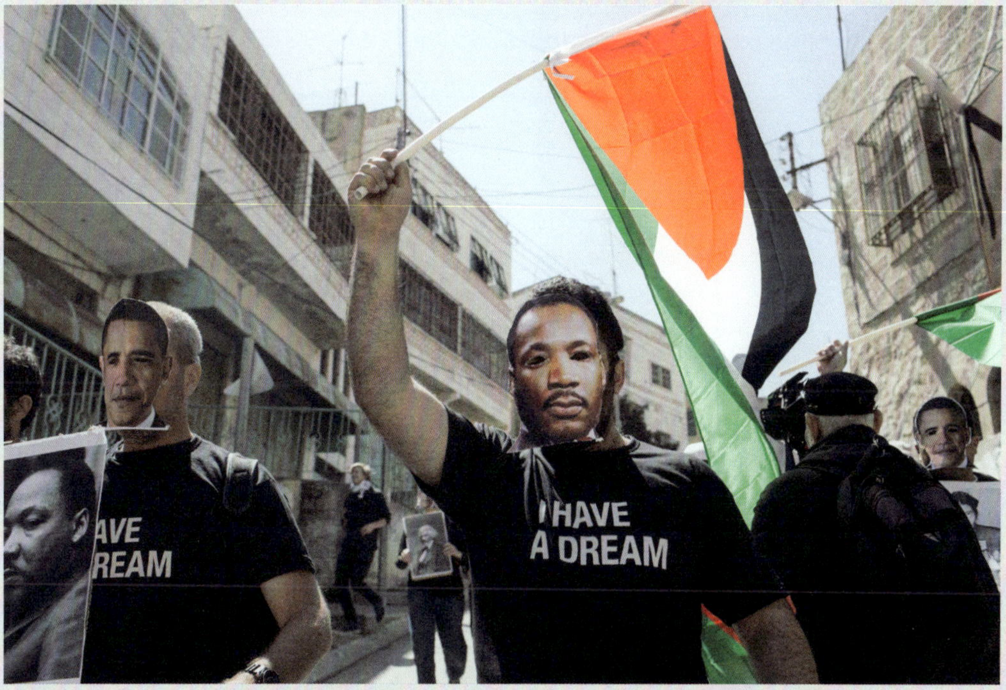

Activist with Martin Luther King, Jr. mask marches during US president's visit to the West Bank, Hebron, 20.3.2013

Hebron, West Bank 22.2.2013

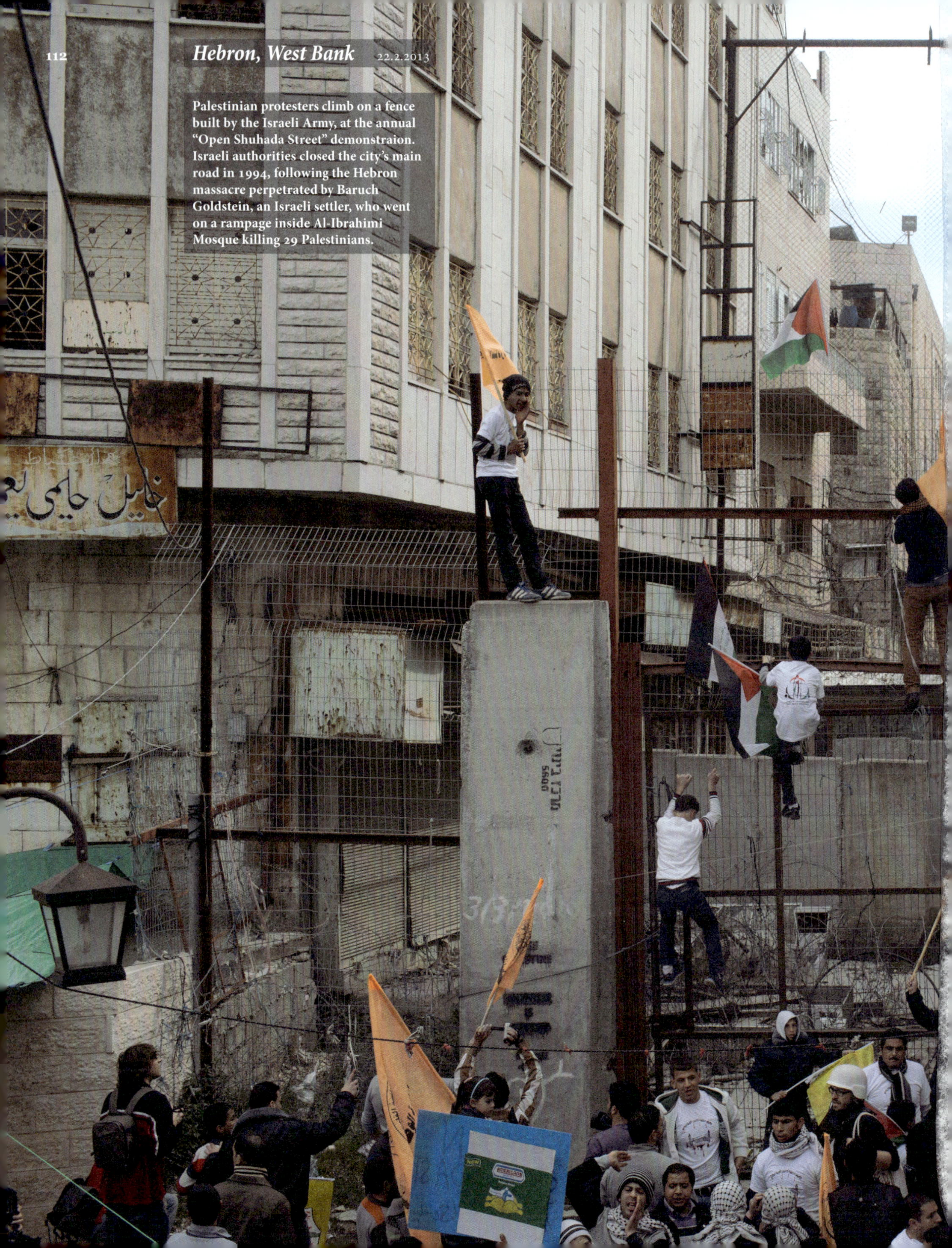

Palestinian protesters climb on a fence built by the Israeli Army, at the annual "Open Shuhada Street" demonstraion. Israeli authorities closed the city's main road in 1994, following the Hebron massacre perpetrated by Baruch Goldstein, an Israeli settler, who went on a rampage inside Al-Ibrahimi Mosque killing 29 Palestinians.

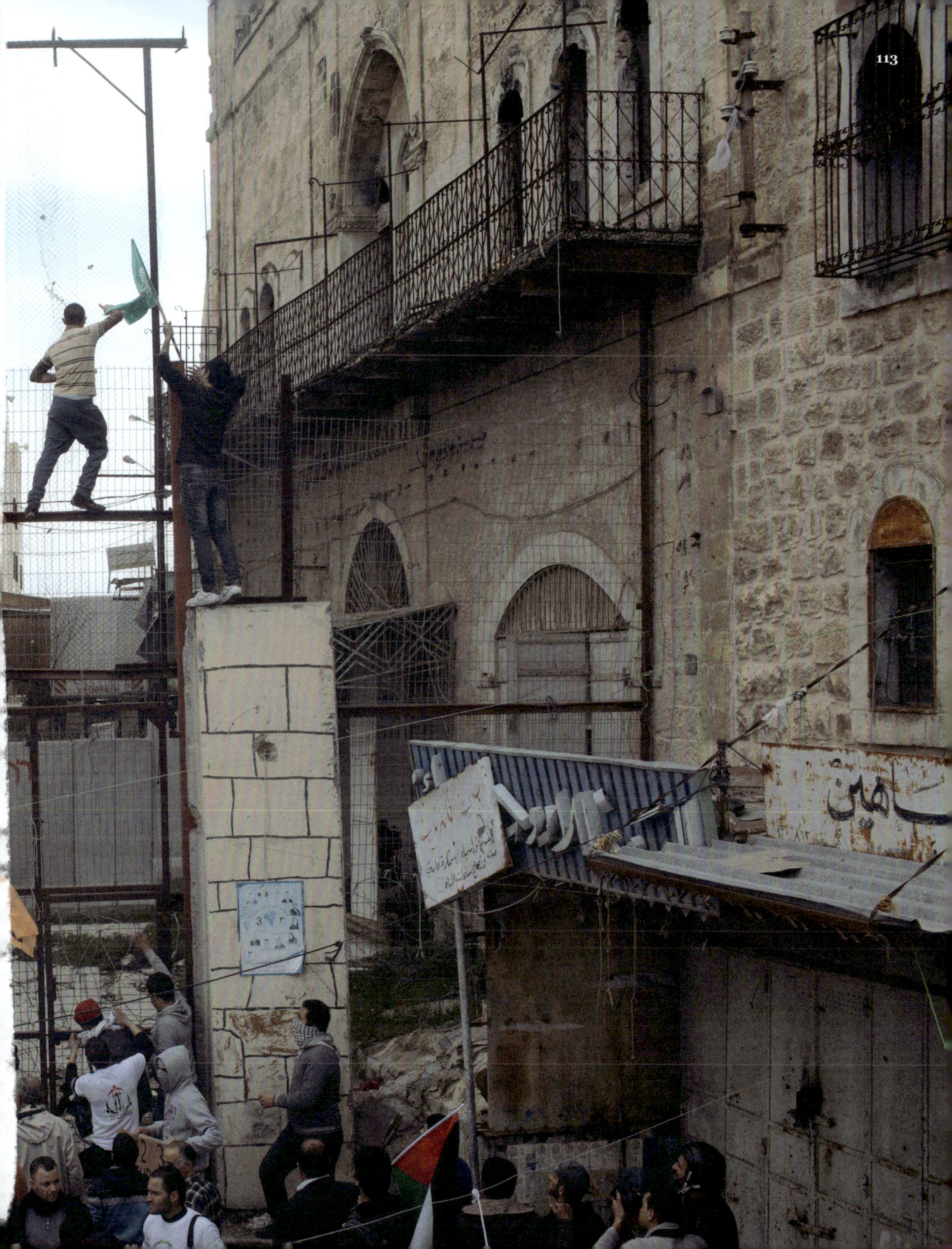

Hebron, West Bank 4.4.2013

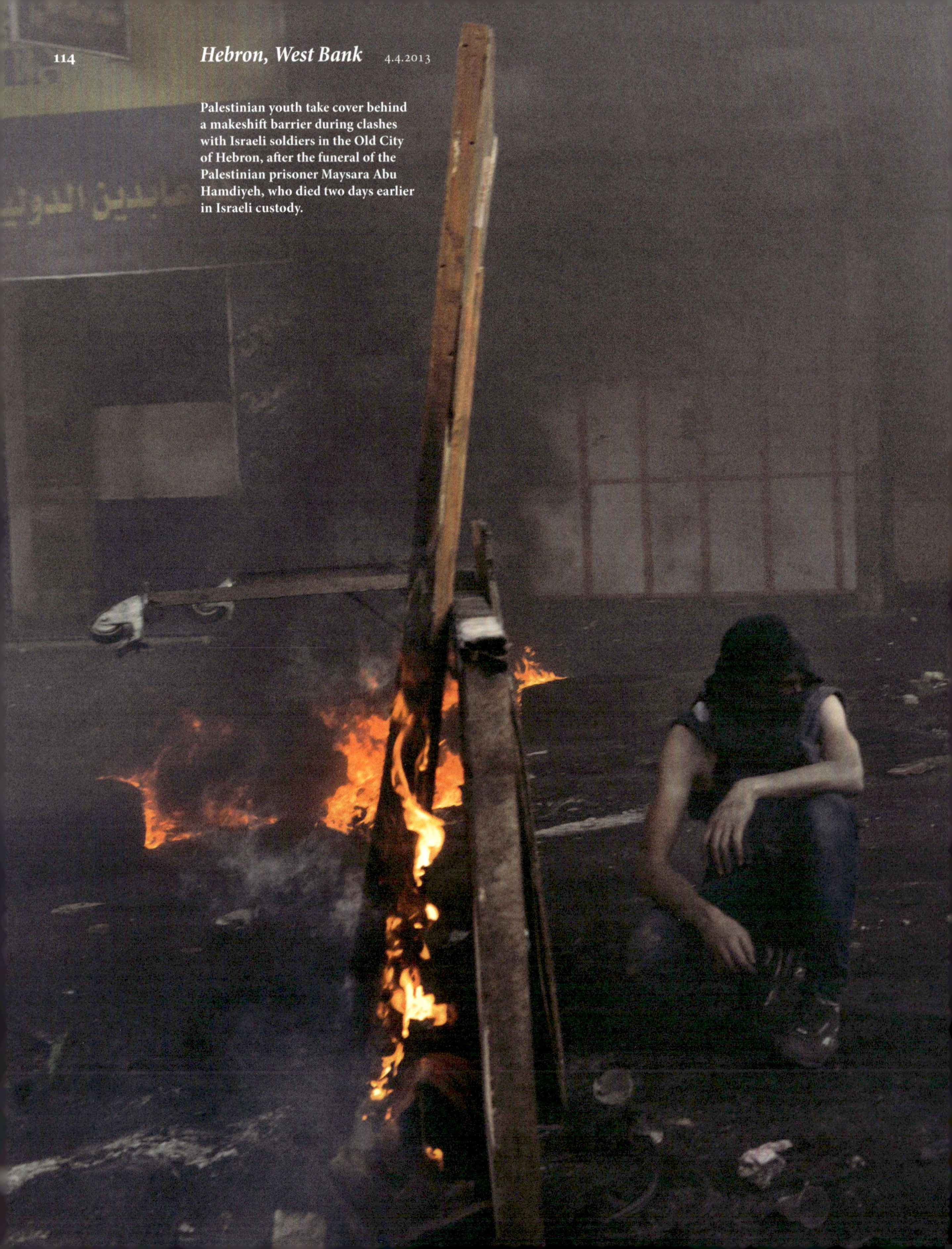

Palestinian youth take cover behind a makeshift barrier during clashes with Israeli soldiers in the Old City of Hebron, after the funeral of the Palestinian prisoner Maysara Abu Hamdiyeh, who died two days earlier in Israeli custody.

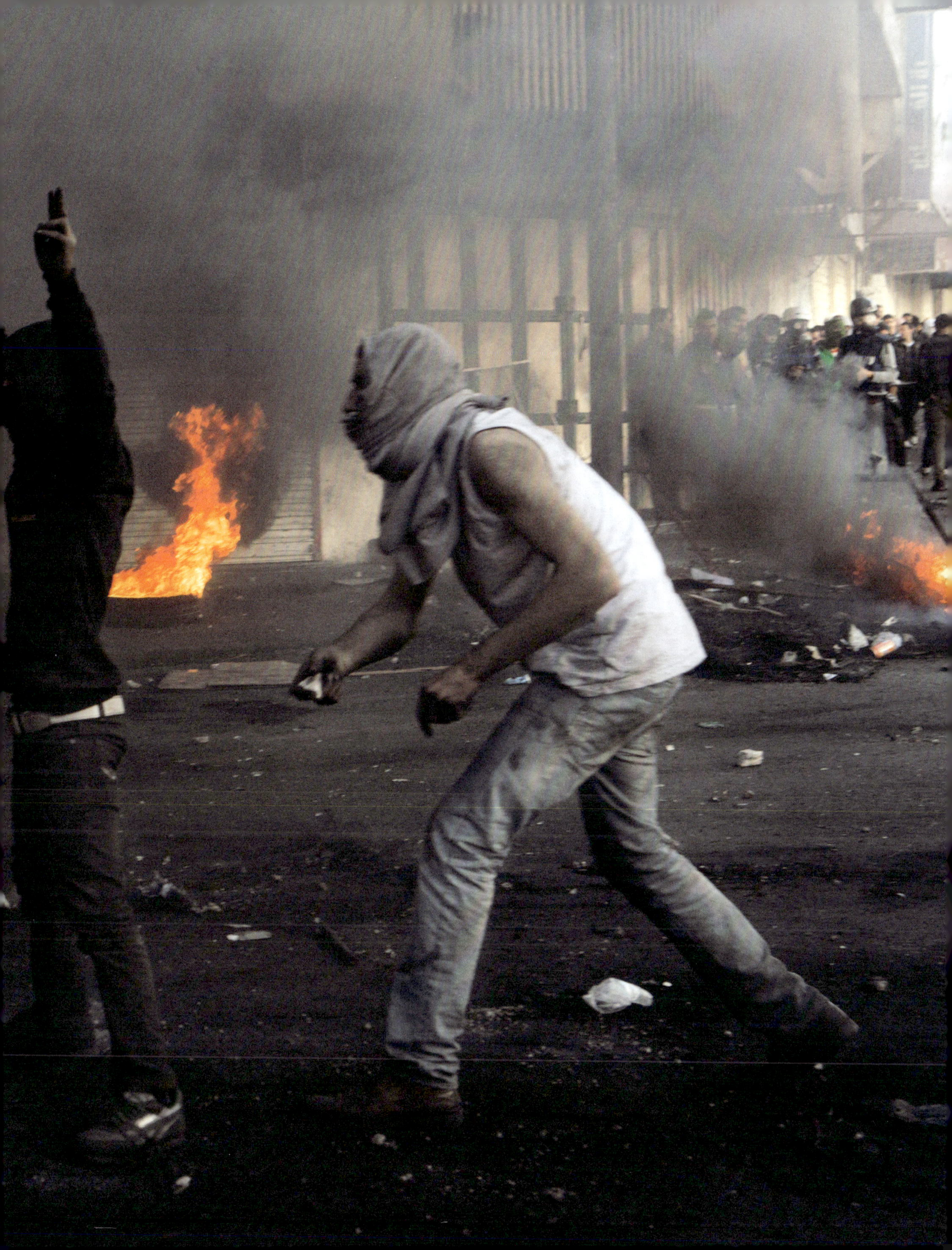

Hebron, West Bank 5.9.2007

An Israeli soldier tries to prevent an Activestills photographer from taking pictures near an army roadblock in the city of Hebron, while an Israeli settler attacks co-founder of the left-wing group Breaking the Silence, Yehuda Shaul.

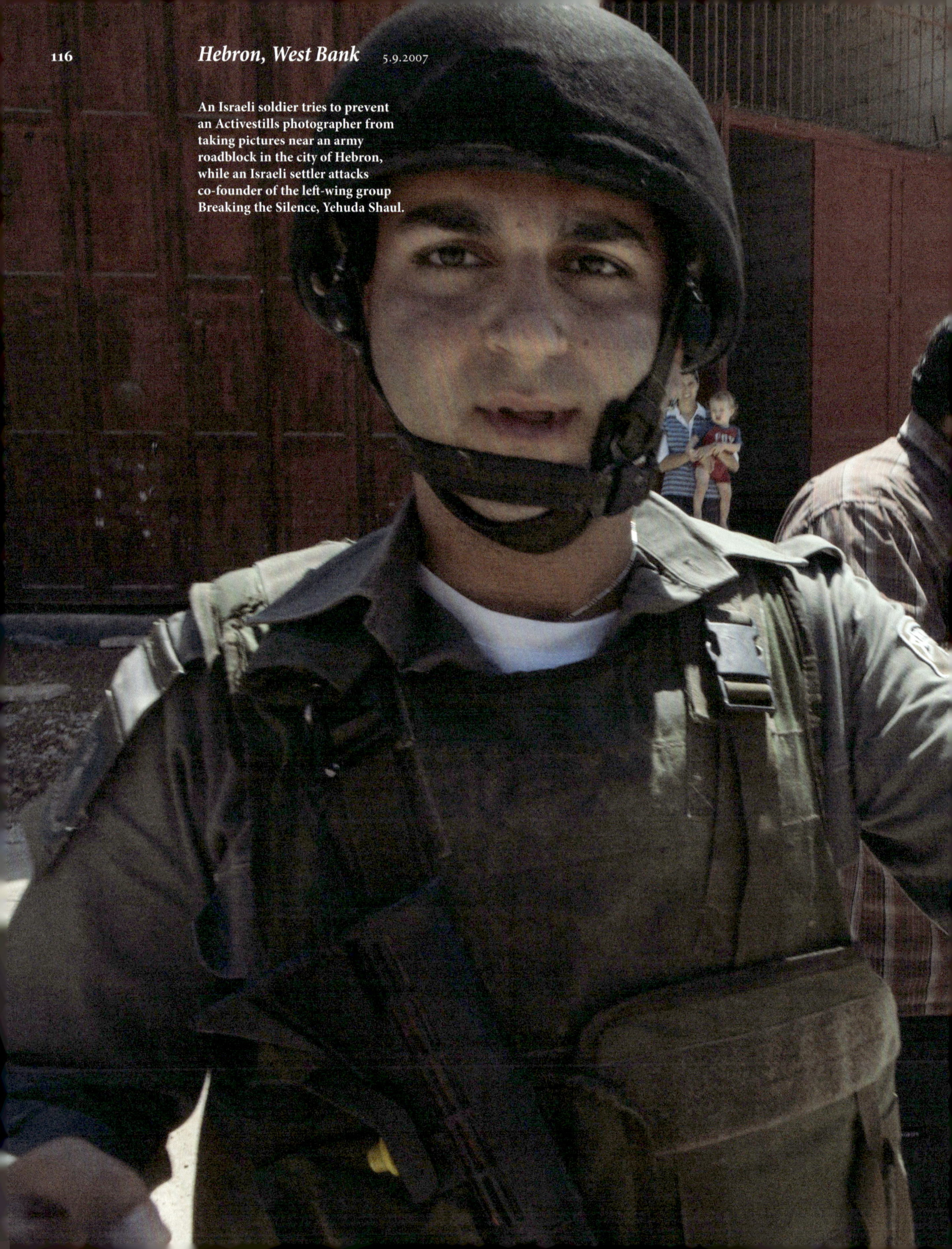

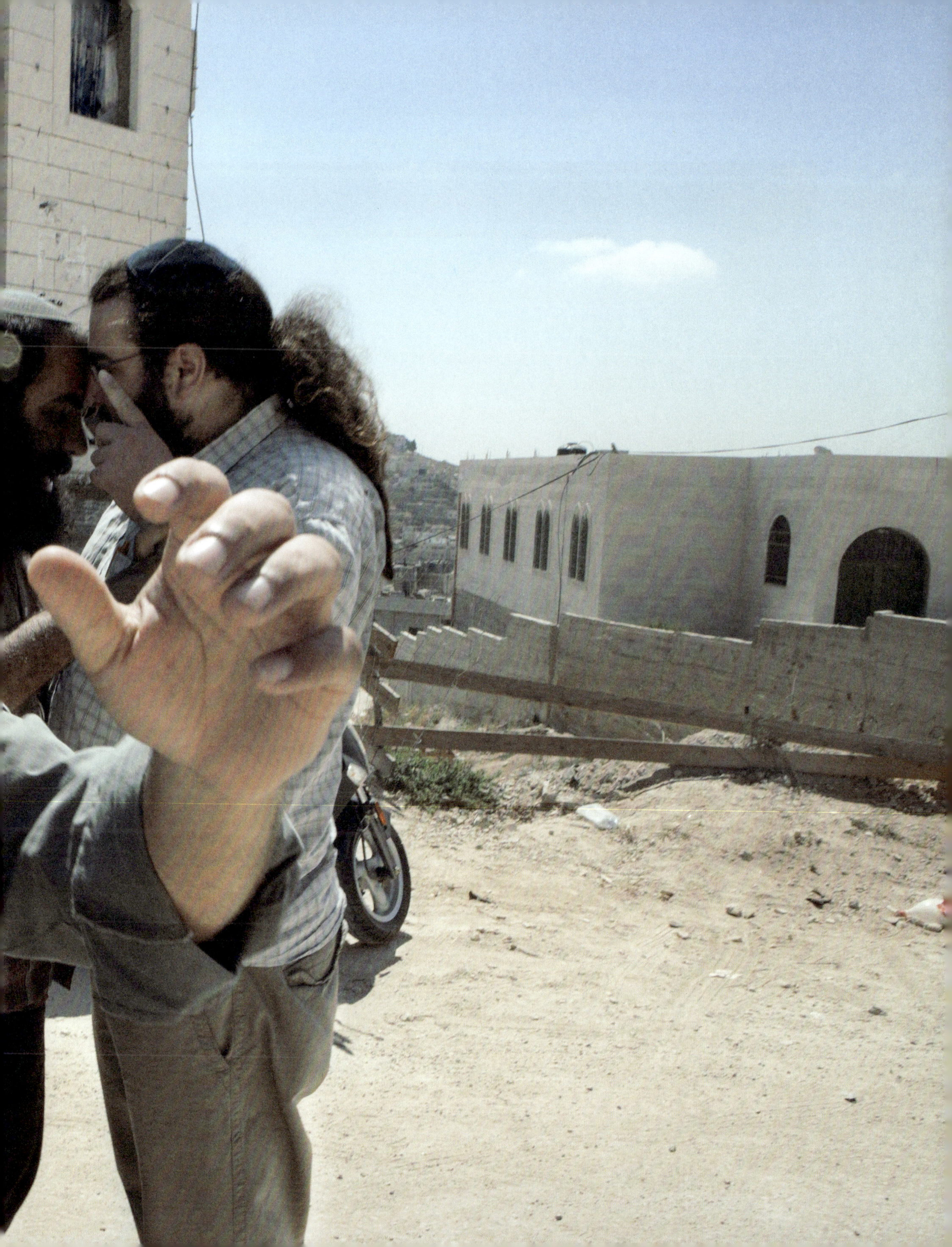

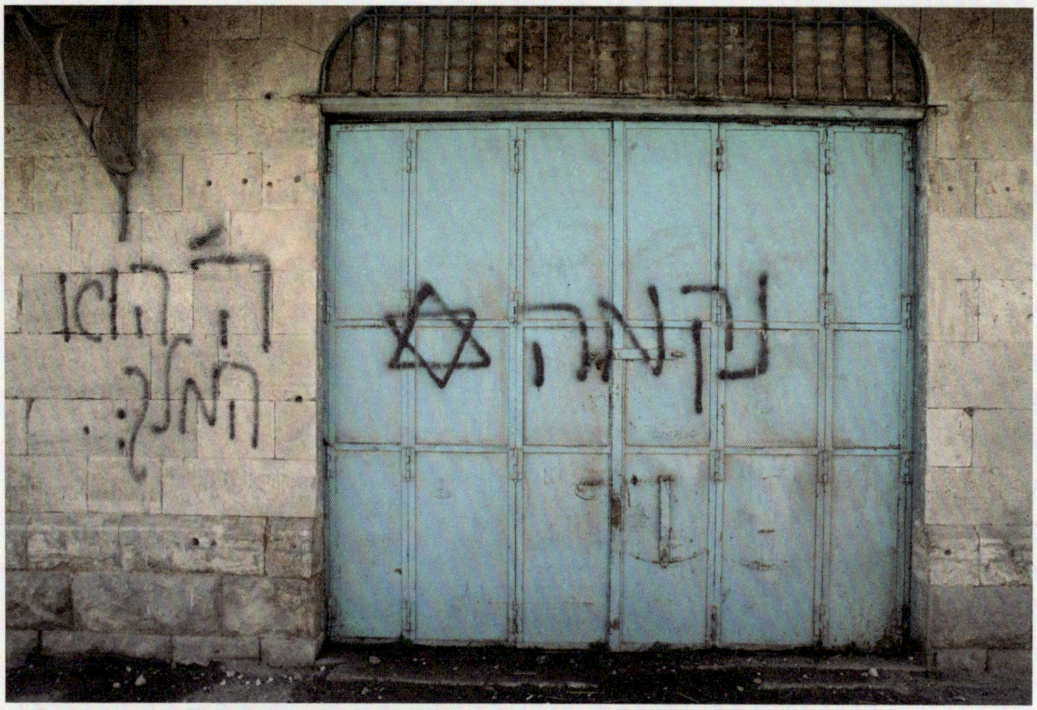

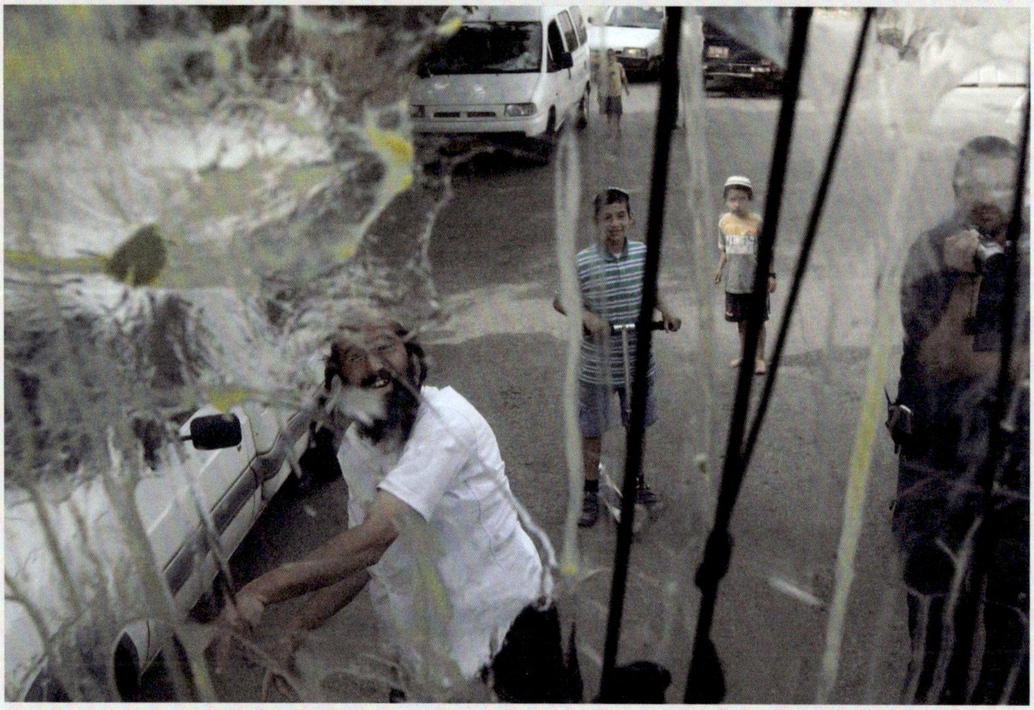

1. Grafitti of the Star of David, with the word "revenge" written in Hebrew, sprayed on the door of a Palestinian-owned shop, 24.1.2007 / **2.** A settler throws eggs at a bus of activists from the left-wing group Breaking the Silence, 25.4.2008

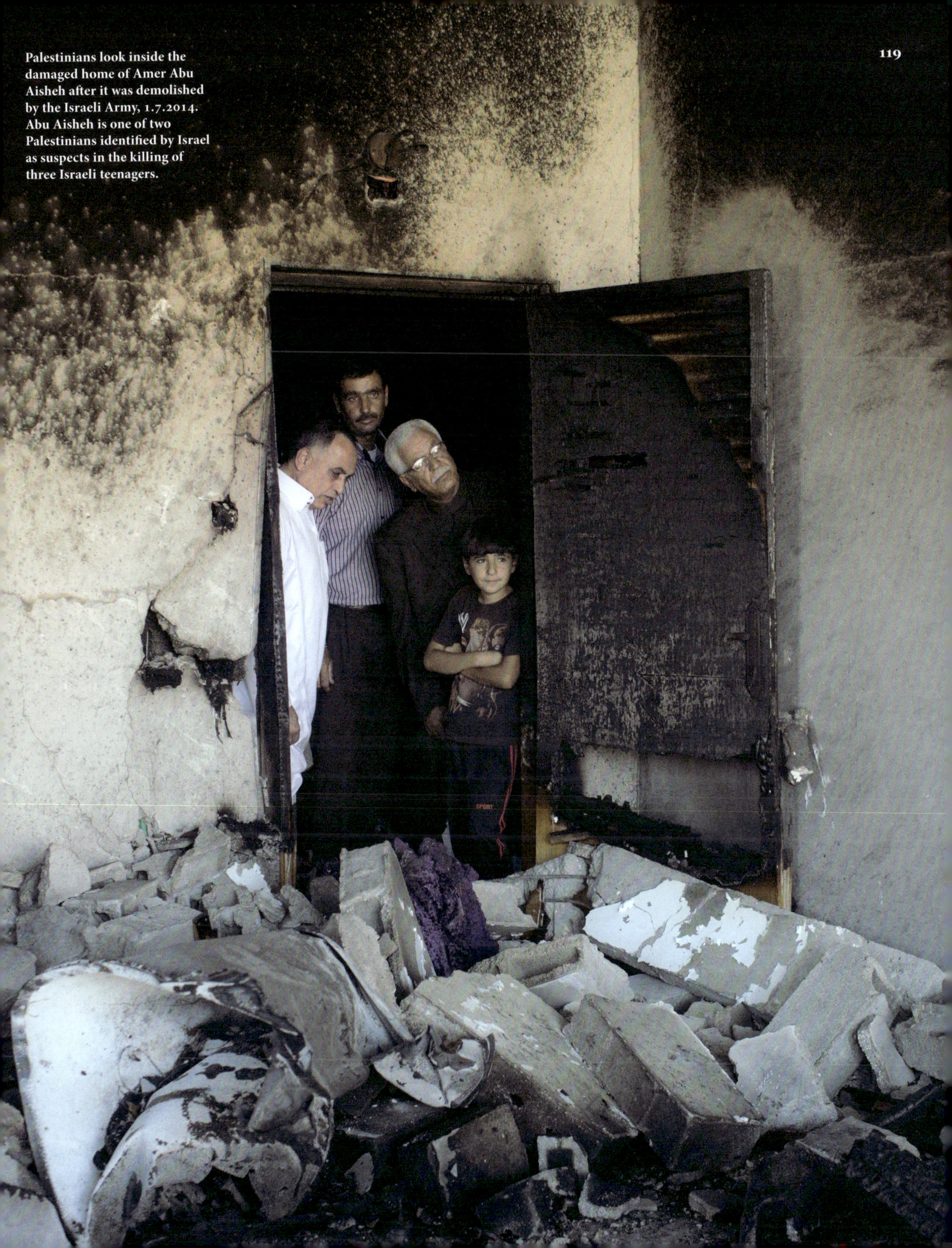

Palestinians look inside the damaged home of Amer Abu Aisheh after it was demolished by the Israeli Army, 1.7.2014. Abu Aisheh is one of two Palestinians identified by Israel as suspects in the killing of three Israeli teenagers.

Abdallah Abu Rahmah

I saw Activestills trying to support us, trying to be a part of our struggle. It was important for us in Bil'in to get the truth out to the world. When I was in jail, Activestills photos were shown to the judge to give him a true picture of the actual event. Every time I was arrested I found a photographer from Activestills following me, supporting me in jail. When I was accused of throwing stones, the photos from that protest succeeded in proving that there were no stones thrown during the action. I was released two or three weeks after that hearing.

This photo is special for me, because it is very difficult to take a photo from inside the jail or inside Ofer military court.[1] Activestills photographer Oren Ziv succeeded and the photo was made into a poster that was sent all over the world. The "*Shabas*" [Hebrew acronym for the Israeli Prison Service] used to allow the Palestinian prisoners to be photographed inside jail. If I remember correctly, we even had to pay for the photos. It was like a business for them. Sometimes the photos were taken in the canteen of the prison. I wanted to have a photo as a memento for me and my children. But this one by Oren serves as the best memory for me.

Activestills members took part in the struggle in Bil'in and their photographs became symbols of the struggle. When I think about our success in Bil'in, it was a joint effort that combined many elements: the cooperation with international and Israeli activists, the creativity of the protests, and the insistence on working with the media, both independent and mainstream. We are a small village, and it was a big effort to raise media and public awareness for our struggle.

Activestills played an important role in this from the first moment, both at the protests and at night when the Israeli Army conducted raids. TV crews came during the day, filmed for one hour and then left. But the local Bil'in photographers and Activestills members stayed with us, slept in our homes, and helped to spread the photos, to spread the truth, to the Israeli media, social media, and elsewhere. They took photos of the stun grenades, the dogs, and the violence in the night. That is why we trusted them and asked for their support also in direct actions at places like Bab al-Shams, Ein Hijleh and many others.

We learned a lot from each other: Palestinians, Israeli and international activists, journalists, photographers, and lawyers. Some ideas were born from this collaboration. We exchanged and shared our experiences, and that is how we have gained something. Because of all this, today, we have the power to continue.

Abdallah Abu Rahmah is a member of the Palestinian Popular Struggle Coordination Committee and a leading activist of the popular struggle in his village, Bil'in.

1. The Ofer military court is an army court situated in close proximity to Ofer military prison in the occupied West Bank, near the city of Ramallah. It is used by Israel for trials of Palestinians. Journalists require special permits in order to enter the court.

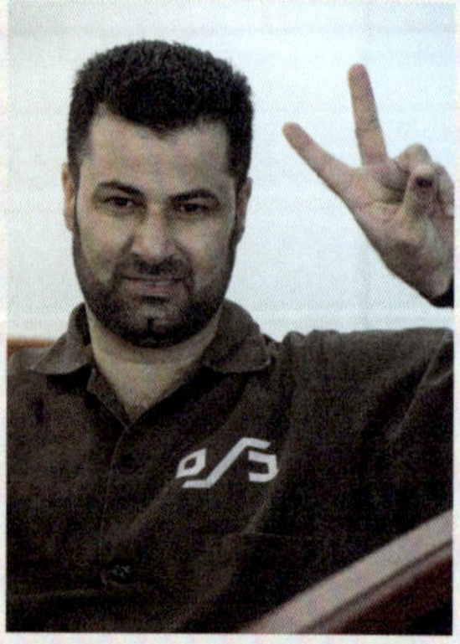

Abdallah Abu Rahmah raises his hand to signal 'V' for victory inside the Israeli Ofer military court before his hearing, West Bank, 15.9.2010. He was convicted of organizing demonstrations against the Israeli separation wall and was sentenced to 16 months in prison.

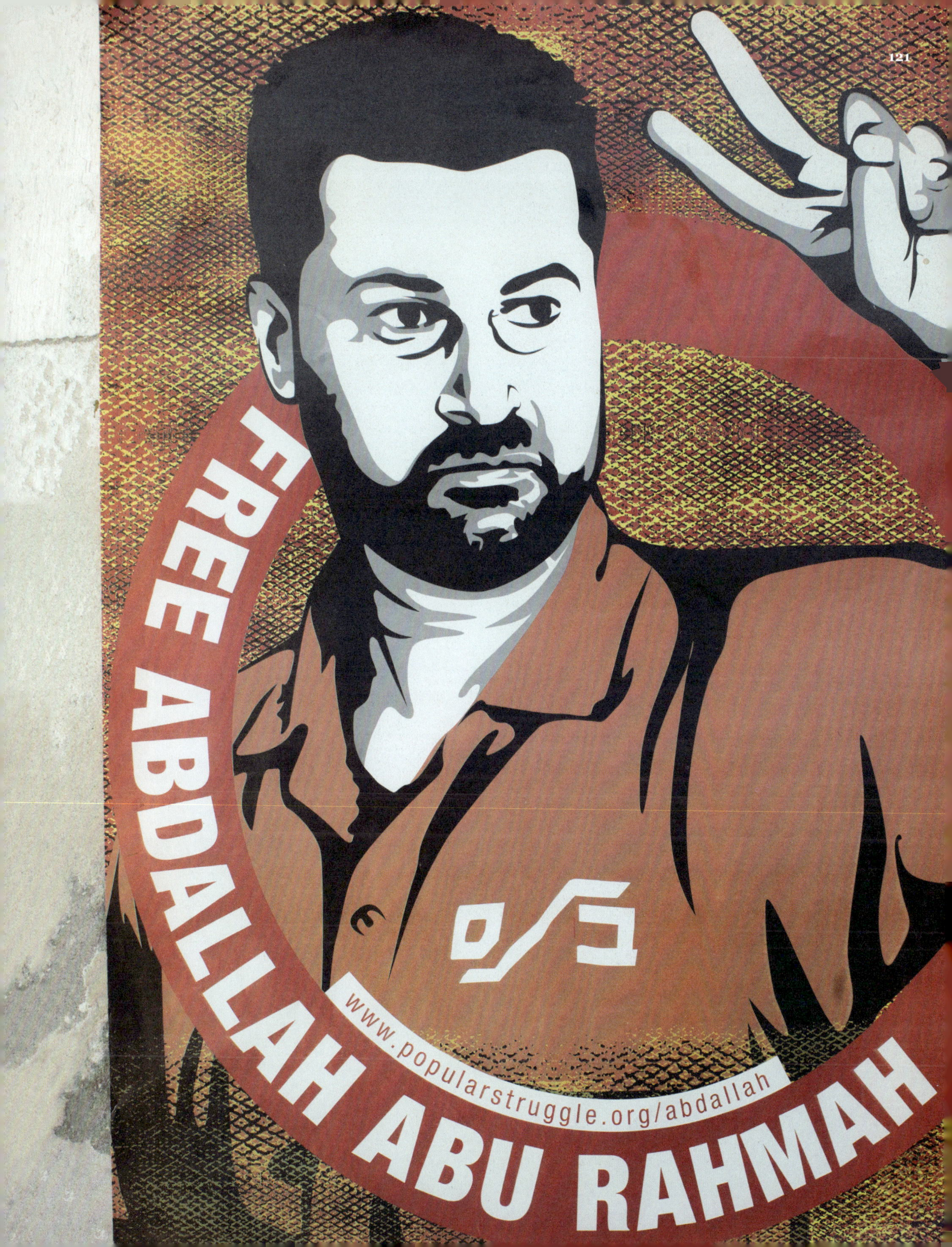
FREE ABDALLAH ABU RAHMAH
www.popularstruggle.org/abdallah

Old City, East Jerusalem 17.4.2012

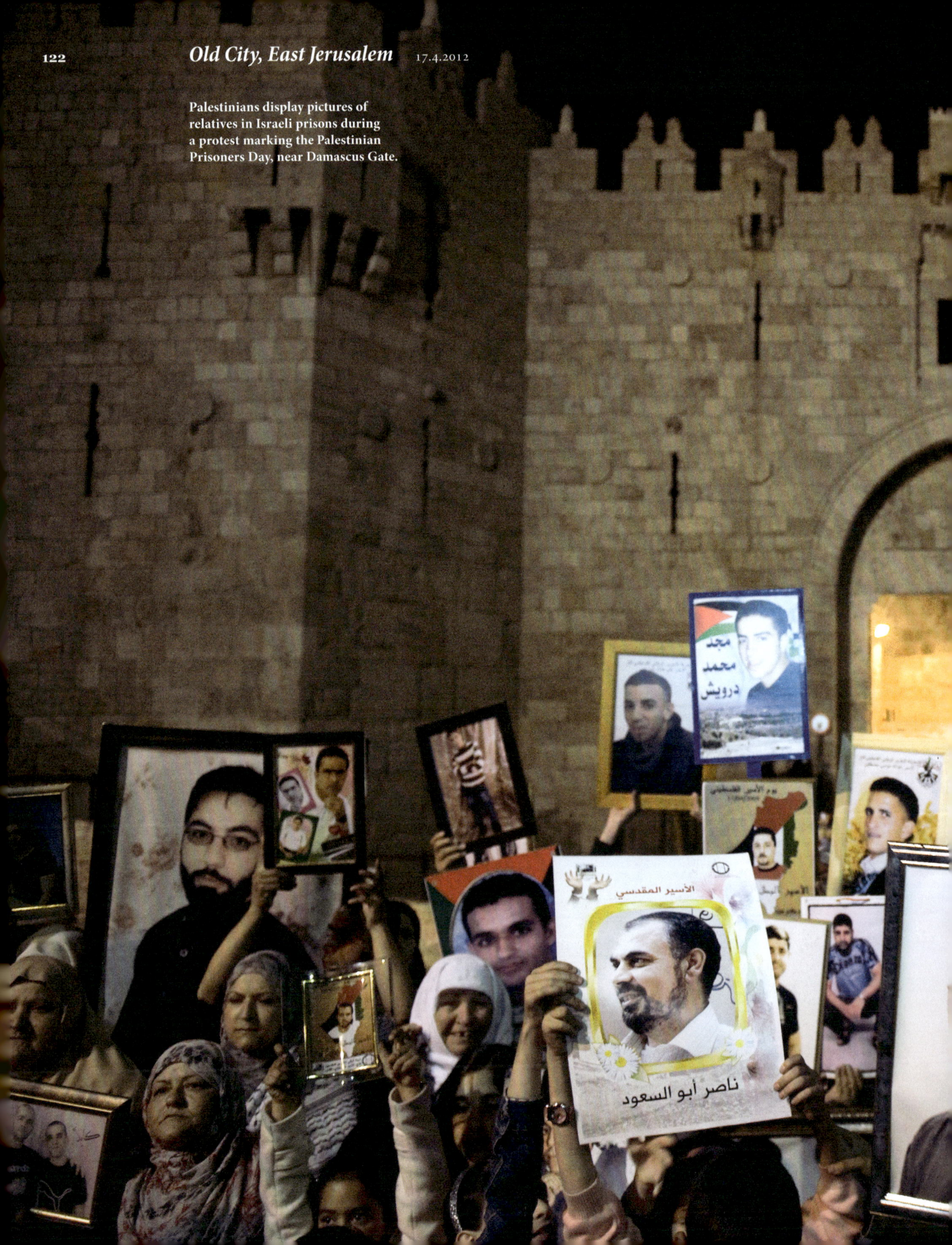

Palestinians display pictures of relatives in Israeli prisons during a protest marking the Palestinian Prisoners Day, near Damascus Gate.

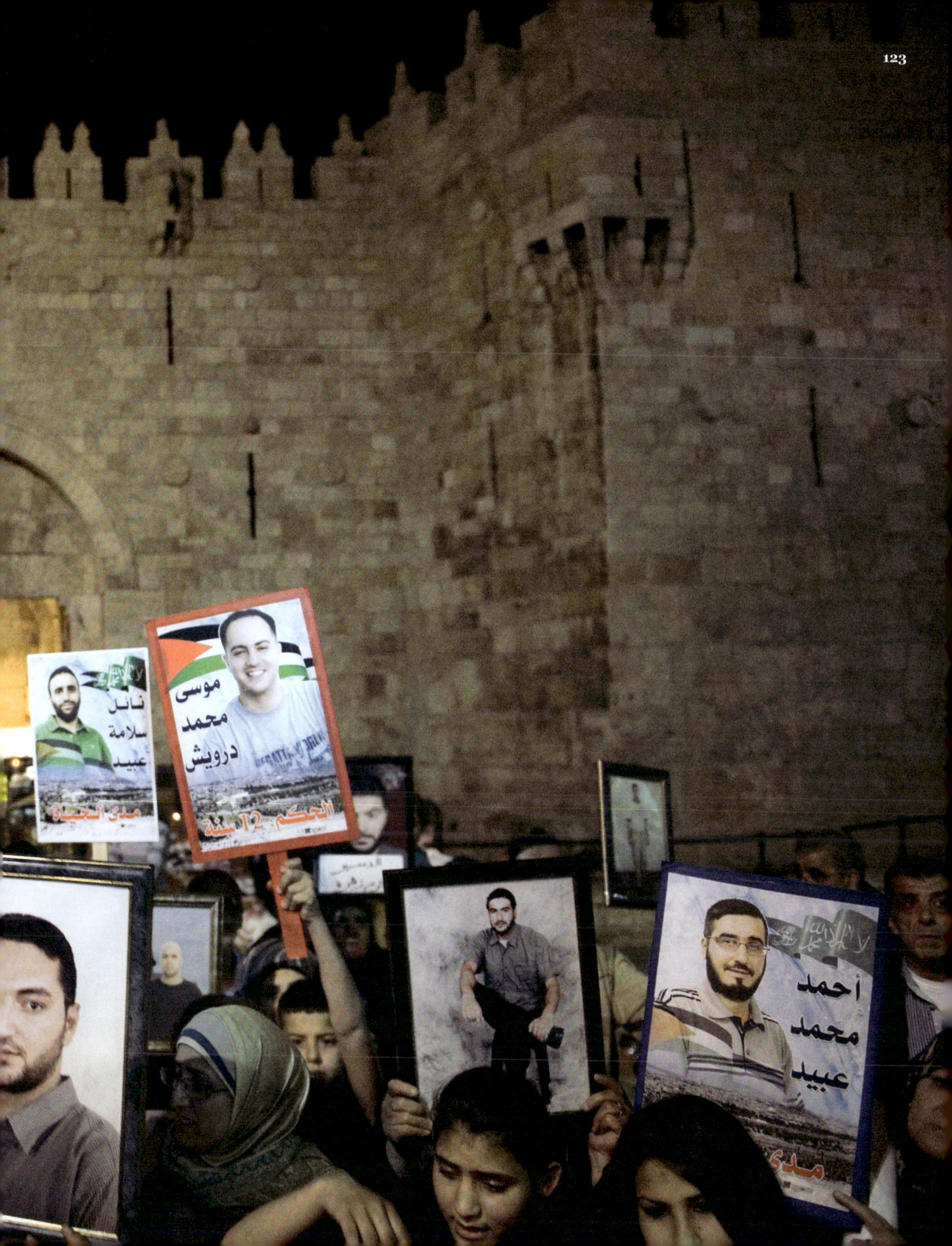
نائل
سلامة
عبيد
مدى الحياة
موسى
محمد
درويش
الحكم 12 سنة
أحمد
محمد
عبيد

Arraba, West Bank 18.4.2012

Khader Adnan plays with his daughter on his first day out of Israeli prison. Israeli authorities released Adnan from administrative detention after he was held for four months without trial. He protested against his administrative detention by holding a hunger strike for 67 days.

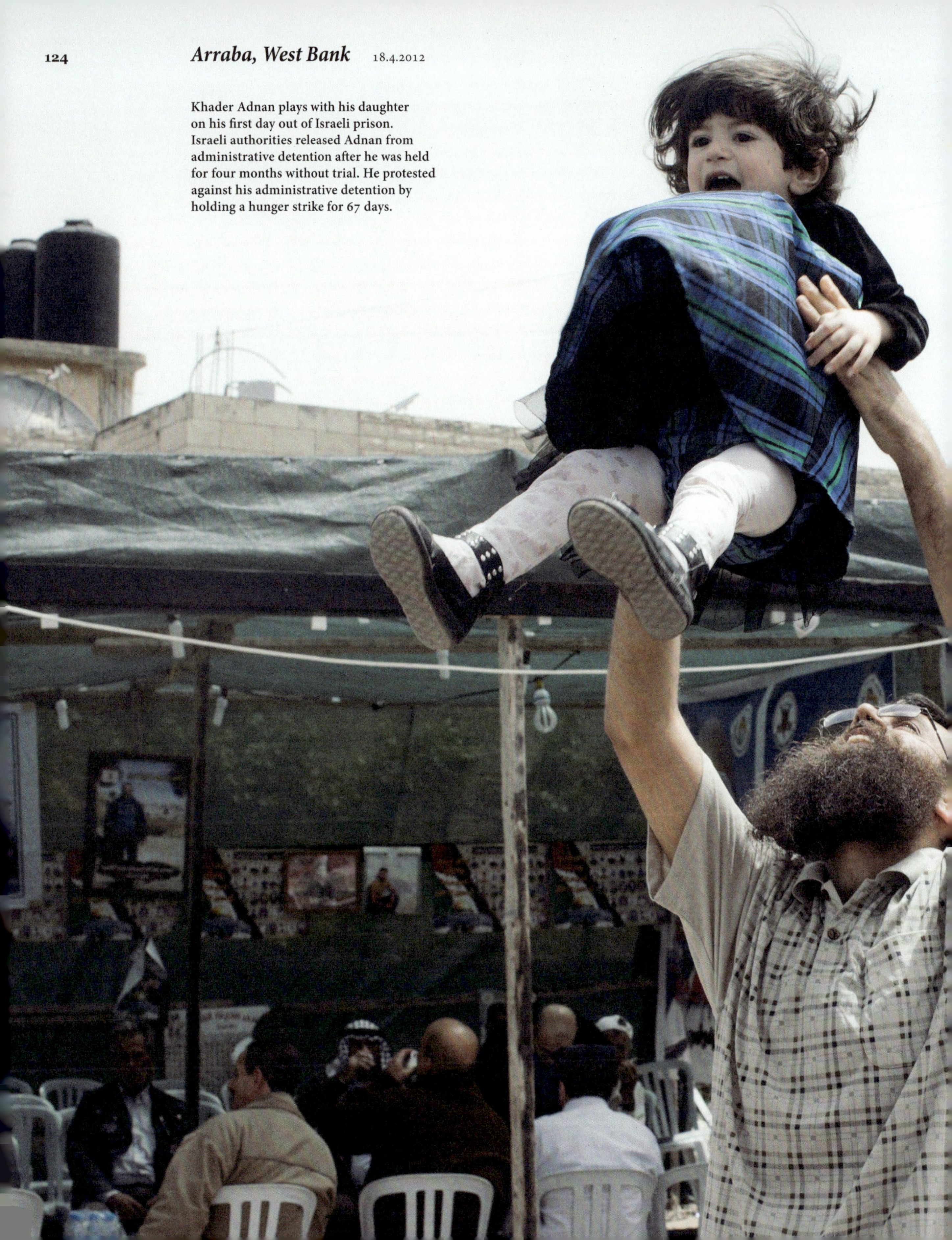

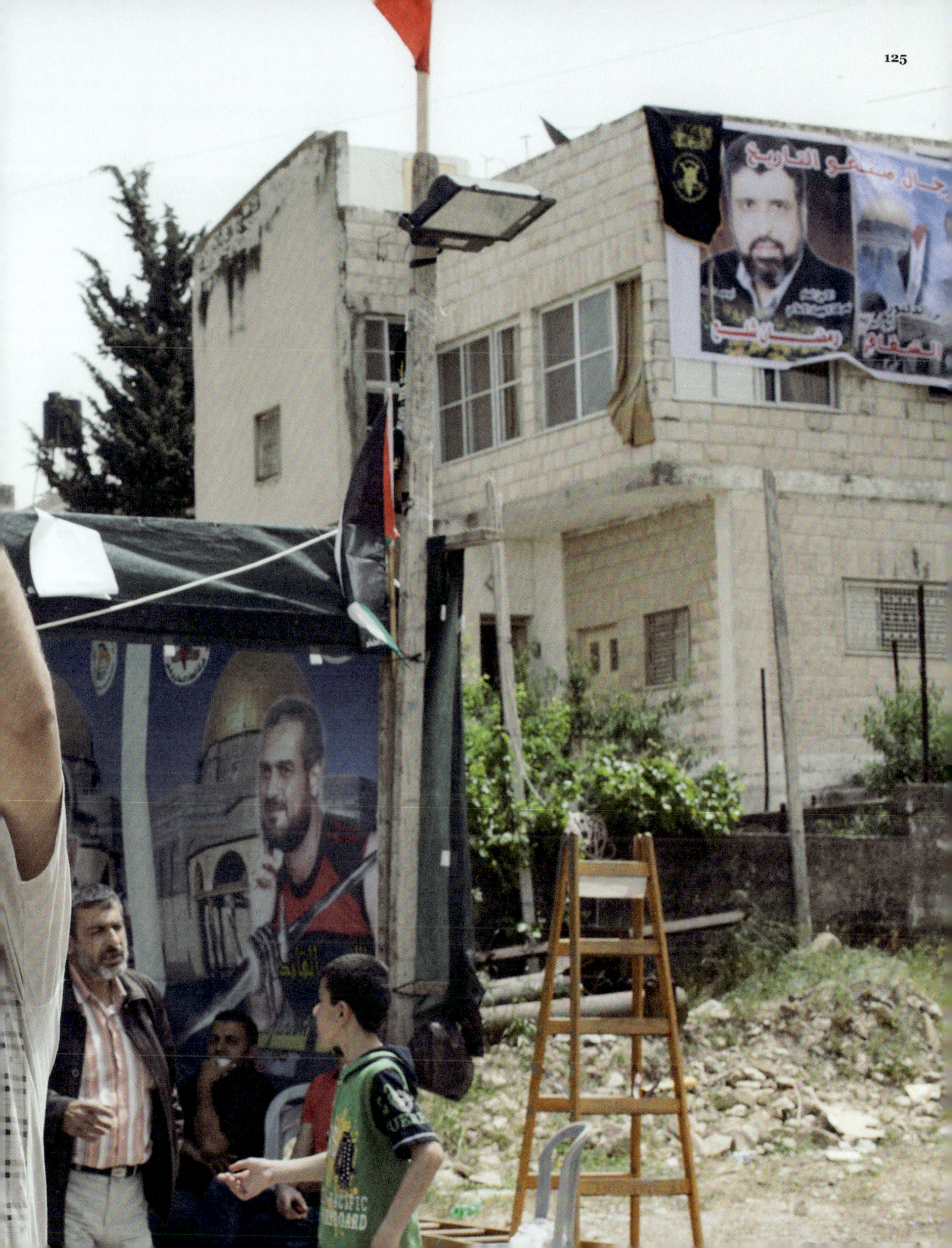

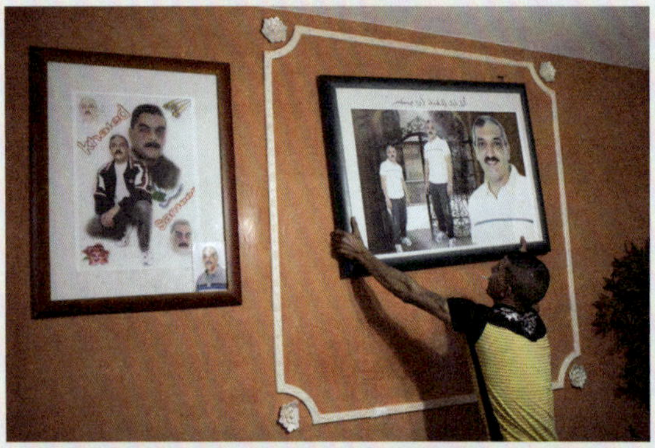

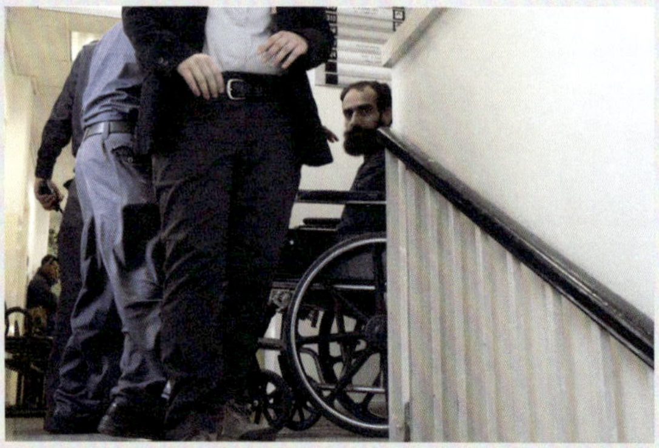

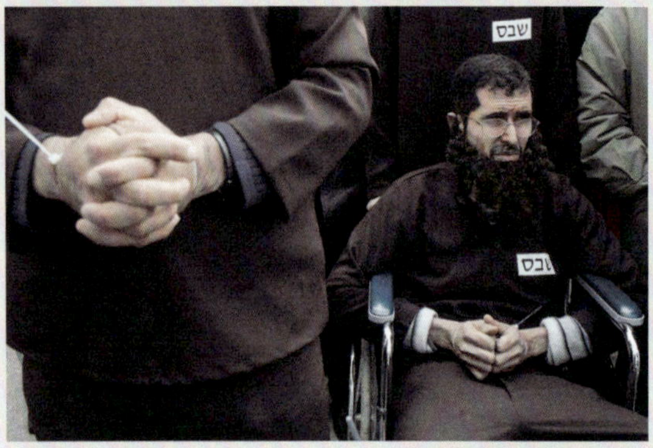

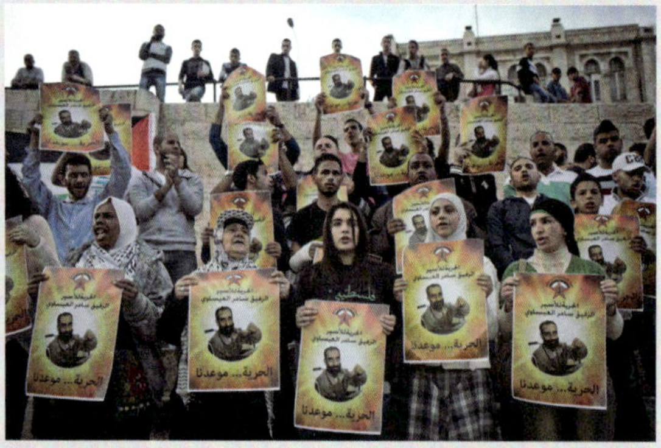

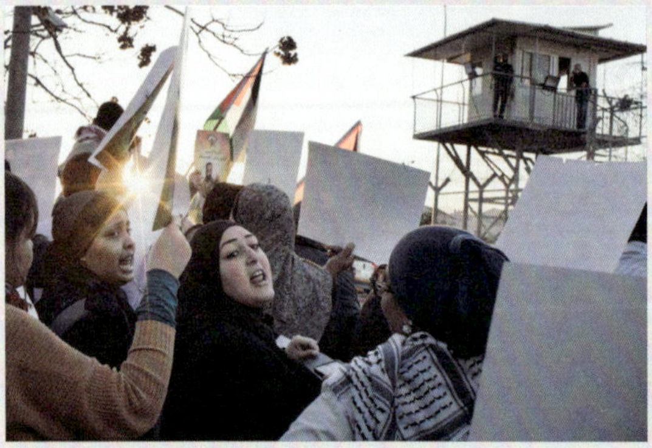

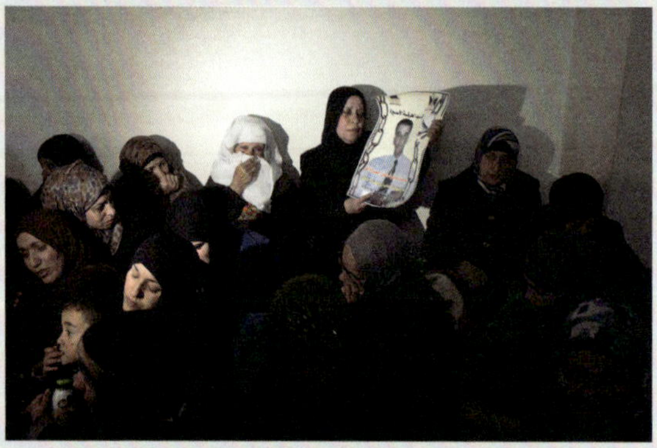

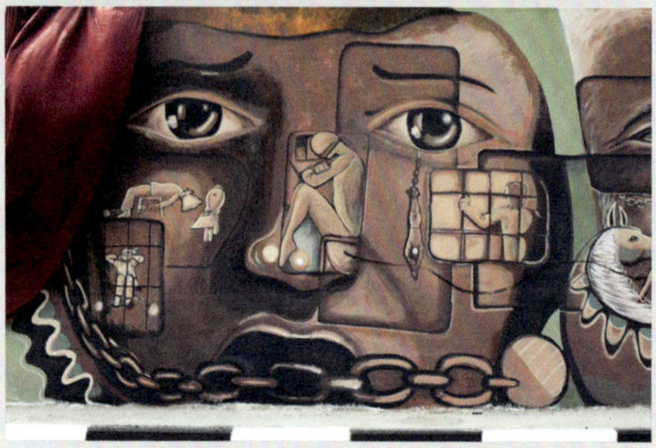

{Top left to right}
1. Relatives prepare for the homecoming of Haled Muheisen, released from Israeli prison, Al-Issawiya, East Jerusalem, 17.11.2011 / **2.** Palestinian hunger-striker Samer Issawi before his court hearing, West Jerusalem, 19.2.2013 / **3.** Protesters stage a solidarity action with hunger-striker Khader Adnan, Bil'in, West Bank, 17.2.2012 / **4.** Solidarity vigil with Samer Issawi, Jerusalem's Old City, 12.3.2013 / **5.** Solidarity vigil with Samer Issawi, outside Ramle prison, Israel, 4.2.2013 / **6.** Funeral of Palestinian prisoner Arafat Jaradat, Sa'ir, West Bank, 24.2.2013 / **7.** Graffiti welcoming Khader Adnan, Arraba, West Bank, 18.4.2012

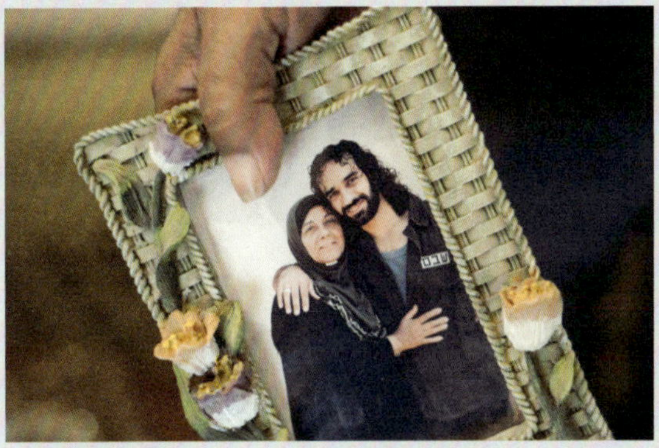

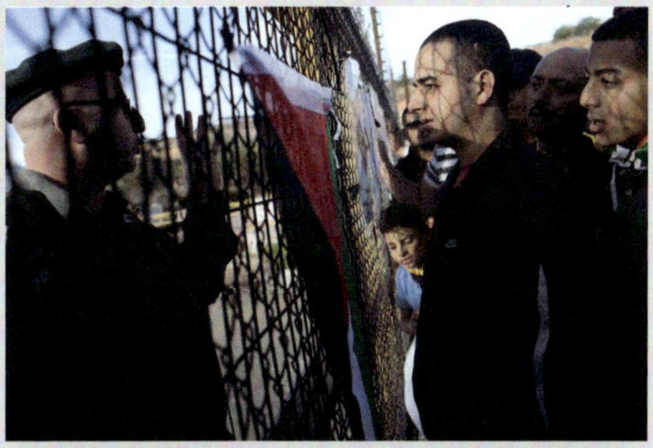

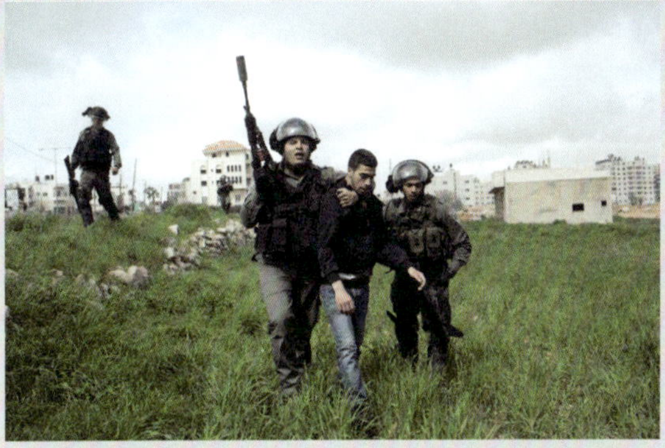

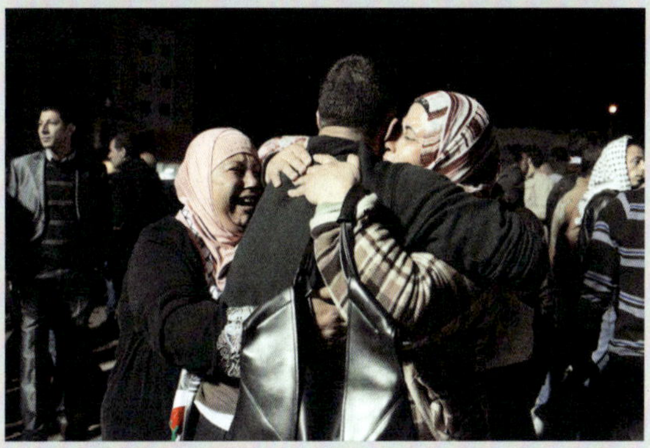

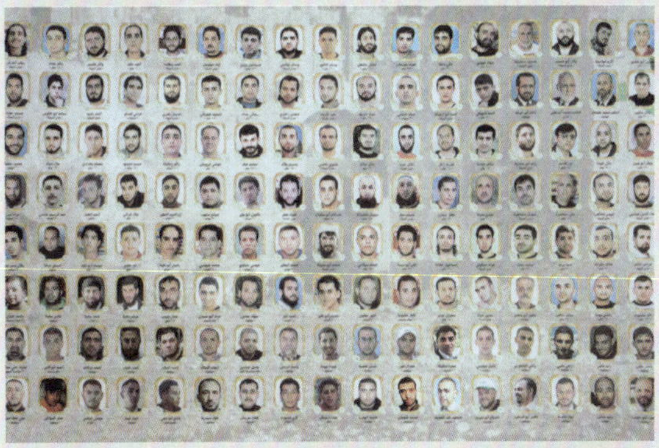

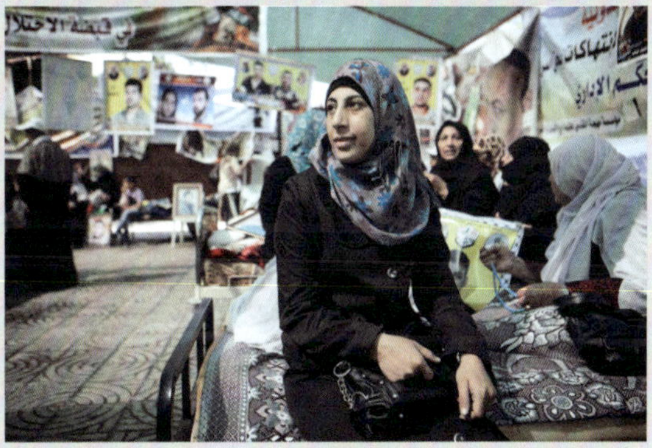

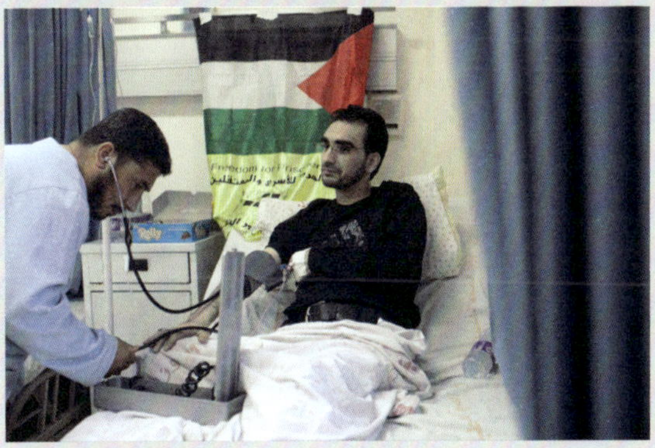

{Top left to right}
1. Tariq Issawi holds a photo of his wife, Layla, visiting their son Samer in an Israeli prison, 10.10.2012 / **2.** Palestinians await a prisoner exchange, Ofer military prison, West Bank, 18.10.2011 / **3.** Soldiers arrest a Palestinian, Ofer military prison, West Bank, 28.2.2013 / **4.** Palestinians celebrate prisoners' release, Ramallah, West Bank, 19.12.2011 / **5.** Poster of Palestinian prisoners carried at a protest, Ramle, Israel, 3.5.2012 / **6.** Palestinian hunger-striker Hana Shalabi inside a solidarity tent in Gaza City, Gaza Strip, 7.5.2012 / **7.** A doctor checks Thaer Halahleh, after he ended a 78-day hunger strike, Hebron, West Bank, 6.6.2012

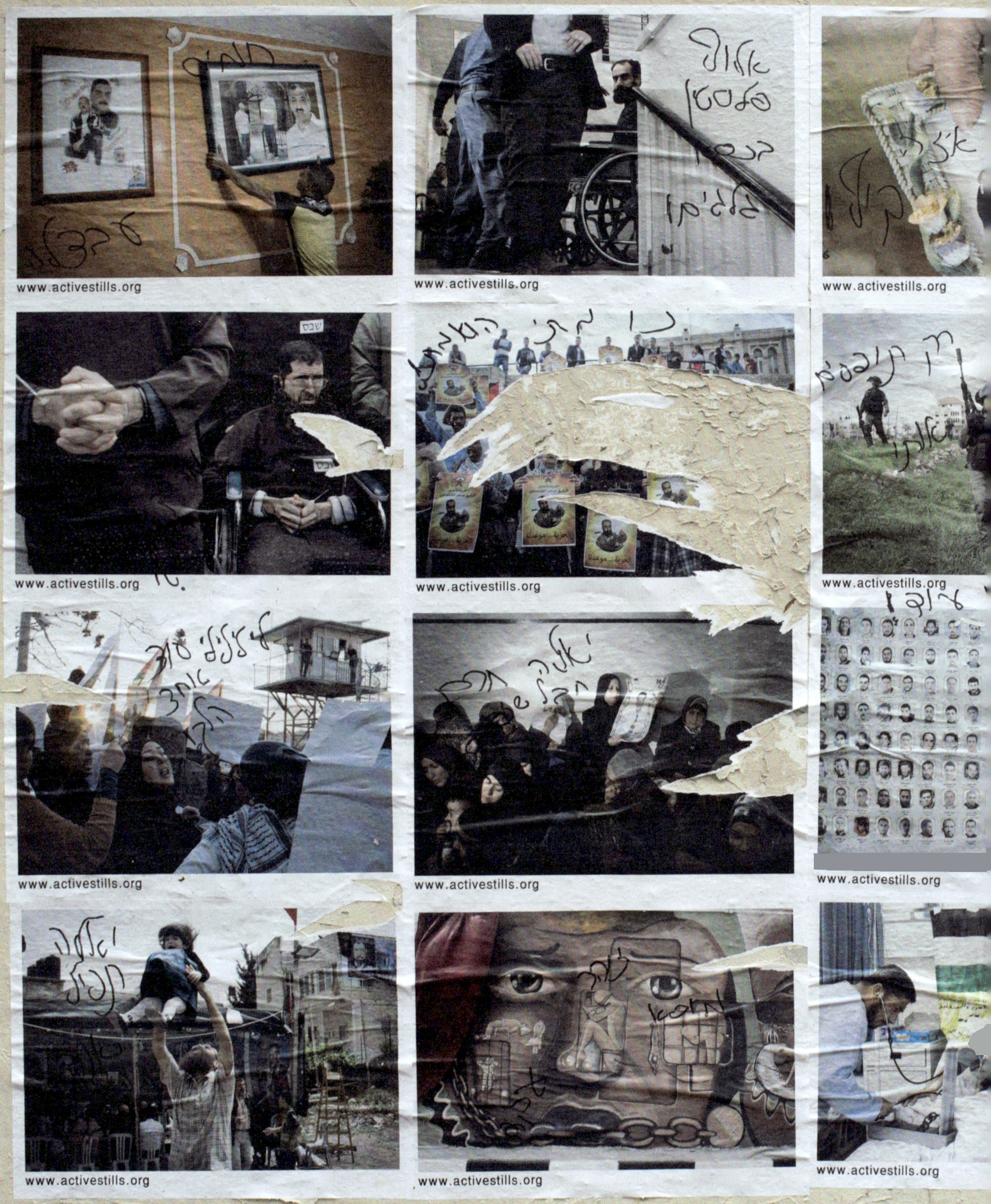

Racist comments in Hebrew on an Activestills street exhibition hung in Tel Aviv the previous night, in solidarity with Palestinian Prisoners Day.

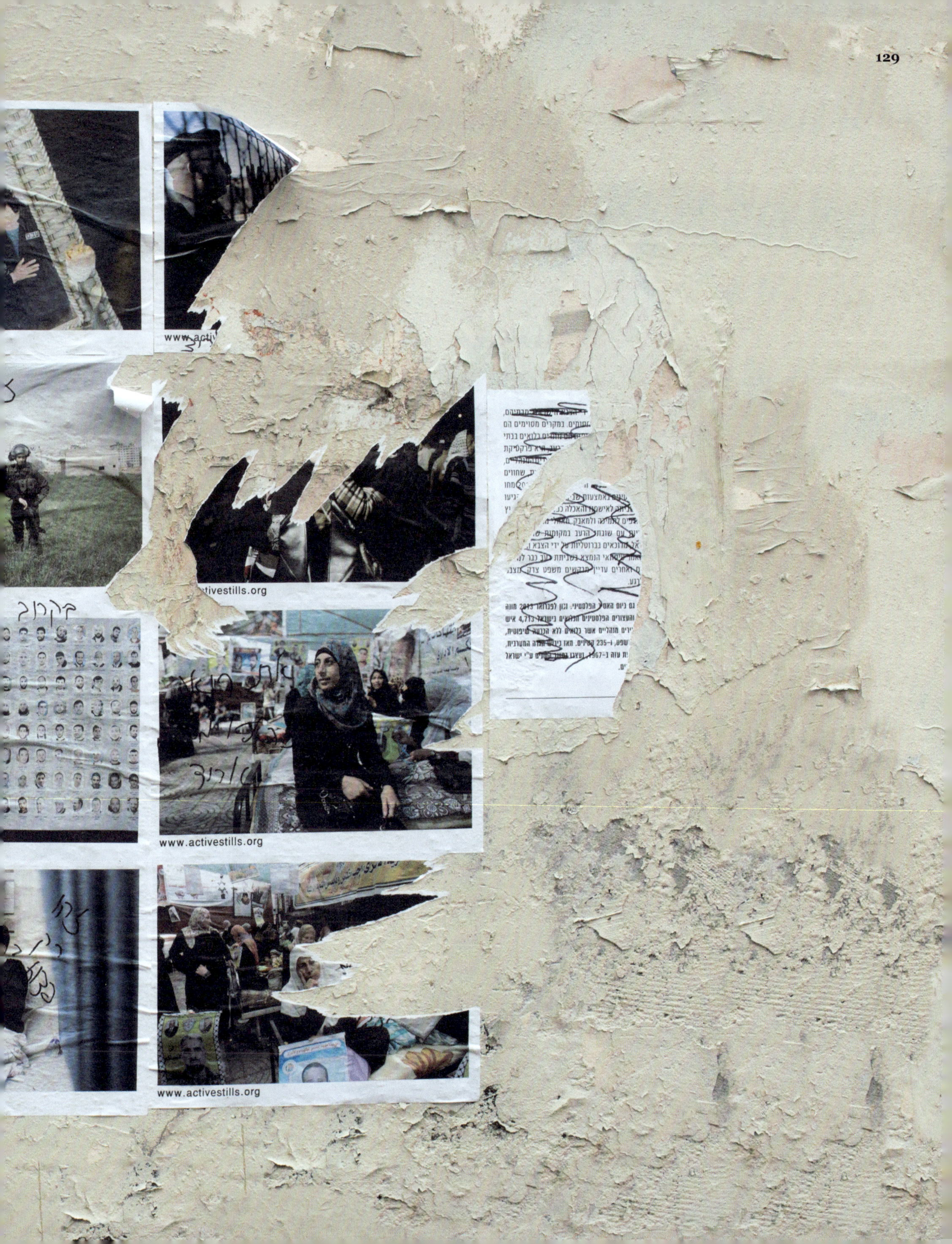
activestills.org
www.activestills.org
www.activestills.org

Monim Mandela

The group that walked the March For Freedom had one goal.[1] We wanted to show the world that we are not escaping from Holot detention center, but protesting against our unjust imprisonment in peaceful ways. We asked to be recognized as refugees, as human beings who had not committed any crime. Our only deed was to run away from war. We wanted the Israeli public to see us as such, and so we decided to walk straight to Jerusalem and protest in front of the Israeli Parliament, to make a political statement against Israel's asylum policies.

I was imprisoned under the infiltrators law for a year and a half, and that December day was the first day for me outside of prison since I crossed the border from Egypt into Israel.[2]

I suffered a lot of violence on my journey here, and unfortunately violence continued inside prison. But I'm not a violent person, and my community isn't either. By staging this march, we wanted the Israeli public to understand that we are not a threat to it, but a peaceful community of refugees.

We arranged our messages to the media before walking out of prison and were ready to answer questions. Despite the Israeli media's efforts to portray us as lawbreakers, we continued throughout the three-day event to try and explain our act of civil disobedience. We wrote our signs in English and asked our Israeli supporters to help us write them in Hebrew too. We continued to answer questions even when we understood that most of the Israeli media was against our protest.

After we were arrested and sent back to prison, there was great disappointment, but at the same time we knew we had achieved a great deal. We saw the newspaper headlines, and the solidarity shown with our act that spread on social media, both within the local community and internationally. I was personally very encouraged by the fact that the Eritrean and Sudanese communities acted together. It gave me hope for the future. Of course, we didn't think that with one act we will solve everything. The road is very long.

Monim Mandela is a Sudanese asylum seeker and one of the organizers of the March For Freedom. He currently lives in Ashkelon, Israel. He is still waiting to be recognized as a refugee by the Israeli authorities.

1. March For Freedom is the name given to the three-day march from the Holot detention center in the southern part of Israel to the Israeli Parliament in West Jerusalem, staged by 150 African asylum seekers from Sudan and Eritrea on 15–17 December 2013. Upon reaching Jerusalem, all the participants were arrested by the Israeli immigration police and sent back to prison. The event triggered a wave of solidarity protests of the African community in Israel and its supporters, culminating in the biggest protest ever staged by asylum seekers; it was attended by over 30,000 people who convened in Rabin Square in Tel Aviv on 5 January 2014.

2. The Prevention of Infiltration Law was enacted in 1954 and allows the Israeli government to deport or imprison an infiltrator before or after conviction. As growing numbers of African asylum seekers escaping genocide in Sudan and military incursion in Eritrea reached the Israeli borders in 2006, the government passed an amendment to the law that would allow Israeli immigration police to imprison asylum seekers without trial for varying periods of time in what is termed an "open prison."

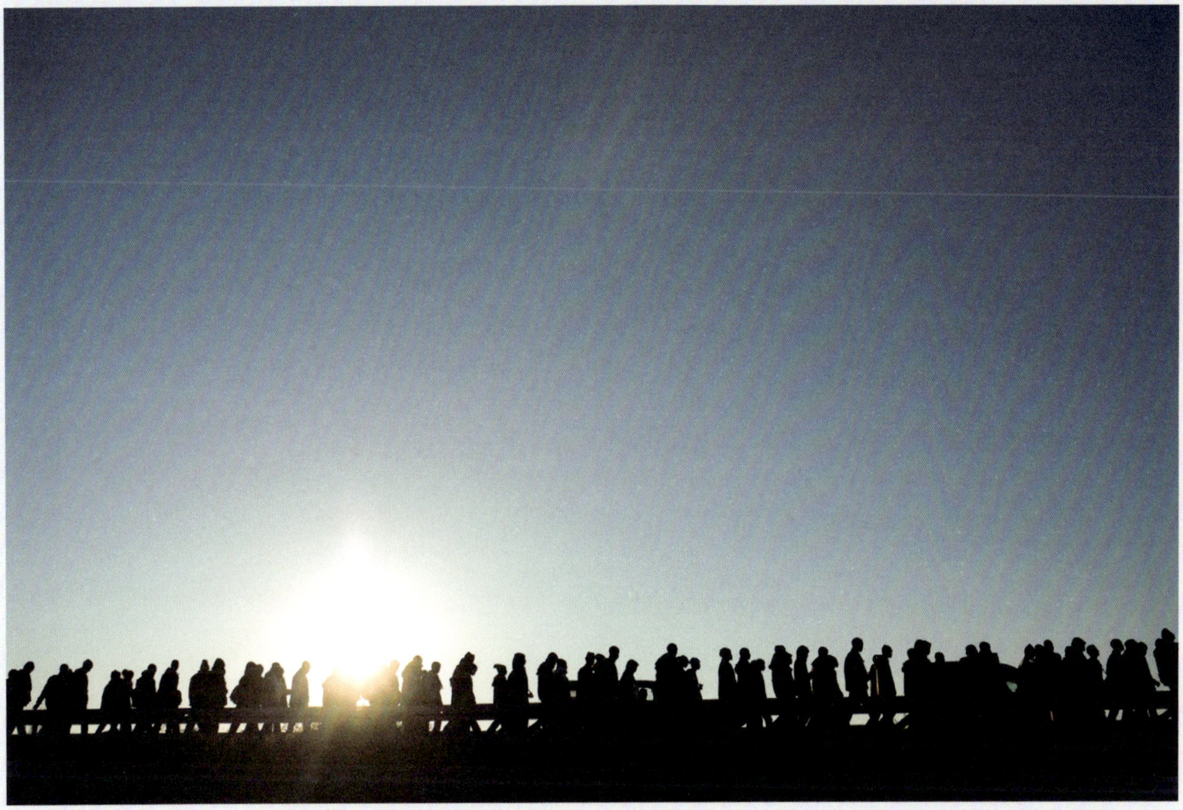

African asylum seekers at the March For Freedom from Holot detention center
to West Jerusalem, Negev Desert, Israel, 16.12.2013

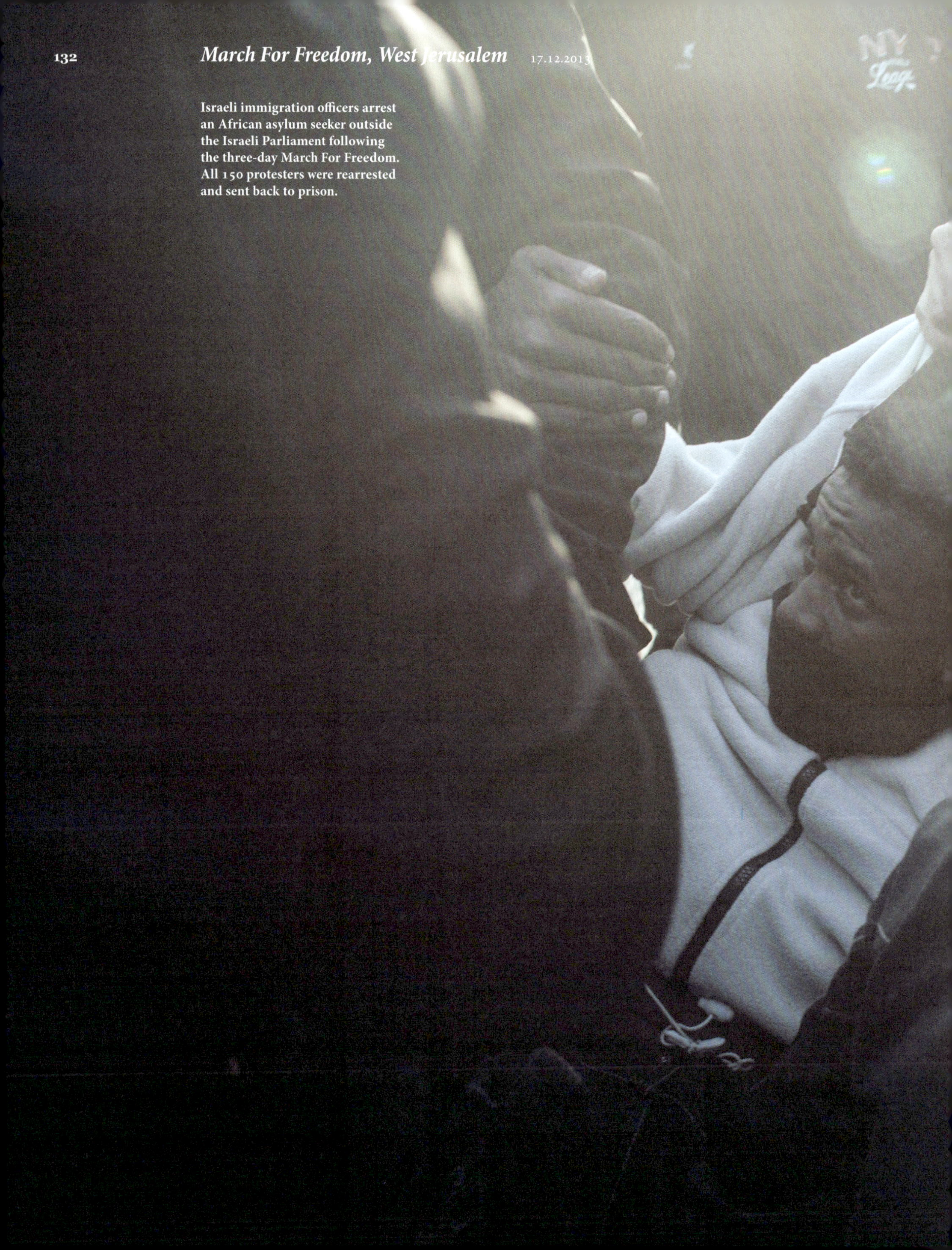

Israeli immigration officers arrest an African asylum seeker outside the Israeli Parliament following the three-day March For Freedom. All 150 protesters were rearrested and sent back to prison.

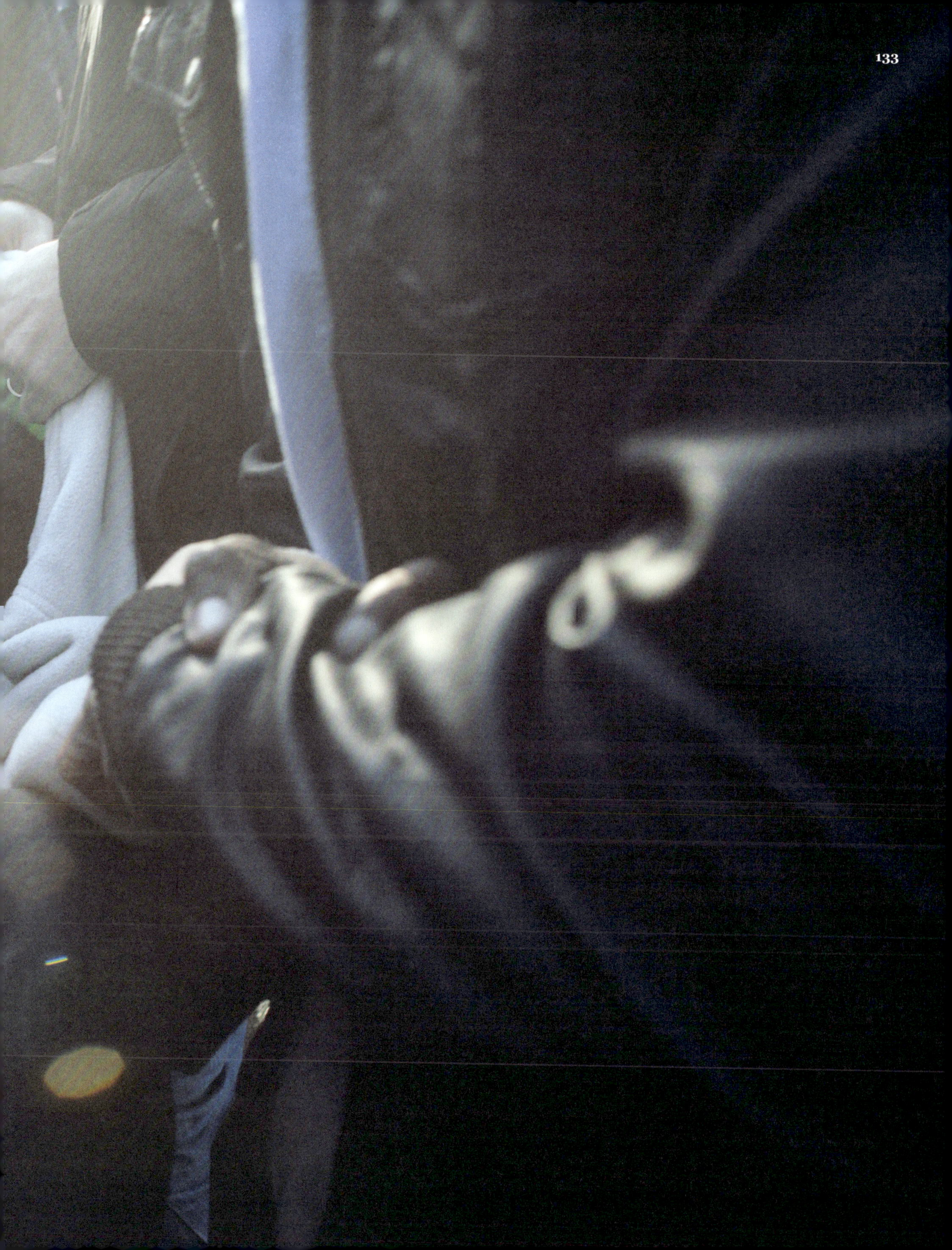

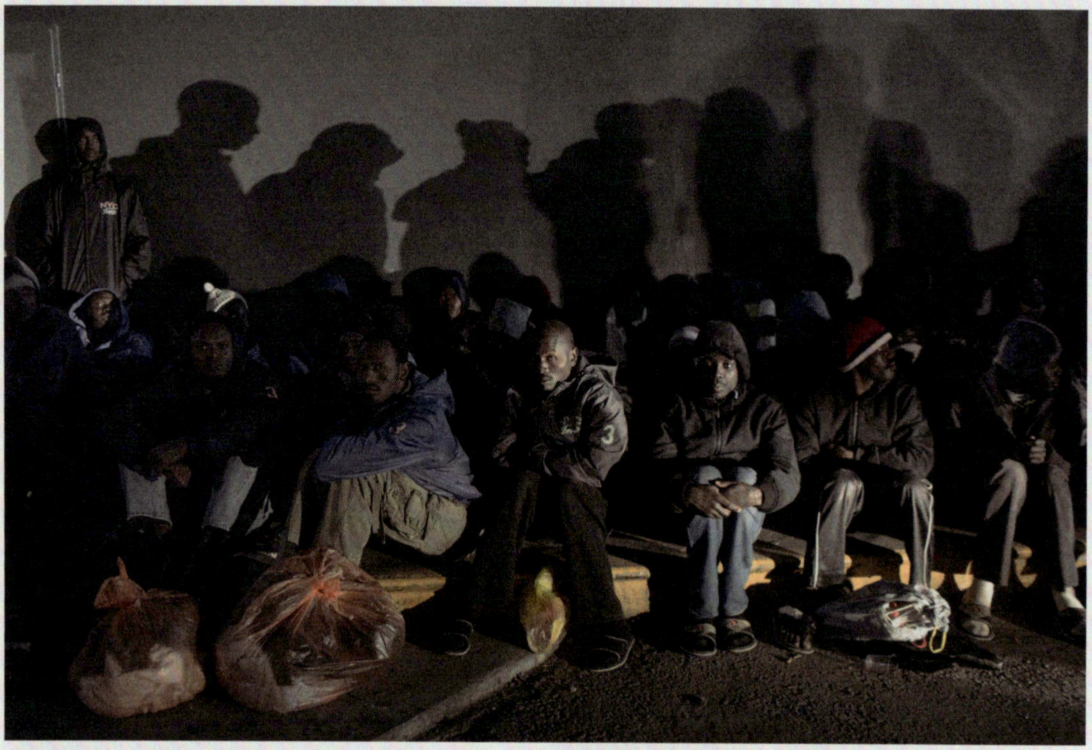

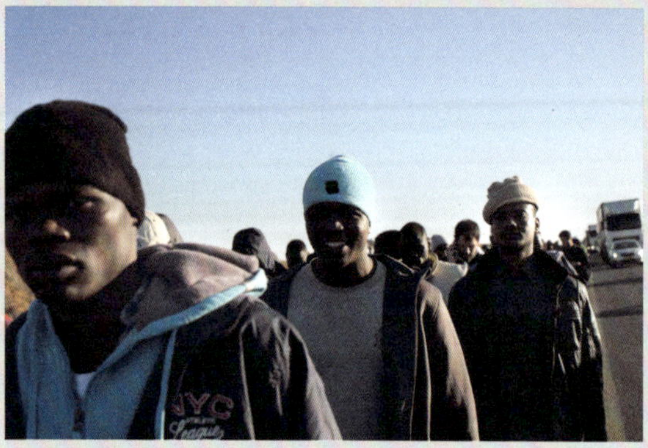

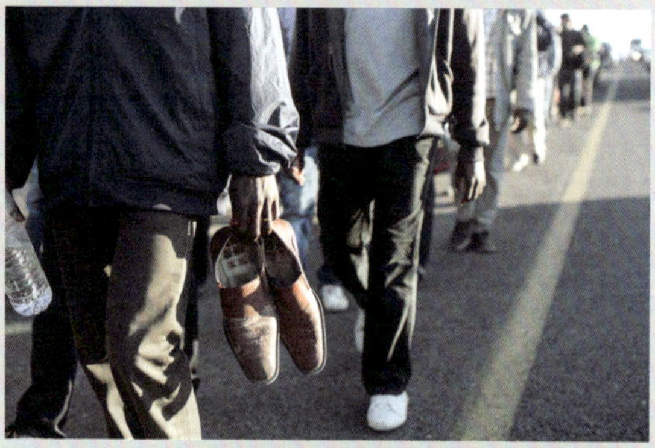

{Top left to right}
1. African asylum seekers gather outside the central bus station in the southern city of Be'er Sheva, after marching six hours by foot from the Holot detention center, Negev Desert, 15.12.2013 / **2+3.** African asylum seekers march to Jerusalem on Road 40, Negev Desert, 16.12.2013 / **4.** Activists try to prevent Israeli immigration police from arresting African asylum seekers in front of the Israeli Parliament, West Jerusalem, 17.12.2013

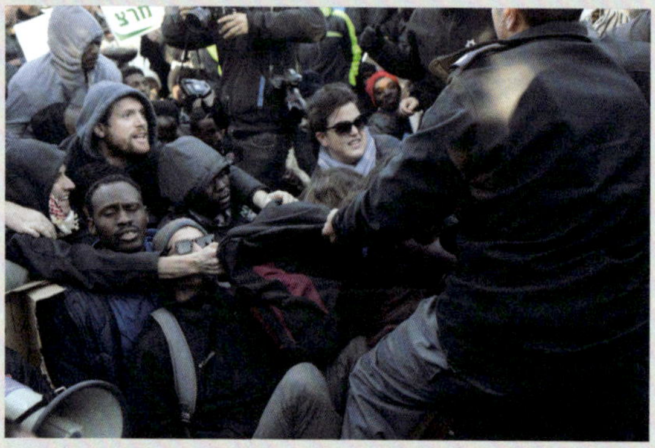

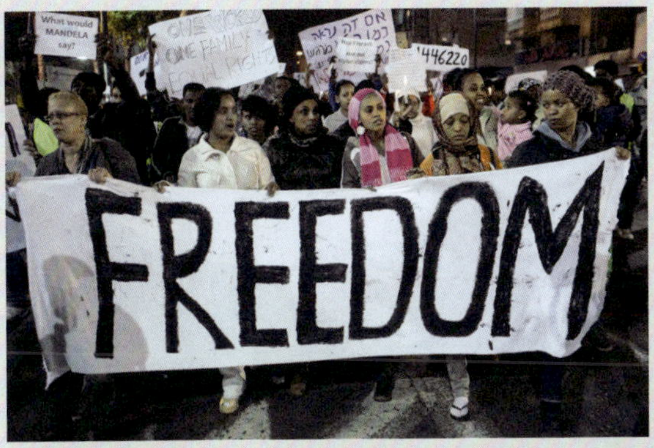

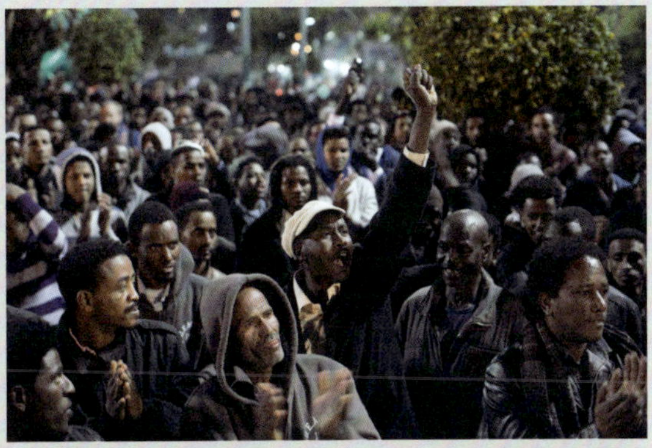

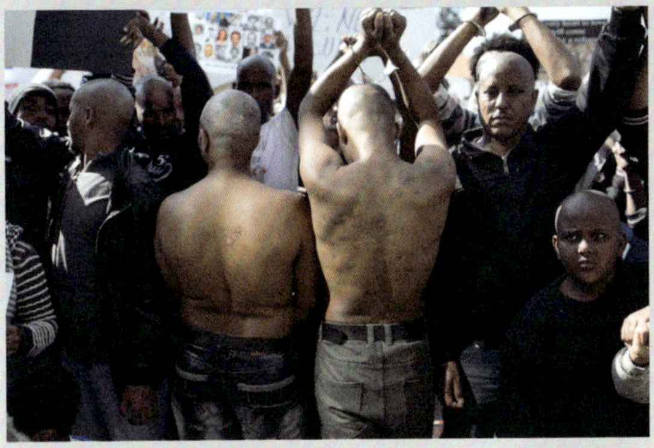

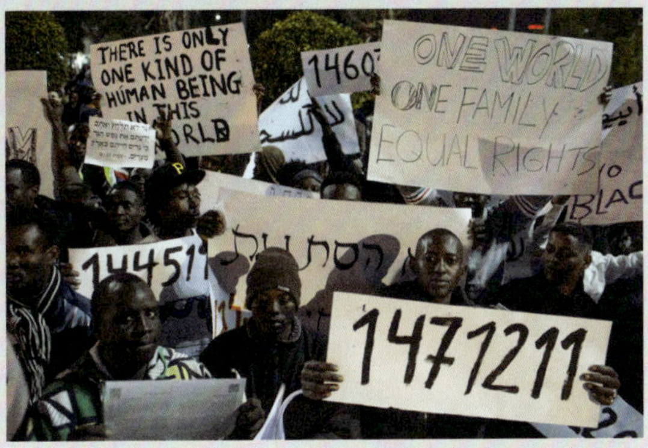

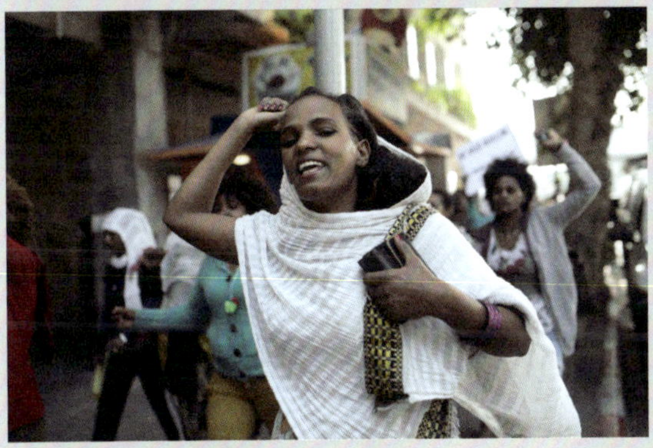

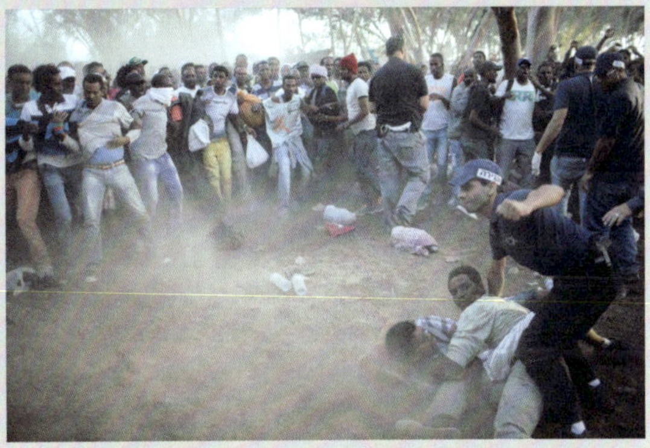

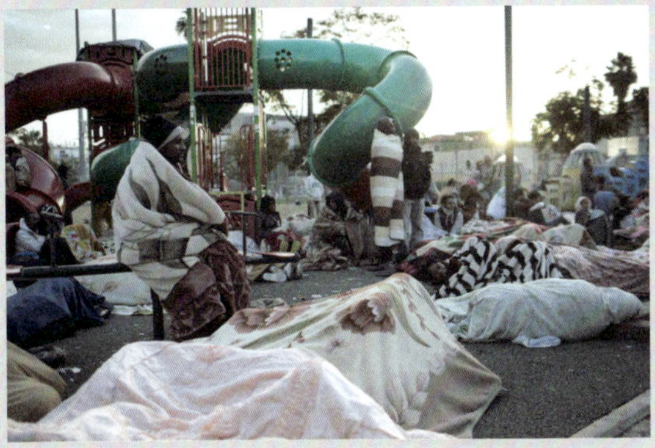

{Top left to right}
1. The African community protest in solidarity with imprisoned asylum seekers, Tel Aviv, 28.12.2013 / **2.** Community gathering in Levinsky Park, Tel Aviv, 21.12.2013 / **3.** African asylum seekers show scars of torture inflicted by Egyptian smugglers in the Sinai Desert, Tel Aviv, 11.2.2014 / **4.** Solidarity protest, Tel Aviv, 28.12.2013 / **5.** Solidarity protest, Tel Aviv, 15.1.2014 / **6.** Israeli immigration police arrest African asylum seekers near the Israeli-Egyptian border, 29.6.2014 / **7.** African asylum seekers stage a sit-in protest calling for recognition of their refugee rights, Tel Aviv, 3.2.2014

Reuven Abergel

Reuven Abergel is an activist for public housing and Mizrahi rights in Israel, and is a co-founder of the Israeli Black Panthers.

When Activestills photographers asked me to write a text for this book, they sent me photographs of protests where I can be seen in the picture. In some of them, I am holding their photos; in another, I am serving as a judge in a popular court for public housing, a community-media event that the women struggling for public housing organized in order to raise public awareness of Israel's crumbling welfare services. I looked over the photographs and then I asked them to send me one of a hole in the Israeli separation wall, a hole that had been made by young Palestinian activists on the Palestinian side in the Abu Dis neighborhood in East Jerusalem. I know that place well. I grew up in Musrara, a neighborhood on the seam between East Jerusalem and the western part of the city, which was also where the Israeli Black Panthers movement started, a movement that sought to right the wrong that had been done to the Mizrahim, the Jews who emigrated from Arab countries to Israel in the 1950s. I look at these pictures and find myself writing:

Soldiers have been stationed atop your walls Jerusalem,
All day and all night,
Walls that separate Mizrahim from Ashkenazim,
Walls that separate long-time residents from newcomers,
Walls that separate Palestinian citizens of Israel from Jewish citizens,
Walls that encircle villages and cities under occupation.

The wall of the Old City in Jerusalem surrounds the collective memory
Of the inhabitants of this land from time immemorial, and today
It casts a heavy shadow over the words written in the declaration of
independence of the State of Israel, "A Jewish and democratic state."

The Jewish People has built walls inside its heart,
The longest and highest wall, between us and the Palestinians,
Walls that surround the prisons inside which Palestinians
Who are struggling to end the occupation are jailed,
And also Ethiopian, Russian, and Mizrahi youth,
Who were unable to find a home here.

We have built walls between us and Arab countries
With whom we have signed "peace" agreements, Egypt and Jordan,
We have built walls against the judicial system and the Parliament,
We have built walls against compassion, against morality,
Against solidarity, against the poor,
Against human rights organizations.

Watchmen have been placed atop your walls Jerusalem,
Every day and every night,
Walls
That separate us
From everything that is of value.

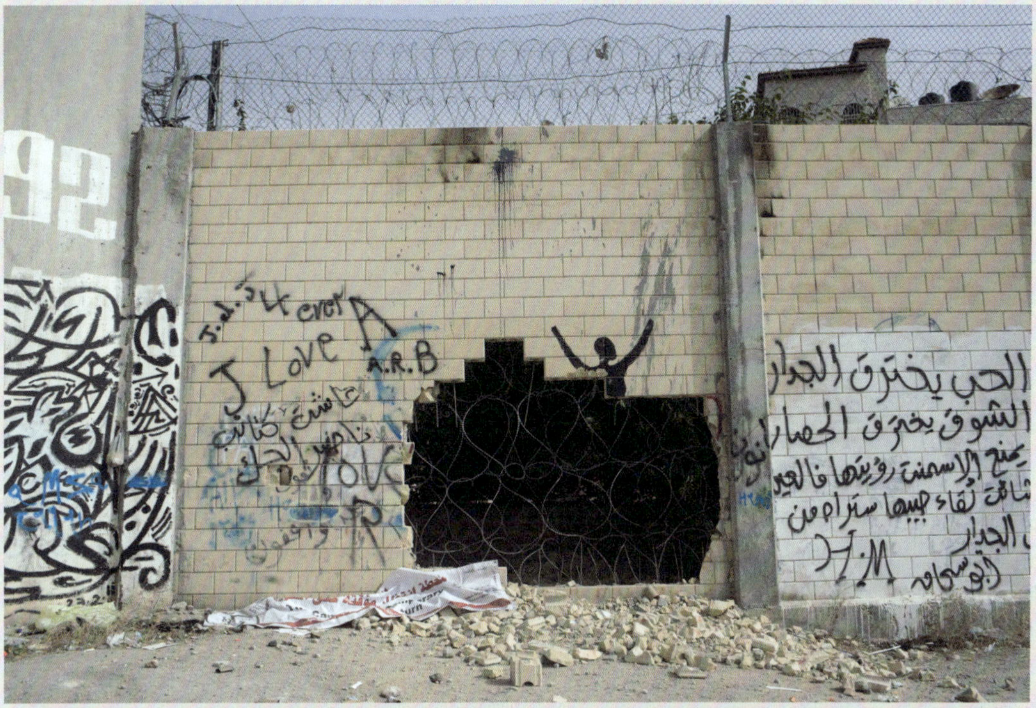

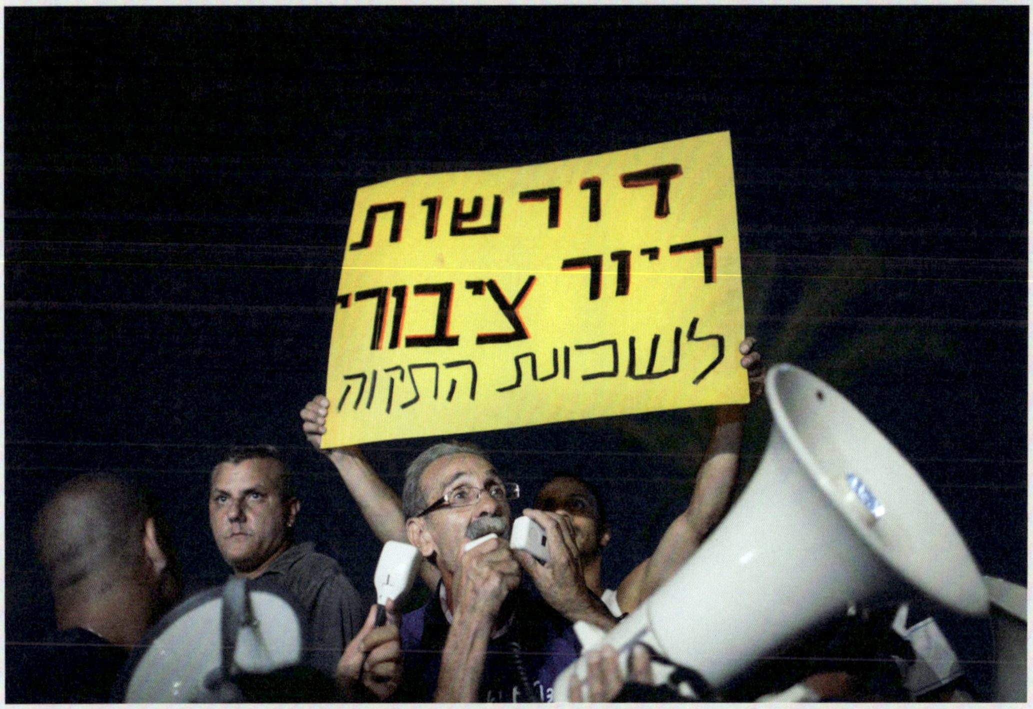

1. An opening in the Israeli separation wall between the East Jerusalem neighborhoods of Ras al-Amud and Abu Dis, 18.5.2013 / **2.** Reuven Abergel speaks at a protest for social justice in the city of Bat Yam, Israel, 10.8.2011. The sign says: "we demand [in female tense] public housing for the Hatikva neighborhood."

West Jerusalem 30.4.2015

Israel's Ethiopian community demonstrates against police brutality and racism, following a series of incidents involving police violence directed at Ethiopian youth.

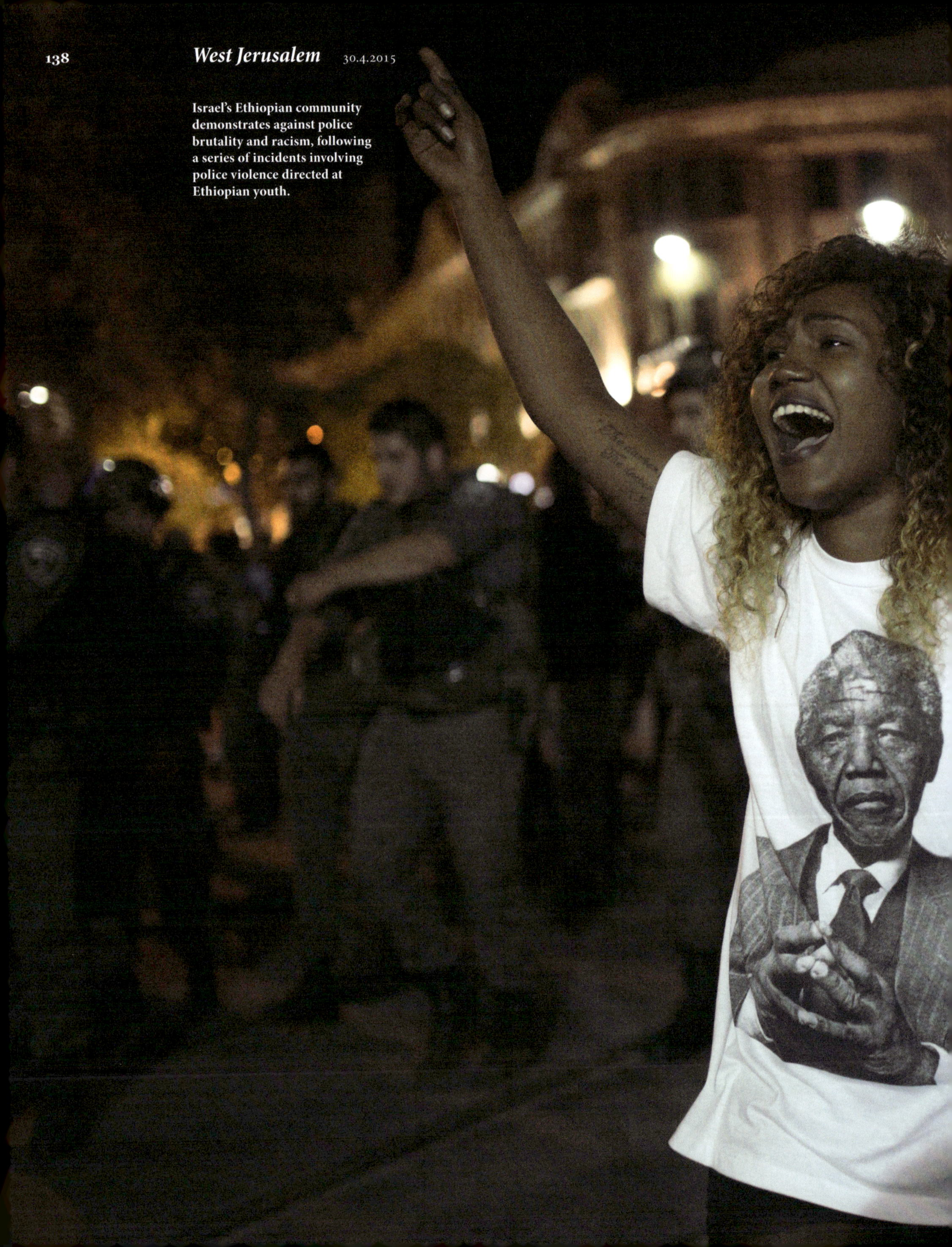

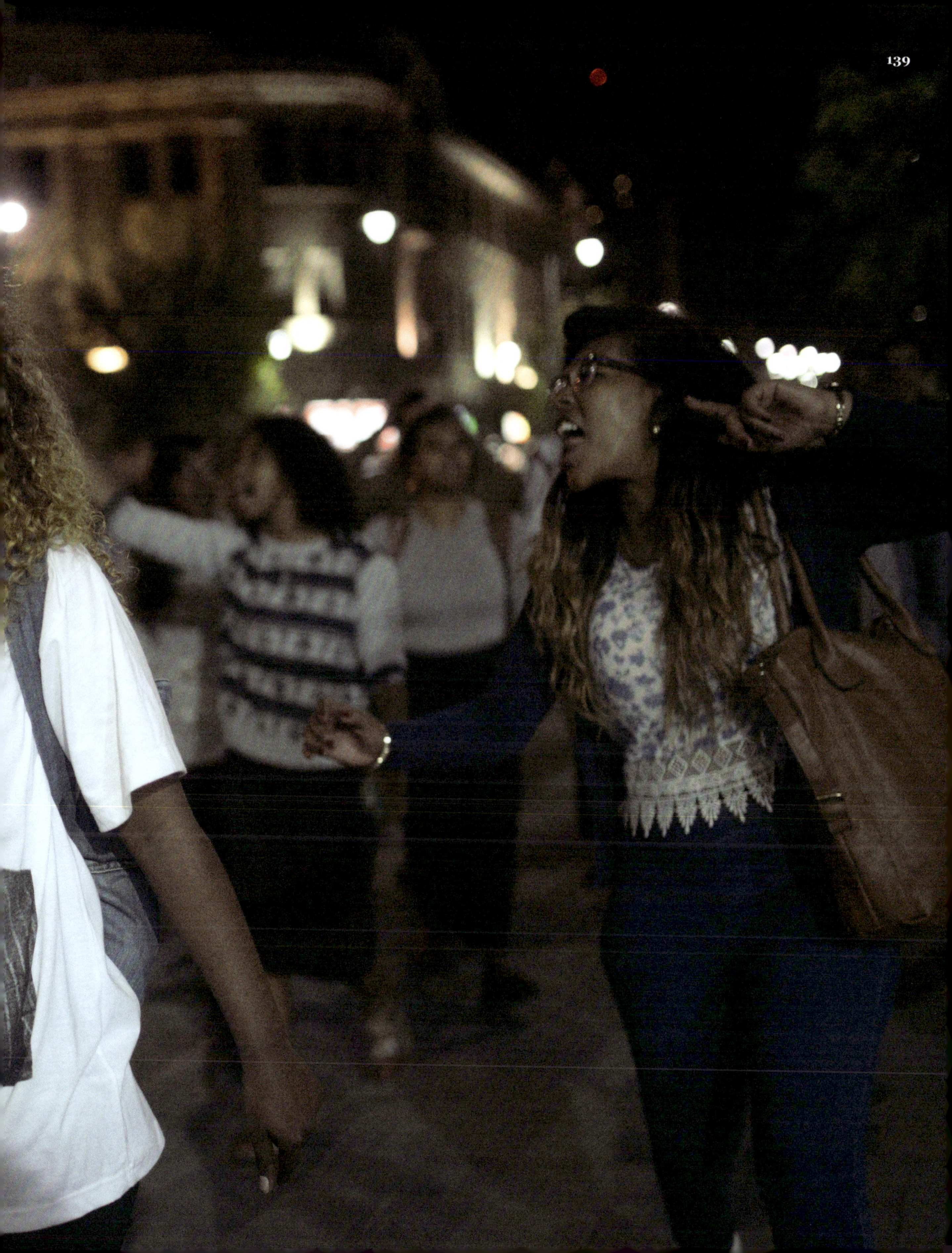

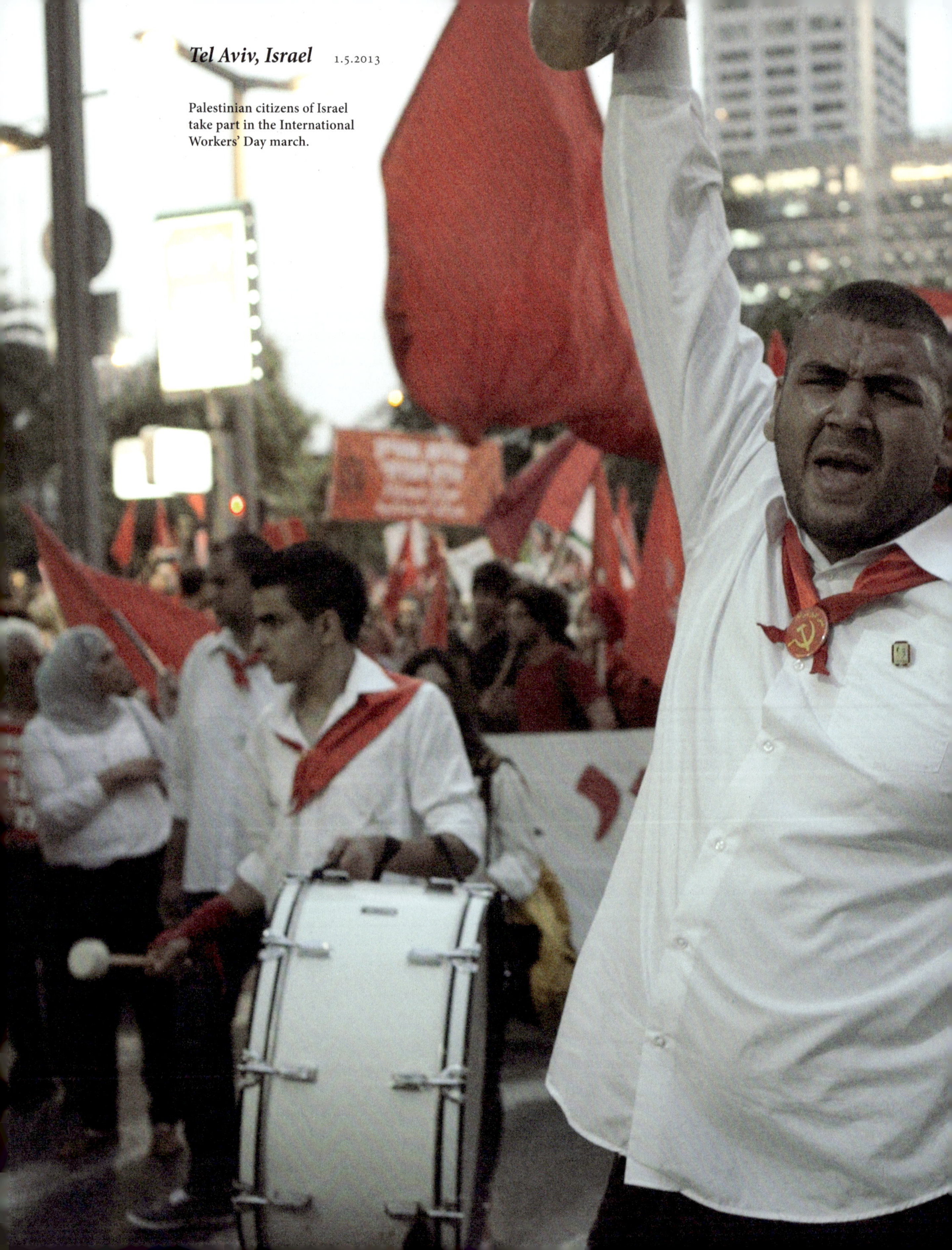

Tel Aviv, Israel 1.5.2013

Palestinian citizens of Israel take part in the International Workers' Day march.

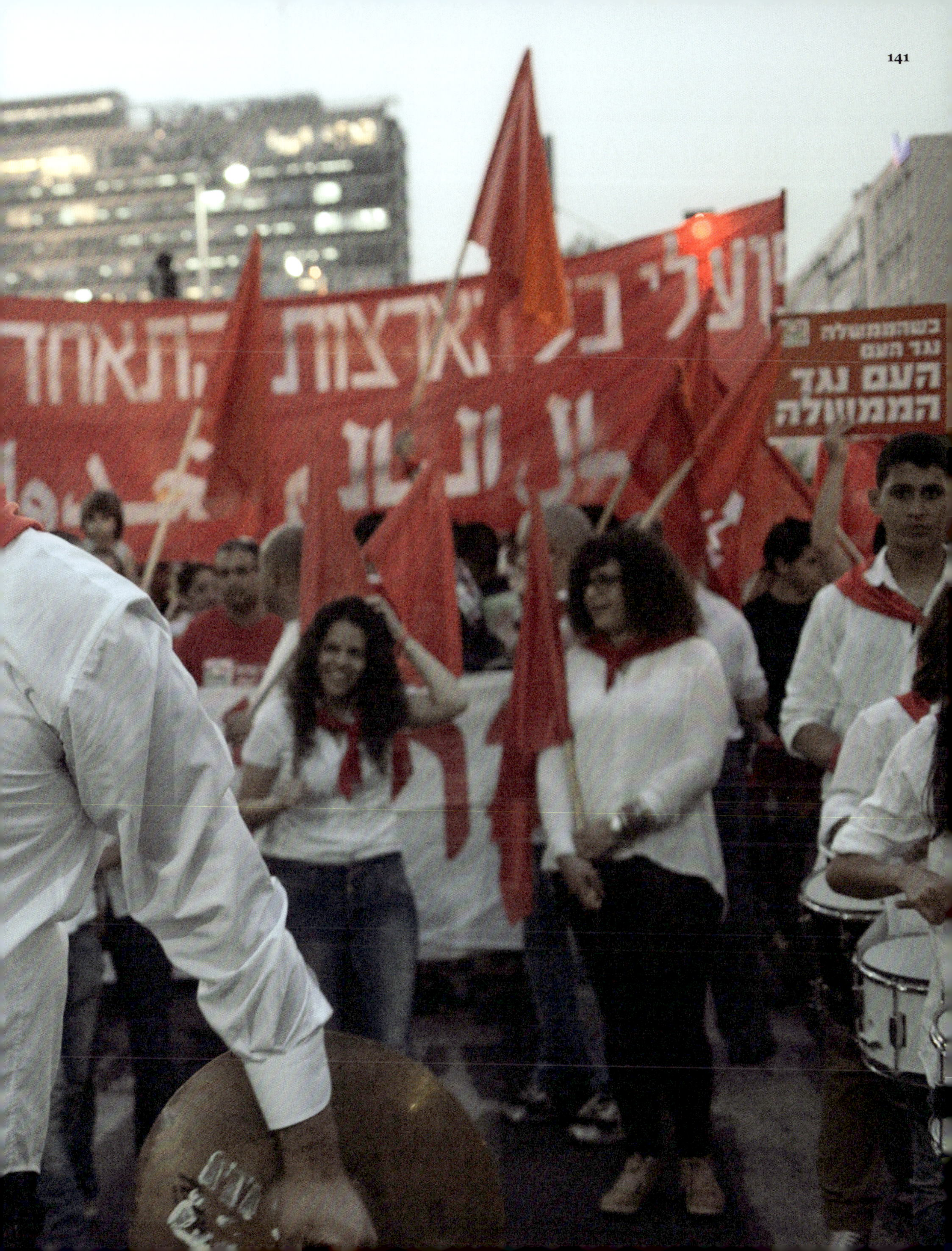
ארצות
כשהממשלה
נגד העם
העם נגד
הממשלה

Carmen Elmakiyes-Amos

It was a special day, and I remember this moment in the eviction. In this photo, we see the first resistance in Giv'at Amal to the eviction of residents from their homes. The earlier evictions took place without any opposition or media racket. This rough eviction is of Rivka Hayilovsky, a 60-year-old woman who had lived her entire life in the Giv'at Amal neighborhood. Rivka stood bravely facing the eviction forces, with the activists and the neighborhood residents alongside her.

I was affected by both the defiance and emotion of the residents, who saw that it is possible to resist and that there are activists who care to join their struggle, and at the same time, it was a not-quite-so-simple experience, where all of us—activists and residents—sustained heavy physical blows at the hands of the police. Seeing old women being beaten by the police is a pain that stays with you forever. It's a trauma that neither one's reason or soul can process.

Like with all the other evictions, I went to this one with my camera ready to shoot. In the middle of the picture you see me starting to film at the moment when the police start trampling on the activists and the residents. Not visible in the picture is my own internal doubt every time I photograph an eviction or some other civil injustice. On the one hand, I want to document the police brutality and the nonviolent protest of the courageous residents, and on the other, I want to sit on the ground and resist. And for me, this is the hardest question: photograph or get involved.

I document the evictions in the neighborhood and many other events connected to the gentrification process. I see photography as an integral part of the struggle, and think it is very important who the photographer is. I am connected to the struggle and to the camera in my very soul, and I feel as if I am bound to documenting the tremendous injustice that is taking place on the backs of these Mizrahi residents, whom the government views as second-class citizens. It is lending a hand to expel them from their homes after 60 years, just so that someone can get even richer than they already are. I look at this photograph and think, what's going on in the minds of these tycoons who decide to bring this huge police force in order to evict a 60-year-old woman from her home?

Carmen Elmakiyes-Amos is a political-social activist. She is involved in the movement Ahoti [My Sister], and is one of the founders of the group Lonehmadim-Lonehmadot,[1] an independent organization seeking to promote discourse about Mizrahi identity, and equality among ethnic groups in Israeli society. The group views itself as continuing the social political path of the Israeli Black Panthers.

1. The name "Lonehmadim-Lonehmadot" [Hebrew for "not nice persons"] comes from a comment made by Israeli Prime Minister Golda Meir of the Labor Party, in response to the Israeli Black Panthers' actions and protests over discrimination against Mizrahim [Jews descended from Arab or Muslim countries]. Meir described the group in the Israeli media as "not nice persons."

{Opposite page}
Carmen Elmakiyes-Amos [in the middle of the frame holding a camera] films as activists and residents are being pushed by police forces during an eviction of six families, Giv'at Amal, Tel Aviv, Israel, 27.3.2014

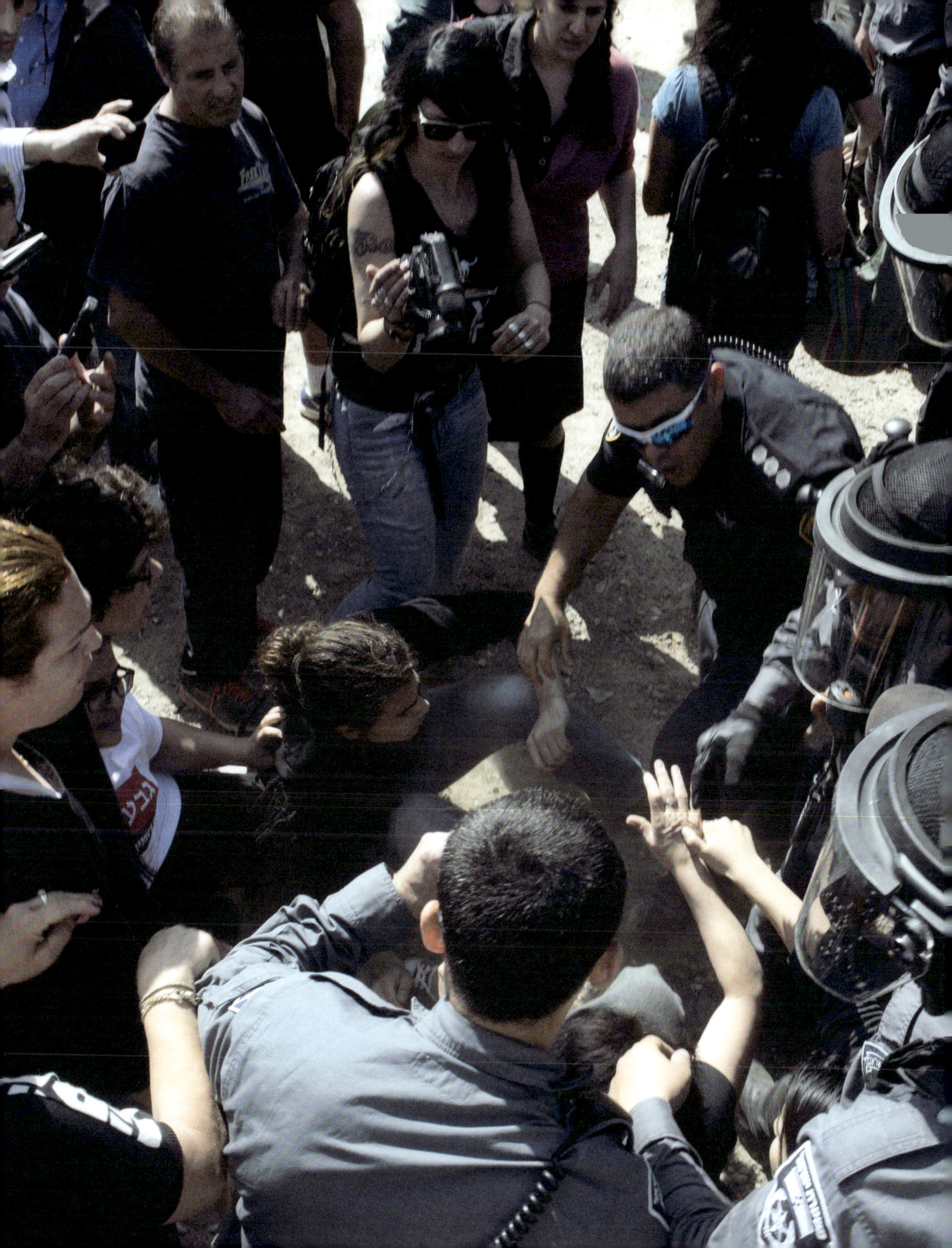

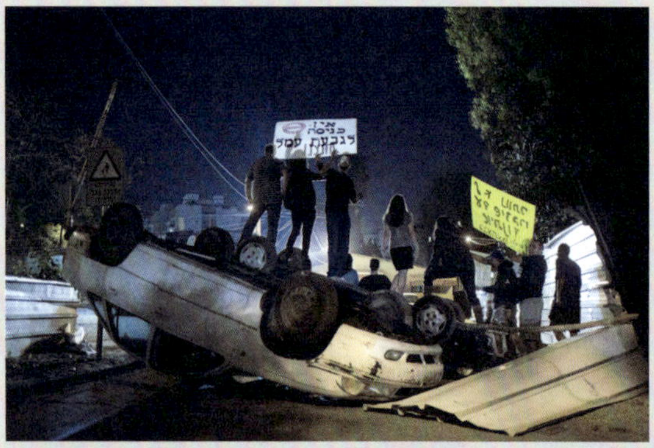

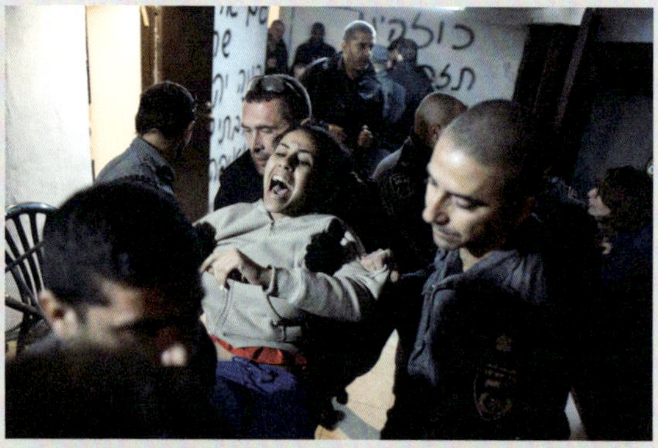

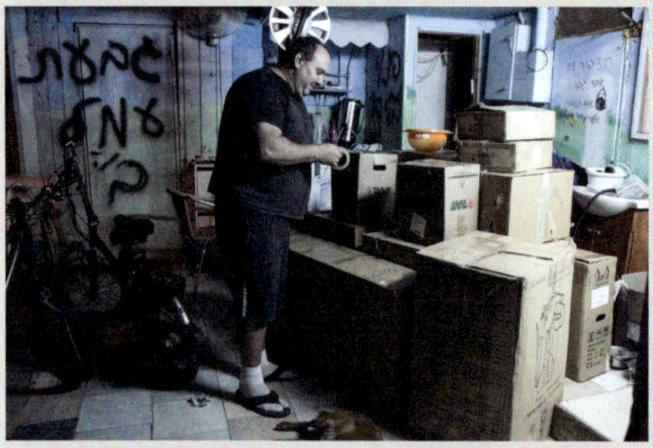

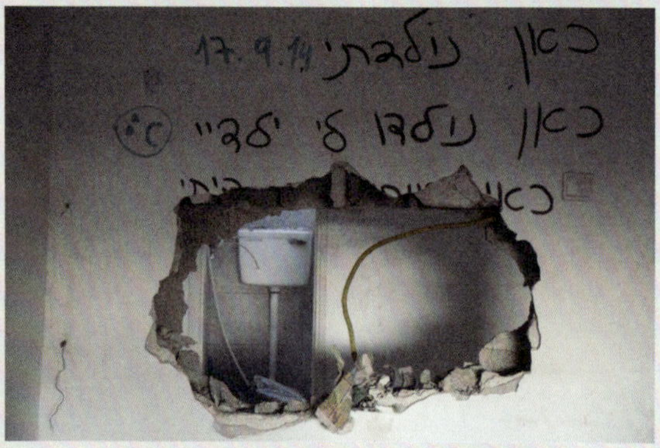

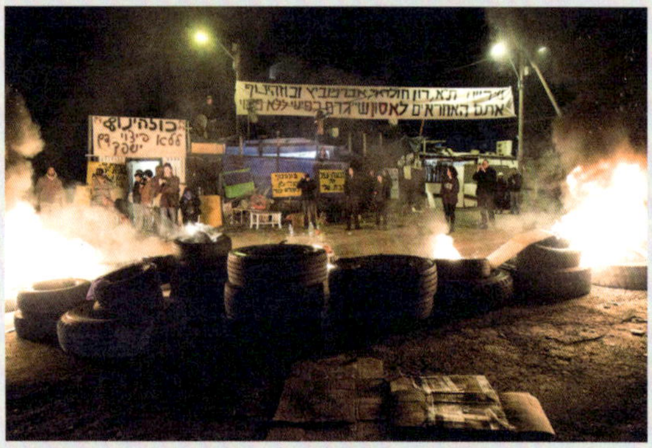

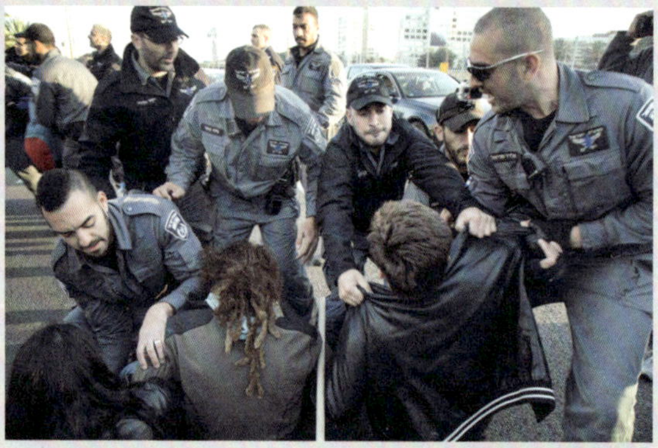

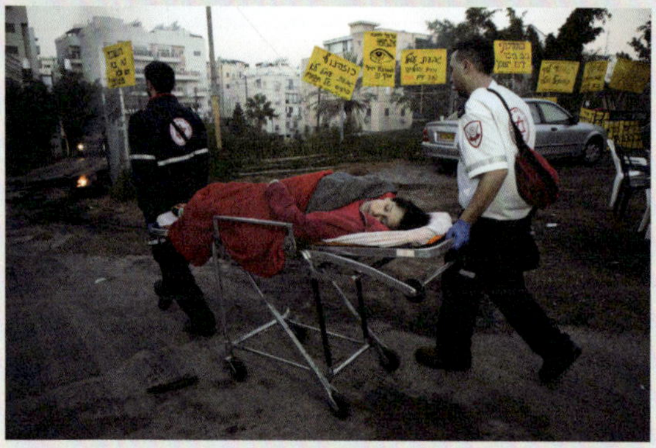

{Top left to right}
1. Residents block the entrance to the neighborhood the night before an eviction, 22.4.2014 / **2.** A resident detained by the police during an eviction, 29.12.2014 / **3.** Ziv Koifman packs his family's belongings, 28.12.2014 / **4.** Graffiti on walls of a destroyed home: "I was born here, my children were born here," 21.9.2014 / **5.** Burning barricades, 29.12.2014 / **6.** Israeli police evacuate protesters as they block a highway close to the neighborhood, 29.12.2014 / **7.** An injured resident being evacuated, 29.12.2014

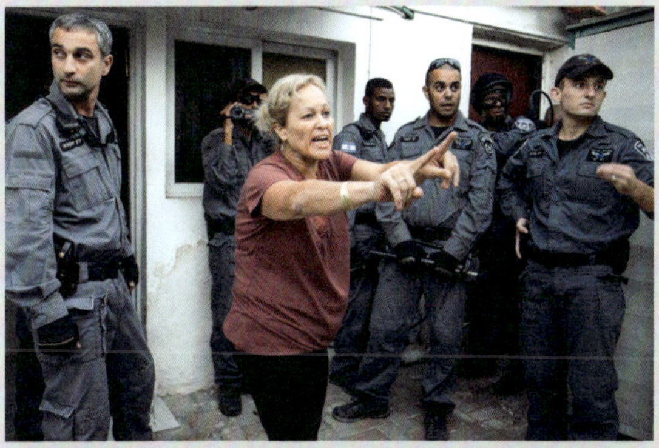

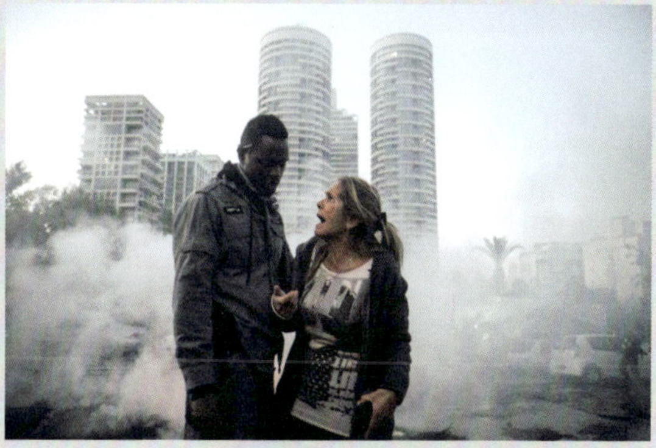

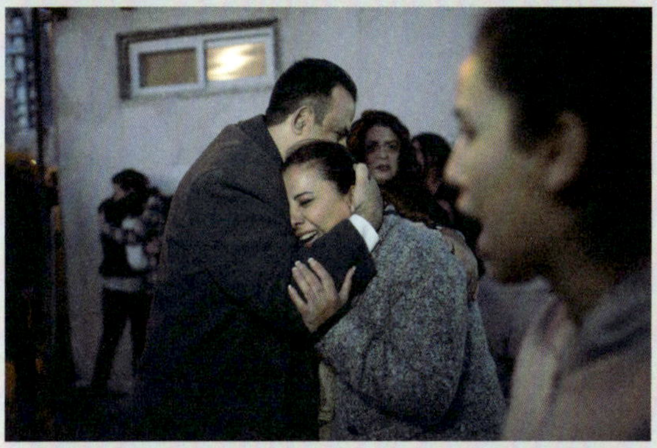

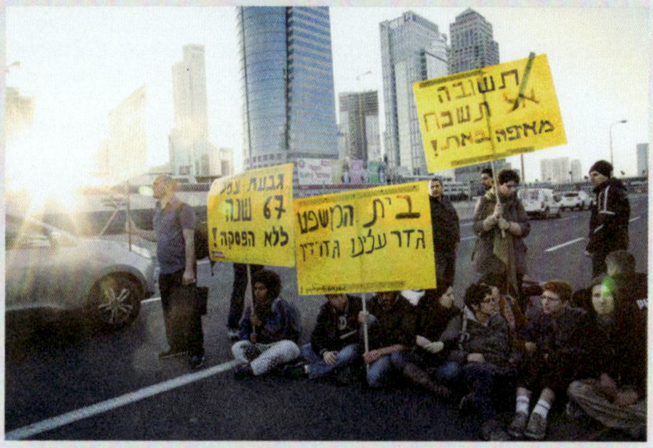

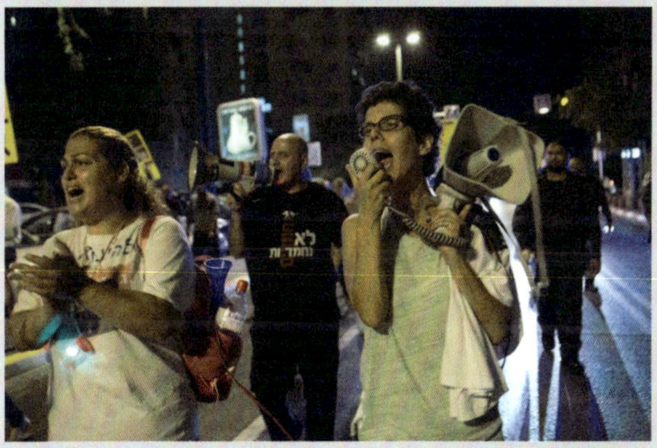

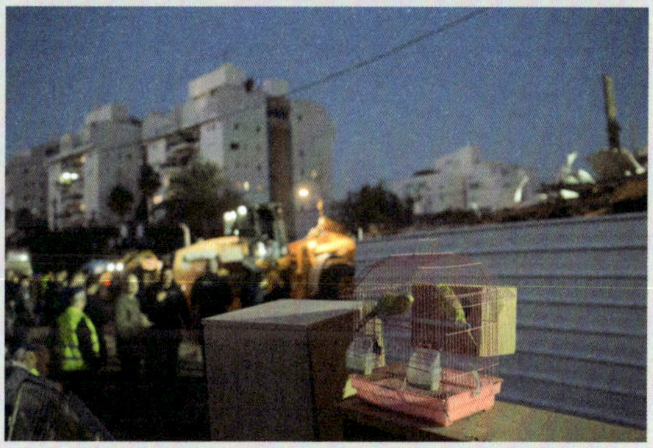

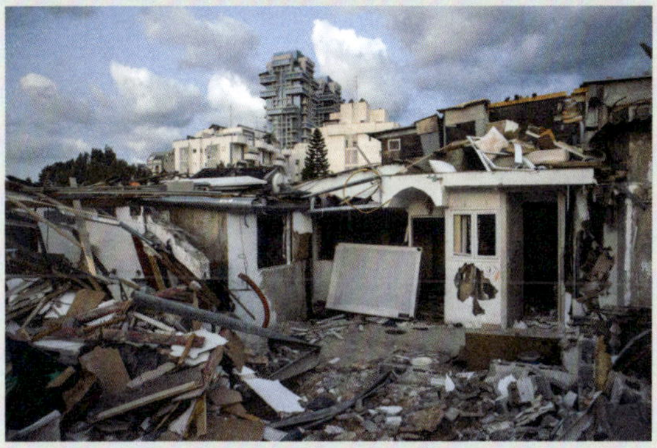

{Top left to right}
1. A resident tries to prevent police from evicting a home, 17.9.2014 / **2.** A resident confronts a policeman, 29.12.2014 / **3.** Residents comfort each other, 29.12.2014 / **4.** Activists block a highway to publicize the eviction of eight families, 29.12.2014 / **5.** Residents protest against house evictions, 15.9.2014 / **6.** Birds in a cage near the belongings of evicted residents, 29.12.2014 / **7.** A home destroyed by a private contractor, 21.9.2014

Chen Misgav

This photo was taken during a demonstration in front of Tel Aviv's town hall in January 2012 (top right). The cold and rainy winter didn't stop the few hundred activists from joining the residents of the city's neglected Hatikva neighborhood to demonstrate against the evacuation of their protest tent-camp. Situated in a park in the middle of this south Tel Aviv neighborhood, this protest camp was the last to survive of the 2011 massive tent-camps that were spread across Israel in the wave of social demonstrations that brought thousands of citizens into the streets protesting against impossible housing fees.

Unlike people from other protest camps, Hatikva residents had nothing to lose. They were people with no other options and during this protest they wanted the municipal representatives to look them in the eye as they asked for solutions to their welfare problems.

I joined this protest—like many others during that summer, which turned to autumn and then winter—as both an activist and academic researcher. At the time, I was doing my fieldwork for my PhD dissertation. The research I conducted was about activism and public space. Considering myself a "militant ethnographer," I felt obligated to participate in the demonstrations and other activities. Needless to say, I also identified with the protesters, wanting to reveal injustice and, through the voices of the protesters, to raise claims and arguments.

This complex *positionality* made my own body an inseparable part of my research. I felt it many times during my activity. One such moment can be seen clearly in the photo that Activestills' Oren Ziv took when I was arrested during this protest. The megaphone that I was holding fell to the ground as a few policemen in black uniforms threw me down.

At this particular moment when the photo was taken, in the huge mass of protesters confronting the police, yelling and trying to pull me out of their hands, I was an activist. When I hit the floor, I lost my glasses and then fainted. A few minutes later, I remember waking up with water on my face and sitting next to me were more activists who had been arrested and handcuffed. I spent the night at a police station, and in the morning, I saw my photo on the Internet on a few radical websites that reported about the demonstration.

At first, I was terrified looking at this photo. I moved again into my academic position and felt odd seeing myself as a representative of the event. In the midst of the action, I didn't pay attention to the photographers and couldn't even think about the event's representation. However, later I understood the feeling caused by looking at this photo—it was the double positionality: first as the object of representation, and second as a researcher who tries to understand these representations. Looking at myself in the photograph made me think that in order to do our duty and bring social and political change, we must be involved fully, in body and in mind.

Chen Misgav is currently a post-doctoral fellow at Ben-Gurion University and a research fellow at the Minerva Humanities Center at Tel Aviv University. He writes about urban politics, gender, sexuality, activism, and protest movements.

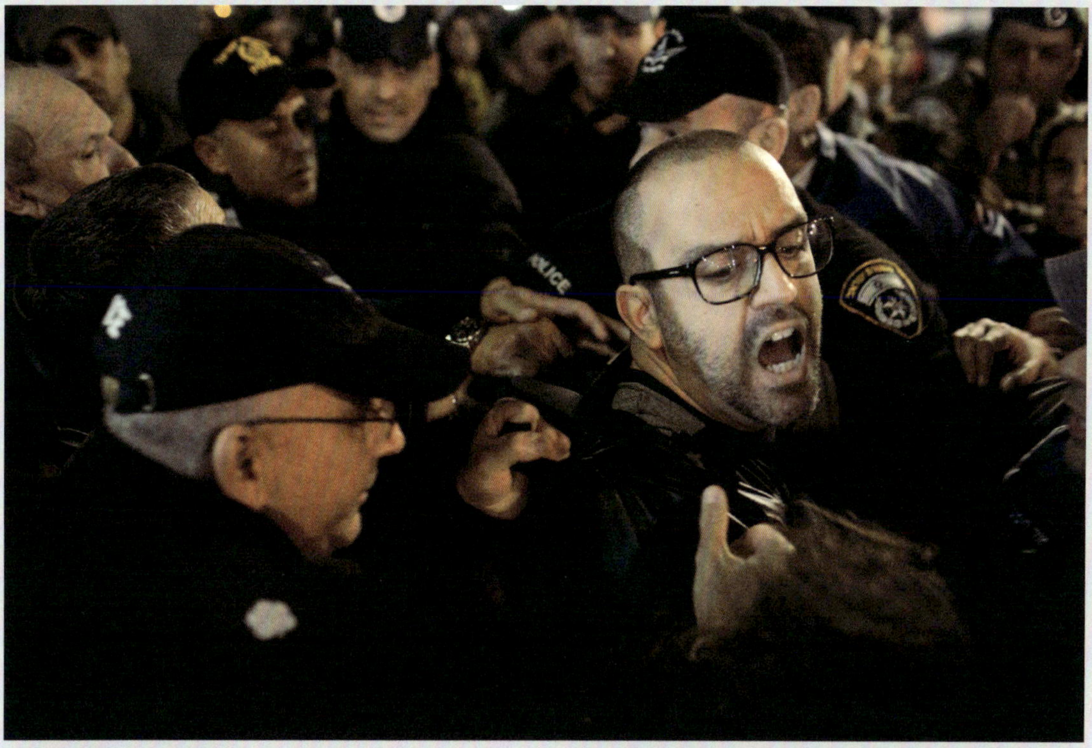

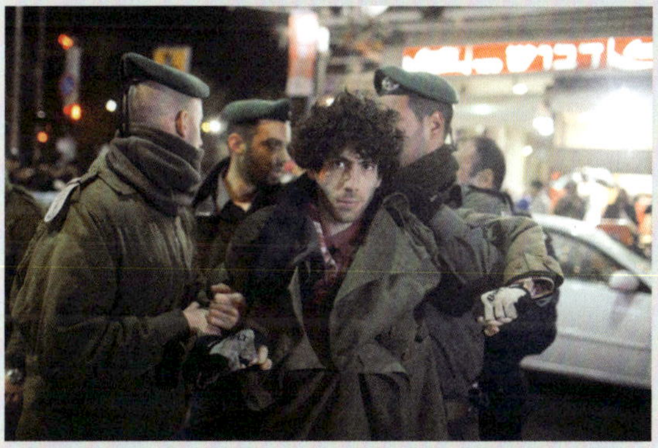

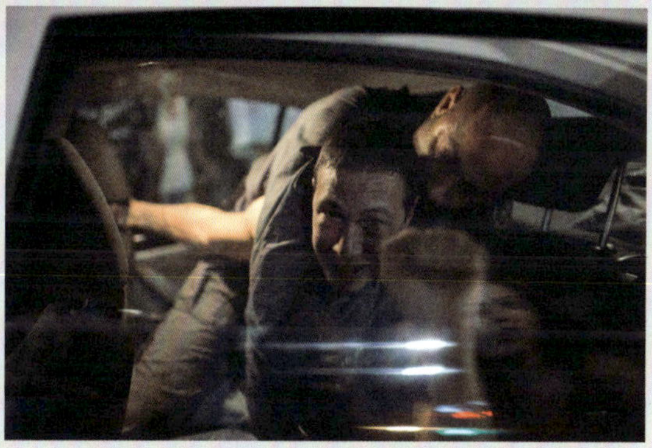

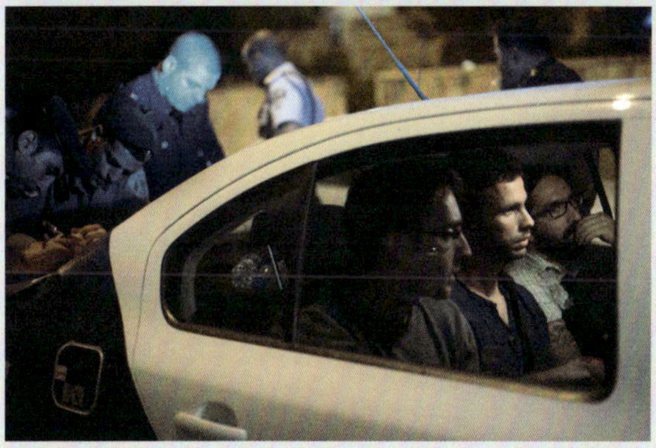

{Top left to right}
1. Police arrest Chen Misgav in front of the Tel Aviv municipality during a social justice protest, Tel Aviv, 15.1.2012 / **2.** Arrest, social justice protest, Tel Aviv, 22.1.2012 / **3.** Arrest, social justice protest, Tel Aviv, 23.7.2011 / **4.** Arrest, social justice protest, Tel Aviv, 13.9.2011

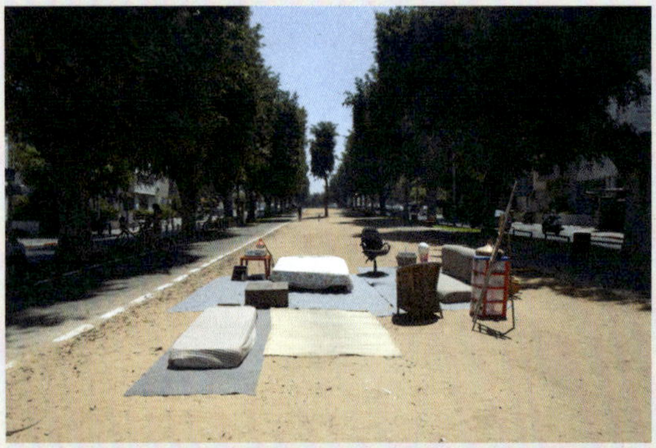

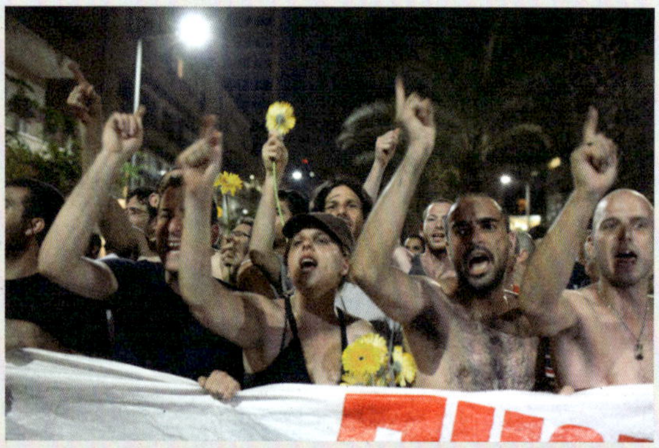

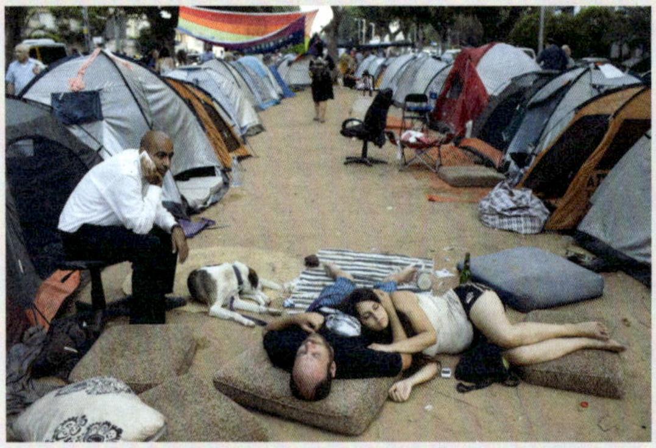

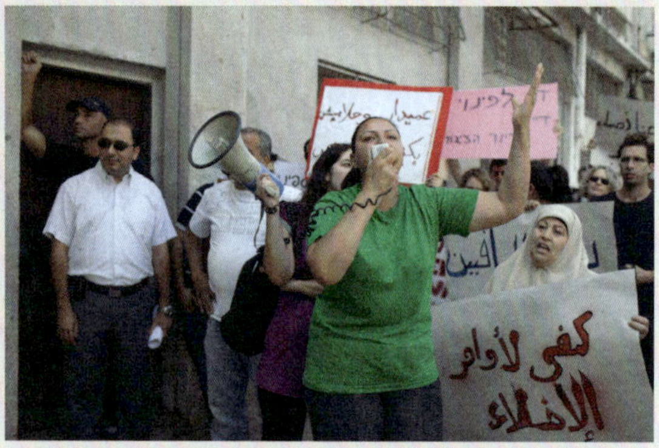

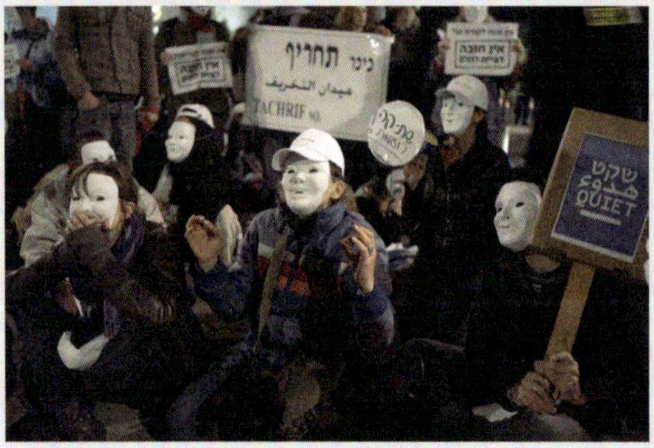

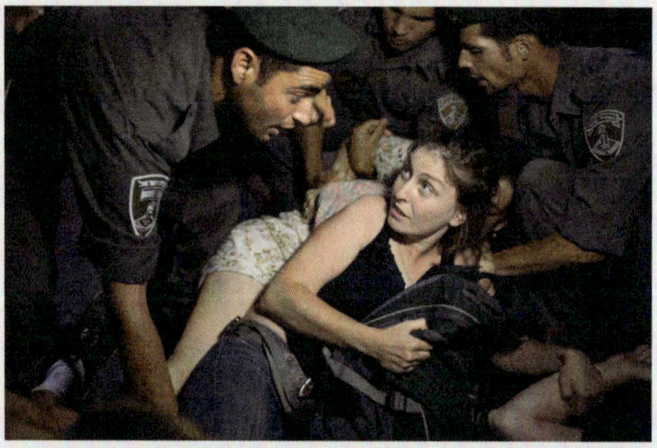

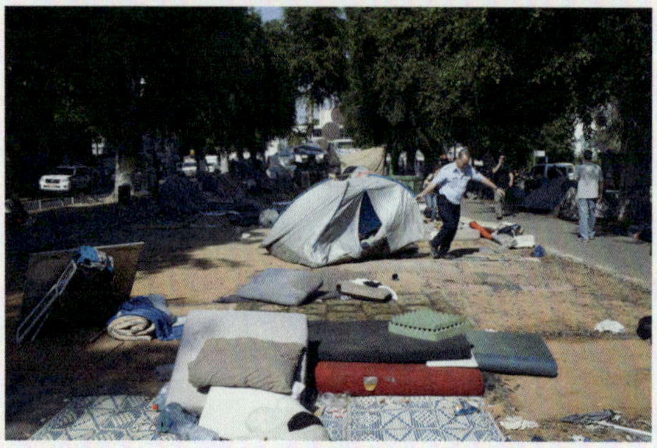

{Top left to right}
1. Daphni Leef's initiation of a protest tent camp for social justice, Rothschild Boulevard, Tel Aviv, 14.7.2011 / **2.** Protesters march, 21.7.2011 / **3.** Protesters in Rothschild Boulevard tent camp, 20.7.2011 /**4.** Palestinian citizens of Israel protest against the privatization of public housing services, Jaffa, 21.9.2011 / **5.** Israelis take part in a silent protest, Tel Aviv, 2.2.2012 / **6.** A protester evacuated by an Israeli border policeman during a road blockade, Tel Aviv, 23.7.2011 / **7.** Eviction of Rothschild Boulevard tent camp, 3.10.2011

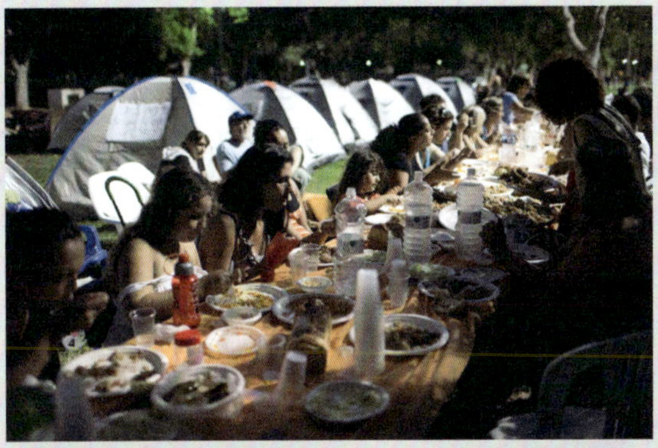

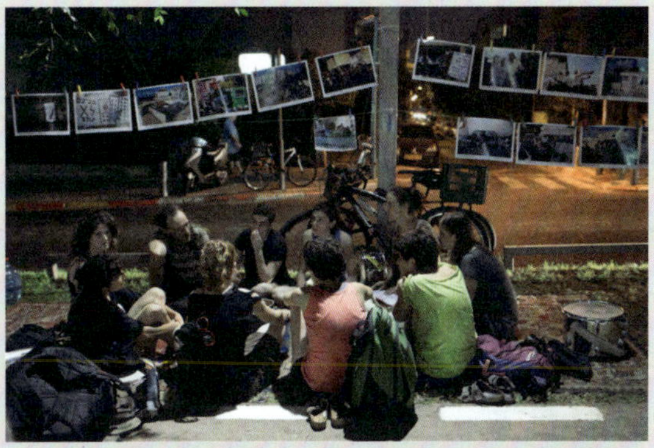

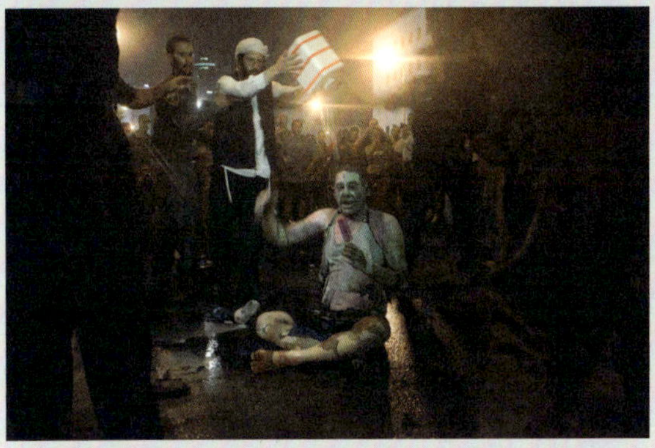

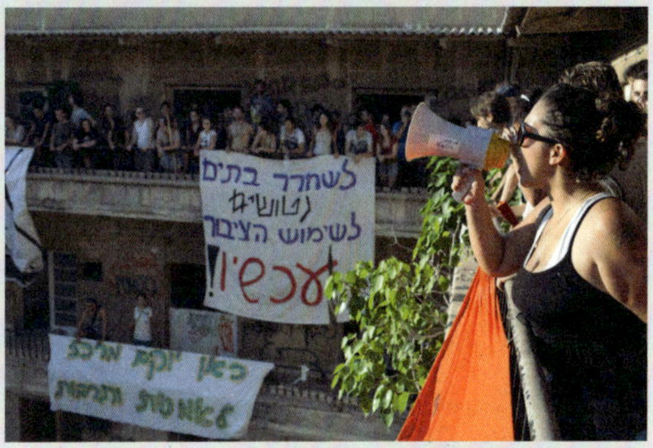

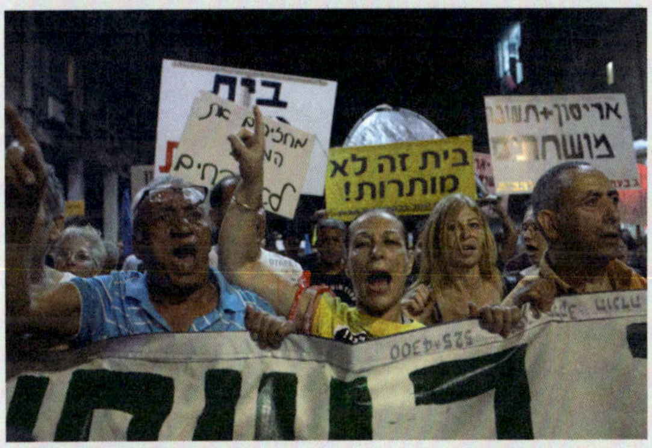

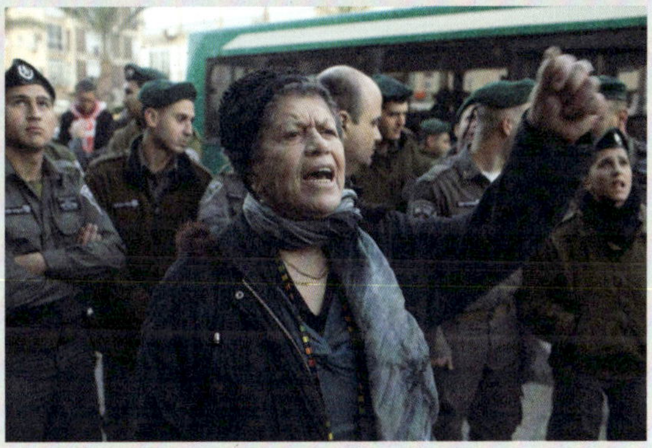

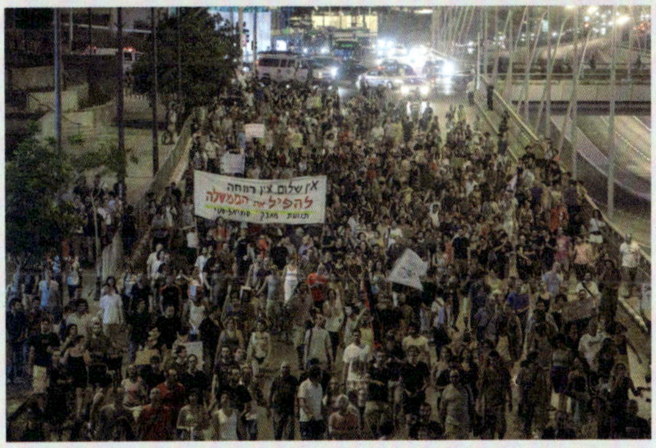

{Top left to right}
1. Communal dinner in Levinsky tent camp, Tel Aviv, 29.7.2011 / **2.** An Activestills exhibition on the issue of housing, Rothschild Boulevard tent camp, Tel Aviv, 20.7.2011 / **3.** Bystanders pour water on Moshe Silman after he set himself on fire during a protest, Tel Aviv, 14.7.2012 / **4.** Protesters squat in an abandoned building, Tel Aviv, 22.8.2011 / **5.** Protesters commemorate a year since Moshe Silman's self-immolation, Tel Aviv, 13.7.2013 / **6.** A woman protests against the eviction of Hatikva tent camp, Tel Aviv, 15.1.2012 / **7.** Protesters march to commemorate Moshe Silman, Tel Aviv, 21.7.2012

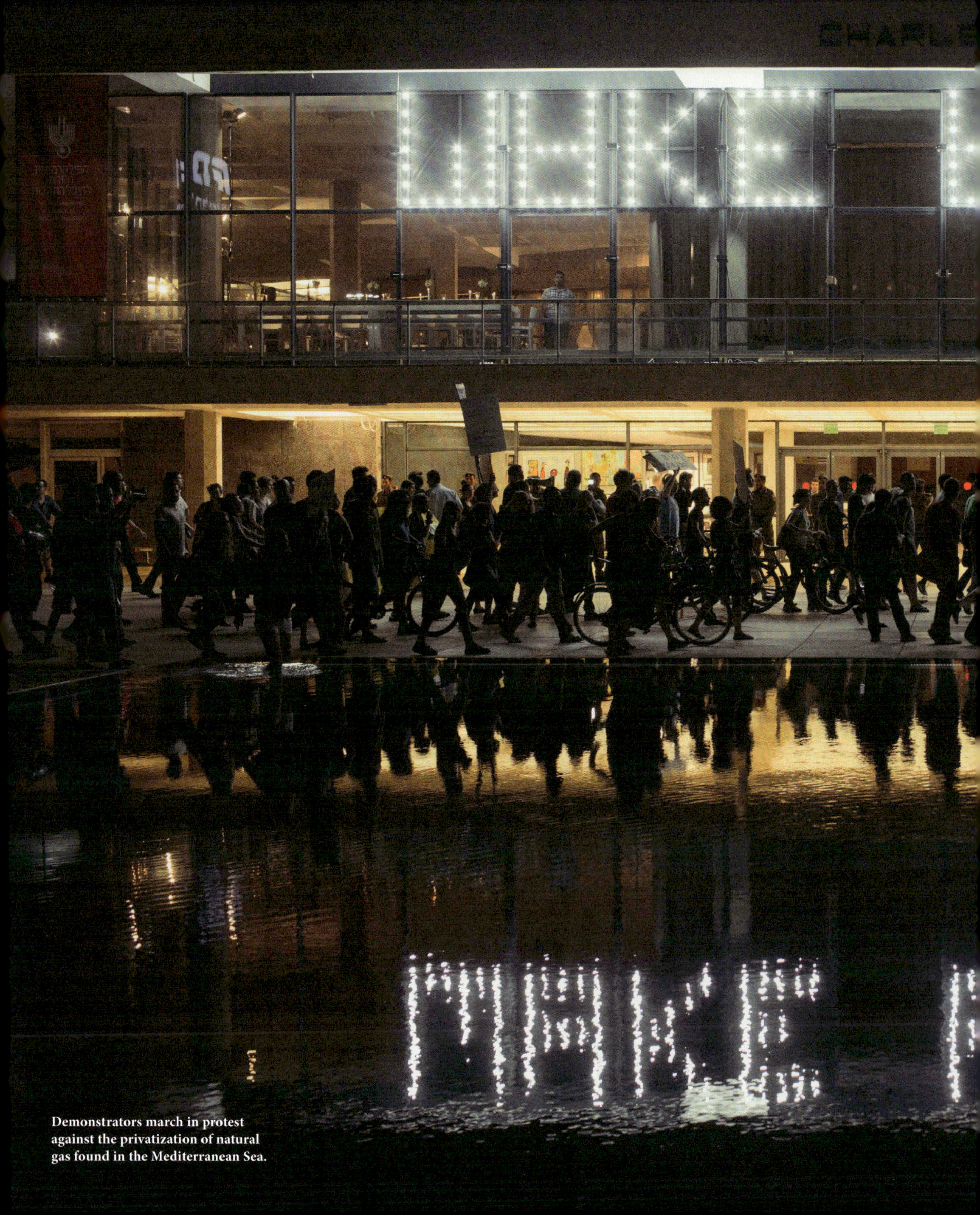

Demonstrators march in protest against the privatization of natural gas found in the Mediterranean Sea.

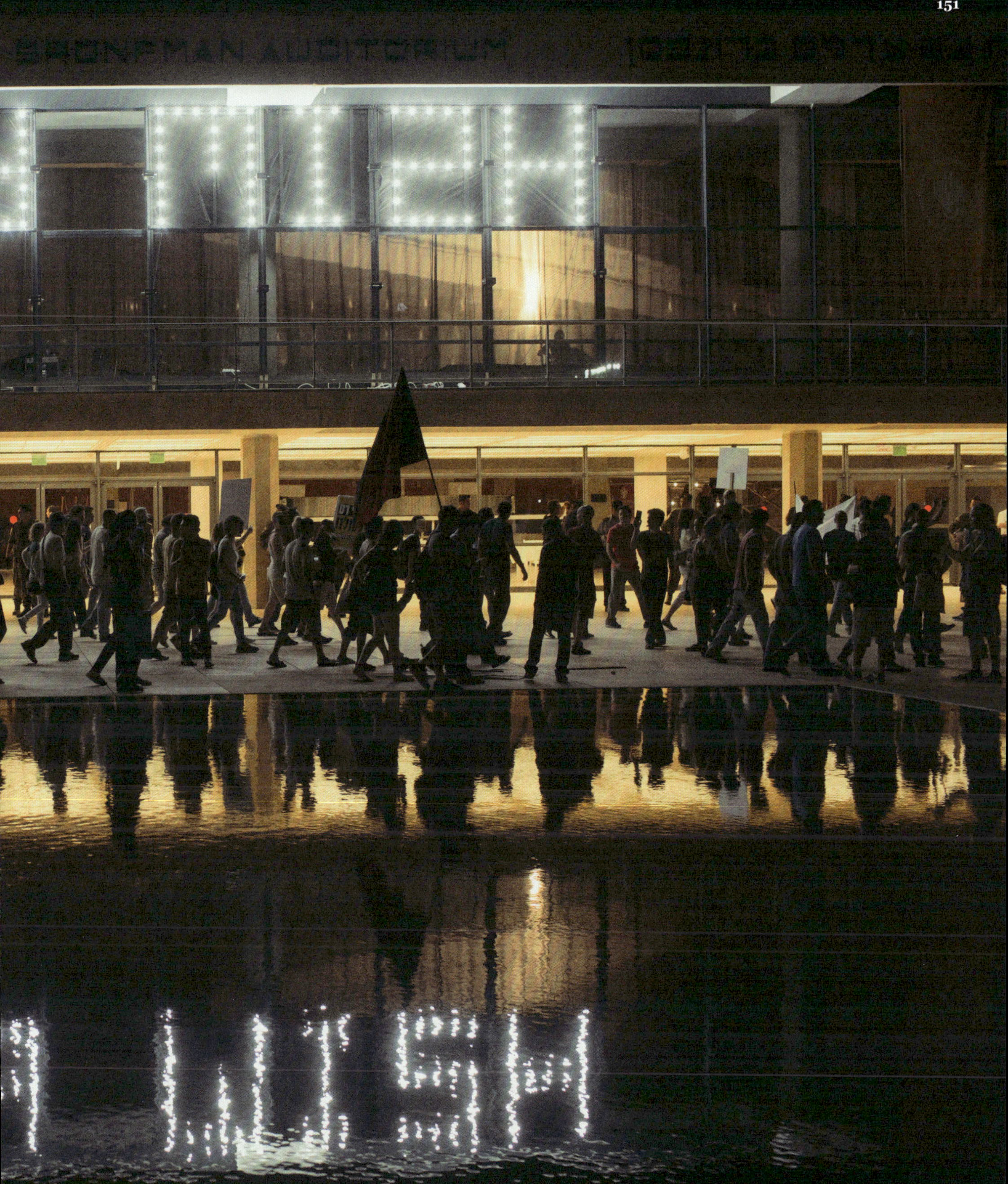
BRONFMAN AUDITORIUM

Lilach Ben David

Lilach Ben David is a transsexual, bisexual, and feminist activist. She is a regular contributor to the *Local Call* magazine, where she writes mainly about Israeli left-wing movements.

Notes on Photographing Transgender Bodies, and a Thank You

I'm sitting with my sister-out-of-choice at a cute café in the middle of the city of Givatayim. She is dressed as usual in a mix of blazer and skirt, with some hair peeking out over her bra-line and uneven lipstick. We speak about politics, gossip about the LGBTQ community, trying to figure out what we are doing with our lives. Suddenly, a flash! That a--hole on the other side of the café window took a picture of her! In seconds I was on my feet. I went inside and screamed at him in front of all the customers, in front of his wife and children that—what did he think he was doing! And that he is going to erase that picture right now! And that we are not his circus! At first, he puffed himself up like some peacock and tried to threaten me. Afterwards, he erased it. In the end, he even came over and apologized.

Two weeks ago I accidentally bumped into a wonderful, delicate trans-girl, whose so-called "friends" had spread pictures of her from before her transition on WhatsApp, which made their way to all the kids in the town where she lives. Exposing "before" pictures of trans people is one of the cruelest and most painful gender-disciplining practices because it tells the story of "exposing the truth," a story according to which the way we choose to live our lives and express ourselves to the outside world is a lie, while pictures from the past reveal what society believes to be the "truth" about who we are.

The photograph captures not only the photographed object. Photography also immortalizes a point of view, the angle of a gaze, an attitude, and a perspective. Photography also always expresses the ideological position of the photographer. With the tremendous power of photography, people who assumed the role of the police in the tyrannical reality of gender can photograph our bodies, transgender people, and force upon us stories of contempt, humiliation, mockery, ridicule, and dehumanization.

But there is another kind of photography. When Keren Manor photographed us marching along Allenby Street on that Saturday night when we set out to "take back the night" in response to another horrific transphobic assault, her lens captured more than just a historic moment for the transgender community in Israel. From a political place of respect and shared destiny, the photographer chose to be there in order to immortalize our anger, our pride, our solidarity, and our political demand for gender freedom. She captured not only the beauty within us and the power of our struggle, but also our humanity. Thank you for this, Keren. Humanity is a much better subject for a photograph than humiliation.

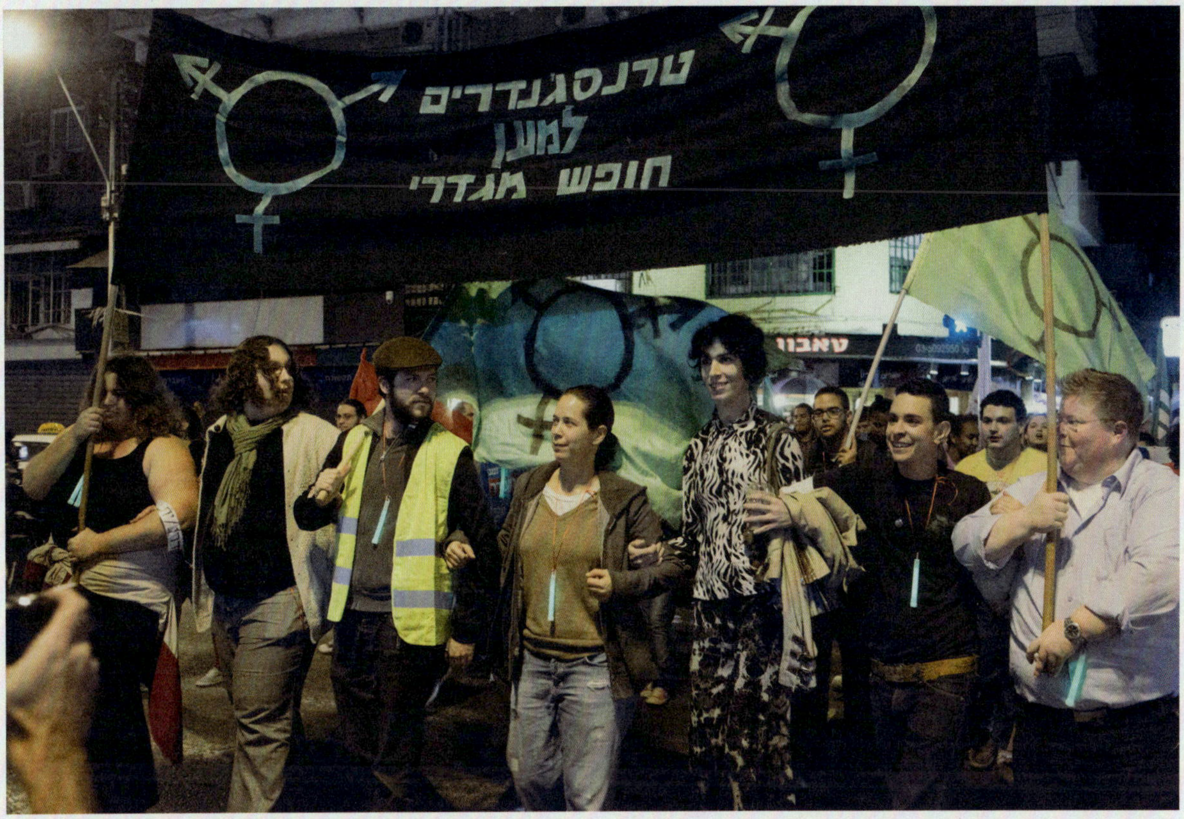

Israeli LGTBQ activists [Lilach Ben David second on the left] protest against hate crimes and police violence, Tel Aviv, 16.1.2014. Following a brutal attack in south Tel Aviv perpetrated against a transgender woman by eleven off-duty border police, during which they sprayed her with pepper spray and shot her with a Taser gun, the Gila Project for Transgender Empowerment organized a march under the banner “Taking Back the Night.” Over a thousand protesters participated in the march, the largest demonstration in the history of the transgender community in Israel.

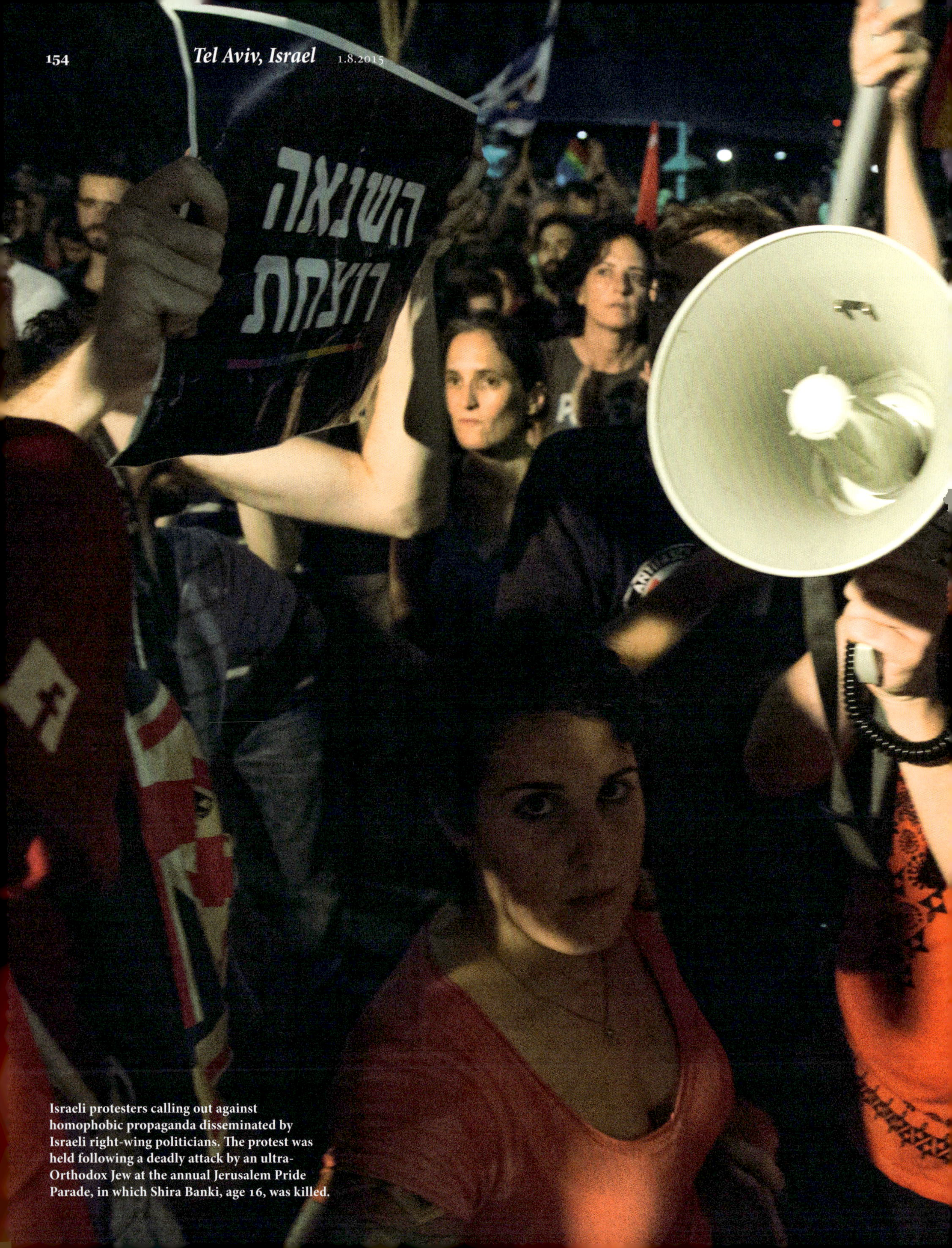

Israeli protesters calling out against homophobic propaganda disseminated by Israeli right-wing politicians. The protest was held following a deadly attack by an ultra-Orthodox Jew at the annual Jerusalem Pride Parade, in which Shira Banki, age 16, was killed.

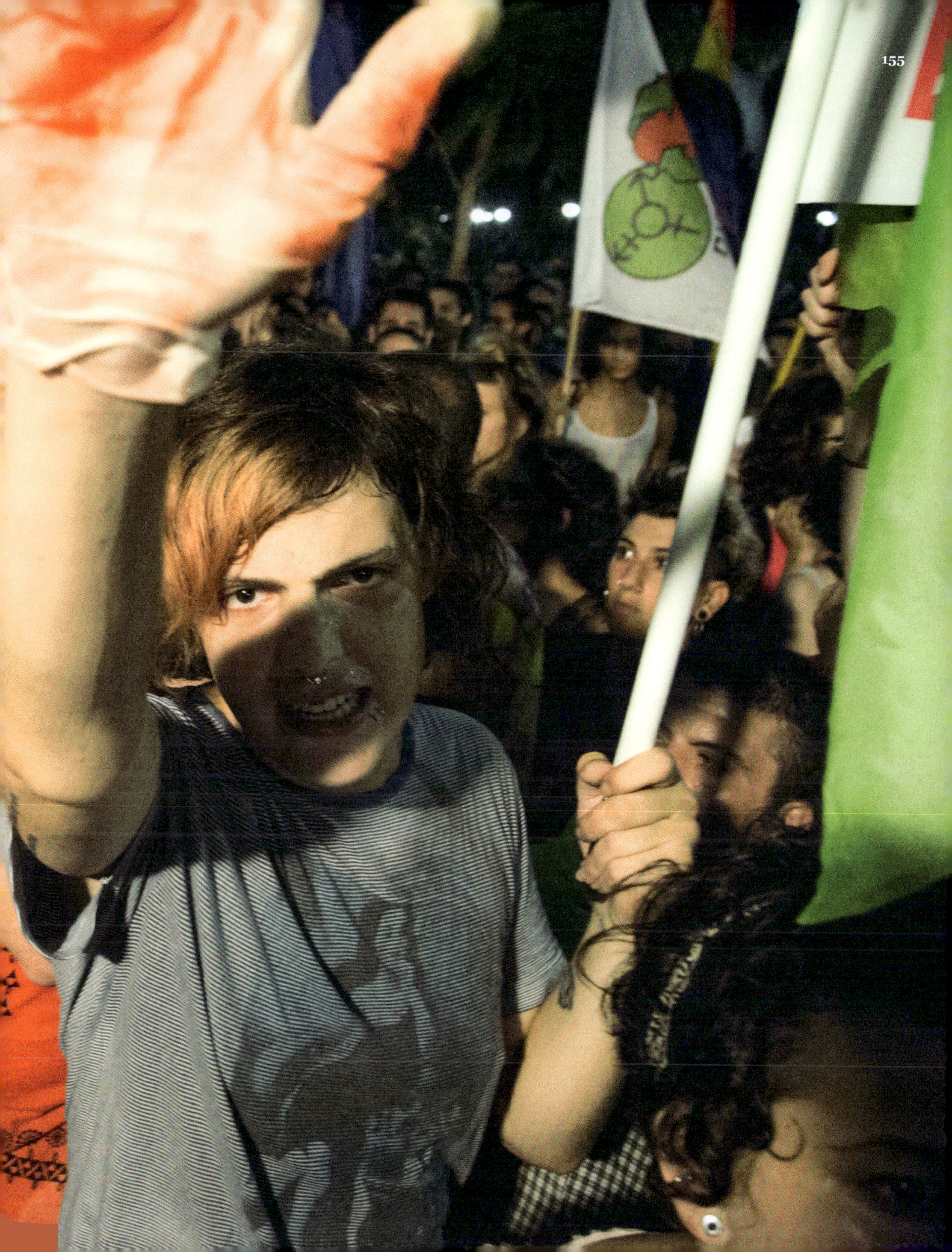

Tel Aviv, Israel 25.2.2012

Members of the Queer community in Tel Aviv at a party in the Rogatka Vegan Bar.

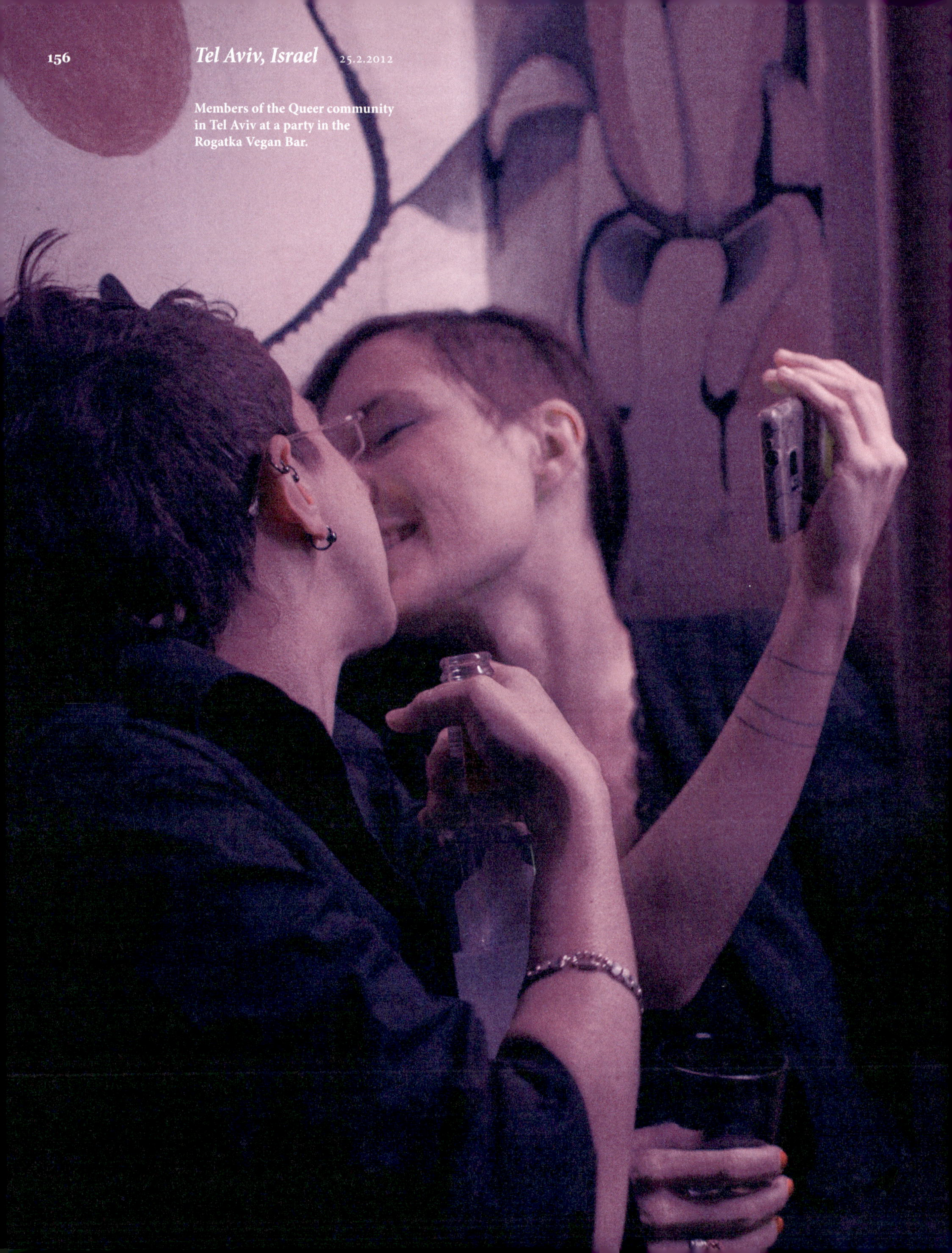

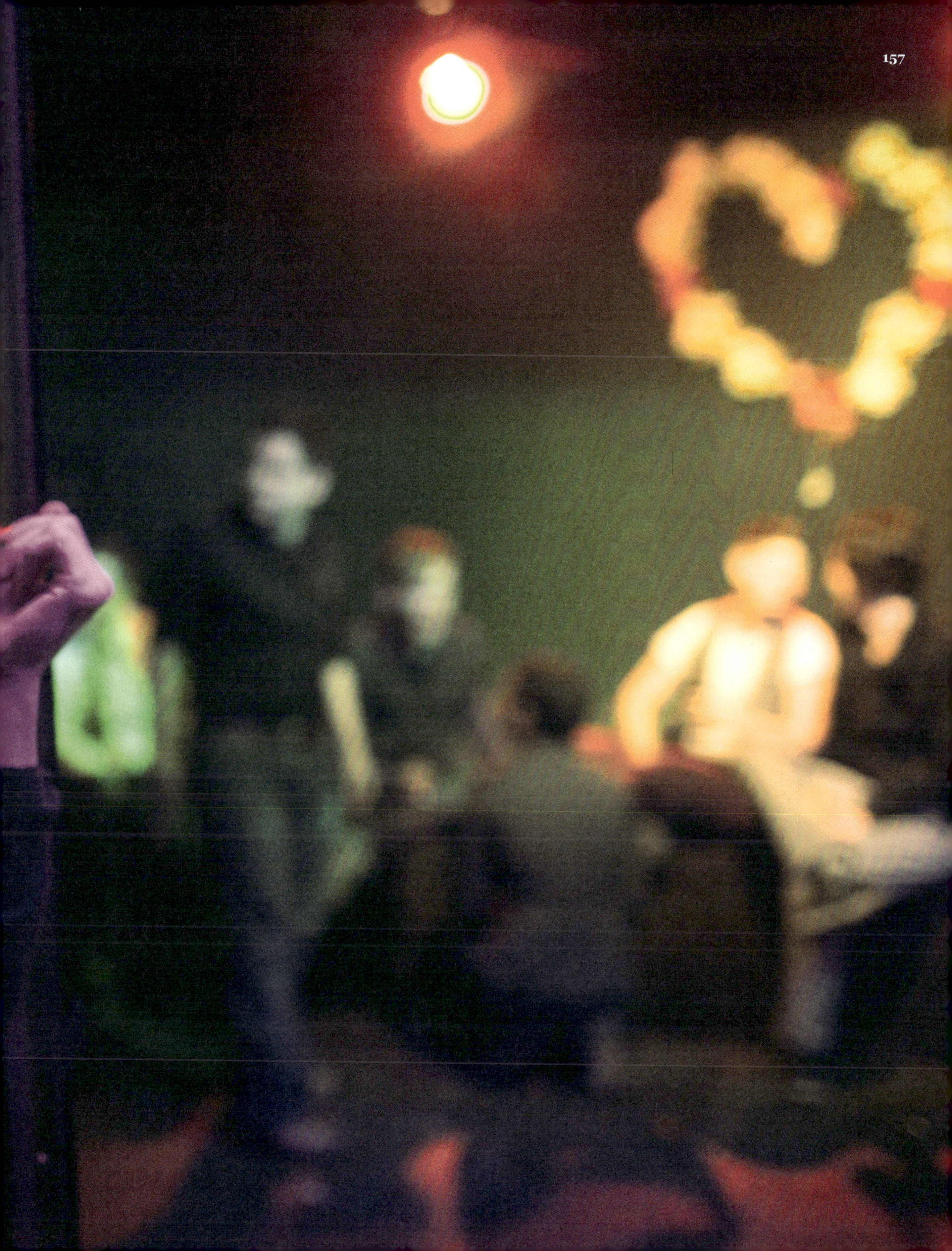

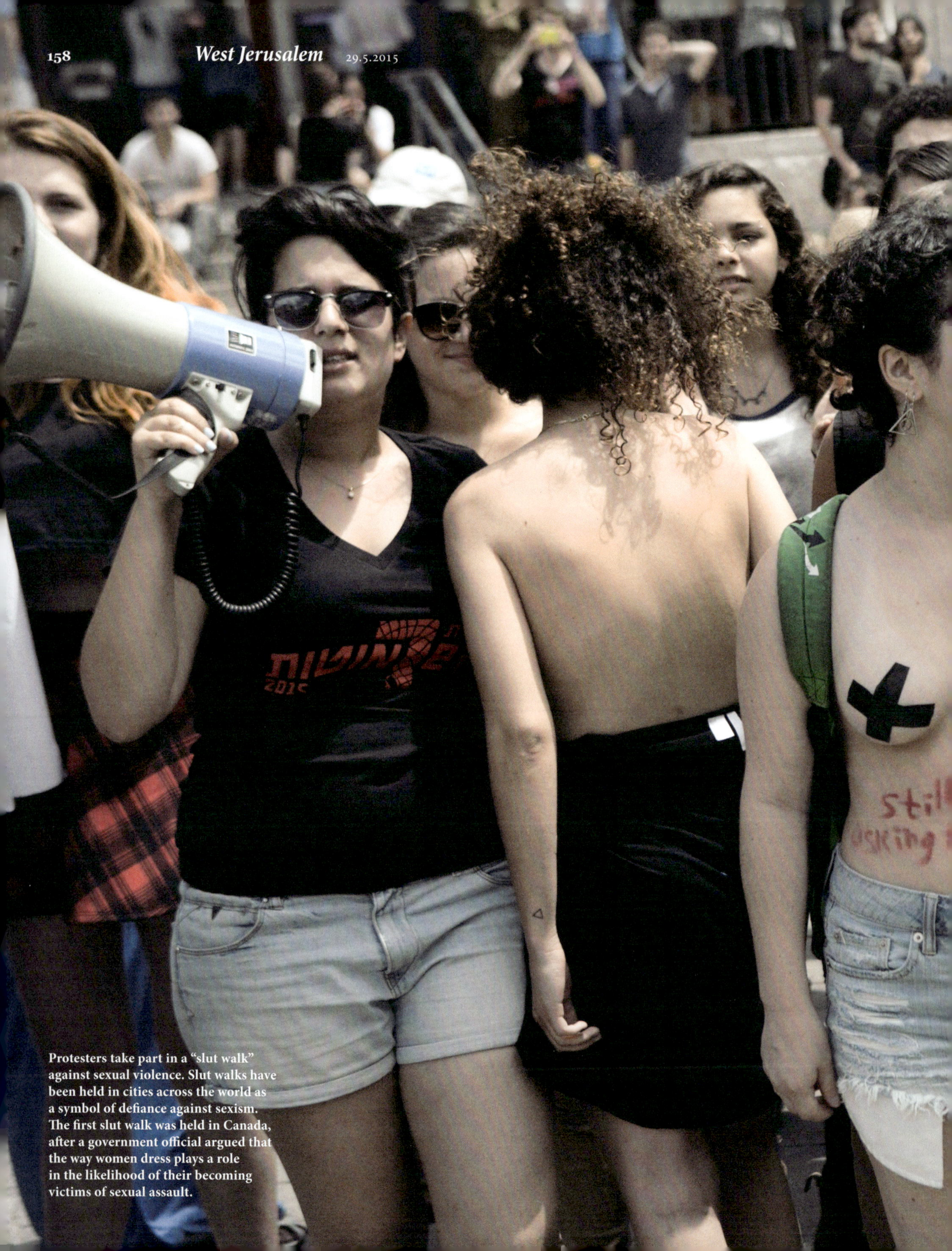

Protesters take part in a “slut walk” against sexual violence. Slut walks have been held in cities across the world as a symbol of defiance against sexism. The first slut walk was held in Canada, after a government official argued that the way women dress plays a role in the likelihood of their becoming victims of sexual assault.

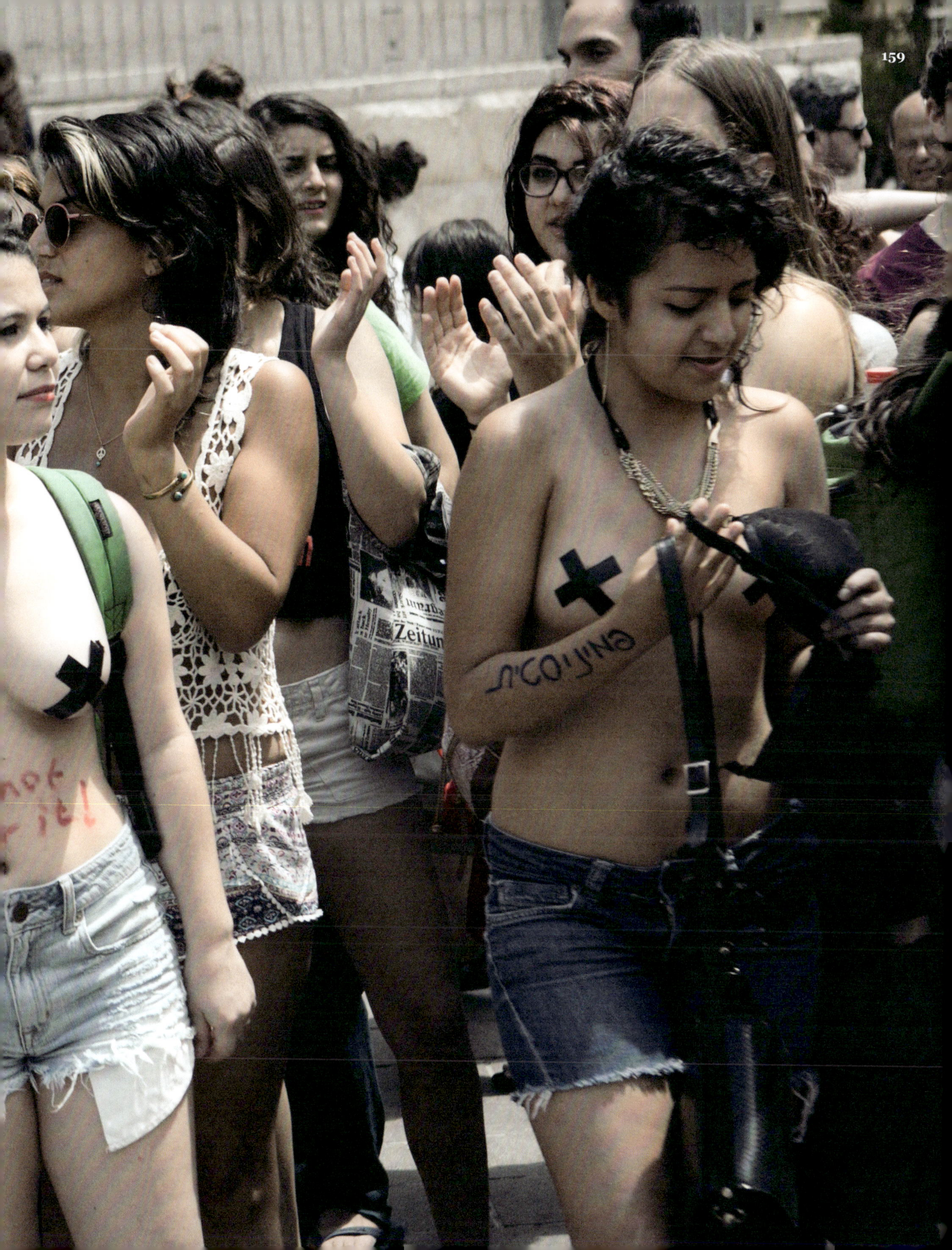
Zeitun
not

Adi Winter

Adi Winter is a political activist for women's rights and animal rights and is the spokesperson for the Israeli Society for the Abolition of Vivisection (ISAV).

On 7 July 2011, I was convicted of unlawful gathering after blocking a roadway during a protest that had taken place four years before against the plea bargain that was being offered by the Attorney General to Moshe Katsav, then the president of Israel. The protest, in June 2007, was organized by a coalition of 27 women's organizations in response to the deal then offered to the president, that he admit to having conducted an affair with one of the complainants and in return the charge of rape would be dropped. At the end of the demonstration, over a thousand female demonstrators blocked a road in Tel Aviv—six of us were arrested and charged. The judge sentenced me to a three-year suspended sentence with three months' probation and a 3,000-shekel fine or three months in jail. Here is what I said in court:

Following my conviction, this is the stage where I am expected to show remorse and ask for mitigation of my sentence. Allow me to do so because indeed I am not without remorse. I am being tried because of my choice to demonstrate against the plea bargain offered to the President, which has silenced the women who bravely raised their voices [against sexual harassment]. As a feminist activist for human rights and animal rights, I view the Katsav trial as one among countless examples reflecting a sick society that oppresses the weak, whoever and wherever they are. As a woman in a man's world, I live in a place where I do not feel safe in my city, on the street, in the stairwell, and not even in my own home. Women are subjected to harassment on a daily basis, live constantly with an obsession about their appearance, a reality that shapes us as silent and helpless. This society reminds me time and again of how it views my place and role in it. Who among us sitting here today truly feels that she is good enough?

Along with this I also always remind myself that along with being a woman, as a Jew in the State of Israel, I have privileges, I am part of an occupying nation. Whether I want or not, I have privileges, such as the ability to bargain [with the authorities] and to pay a lower price for what the State defines as my crimes. I know how to read. I have running water and food; most people in the world do not have these privileges. Even as a human being I have unbelievable privileges compared with the millions of animals that are tortured, used, and slaughtered every day for human caprice—it is my duty to act as their voice. With these privileges comes responsibility, the responsibility to struggle together for their liberation which is also ours.

Civil disobedience is a legitimate and necessary part of any struggle for freedom. No one wants to go to prison. I too am fearful, but more than my fear of incarceration I fear closing off my heart. I feel alone now but know that I am not. One after the other, we stand here, decade after decade, century after century, standing and crying out: no more, not in my name, I will not be silent, and I will not turn my gaze away from oppression. One after the other on the witness stand we say, "Given the chance again, I would do the same thing."

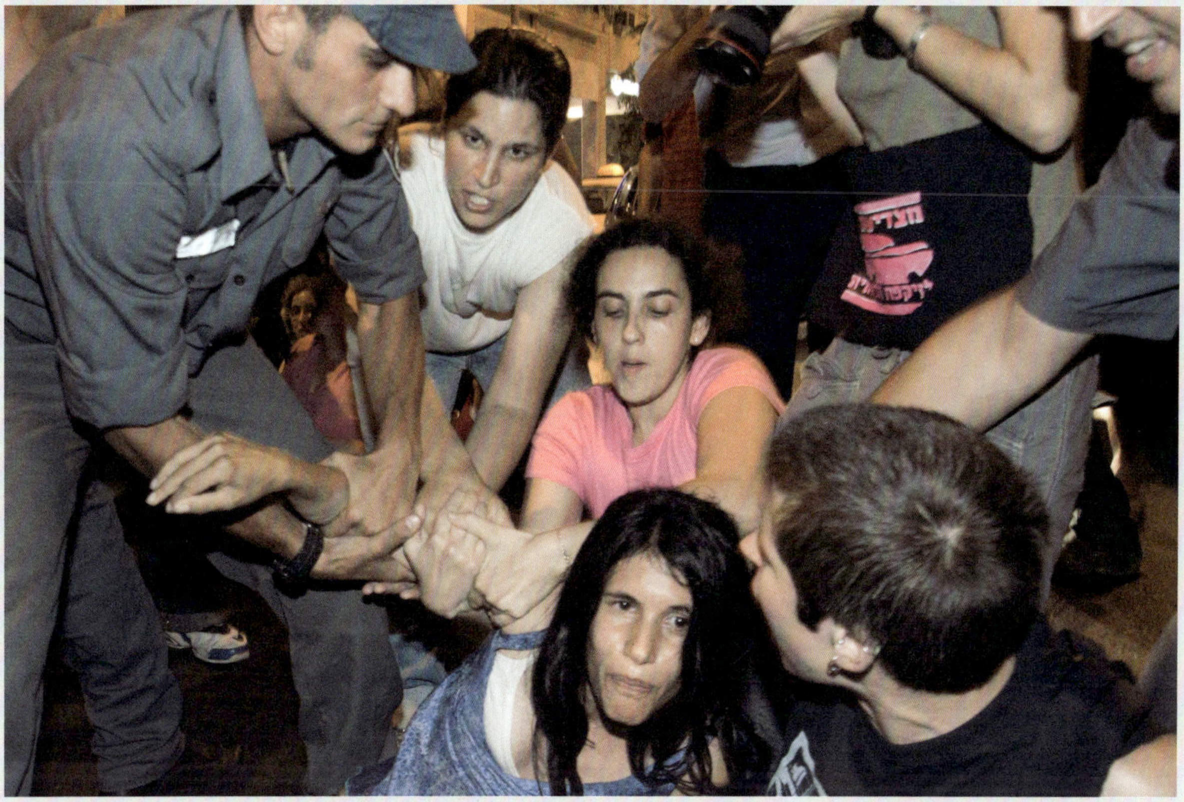

Adi Winter and a fellow activist being arrested during a protest against Moshe Katsav's plea bargain, Tel Aviv, 30.6.2007

I have regret. Regret that if I stand here on trial today, apparently I have not done enough. So long as we live in a society where women are harassed and live with low self-esteem, so long as there is an occupation, so long as animals are kept in cages, we have not done enough and there is much more work ahead. If the court will decide to lock me up behind bars, I will cope. I do not want to allow fear to overcome doing what is right, as Martin Luther King, Jr. said, "Society's punishments are small compared to the wounds we inflict on our soul when we look the other way."

The protest at which I was arrested was one of the most empowering that I have ever attended, and I am proud to be a part of a movement which succeeds in creating such an event of solidarity.

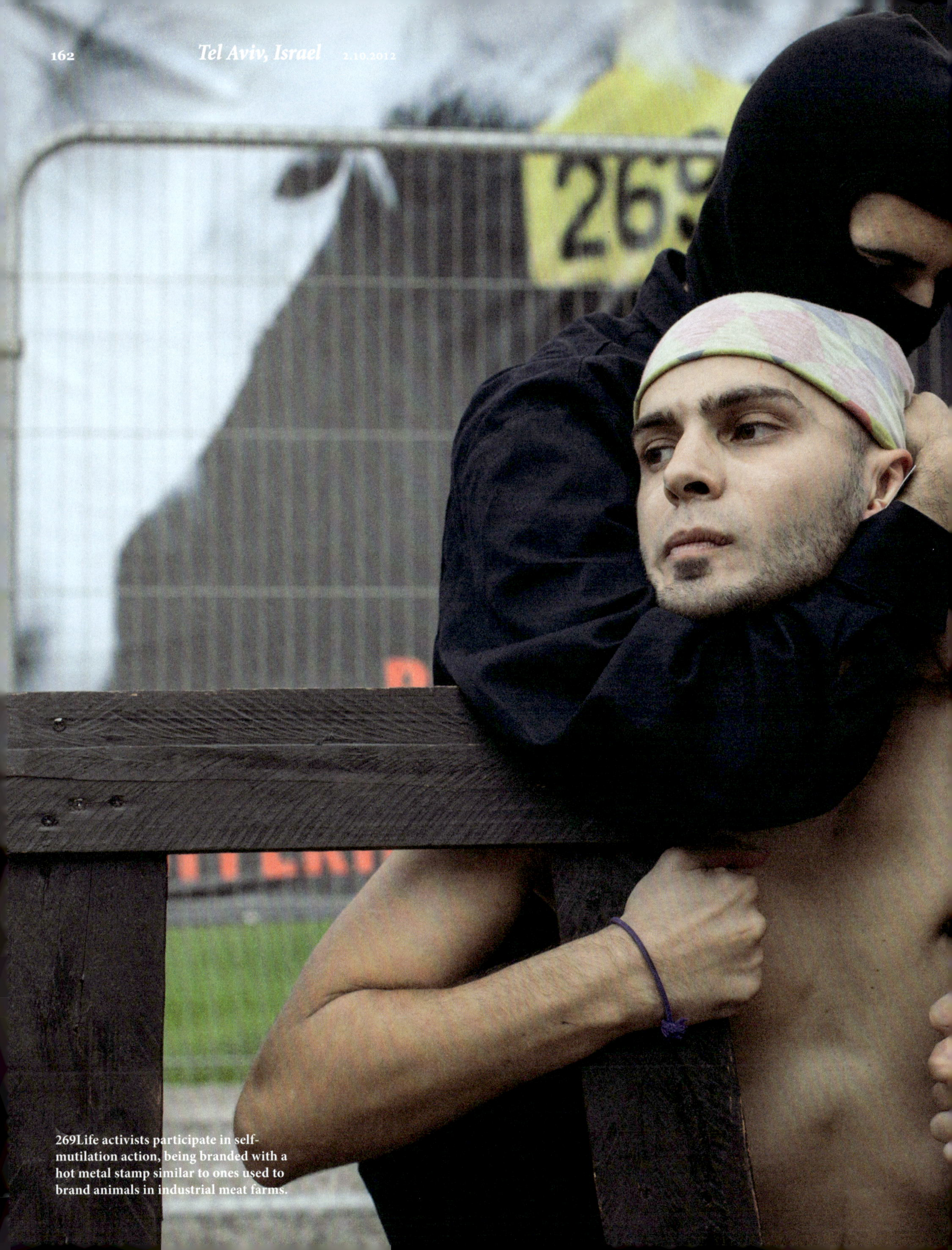

269Life activists participate in self-mutilation action, being branded with a hot metal stamp similar to ones used to brand animals in industrial meat farms.

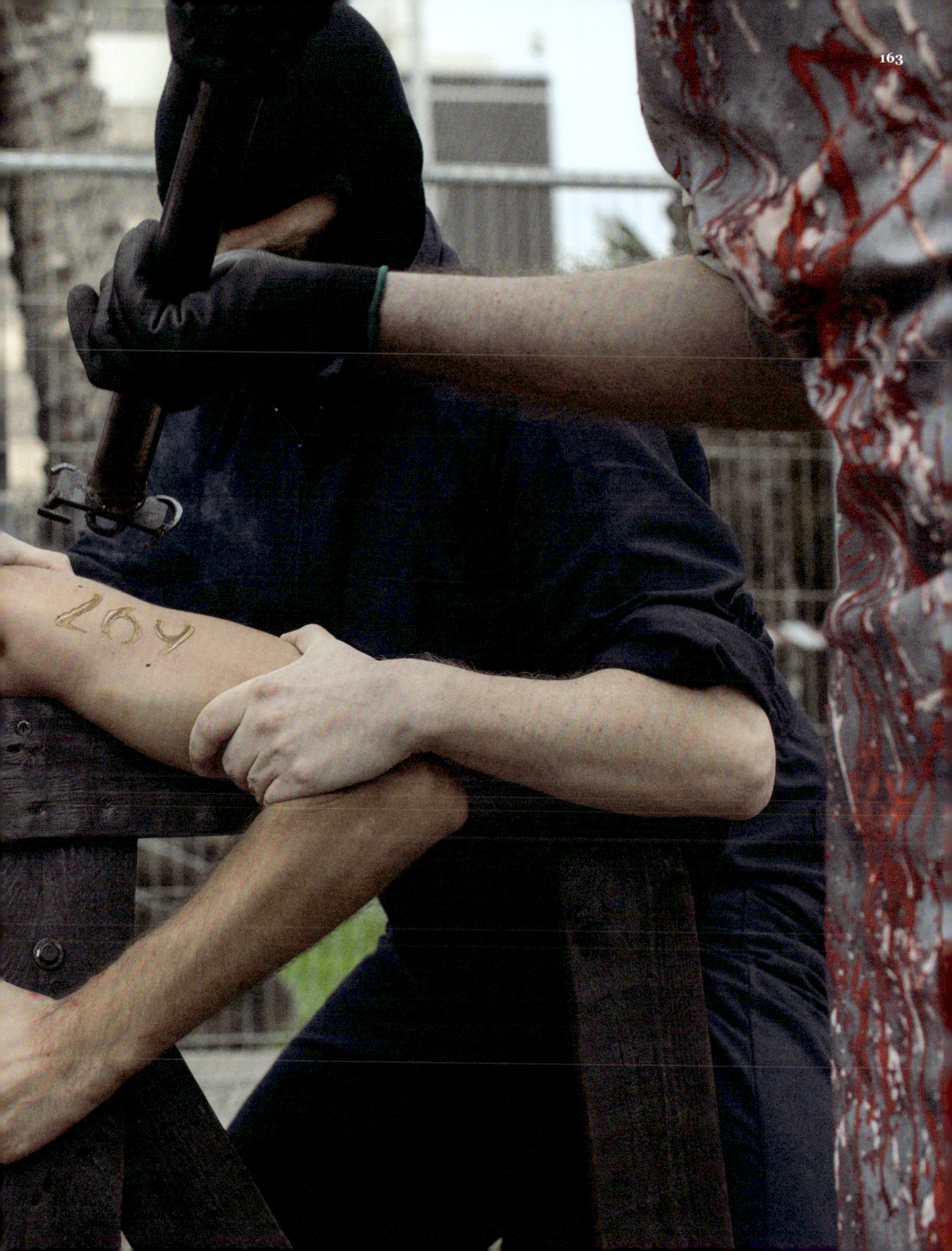

Santiago Gomez

Santiago Gomez is an Israeli animal liberation activist.

It seems the cards ought to be stacked high against Israelis working to end institutionalized violence toward animals. Not only is Israel among the largest consumers of meat per capita in the world, it is also a rather violent place in general—ranked 14th most dangerous country in the Global Peace Index,[1] between Zimbabwe and Colombia—as well as proud parent to the longest military occupation in modern times, with a long list of wars, intifadas, and armed conflicts under its short cartridge belt. And that's without counting various other ills, such as the economic ultra-violence entailed in having one of the highest poverty rates in the West.[2]

And yet, in the midst of all sacrificial jingoisms and harsh theologies of domination and dominion, animal rights activists have been making unprecedented headway these past few years; not top-down via laws or bans, but rather horizontally, by making animal rights, and ethical veganism in particular, a prominent feature of Israeli public discourse.

At this point, it should perhaps be stressed that "Israeli public" refers to Arab citizens as much as to Jewish ones. A 2015 *Ha'aretz* poll even found a higher percentage of vegetarians and vegans among Palestinians with Israeli citizenship than among Jews. And just like every other poll and study done in the last five years, it also confirmed that Israel has by far the most favorable vegans-to-population ratio of any country in the world.[3]

How have local activists achieved this quotidian quantum leap? Well, I've been a part of the Israeli animal rights movement since the early 1990s, seen it grow from a small subcultural appendage of the euphoric idealism that shifted protest paradigms beneath the Oslo Accords years (1992–94), to a formidable fighting force that has earned its place in the heart of today's mainstream—and even I am at a loss for an answer. Perhaps there's a multi-linearity at play here that is not yet distant enough for us to trace.

However, if there's one thing we can already surmise, and quite clearly too, it's that the rise in aggressive and confrontational—and controversial!—forms of activism proved to be the key factor in pushing our message center stage. "Israeli vegans are often at odds with the Hindu or hippie vegan culture," a worried food sociologist at Tel Aviv University told AFP news agency in 2014, "and instead employ a rhetoric of force which favors violent activism. "His mistaking militancy for violence notwithstanding, it is true that after years of sweetening pills and softening blows, of kowtowing and coat-tail riding and treating animal liberation like maudlin politics or a mere appendix to larger (and always human-centered) agendas, we finally understood that a person can only experience holocausts for what they are once he/she sees other people responding to them as holocausts; anything else merely lets more cognitive dissonance in.

"Be realistic, demand the impossible!" counseled *les Enragés* of '68, and half a century later, 2,000 miles away, Israel's animal liberationists seem to have taken the old revolutionary adage to heart.

1. See "Global Peace Index 2014: every country ranked," The Guardian, http://www.theguardian.com/news/datablog/2014/jun/18/global-peace-index-2014-every-country-ranked, accessed 29.3.2016.

2. See "Poverty Report / Israeli Has Highest Poverty Rate in West," *Ha'aretz* [English], http://www.haaretz.com/israel-news/.premium-1.690901, accessed 29.3.2016.

3. See "Veganism on the Rise Among Israeli Arabs," *Ha'aretz*, http://www.haaretz.com/israel-news/.premium-1.675472, accessed 29.3.2016. See also "Israelis growing hungry for vegan diet," JTA, http://www.jta.org/2014/10/15/life-religion/israelis-growing-hungry-for-vegan-diet, accessed 29.3.2016.

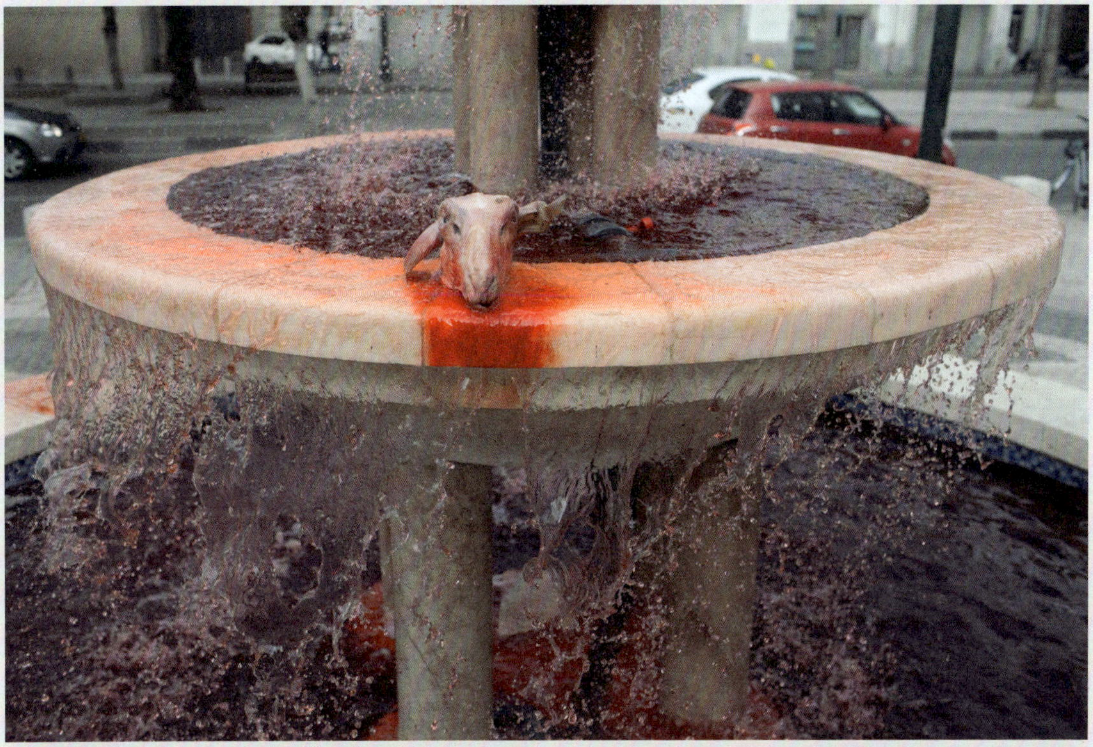

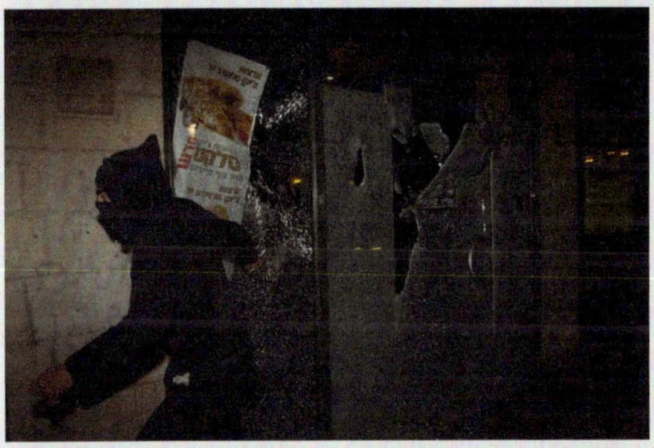

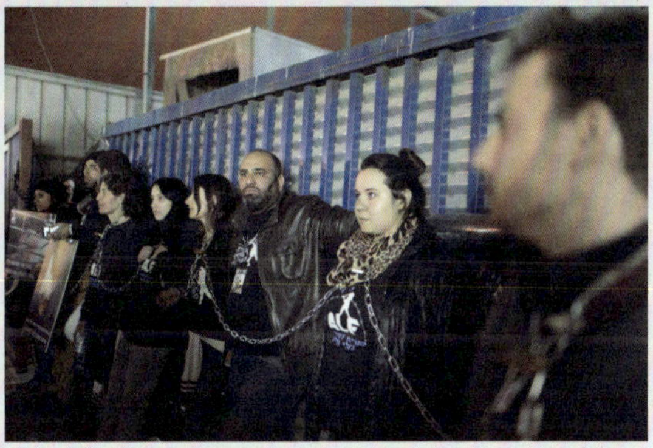

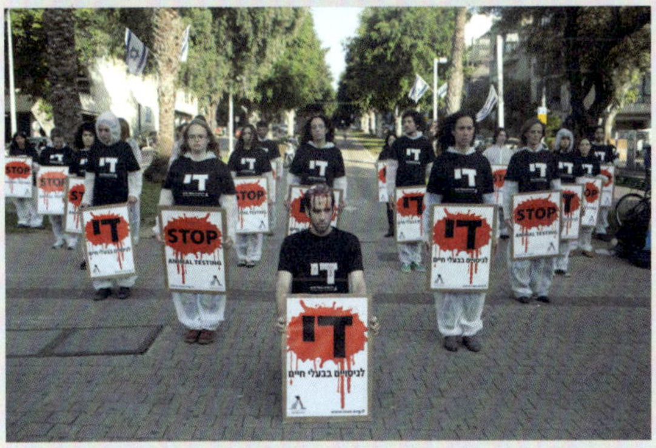

{Top left to right}
1. A goat's head left in a fountain, Jaffa, Israel, 5.3.2013 / **2.** An Israeli activist breaks a McDonald's fast food restaurant window during an animal rights action, Jaffa, Israel, 19.10.2007 / **3.** Members of the Israeli Animal Liberation Front block the entrance to a slaughterhouse, preventing a truck loaded with chickens from entering, Kfar Habad, Israel, 27.2.2014 / **4.** Activists protest against animal testing, Tel Aviv, 23.4.2013

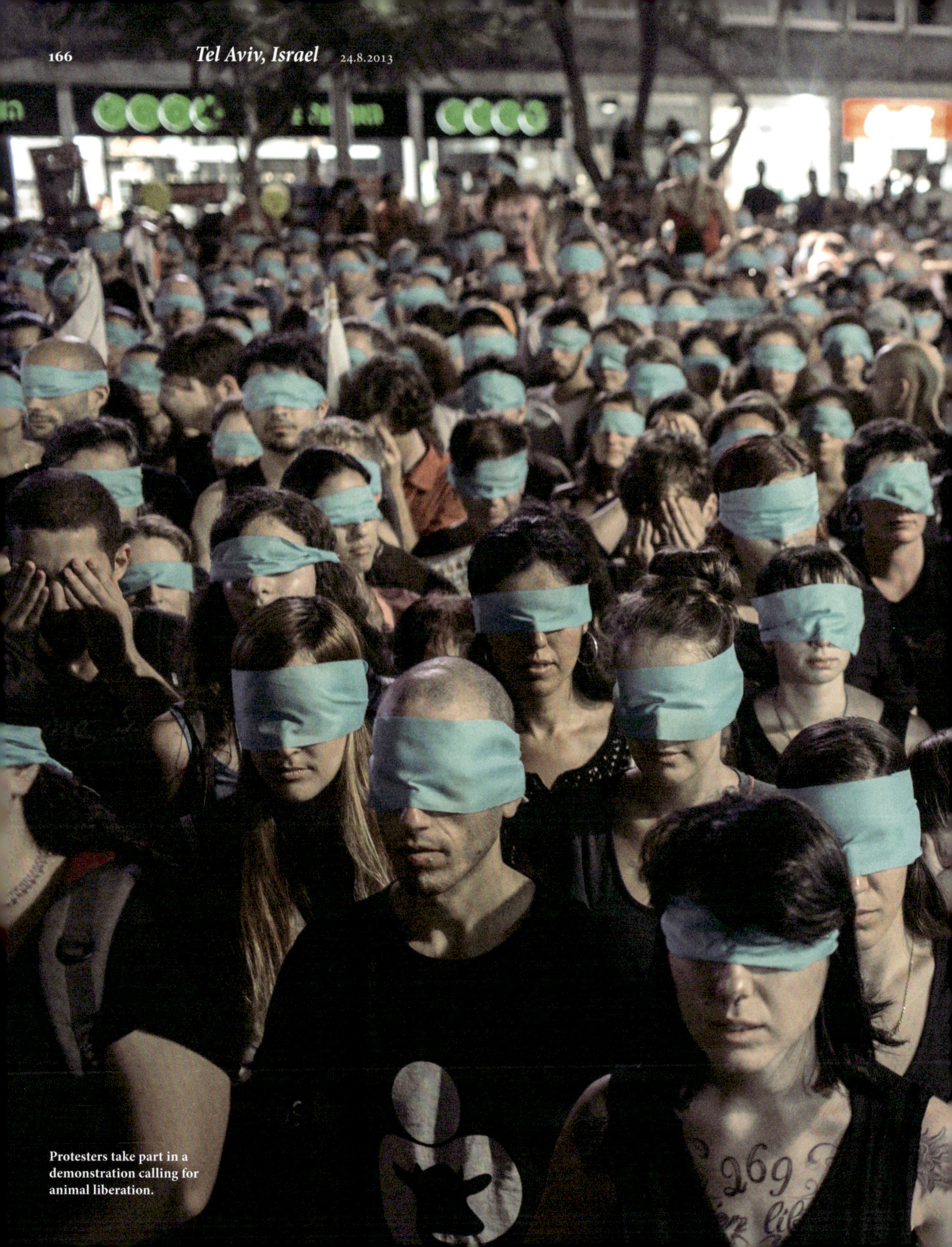

Protesters take part in a demonstration calling for animal liberation.

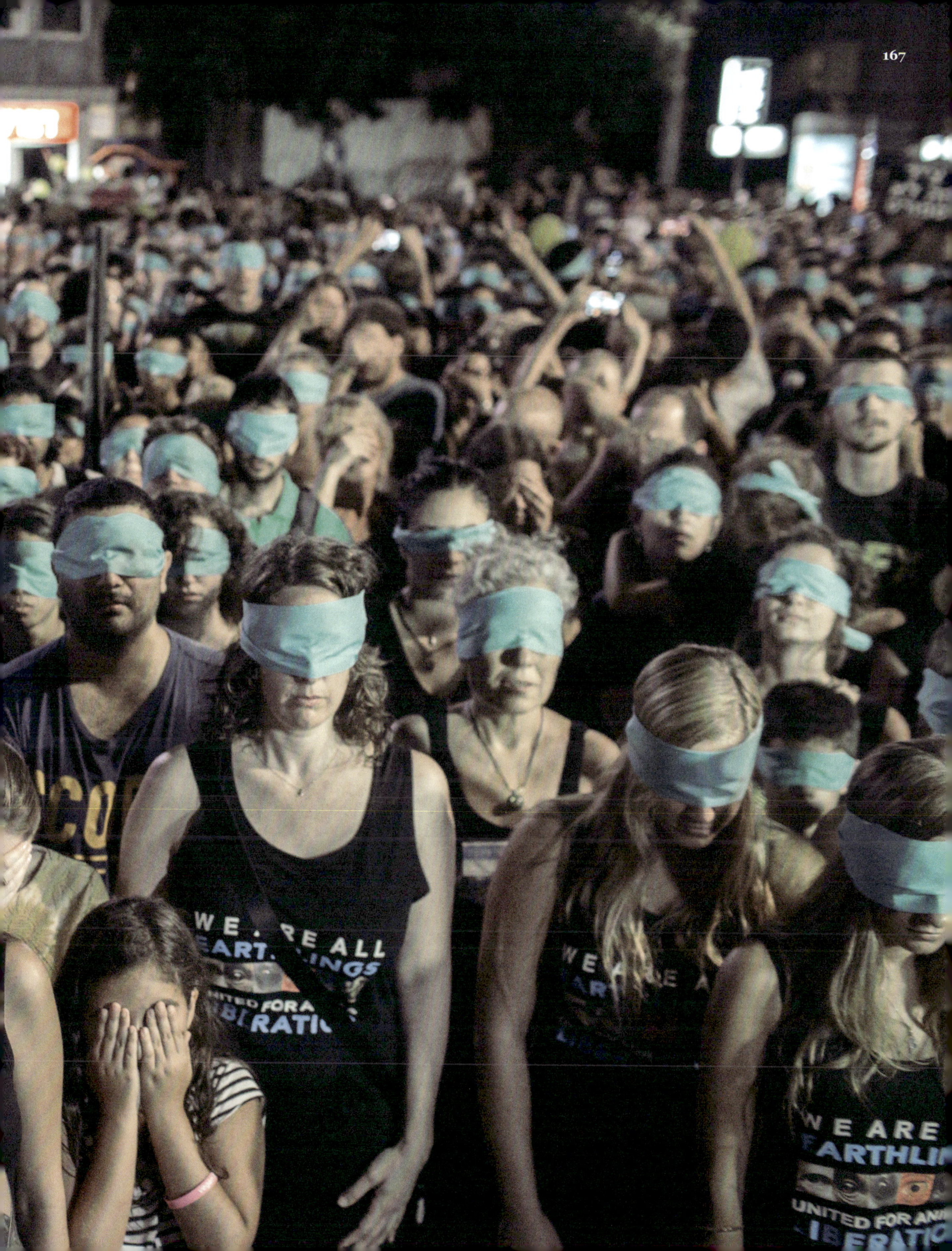
WE ARE

Stills

Toward a Theory of Activist Photography: Community, Performativity, and Affect

Al-Ma'asara, West Bank 22.10.2010

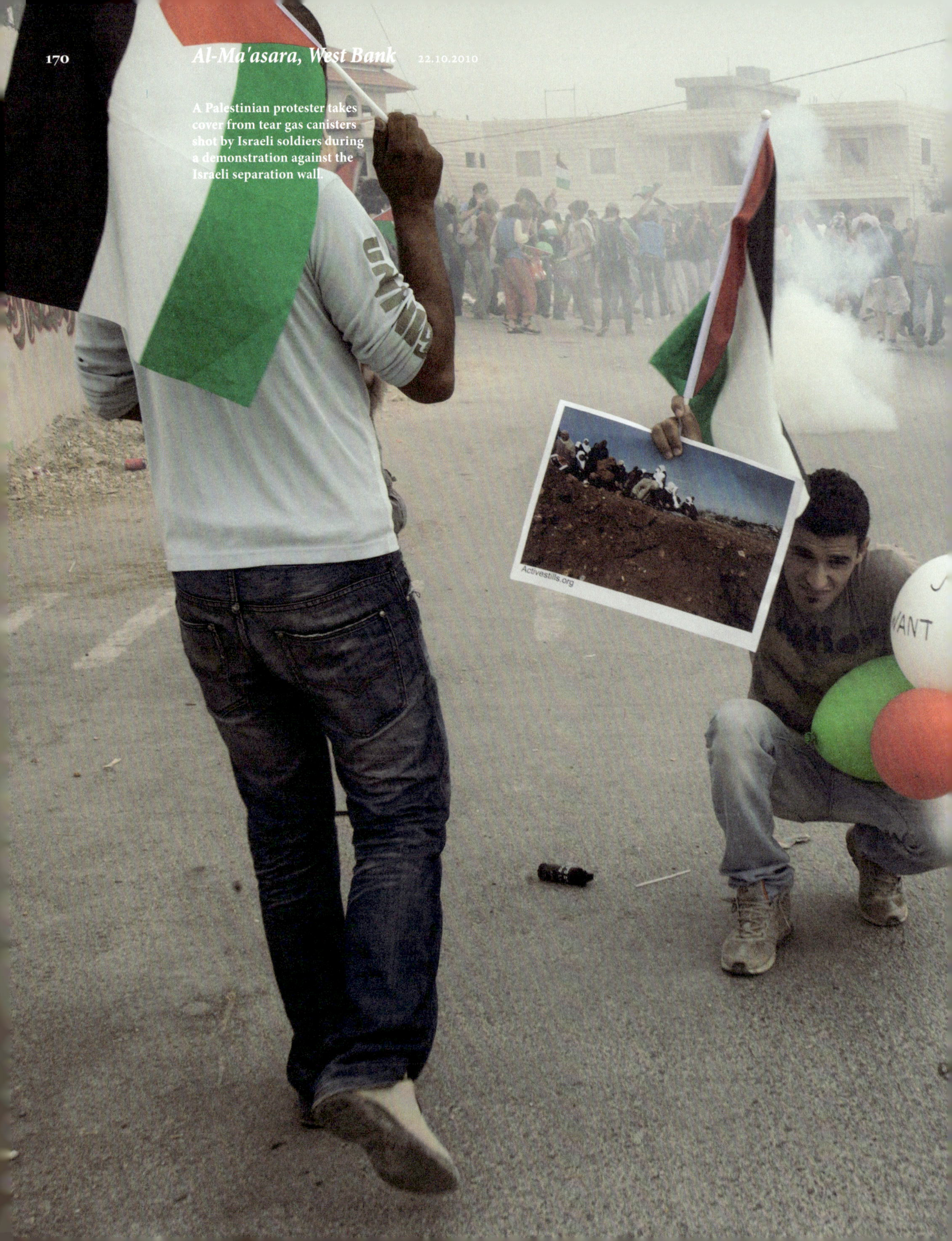

A Palestinian protester takes cover from tear gas canisters shot by Israeli soldiers during a demonstration against the Israeli separation wall.

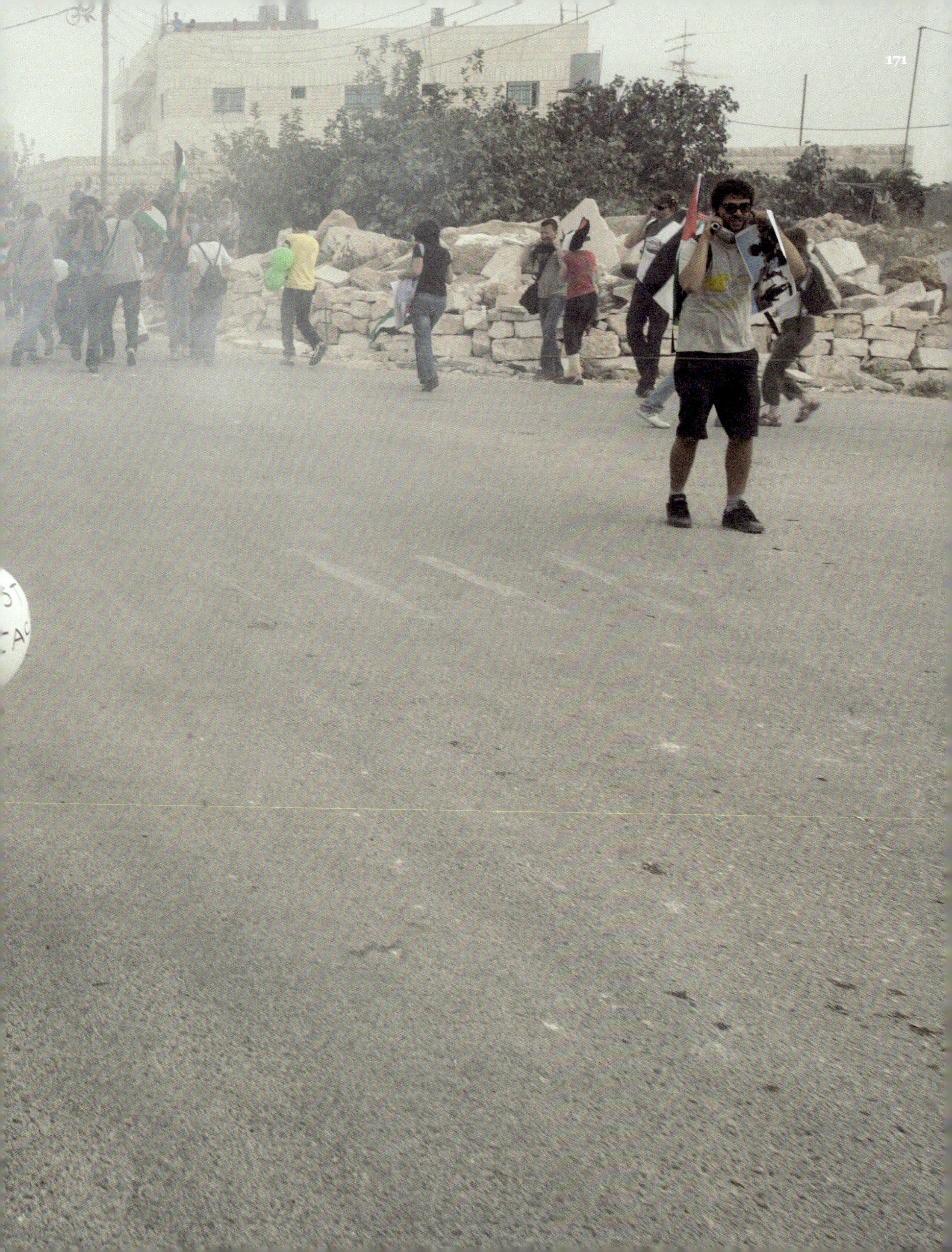

Tel Aviv, Israel 12.5.2010

Bedouins from the villages of Al-Araqib and Damash in the Negev Desert protest against displacement.

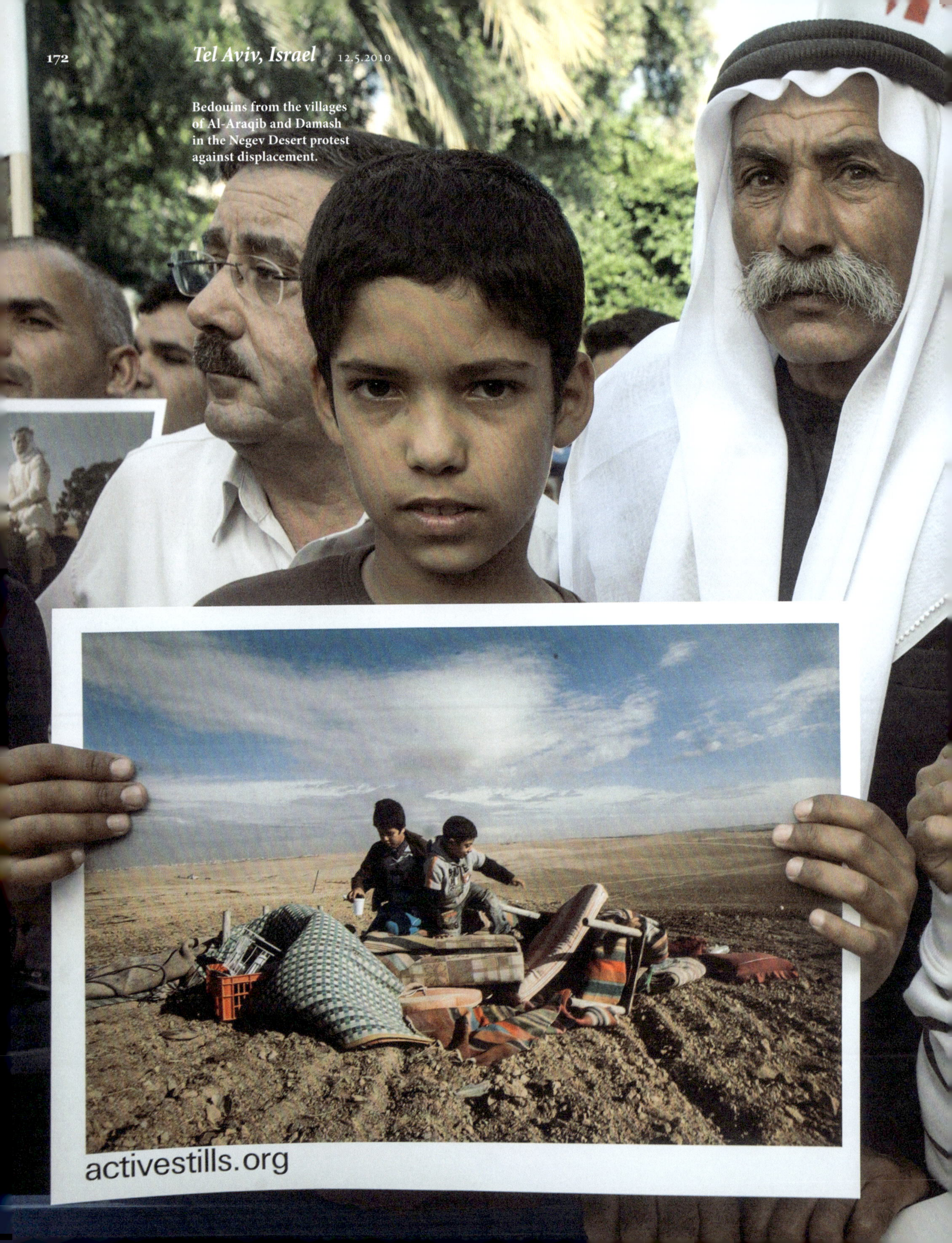

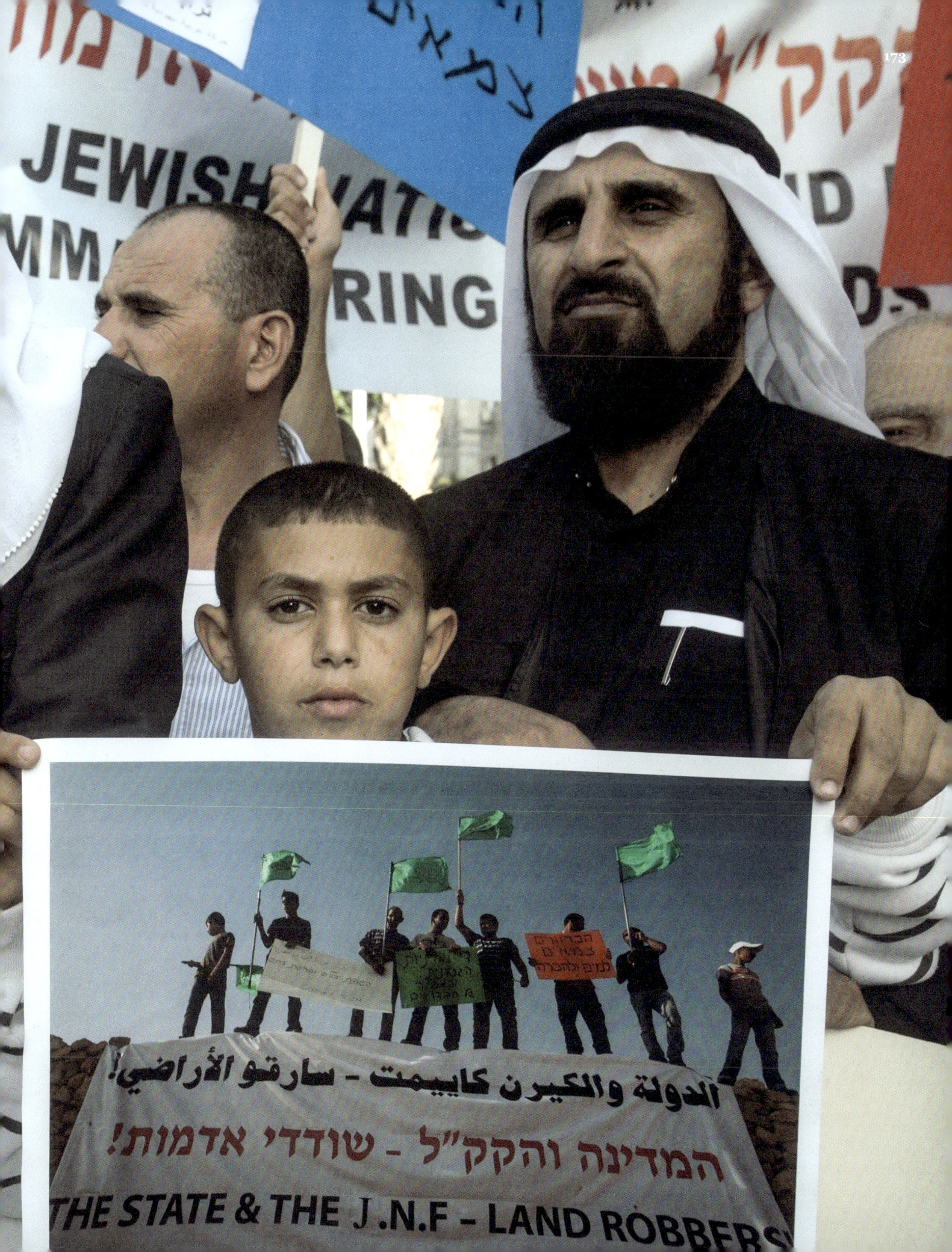

الدولة والكيرن كاييمت - سارقو الأراضي!
המדינה והקק"ל - שודדי אדמות!
THE STATE & THE J.N.F - LAND ROBBERS

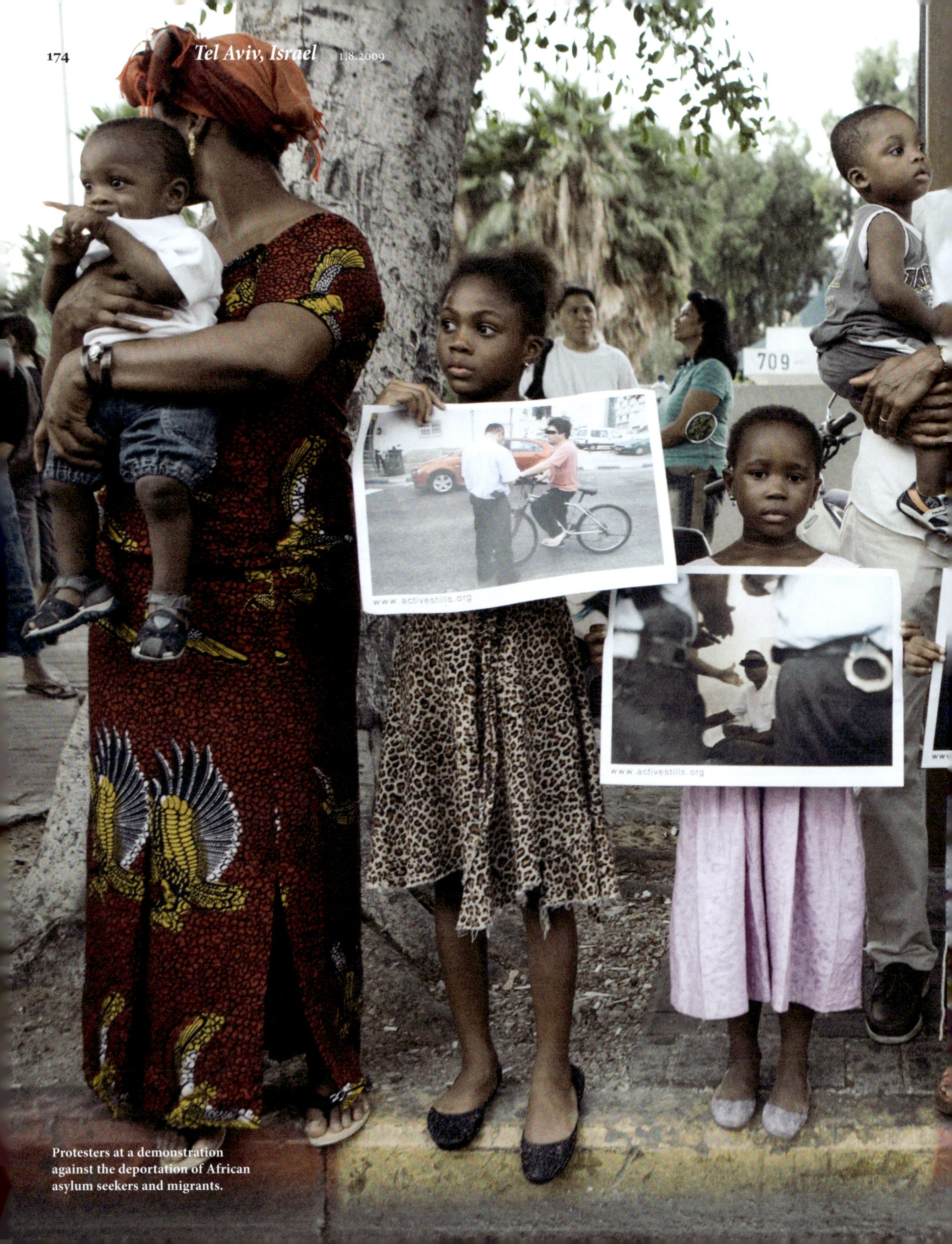

Protesters at a demonstration against the deportation of African asylum seekers and migrants.

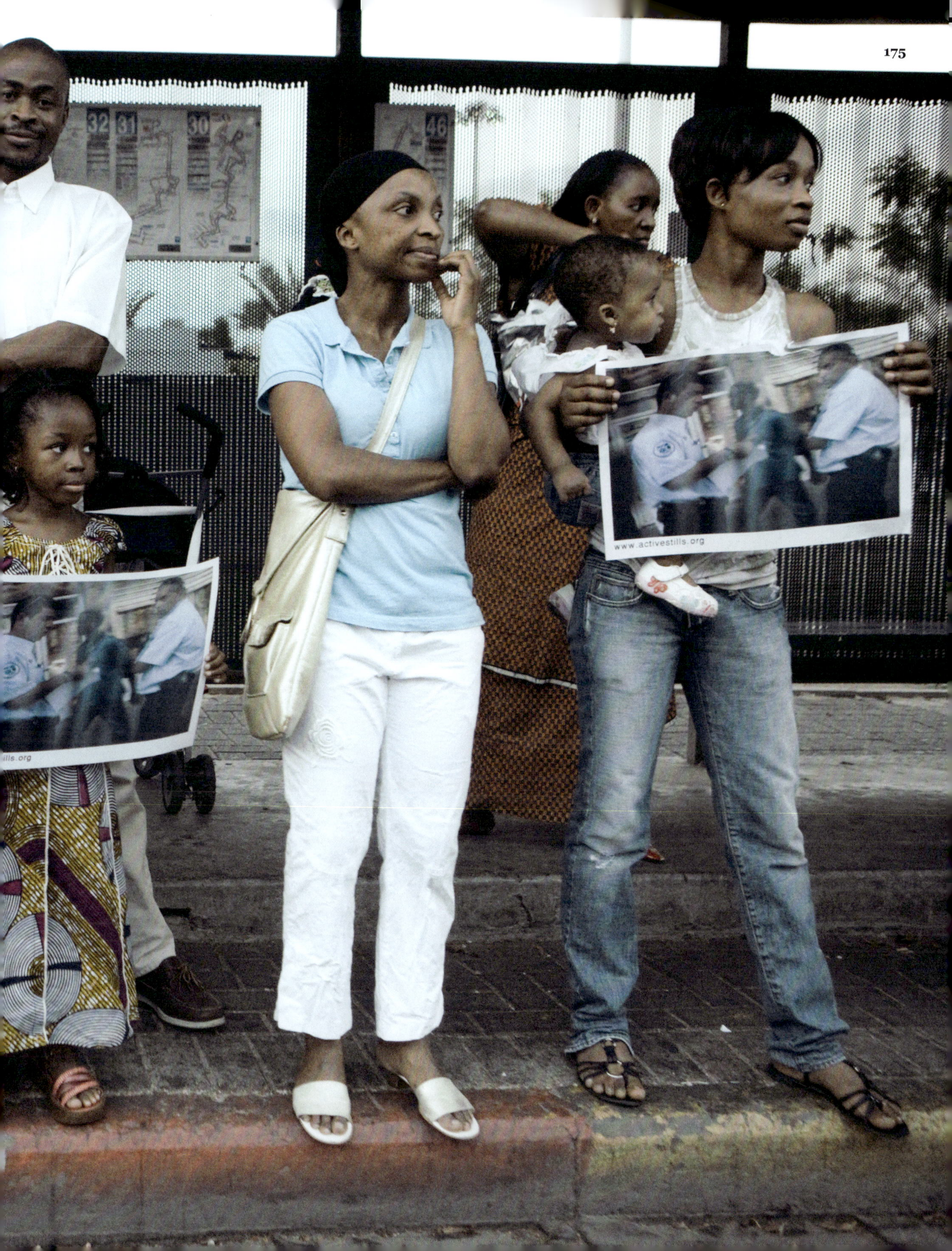
32
31
30
46
www.activestills.org

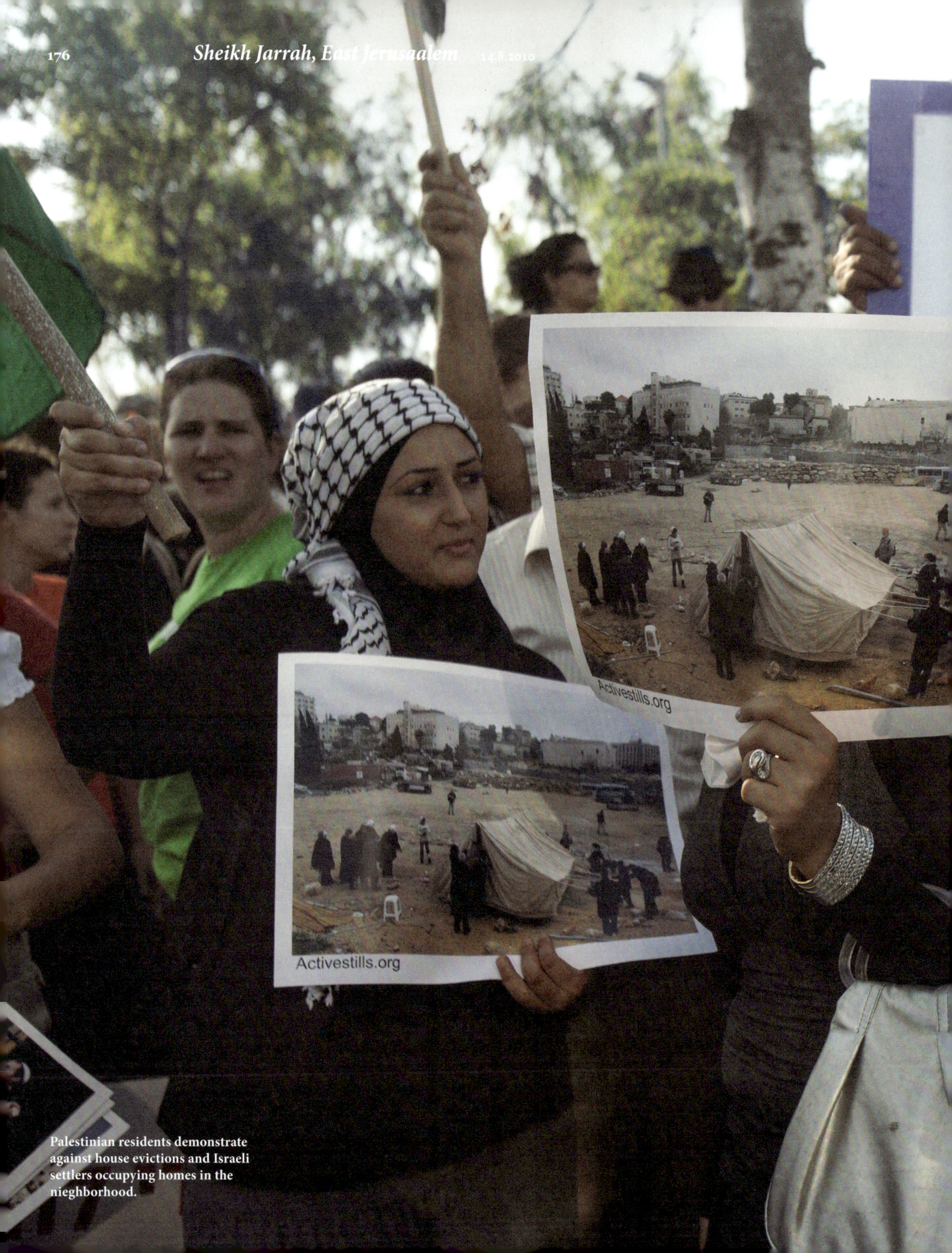

Palestinian residents demonstrate against house evictions and Israeli settlers occupying homes in the nieghborhood.

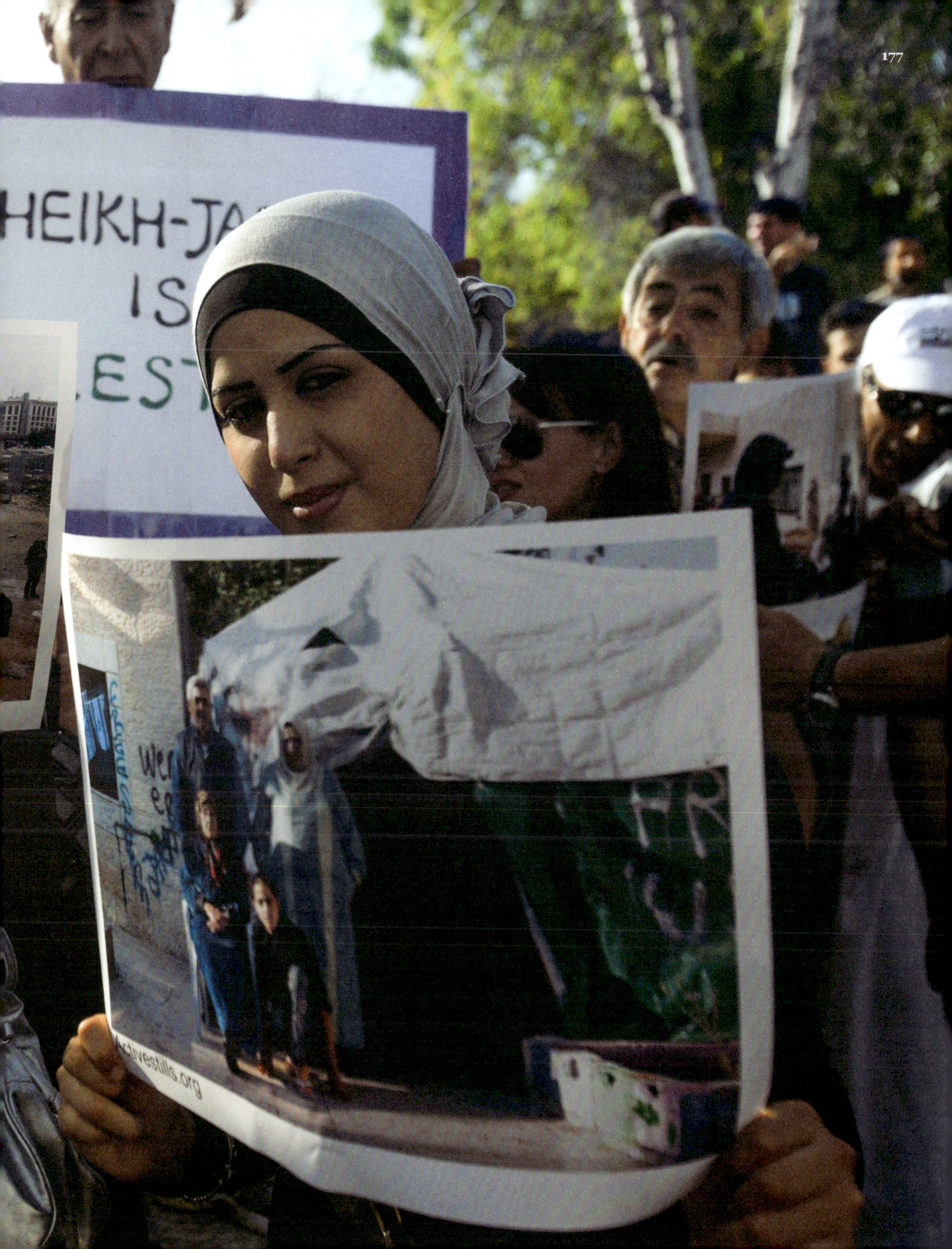
HEIKH-JA
IS
LEST
Activestills.org

Supporters and residents protest against the eviction of the Kfar Shalem neighborhood.

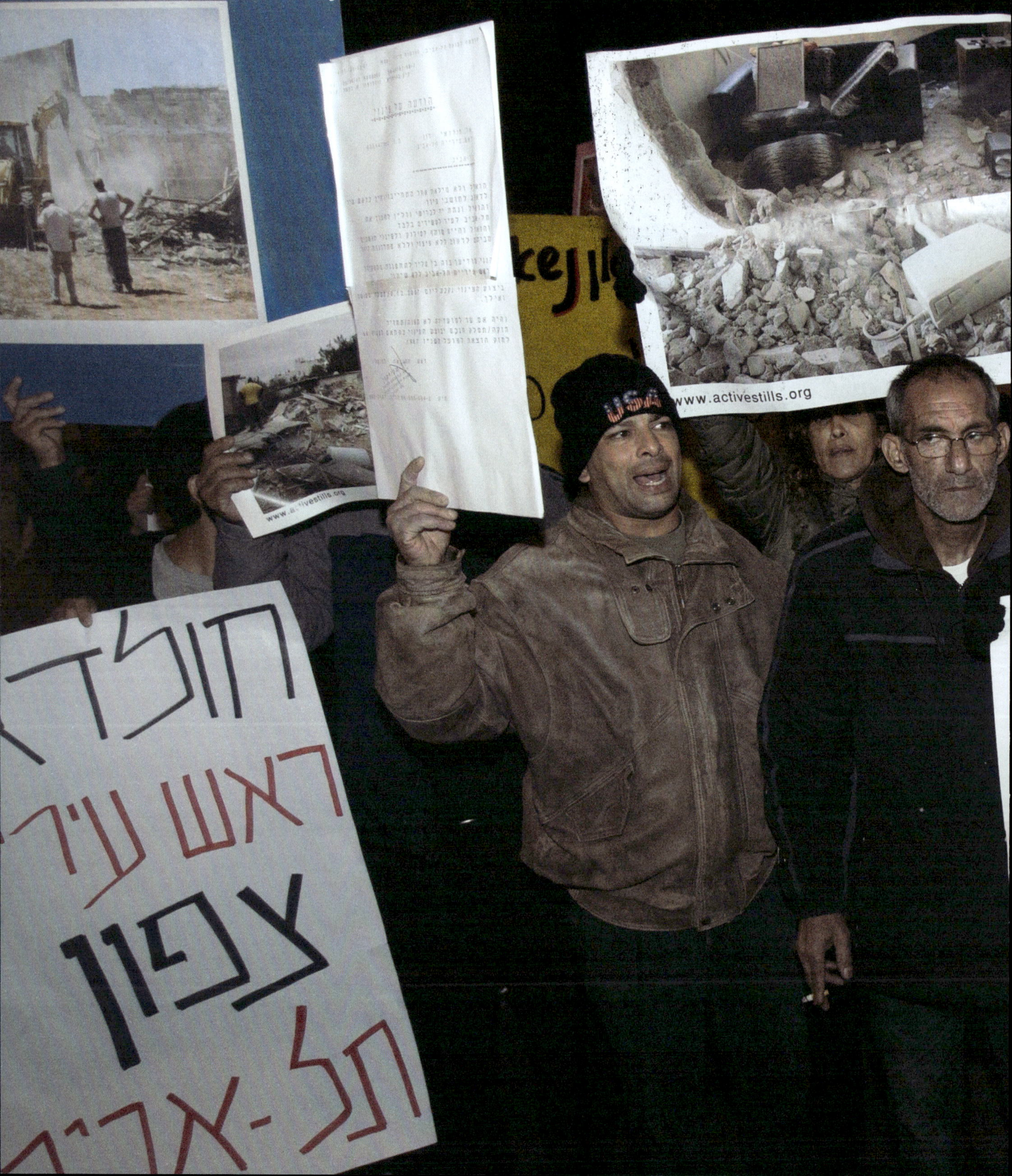

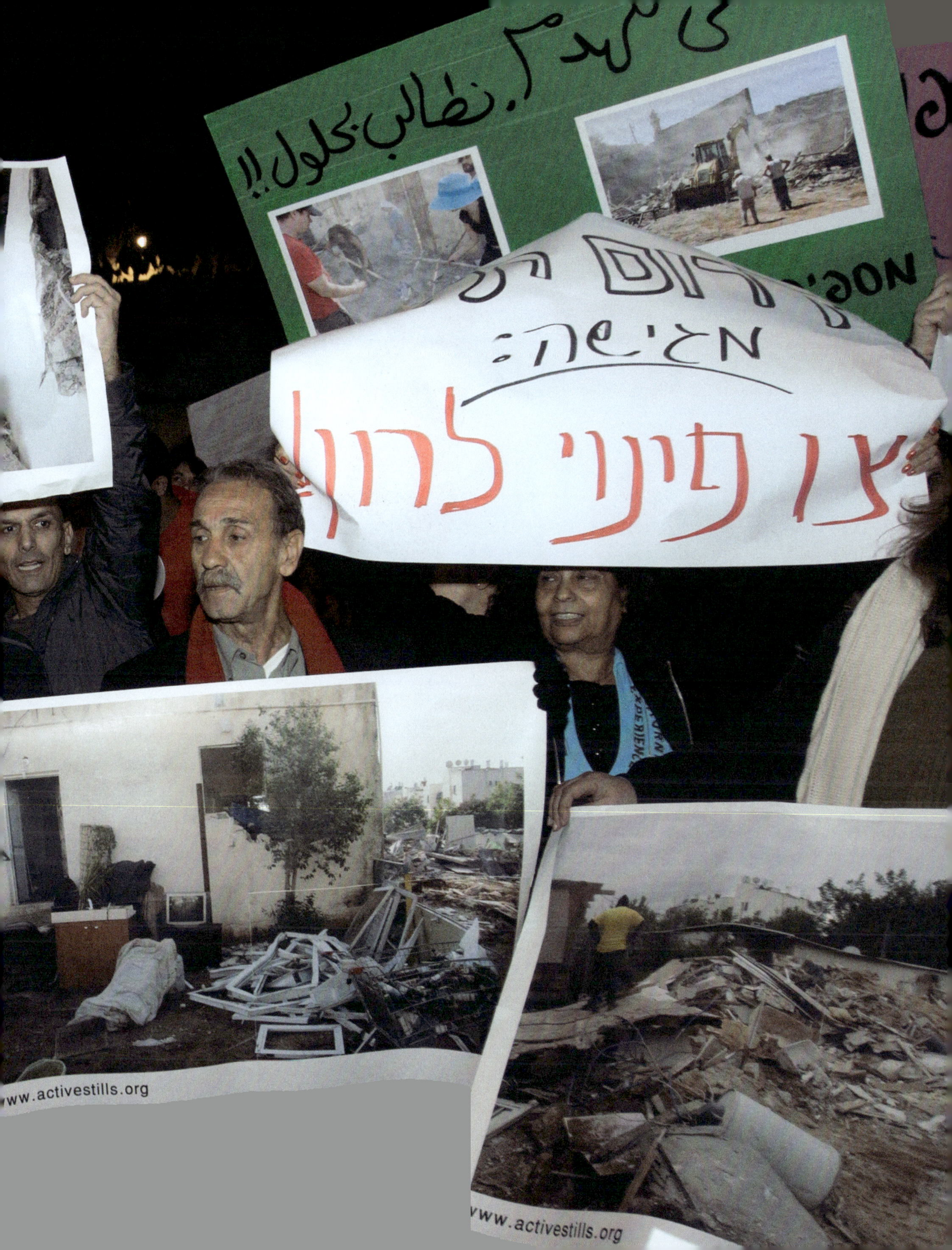

نطالب بحلول!!
מגישה:
www.activestills.org
www.activestills.org

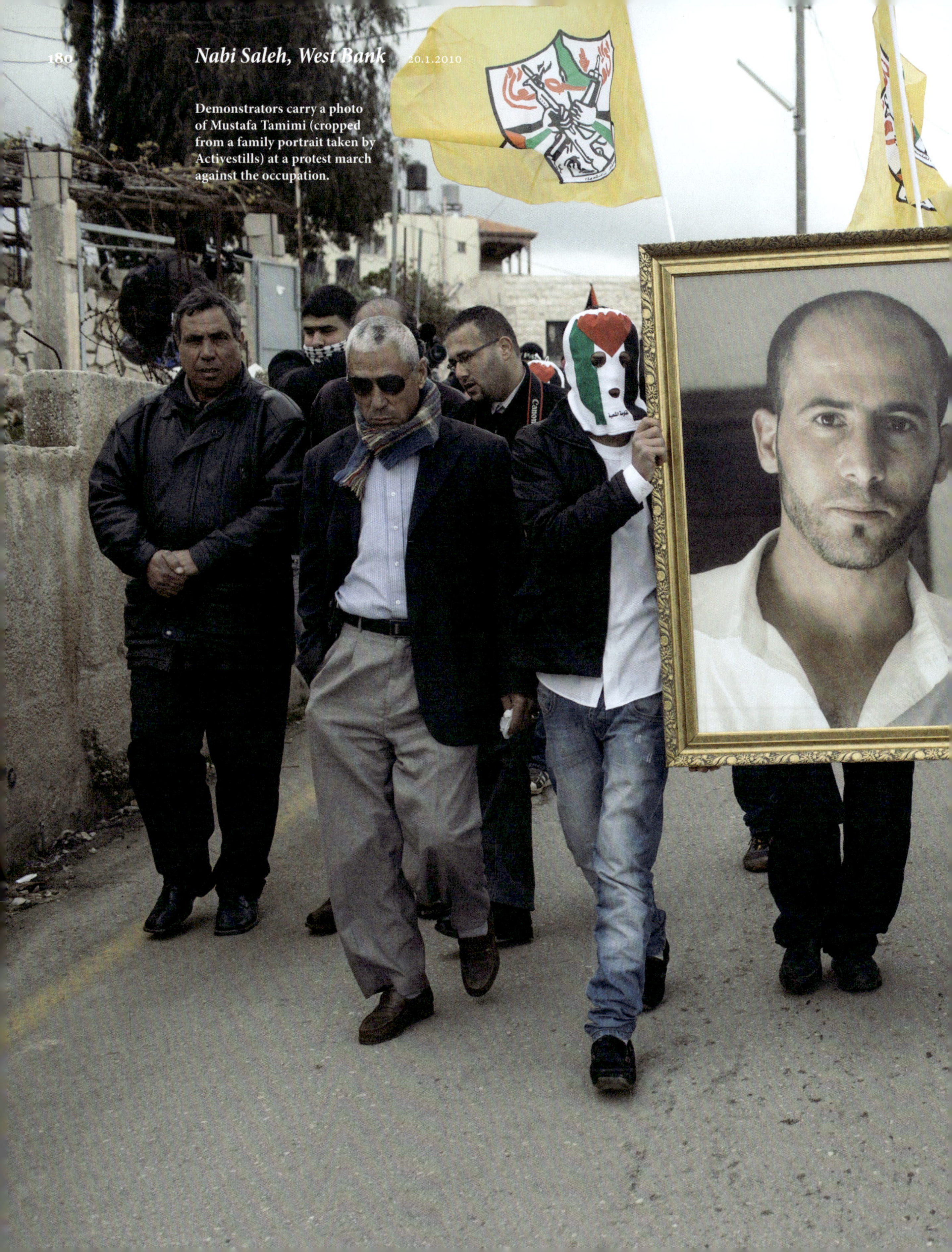

Demonstrators carry a photo of Mustafa Tamimi (cropped from a family portrait taken by Activestills) at a protest march against the occupation.

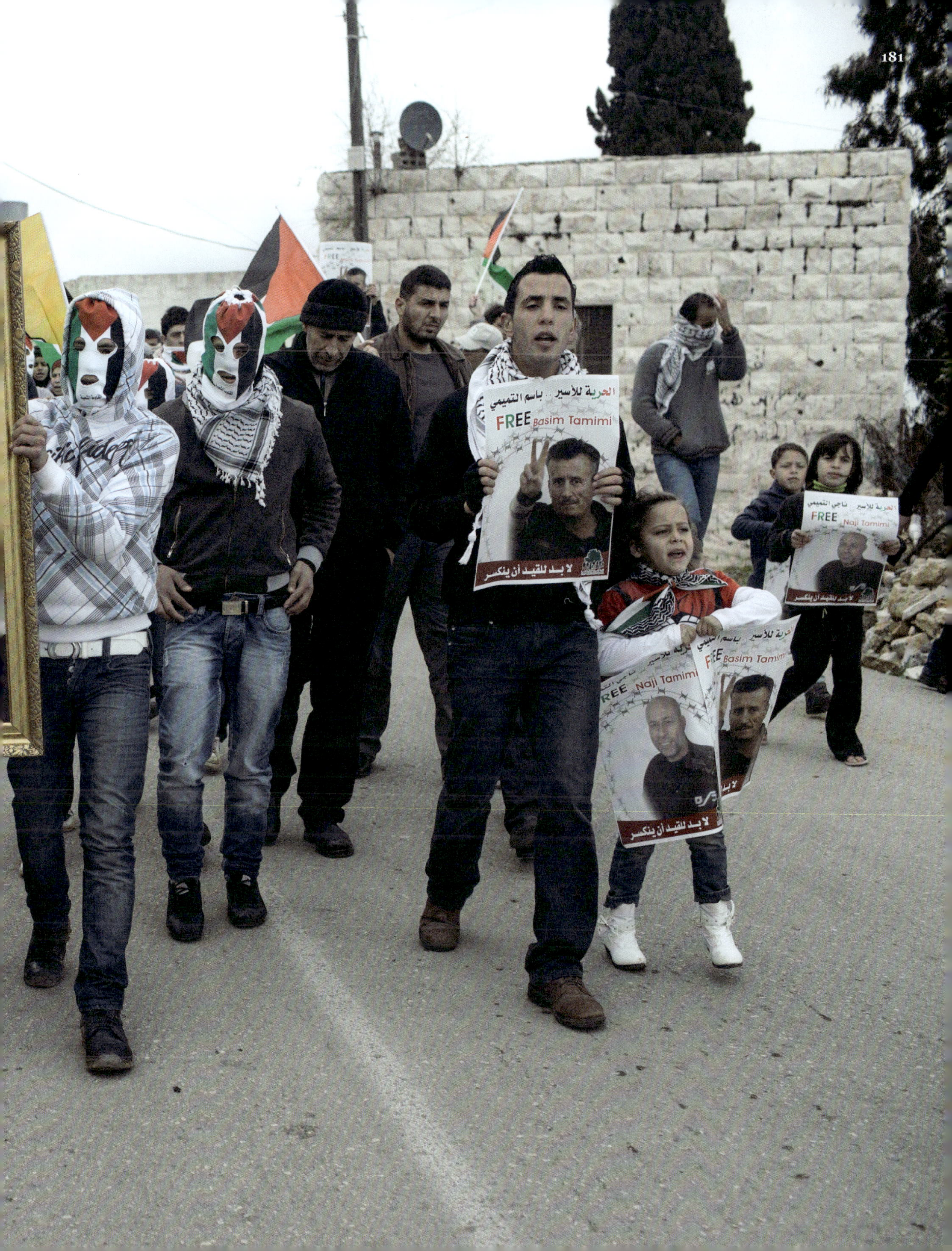
الحرية للأسير .. باسم التميمي
FREE Basim Tamimi
لا بد للقيد أن ينكسر
ناجي التميمي
FREE Naji Tamimi

Surviving Images and Images of Survival: On Activestills' Photographs of Protest

Vered Maimon

Activestills' work points to a major change in the political and critical viability of photography within global visual culture. In the current moment, it is no longer in its status as a "document" or irrefutable indexical form of evidence and testimony that photography acquires its prominent role, but in its capacity to foster *belief* in specific framings of the real, what Judith Butler calls "frames of war and violence."[1] That is, in its ability to relay political and ethical affects that are inseparably sensorial, perceptual, and material. This change led scholars such as Margaret Olin, Ariella Azoulay, and Thomas Keenan to insist on the need for a theoretical and critical shift in the field of the history and theory of photography, and particularly within scholarship on documentary photography.[2] Keenan explains the urgency and necessity of this shift in his seminal essay "Mobilizing Shame":

> What would it mean to come to terms with the fact that there are things which happen in front of cameras that are not simply true or false, not simply representations and references, but rather opportunities, events, performances, things that are done and done for the camera, which come into being in a space beyond truth and falsity that is created in view of mediation and transmission?[3]

Thus rather than focusing on the representational aspects of photography (the relation between the image and its referent), these scholars emphasize its *performative* roles (the intersubjective relations between viewer or user and image).

In relation to these observations, it becomes clear that Activestills' photographs acquire their political currency and meaning not simply because they document protesting communities and acts of military and state violence that are inflicted on them. Their power resides not simply in what is seen in them, but mainly in their *operative* mode of transmission, circulation, and dissemination. Their images are thus performative rather than representative since they are subject to continuous acts of reinscription and repetition through which sovereign strategies of possession (of land and territory) and control (of subjects and populations) are challenged. I argue in this essay that it is precisely in their dynamic and multiple roles as simultaneously material objects, visual images, and tactile surfaces that the photographs enact an urgent call for political forms of agency and solidarity.

The Afterlives of Images

More than anyone else, it was Aby Warburg who, as part of his effort to expand the study of art into the study of images in all their forms, developed the notion of *nachleben* or the "survival" of images. His concern was thus with the "afterlife" of images, what Georges Didi-Huberman calls "heterochronies."[4] Warburg resisted formal modes of analysis that consisted in the visual identification and decipherment of stylistic and iconographical motifs through which visual objects are conceived as fixed, self-contained, and "passive" documents of history. Instead he saw images as *agents* of communication and transformation. The meaning of images for Warburg was thus determined by their function and use as part of their *operative* mode of historical transmission. Warburg emphasized the psychological and expressive function of images, their emotional efficacy, as part of civilization's relentless and inherently unresolved struggle against fear, myth, and superstition. For him, images do not simply "represent" or depict the oscillating struggle between magic and logos, but are active forces within it as instruments of "psychological orientation" and means of *survival*.[5]

Warburg's legacy has recently been evoked in relation to the current politicization of the field of visual studies, and the emergence of new digital technologies of production, dissemination, and circulation of images.[6] Yet, this recent reconsideration of his legacy also makes it clear that his psychological theory of perception and emotion needs to be significantly rethought. While Warburg emphasized the role images have in the self-preservation of human civilization as part of the affirmation of life as an immanent biological, cultural, and psychological force, in the current moment, it is mainly in relation to the political and economic condition of *precarity* that the survival of images, their active and fluctuating modes of circulation and transformation, becomes inseparable from strategies and acts of survival. Life, as Butler argues, is no longer conceived as ontologically given or as a function of a universal psychological impulse, but as a *condition of co-dependency* through which the possibility of being materially and economically sustained relies "on social and political conditions, and not on a postulated internal drive to live."[7]

Precarity is thus not an existential fact marking human finitude and mortality, but a politically and economically induced condition through which a differential allocation of resources and protections is set and defended. For Butler, the term "precariousness" marks a political and social ontology which is not concerned with

> ... fundamental structures of being that are distinct from any and all social and political organization. On the contrary, none of these terms exist outside of their political organization and interpretation. The "being" of the body to which this ontology refers is one that is always given over to others, to norms, to social and political organizations that have developed historically in order to maximize precariousness for some and minimize precariousness for others.[8]

Since precarity has become the underlying condition of life under globalization, Butler insists on the need to reconsider the possibilities and ends of political forms of resistance. While political action, as Hannah Arendt famously argued, requires the space of appearance, this space cannot be assumed to be given as a kind of vacant stage on which subjects exercise their rights for communication and debate. This space only comes into being and is actively created when subjects, who are often devoid of rights, collectively exercise their right to have rights not out of a "natural" law or a metaphysical principle, but out of their political state of precariousness and continuous exposure to violence.[9] In the current political moment, Butler argues, assembled bodies articulate a new time and space for the popular will through performativity not only of speech, but also of bodily action, gesture, movement, congregation, and persistence, and with these actions they reconfigure "what will be public and what will be the space of politics."[10] Thus, it is precisely when exposed bodies occupy and persist in a space without protection that they exercise a right for support of sociality, belonging, care, mobility, and livelihood. As Butler states: "political claims are made by bodies as they appear and act, as they refuse and as they persist under conditions in which that fact alone is taken to be an act of delegitimation of state power."[11] Contemporary demonstrations and modes of resistance are thus configured today as interventions within the spatial organization of power in order to performatively stage, on the one hand, the continuous exposure to violence of those who are considered to be "non-subject" by sovereign power, *and* on the other, the need for support and protection for the maintenance of the right for life *for all*.

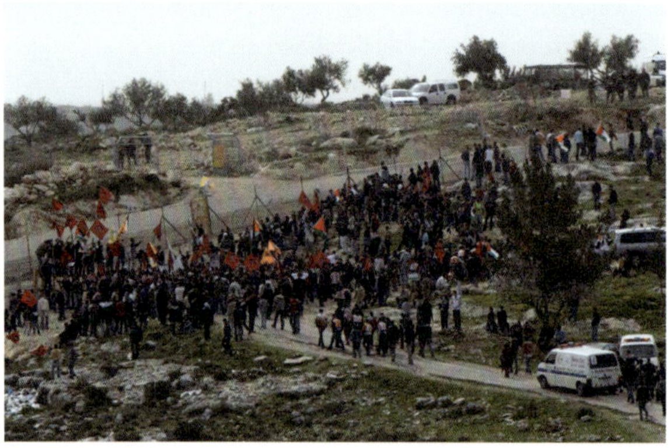

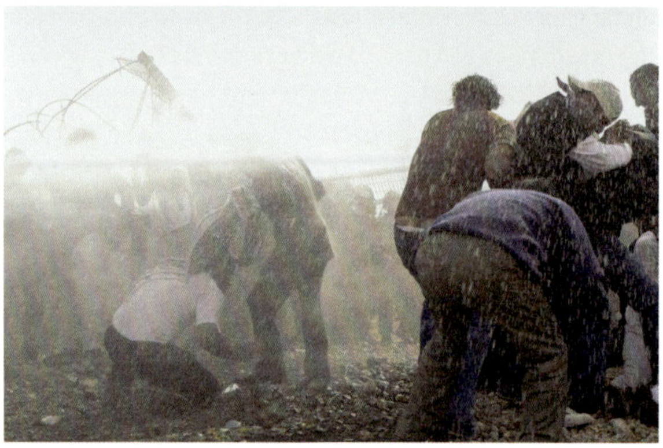

Fig. 1. Protesters at the construction site of the Israeli separation wall during a demonstration, Bil'in, West Bank, 22.2.2008
Fig. 2. Protesters take cover as the Israeli Army sprays them with a water canon, Bil'in, West Bank, 23.2.2007

Based on this formulation of political resistance, I argue that Activestills' photographs of the weekly demonstrations in Bil'in and other Palestinian villages are performative rather than simply documentary because they are not meant to "represent" the Palestinian struggle, but to actively create a space of appearance and intervention through which the Palestinians can be recognized as subjects of political rights [**Fig. 1**]. Since 2005, there have been weekly unarmed demonstrations in Bil'in against the Israeli separation wall and the confiscation of lands that are organized by the local popular committee.[12] Different Israeli and international human rights groups often take part in the demonstrations. Yet, in contrast to press photographs of Bil'in, Activestills images are not meant to create journalistic images of victimhood or heroism, but to expose precarity as an outcome of political policies and military strategies. That is, the presence of the collective's cameras is not conceived to be "external" to the events that are photographed, but aims to challenge the communicative rational ideal of liberal public space as grounded on equality and transparency. Their images capture the demonstrations not as "news items," but as bodily acts of exposure to military violence toward subjects, acts that by their sheer continuous persistence undermine the legitimacy of state power [**Fig. 2**]. Like the demonstrations, Activestills' photographs expose political public space as one that is structured by antagonism and differential allocation of resources, and thus actively take part in the reconfiguration of political space by subjects who collectively insist on exercising their right to have rights.

Persistence and survival are thus the enabling conditions of *both* the struggle and the photographs. The survival and persistence of the images hinges on their transmission and circulation through which the struggle, its ends, and costs, are not just visualized, but perpetually propagated and mobilized. That is, the images "survive" and acquire multiple "afterlives" because, as Warburg argued, they are operative. Their meaning thus derives not simply from any specific iconographic, formal, or stylistic conventions they employ, but because they have material, sensorial, and emotional efficacy—they are *affective*—they produce social effects and enable political forms of agency. As anthropologists Benjamin Lee and Edward LiPuma recently argued, in the current moment, circulation and exchange can no longer be seen as processes that simply transmit meanings, but as "constitutive acts in themselves." They coined the term "cultures of circulation" in order to argue that circulation needs to be considered as a cultural process with its own forms of abstraction, evaluation, and constraint, which are created by the interactions between specific types of circulating forms and the interpretative communities built around them.[13]

This argument suggests that issues of subjectivity, agency, and performativity cannot be adequately addressed through an exclusive emphasis on representation. Rather, they must also address specific mediums of public address, social modes of communication, and different platforms of exchange through which political struggles and forms of agency are not simply documented as pre-given, but are enacted or performed as part of *actual lived experience* and unfolding movements of alliance and antagonistic dissent.

The role of Activestills' images as means of survival and their multiple "afterlives" within the lives of the protesting communities they take part in forming can be best demonstrated through images of the leaders of the non-violent struggle in Bil'in, Adeeb Abu Rahmah and Abdallah Abu Rahmah, the former bullied by soldiers and the latter detained and put on trial at the military court in Ofer prison [**Figs. 3, 4**]. These images appear not only in the collective's archive, Facebook page, Twitter account, and Flickr online photo-stream, but also on banners that are hung on public buildings in Bil'in and other villages, and are also used as graphic components together with texts in posters and placards held by demonstrators. The images become a form of currency, an animating force through which the very effort to eliminate the rights of the struggle's leaders by incarcerating them in a military prison in which their rights are voided, only intensifies their resistance and the validity of their political demands for rights and support.

In the case of the photograph of Abdallah Abu Rahmah, wearing the brown uniform of Ofer prison [**p. 120**], it is striking how the very *act* of photographing him becomes a performative gesture that challenges his condition as "non-subject" deprived of political rights. While the uniform with its white Ofer prison logo is part of a mechanism that subjects him to disciplinary strategies of individualization and control, the image stages a refusal for this condition. This "event" occurs not only because of his gesture in the picture, but because in his direct gaze toward the camera Activestills' photographer Oren Ziv has placed in front of him, he is addressing *not* the military judges, who take (an illegal) part in the dispossession of his rights and land, but a public and a community of co-supporters, both actual and virtual, who will recognize him now or in the future (due to the continuous circulation of

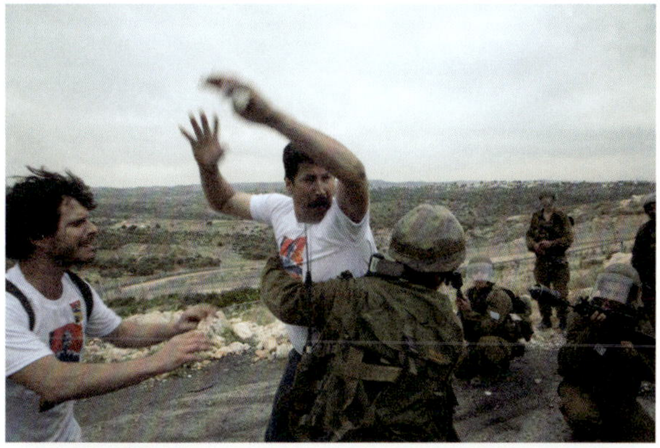

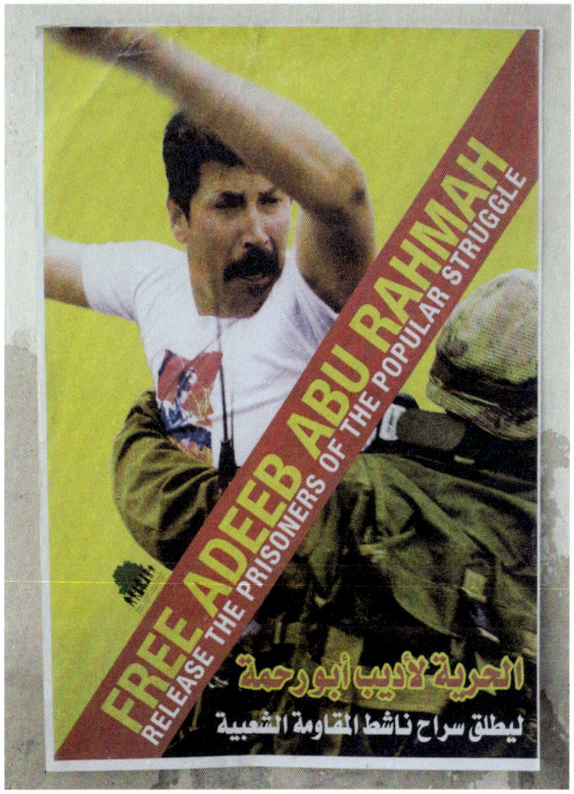

Fig. 3. Adeeb Abu Rahmah detained by Israeli soldiers, 24.4.2009
Fig. 4. A poster printed by the Palestinian Popular Struggle Coordination Committee in solidarity with Adeeb Abu Rahmah

the image) as a *subject of rights*. The point is not to "return the gaze" of the "victim," thus conferring on him "dignity," but to operatively *transmit* his acts of defiance beyond the confines of the occupation's military institutions of oppression. The aim of the photograph is thus not simply

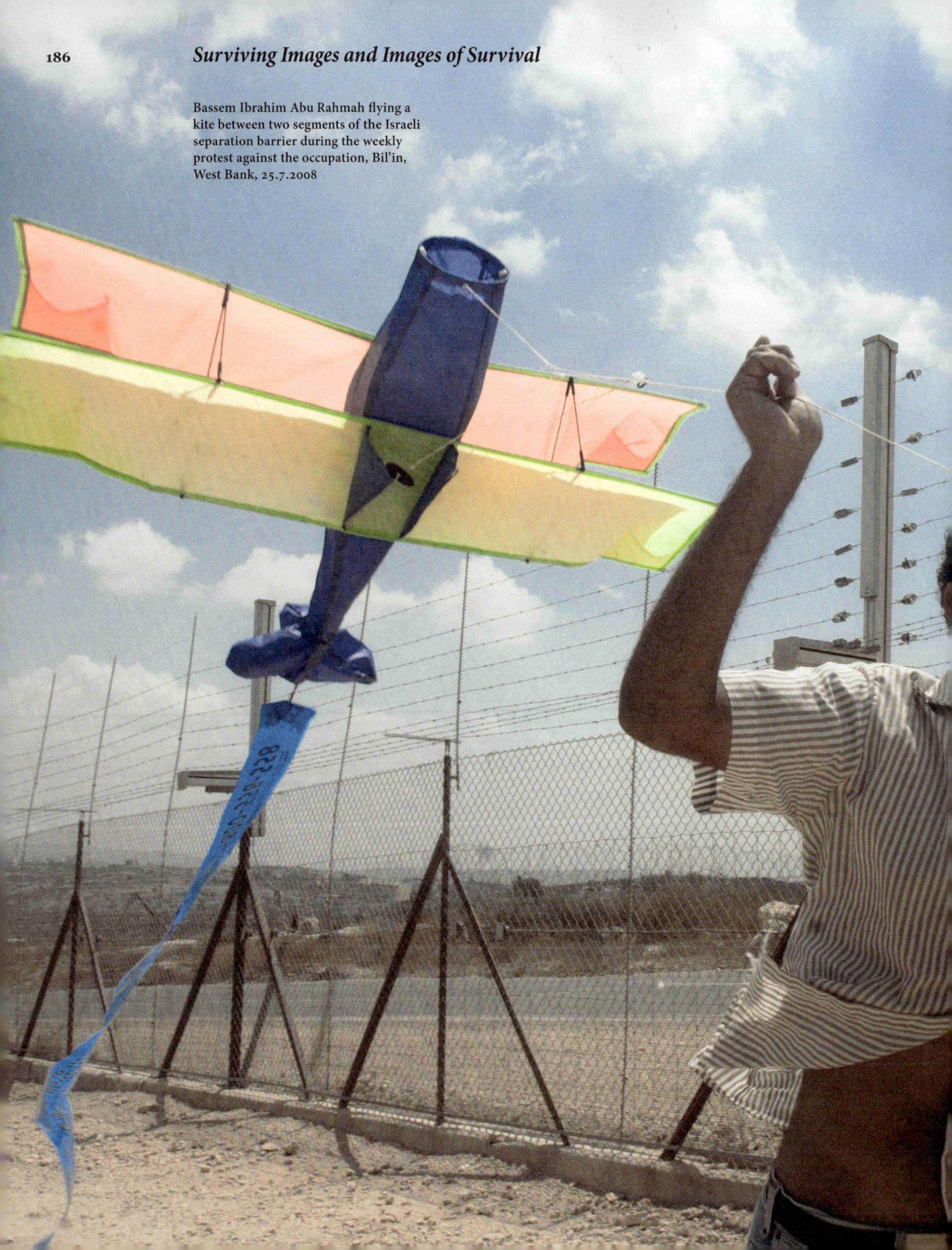

Bassem Ibrahim Abu Rahmah flying a kite between two segments of the Israeli separation barrier during the weekly protest against the occupation, Bil'in, West Bank, 25.7.2008

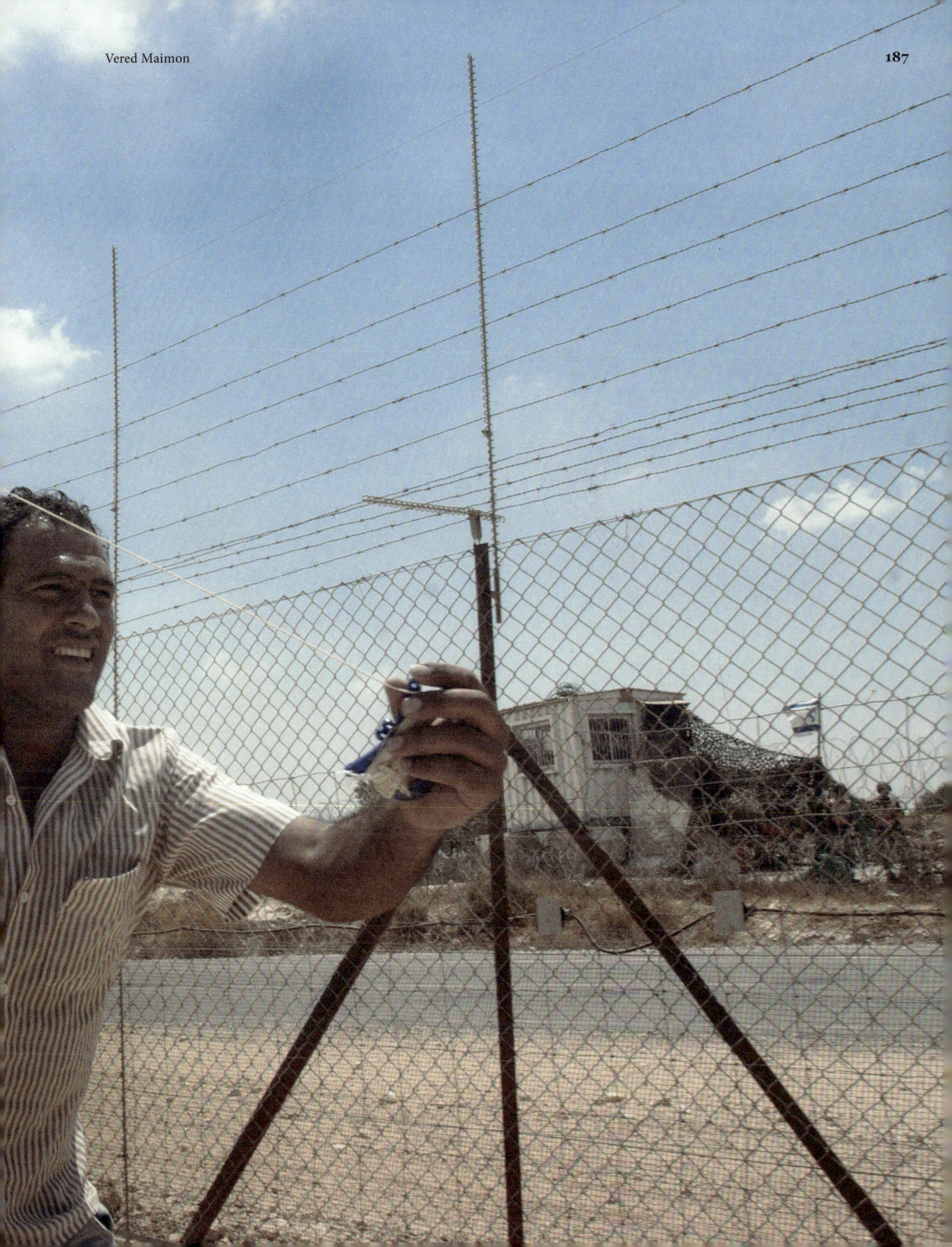

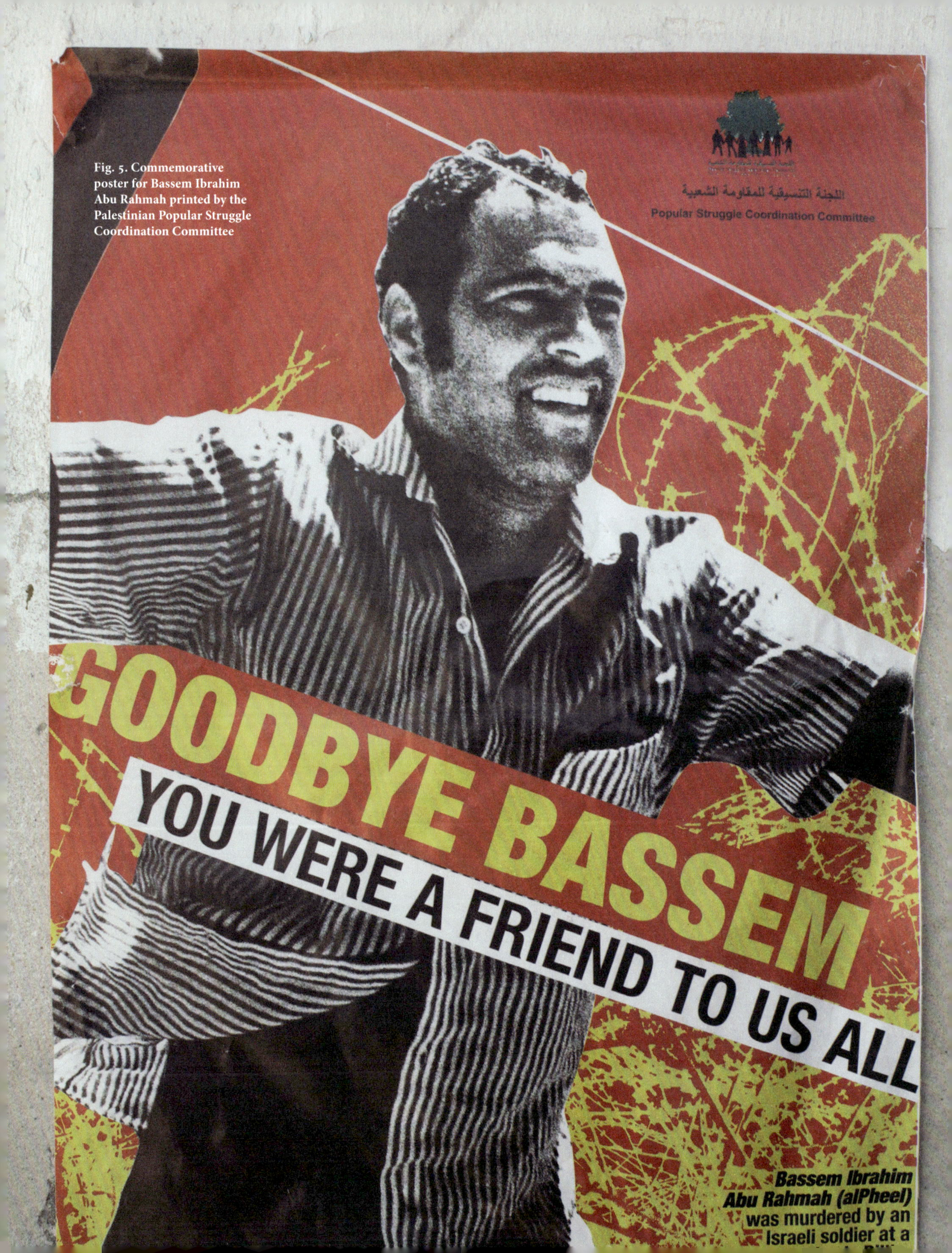

Fig. 5. Commemorative poster for Bassem Ibrahim Abu Rahmah printed by the Palestinian Popular Struggle Coordination Committee

to "represent" Abdallah Abu Rahmah and, in this way, perhaps, unintentionally repeat his victimization as is often the case in documentary photography,[14] but to further communicate his acts of protest and resistance to the occupation by creating a space of appearance (even in a military court!) through which political agency and solidarity are enacted as part of a continuous struggle against precarity and ongoing violence.

Another extraordinary example is the image of Bassem Ibrahim Abu Rahmah, who was killed in 2009 by an Israeli soldier during a demonstration in Bil'in. A photograph taken by Activestills of him flying a kite alongside of the separation barrier **[pp. 186–87]** appears in a poster commemorating his death **[Fig. 5]**. The poster was then hung outside his house and throughout the village **[Fig. 6]**, as part of a memorial marking the site of his death, together with empty tear gas canisters that caused his death **[Fig. 7]**, and later was turned into a placard and a shield used to protect demonstrators from tear gas grenades **[Figs. 8, 9]**. The photographs take an active part in the continuous mobilization and propagation of the struggle, through its appropriation by the community it makes visible and transmission between different surfaces of display and exchange. As part of this process, the image becomes an inextricable part of bodily gestures and acts, and in this way, it becomes an agent for transformation and political change, rather than a "fixed" representation of resistance.

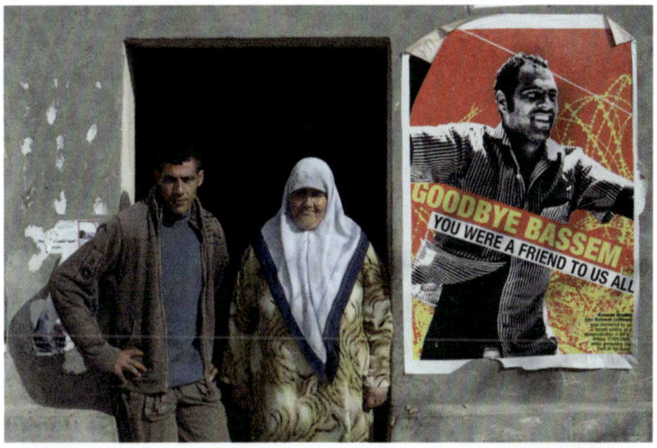

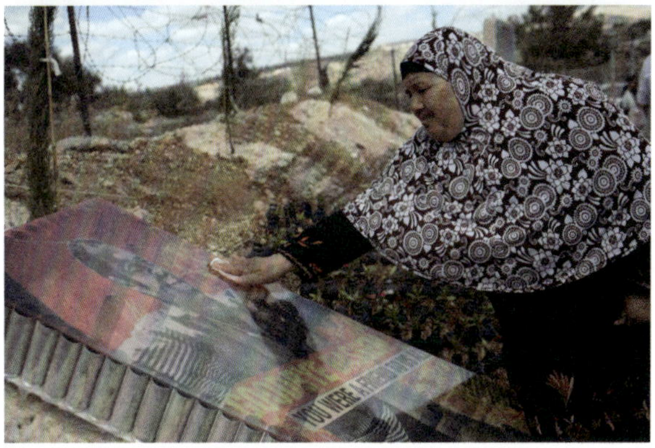

Fig. 6. Subhiya Abu Rahmah, the mother of Bassem, and his brother Ashraf pose for a portrait in front of their home, 7.4.2010
Fig. 7. Subhiya cleans the memorial monument to her son at a ceremony marking the eighth year of the popular struggle in Bil'in, 4.10.2013

The flat posters, banners, placards, and shields that enable the circulation of the images of Bassem Ibrahim Abu Rahmah, beyond their digital circulation online, demonstrate their roles as *tactile* signs and *material* objects rather than simply visual images that are read or consumed through contemplative spectatorship. This movement and transformation of the images can be best understood through anthropologist Christopher Pinney's concept of "surfacism" as part of his work on Indian and African popular postcolonial photography. Pinney argues that through preoccupation with the materiality of the image and its surface, "the photographic image becomes a site for the self-fashioning of postcolonial identities."[15] These practices challenge colonialist mobilizations of photography as part of administrative and identificatory strategies of surveillance and control of colonized populations, by redefining the photograph not as a "neutral" or "transparent" window onto the world, but as "a surface, a ground, on which presences that look out toward the viewer can be built." This is what Pinney calls "visual decolonization" through which collage and montage techniques "transpose the focus of photographic images from the space between the image's window and its referents to the space between the images' surfaces and their beholders."[16] The meaning of these photographic images, emphasizes Pinney, cannot be attributed solely to their status as indexical traces of "past events," rather they become, spatially and materially, multilayered and complex artifacts that are open to multiple acts of inscription and repetition. The movement and transformation of Activestills' photographs (by *both* their subjects and viewers) into complex material objects and tactile surfaces, further supports Pinney's argument

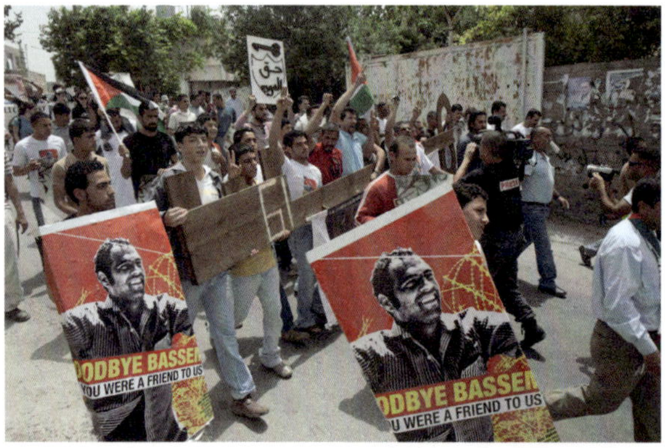

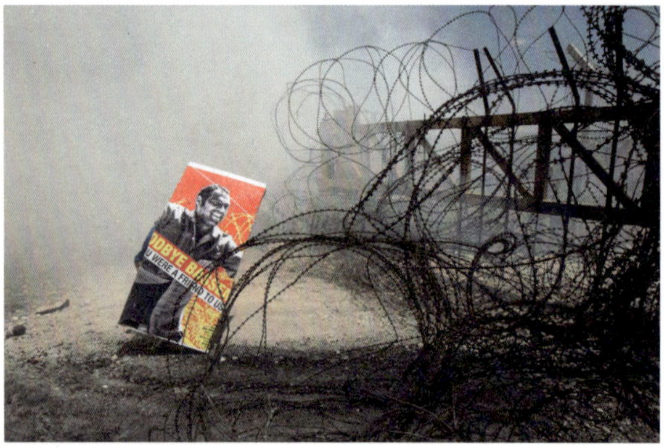

Fig. 8. Protesters marching with carton shields, Bil'in, 15.5.2009
Fig. 9. A protester in a cloud of tear gas, Bil'in, 29.5.2009

because these images are not simply irrefutable fixed "documents" (photographs *of* protest), but *active* components in a collective political struggle (*protesting photographs*), which acquire their meanings and roles through their multiple "afterlives" as means of survival for specific communities whose lives are marked by precarity and continuous exposure to violence.

Affective Communities

In their movement and circulation, Activestills' photographs mark a new threshold in the history of documentary photography. While their images are often gestural and dramatic due to the confrontational and violent nature of the events they depict, they refrain from any visual iconographic rhetoric of suffering and destitution. These images are not meant to solicit emotions such as empathy, compassion, shame, or guilt or to "shock" the viewer, but to disrupt the "affective economies" through which, as part of Israel's segregation policies, the Palestinians are constituted as vulnerable "disposable" non-subjects. In her book *The Cultural Politics of Emotion*, Sara Ahmed argues that emotions are not interiorized characteristics of individual or collective bodies but what operates through specific forms of circulation to "make" or "shape" the surfaces and boundaries of bodies. She shows that emotions suggest *contact* not essence, that is, what individuals feel toward objects or subjects depends not on their qualities (good or bad), but on whether they are perceived as beneficial or harmful to them. "Contact involves the subject, as well as histories that come before the subject. If emotions are shaped by contact with objects, rather than being caused by objects, then emotions are not simply 'in' the subject or the object." Having an emotion thus means associating it with "the very affect of one surface upon another, an affect that leaves its mark or trace. So not only do I have an impression of others, but they also leave me with an impression; they impress me, and impress upon me."[17]

This suggests that emotions cannot be reduced to bodily sensations because they involve thought and judgment toward another body's capacities. Ahmed points out that while one tends to think about emotions as immediate sensorial or bodily reactions this, in itself, is not a mark of a lack of mediation. Contacts are shaped by histories which determine (re)actions or relations of attraction and repulsion in relation to subjects and objects, and involve "affective forms of reorientation" or "affective economies" through which emotions are attached to or subtracted from collective subjects through their accumulated histories of circulation. Thus, rather than residing in groups or individuals, emotions are operative because they "produce the very surfaces and boundaries that allow the individual and the social to be delineated as if they are objects."[18] Ahmed's analysis suggests that emotions *do things* as part of specific economies through which concrete values accumulate, and constitute certain bodies *as* vulnerable and immobile. Emotions *bind* subjects together by delimiting them from those who are considered non-subjects.

Ahmed's reformulation of emotions as accumulated social affects adds support to Lee and LiPuma's argument that circulation processes do not simply transmit preexisting meanings, but function as constitutive cultural forces with their own identitarian forms of abstraction and evaluation. It also further explains the operative aspects of Activestills' images because their aim is not to "represent" the Palestinians as "Others" and in this way to trigger empathy toward them, but to repartition and realign material and perceptual divisions and demarcations so that "those who have no part" can be *recognized* as subjects of political rights who are entitled to support and protection from violence. This motivation becomes particularly evident in the images' mode of production. The collective members include Israelis *and* Palestinians as well as Europeans and Americans. And when photographing the demonstrations in the West Bank, Activestills' Israeli members always stand on the Palestinian side opposite the Israeli soldiers, thus forcing them to acknowledge political solidarity that undermines the racist partition of space **[Figs. 10, 11]**. The very presence of Israeli demonstrators in Bil'in complicates the exclusive infliction of violence and is meant to counter precarity with support and care. Thus, alongside images that show exposure to violence, Activestills photographs also focus on images of Israeli, Palestinian, and international solidarity, as well as on collective care **[Figs. 12–14]**. The images emphasize interdependency and contact in order to reorient and counter the "affective economies" through which the boundaries between surfaces and bodies are created in a way that constitutes the Palestinian bodies as vulnerable and immobile and the Israelis as armored and active **[pp. 194–95]**. In this way precarity becomes a common condition that realigns political subjects rather than separates them, while solidarity is configured as a political weapon *and* as the underlying condition for the production of images of struggle.

The effort to repartition and realign material and perceptual divisions also underlies Activestills' modes of public display of their images, as writers in this collection point out.[19] The collective frequently organize exhibitions in public spaces in major cities in Palestine/Israel and in the spaces where the struggles for rights take place. The motivation behind these street exhibitions is not simply to expose the "secret" of the occupation, but to reorient the way it is presented and conceptualized by intervening in the spatial organization of power according to which Israeli citizens enjoy the rights of movement and protection while these rights are withheld from the Palestinians. To bring

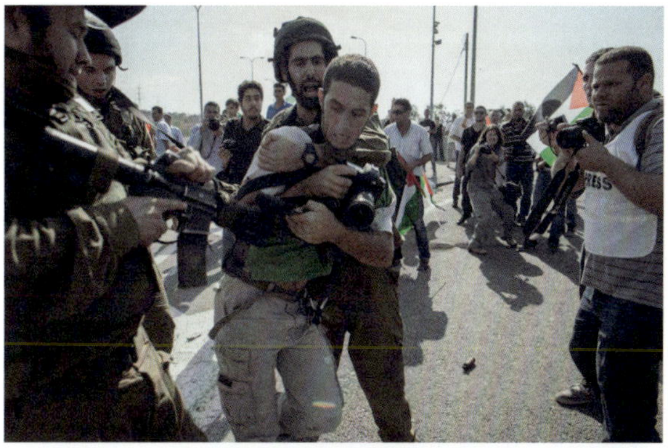

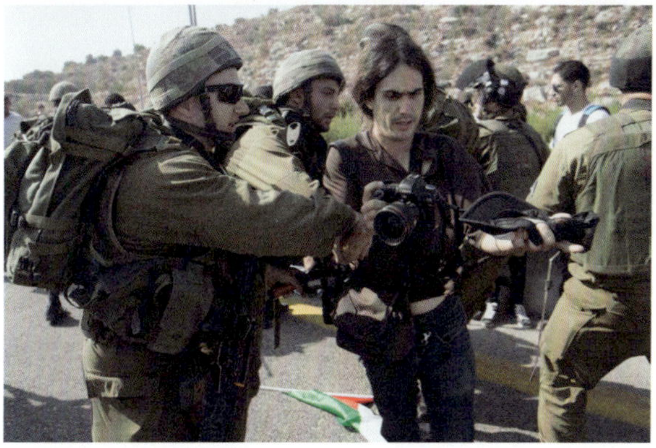

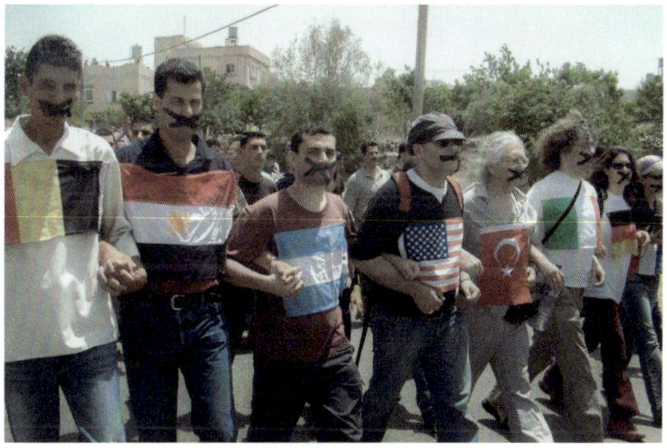

Fig. 10. Israeli soldiers try to arrest Activestills photographer Yotam Ronen at a protest against settler violence, 16.10.2012 / **Fig. 11.** Israeli soldiers try to arrest Activestills photographer Oren Ziv during the same action noted above / **Fig. 12.** Palestinian and Israeli protesters march with flags of different states, calling for international intervention against the construction of the Israeli separation wall, 20.5.2005

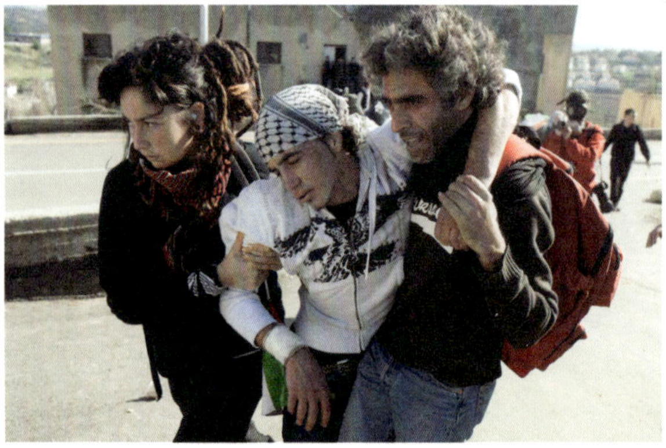

Fig. 13. Protesters help a fellow Palestinian activist injured by a rubber bullet during a protest in Nabi Saleh, West Bank, 22.1.2010

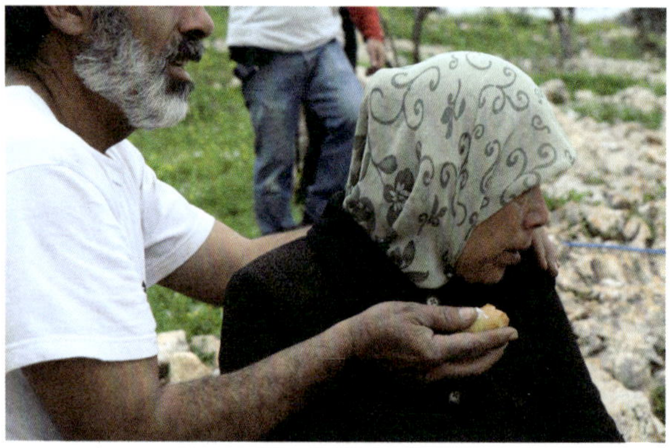

Fig. 14. A Palestinian activist helped by her husband after inhaling tear gas, Bil'in, 23.2.2007

Bil'in to Tel Aviv in the form of street exhibitions means changing the medium of public address and communication platform as a way to materially and perceptually demonstrate what Ahmed defines as the affect of one surface upon another, an affect that leaves its mark or trace on both sides of the conflict. These public displays thus counter the general convenient view that the violence of the occupation leaves no trace outside the West Bank. Instead they suggest dependency and the recognition that rights that are not *shared* cannot be defined as rights at all since the very notion of human rights is politically intelligible only as a general and universal condition. Appropriating rights exclusively to oneself abolishes the very ground on which political and ethical claims can be made.

These strategies of production and display differentiate Activestills' photographs from other major photographic projects depicting political demonstrations, such as Chris Marker's book and exhibition *Staring Back* (2007), or Allan Sekula's slide projection and book *Waiting for Tear Gas* (1999-2000).[20] These photographic projects document resistance but they are not meant to enable and actively reinforce political agency or to propagate struggle. They are more representational than performative because they are ultimately meant to be looked at and not to be *used* by specific communities as part of an effort to intervene in the partitions and "affective economies" through which the boundaries between subjects are made. While Marker's and Sekula's images register how the condition of collectivity can be elusive and dispersive, and therefore ultimately unrepresentable, Activestills' photographs take part in the formation of *specific* protesting communities and their struggles. Their images are meant to be touched, held, carried, and worn and, in this way, to trigger and propagate affects between, and through, bodily gestures and acts.

In conclusion, the significance of Activestills photographs lies not in their "documentary" or indexical "evidentiary" status, but precisely in the opening of a space that questions political, social, and perceptual partitions as these manifest themselves in normative frames of violence and the affective economies these produce. Their photographic work suggests that understanding photography's role within contemporary global visual culture necessitates a shift in the frame and the ends of analysis within the theory and history of photography—from problems of reference to those of circulation and transmission; from notions of irrefutable (indexical) authentication to ones of belief and accumulative affects; and finally, from the focus on images and their institutional "constructed" modes of representation to an analysis of their performative modes of reinscription through which political forms of agency are both contested and made possible in the current moment.

1. Judith Butler, *Frames of War: When is Life Grievable* (London and New York: Verso, 2010).
2. Margaret Olin, *Touching Photographs* (Chicago, IL: University of Chicago Press, 2012); Ariella Azoulay, *The Civil Contract of Photography*, trans. Rela Mazali and Ruvik Danieli (New York: Zone Books, 2008), and her more recent *Civil Imagination: A Political Ontology of Photography* (London: Verso, 2012); Thomas Keenan, "Mobilizing Shame," *The South Atlantic Quarterly* 103:2/3 (spring/summer 2004): 435–49.
3. Keenan, "Mobilizing Shame," 435.
4. Georges Didi-Huberman, "The Surviving Image: Aby Warburg and Tylorian Anthropology," *Oxford Art Journal* 25:1 (2002): 59–70.
5. See the essays collected in Aby Warburg, *The Renewal of Pagan Antiquity: Contributions to the Cultural History of European Renaissance*, trans. David Britt (Los Angeles, CA: Getty Research Institute for the History of Art and the Humanities, 1999). See also Aby Warburg, *Images from the Region of the Pueblo Indians of North America*, trans. Michael P. Steinberg (Ithaca, NY: Cornell University Press, 1995).
6. See Nicholas Mirzoeff's introduction to the third edition of *The Visual Studies Reader* (London and New York: Routledge, 2013). See also W.J.T. Mitchell's essay in the collection, "There are No Visual Media," in which he argues that visual culture needs to move beyond the emphasis on the visual and the "scopic wars" into "a more productive critical space, one in which we would study the intricate braiding and nesting of the visual with the other senses, reopen art history to the expanded field of images and visual practices which was the prospect envisioned by Warburgean art history": ibid., 13.
7. Judith Butler, *Frames of War*, 21.
8. Ibid., 2–3.
9. Judith Butler, "Bodies in Alliance and the Politics of the Street," in *Sensible Politics: The Visual Culture of Nongovernmental Politics*, eds. Meg McLagan and Yates McKee (New York: Zone Books, 2012), 124.
10. Ibid., 120.
11. Ibid., 124.
12. Bil'in is an agricultural village of about 1,800 residents that is located twelve kilometers west of the city of Ramallah in the West Bank. Since the 1980s about 55 percent of Bil'in's agricultural lands have been confiscated for the construction of Modi'in Illit settlement. In 2005, Israel began constructing a separation wall on Bil'in land cutting the village in half, its houses on one side and agricultural lands on the other, in order to put Modi'in on the Israeli side of the wall.
13. Benjamin Lee and Edward LiPuma, "Cultures of Circulation: The Imaginations of Modernity," *Public Culture* 14:1 (winter 2002): 192.
14. On victimization in relation to documentary photography, see Martha Rosler's canonical essay "In, Around, and Afterthoughts (on Documentary Photography)," in *The Contest of Meaning*, ed. Richard Bolton (Cambridge, MA: The MIT Press, 1989), 303–40.
15. Christopher Pinney, "Notes from the Surface of the Image: Photography, Postcolonialism, and Vernacular Modernism," in *Photography's Other Histories*, eds. Christopher Pinney and Nicholas Peterson (Durham, NC and London: Duke University Press, 2003), 219.
16. Ibid., 219.
17. Sara Ahmed, *The Cultural Politics of Emotion* (New York: Routledge, 2004), 6.
18. Ibid., 10.
19. See Simon Faulkner's and Meir Wigoder's essays in this volume.
20. On Marker's book and exhibition *Staring Back*, see my essay "Towards a New Image of Politics: Chris Marker's *Staring Back*," *Oxford Art Journal* 33:1 (March 2010): 81–101; on Sekula's slide projection and book, see Benjamin J. Young, "On Strike: Allan Sekula's Waiting for Tear Gas," in *Sensible Politics: The Visual Culture of Nongovernmental Politics*, eds. Meg McLagan and Yates McKee (New York: Zone Books, 2012), 149–81.

Bil'in, West Bank 18.2.2011

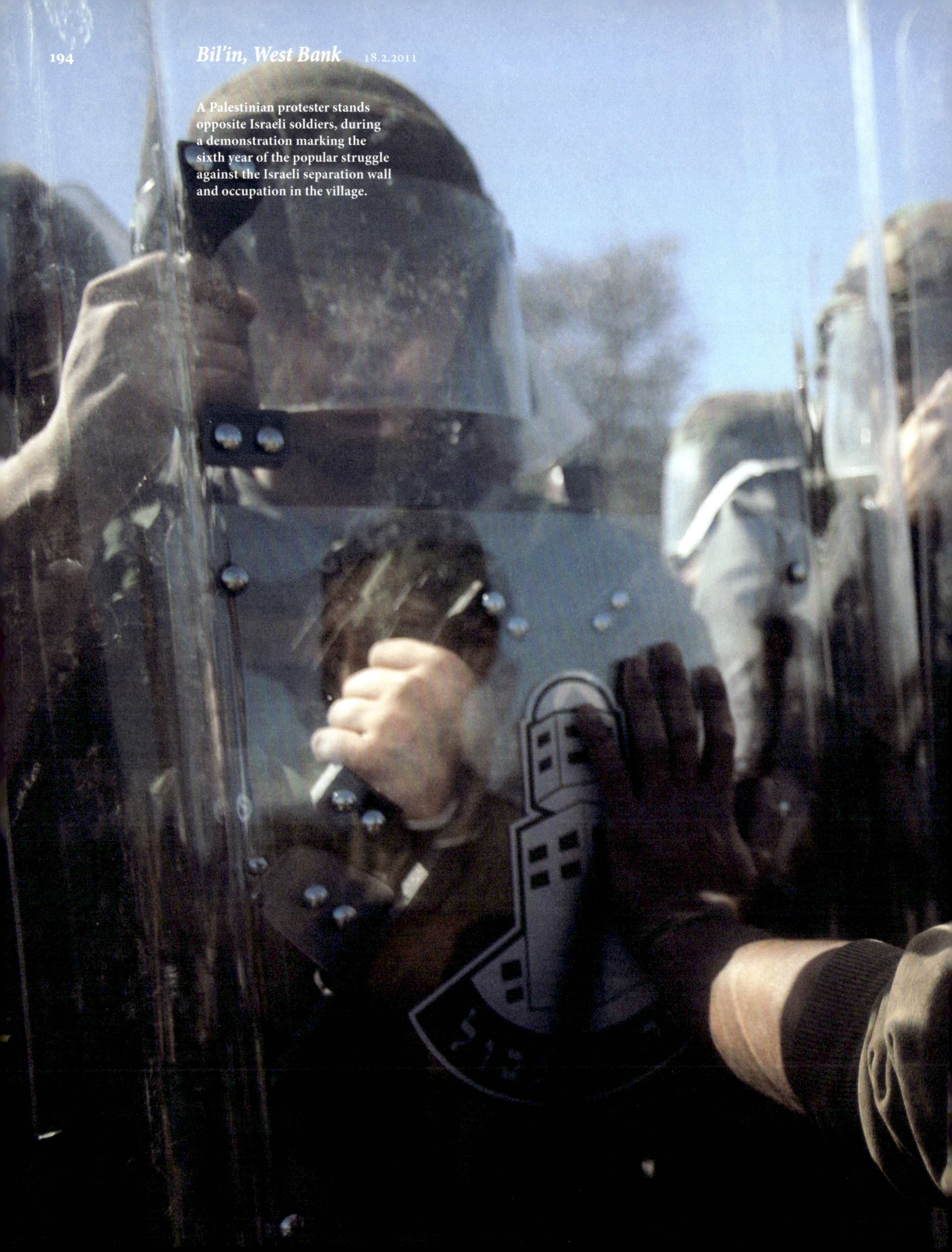

A Palestinian protester stands opposite Israeli soldiers, during a demonstration marking the sixth year of the popular struggle against the Israeli separation wall and occupation in the village.

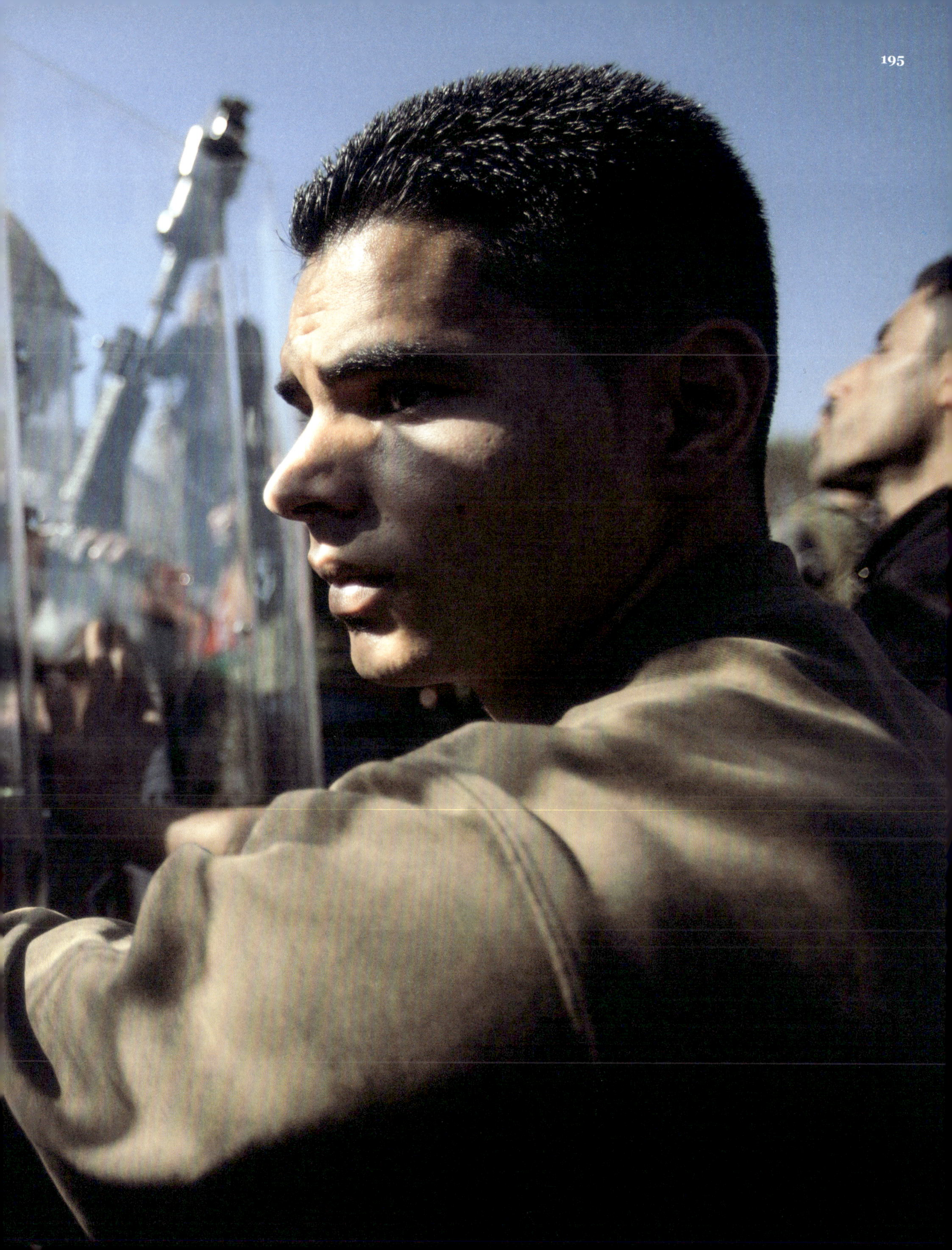

Communities of Touch: Photography's Spaces of Appearance

Meir Wigoder

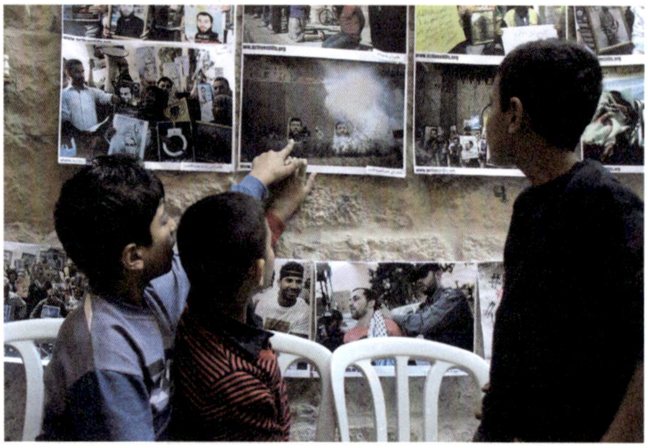

Fig. 1. An Activestills exhibition displayed near the house of the Palestinian hunger-striker Hassan Safadi, in tribute to his release from Israeli prison, Nablus, West Bank, 29.10.2012

From where should one start writing about the subject of *photographic-activism*? From what sound bite can one start to discern the way by which mute photographs make the speech acts resonate of political protests, social gatherings, sit-ins, and marches of the disenfranchised, occupied, and undocumented citizens who desperately want to be heard? At first, my inclination was to write about the role that vigilance plays in the witnessing activities of the Activestills collective. I then came across photographs in their archive that show how they exhibit their own work in public spaces during scenes of protest and how their photos are used by protestors for demonstrative purposes in order to call attention to their struggles.[1] These photos posed a critical challenge for me. I wanted to find a way to explain how photographs become *performative* once they *re-appear* in public spaces of protest, in which the demonstrators become the spectators of their own actions that had been documented in previous acts of protest.

Once I understood that I was interested in the ways by which Activestills make records of their own work, just as artists do in site-specific installations that will not last forever, I needed to rethink the photographic paradigm by which to study the subject. I realized that it was neither the topics of the Activestills testimonies that I should investigate (even though they are significant documents of Israeli human rights violations), nor the qualities of their photographs per se (which are excellent by any photojournalistic standards); rather, I should start by making a theoretical distinction between *witnessing* (an act of observing and documenting reality by bystanders) and *displaying* (a curatorial act in which photographs are chosen to be shown to a public that is imagined in advance). Under such circumstances, it is also important to distinguish between exhibitions that take place in urban spaces in which pedestrians pass by randomly, and photographic displays that are created as an act of solidarity with a community whose members are protesting and demanding their civic rights [Fig. 1]. We must also distinguish between the act of *showing* (in which subjects within the photographs are holding and displaying images and slogans to call attention to their political demands), and the act of *recording* (in which photos are presented within photos), which attests to the way in which Activestills document their activities. Here the emphasis is on the way their own photographs are exhibited in public and displayed on banners during scenes of protest; such records are somewhat reminiscent of the way filmmakers make production stills of their work in order to attest reflexively to the process of filmmaking and in order to publicize their work.

All the above lead me to the main focus of the essay: the attempt to understand how the performative act of displaying photos creates a sense of *communality*, in which the subjects of the photos become spectators of their own struggle upon viewing the photo exhibitions presented to them in public spaces during further scenes of protest and social gatherings. Following are some examples of the way in which Activestills have circulated, exhibited, and documented their own work: 1. In the village of Bil'in, Palestinian civic protest against the construction of the Israeli separation wall has been prolonged and has relied on rituals of performance to which both the Palestinian demonstrators and the Israeli soldiers adhere. The Palestinian and foreign activists use Activestills photos of their struggle for PR purposes on their own websites: in a demonstration to support a legal injunction against the construction of the wall on Palestinian lands in Bil'in, demonstrators placed Activestills photos on placards and displayed images of the wall and the disputed terrain as visual evidence outside the court. 2. Photographs of demolished houses in Bedouin communities, in the south of Israel, were handed to the local Bedouin not only in order to use them in demonstrations and for PR purposes, but also in order to keep count of how many homes had been destroyed in the Negev, as many of these actions were not reported by the commercial media. 3. Their photographs of Israeli youth refusing to enlist in the army (portraits and records of the day they turned up to enter prison, and the demonstrations outside the prison calling for their release) were also displayed in support of conscientious objectors as part of a symposium on the subject. 4. Their photos have been displayed on the Israeli separation wall during an exhibition to mark the fortieth anniversary of the Israeli occupation of the West Bank and Gaza in 1967 [pp. 78–79]. 5. Other exhibitions were set up in rallies organized by refugees from Eritrea and Darfur who were demanding to not be repatriated and to receive a legal permit to remain in Israel [Figs. 2, 3].

Once we focus on the photos that are records of the way Activestills display their work, we realize that we must also shift our discussion from the *subject/object* relations of vision to a discussion of the *seeing/showing, witnessing/displaying* paradigms in photography. Such a shift leads to a surprising understanding: these kinds of records that mirror the act of witnessing, being witnessed, and observing the actions of civic protest, have no resonances in the modern narcissistic practices of photography and art. Instead of the expectation we have from seeing photos-within-photos, which leads to effects of *duplication* and *repetition* (these are mainly associated with the *mise en abyme* effects in art, in which the ground of the image is undone by a vertiginous and dizzying effect that places in question the integrity of the surface and the entire existence of the object), we have, in our case, a reflexive act that takes on a political turn: the duplication of photos-within-photos only strengthens the impact of the evidence by showing us that photographs are not passive objects. Indeed, in the hands of the subjects that are protesting for their civic rights, they become weapons that can *face us* and challenge our moral and ideological beliefs. The internal and external mirroring play of photos-within-photos makes us realize their critical and political value: if we were to employ a *rhythm-analysis* (to use Henry Lefebvre's term that defines how spatial trajectories and tempos of pedestrians can indicate the urban socio-economic relations of particular areas of a city) for such displays of photos in relation to how they influence their spectators, we would be able to analyze how different locations, divergent backgrounds, and a variety of methods for hanging photos on street walls, fences, and tents, attest to the ways in which public spaces have been taken over for a brief period for a purpose they were never intended to serve in daily life.[2]

I now turn briefly to theory in order to understand how such spaces facilitate political and social gatherings

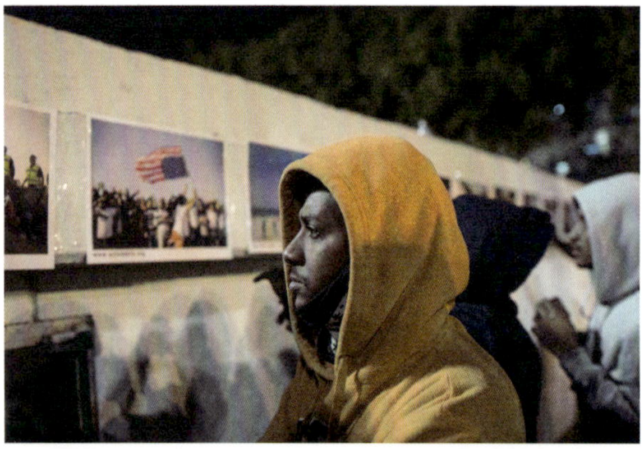

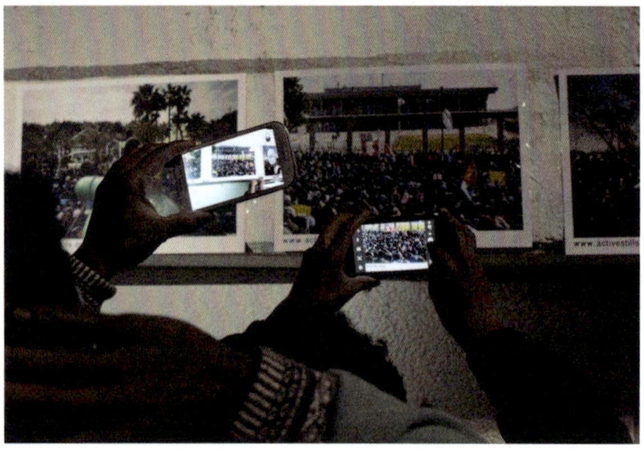

Figs. 2-3. African asylum seekers look at an Activestills exhibition in Levinsky Park, Tel Aviv, 3.2.2014

in which photos are displayed. In *The Human Condition,* Hannah Arendt contrasts the intimate private realm (which is related to the family and to solitary thoughts that get expressed outwardly via storytelling and conversing) to the public realm (which is characterized by everything that is seen and heard by everybody). The spaces of appearance are formed by different kinds of group gatherings, and especially by the sharing of speech and action, which give people a sense of purpose and power. The following passage cited from Arendt's book provides the basis for discussing the representation of group gatherings in the Activestills photos:

> The space of appearance comes into being whenever men are together in the manner of speech and action, and therefore predates all formal constitution of the public realm and the various forms of government, that is the various forms in which the public realm can be organized. Its peculiarity is that, unlike the spaces which are the work of our hands, it does not survive the actuality of the movement which brought it into being, but disappears not only with the dispersal of men—as in the case of great catastrophes when the body politic of a people is destroyed—but with the disappearance or arrest of the activities themselves. Wherever people gather together, it is potentially there, but only potentially, not necessarily and not forever.[3]

There are two principal points here that can serve our topic of analysis. First, Arendt does not consider the role of space and place as a condition for the creation of spaces of appearance. Second, a crucial point is that the formation of such gatherings relies on *simultaneity* and on the dispersed *potentiality* of the gatherings that makes such exchanges of speech and action temporary and transient.

In Judith Butler's essay, "Bodies in Alliance and the Politics of the Street," Arendt's thoughts on the emergence of *spaces of appearance* are redefined in the context of Butler's own interest in the performative body, especially in relation to the formations of the protesting crowds in the wake of the Arab Spring and the Occupy movements. She writes that "for politics to take place, the body must appear," and this can only take place through the recognition that our interaction in the public space is not only governed by a visual criterion of seeing each other but also by the way our voices and our actions define for each other the place where we share our actions: "who we are, bodily, is already a way of being 'for' the other, appearing in ways that we cannot see, being a body for another in a way that I cannot be for myself, and so dispossessed, perspectivally, by our very sociality." This entails reliance on the other's shared presence and on their gaze as well: "I must appear to others in ways for which I cannot give an account, and in this way my body establishes a perspective that I cannot inhabit."[4]

Butler parts from Arendt's definition of the spaces of appearance in one major respect: she argues that the space where groupings are formed does matter. One must ask, therefore, how such a plurality of persons is formed: "who enters this plurality, and who does not, and how are such matters decided?" Likewise, one must ask "where are we when we appear?" which leads to the idea that "the body, defined politically, is precisely organized by a perspective that is not one's own and is, in that sense, already elsewhere, for another, and so in departure from oneself."[5] The specific choices of locations for such gatherings are crucial for establishing the meaning of the events. A great many locations chosen by Occupy and other revolutionary gatherings in the Arab Spring were selected because they had highly symbolic meanings for the sovereign powers against which the demonstrators were rebelling. Butler writes that:

... the bodies on the street redeploy the space of appearance in order to contest and negate the existing forms of political legitimacy .... These are subjugated and empowered actors who seek to wrest legitimacy from an existing state apparatus that depends upon the public space of appearance for its theatrical self-constitution.[6]

In addition, we must mention Jean-Luc Nancy's thoughts on the subject, which also take into consideration Arendt's writings on our topic.[7] The way in which Butler uses the word "together," in her description of the way social gatherings and political protests are formed, resonates, albeit differently, with the way Jean Luc-Nancy characterizes the "Spectacle of Society," in his book *Being Singular Plural*. Here the word "together" is replaced by the notion of "we," which raises similar questions to those Butler addressed: What type of space and time does this "we" encompass? Is it something globalized, amorphous, and general, or does it rely on an assembly of persons in a concrete place that makes the participants *simultaneously* visible to each other? Nancy writes that "We can never simply be 'the we,' understood as a unique subject, or understood as an indistinct 'we' that is like a diffuse generality. 'We' always expresses a plurality, expresses 'our' being divided and entangled." This "we" has theatrical connotations as well. However, it "is not a stage in the sense of an artificial space of mimetic representation" but "in the sense of the opening of a space-time for the distribution of singularities, each of whom singularly plays the unique and plural role of 'self' or the 'being-self.'" [8] It is important to make clear that this self is not an individual that exists prior to the formation of the community, and not the self that exists in the private realm, in contrast to the public realm, in the Arendtian sense. Singularity, for Nancy, exists only in relation to the way in which we first of all exist for each other, and in relation to each other, even if no direct contact is made between us in the spaces we share. In other words, each one exists only in relation to the multiplicity of other singularities that share a *common being* and a *co-presence* in the world. Nancy puts it in this way:

Being gives itself as singular plural and, in this way, organizes itself as its own stage. We present the "I" to ourselves, to one another, just as "I," each time, present the "we" to us, to one another. In this sense, there is no society without a spectacle; or more precisely, there is no society without the spectacle of society.[9]

I want to coin the term "communities of touch" here in order to define the ways in which communal gestures make us aware of being together, in contact and in separation, just as our skin defines the limits of our bodies in a shared world. Under such circumstances, even our gazes and voices can touch each other in a sense of solidarity during formation of the protests and social gatherings that often take place spontaneously and dissipate just as quickly. Touching also resonates with several aspects of the cultural and political climate of the country I live in. First, the bodily proximity between people, in which speech and action prevails, is far closer in Middle-Eastern societies than in other Western countries; speech often includes gestures of touching even if the interlocutor is a stranger to us. Second, touching can also abruptly erupt as a form of violence that testifies to the heated emotional climate of a conflictual society that is becoming less and less tolerant. Finally, in the context of the Activestills "production stills," as I prefer to call them, it refers to how the spectators of their exhibitions tend to point at and touch photos with a degree of familiarity and irreverence, in contrast to the more sterile prevailing practice of viewing images in private galleries and museums, where the approach is based on the warning "Do Not Touch." Even more significantly, the act of solidarity in which Activestills pursue sharing their photos with the subjects of the struggles they document, shows how photos are no longer singular commodity objects but actually turn into forms of leaflets that are distributed by hands, pasted on walls with brushes, held up over the heads of protesters in demonstrations, and displayed in locations that have never been used before for such exhibition purposes. For this reason, one is unable to look at the *records* of the Activestills photo-displays without being literally moved by the variety of gestures that point, hold, hang, and paste photos on many different types of surfaces.

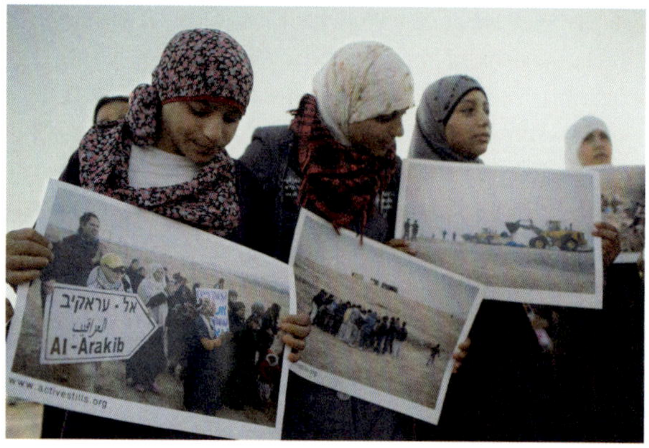

Fig. 4. Residents of Al-Araqib hold Activestills photographs at the protest marking one year since the demolition of the entire village by the Israeli authorities, Lehavim Junction, Negev, Israel, 27.7.2011

In their archival records, we can isolate gestural notations upon the "music sheet" of spectatorial encounters, as the subjects of the photos look at their own actions being depicted in the exhibited photos: groups of refugees from Darfur and Eritrea are seen walking along a prison fence at Holot, where refugees are incarcerated, as they look at photographs that hang on the fence and reveal highlights from previous acts of protests in which they had demanded their freedom and right to be recognized as political refugees [**pp. 11–12**]. Some stop by the photos and point at faces that they may have recognized. By doing so, they enact the indexical gesture of the finger that represents the photographic deictic on which all testimony relies. Hands hold mobile phones to photograph some of the exhibited photos in another exhibition organized in south Tel Aviv for the refugees—their camera gestures appropriate the displayed photographs as acts of ownership over the images in order to send and share the photos with friends. Other photographs are hung on a washing line in a large tent that has been erected to welcome a Palestinian hunger striker released from jail. The photographs are hanging because the tent has no proper walls, and this reminds us of the Israeli Army tent camps that have been converted into spaces of confinement for administrative detention prisoners, who never know when they might be released. Hanging photographs, in which pegs are used as weights at the bottom of the photos to stabilize and straighten the images on display, evoke the quintessential impression of touch, denoting the flimsy existence of the images in a makeshift space that has been set up to welcome the guests who will form groups of sociability and will then disperse.

I focus now on a single image as an example of how we can analyze other Activestills photographs that contain their own photos: a group of Bedouin girls are holding Activestills photos during a demonstration commemorating the demolition of Al-Araqib village in the Negev, in southern Israel [**Fig. 4**]. My attention is drawn to the gestures of the Bedouin girls who are not holding up the photographs as is customary in demonstrations, but are actually clutching them closer to their bodies. The three girls are seen slightly from below, which accentuates their faces and the photos they hold against the backdrop of the sky. The perspective creates the impression that the photos in their hands are touching each other and even appear to overlap (this almost resembles an amateur panorama, created by joining photographs of a similar location along the same horizon line.) One girl, in the center, is distracted because she is looking to see what photograph her friend is holding, and her own photograph is consequently slightly skewed. By looking sideways, she reminds us that it is impossible both to display a photograph and also to see it. In other words, just as the girls cannot both act and see themselves protesting, and thus they need their *co-presence* in order to share their own space of appearance, so the photographer cannot see himself viewing the protest, and thus the act of photographing one's own photos is a reflexive act that calls attention to the photographer's presence too. To put it differently, it is not only the photographer who is providing the Bedouin girls with the sense of their own presence in the scene; it is also their act of displaying the Activestills photos that enables the photographer to feel that he, or she, is taking part in the event.

The two photos being held on the right side of the image show the actual event of the destruction of Al-Araqib village: one photo, furthest right, shows a bulldozer participating in the act of destroying a home in a village of 300 inhabitants and an estimated 46 buildings.[10] In the center photo, held by the girl who is slightly distracted, a group of people are huddled in the location where the demolitions are taking place. The round shape they form with their bodies reminds us that even if homes are destroyed, the *body politics* and gestures of a community can create their own physical insignia to show that they intend to remain steadfast in their struggle to save their lands. The idea of an *absently present* community is especially represented in the third photo, held by the Bedouin girl on the left side of the image: in the photo, we see a person holding a mock state highway sign during a demonstration against the destruction of the Bedouin village. The state highway sign, in Hebrew, Arabic, and English, reads "Al Arakib" and is meant to remind us, both symbolically and concretely, that such signposts do not exist for dozens of Bedouin communities that are considered as "unrecognized villages," because the Israeli state has claimed its own ownership of these lands and does not recognize the Bedouin's legal claims on it. Consequently, these villages are not on official maps, they have no paved roads leading to them, and they have no running water or electricity. In sum, we are presented with a multi-layered photograph that condenses on its surface (not as a palimpsest) a *simultaneous* co-existence of different terrains and gestures that contrast signs of destruction and of protest: horizontal patches of a desert that has been flattened by bulldozers and the upright postures of protesters that show how communities remain committed to their struggle during acts of state violence. To reiterate, the plurality of spaces of *co-appearance*, in the several photos that are displayed separately in a single location of protest, highlight a *timeline* of the Bedouin's endless struggle over their disputed lands.

In sum, I want to remind the reader that the main theme of this essay has been how Activestills record the formations of the spaces of appearances, which are partly created by the curatorial gestures of exhibiting their photos in social and political gatherings. *The communities of touch*, as I refer to the gestures that create connections between the exhibited photos and the social gatherings, could not be understood without the references to Arendt's, Butler's, and Nancy's writings on the *spaces of appearance* and the *spectacle of society* (but not *the society of the spectacle*). I have chosen not to discuss, for lack of space, a significant keyword that features in the three theoretical texts: "*between*" denotes the spaces among "men," "bodies," and "singularities" that signify the essence by which everyone comes together but each one also remains separate. This is not in any way similar to the way in which some theorists have discussed the character of *fusional crowds*.[11] For Arendt, the groupings of people in the space of appearance, through speech and action, rely on what lies "between them"; for Butler, the performative power of demonstrations must take into account the spacing "between bodies"; while Nancy's notion of "co-appearance" relies on the in-between that connects and separates singularities by means of actions and inaction, as they stand *side-by-side* and do not even have to look at each other.

The notion of *between* can be a useful term to summarize and characterize the work of Activestills: First, their curatorial decisions involve hanging photos side-by-side, which influences the way in which the spectators look at them. For example, rather than favoring the single iconic photograph as an exemplar of the news event, they prefer to display several photos in deliberate arrangements, as in the photojournalistic *photo-essay*. In many of their street exhibits, they have adopted the grid format for hanging photos: here, the spacings play a crucial role in creating an overall effect that relies on the relations obtaining between the photos and not on any particular image. Second, the logic of the grid exists in the digital archive as well: here, the photos are arranged as thumbnails in a tier system that relies on categories, dates, and subjects that receive a different meaning once they have been uploaded and stored as historical documents rather than as singular testimonies of political events. Likewise, the collective character of Activestills encompasses a relationship between the individuals and the group: on the one hand it has to accommodate the different agendas and particular styles of each photographer, while on the other hand these have to be committed to a similar political goal. In sum, my correlation between the *in-between* spaces of gatherings, the formal *spacings* of photos in exhibitions, the *thumbnail* photos in the archive, and the *aggregate* character of a photographic collective, can be compared to how Butler describes the interaction of bodies in street demonstrations: "No one body establishes the space of appearance, but this action, this performative exercise happens only 'between' bodies, in the space that constitutes the gap between my own body and another's"; and for this reason, "my body does not act alone, when it acts politically. Indeed, the action emerged from the 'between.'"[12]

I want to end by touching upon the overall subject of all the protests that Activestills have documented, and especially those in which their photos were used as part of a participatory action that evokes the solidarity of *being-in-common* with the subjects of the struggle. I take my cue from Jean-Luc Nancy's essay "Sharing Freedom: Equality, Fraternity, Justice," in which he notes the significance of the moment of the *initiality of freedom* that must always constitute a new form of beginning: "Freedom cannot be awarded, granted, or conceded according to a degree of maturity or some prior aptitude that would receive it. Freedom can only be taken: this is what the revolutionary tradition presents." Freedom is thus an "initiality of being" that sets things into position and relies on sharing "*in the space of relation*".[13] Nancy claims that "it is the simultaneous breaking into the interior of the individual and of the community, which opens the specific space-time of initiality."[14] I take this to mean, in the wake of the Arab Spring and the sporadically and unorganized Occupy movement sit-ins all over the world, that the spontaneous practices of being-in-common and the performative bodies forming interactive actions in street protests always rely on a contemporaneous moment that *each time* gives the impression of a new beginning that is meant to signal a revolutionary sign of hope for the future.

In light of all the above, I would like to propose a different grammatical tense for the type of *activist photography* I have been discussing: we must depart from Roland Barthes's *present-past* tense, which is typified by a verifiable index that is concerned with melancholy and memory. Nor do I exactly mean the *future conditional* tense, reflecting the hope that many of the photos of Activestills will remain in the archive to serve as documentary evidence of human rights violations at a future date, when they will provide evidence in international human rights courts of justice. In a more abstract sense, I believe that the *re-emergence* of the exhibited photos in the spaces of appearance functions as a beacon of future events that are yet to take place; or, in other words, they are actually moments of visitation from the future in the present that give us a sense of hope for changes that have failed to occur in the present—these moments represent the photographic tense of *what is to come.* Let me frame this point differently. Some writers have written disparagingly of the lack of changes in the aftermath of the Arab Spring and the Occupy Movement protests—democracy has not reached these Arab countries and, in the case of Occupy, the protests were not sufficiently focused. Other writers, in contrast, see in these events promising signs that rely on a different perspective of time: Nancy, for example, rejects the views of those who belittle the failure of past revolutions that have not brought about change, by arguing that a "revolution does not at all exclusively signify the taking of power by a political faction." Rather, it signifies "the opening of decision, the community exposed to itself."[15] Such abrupt and fragmented moments of communal exposure remind us that freedom is not simply a project to be embarked upon, not simply something to attain, not something governed only by conditions, but in fact is an affirmation of the very *hic et nunc* of the spirit of equality, freedom, and fraternity. For this reason, I believe that the crux of Activestills' contribution lies not only in their vigilant approach to testimony, but also and mainly in their sense of solidarity with their subjects, based on the politics of "initial freedom." Nancy characterizes such a revolutionary spirit and the yearning to share freedom as an action that always takes place on the surface of beginnings; in other words, the principle of sharing relies on the fact that "freedom cannot be finished."[16]

1. The photographs under discussion are stored in the Activestills archive under the following categories: "Activestills Exhibitions," "Activestills Street Exhibitions," "Photographs": http://www.activestills.org/archive.php.
2. See, for example, Henri Lefebvre, *Rhythm Analysis: Space, Time and Everyday Life* (London: Bloomsbury Revelations, 2003).
3. Hannah Arendt, *The Human Condition* (Chicago, IL: University of Chicago Press, 1998), 199.
4. Judith Butler, "Bodies in Alliance and the Politics of the Street," accessed 2.1.2016, http://www.eipcp.net/transversal/1011/butler/en.
5. Ibid.
6. Ibid.
7. For a comparison between Nancy's and Arendt's ideas on this subject and the sense in which Nancy's concept of sharing the world and "being-with" relates to Martin Heidegger's *Mitsein*, see Howard Caygill, "The Shared World—Philosophy, Violence, Freedom," in *Jean-Luc Nancy: The Sense of Philosophy*, eds. Darren Sheppard, Simon Sparks, and Colin Thomas (London: Routledge, 1997), 19–31.
8. Jean-Luc Nancy, *Being Singular Plural*, trans. Robert D. Richardson and Anne E. O'Byrne (Stanford, CA: Stanford University Press, 2000), 65 and 66.
9. Ibid., 67.
10. For more information on the demolition of Bedouin homes and the legal status of "unrecognized villages," see: http://972mag.com/tag/al-arakib/.
11. The idea of the fusional crowd is often related to ideas about the revolutionary crowd and to scenes of mobs and riots. The most well-known book on the subject is Elias Canetti, *Crowds and Power*, trans. Carol Stewart (New York: Farrar, Straus and Giroux 1984); a different approach that is far more relevant to the formation of the political crowds in relation to seriality is discussed by Jean-Paul Sartre. See Jean-Paul Sartre, *Critique of Dialectical Reason: Theory of Practical Ensembles*, trans. Alan Sheridan-Smith (London: NLB, 1976); 345–51; for a short commentary on "the group in fusion" and its relation to seriality, see Denis Hollier, *The Politics of Prose*, trans. Jeffrey Mehlman (Minneapolis: University of Minnesota Press), 29–33.
12. Butler, "Bodies in Alliance." On the relations between performativity, bodies, and demonstrations, see also Judith Butler and Athena Athanasiou, *Dispossession: The Performative in the Political* (Cambridge: Polity Press, 2013).
13. Emphasis added, MW. The relational space between bodies, which makes the action of freedom possible, is discussed by Butler in her interpretation of Arendt's text on the spaces of appearance: "Freedom does not come from me or you; it can and does happen as a relation between us or, indeed, among us. So this is not a matter of finding the human dignity within each person, but rather of understanding the human as a relational and social being, one whose action depends upon equality and articulates the principle of equality" (Butler, "Bodies in Alliance").
14. Jean-Luc Nancy, "Sharing Freedom: Equality, Fraternity, Justice," in *The Experience of Freedom*, trans. Bridget McDonald (Stanford, CA: Stanford University Press, 1993), 77 and 79.
15. Idem, "Fragments," *The Experience of Freedom*, 164.
16. Idem, "Sharing Freedom," 80. On the significance of beginnings, in relation to our need to act and insert our character among others through speech and action, see Hannah Arendt's *The Human Condition*, 175–218.

Holot Detention Center, Negev Desert, Israel 17.2.2014

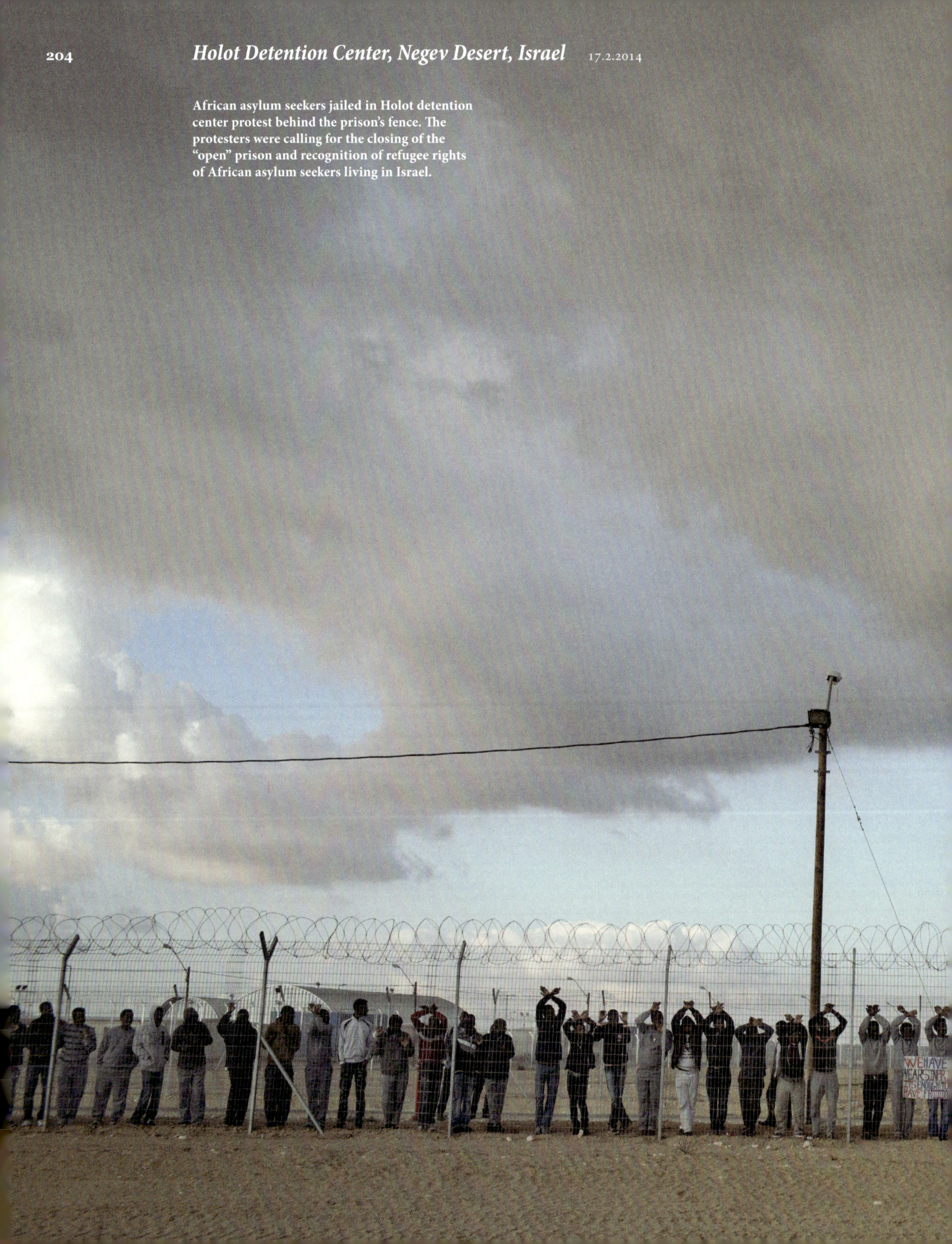

African asylum seekers jailed in Holot detention center protest behind the prison's fence. The protesters were calling for the closing of the "open" prison and recognition of refugee rights of African asylum seekers living in Israel.

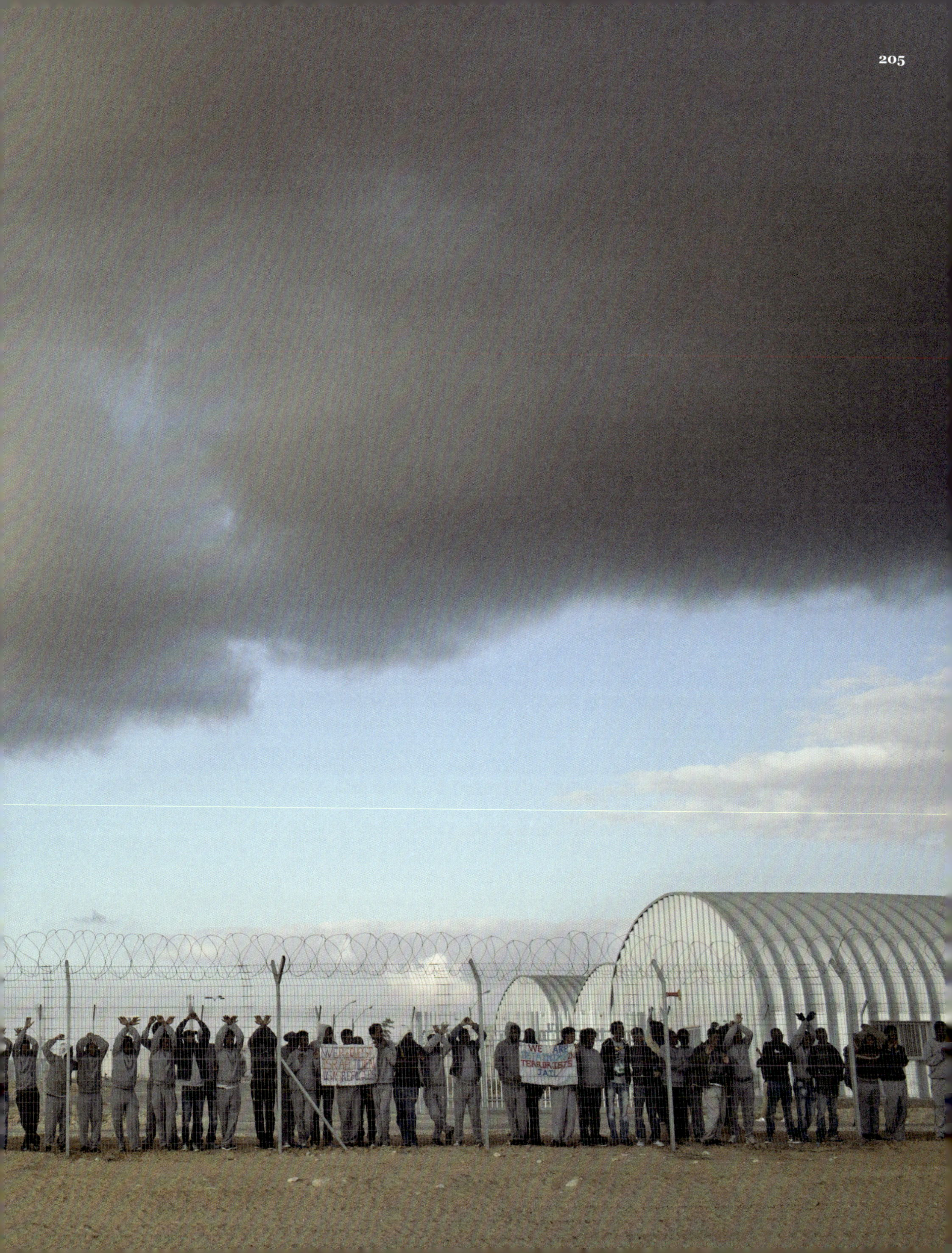
WE REQUEST
REFUGEES
WE ARE
TERRORISTS
JAIL

Before the Law

Sharon Sliwinski

I wonder what they dream about, these men who are trapped between worlds, unable to go forward and unable to go back. When night comes, do they dream of elsewhere? Does A.A.M.S. dream of his family: his mother, his wife, and his two children whom he last saw some years ago at the Kalma refugee camp in Darfur [**Fig. 1**]? Does his father, who was murdered by the Janjaweed, figure in his night visions? Or, after so many years of imprisonment, does one only dream of prison? Helplessness can weigh heavily on the soul. Solomon Hagos ruminates about the girl who was raped by the Bedouin smugglers who trafficked a group of his fellow Eritreans across Sinai; not the girl he managed to save from their lust, but the other one—the one who confided to him about what they did to her [**Fig. 2**]. Zerei Gebresilasi seems to have good reason to worry about the thoughts that come at night in this place which he can neither leave nor make a new home [**p. 208, top left**]: "There are people who have gone crazy here. In Saharonim prison at least you know that you have to stay in one place and you can't get out. Here, they give you the option to leave, but they tell you that you must come back."

"Here" is the Holot detention center—a so-called "open facility" that, like Saharonim, is located in the harsh, remote region of the Negev desert. Twice a week, African asylum seekers in Israel are summoned to a parking lot in Tel Aviv where they are loaded onto buses and driven inland to this detention center. Holot holds several thousand men, and most of them are from Sudan and Eritrea. These men are refugees who have fled torture, kidnapping, and worse in their countries of origin. All have been detained under Israel's recently amended Prevention of Infiltration Law, which defines all irregular border-crossers as "infiltrators." The original 1954 law was designed to prevent the reentry of Palestinian refugees. While the principal target of the amended law seems to have changed, its central character has not.

Holot is run jointly by the Israeli Prison Service and the Interior Ministry. By all accounts, the conditions in the center are terrible: the provisions are woefully inadequate, the rules and regulations—including twice-daily roll calls—are impossibly strict, and any violation can carry severe punishments, including transfer to other prisons.

In September 2014, the Israeli High Court of Justice ruled that Holot must be closed within 90 days

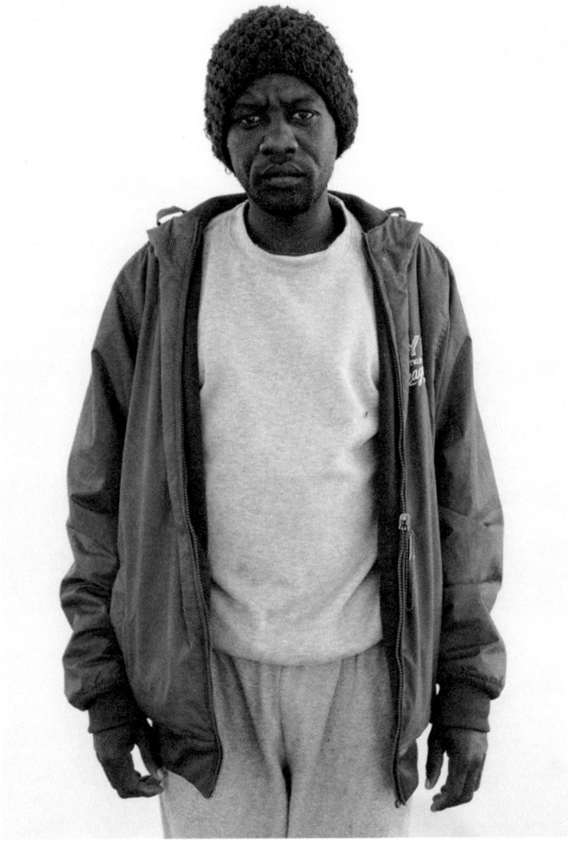

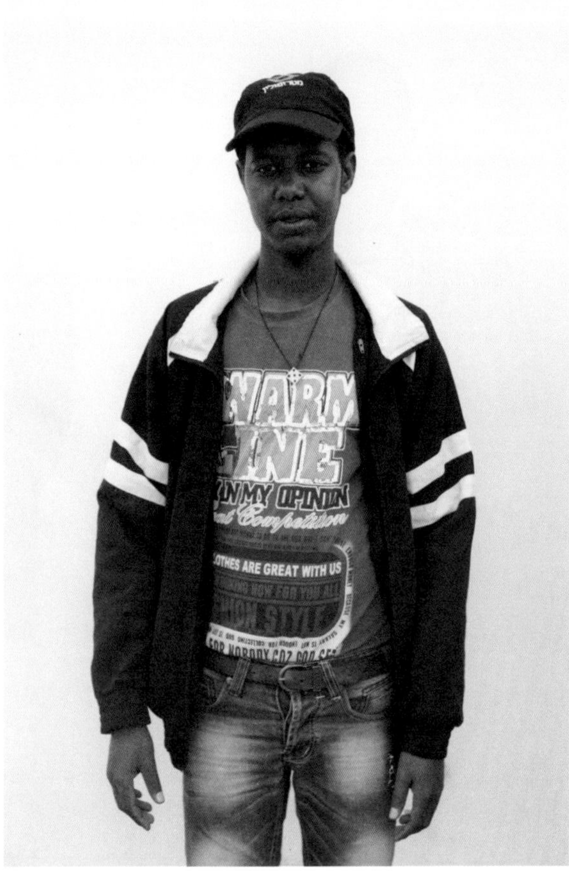

Fig. 1. A.A.M.S.: "I am 38 years old, married and a father of two children. I was born in Niala, South Darfur. My father was murdered during an attack on our village in 2003. We had to run away and seek refuge in the Kalma refugee camp. My mother, wife, and children still live there today. I miss them very much and I don't know what their situation is. I came to Israel to seek protection but I was imprisoned. I have been in prison for almost two years. I don't want to be in prison any more."

Fig. 2. Solomon Hagos: "I was a soldier in Eritrea. During my military service I was sentenced to three years in prison although I had not committed a crime. I succeeded to escape from prison after four months. I joined a group of 80 people who escaped from Sudan to Sinai. After we gave the money to the smugglers they told us it was dangerous to depart for Israel just then. We waited another week. There was a girl there who the Bedouin called over. They said that they wanted to talk to her. they wanted to talk to her; when she came back she told me she had been raped. Afterwards they wanted to take another girl aside, but I argued with them. After a week, all the 80 people were released but the Bedouin kept me with them in the desert for another eleven days."

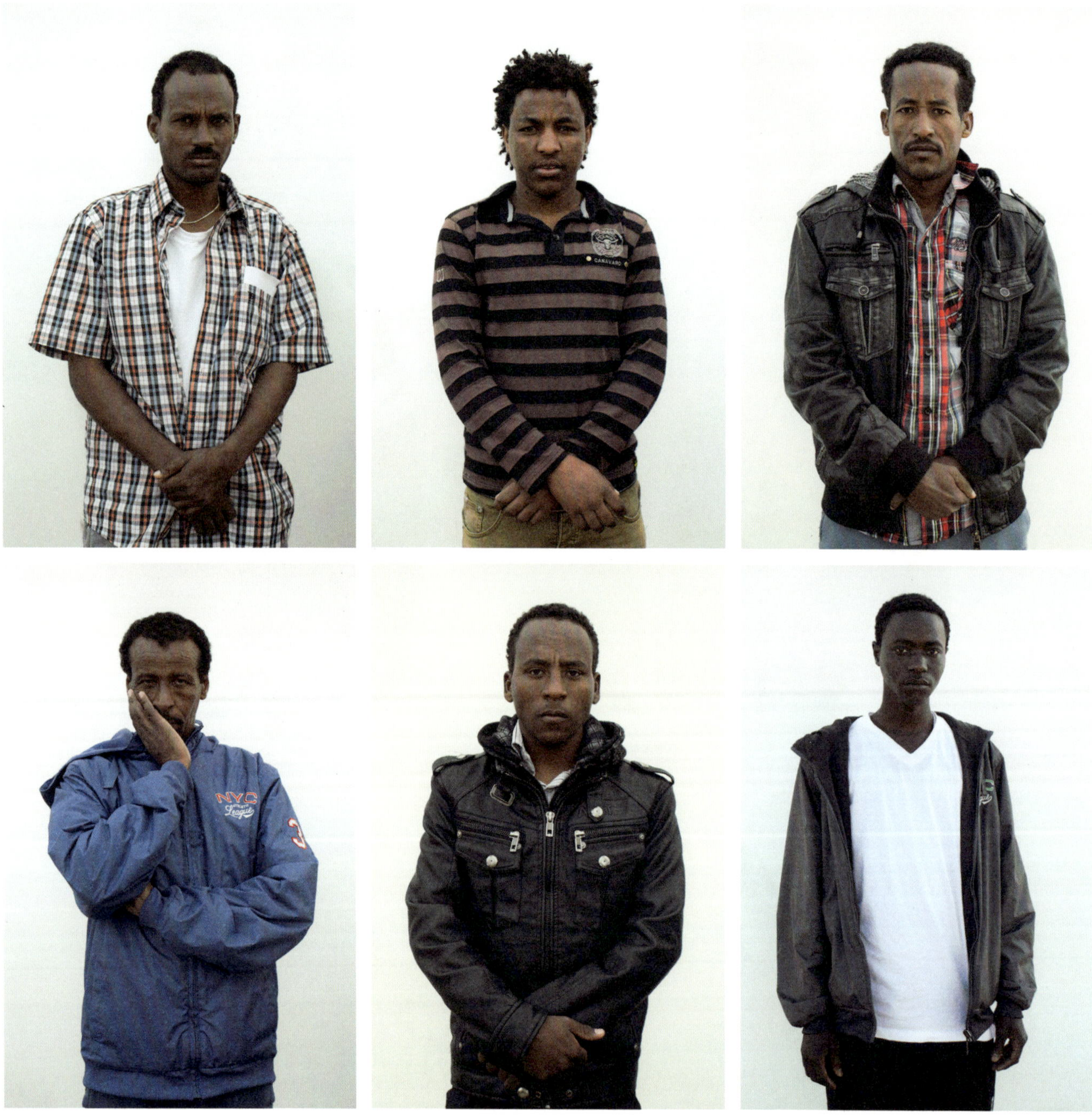

This portrait series was taken outside the Holot detention center for African asylum seekers. Under current Israeli law, people's only hope for release is if they agree to be deported back to their home countries from which they fled.

{Top left to right} Zerei Gebresilasi [Eritrea] / Haben [Eritrea] / Yunas [Ertirea] / Abadom Girogis [Eritrea] / Araya Fishazion [Eritrea] / S.Y.A.J. [Niala, Darfur].

and that the state must release all the prisoners. The Interior Ministry largely ignored the ruling until August 2015, whereupon some 1,200 men were finally released. But the release forms arrived with further constraints: the "infiltrators" were given a two-month permit, but forbidden from working or living in Tel Aviv or Eliat—the two cities where the majority of their refugee communities are located. At the end of these two months, they need to return to the Interior Ministry to request renewal of their conditional release visas. The government has not revealed what the punishment would be for violating these constraints. This represents a subtle change of strategy: where the state initially sought to detain and contain these "infiltrators," now it sets them in perpetual motion, preventing them from ever making a home. These men are hopelessly trapped in the circuitous logic of Israeli law—mercilessly subject to the imperatives of the state and simultaneously barred from access.

To wonder about their dream-life is to speculate about where the boundaries of the law end. How do one's lived conditions come to permeate one's subjectivity? Is there a part of interior life that is protected from the perverse reach of the law? What acts of imagination can stage or even perhaps suspend the force of law? And more to the point of this book—how might photography be mobilized to intervene in this form of sovereign violence?

Oren Ziv's portraits portray each of these men in agonizing solitude, their bodies seemingly suspended in space by a flat grey-white border. This simple framing serves to underscore each subject's precarious legal status: each figure is caught in a liminal state, mounted in a kind of perpetually suspended sentence. They can neither move forward with their lives nor go back. The inhospitable place that holds them is a gateway to nowhere.

Each time I study Ziv's portraits, trying to glean something from the men's inscrutable faces, I think of Franz Kafka's strange, short parable, "Before the Law." In fact, this is the title I've always silently attributed to the series—especially when the photographs are presented in tableau form [**opposite**]. Kafka probably would never have imagined the protagonist of his story as an Eritrean or Sudanese civilian fleeing his war-torn homeland to come to the gates of Israel, but this is part of the story's prescience, its surprising malleability. Any one of these men could easily play the part of Kafka's "man from the country," a man who has come to one of the gates of the Law to ask for admittance. In Kafka's story, the man from the country is met by a huge, Cossack-looking gatekeeper who imposes himself between the man and the open doorway. The gatekeeper does not deny that admittance may be granted at some point: "It is possible," the gatekeeper intones, "but not now." This enigmatic response sustains the man's hope and he decides to stay at the gate to wait. He is trusting, believing that "the Law should be accessible at all times and to everyone."

The man settles in to wait to be admitted to the Law, spending his days sitting on a stool outside the gateway. He becomes fixated by the radiance that seems to stream out from the doorway that remains tantalizingly open. But the days turn into years. The man frequently queries the gatekeeper who always replies that he cannot be let in ... yet. Bribes do not work, childish pleading does not work, nothing works, and the man begins to curse his luck. Kafka's parable abruptly ends when the man, who has grown old and stiff, musters just enough energy to ask the gatekeeper why, in all the years he has waited, no one else has ever appeared to ask for admittance at the gates of the Law? The gatekeeper roars into his ear: "No one else could ever be admitted here, since this gate was made only for you. Now I am going to go and shut it!"[1]

As Jacques Derrida has pointed out, Kafka's haunting parable carries all the merits of a narrative while also offering a potent commentary on the force of sovereignty, which is to say, it puts the protagonists into a literary relation.[2] This might seem like an obvious, or perhaps even trivial point, but its significance becomes clear when juxtaposed to the *fiction-less* quality of the law. The foundation of the law's force lies precisely in the fact it is *not* a fiction. There is no obvious author of the law; its claim to absolute authority is established through universal, categorical pronouncements. The man from the country states what most of us believe to be true: the law should be accessible to all people at all times. But the tragedy here, if I can put it that way, is that he fails to grasp that it is precisely this universality—this *authorlessness*—that prevents him from accessing the law. The law derives its authority precisely by holding its subjects in place: to be recognized as a subject-of-law is to be perpetually held *before* the law.

It also bears pointing out that this is also photography's mode of operation. In a disquieting way, all these men—A.A.M.S., Solomon, Zerei, and the rest—have been frozen before the spectator, held in suspended animation by Ziv's camera. This confining mode of representation is precisely what draws the ire of critics: photography—and documentary photography in particular—turns on a myth of objectivity. It operates by exerting a kind of visual tyranny over its subjects—a tyranny that bears an uncomfortable similarity to the way that sovereign states are able to suspend the status of certain subjects, holding individuals interminably before the law.[3]

But this is also photography's great potential: Ziv's effort to render these individuals visible—to make their visage public, to make them *appear* alongside their brief testimonial statements—effectively illuminates the politics of disregard that lies at the heart of the infiltrator law. By willingly entering into a visual and textual relationship with these men, Ziv calls into question the *author-ity* of this law. We might compare his gesture to Kafka's literary act—a gesture that seeks to sniff out the law's attempt to conceal its own origins, a challenge to the authority upon which it rests. Circulating these photographs can be read, moreover, as an attempt to intervene upon the law's efforts to make these individuals disappear. But this circulation also issues a potent challenge: the images place the spectator in the position of Kafka's gatekeeper. With our back to the law, we are positioned to face these men "from the country." Our gaze, however sensuous and compassionate, can only serve to defer their entrance, to withhold the men's passage. In this way, Ziv effectively entangles the politics of spectatorship within the prohibitions of the law. He challenges us, like Kafka, to consider our rapport, to question how our modes of looking and thinking silently sustain and comply with the operations of sovereign power.

Like Kafka's parable, the Holot detention center is a world populated entirely by men. Or perhaps it is more accurate to say that Holot is a world bereft of women. This is the paternal logic embedded in the law of hospitality, the way the sovereign state operates like the head of household, the figure who possesses the authority to extend or refuse hospitality to the stranger.[4]

In contrast to the hostile welcome issued by the Israeli state, the Women in Black seek to tender their own particular model of civility and hospitality **[opposite]**. One could also give the title "Before the Law" to Keren Manor and Shiraz Grinbaum's portraits of these courageous women. In this case, the title would work like a kind of counterpoint, a signal of the way this group offers a rather different melody to the state's martial song of sovereignty.

Every Friday since 1988, these women have stood with their characteristic black signs in the main squares of cities and at highway junctions. The movement began as a response to the human rights abuses perpetuated by Israeli soldiers in the occupied Palestinian territories. Many of their signs call for an end to the occupation. They wear black clothing to signal that they are in a state of mourning for the victims of the conflict. The women's regular appearance represents a kind of vigil, a persistent effort to honor the dead. They share a kinship, in this respect, with the Mothers of the Plaza de Mayo, whose children were disappeared during the Dirty War in Argentina. The enduring public protest also recalls the Black Sash movement in South Africa—the group of white women who tirelessly stood in the streets with signs protesting against the apartheid regime. Each of these groups occupy public space in a regular, weekly ritual, a gesture that seeks to make the state's violence legible, or indeed grievable, in Judith Butler's terms.[5] This demand-for-justice-cum-public-work-of-mourning seems to have a distinctly gendered dimension. As one of the Women in Black's founders, Edna Glukman **[opposite, top left]** recalls:

> In the beginning, the right-wing protesters started to attack us during the vigils. We sewed big black banners and with small white letters we wrote slogans against the occupation, as well as for justice, peace, and women. By the time we began writing the word "women" on our banners, it was already starting to become a women's movement.

These women endure significant abuse—they are spat at, verbally harassed, and sometimes even physically attacked—and they subsequently have become a symbol of persistence and resilience in the country. Their relatively simple gesture of taking to the street should remind us of the remarkable potency of nonviolent resistance: the determination and willingness of individuals to use their

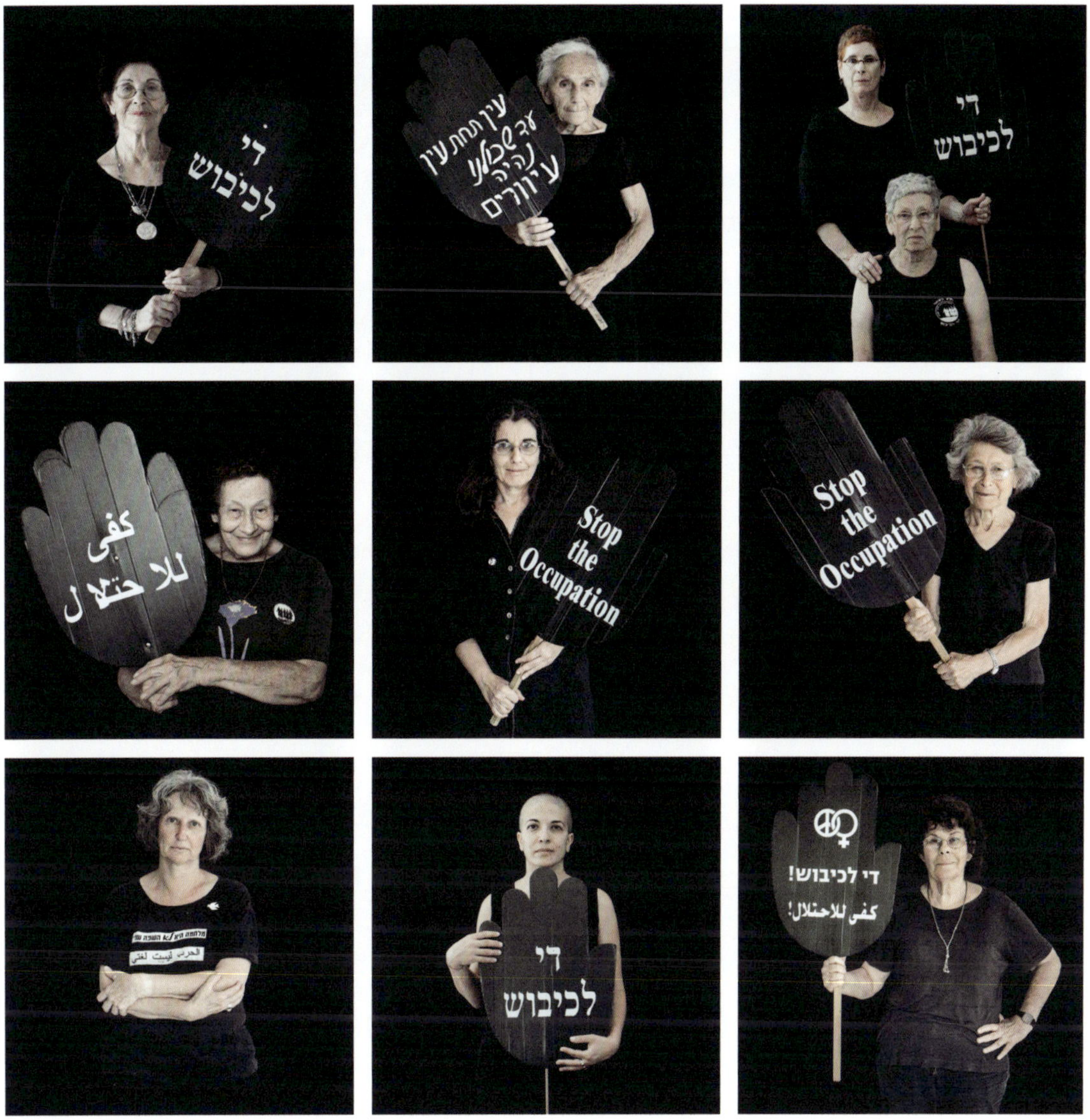

In honor of International Women's Day 2013, Activestills paid tribute to more than a quarter century of anti-occupation activism by the Women in Black group in Israel. Every Friday since 1988, these women have stood in the main squares of cities or at highway junctions with signs calling calling for an end to the Israeli occupation.

{Top left to right} Edna Glukman holding a sign in Hebrew that says: "Stop the Occupation" / Stela Tzur holding a sign in Hebrew that says: "An eye for an eye until all of us will be blind" / Dafna Kaminer (sitting) and Tamar Leahn /Aliya Strauss holding a sign in Arabic that says: "Stop the Occupation" / Orly Nathan / Yenina Altman / Varda Sivan / Vered Madar / Edna Zaretzki Toledano.

bodies as a medium to render injustice visible. This basic and yet powerful gesture also sustains and nurtures the public sphere, a domain that Hannah Arendt characterized as *a space of appearance*.[6] For Arendt, the public sphere is the central organ of the human condition. She described it as a theater of resonance, a place that sustains the possibility of seeing and being seen, or hearing and being heard. The Women in Black claim this fundamental agency: the power to appropriate and transform public space into an amphitheater of justice.

Whereas Oren Ziv frames his detainees with a flat grey-white border, Manor and Grinbaum shroud the women in blackness, using light to dramatically accentuate their subjects' own strategy of theatrically mobilizing their bodies to illuminate human affairs. In these pictures, the women seem to possess their own light source that is in stark contrast to the dark times in which they live. It is as if they have harnessed something of that radiance that seems to fixate Kafka's man from the country—the illumination that comes from beyond the gates of the law.

Perhaps most importantly, the photographers remind us that the power of such illumination often comes less from abstract theories and concepts than from women and men who, in their lives and work, are determined to kindle and protect this space of appearance in spite of all. They show us that the *polis*, properly speaking, is not equivalent to the state, but rather lies in that space between people who act and speak together for a common purpose. Taken together, these photographs issue a warning: not everyone has access to this space of appearance. But they also serve as a reminder of our fundamental human agency: each one of us provides the guarantee for the other's presence in the human world, just as our presence, in turn, is guaranteed by the other.

1. Kafka's parable "Vor dem Gesetz" ("Before the Law") was first published in 1915 in the independent Jewish weekly, *Selbstwehr*. I've drawn from the English translation published in *The Metamorphosis, In the Penal Colony, and Other Stories*, trans. Joachim Neugroschel (New York: Simon and Schuster, 1993), 249–51.

2. Jacques Derrida, "Before the Law," in *Acts of Literature*, ed. Derek Attridge (New York: Routledge, 1992), 181–220.

3. Critiques of documentary photography are manifold. I am thinking in particular of Martha Rosler's "In, Around, and Afterthoughts (On Documentary Photography)," in *The Contest of Meaning: Critical Histories of Photography*, ed. Richard Bolton (Cambridge, MA: MIT Press, 1989), 303–42.

4. See, for instance, Jacques Derrida's seminar on the "Foreigner Question" in *Of Hospitality, Anne Dufourmantelle Invites Jacques Derrida to Respond*, trans. Rachel Bowlby (Stanford, CA: Stanford University Press, 2000), 3–74.

5. Judith Butler, *Frames of War: When Is Life Grievable?* (New York: Verso, 2009).

6. Hannah Arendt, *The Human Condition* (Chicago, IL: University of Chicago Press, 1958).

{Opposite page}
African asylum seekers protest,
Tel Aviv, 16.12.2008

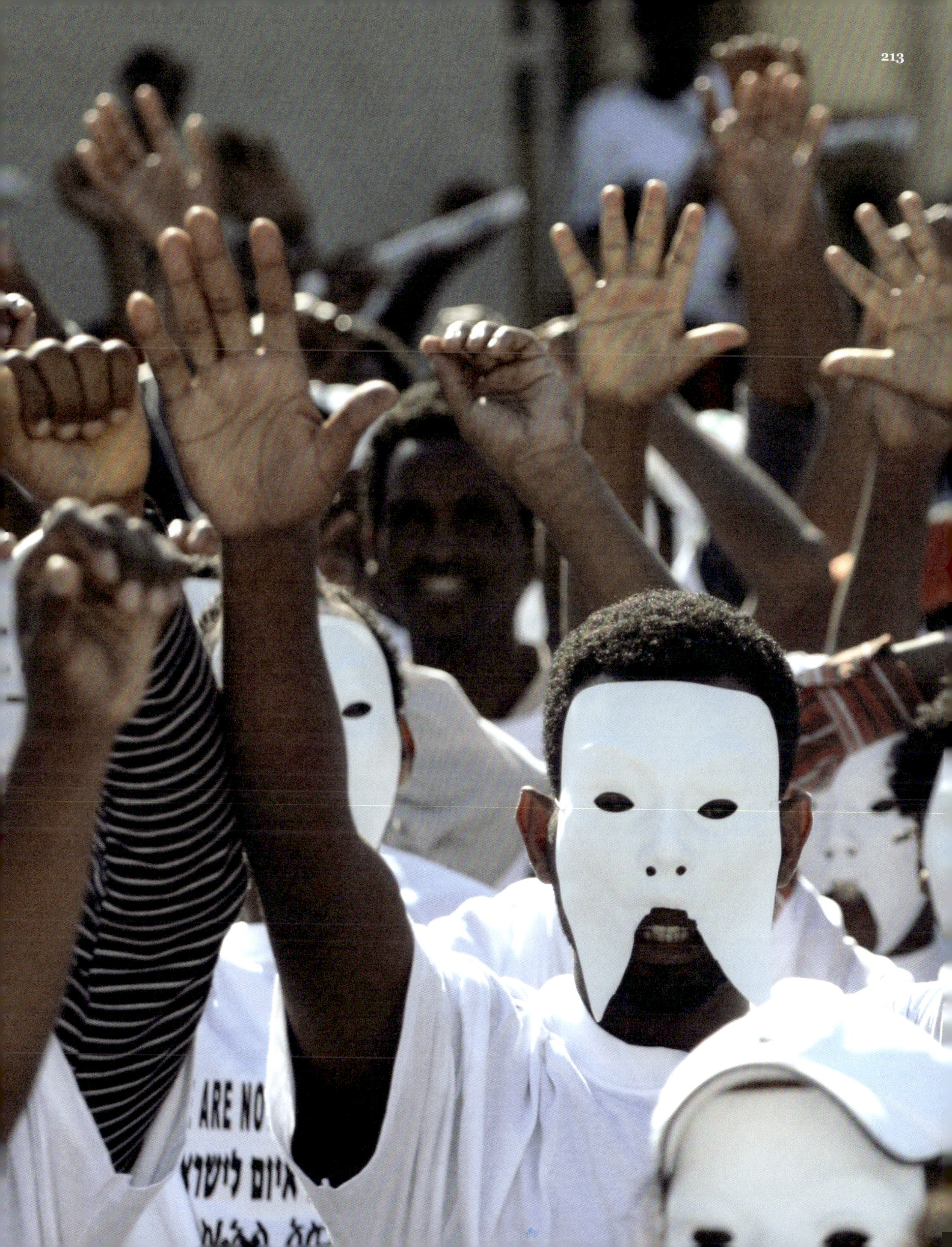
ARE NO
איום לישרא

Being There

Ruthie Ginsburg

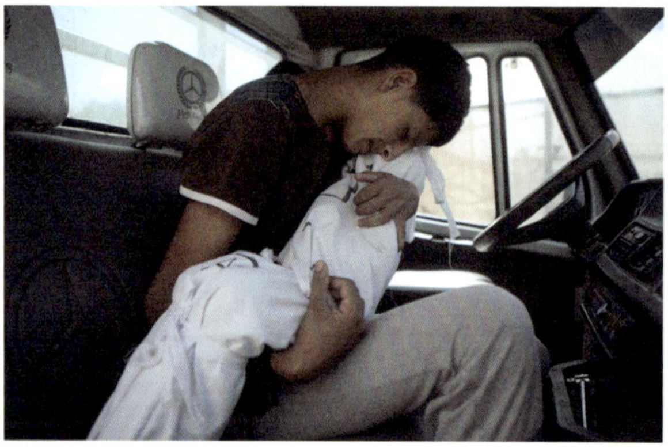

Fig. 1. Mohammad Madi holding the body of his niece Jana, Rafah, Gaza Strip, 3.8.2014

During the Israeli military operation Protective Edge (summer 2014), Anne Paq, a member of Activestills, photographed a man in a field in Rafah, in Gaza [**Fig. 1**]. The man, seated inside a truck, clings to a small body wrapped in a white sheet. Paq thought she was photographing a young father in mourning embracing his dead child, but after learning the names of the victims of the Israeli military operation, she understood that the child's entire immediate family had been killed and that the man in the photograph was Mohammad Madi, the girl's uncle whom Paq had seen and photographed that same day. Due to the huge number of victims and the lack of space in the hospital morgues, bodies were being stored in a cooling facility used for vegetables and flowers.[1] Madi had come to take his niece from the facility, which was, by then, overloaded with bodies. Overwhelmed by the destruction wrought by Operation Protective Edge, Paq decided to trace the victims' families in order to "give them a face." She located 50 families and photographed pictures of the ones who had died, as part of the documentary project "Gaza's Obliterated Families" [**p. 264**]. Visiting Madi's family, she learned that six family members had been killed, including three children. In a photograph of a mobile phone screen, we see Jana and Hala, who were just two and four years old when they died from a missile that hit their home [**Fig. 2**]. The photograph of the two girls evokes a sense of intimacy. In a printed or digital family photo album, such a picture offers an image of happiness and joy, but since the summer of 2014, it has signified loss.

Paq's project aims to tell the stories of some of the thousands of Palestinians who were killed during the Gaza war.[2] It encompasses unusual images in Activestills' archive. While most of the photographs of the Activestills group document civil encounters and demonstrations, the images in this project call to mind a still life. Portrait photographs of the victims are photographed like objects, arranged on rocks, on top of a bed cover, held in someone's hands, as a screen saver on a mobile phone. The photographs were taken in the places where the deceased were killed. Embodied in the work is this dialectic between the subjects (the photographed) and objects (the photographs), between the un-presented and the represented. In a related matter, in August 2014, the Israeli Broadcasting Authority and the High Court of Justice denied the appeal of the human rights organization B'Tselem to broadcast the names of children killed during the strikes in Gaza.[3] While B'Tselem claimed that it was engaging in information distribution, its opponents regarded the proposed action as a political statement, claiming that it pointed to the Israeli government as being held accountable in the children's deaths, rather than Hamas. Showing victims' faces and names in an appeal for accountability is a familiar practice utilized in civil struggles worldwide. In Argentina, the Mothers of the Plaza de Mayo carry photographs of their missing children, as do the mothers of Palestinian political prisoners in demonstrations against the occupation [**Fig 3**]. Viewed in this light, Paq's project can be seen as an activation of images in a political manner. In the project's publication, she wrote: "One of the aims of the project is to raise awareness of these families and support their call for justice."[4] Like other photographs taken and published by Activestills, it urges the display of what has been banished from public sight.

In our conversation, Paq explained that the project turned out to be a project for the family members in Gaza who remained after the loss of their loved ones.[5] She challenged the common notion of the "decisive moment" in photojournalism by focusing on the survivors displaying photographs of their dead family members.[6] Even though the survivors are not pictured, the images are just as much about them as they are about the deceased individuals in the photographs. This idea motivated Paq to get to know bereaved Palestinian families and to return several times to visit them in the Gaza Strip. Becoming familiar with the people being documented is an integral part of Activestills' practice. The photographers make an effort to connect with the community they photograph either by visiting before or remaining after an event such as a demonstration, or by continuing to be in contact, as Paq was. They always offer the communities the photographs for their own use. While Activestills' photography emerges, in part, from communal connections, it also aims to create connections among the diverse civil struggles of oppressed communities in Palestine/Israel. I would argue that Activestills' approach can be viewed in light of recent theoretical debates about the political role of photography. Referring to David Green and Joanna Lowry's essay "From Presence to the Performative: Rethinking Photographic Indexicality," I suggest that we view the indexical property of photography as shifting attention from "it was there" to "being there."[7] Another aim of outlining the political essence of a particular situation as "being there" is to overcome the prevailing terms of public discussions on photography that are divided between skepticism and certainty. Nevertheless, focusing on "being there" does not undermine the importance of Activestills' archival or curatorial work (through their street exhibitions); rather, it serves to illuminate this special way of documentation, which intersects with the other political constructs featured in their work.

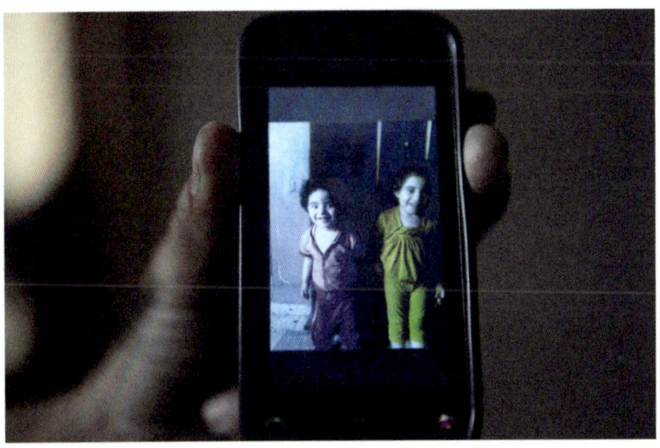

Fig. 2. Photo of Hala and Jana on Mohammad's mobile phone, 19.11.2014

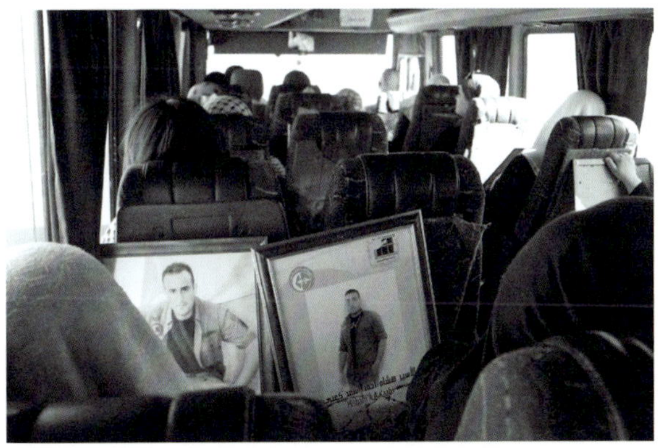

Fig. 3. Palestinian mothers on their way to a solidarity protest with Palestinian prisoners, Nablus, West Bank, 29.3.2013

A Shift from "It Was There" to "Being There"

Conventionally, the political role of photography has been based on the medium's indexicality. The photograph is thought to be an analog, a trace of what was in front of the camera lens at the moment the photograph was taken. It therefore indicates its referent's reality, or in other words, a photograph can portray a sense of reality that the viewer can evaluate. Kaja Silverman notes that the scholarly debate about photographic indexicality is divided between those who stress its constructedness and those who emphasize its evidentiary value. While the former see photographs as an outcome of a particular cultural setting and psychological reaction, the latter tend to believe in photography's transparent qualities. She writes: "if a photograph can prove 'what was,' then it is the royal road to certainty—the means through which we know and judge the world."[8] Green and Lowry point to the destabilization of the privileged status of photography as "an arbiter of truth and reality" with the rise of digital technology in the 1980s and the new ways of processing an image. Like Silverman, they see the photograph's indexicality at the heart of the issue. Reminding us that Roland Barthes in *Camera Lucida* connected the photograph's indexicality to memory, death, and mourning in a way that is difficult to untangle, Green and Lowry turn to the writings of American pragmatist philosopher C.S. Peirce, who had considered indexicality before Barthes and argued that the indexical sign had "less to do with its causal origins and more to do with the new way which it pointed to the event of its own inscription."[9] Green and Lowry argue that photographs are not just indexical because of a physical-chemical occurrence where light is documented in an instant on a photosensitive strip of film, "but because, first and foremost, they were taken. The very act of photography, as a kind of performative gesture which points to an event in the world, as a form of designation that draws reality into the image field, is thus itself a form of indexicality."[10]

Hence, they do not refute the suggestion that the familiar form of indexicality (the physical trace of an event) is specific to photography, but rather they add another form—the performative gesture that points toward it, which I call "being there."[11] While these authors turn to the artistic practice of photography to demonstrate the performative gesture of photography, I wish to address its political role by looking at the work of Activestills. Shifting attention from the evidentiary force of photography to its performative power opens up new ways to sketch its activation, that is, its role in political engagement. With Activestills, this engagement is also a form of solidarity with the documented community. My notion of political photography emphasizes the role of Activestills' images in creating a conjunction between oppressed communities, therefore undermining the foundations of the Israeli regime that is built on differentiations and separations.

On Activestills' website, a weekly visual report appears under the title "Happening Now Stream." Unlike "Gaza's Obliterated Families," the photographs here are a form of reportage: viewed in succession, they show a flow of events, intertwining information from different places and civil encounters. For example, a page from July 2007 featured a protest against the closing of the investigation into Abir Aramin's killing in Jerusalem, harvest work in the field of the Jabari family in Hebron, home rebuilding in Jaffa, homeless Israeli women demonstrating in Jerusalem, a demonstration against the Israeli separation wall at Bil'in, and Israeli activists protesting at Kfar Shalem, a neighborhood in south Tel Aviv. Though it may seem like a photojournalistic montage, that is, a series of documentary photographs of political events occurring in Palestine/Israel, this is not the case. There is no hierarchy governing the photographs' representations, and no one photograph shows a given event, but rather, several do, which is an unusual way to portray news. In some cases, more than one of the collective's photographers is compiling the visual report. Therefore, we see the event from more than one camera's vantage point on the same web page. The collective does not try to depict an "objective" point of view, as would be expected from a photojournalist; rather, each photographer offers his or her own perspective. Keren Manor recollected:

> In the first years, we were looked at as outcasts by other photojournalists, who argued that we are not professional photographers because we are political, because we declare that we are political. We were not photographing from a remote hill but rather we were part of the situation.[12]

Their point of view is also expressed through the events they choose to cover. Most of the documentation is

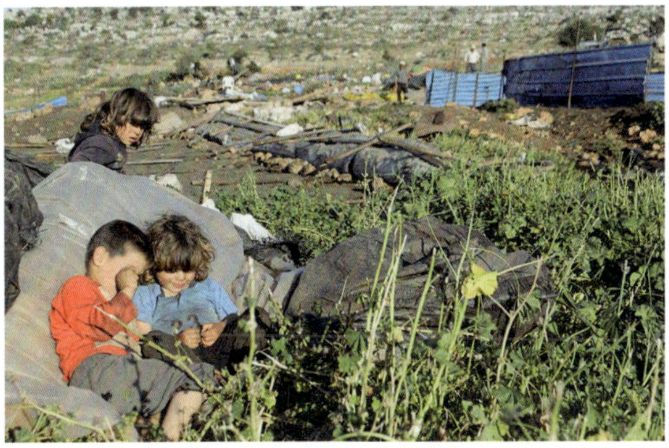

Fig. 4. Palestinian children sit near homes demolished by the Israeli authorities in the village of Kufr a-Dik, West Bank, 16.4.2012

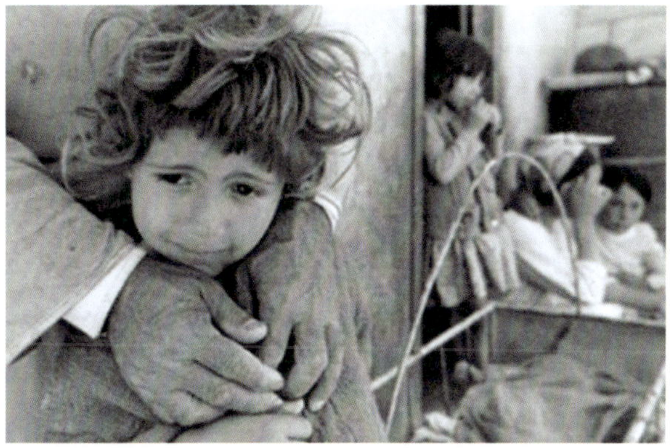

Fig. 5. A Palestinian family in a refugee camp, date unknown [Photographer unknown, courtesy of the Palestinian Return Center]

centered on civil struggles as Activestills members feel that they are part of these struggles, especially when they contribute by means of the photographs they take. Even if in most of the cases that the group's members document, it is not "their own struggle," they identify with civil resistance. Yotam Ronen addressed how documenting helps him express his solidarity, even if he is in a privileged position with regard to the concrete struggle:

I am a white (Ashkenazi) male; therefore, most of the struggles are not my struggles. I am straight, I am not a woman, and nothing has been taken from me. Coming from a disposition of solidarity and identification with the struggle makes it be, in a way, my struggle.[13]

Shiraz Grinbaum concurred:

In Activestills' photographs, I see a combination of acts: exposing, embracing (the people and the situation), and urging. We come to 'be there,' and the photographs indicate that we were there. Many photographs show the same scenes over and over again. I see that referring to the tension between 'it was there,' 'that' happened, and 'I was there.' The tension is both ethical and phenomenological.[14]

The sense of "being there," which constructs the experience of the photographers, repudiates the distinction between the documentation and the documented, between the photograph and the photographed, and it acknowledges that the group's photographic practice is a political performative gesture.

Complexities of Access

"Being there" also seizes upon the intricate relationships bound up with the Palestine/Israel geopolitical situation and forms the basis of the image making and image assembly in Activestills' work, as can be seen, for example, in Ahmad Al-Bazz's photograph from Kufr a-Dik [**Fig. 4**].

Al-Bazz took the photograph of Kufr a-Dik village not long after the Israeli Army demolished the house of the children seen in the image. The expanding settlements of Bruchin, Alei Zahav, and Pedu'el were making everyday life impossible for the Bedouin families living nearby. In spring 2012, Al-Bazz documented the destruction of three tents and three water wells that were being used by the Palestinian farmers. Most of the farmland of these Bedouins was in Area C, an area under Israeli control. Palestinians were unable to acquire any sort of building permit, even though their livelihood depended on this land. Israeli authorities claimed that they were demolishing the houses for security reasons. One of the farmers responded: "I don't have any guns or tanks, just my trees. Staying in Area A is like living in a small prison."[15] Palestine/Israel's territorial division between the occupied Palestinian territories and Israel (within the area defined by the Green Line), division of the territory in the West Bank after the 1993 and 1995 Oslo Accords into areas A (under Palestinian control), B (mixed control, where the Israeli forces are responsible

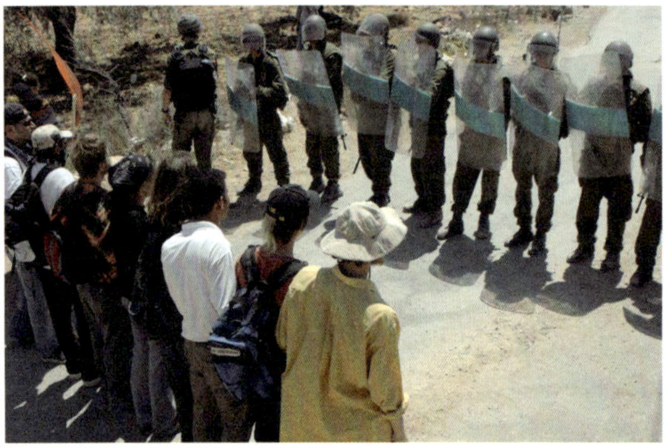

Fig. 6. Protesters confront Israeli soldiers during a demonstration against the Israeli separation wall, Bil'in, 5.8.2005

for security), and C (under Israeli control), and the 2005 disengagement from Gaza, have harmed the Palestinian community. They also affect the ability of "being there" for Activestills photographers as the right of entry to the various territories differs for the members of the collective. Access to areas outside of the West Bank is denied to Palestinians, while Area A is inaccessible to Israelis and the Gaza Strip is completely closed to all except for international photographers who may enter all the zones in Palestine/Israel. Al-Bazz commented that as a Palestinian, "I can move [around] in about twenty percent of the country. I cannot enter Gaza and I cannot visit the destroyed Palestinian villages from '48."[16] But the photographs can.

Al-Bazz pointed out that the child in the Kufr a-Dik photo resembles the Palestinian girl in an iconic photograph of the Nakba[17] that was taken in a Palestinian refugee camp after 1948 [**Fig. 5**]. Robert Hariman and John Lucaites, writing about the power of iconic photographs in American culture in their book *No Caption Needed*, argue that these kinds of photographs "have more than documentary value, for they bear witness to something that exceeds words. Objects of contemplation bearing the aura of history, or humanity, or possibility, they are sacred images for a secular society."[18] While the authors aimed to fill in the gaps resulting from the lack of captions, the book's title is an apt characterization of the photograph of the Palestinian girl. The photograph, without any indication of where it was taken or the name of the girl or the photographer, is featured in websites devoted to Palestinian political heritage.[19] Despite the different background scenes, there are many similarities between the 1948 photograph and Al-Bazz's photograph from 2012: in both, a child (or children) appears in the left foreground with the visual field receding sharply at right and the introverted gaze of the girls lending the images a sense of sadness. The photographs, as such, seem to escape restrictions that are placed on people, especially as regards their movement and access. Though Al-Bazz, as a Palestinian living in the West Bank, is prevented from reaching the ruined Palestinian villages of 1948, the photograph does. In echoing the image from 1948, his photograph shows the connection between the events of the past and the present, and thus the Nakba is portrayed as an ongoing event.[20] In our discussion, Al-Bazz pointed to the connection between civil struggles against displacement and house demolitions on both sides of the Green Line in Activestills' work. The Kufr a-Dik photographs are visible in the collective's archive alongside photographs from Al-Araqib, in the Negev, the southern part of the country, and Iqrit in the north. By presenting photographs of these civil struggles together, they create connections among the different regions and link the past (1948) to the present.

The barriers imposed by the political situation affect not only the movement of the Activestills photographers but their economic opportunities as well. For Palestinian and Israeli photographers to be working together is exceptional, given the expansion of BDS (Boycott, Divestment and Sanctions against Israel). Al-Bazz explained that his work in Activestills and his support for BDS are not contradictory actions, as long as he focuses his documentation on the Israeli occupation. He will not contribute photographs to Activestills' website that depict issues besides the occupation. The economic gap between the occupied territories and Israel makes pro bono work for Activestills something that few Palestinian photographers can afford to engage in. Palestinian photographers will probably prefer to work for a news agency such as AP for economic reasons, rather than work independently for the collective. Thus, "being there," as representing an assembly of diverse views portrayed by photographers of various identities, is intertwined with the Palestine/Israel political situation and its economic implications. The divergent view that Activestills attempt to render is influenced and framed by the Israeli occupation.

Photography and Activism

"Being there" with the community is part of Activestills' intertwining of activism and photography. As Oren Ziv explains, "Most of the photographers think we are activists and most of the activists think we are photographers. In the ongoing work, you would not notice that I photograph differently. The question is what you do with the photographs afterwards."[21]

Three photographs by Yotam Ronen taken in Bil'in demonstrate the tension that comes from "being there," and engaging in activism and photography; the strain of delivering an image and being a dissident; of looking from the correct angle and protesting; of observing and being in the midst of the chaos.

Ronen regards this photograph from summer 2005 as the first of his photographs to have captured the dynamics of the protests in the village of Bil'in [**Fig. 6**]. The photo shows a group of Palestinians and activists standing opposite a group of Israeli soldiers. An oblique line divides the picture and signals the tension between the opponents. The other two images from the same political struggle, but not from the same day, show Ronen repositioning himself from activist to photographer [**Figs. 7, 8**].

These two photographs document a situation that is common at encounters between activists and the Israeli Army in the West Bank: activists are arrested by the Israeli Army. The scene of two groups confronting each other captured in the first photograph occasionally escalates into the situation in the two next photographs. In the second photograph [**Fig. 8**], photographers can be seen in the background framed by the scene of the arrest in the foreground, as if they are the subject of the picture, rather than the scene of the arrest captured by Ronen's camera. The bodies of the Israeli soldiers function like vertical pillars on either side of the body of the protester, whose semi-recumbent pose seemingly acts as a base for the two photographers who stand in the distance. From their dress, the photographers and protesters appear to be affiliated with the same group, though their poses make clear the differences in their actions. Although the focus of the camera lens is the activist who is being dragged, the photographers in the background are at the center of the picture.

The protester being arrested in the photograph is Ronen's brother. Their family relationship highlights the distinction between the role of photographer and protester, as Ronen revealed:

> My instinct when the soldiers arrested my brother was to help him. I saw that he was being dragged. I had stopped, around that time, being involved in the same manner. I remember the ability I developed to detach myself from the situation. I knew he would be arrested and then released, and I preferred to photograph and not to be in the same situation. Maybe these photographs represent the course I went through. I want to take part in these struggles, but I am a photographer.[22]

There is, indeed, a distinction between activism and photography; however, they merge in Activestills' essential act of "being there." Although most of the collective's members acknowledge that they have undergone a process of evolution in how they conduct themselves,

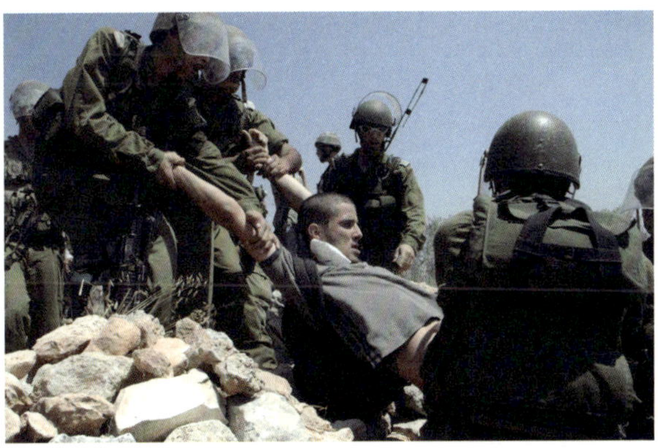

Fig. 7. Bil'in, 26.8.2005

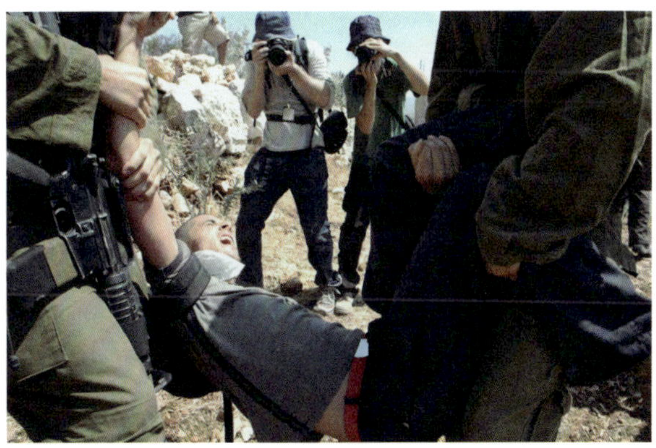

Fig. 8. Bil'in, 26.8.2005

they still go to political events as activists and not solely as photographers. Therefore, most of the members do not separate the two roles. With the increased incidence of physical violence and arrest of activists during demonstrations, including of Israeli activists by Israeli soldiers, Activestills photographers now often shield themselves. Manor sees it this way:

> I detach myself from my activist friends, though in a way I am in a different position. It was not a collective decision, but one used a gas mask, and one a bulletproof vest, and we saw that we could continue to photograph, and not run away, even when the soldiers were shooting. At first, I thought I should not shield myself, but I decided to photograph and I have to separate what I have to do as a photographer from what I have to do as an activist.[23]

The camera was regarded by early commentators such as Walter Benjamin as a form of prosthesis, an instrument that enlarges vision. Photography, he noted, presents us with more; it also presents to us how much we do not see.[24] Prosthesis indicates impairment, not just a technical device that expands the power of the photographer/observer. Manor's thinking on the relation between photography and activism designates something similar—the advantage and disadvantage of the photographer's positioning within the political engagement of a protest. "Being there" as a photographer expands the event with the images she produces and enables us to see, but it also exposes the limits of political engagement. The photographer's position brings to mind the vulnerability of activism and the precariousness of its outcomes (including its visual documentation). Attempting to seize in words the relation between activism and photography in Activestills seems destined to fail. In "being there," at an event, as Manor and Ronen point out, they sometimes find themselves having to detach their activism from their photography, yet their motivation for "being there" is a combination of the two.

Final Remarks

My understanding here is based on a multi-layered study that combines discussions with the photographers of Activestills, examination of their photographs, and the political context that marks their work. Green and Lowry suggest a broader perspective on the connection between photography and the photographed image and our way of comprehending this connection. The authors rethink this relationship by offering an analytical framework of engagement that looks at photography's indexicality as a performative gesture. With the help of their framework, I have suggested that we perceive Activestills' photographic political work as "being there," rather than adopting the common Barthesean "it was there" notion of photography's indexicality. Activestills' "being there" is aligned in solidarity with the oppressed communities they document. However, the political situation in Palestine/Israel affects their work even as it is documented in it. The intricate relations between activism and photography and its dynamics are stirred by the collective's way of engagement, which also indicates their uniqueness. Oren Ziv's observation offers a fitting final commentary on the inimitable work of Activestills:

> Reporters are never there. You are there because you have to take a photograph. To be there is a basic element of the work. To be there is to support the people. When I worked for a newspaper, I was there in places I did not want to be. It is essentially different to go to Al-Araqib village and to be there because you want to. Photojournalists work with a clock—when they have what they need they leave. We work differently. I go to a place; I am with the activists; I am there until the end.[25]

1. Amira Hass, "In Rafah, Hospital Morgues Cannot Hold All the Bodies," *Ha'aretz*, 3.8.2014, http://www.haaretz.com/news/diplomacy-defense/.premium-1.608532.

2. According to the United Nations Independent Commission of Inquiry on the 2014 Gaza Conflict, "In the 51 day operation, 1,462 Palestinian civilians were killed, a third of them children." See http://www.ohchr.org/EN/NewsEvents/Pages/DisplayNews.aspx?NewsID=16119&LangID=E.

3. Revital Hovel, "B'Tselem Loses Supreme Court Bid to Broadcast Names of Children Killed in Gaza," *Ha'aretz*, 15.8.2014, http://www.haaretz.com/news/israel/.premium-1.610477.

4. Activestills, "Photos: The Palestinian Families Obliterated in Just 51 Days," 26.8.2015, http://972mag.com/photos-the-palestinian-families-obliterated-in-just-51-days/110877.

5. Conversation with Anne Paq via Skype, Tel Aviv, 2.10.2015.

6. The "decisive moment" refers to the title of the book (1952) by Henri Cartier-Bresson, expressing the view that the photographer seeks to capture the essence of an event via a singular still photograph.

7. David Green and Joanna Lowry, "From Presence to the Performative: Rethinking Photographic Indexicality," in Joanna Lowry, David Green, and Jan Baetens, *Theatres of the Real* (Manchester: Photoworks, 2009), 47–60.

8. Kaja Silverman, *The Miracle of Analogy or The History of Photography*, Part 1 (Stanford, CA: Stanford University Press, 2015), 4.

9. Green and Lowry, "From Presence to the Performative," 48.

10. Ibid., 48.

11. For Activestills, "being there" is the communal essence of their practice. "Being there" may also be realized using technological means, such as the use of surveillance cameras. This notion encompasses the panoptic character of CCTV: it does not require a "true vision" of an event but rather, it is sufficient to show that it was photographed.

12. Conversation with the author, Tel Aviv, 2.9.2015.

13. Conversation with the author, Tel Aviv, 2.9.2015.

14. Conversation with the author, Tel Aviv, 2.9.2015.

15. Aura and Robin, "Israeli Army Demolish Houses and Wells in Kufr ad Dik," 17.4.2012, http://palsolidarity.org/2012/04/israeli-army-demolish-houses-and-wells-in-kufr-ad-dik.

16. Conversation with the author, Huwwara, 22.9.2015.

17. Nakba, meaning disaster or catastrophe in Arabic, is the word used for the expulsion of more than 700,000 Palestinians from their homes (villages) during the 1948 war.

18. Robert Hariman and John Louis Lucaites, *No Caption Needed: Iconic Photographs, Public Culture, and Liberal Democracy* (Chicago, IL: University of Chicago Press, 2007), 2–3.

19. See http://www.prc.org.uk/portal/index.php/activities-news/press-release/3201-palestinian-nakba-in-pictures.

20. The Israeli policy aimed at displacement of Palestinians, and that included demolition of houses, began in 1948 as an attempt to "Judaize" the land, and as the photographs of Al-Bazz and others have shown, has continued ever since. See *"We Never Finished 1948": The Continuing Campaign of Internal Displacement in Israel/Palestine* (Israel/Palestine: Activestills and the Israeli Committee Against House Demolitions, 2011).

21. Conversation with the author, Tel Aviv, 1.9.2015.

22. Conversation with the author, Tel Aviv, 26.9.2015.

23. Conversation with the author, Tel Aviv, 2.9.2015.

24. Walter Benjamin, "Little History of Photography," in Walter Benjamin, *Selected Writings*, Volume 2, Part 2, 1927–1934, trans. Rodney Livingstone et al., eds. Michel W. Jennings, Harol Eiland, and Gary Smith (Cambridge, MA: Belknap Press of the Harvard University Press, 1999), 507–40.

25. Conversation with the author, Tel Aviv, 1.9.2015.

Qalandiya Checkpoint, West Bank 24.7.2014

A Palestinian protester takes cover as Israeli soldiers fire live ammunition during a demonstraion against the Israeli offensive on the Gaza Strip. Over 20,000 Palestinians took part in the protest, two were killed, and more than 200 were injured.

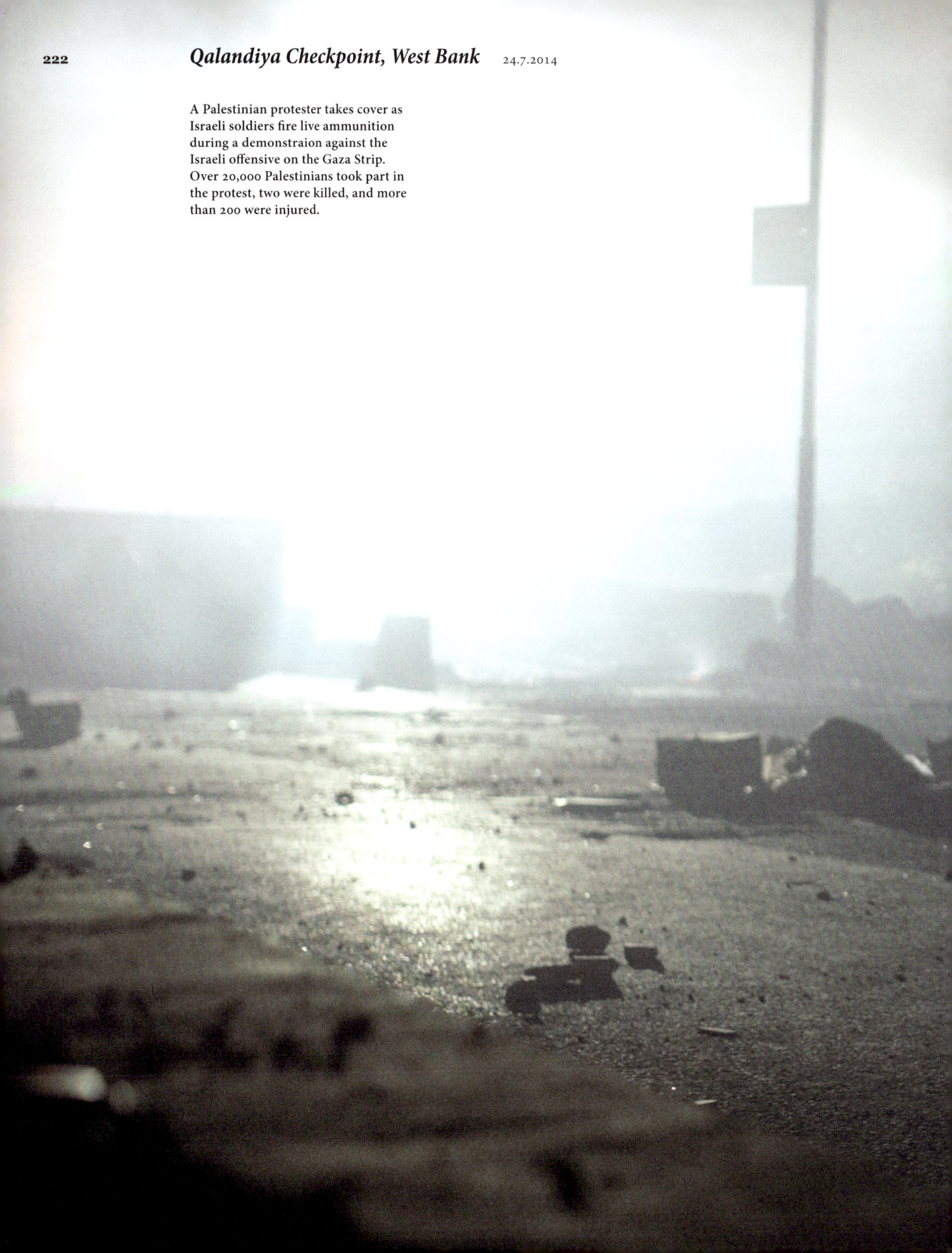

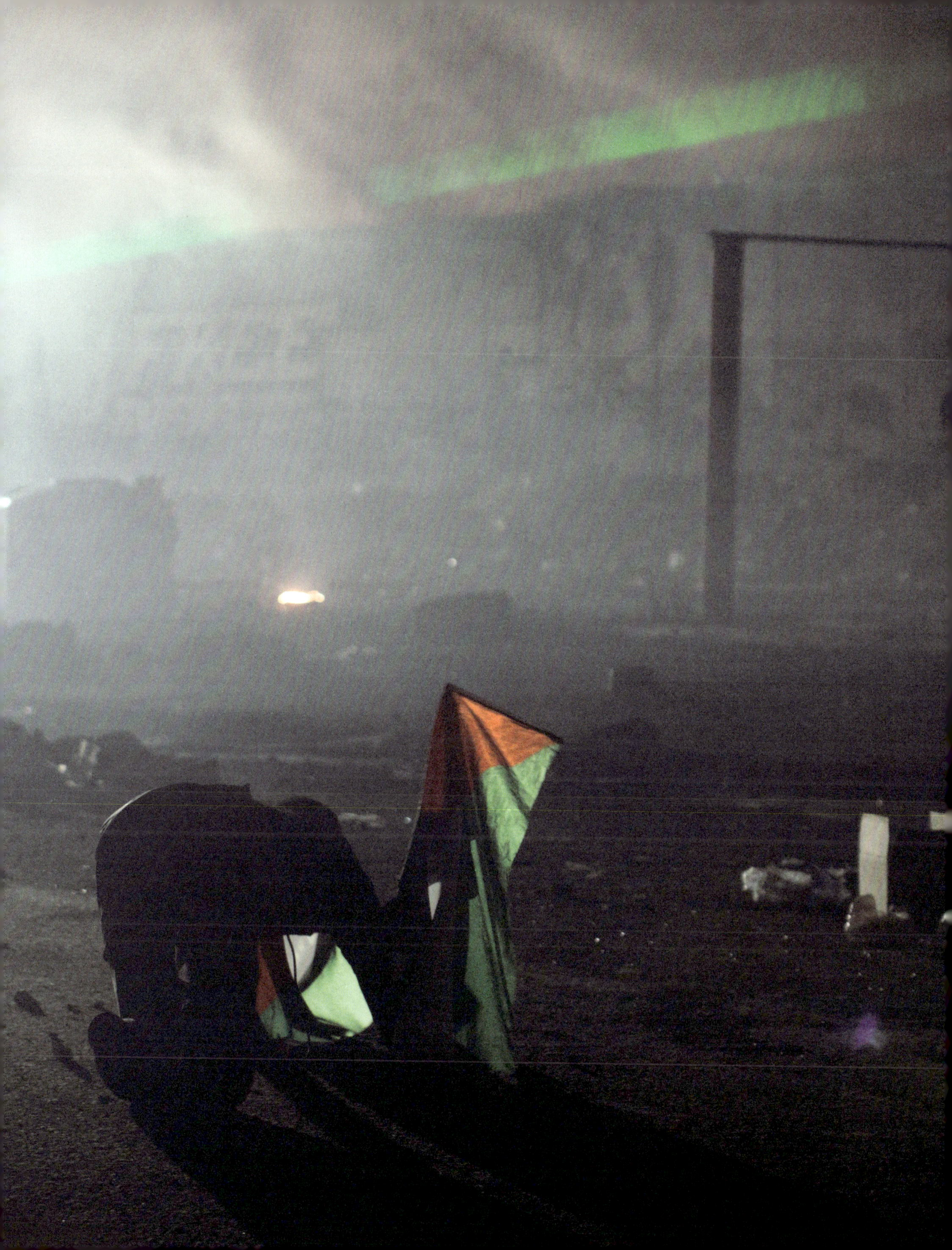

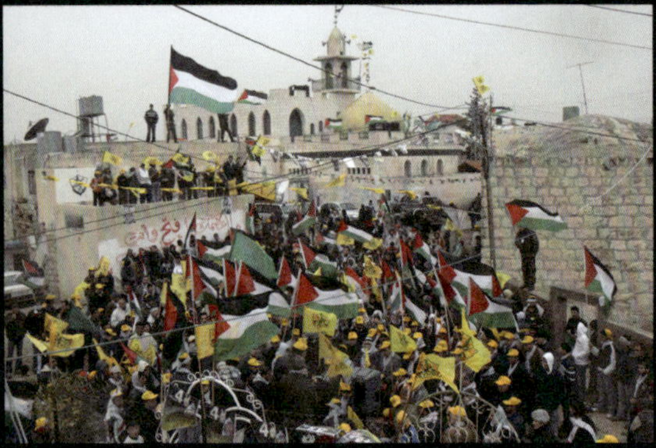

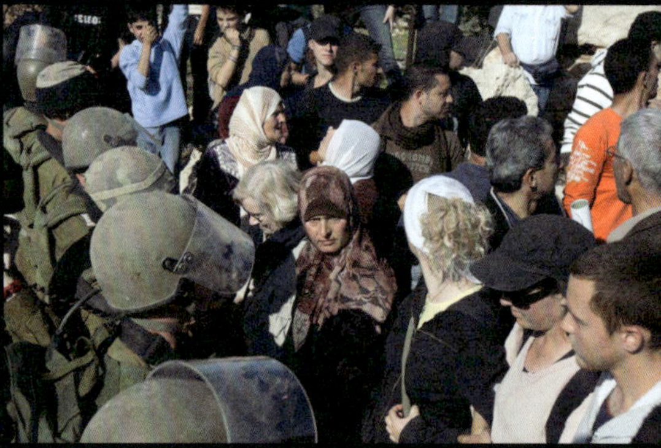

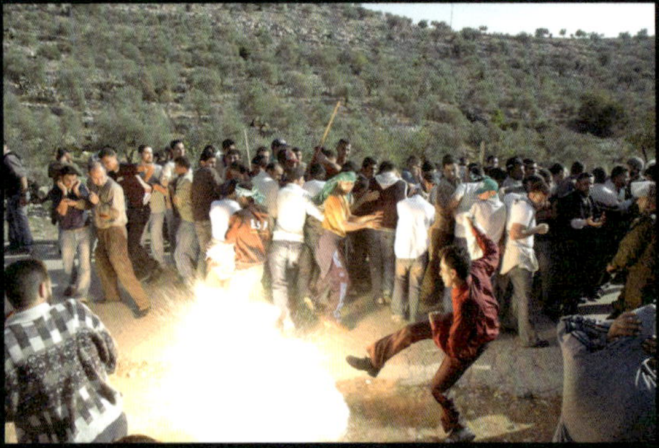

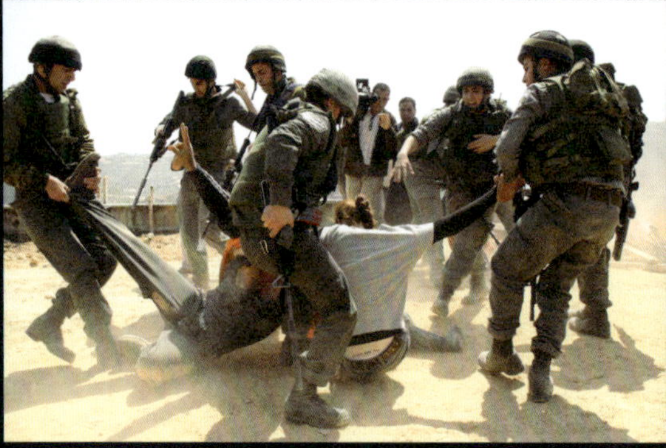

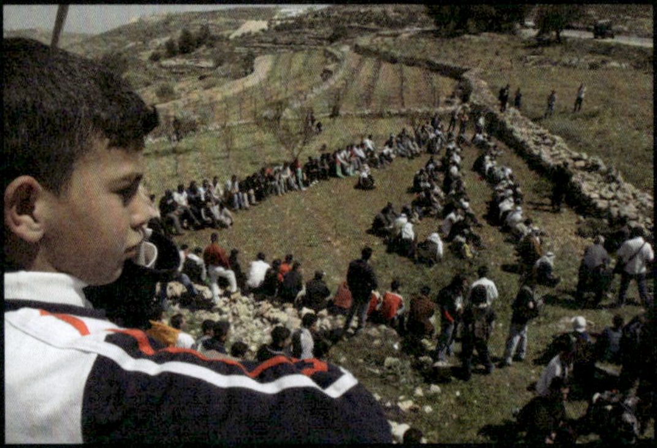

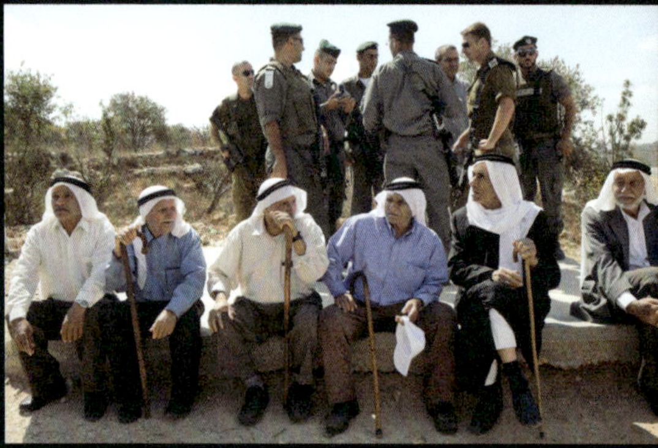

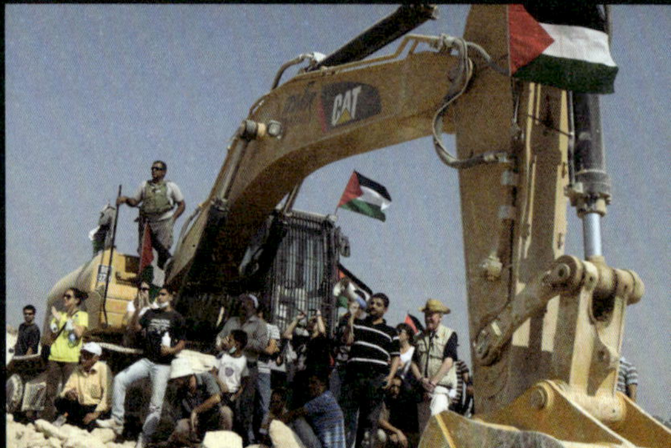

{Top left to right}
1. Protesters gather before a protest, Bil'in, West Bank, 5.1.2007 / **2.** Protesters during an action against the Israeli separation wall, Jayyous, West Bank, 16.11.2008 / **3.** Protest against the Israeli separation wall, Abud, West Bank, 25.11.2005 / **4.** Protest against the Israeli separation wall, Al-Ma'asara, West Bank, 12.4.2007 / **5.** Land Day commemoration protest, Al-Ma'asara, West Bank, 30.3.2007 / **6.** Protest against the Israeli separation Wall, Biddu, West Bank, 30.8.2009 / **7.** Protesters prevent the construction of the Israeli separation wall, Al-Walaja, West Bank, 4.8.2010

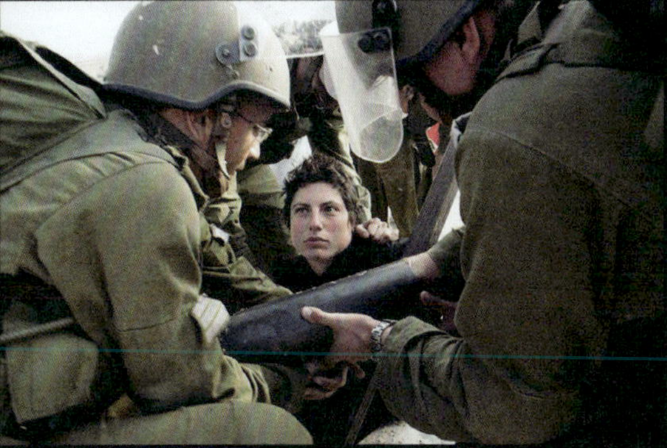

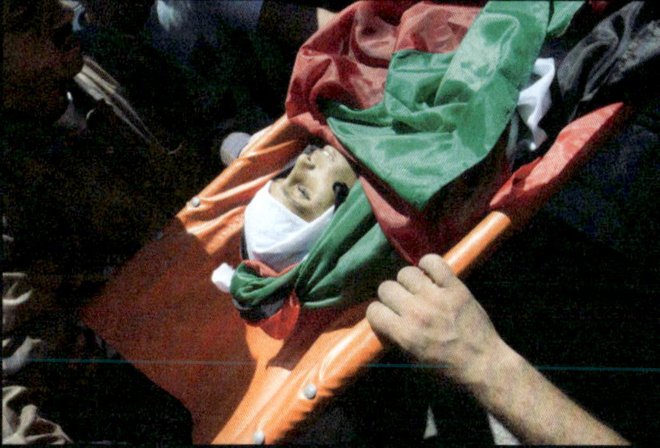

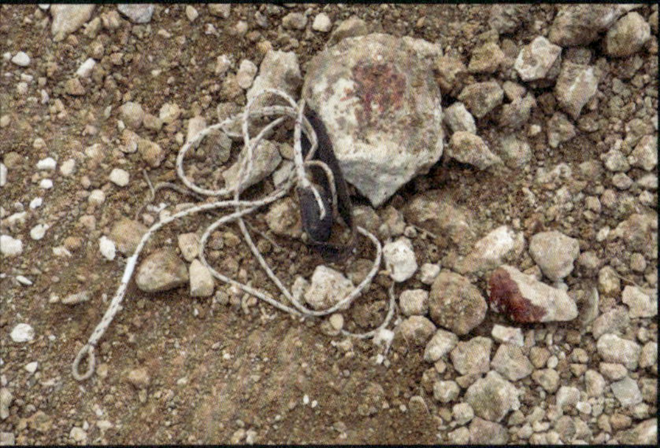

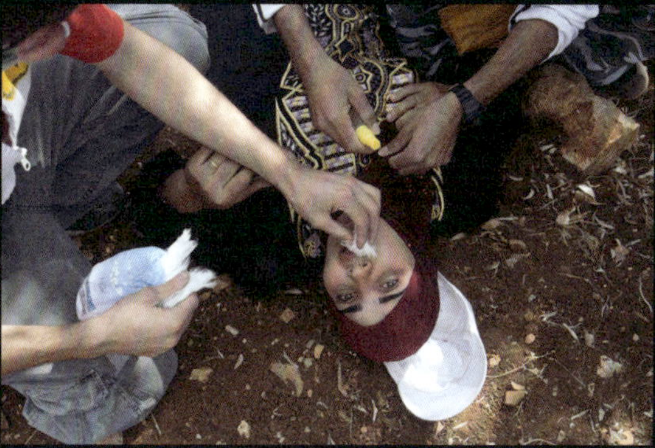

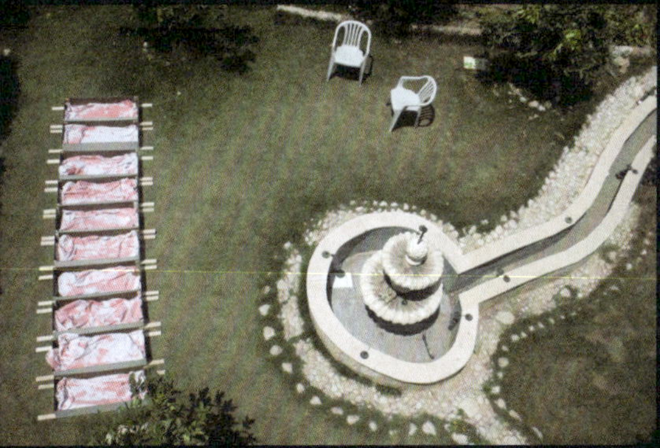

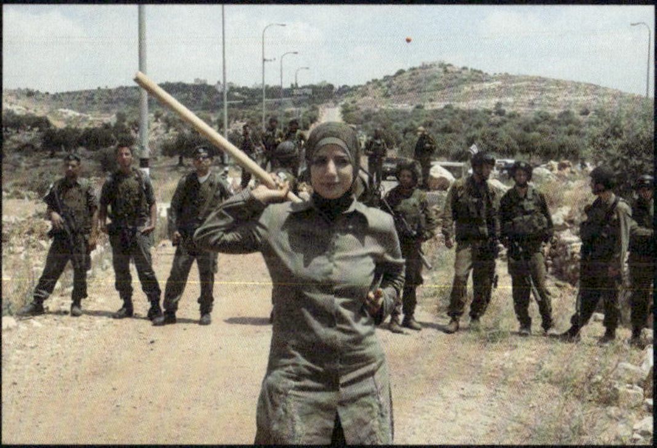

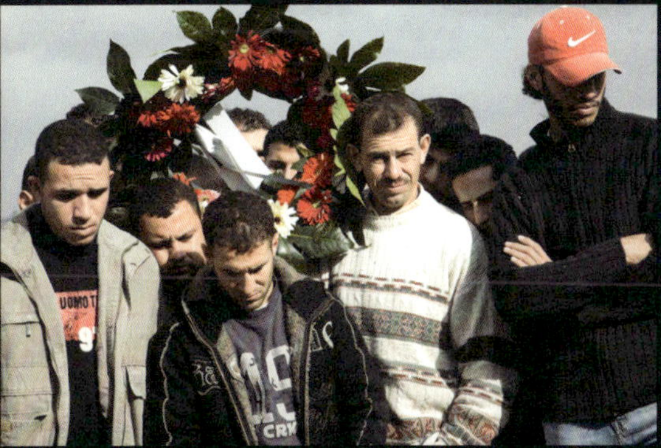

{Top left to right}
1. A protester chained during a protest, Bil'in, West Bank, 4.11.2005 / **2.** The funeral of Ahmed Yusef Mousa, Ni'lin, West Bank, 30.7.2008 / **3.** A slingshot belonging to a Palestinian protester, Ni'lin, West Bank, 4.12.2009 / **4.** A protester suffering from tear gas, Ni'lin, West Bank, 10.10.2008 / **5.** Mock corpses ready for burial staged by protesters, Bil'in, West Bank, 16.6.2006 / **6.** Protester at an action against army roadblocks, Shufa, West Bank, 10.5.2008 / **7.** Funeral of Arafat Khawaja, Ni'lin, West Bank, 29.12.2008

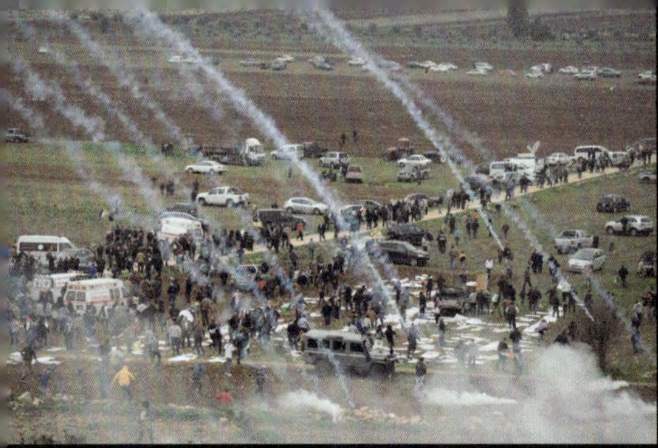

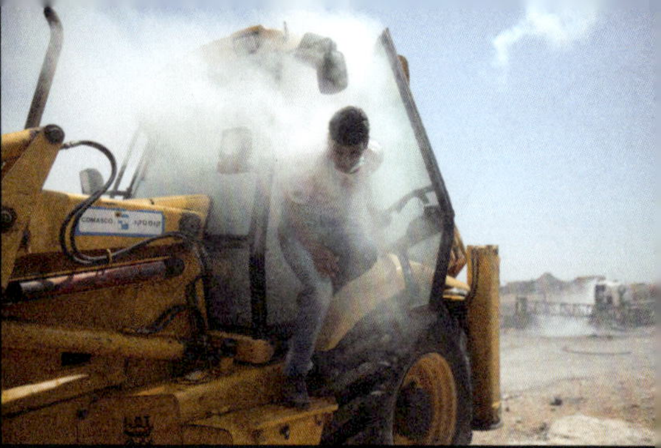

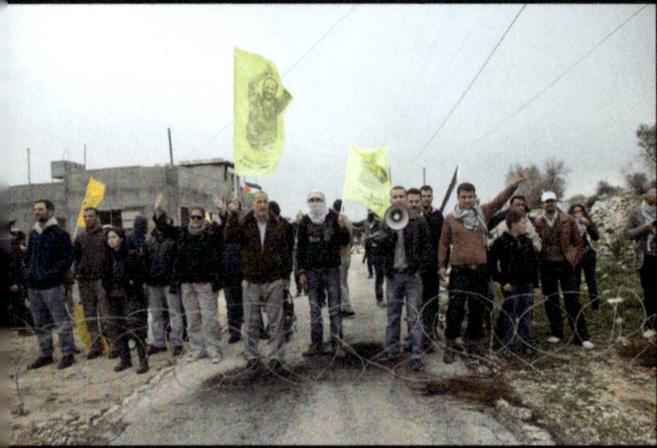

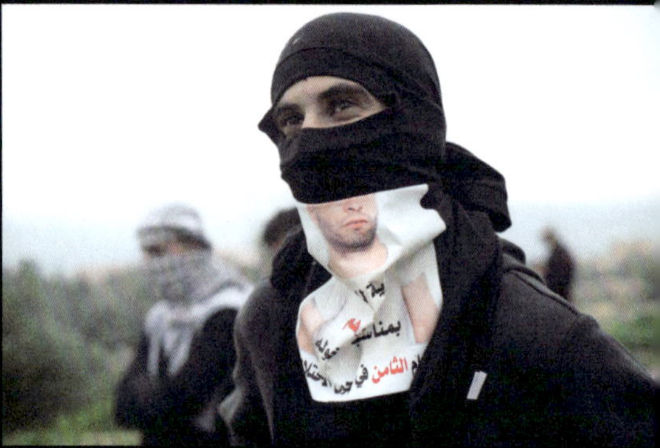

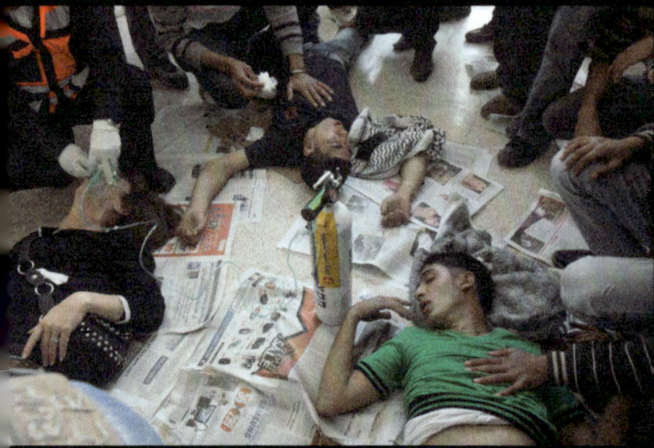

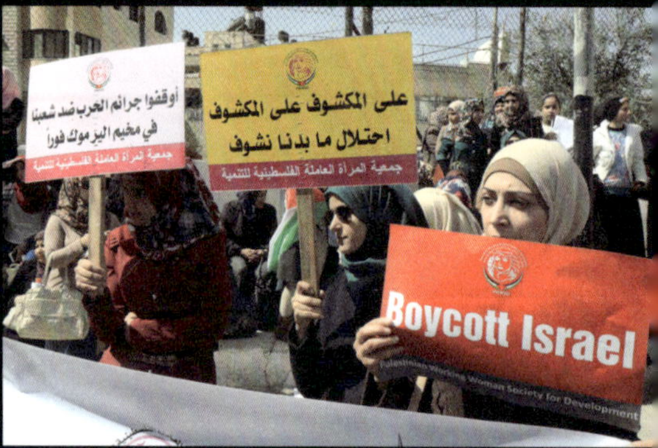

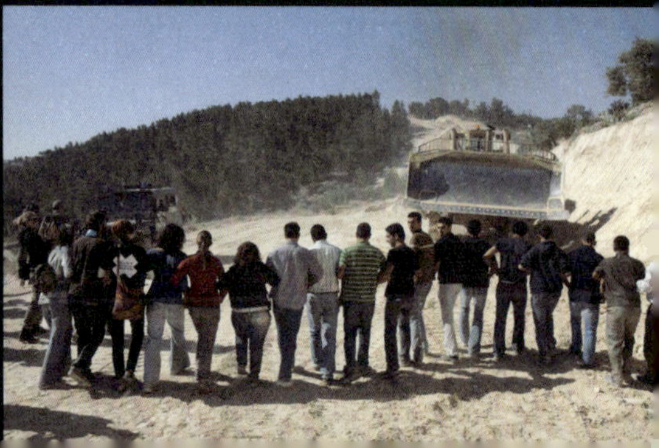

Top left to right}
. Protest commemorating the death of Palestinian ninister Ziad Abu Ein, Turmus Ayya, West Bank, 9.12.2014 / **2.** A Palestinian protester escaping a oulldozer at a direct action, Bil'in, West Bank, 24.6.2011 / . Protesters, Kafr Qaddum, West Bank, 30.12.2011 / . Protester, Kafr Qaddum, West Bank, 19.12.2014 / . Protesters treated at a clinic during Nakba day protest, Qalandiya, West Bank, 15.5.2011 / **6.** Protesters mark nternational Women's Day, Qalandiya Checkpoint, West Bank, 7.3.2015 / **7.** Protesters at a direct action against the sraeli separation wall, Al-Walaja, West Bank, 6.5.2010

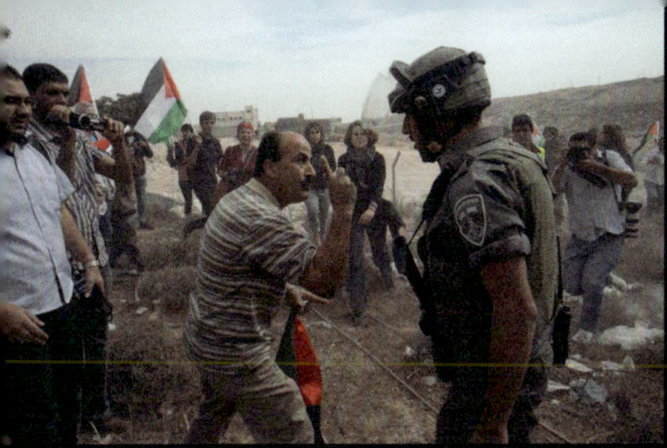

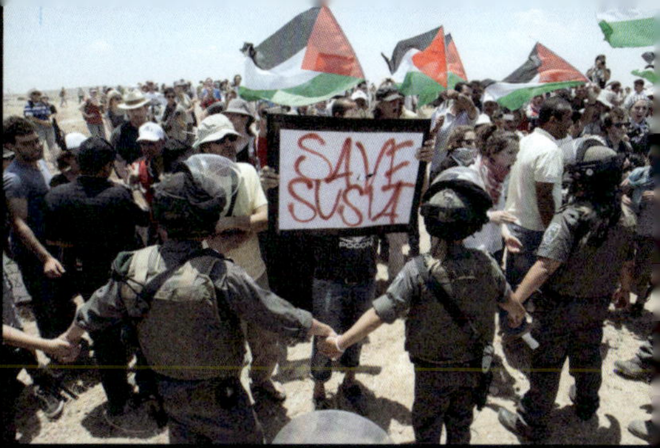

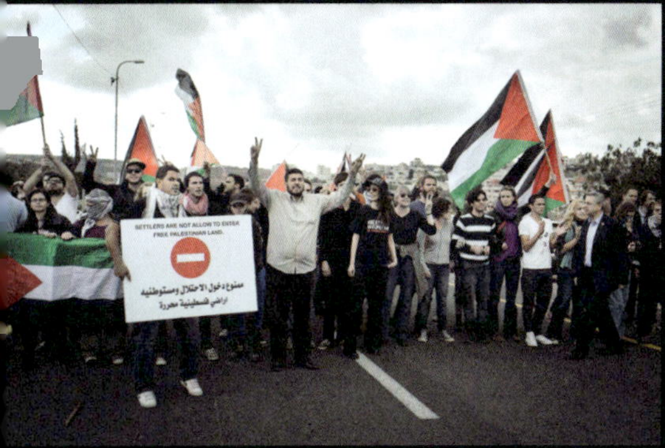

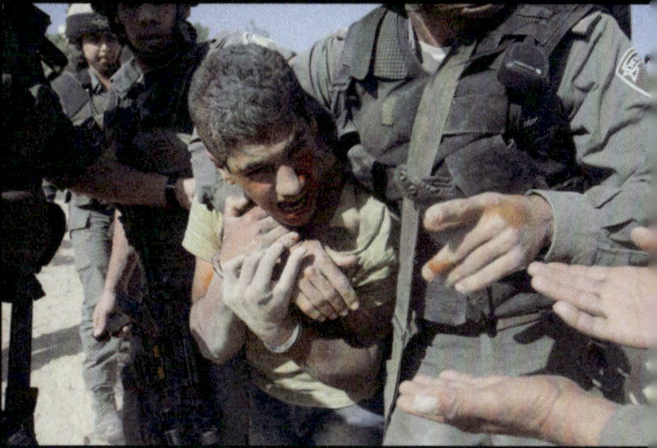

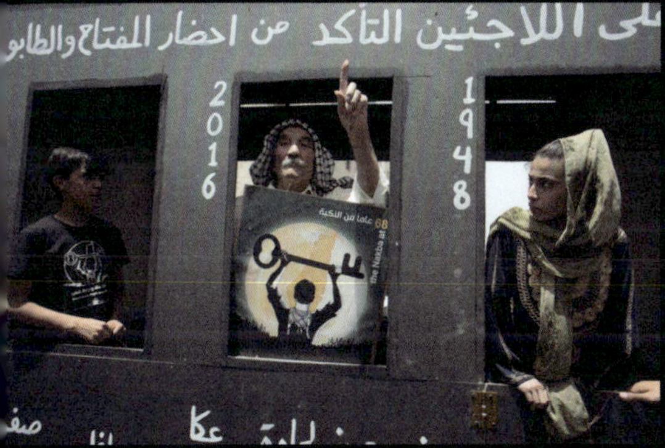

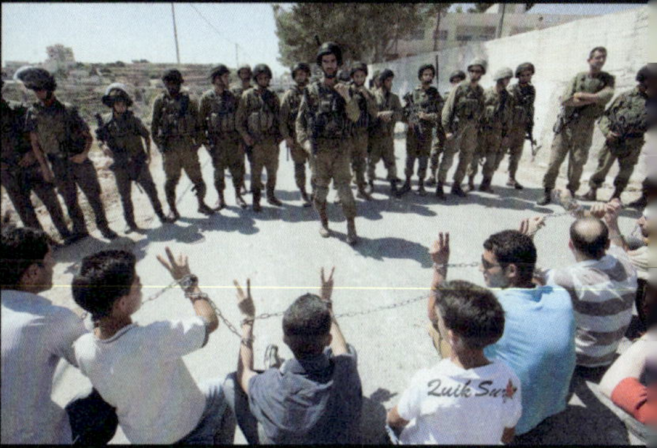

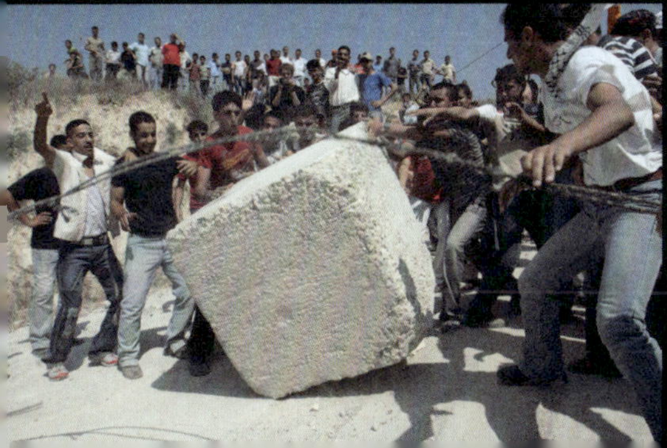

{Top left to right}
1. Action against settlements, Sha'ar Binyamin settlement, West Bank, 24.10.2012 / **2.** Protest against the demolition of Susiya village, West Bank, 22.6.2012 / **3.** Protesters block Road 60 at an action against movement restrictions for Palestinians, West Bank, 14.11.2012 / **4.** Palestinian youth arrested at a direct action, Al-Walaja, West Bank, 27.4.201 / **5.** Palestinians inside a makeshift train, symbolically heading to the homes they were forced to leave in 1948, Bethlehem, West Bank, 15.5.2016 / **6.** Protesters stage a sit-in, Al-Ma'asara, West Bank, 14.9.2012 / **7.** Protesters remove an army roadblock, Sarra, W... Bank, 31.8.2007

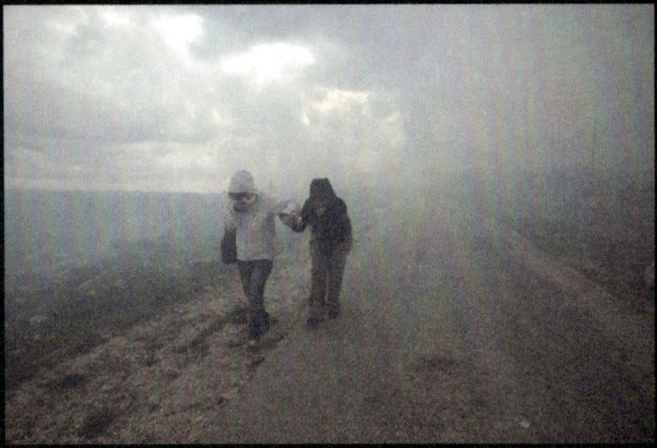

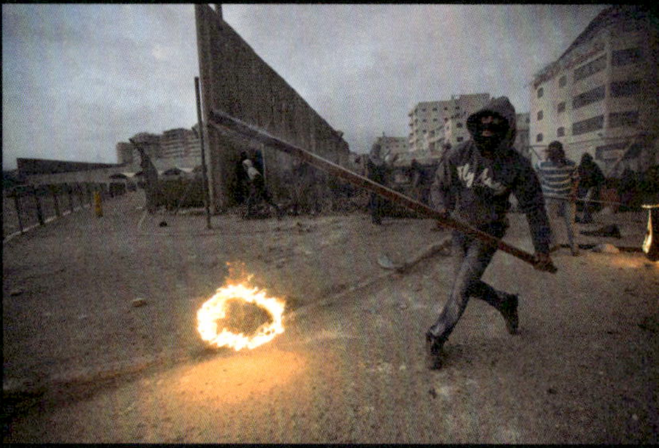

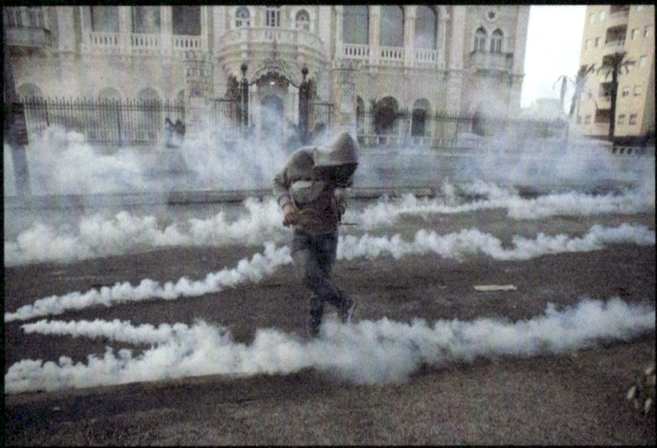

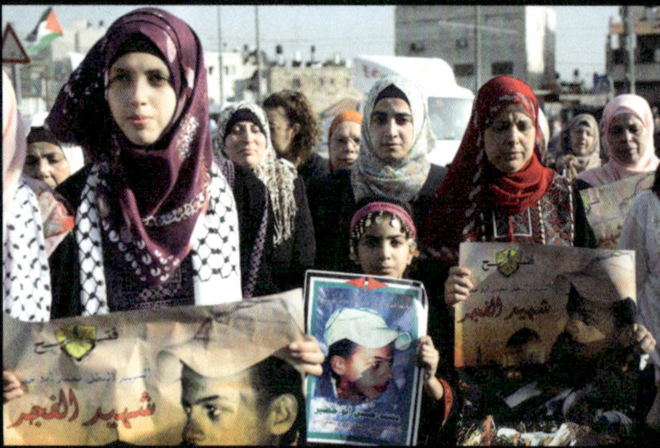

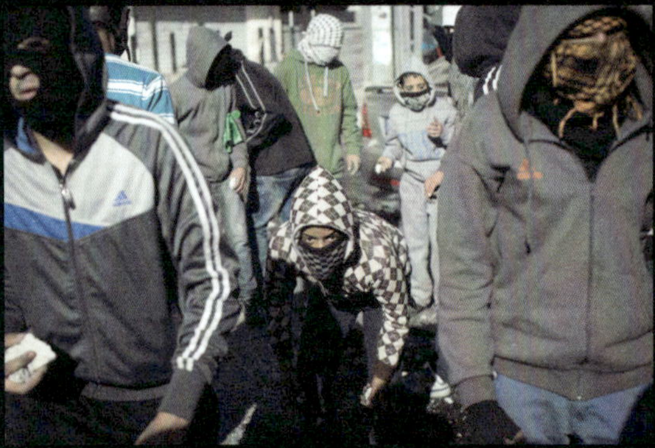

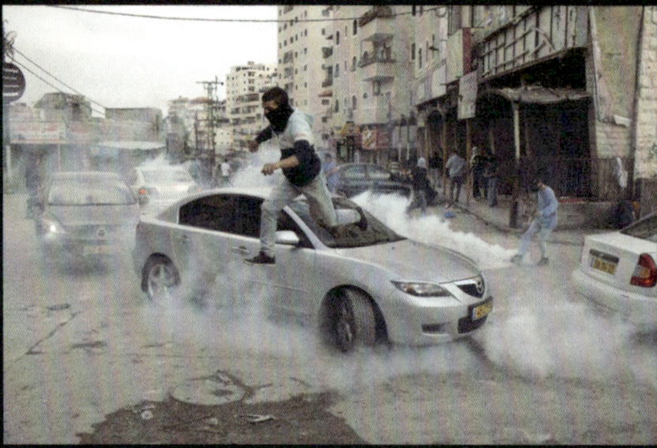

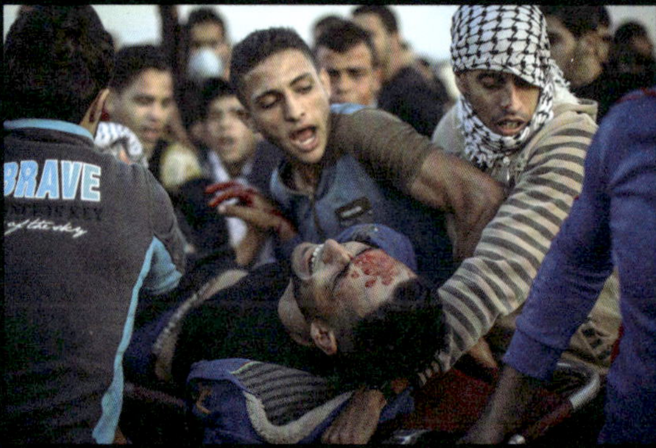

{Top left to right}
1. Protesters suffer from tear gas, Bil'in, West Bank, 20.2.2009 / **2.** A protester at clashes, Shuafat refugee camp, East Jerusalem, 5.11.2014 / **3.** A protester at clashes with the Israeli Army, Bethlehem, West Bank, 20.11.2015 / **4.** Protesters commemorate the murder of Mohammed Abu Khdeir, Shuafat, East Jerusalem, 2.7.2015 / **5.** Protesters at clashes with Israeli border police, Shuafat refugee camp, East Jerusalem, 7.11.2014 / **6.** Protester at clashes with Israeli border police, Shuafat refugee camp, East Jerusalem, 5.11.2014 / **7.** Protester shot by the Israeli Army, Israeli-Gaza border, 16.11.2015

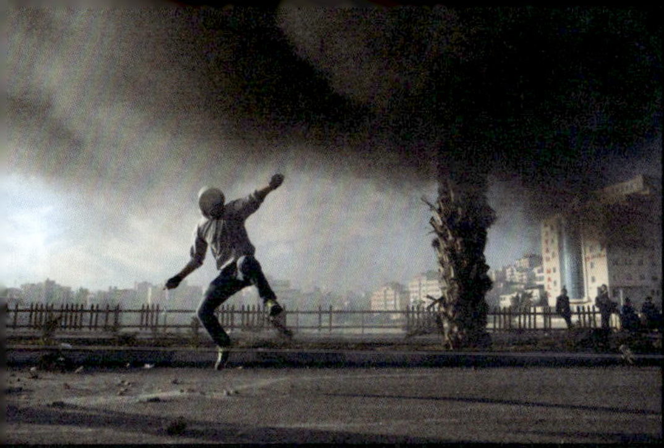

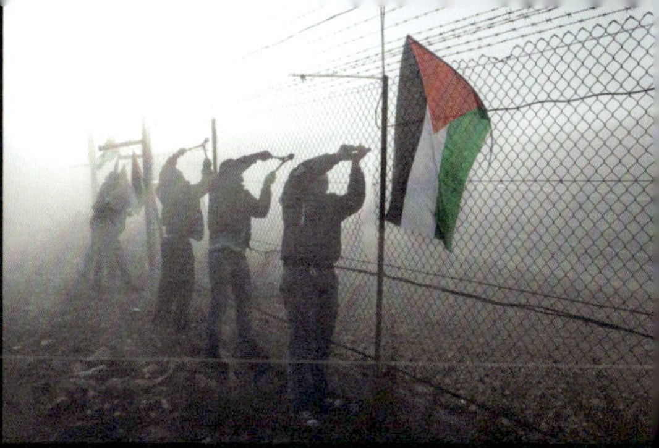

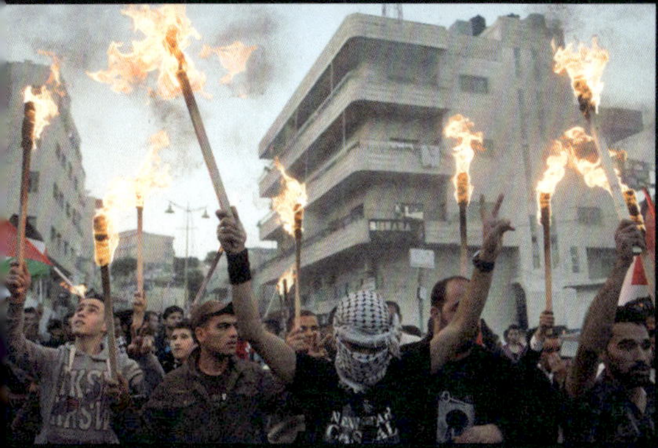

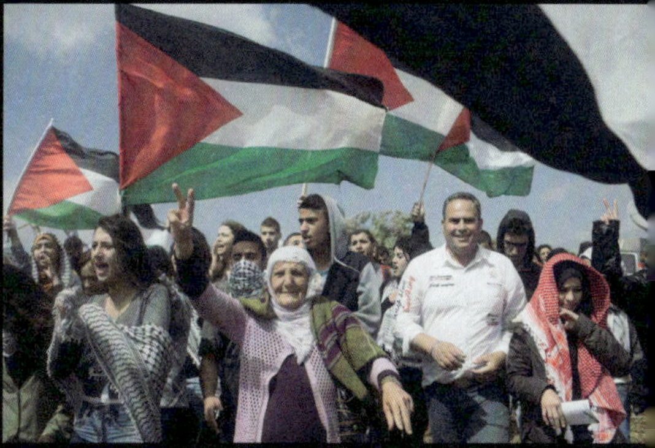

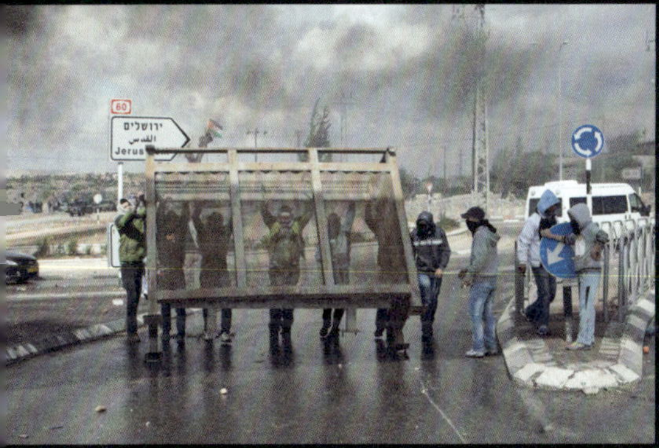

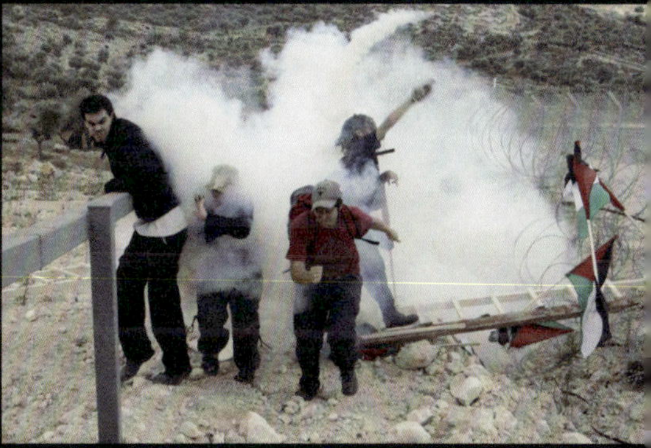

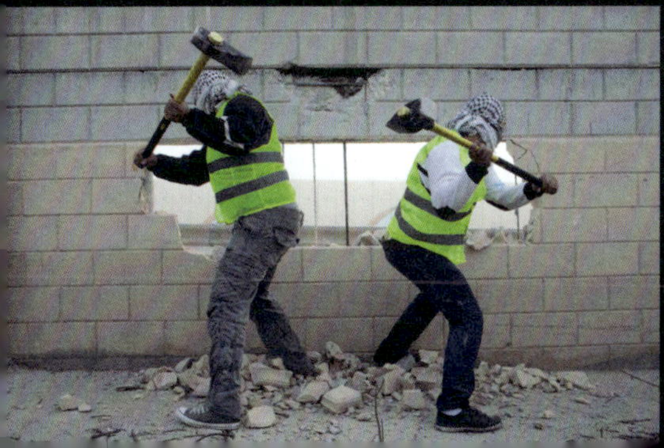

{Top left to right}
1. Protester at clashes, near Israeli settlement of Beit El, West Bank, 20.11.2015 / **2.** Protesters cut a section of Israeli separation wall, Rafat, West Bank, 15.11.2013 / **3.** Protesters march at Nakba day protest, Bethlehem, West Bank, 14.5.2013 / **4.** Palestinian citizens of Israel during March of Return protest, Hadatha village, Israel, 23.4.2015 / **5.** Protesters during clashes after the funeral of Tal'at Ramia, A-Ram, West Bank, 25.2.2012 / **6.** Protesters run from tear gar, Bil'in, West Bank, 27.10.2005 / **7.** Protesters break the Israeli separation wall, Bir Nabala, West Bank, 15.11.2013

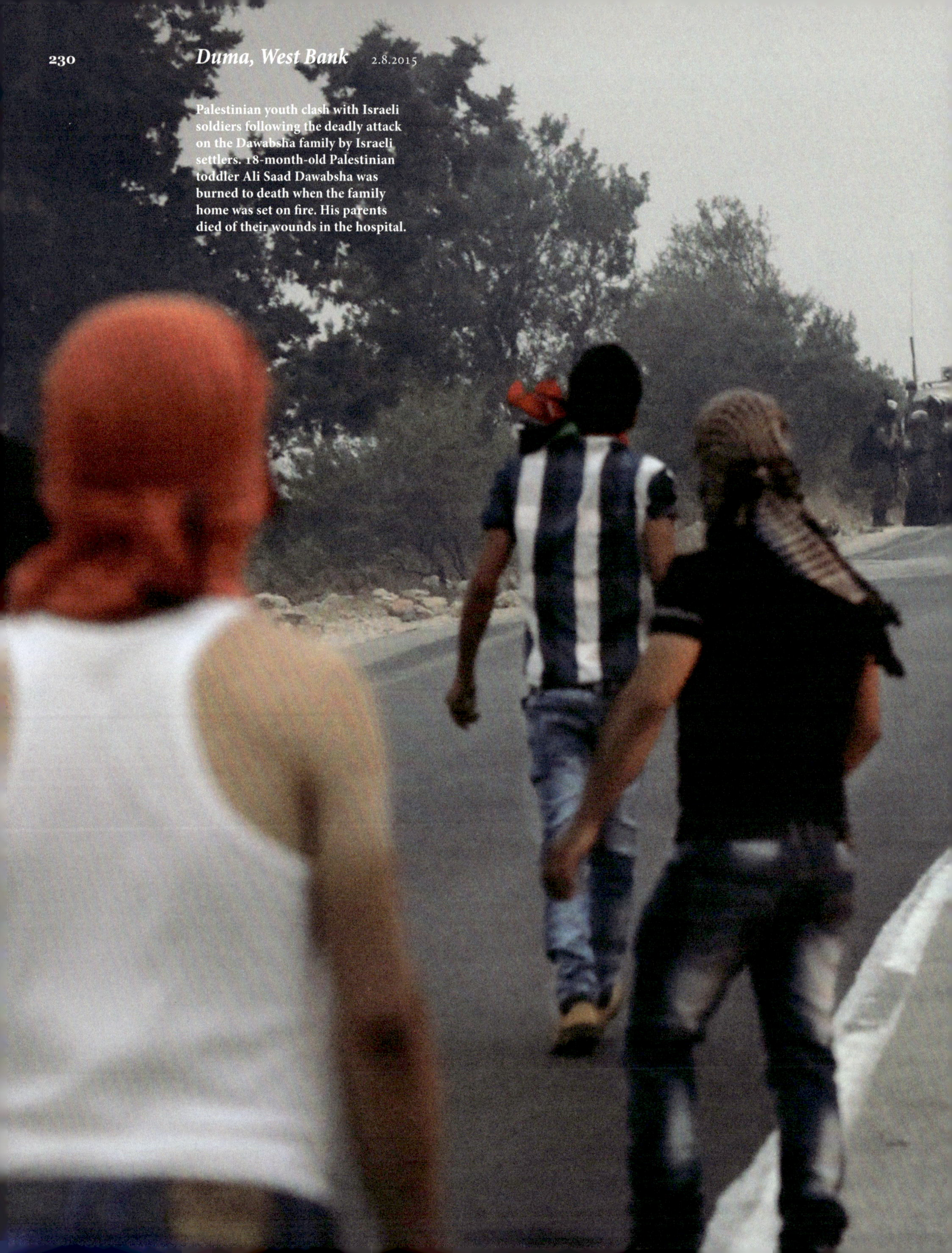

Duma, West Bank 2.8.2015

Palestinian youth clash with Israeli soldiers following the deadly attack on the Dawabsha family by Israeli settlers. 18-month-old Palestinian toddler Ali Saad Dawabsha was burned to death when the family home was set on fire. His parents died of their wounds in the hospital.

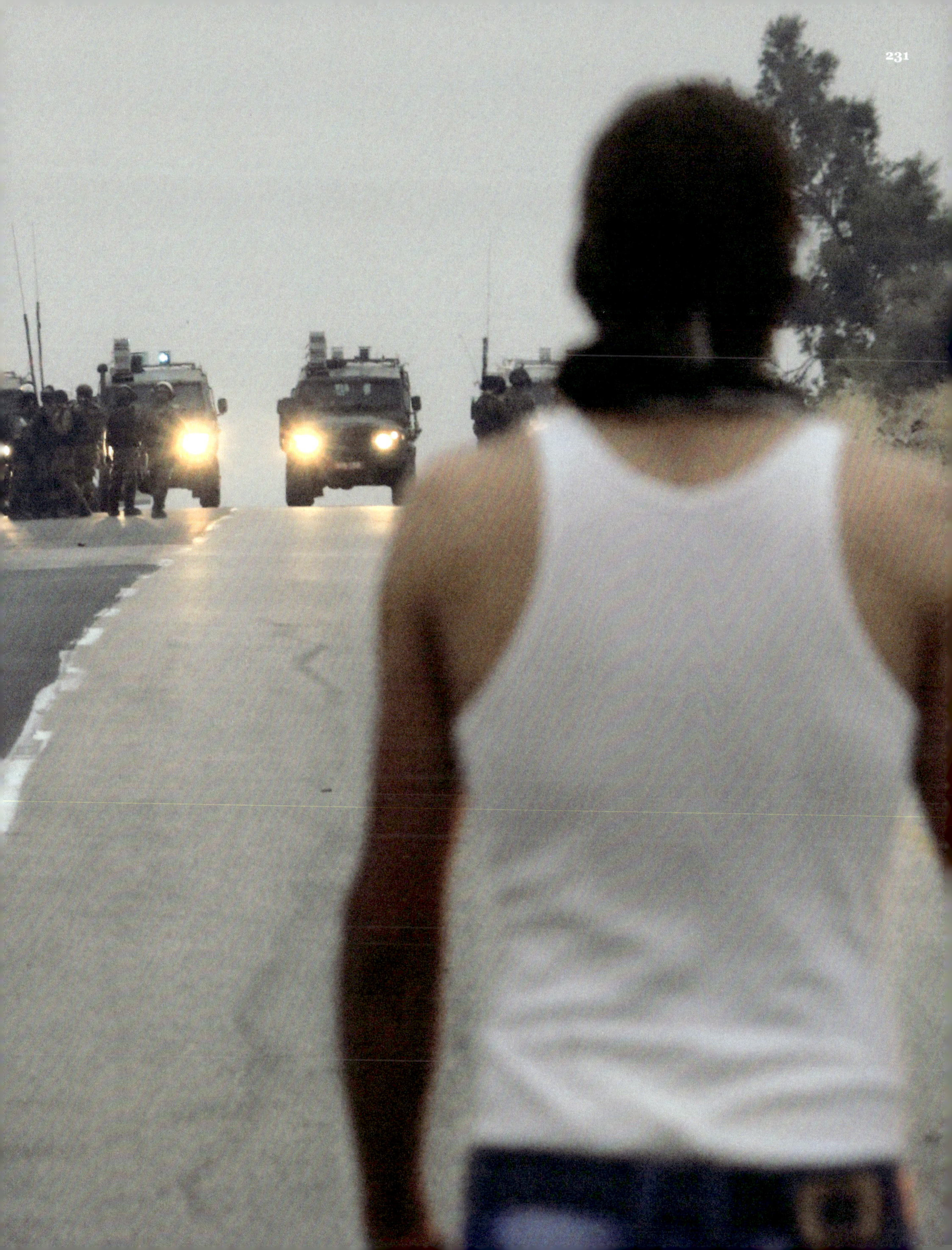

Ahmad Al-Bazz

Why am I a Member of Activestills?

Almost seven years ago I became a fan of Activestills. Today, I'm a member. As a young media student living in the occupied West Bank, I was fascinated by the Activestills collective—a body of activist photographers working in Palestine/Israel with a special focus on the Palestinian struggle.

In my final years of high school, and like everyone else in this agitated country, my interest in politics began to grow as a result of living under the ongoing Israeli military occupation. Back then, while I would explore the Internet, visiting Activestills' website was one of my weekly habits. I also enjoyed collecting my favorite pictures from their archive and organizing them in folders on my laptop. I sensed something unique in their work, maybe because of their wide coverage of the actions, or the "activist soul" that came through in the photographs.

I admit that at first I felt angry when I realized that most of Activestills' members were Israeli. It was a shock because I used to consider every Israeli, without exception, a colonialist. Over time, some of my ideas have changed, and the range of "exceptions" has become broader.

In 2010, I began to study media at a local Palestinian university in the West Bank and at the same time started working on my photography skills, which I had already been practicing as a hobby for a few years. I also decided to dedicate more time to activist work in the popular struggle. I volunteered in different groups and campaigns inside and outside the university campus. My favorite destinations were the weekly demonstrations against the Israeli occupation that were taking place in several villages. Every Friday I would take my camera to document the actions and in this way I was able to connect my interest in photography with my activist work.

On a cold day in 2012, I happened to meet Anne Paq, a member of Activestills, in the West Bank village of Nabi Saleh. I was excited to finally meet someone from Activestills in person. Making the best of my not very fluent English, we had a short conversation, during which I overcame my inhibition and asked to join Activestills. A few weeks later, my student-dream became a reality when I was invited to attend my first Activestills meeting.

Israeli-Palestinian Cooperation?

Activestills was more than a platform to publish my pictures. I also felt very close to the collective's members. I found we had many ideas and beliefs in common but, naturally, also some inevitable differences. Making the decision to become a member of the Activestills collective was not simple; as a matter of fact it was complicated, as is everything in this country.

The joint struggle was welcomed by broad segments of Palestinians, especially by the residents of villages struggling weekly against the occupation. However, joint Israeli-Palestinian work is not that popular in Palestine for a variety of reasons. Many Palestinians have chosen to avoid "normalization with Israelis."

According to the BDS movement's principles, which are the main reference for Palestinians to judge joint Israeli-Palestinian projects, "normalization" is defined as

> … the participation in any project, initiative or activity, in Palestine or internationally, that aims (implicitly or explicitly) to bring together Palestinians (and/or Arabs) and Israelis (people or institutions) without placing as its goal resistance to and exposure of the Israeli occupation and all forms of discrimination and oppression against the Palestinian people.[1]

1. http://pacbi.org/etemplate.php?id=1850.

This definition is endorsed by the overwhelming majority of Palestinian civil society. However, there is one exception to Israeli-Palestinian joint work that is compatible with the resistance framework of the BDS movement:

> For a Palestinian-Israeli relationship not to be a form of normalization two basic conditions must be met: (1) the Israeli side must support full and comprehensive rights for all Palestinians in accordance with international law, and (2) the relationship itself must involve a form of resistance to Israel's occupation and violations of international law … the only normal relationship between those from the oppressor community and those from the oppressed community is co-resistance, not co-existence. Co-existence can only happen (ethically speaking) after the end of oppression, when both sides can enjoy equal rights.[2]

2. http://pacbi.org/etemplate.php?id=1749.

I am a strict adherent of the BDS principles. My decision to join the Activestills collective was taken after carefully checking those standards, and while I absolutely reject the "colonization of minds," which can happen by getting involved in Israeli-Palestinian projects that try to normalize the abnormal—relations between the oppressed and the oppressor while still under Israeli colonialism—this is not the case with Activestills.

Why Activestills?

Working in a collective with Israeli, Palestinian, and international members has many merits. In my opinion, reading news on a platform like Activestills' is more credible and trustworthy specifically because of its "multinational" nature. In fact, the geopolitical reality in Palestine/Israel makes this kind of cooperation a highly valuable asset.

Due to the occupation's restriction of movement, as a Palestinian photographer I am able to travel in less than twenty percent of Palestine/Israel (the West Bank only, with the exception of some parts of Area "C"). An Israeli photographer can move freely in about eighty-five percent of Palestine/Israel (Israel within the Green Line and the West Bank, except Area "A"), while an international photographer is able to travel freely almost everywhere in Palestine/Israel (Israel within the Green Line, the West Bank, and, with a permit, also Gaza). This complicated reality has made having photographers from different places a necessity to capably cover the area's issues. We often take advantage of this special ability when we want to create a unique collective photo story for a certain action.

Activestills are not a photojournalism agency, but we feel proud to be considered a main source of images for many reputable human rights organizations, campaigns, activists, and human rights lawyers, among others. It is a great feeling to see your work expanding both locally and internationally. Activestills have helped me broaden my activist networks and have also enabled me to meet more Israelis, considering that at one time I had no contact with any Israelis at all.

Members of Activestills are not paid for their work, which I believe keeps the collective's efforts pure and truthful. The collective is not an NGO; it is not registered in Israel or in Palestine or internationally, which, in itself, is a political statement.

Joining the Activestills collective, my second family, was one of the best things that I did in my life. I am very proud to be part of this group which is committed to the struggle against all forms of oppression in Palestine/Israel.

[Opposite page]
A Palestinian takes part in the inaugural Palestine Marathon, Bethlehem, West Bank, 21.4.2013. Under the banner, "Right to Movement," runners had to complete two laps of the same route, as organizers were unable to find a single course of 42 uninterrupted kilometers under Palestinian Authority control.

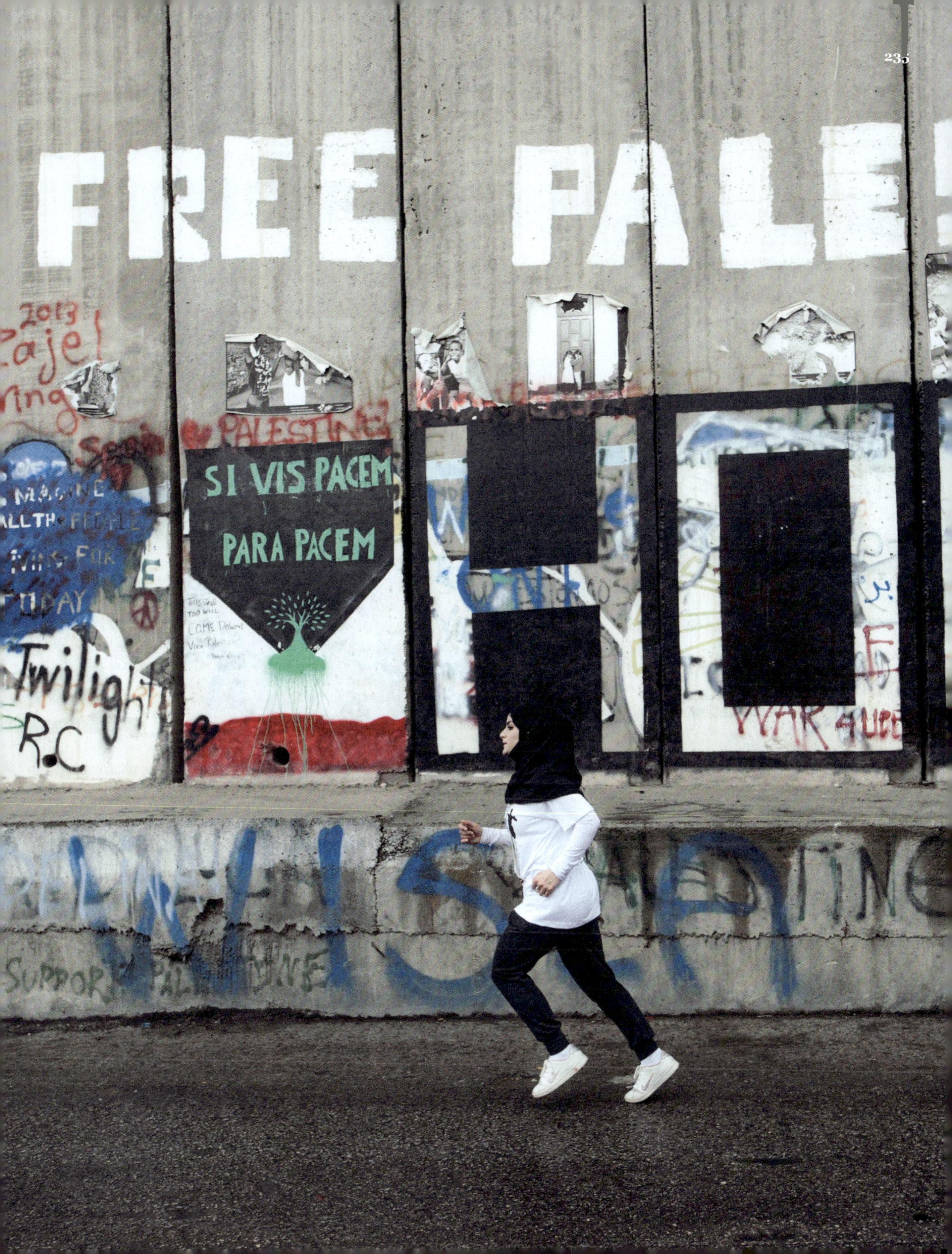
FREE PALE
SI VIS PACEM
PARA PACEM
Twilight
R.C
WAR

Palestinians wait to cross into Jerusalem, on their way to attend Ramadan Friday prayer in Al-Aqsa mosque.

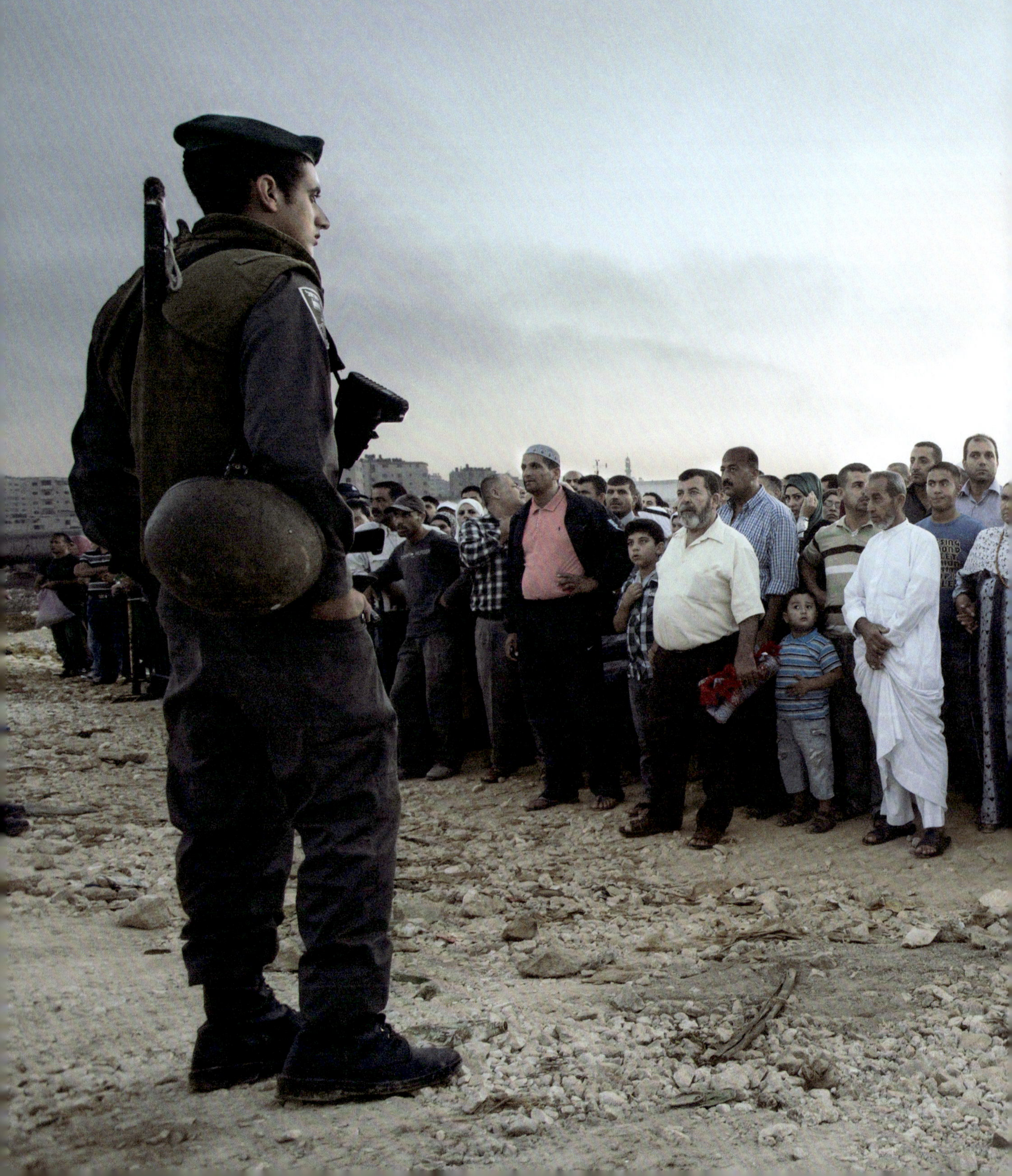

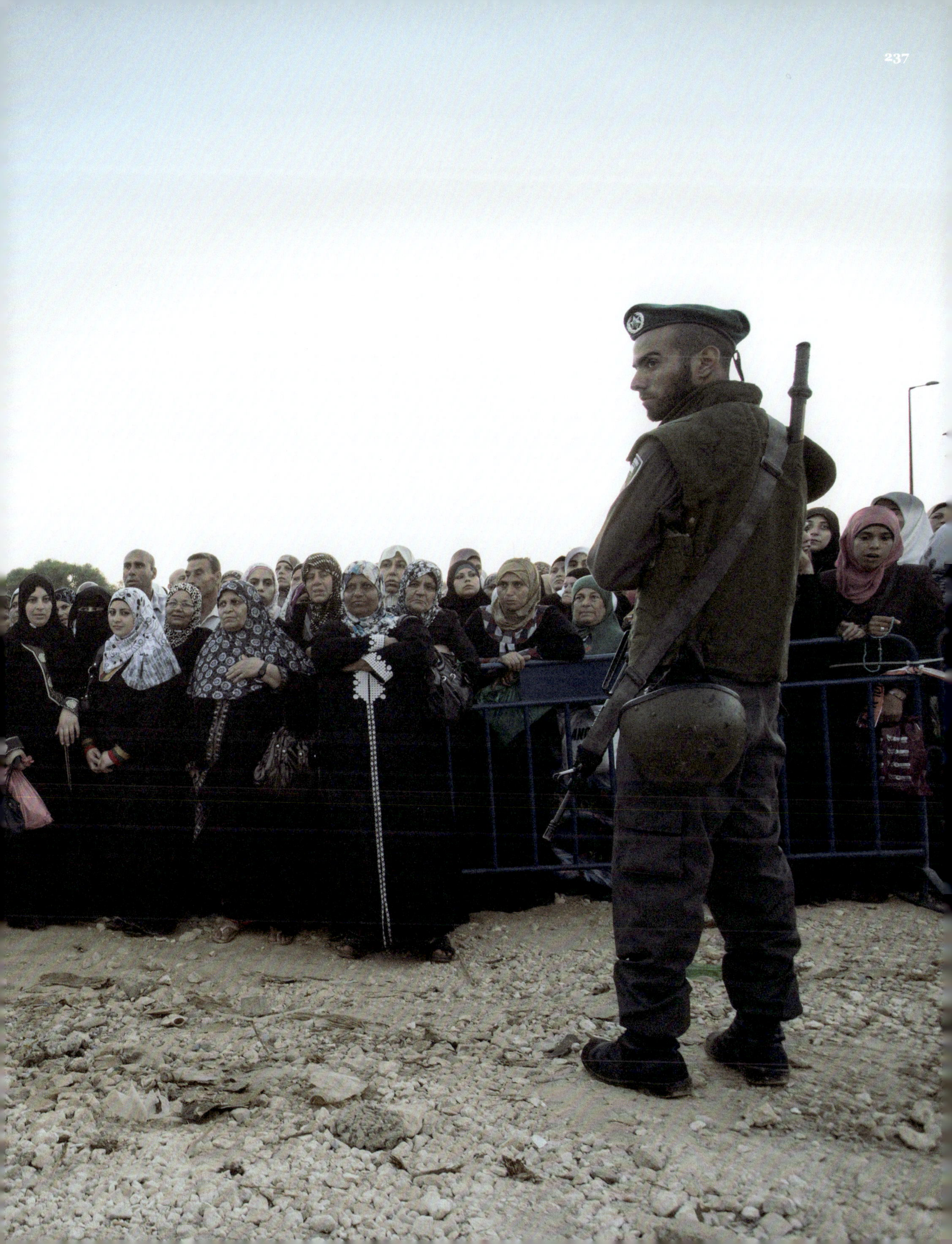

A-Ram, West Bank 19.7.2013

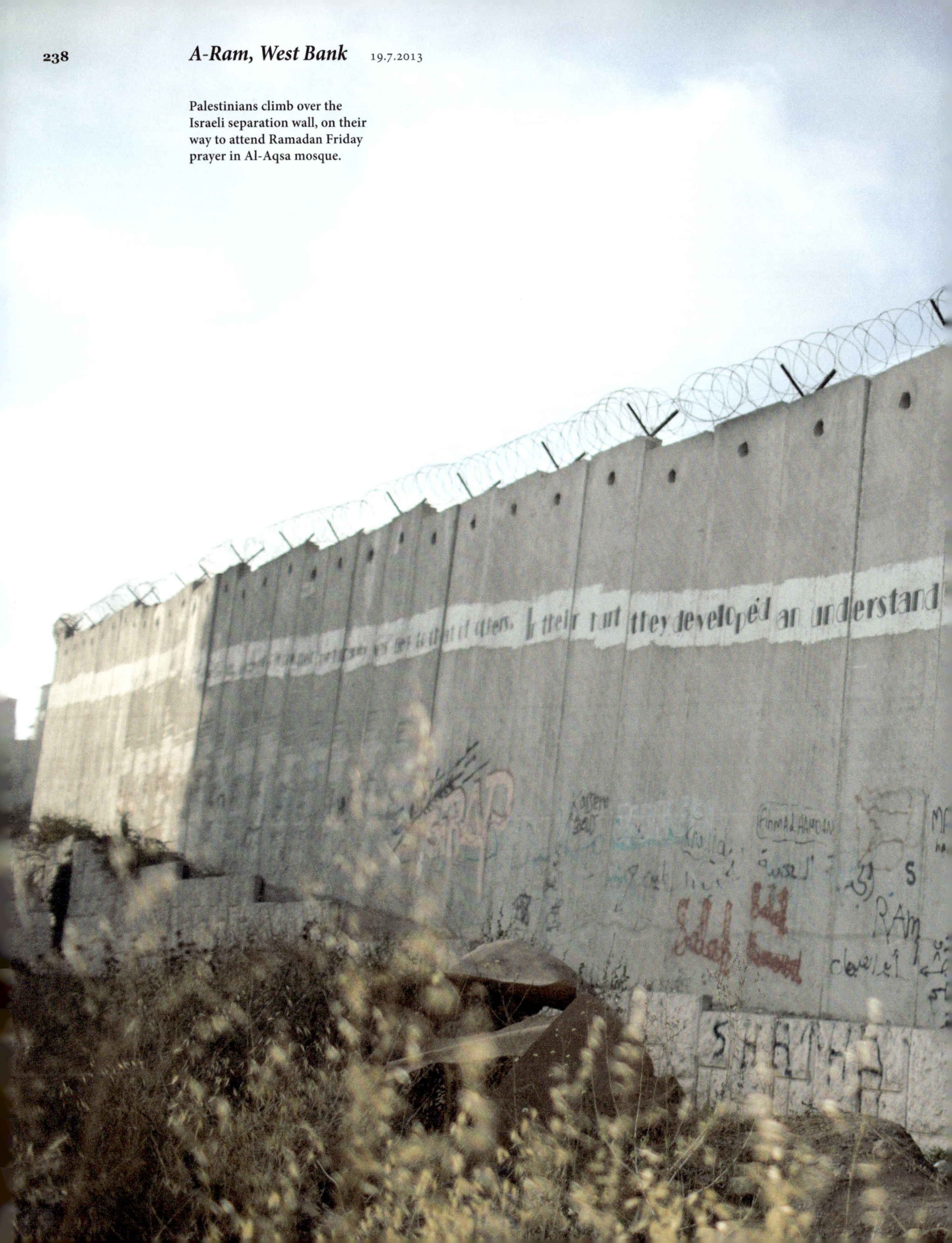

Palestinians climb over the Israeli separation wall, on their way to attend Ramadan Friday prayer in Al-Aqsa mosque.

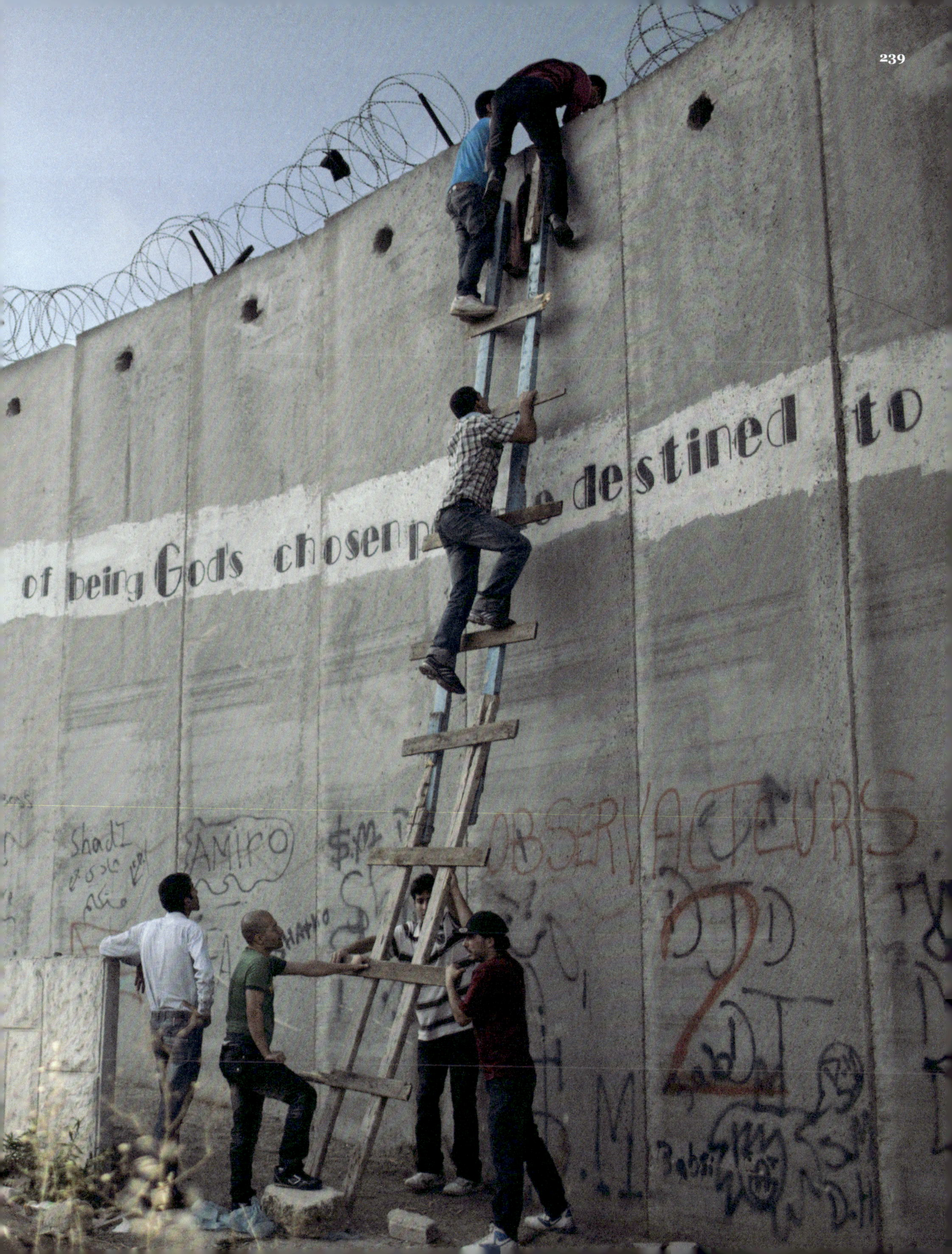
e destined to
of being God's chosen p
OBSERVACTEURS

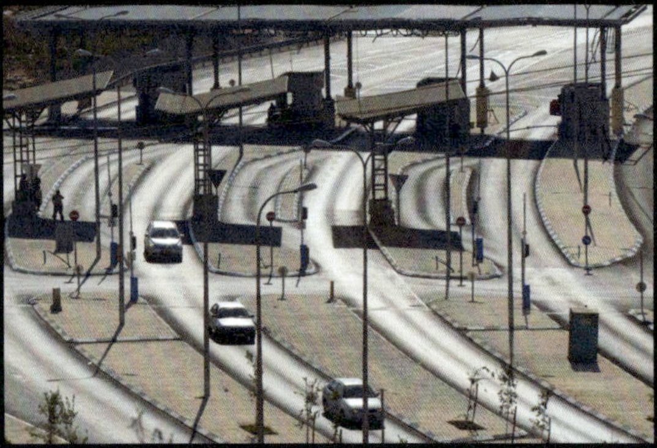

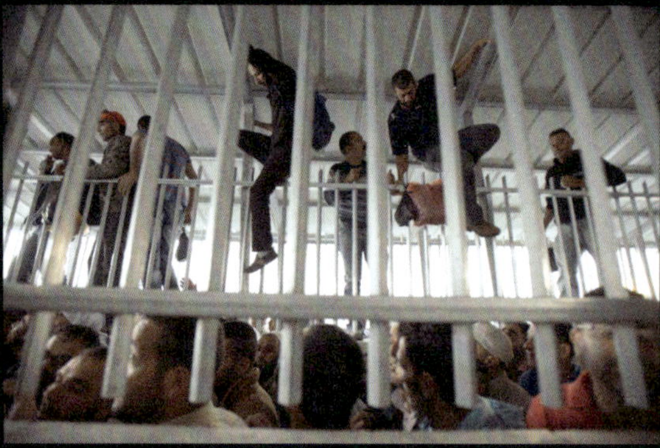

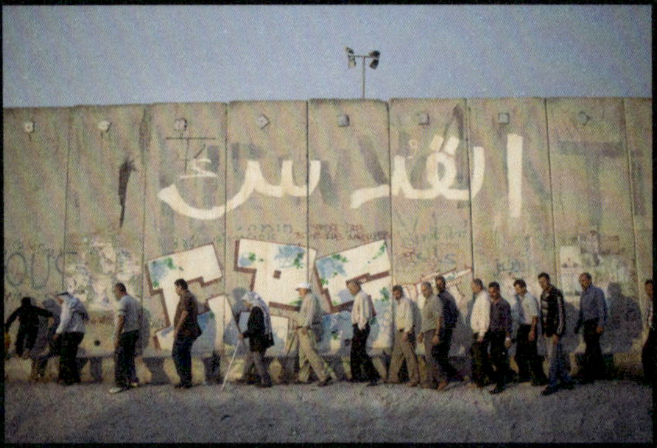

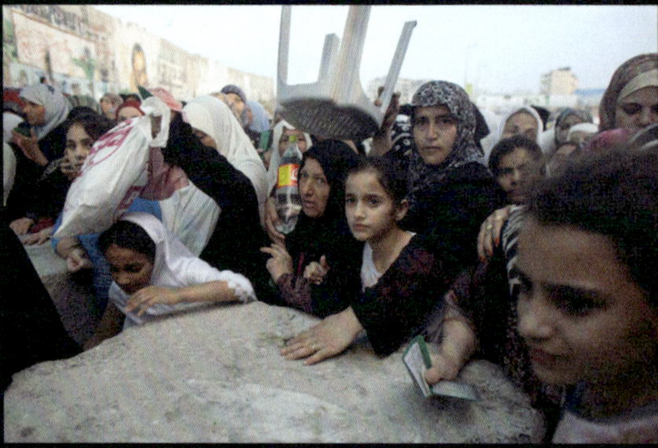

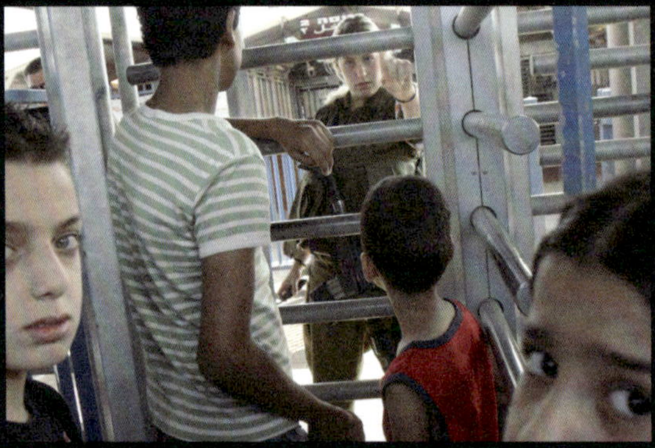

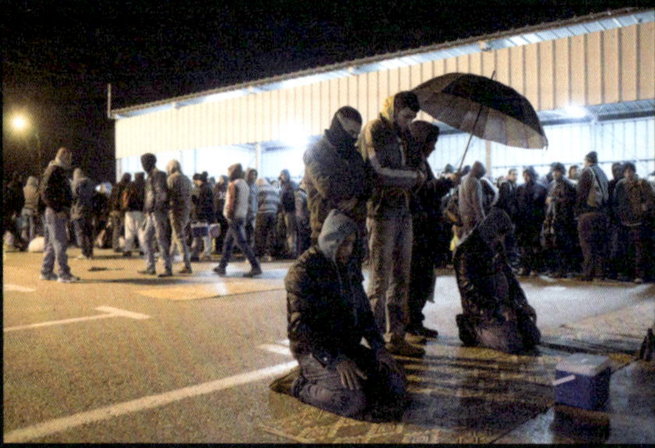

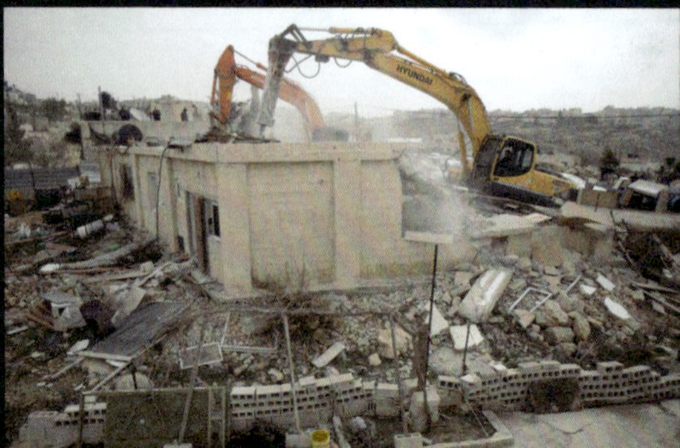

{Top left to right}
1. Israeli cars drive through a checkpoint on Road 60, West Bank, 21.9.2007 / **2.** Palestinians at Bethlehem checkpoint, West Bank, 12.6.2014 / **3.** Palestinians at Qalandiya Checkpoint, West Bank, 26.6.2015 / **4.** Palestinians at Qalandiya Checkpoint, West Bank, 27.7.2012 / **5.** Palestinians at Qalandiya Checkpoint, West Bank, 5.10.2007 / **6.** Palestinians pray at Eyal checkpoint, West Bank, 4.1.2015 / **7.** The home of the Adgluni family being demolished by Israeli authorities, Beit Hanina, East Jerusalem, 27.1.2014

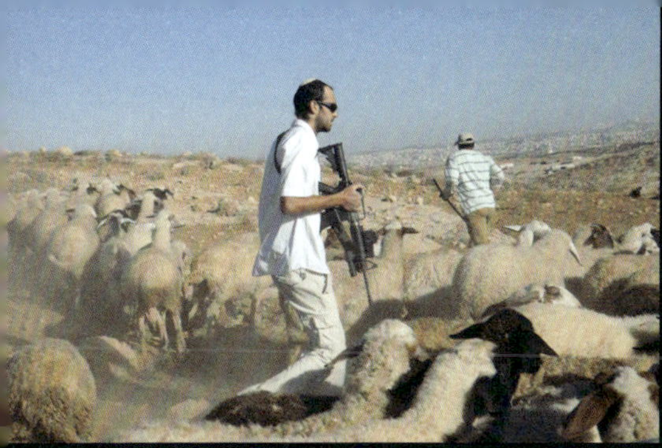

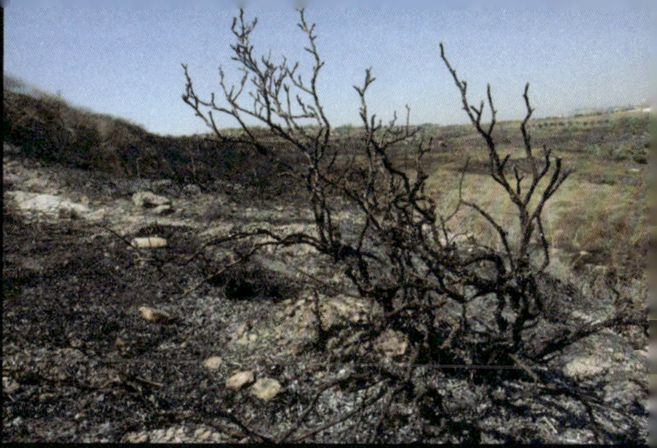

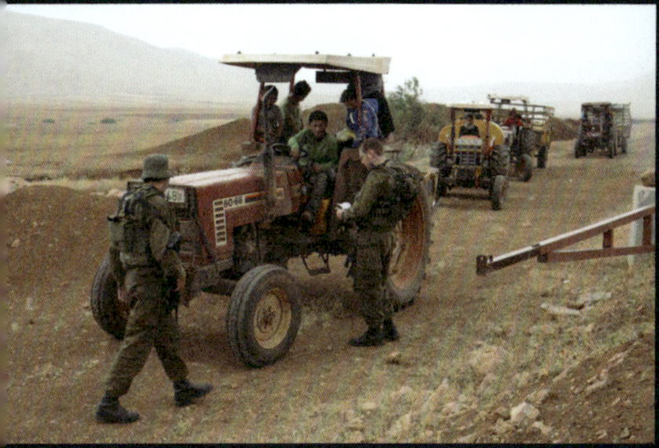

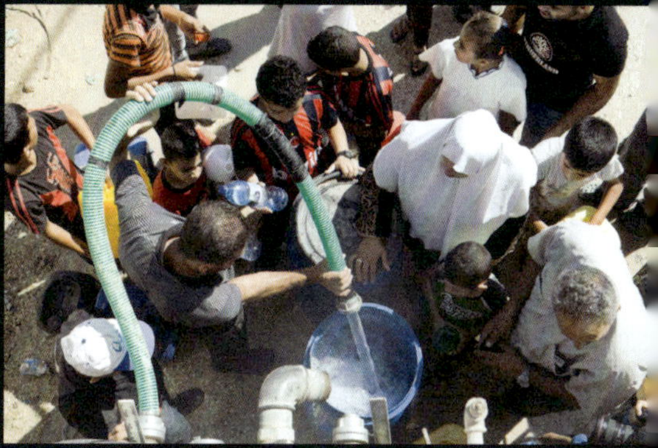

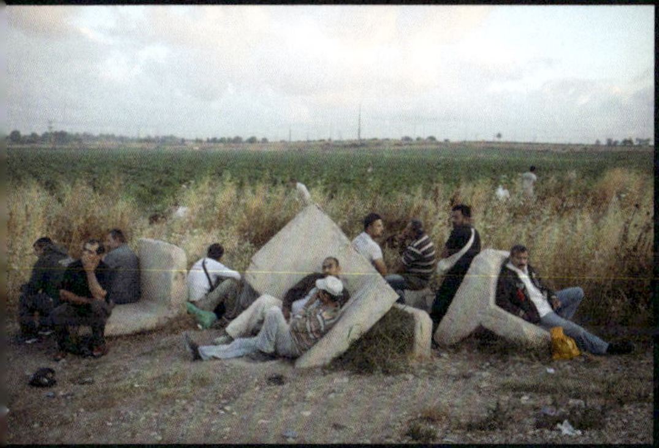

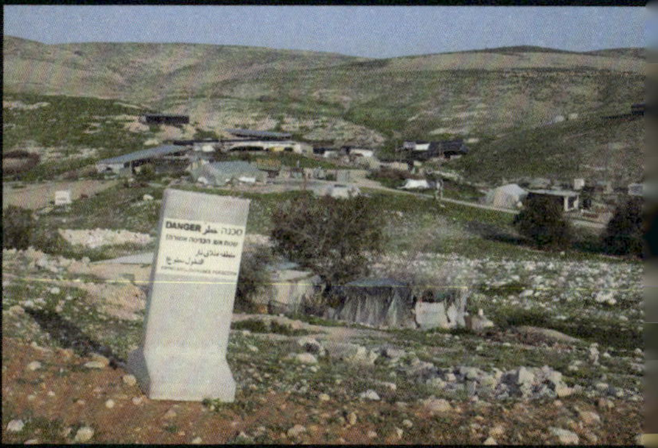

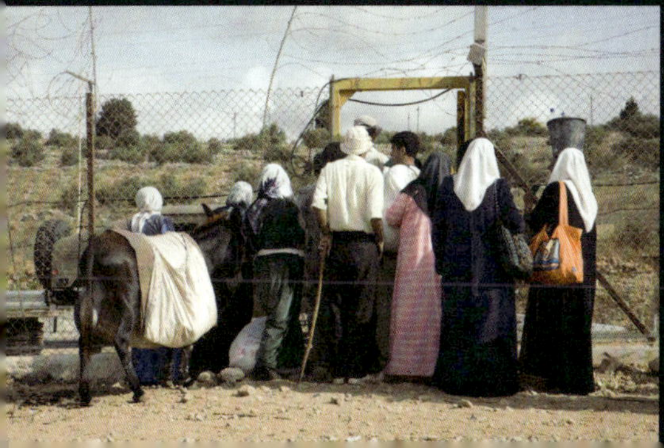

{Top left to right}
1. Israeli settler threatens Palestinian shepherds, Gwawis, West Bank, 18.9.2012 / **2.** Palestinian lands burned by Israeli settlers, Qalqilya, West Bank, 2.6.2009 / **3.** Israeli soldiers check Palestinians at an army gate, Jordan Valley, West Bank, 28.4.2011 / **4.** Palestinians fill water containers Qarawat Bani Zeid, West Bank, 7.8.2009 / **5.** Palestinians wait at Eyal checkpoint, West Bank, 30.5.2012 / **6.** An army roadblock marking a military training area next to a Palestinian encampment, Jordan Valley, West Bank, 14.3.2011 / **7.** Palestinians waiting to pass through an agricultural gate, Al Zawiya, West Bank, 7.10.2008

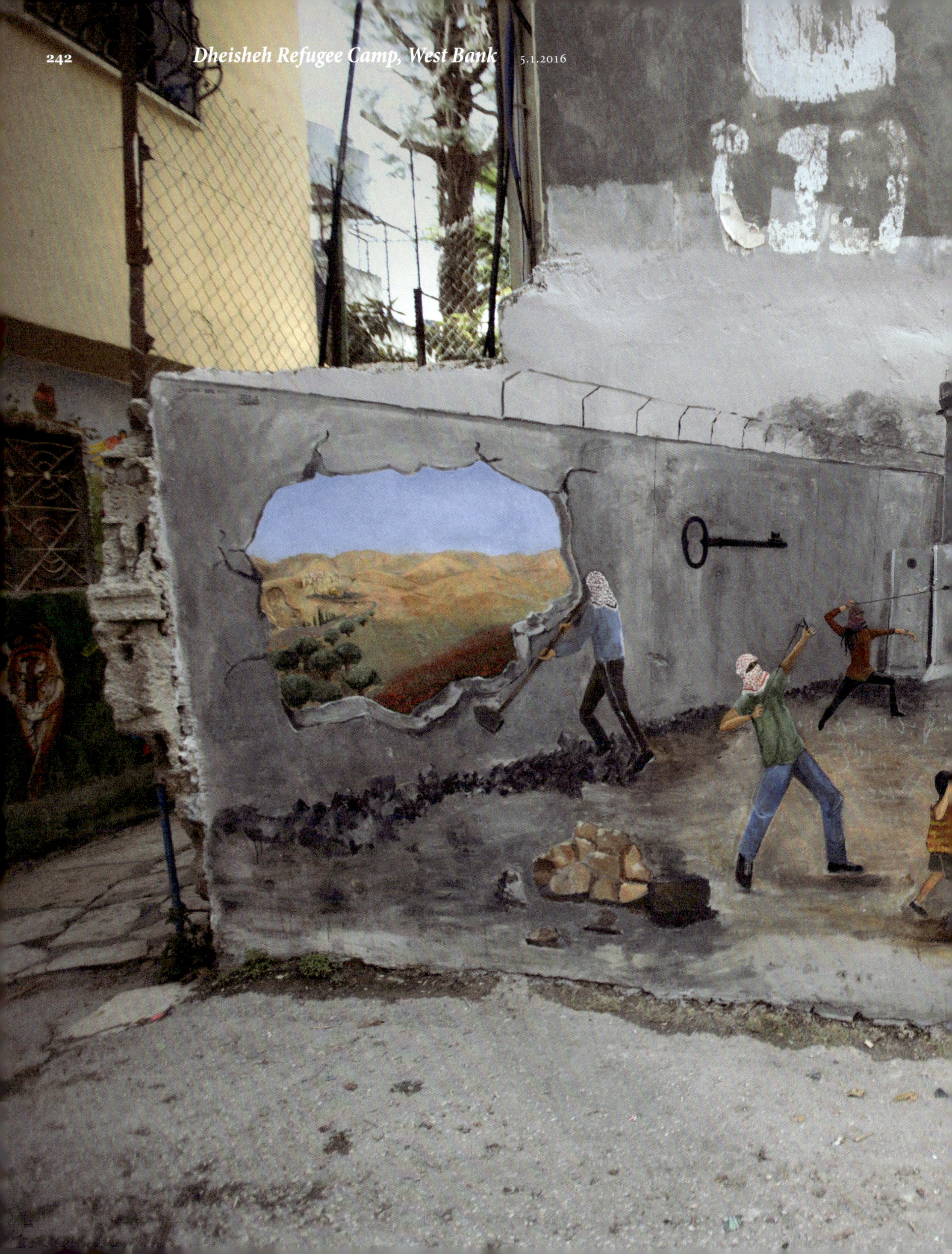

Dheisheh Refugee Camp, West Bank 5.1.2016

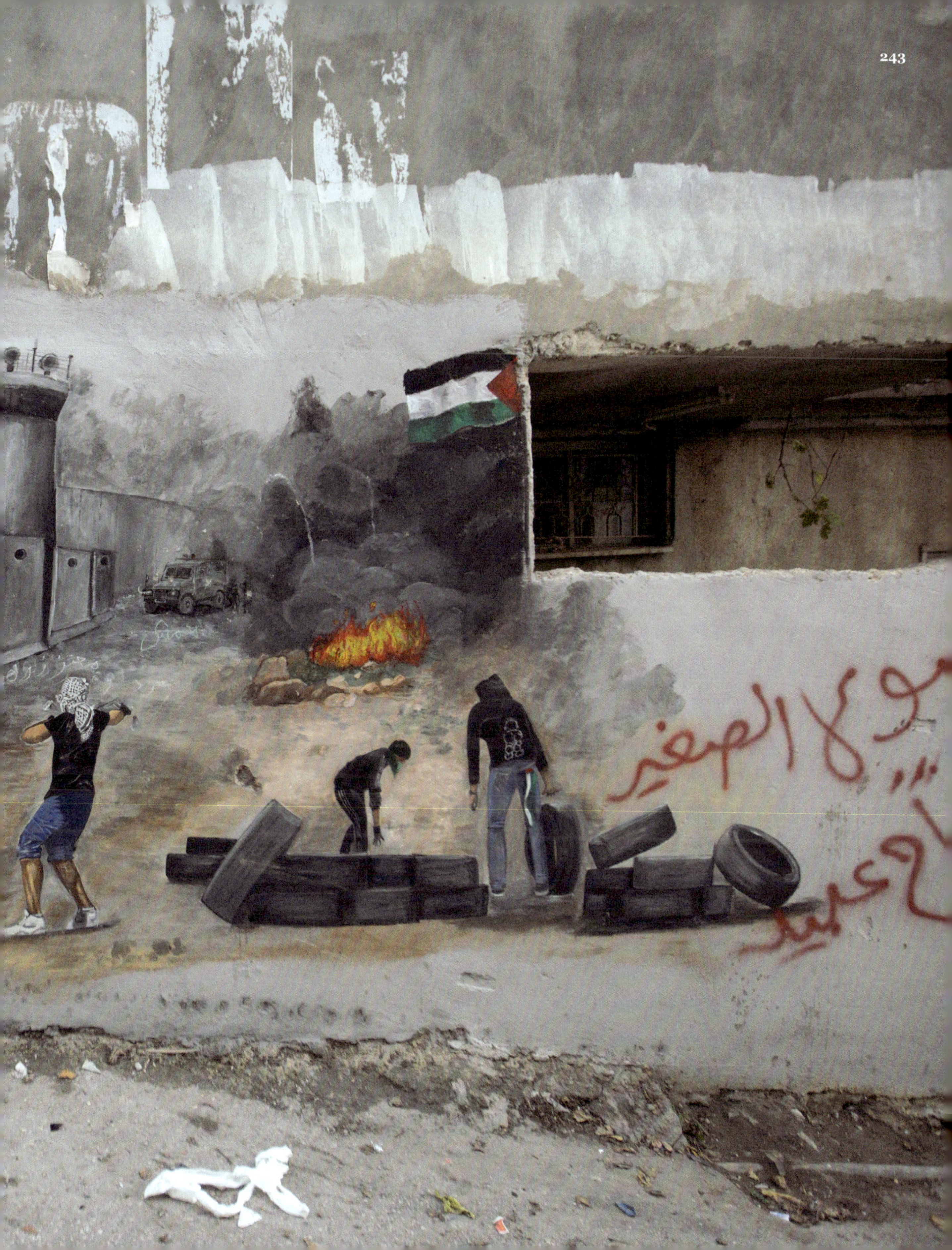

Faiz Abu Rmeleh
Conversation

Oren Ziv: Growing up in Jerusalem's Old City, close to the Al-Aqsa Mosque, you have seen a lot of photographers in your lifetime. What was the moment that made you start taking photographs?

Faiz Abu Rmeleh: I started to photograph in 2009. I had a small digital camera, and I would take pictures on trips and holidays. One day I was coming back from school and I had the camera over my shoulder. When I reached the Damascus Gate I saw a demonstration. I took pictures of the place without paying too much attention to the protest, which was in support of Palestinian political prisoners. Suddenly, someone who knew me called me over and asked that I take pictures. I was afraid to join. I was afraid of the police. But I got over my fear and photographed the bishop of the Greek Orthodox Church, Atallah Hanna, speaking at the demonstration. In the protest I noticed that someone was holding a photograph of a relative of mine who was in an Israeli prison. I took pictures of the people holding the photographs.

Two months later, I heard that another protest was being planned. My cousin, who was a student at Al-Quds University (in East Jerusalem), invited me to video the event. I went there with my camera, but she didn't show up. I started filming and a few seconds later, a policeman came and shoved me and forbade me to photograph. I circled back around the protesters from another place and the police there also stopped me. This made me want to photograph even more.

OZ: And what happened after that?

FAR: I started to think about what I wanted to study. My father was very much against my studying photography. He asked me to work at something else, not only because of the money, but because of the danger. He didn't understand what I could do with it. But I was determined. I worked in a studio doing weddings and portraits. After a few years, my father stopped trying to convince me to find another career, and he also helped me to buy my first really professional camera.

Over the years, I started taking photographer friends on trips to the Old City. One day I went to a protest at Nabi Saleh with Annibal Greco, a Spanish photographer whom I had met at the Damascus Gate. I went with him to the weekly protest there. The army had closed the road to the village that day and there was a lot of commotion. I didn't have any connection to anyone in the village. A taxi driver said that there was a checkpoint a few hundred meters from the entrance to the village and directed us to walk through the valley to reach the mosque. When we got there, the protest had already started, and we immediately began to photograph. I didn't have a helmet or a gas mask. I didn't know what tear gas was. In fact, I didn't know anything. I was wearing regular All Star sneakers, not really meant for running. At some point, I found myself in the middle of a giant cloud of tear gas and a fire had broken out in the fields. Someone came and helped me because I was very dizzy and had fallen. When I returned home, I looked at the pictures I had been able to get and loved them. I printed them and showed them to my colleagues. After this demonstration, I became more involved. I would read on Facebook where the next demonstration was. At the same time, I continued to take pictures in East Jerusalem.

OZ: Did you feel that the camera protected you, or the opposite?

FAR: At first, I had a problem with people, because I was new, and people didn't know me or trust me. They asked me why I was photographing children throwing stones. They were suspicious of me. Also the police didn't really speak to me. There weren't many photographers around back then, or people using smart phones, and if there were, they would take pictures and leave and I would stay. In Al-Aqsa Mosque, they would check at the entrance if you had a camera, not like today. I would go with a permit for the camera so they wouldn't think I had stolen it from somewhere. I would have to insist on my right to photograph. Eventually, people got used to it and they would say about me, "Oh, OK, it's that young guy who takes pictures at Al-Aqsa every Friday." I would post the pictures on Facebook. And all kinds of pages of activists from other countries in the Middle East would post those photos.

Shiraz Grinbaum: And how did you decide to study at Bezalel Academy of Arts and Design?

FAR: I didn't want to study there at all. I was looking into studying in Germany at the time. My friend, who also was looking into studying, arranged a meeting for us with the head of the photography department, Miki Kratsman. I was surprised that the head of a department in an academic institution wanted to meet us, so I went. Neither of us knew Hebrew very well back then. At the meeting, he asked why we had come and what we did. I told him that I was studying German in order to go there to study film. He said to me: "Listen, if I were in your place I wouldn't go to Germany now. If you study here and take everything you will do here and then go, you will know what to do there." I thought a lot about those words: "to do" as opposed to "not doing." That same month I went to a demonstration where I met Oren [Ziv].

It was a Palestinian demonstration that was organized in protest at the settler's Flag March in the Old City.[1] There was an unusually large turnout of people. Lots of families with children came holding Palestinian flags and were waiting for the marchers at the Damascus Gate. The police hadn't prepared for this and it was clear they were not ready. When the settlers arrived, the pushing started. The special riot police unit spread out in two camps. The photographers moved between the two sides. I felt that any minute they were going to disperse the Palestinian protest. Then the tear gas and stun grenades started. The police tried to scatter the crowds, but people kept coming back. When the main contingent of settlers arrived, I came in from the Palestinian side where the police were beating a group of children, some really young. They closed in around the detainees, arresting over forty Palestinians that day. One policeman caught me by the collar and started pointing at me and yelling: "He pushed a policeman, he pushed a policeman!" Everyone jumped on me. Of course I hadn't done anything except take pictures. They beat me very hard that day. I heard the policeman saying, "There's no gas, no gas [for the taser gun], take him to the patrol car." I blacked out for a second and they handcuffed me. I felt that someone was trying to take my camera from me, but my hands were cuffed, so I held on to the camera strap with my teeth. In the midst of all this commotion, I saw that they had arrested someone along with me. It was Oren. We continued to the police car and they put us into it together. I lost feeling in my hands because of the handcuffs and Oren tried to get the police to come over, telling them to loosen the cuffs. When the policeman finally took the handcuffs off, we took the memory cards out of the cameras, out of fear that I would be taken to the police station and have my equipment and images confiscated.

1. The Jerusalem Day march is held annually by Israeli nationalists to celebrate the 1967 Israeli occupation of the West Bank, Gaza and East Jerusalem. The march, which circles Jerusalem's Old City, is called the "Flag March" by the nationalists. In recent years, tens of thousands of settlers, right-wing activists, and Israeli high school students, march through the Muslim quarter of the Old City chanting racist slogans while the Israeli police restrict the movement of the local Palestinian residents and enforce the closing of Palestinian shops in the area.

OZ: Lots of journalists called the police spokesperson that day because they had arrested a few journalists. A high-ranking officer came to see me in the police car, and after I showed him my press ID, and explained to him how I had been arrested, he agreed to free me. Before leaving I told him that you were with me, and had also been arrested for no reason.

FAR: In the end, they released us both and we went back to the Damascus Gate. That had been the most difficult event in Jerusalem for me up to that point. Friends picked me up and we went to look at a view of the Old City. We watched the sunset, and then I went home. My entire family was there waiting for me. When I got home, I threw away all the forms for study abroad and decided that I needed to be here. I need to photograph here. Also, I saw what was going on in the social media and I understood that the police had focused on photographers because they didn't want pictures from the Palestinian demonstration; they didn't want there to be documentation of the strong resistance. The result was the opposite. I understood that I need to do things with the camera that I have. And I understood that if I hadn't had my camera that day, I would have gone out to protest anyway. Soon after I joined Activestills.

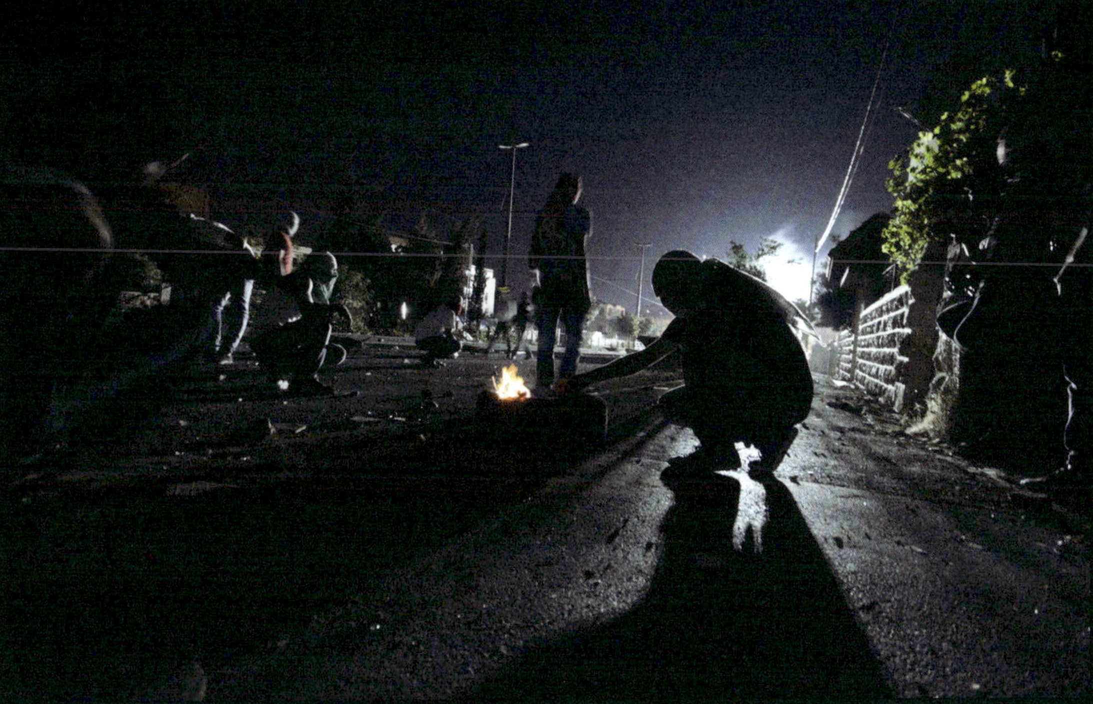

Palestinian youth burn part of the track of the light rail, following the funeral of Mohammed Abu Khdeir, Shuafat, East Jerusalem, 4.7.2014. Abu Khdeir, 16-year-old Palestinian, was killed by Israeli right-wing extremists in an apparent act of revenge for the killing of three Israeli youths by Palestinian extremists. His death triggered massive protests in the East Jerusalem neighborhoods.

OZ: You don't go home when the "event is over." And you also photograph people your age, like in the Shuafat neighborhood. How did you arrive at this?

FAR: The shabab [the young protesters] are my friends. I don't know each one of them well, but I understand them and they understand me. We talk a lot about the situation and about why they protest and for me it gives the image an extra value. In Shuafat, the young protesters allow me to be there, because they believe that the photographs do something.

There are many ways to oppose the occupation. Photography is one of them. And right now art is another way for me. I am expanding the documentary photography into my art now, in my studies at Bezalel. The photographer and the protesters are on the same line. I distinguish between photojournalism and art, but of course there are many connections between the two channels. For example, I work on documentary photographs I took in an artistic context. Many people don't want to see a news photo, but through an art work I can open them up to seeing the same content in another way. If I don't try this, I will feel that I haven't done enough. I feel obliged to take this material and study it. It gives me a sense of power. I want to release all of this from inside myself into something. This, for me, is art.

Al-Aqsa Compound, Old City, East Jerusalem 21.11.2014

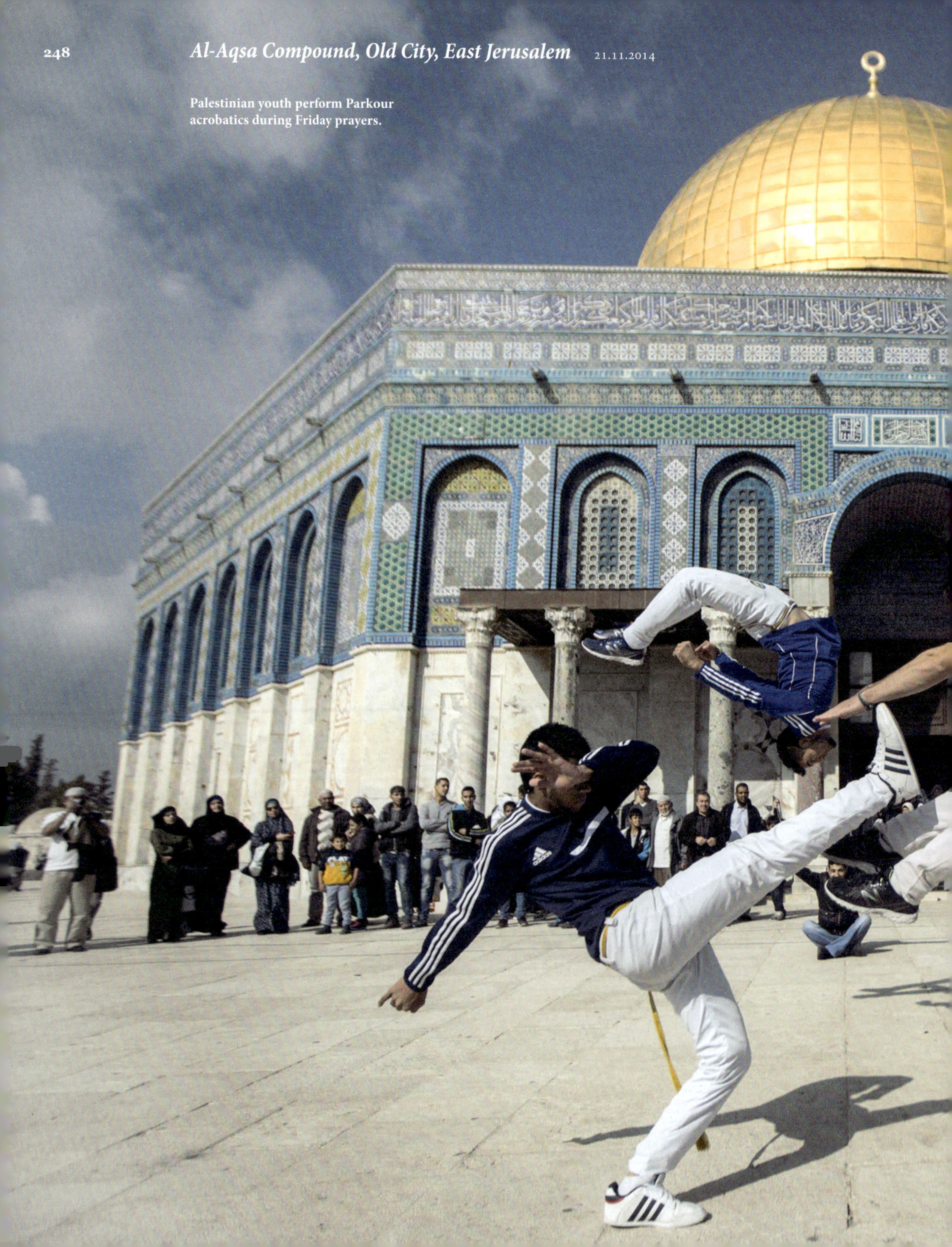

Palestinian youth perform Parkour acrobatics during Friday prayers.

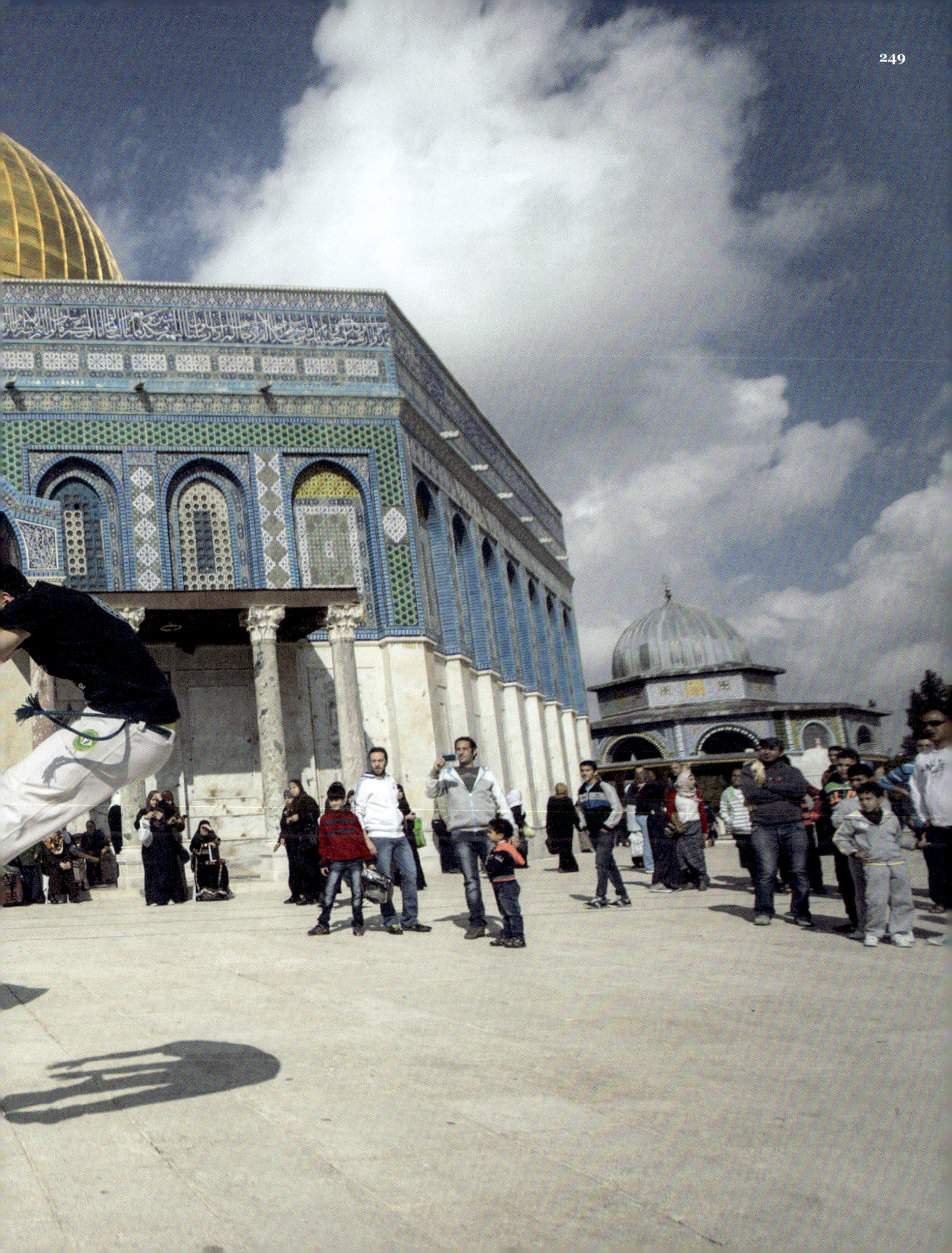

Al-Aqsa Compound, Old City, East Jerusalem

28.6.2016

Palestinians barricade the door to Al-Aqsa mosque during clashes with the Israeli police that broke out after Israelis from the right wing toured the compound.

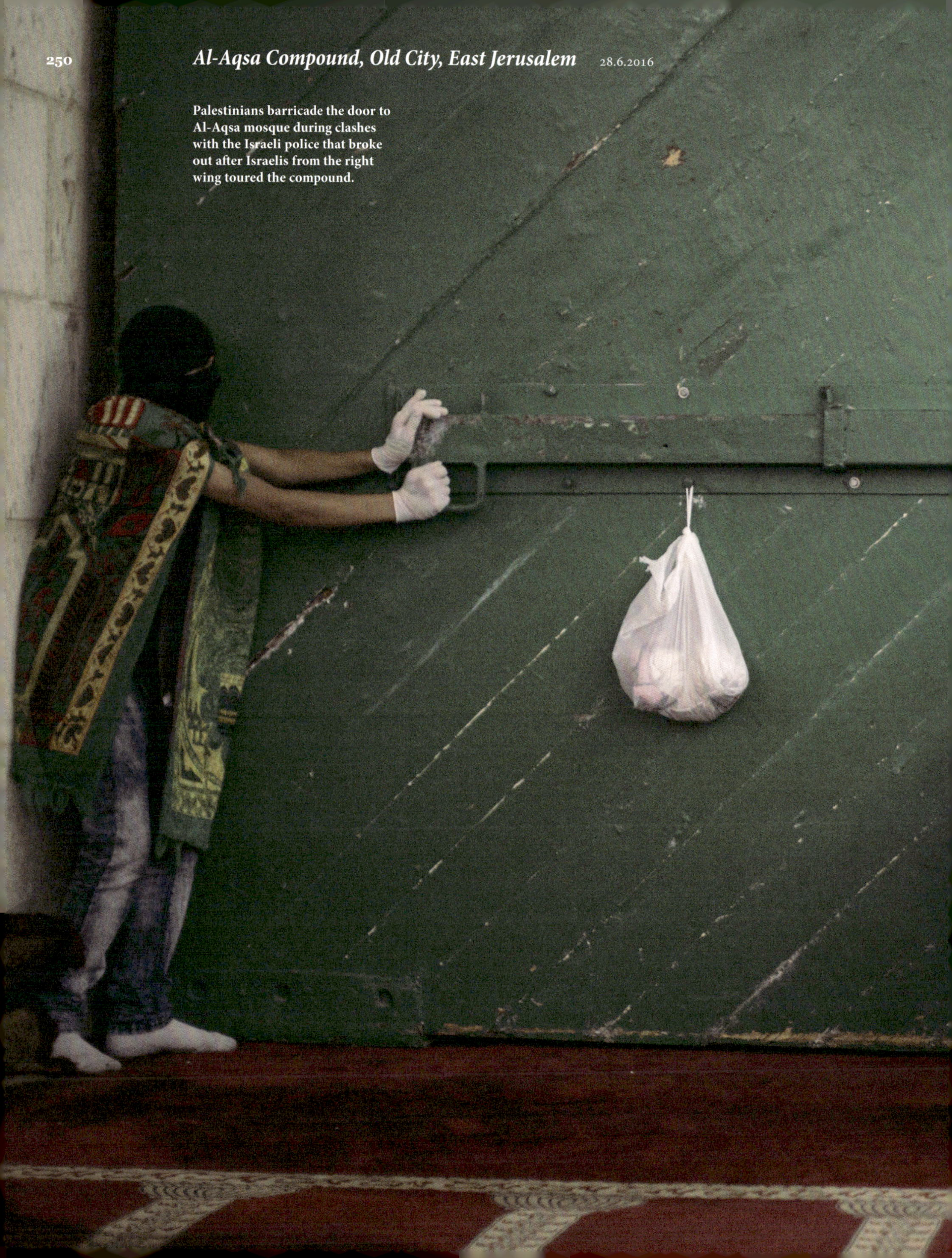

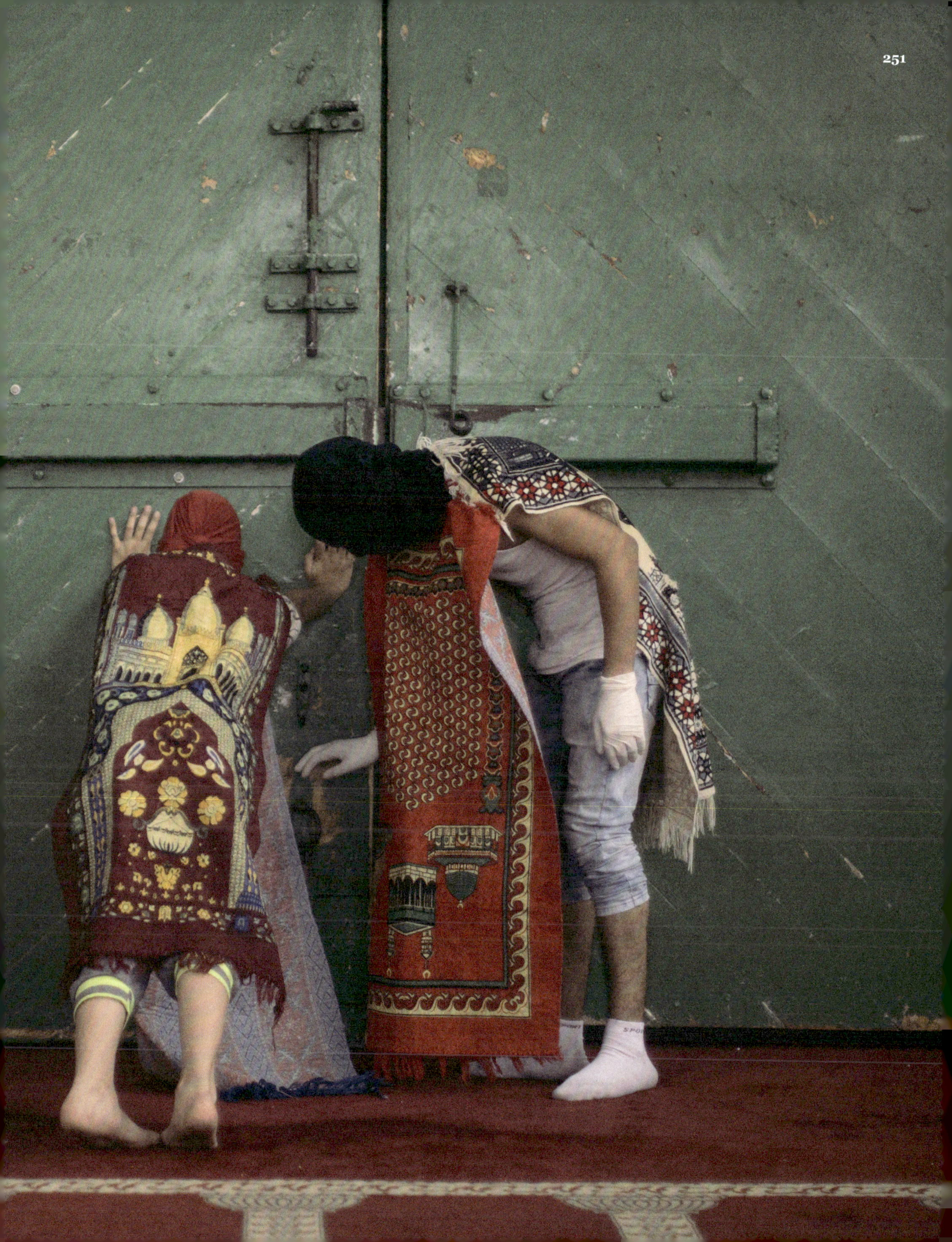

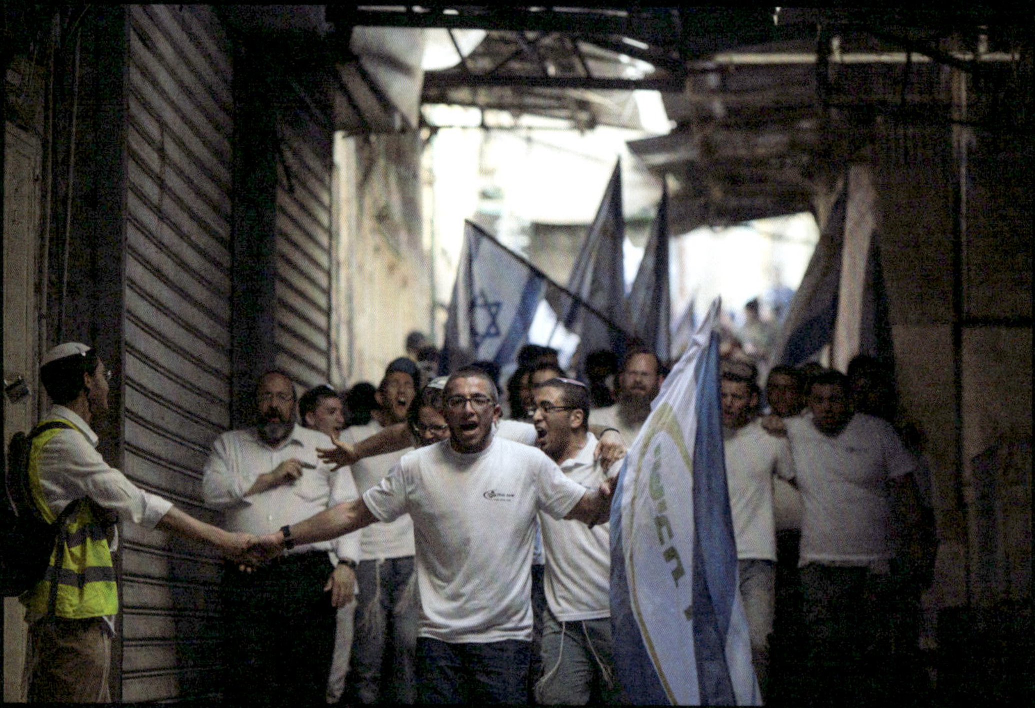

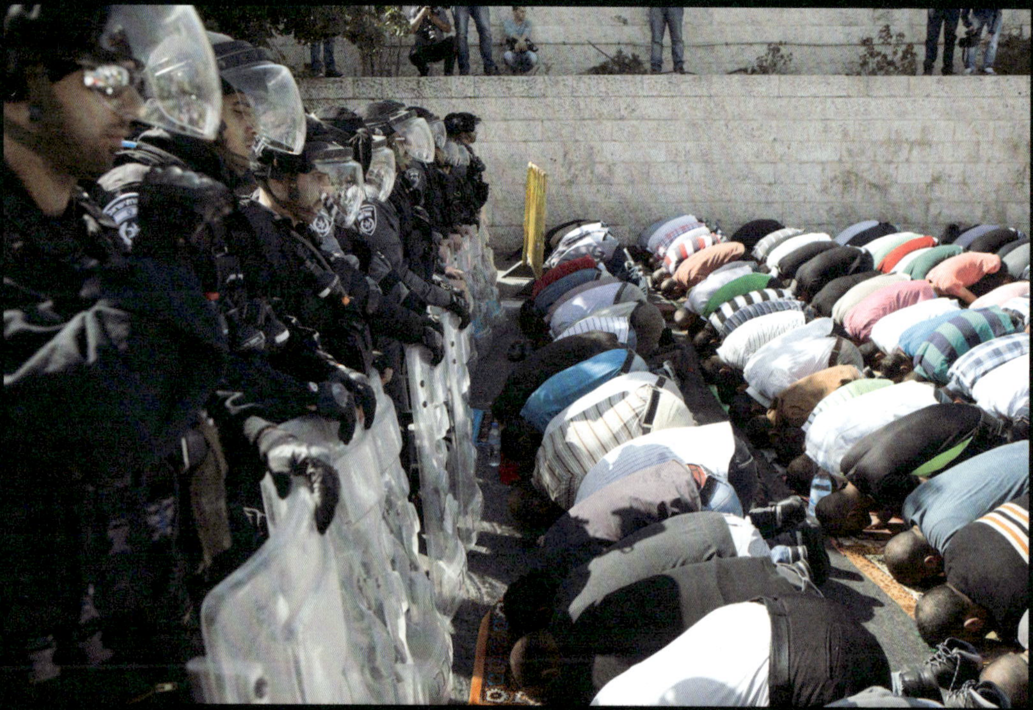

1. Israeli nationalists walk through the Old City of Jerusalem during the Flag March celebrating 48 years of the Israeli occupation of East Jerusalem, 17.5.2015 / **2.** Palestinians perform Friday prayers in Wadi Joz neighborhood outside Jerusalem's Old City, as police block their way to Al-Aqsa mosque, 17.10.2014

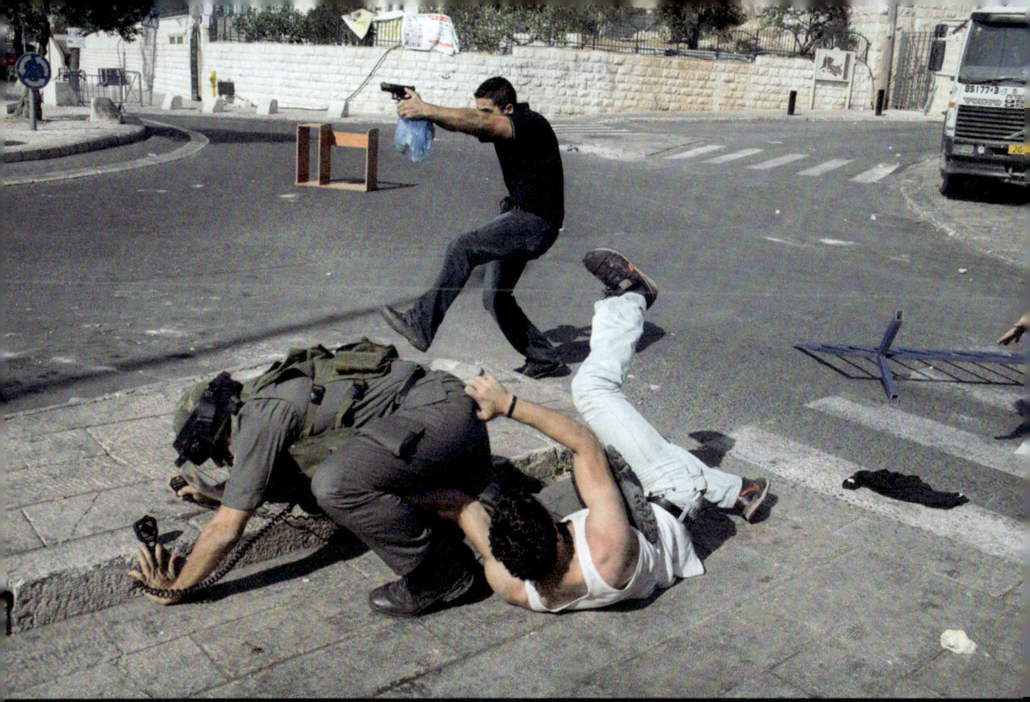

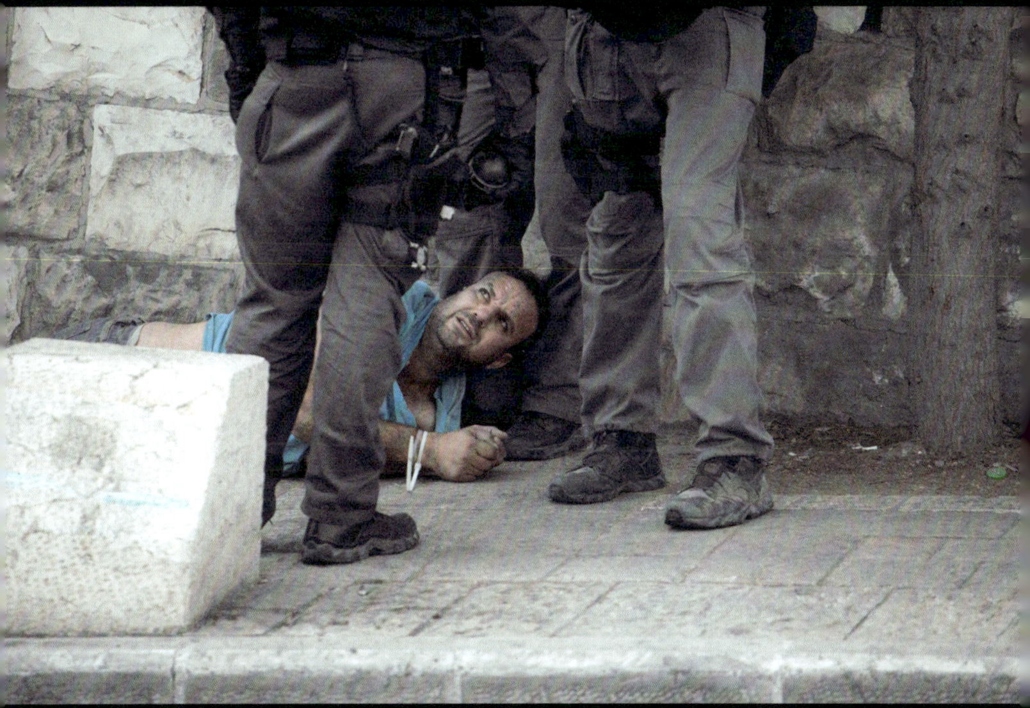

. Israeli uniformed and undercover police arrest a Palestinian youth during clashes in the East Jerusalem neighborhood of Ras l-Amud, after Israel prevented Palestinians under the age of 50 from entering the Al-Aqsa mosque, 27.9.2013 / **2.** A Palestinian protester arrested at a demonstration against access restrictions to the Al-Aqsa compound, 15.10.2014

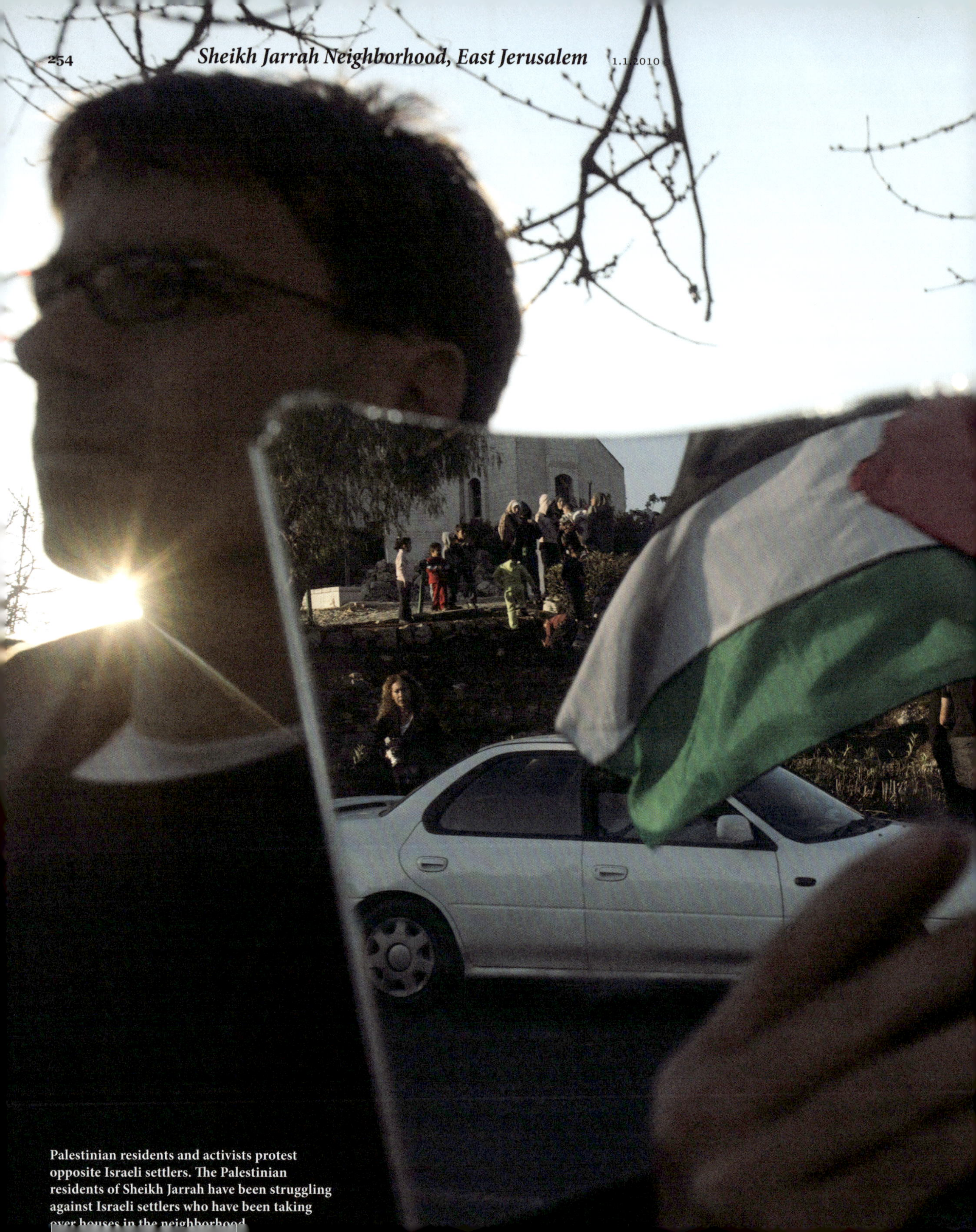

Palestinian residents and activists protest opposite Israeli settlers. The Palestinian residents of Sheikh Jarrah have been struggling against Israeli settlers who have been taking over houses in the neighborhood.

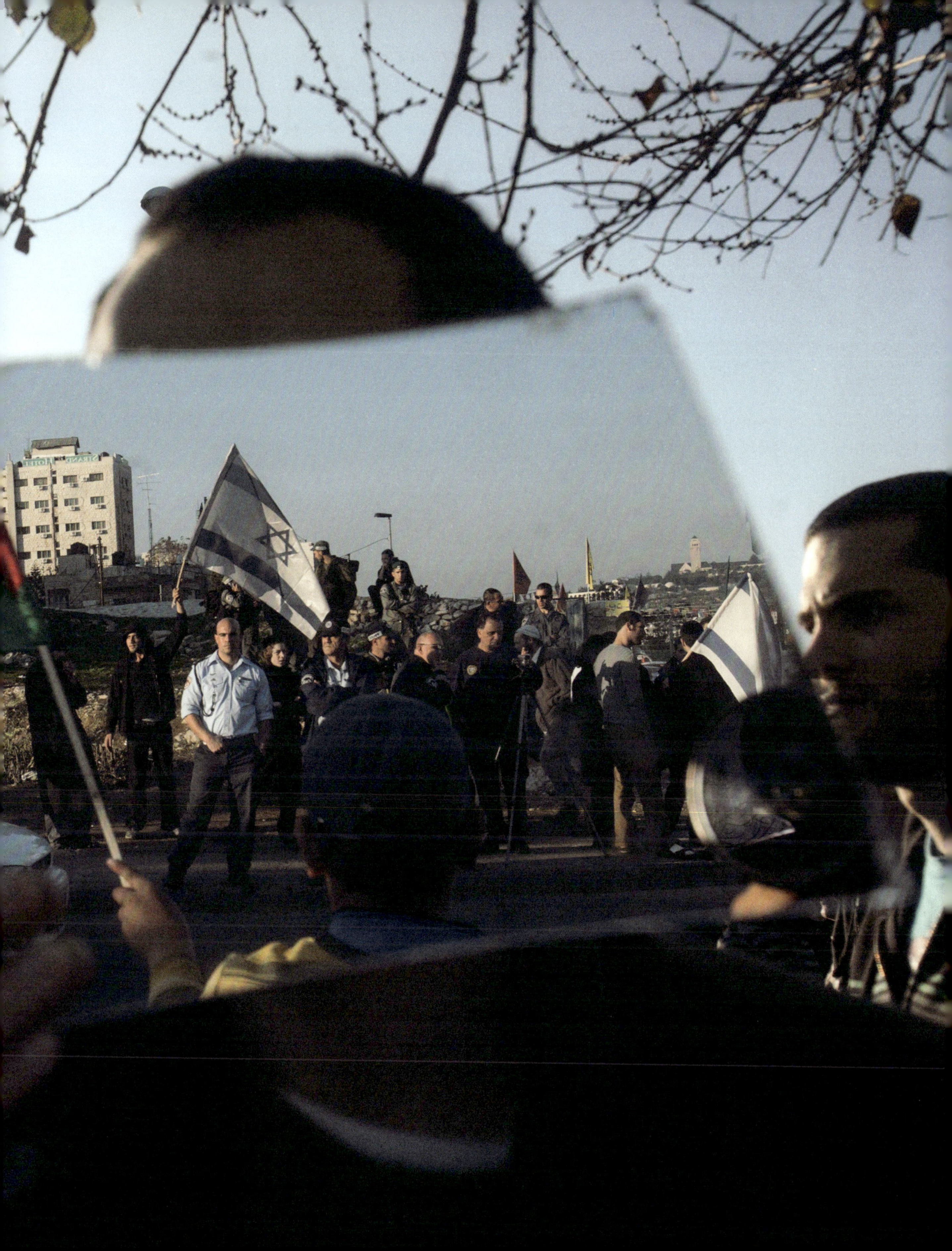

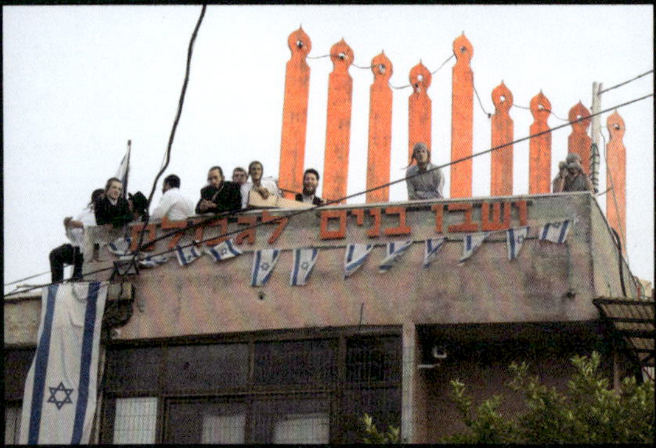

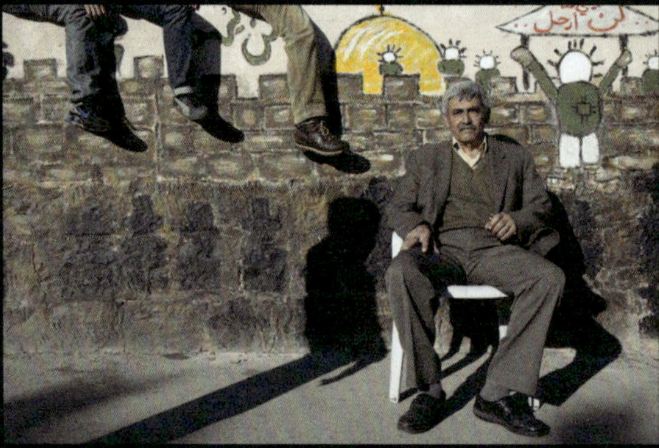

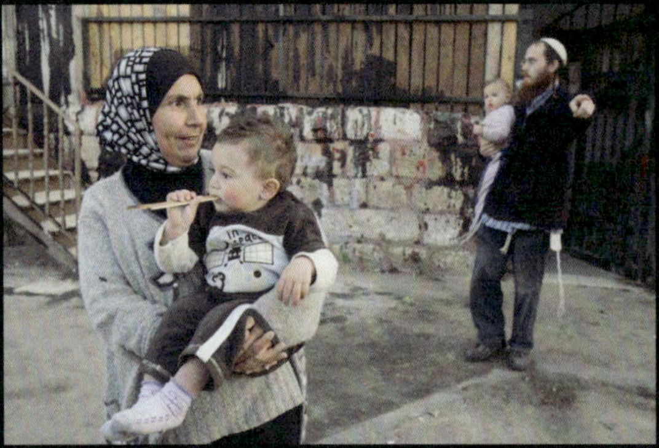

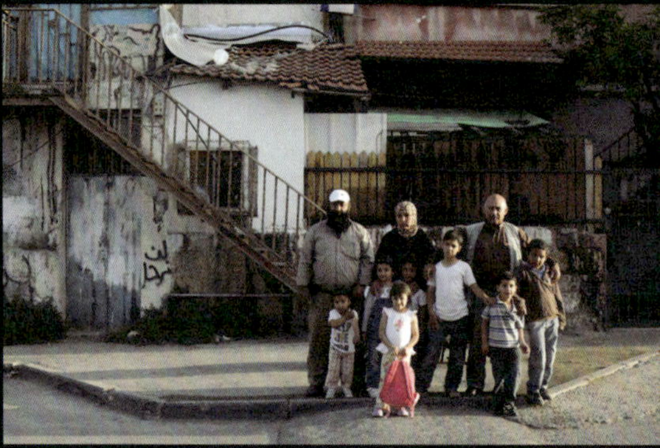

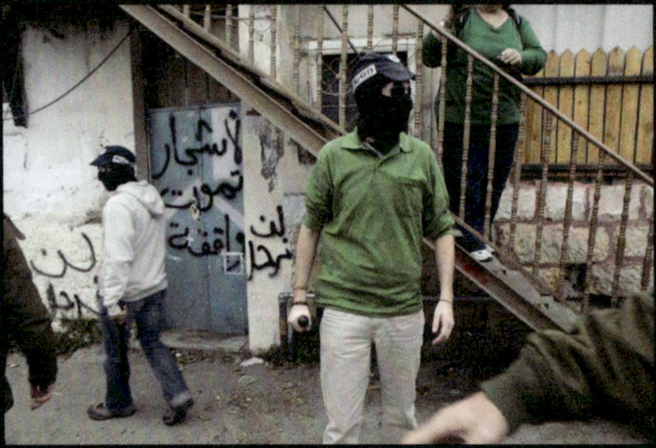

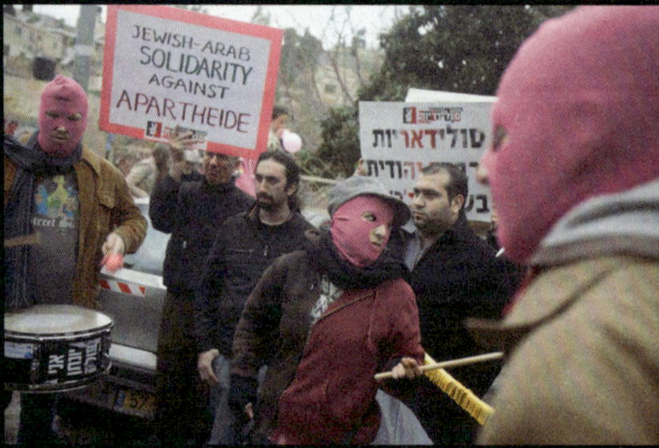

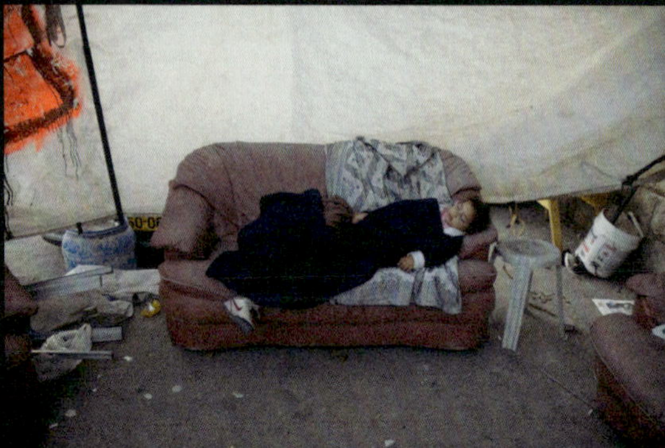

{Top left to right}
1. Israeli settlers stand atop the house of the Palestinian Gawi family, 20.4.2010 / **2.** Nabil al-Kurd sits outside his house, occupied by Israeli settlers, 1.12.2009 / **3.** Israeli settlers harass a Palestinian women, 2.2.2010 / **4.** The Gawi family pose for a portrait in front of their house occupied by Israeli settlers, 27.4.2010 / **5.** Masked Israeli policemen in civilian clothes arrive at a protest, 11.12.2009 / **6.** Israeli activists protest, 11.3.2011 / **7.** A child sleeps inside the tent constructed by the al-Kurd family outside their house, 12.2.2010

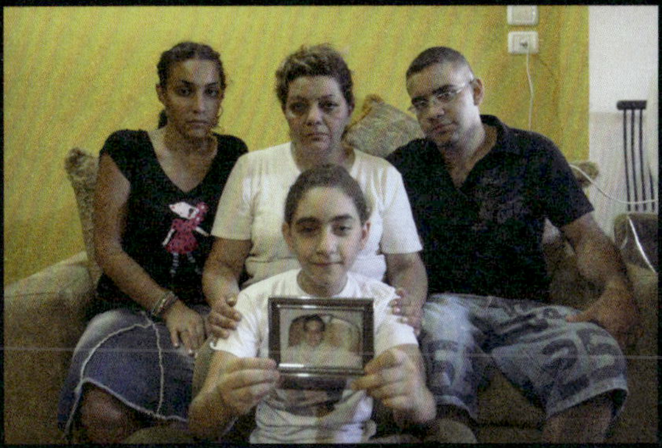
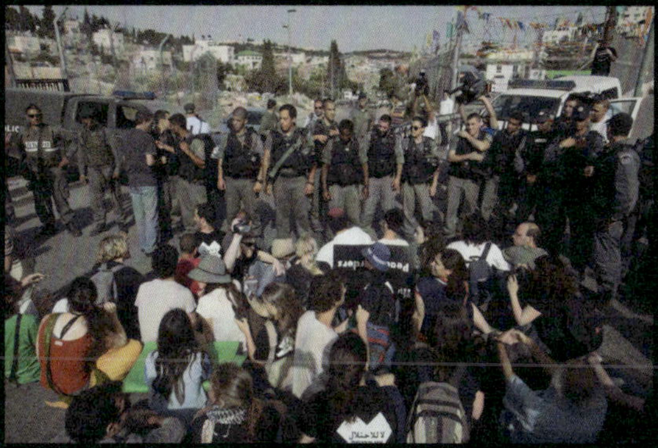
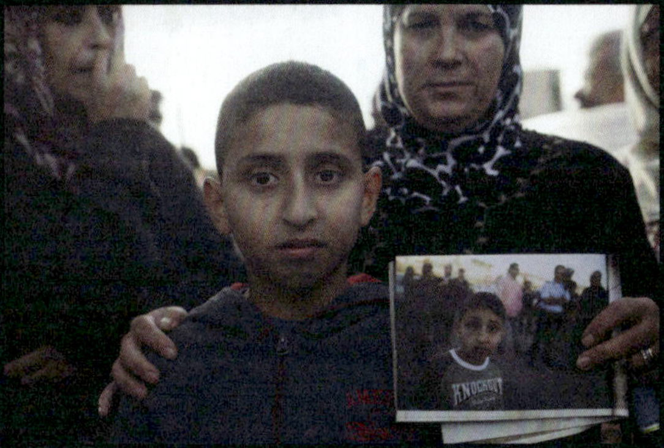
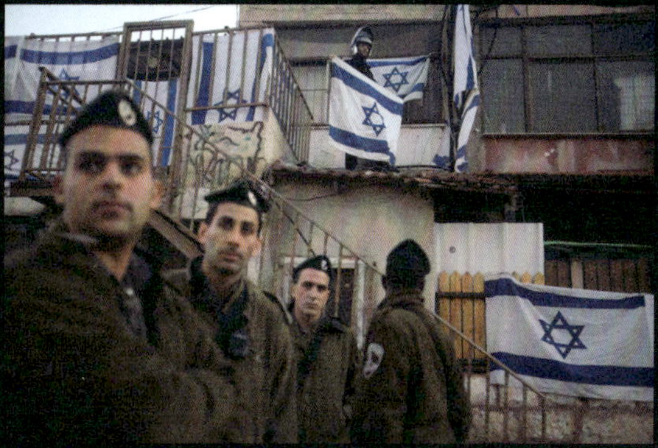
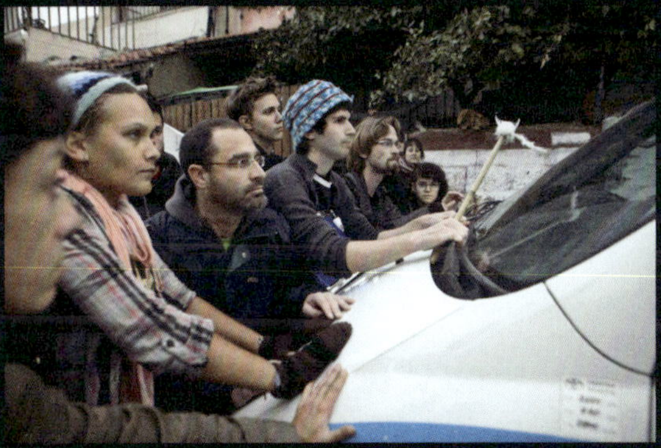
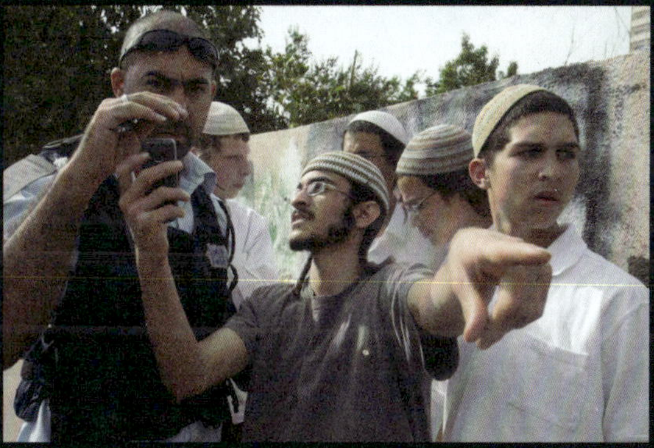
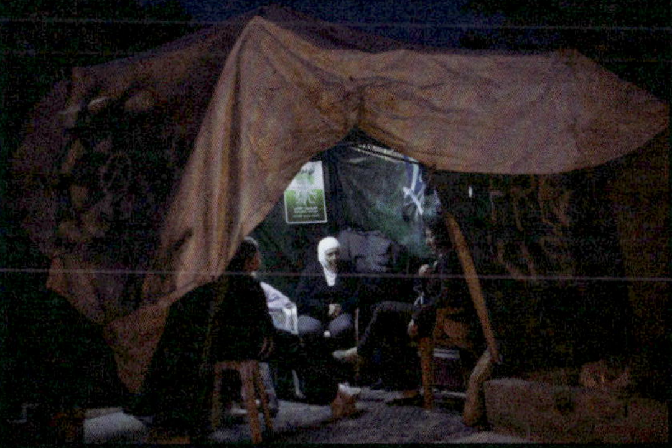

{Top left to right}
1. The Hannoun family poses for a portrait, 9.4.2010 / **2.** Protesters block the main road of the neighborhood, 14.5.2010 / **3.** A child beaten by Israeli settlers shows an Activestills photo of his injury, 29.10.2010 / **4.** Israeli soldiers at a protest, 23.2.2009 / **5.** Protesters block a police car holding fellow-protesters, 11.12.2009 / **6.** Settlers point at local Palestinian residents encouraging the police to arrest them, 20.4.2010 / **7.** Palestinian residents sit in a tent outside their occupied house, 9.4.2010

Tess Scheflan

The House of Contention

On 4 December 2008, Israeli forces evicted the residents of a building known as the "House of Contention," a Palestinian-owned property that had been taken over by Israeli settlers in Hebron.[1] A long period of uncertainty, anxiety, and violence preceded the eviction.

That day I was documenting the events. Shortly after the eviction was completed, dozens of rampaging settlers, mostly masked youth but also adults armed with guns, ran down into the small gorge below the House of Contention. They harassed and intimidated local Palestinian residents and dozens of them surrounded the small house of a Palestinian family located nearby. I picked up my camera to photograph the events unfolding before me. Some of the boys tried to set fire to the Palestinian house by trying to burn the clothesline attached to it. Others smashed windows with sticks and stones. Some tried to uproot the vines in the garden, while yet others climbed to the roof and tried to break the water tank and satellite dish.

After a few minutes of photographing from a distance, I ran toward the house. For years I had felt safe and secure in violent situations like this one. In retrospect, I realize this sense of safety came from my privileges: I was a young, white woman carrying photographic equipment which marked my role as a journalist, I carried an official press pass provided by the Israeli authorities, and my South African accent obscured my Israeli identity.

I ran into the house along with Avi Issacharoff, the *Ha'aretz* newspaper reporter I was working with, followed by a handful of other journalists. Inside were mostly women and children of the Abu Safan family. I could hardly breathe after seeing the terror in their faces and eyes. They thought they were about to die. I cried. One of the women embraced me, and I asked her for forgiveness. I barely photographed anything while I was inside, and eventually Israeli forces came around and convinced the settlers to step back. As the sun set, we left the area. The following day, *Ha'aretz* ran Avi's story, which described the event as a lynch attack that had been averted only by the presence of journalists.

1. For further information about the "House of Contention," see http://peacenow.org.il/eng/ContentionHouse, accessed 29 February 2016.

A few days after this incident, as most Israeli media outlets were losing interest in the story, I returned to the same neighborhood in Hebron with fellow Activestills photographer Oren Ziv joined by *Ha'aretz* reporter Fadi Eyadat. We wanted to highlight the consequences of the eviction on the Palestinian residents in the flashpoint neighborhood of the House of Contention. By then, the house had been sealed off by the Israeli Army and both Palestinians and Israeli settlers were not allowed entrance. During this period, a Muslim cemetery was vandalized, Palestinian children were pelted with stones and injured on their way to school, hate graffiti was sprayed on walls, and there was a heavy military presence. Israeli soldiers walked in and out of Palestinian houses, and some of the houses, especially the rooftops, become improvised army bases.

We were walking down a street near a Palestinian house that was occupied by the Israeli Army, and suddenly a soldier ran toward us and started threatening us. He said that we had no right to photograph although the area was not sealed off by the army. As I picked up my camera, he knocked me to the ground and struck my head with the butt of his rifle. I was evacuated to a hospital in Jerusalem, suffering from a concussion. Since that day, I no longer feel safe. As a photographer, I never regained the confidence I once had before December 2008.

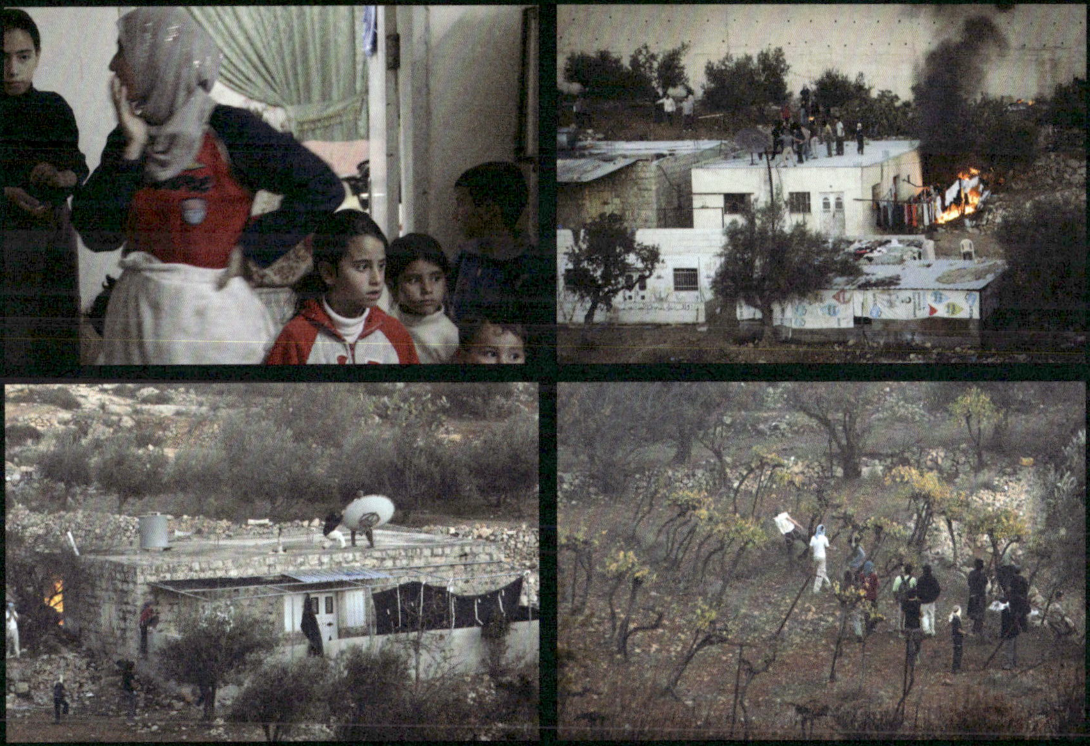

1. Women and children of the Abu Safan family after an attack by Israeli settlers, Hebron, West Bank, 4.12.2008 / **2+3.** Settlers damage a satellite dish on the roof of a Palestinian home, Hebron, West Bank, 4.12.2008 / **4.** Settlers damage a Palestinian vineyard, Hebron, West Bank, 4.12.2008

Hebron, West Bank 4.12.2008

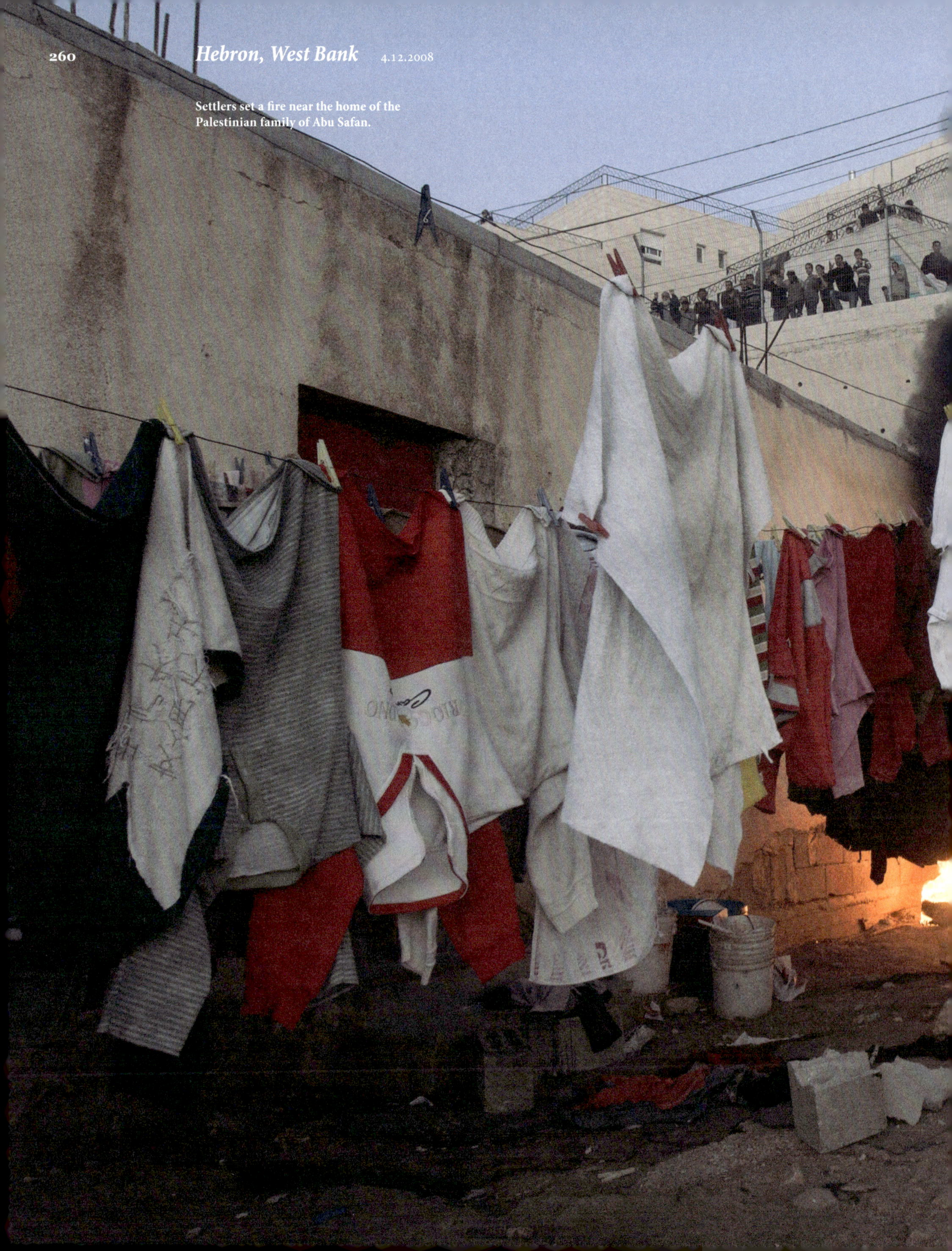

Settlers set a fire near the home of the Palestinian family of Abu Safan.

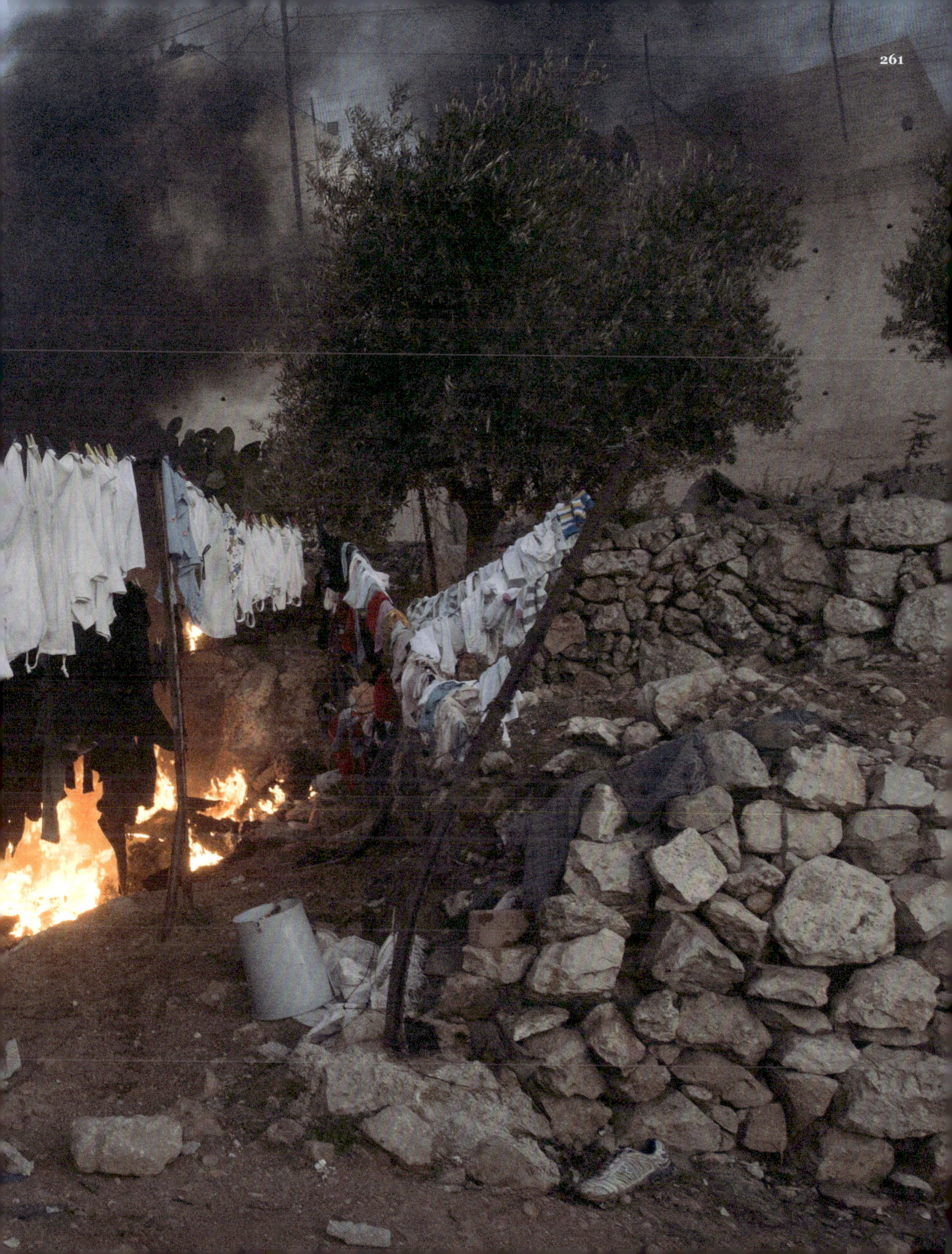

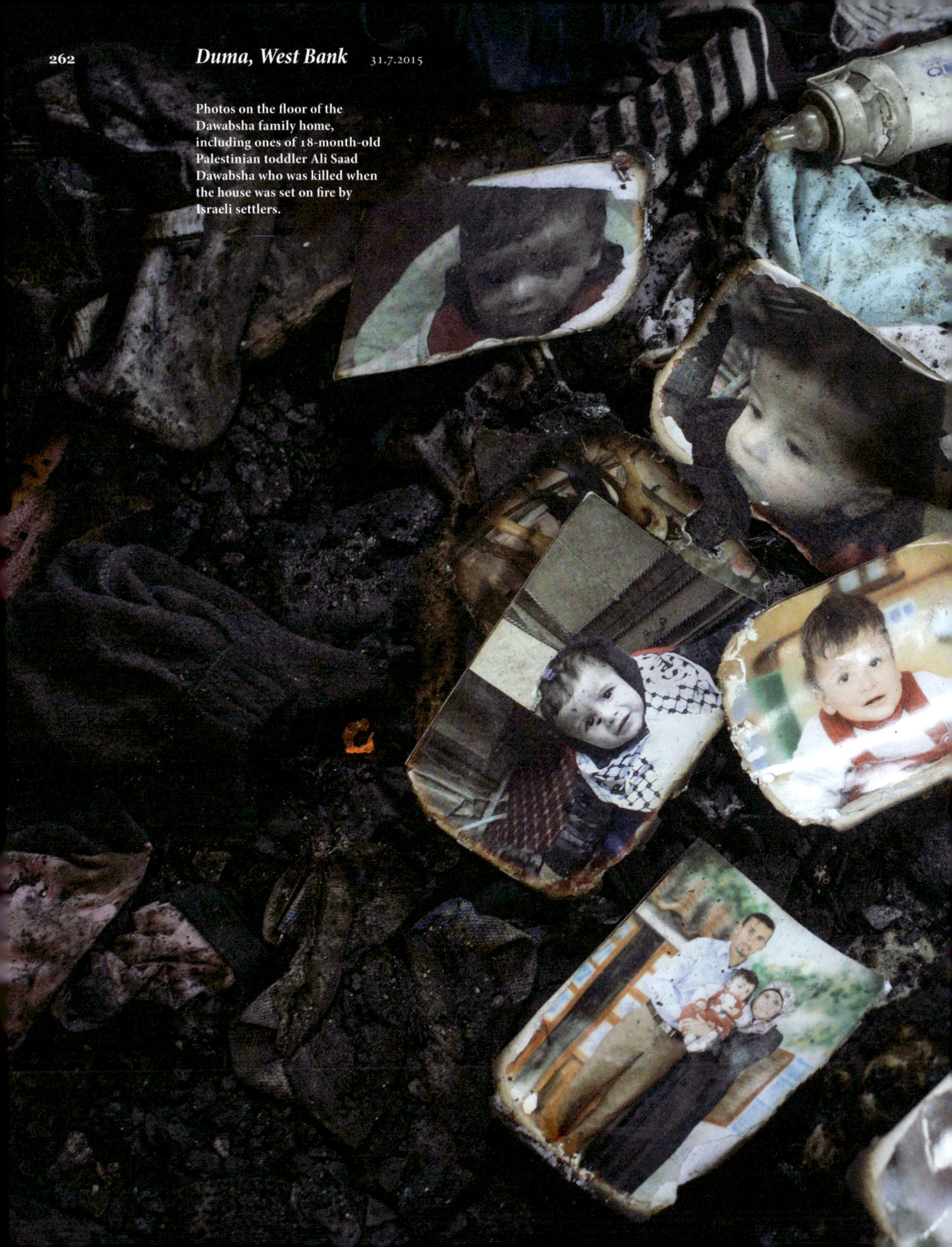

Duma, West Bank 31.7.2015

Photos on the floor of the Dawabsha family home, including ones of 18-month-old Palestinian toddler Ali Saad Dawabsha who was killed when the house was set on fire by Israeli settlers.

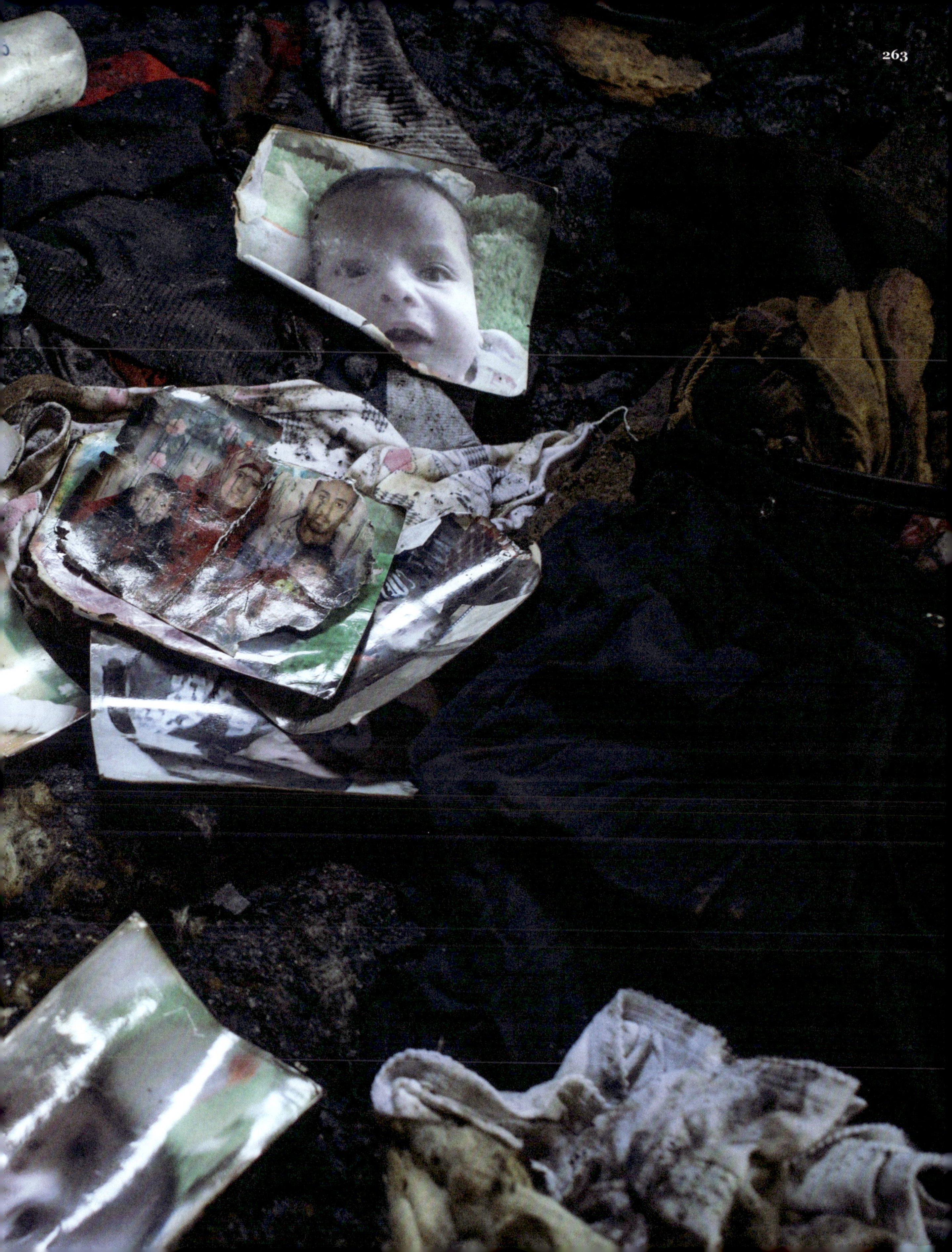

Anne Paq

The Obliterated Families

"Time will ease the pain, but we will not forget our brothers," 18-year-old Ibrahim Al Khalili told me amid the burned-out ruins of his family's factory. Ibrahim had lost eight close members of his family in the Israeli attack on their home.

I was at the Al-Shifa Hospital morgue when the charred bodies of the Khalilis were brought in, the result of the fire in the factory triggered by the bombing of their home next door. Despite the chaos at the hospital that was being flooded with a constant stream of dead and injured, I managed to find out their names and the location from where they had been brought. The Khalilis were only one of the many families in the Gaza Strip that were obliterated in the Israeli attacks in the summer of 2014. According to the United Nations, 142 families lost three members or more, a terrifying statistic. Some families like Ahmad and Asfraf Al Khalili's were completely wiped out.

After the offensive was over, I had the idea to document some of these families, starting with the ones I had encountered during the summer. I wanted to know what had happened to them, what memories did those who survived have of their loved ones, and how were they coping with life after such tremendous loss? A long list of names was published, but I wanted to see what had remained of the people behind the names, to see the destroyed homes, to meet the survivors. I wanted these families to be remembered from the time when they were once complete.

Soon, the project "Obliterated Families" extended beyond my initial intentions. Over the next months, in collaboration with Al Mezan Human Rights Center, I managed to visit and document 50 families. Some lost "only" a few loved ones while others like the Abu Jame family mourned the deaths of 25, including 18 children. How does one survive such immense loss? As the project developed, it became clear that it was going to be as much about the survivors as about the dead. I learned that added to their grief over the loss of their loved ones, is the daily suffering of the survivors who are displaced from homes, living in ruins, with little hope for justice or a better future because of the political stalemate and the Israeli blockade. One of the aims of my project is to raise awareness about these families and their cry for justice.

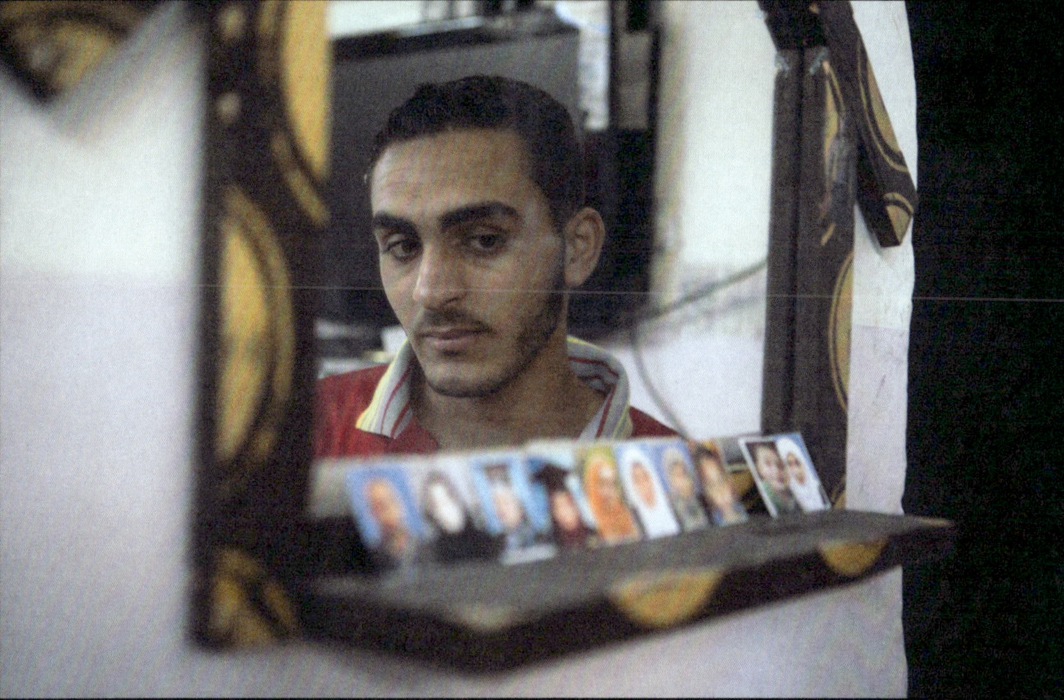

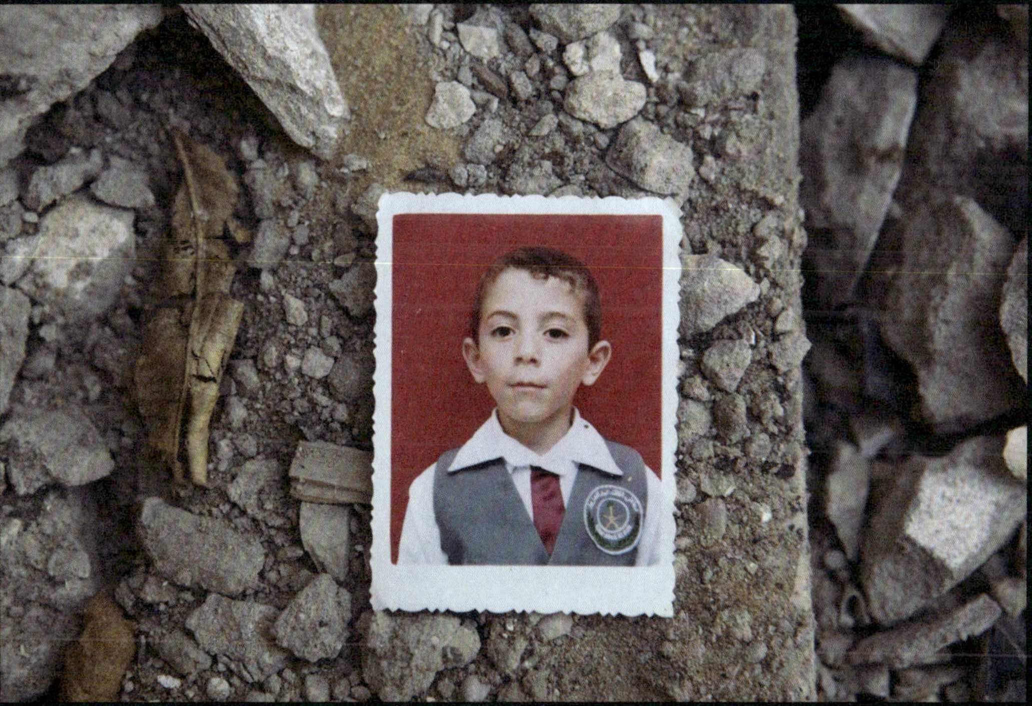

1. Ala Balata, age 18, near photographs of deceased family members killed in an Israeli attack, Jabalia refugee camp, Gaza Strip, 20.9.2014 / **2.** Photo of Abdallah Abdel Hadi Al-Majdalawi, age 13, on the ruins of his home in Jabalia, Gaza Strip, 19.3.2015

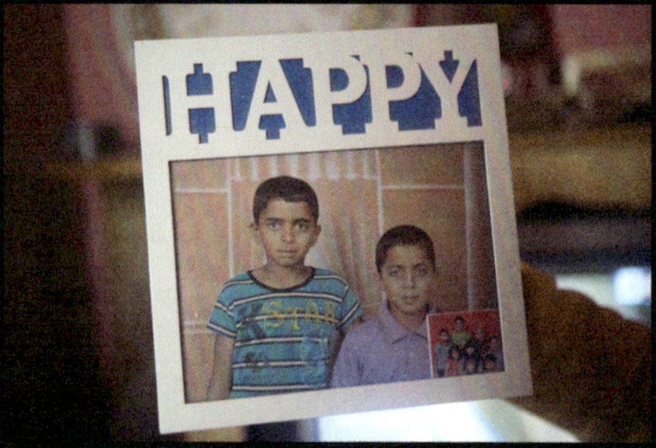

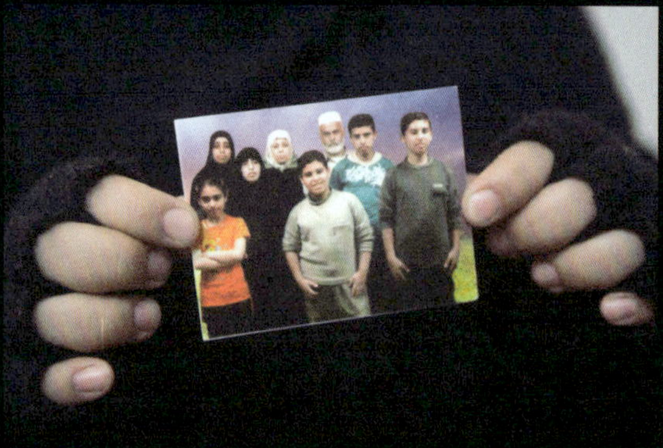

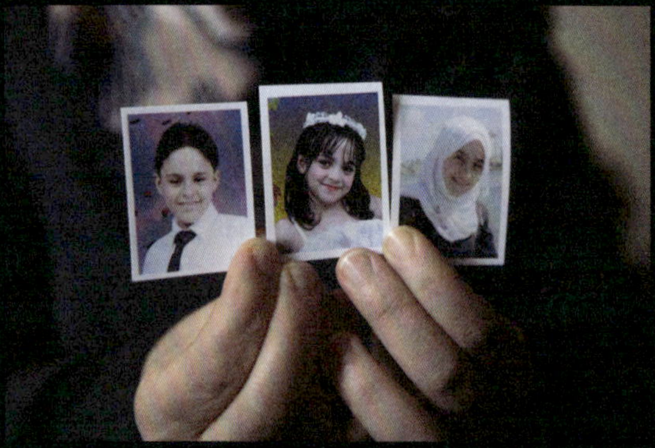

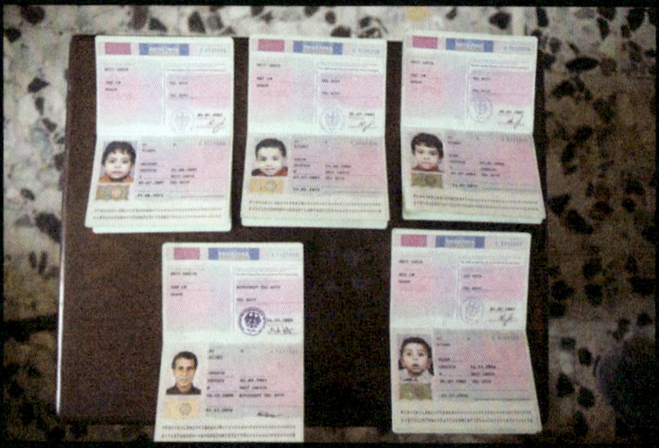

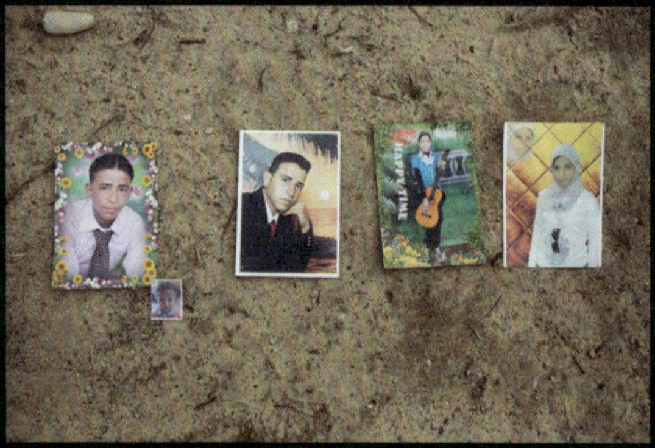

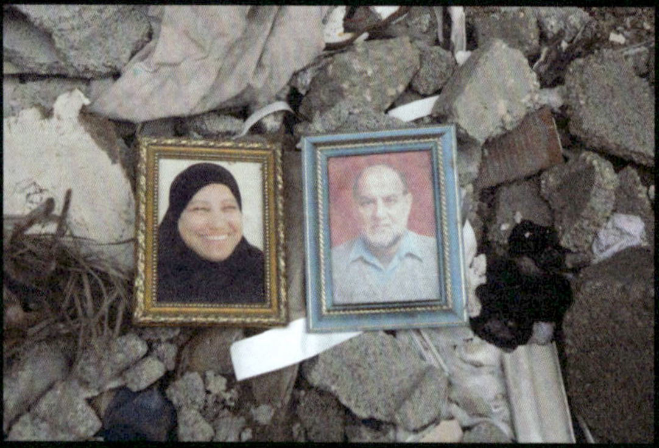

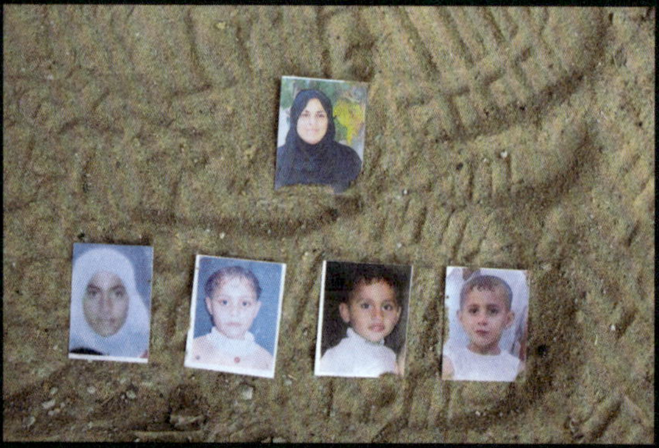

{Top left to right}
1. Photo of Ahmed Mustafa and Mohammed Zo'rob, Rafah / **2.** Photo of the Al-Haj family, from which two members survived, held by Fida'a Al-Haj, Khan Younis refugee camp / **3.** Photos of Mohammed, Yara and Nadeen Al-Farra, held by their mother, Khan Younis / **4.** The passports of Ibrahim al-Kilani and four of his children, Beit Lahiya / **5.** Photos of N'eem Mosa (left), his son Sameeh and his siblings: Abdel Rahman, Samar and Ahlam, Ezbet Beit Hanoun / **6.** Photos of Ibrahim and Jamila Abdullah Abu Itta, Jabalia refugee Camp / **7.** Photos of the Jouda family: Rawia (top), Tasneem, Raghad, Osama, and Mohammed Issam Jouda, Gaza Strip

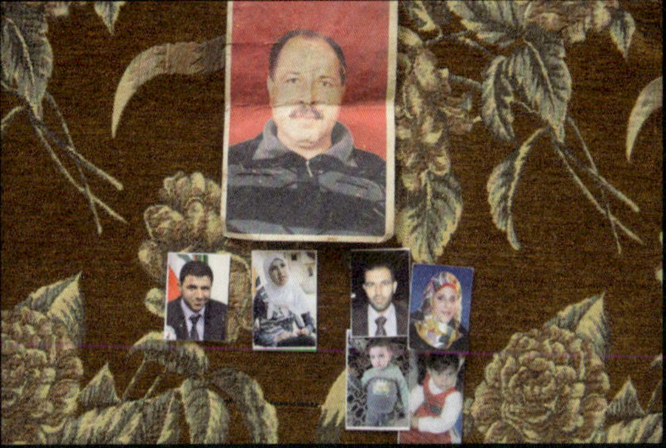

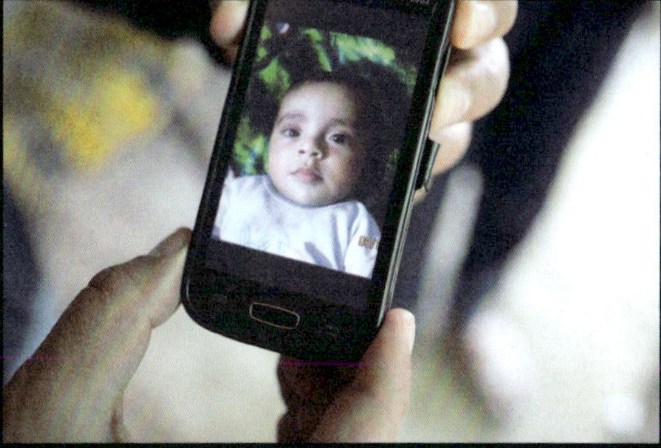

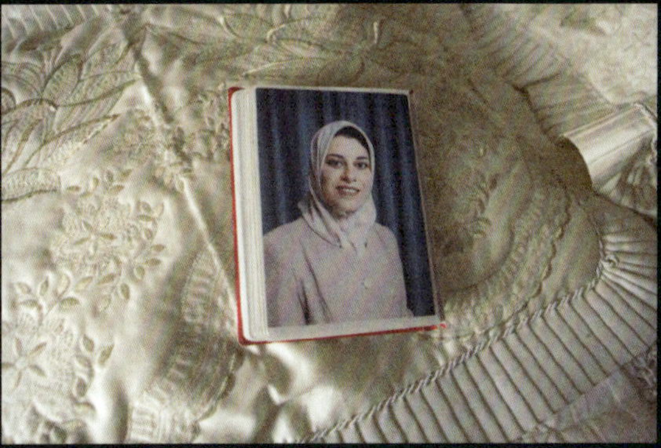

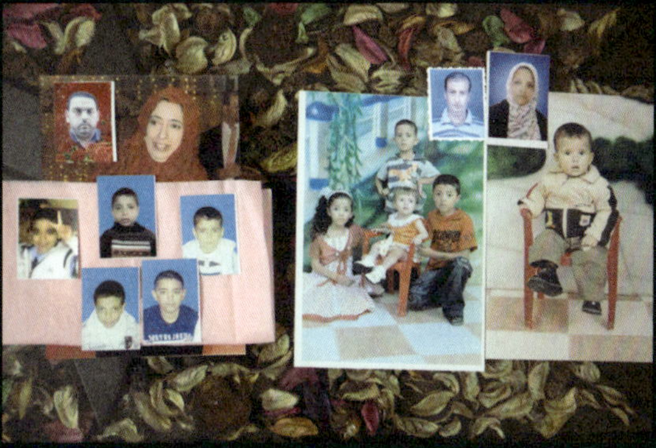

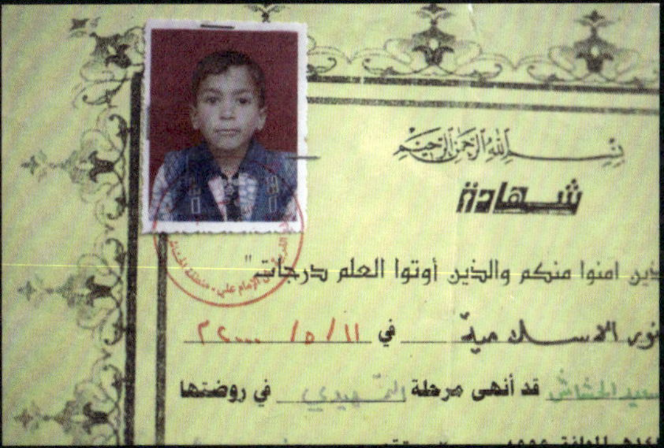

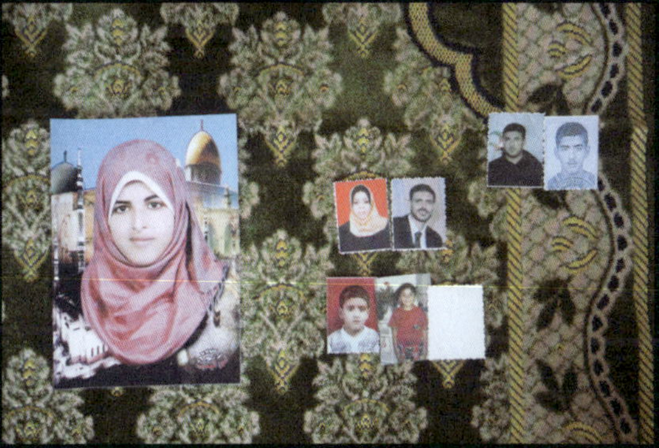

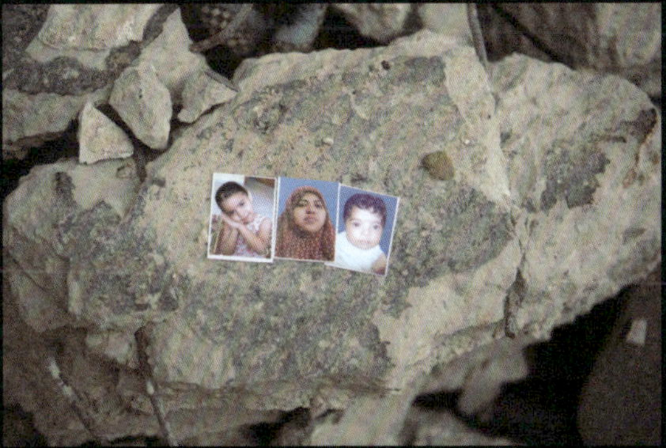

{Top left to right}
1. Photos of members of the family of Mohammed Atta Mahmoud A-Najjar (top frame), Khan Younis / **2.** Photo of Abdel Hadi Hayyel Abu Dahrouj, age 2, A-Zawaydeh village / **3.** Photo of Taghrid Shabaan al-Kilani, Beit Lahiya / **4.** Photos of 14 members of the Abu Amer family, Bani Suheila / **5.** A school certificate of Mohammed Al-Hashash, Rafah / **6.** Photos of the Alouh family, Deir al-Balah / **7.** Photos of Aseel Mohammed Al-Bakri, her mother Ibtisam Ibrahim Al-Bakri, and her sister Asmaa, age 5 months, Al-Shati' refugee camp

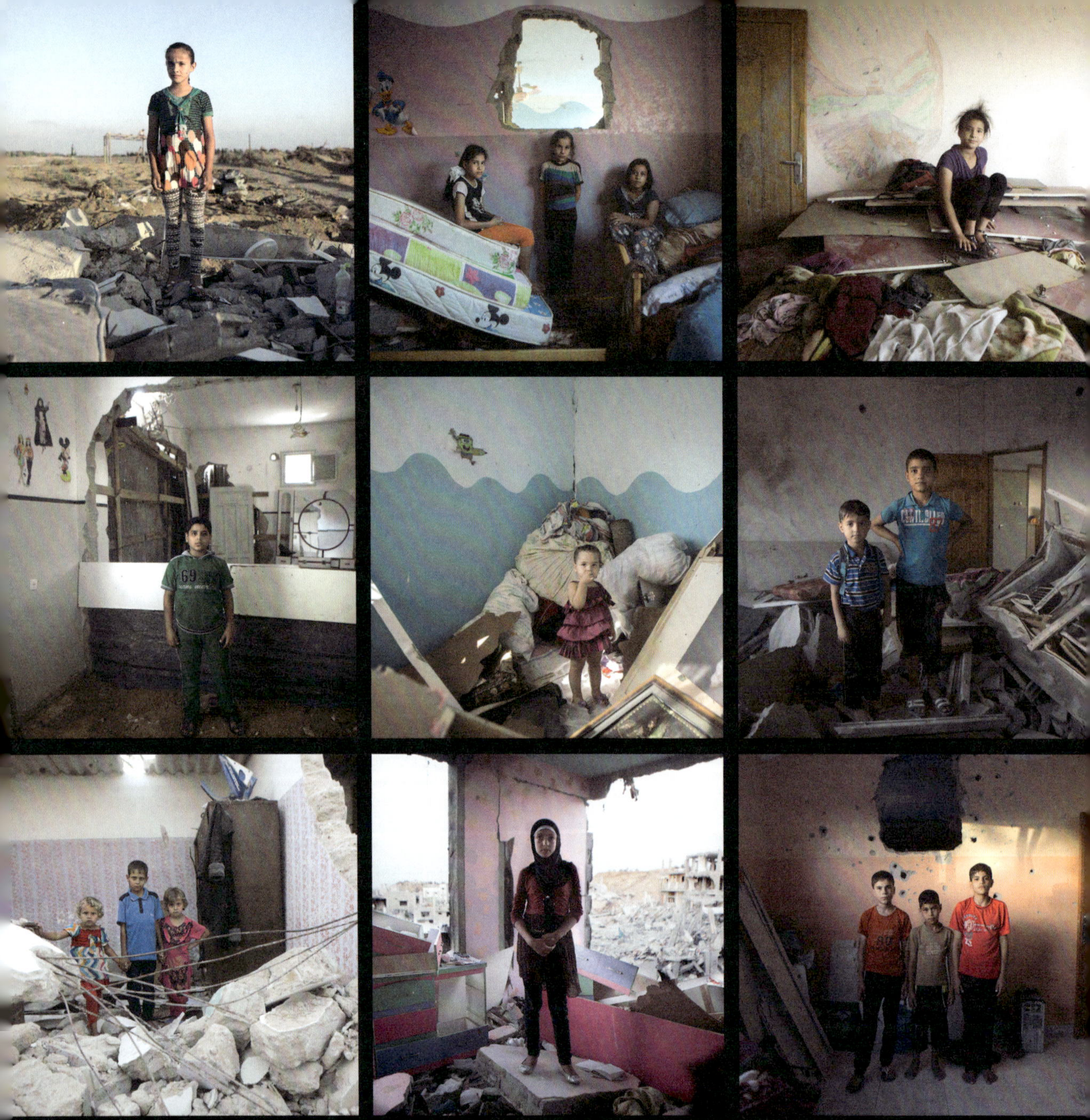

his project portrays Palestinian children in their bedrooms, which were destroyed during the 2014 Israeli military offensive on the Gaza Strip.

Top left to right} **1.** Mayssa / **2.** Shaed Naeem (left), Tasneen, and Saja / **3.** Shorouk / **4.** Obeida / **5.** Asma Nofal / **6.** Abdallah (left), and his brother, Ahmed / **7.** Mariam (left), her brother, Abdel Raman, and sister Eman / **8.** Samah Afanah / **9.** Fadi Naïm (left) and his brothe[rs] Jalal (center) and Basel

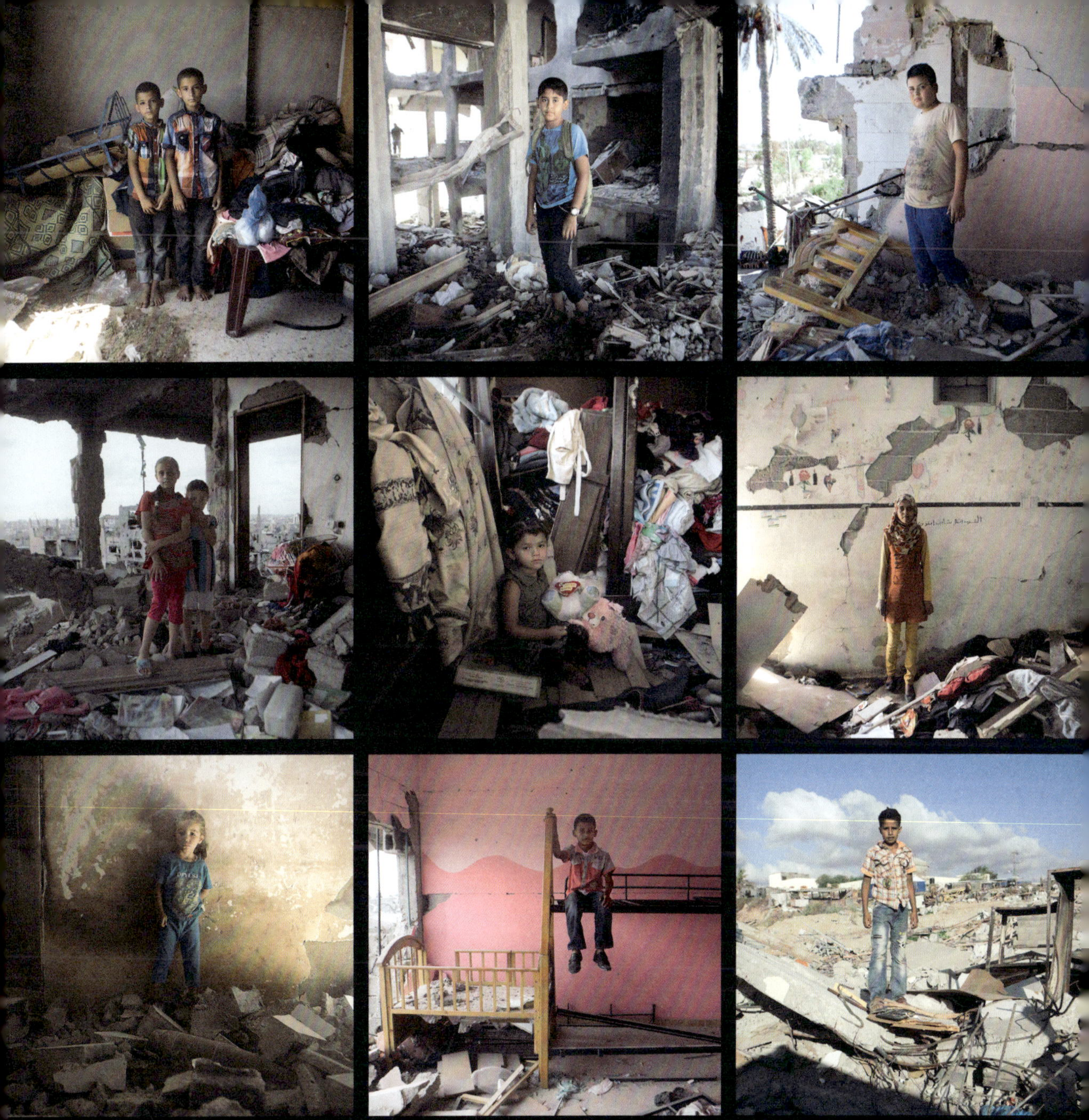

Top left to right} **1.** Ibrahim Al-Hu and his twin brother Abdalah / **2.** Mohammed / **3.** Mohammad /
4. Sanabel and her sister, Haifa / **5.** Shaed Alyazi / **6.** Nisma / **7.** Malak / **8.** Khalil / **9.** Saber

Basel Alyazouri

Learning to Photograph while Running

The 2014 Israeli war on Gaza was my first intense photographic experience. I used to cover day-to-day life before the attack and then, when it came, I had to be in the field—not only to support other photographers, but also as a professional. For me, it was also to help people, not just to get the word out. On the photography side, it was extremely hard at the beginning. I had to learn on the fly.

Sometimes you have to decide whether to take the photo or run for your life. The first day of the attack I went to Shujaiyeh [one of the worst-hit areas during the war]. There was a bombing near the cemetery while people were burying martyrs. Fifty meters from us missiles were falling. I just ran, without taking any photos. Later on, I got used to it and learned to take photos while running.

My work was different from Anne's [Activestills' Anne Paq], because I was in situations where the photography wasn't the first priority for me. For example, the place I love the most in Gaza, Khuza'a, was totally destroyed. I used to go there before the war to chill out—it was an open space, full of farms and trees. During the attack you couldn't even see it because the army had erected hills of sand around it. The first time I went there, I couldn't believe my eyes. The amount of destruction was unimaginable. The family of a very good friend of mine lives there. So the first thing I did was to run to check on their house. Only then did I pick the camera back up.

During these months I realized that living through the war as a normal person, like I had in 2009 and 2012, makes you feel more afraid than being out in the field with your camera. We have a saying here in Gaza, "Come to the bombing; don't let the bombing come to you." It is much harder to sit inside and hear the bombs falling around.

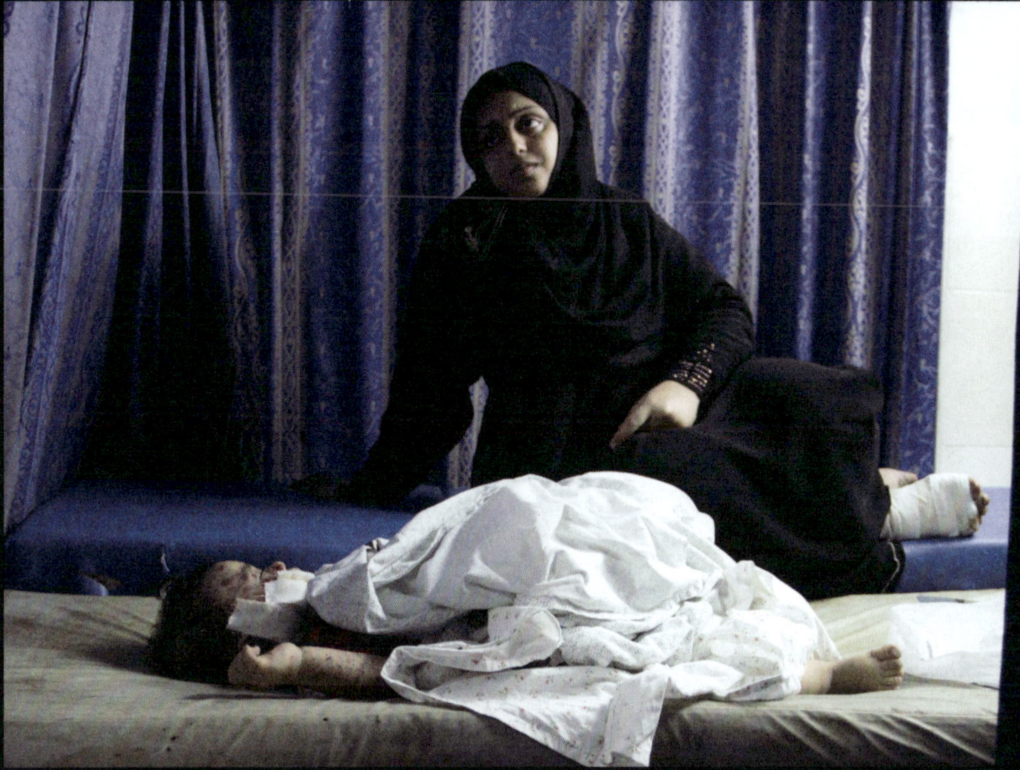

An injured Palestinian child awaits treatment at Al-Shifa Hospital in Gaza City, 30.7.2014

When it was over, it felt like waking up from a dream. The brain is unable to translate such a tragedy. There are many things that I have forgotten, but there are moments that are ingrained in my memory in the form of a photograph. Like one of a woman sitting by her injured child at Al-Shifa Hospital. They had just survived a bombing in which Israeli missiles left an entire street in ruins.

After the ceasefire, Anne and I went to cover areas we couldn't reach before, like Beit Hanoun, Rafah, and many others. Then the real shock hits you, when you start walking in the streets and see all the rubble and ruins.

Together with Anne, I tried to focus on people who didn't get any help. There are still massive numbers of people who don't receive any kind of aid. The most difficult thing is realizing that however harrowing the story you're covering is, the one you will work on tomorrow will be even worse.

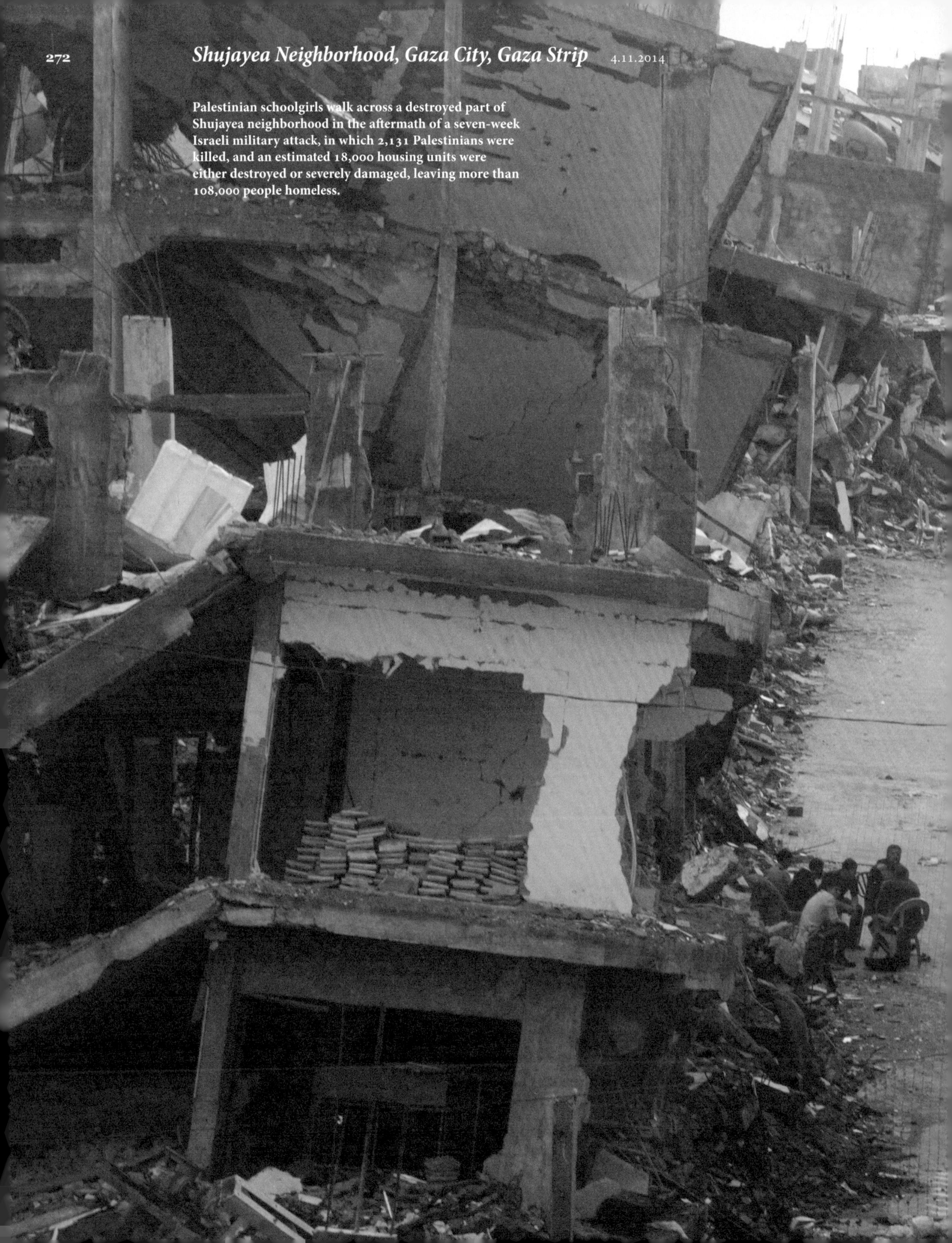

Shujayea Neighborhood, Gaza City, Gaza Strip 4.11.2014

Palestinian schoolgirls walk across a destroyed part of Shujayea neighborhood in the aftermath of a seven-week Israeli military attack, in which 2,131 Palestinians were killed, and an estimated 18,000 housing units were either destroyed or severely damaged, leaving more than 108,000 people homeless.

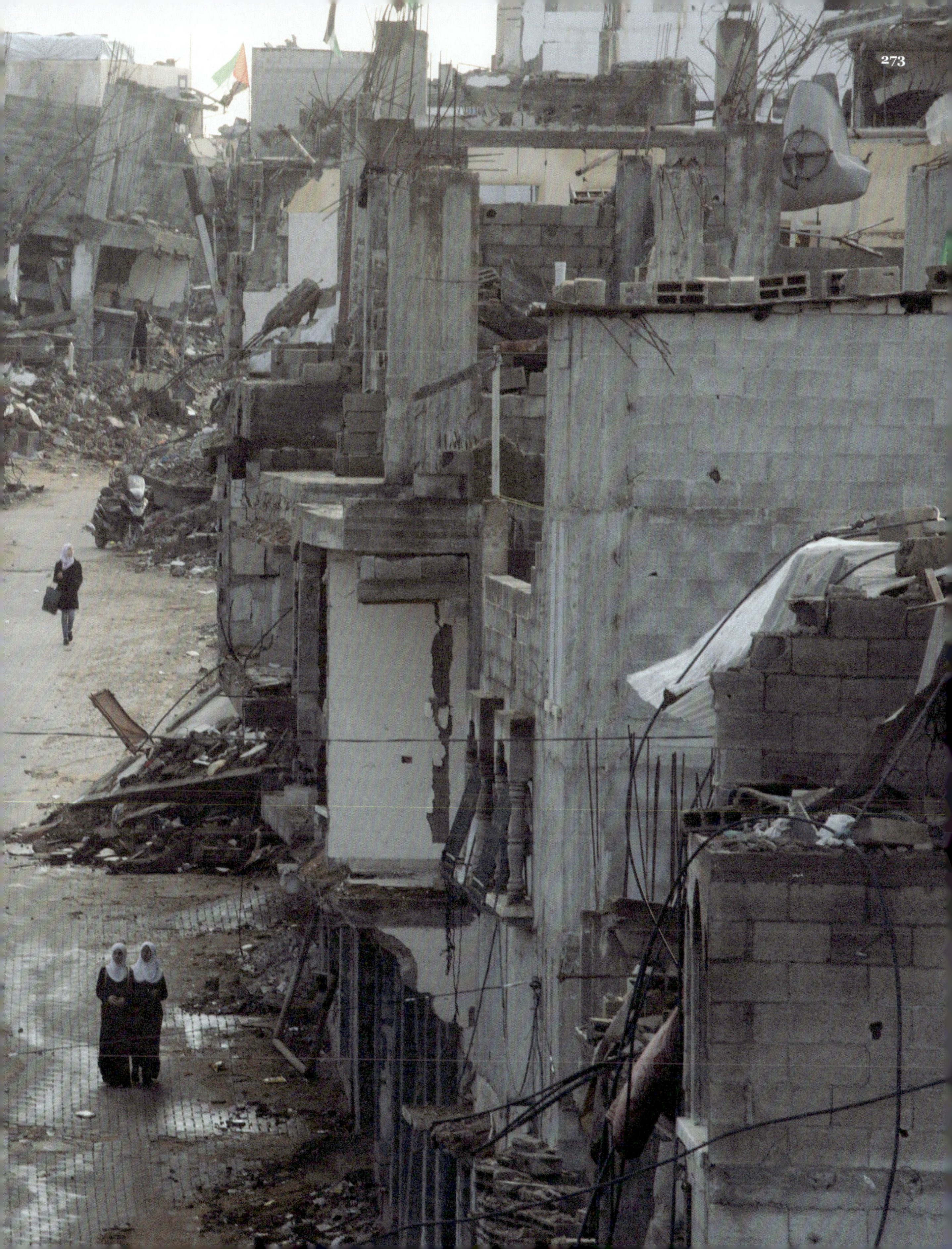

Jabalia, Gaza Strip 16.11.2012

Palestinians mourn the death of Mahmoud Raed Saddllah, age 4, killed in an Israeli attack.

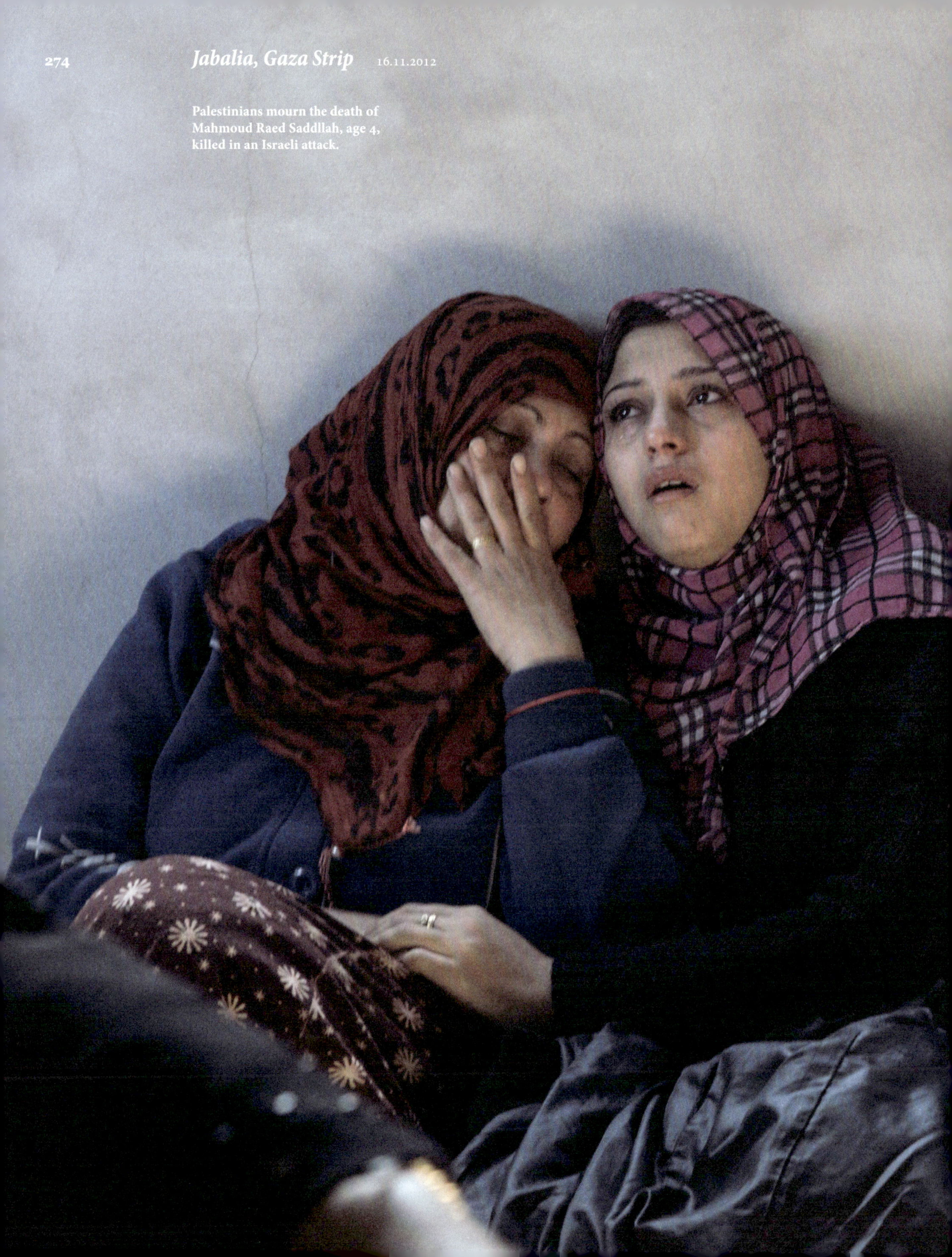

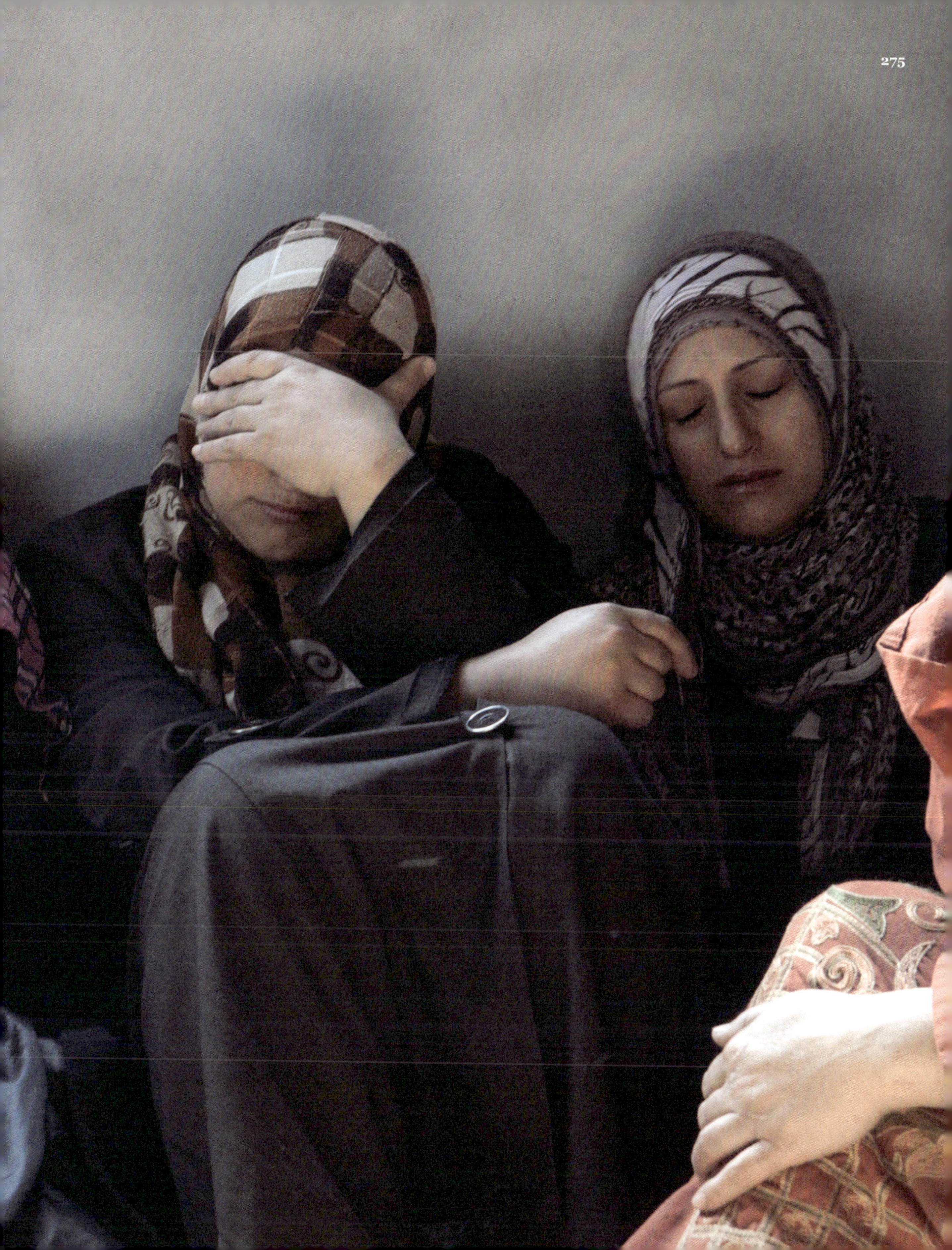

Shujayea Neighborhood, Gaza City, Gaza Strip 15.9.2014

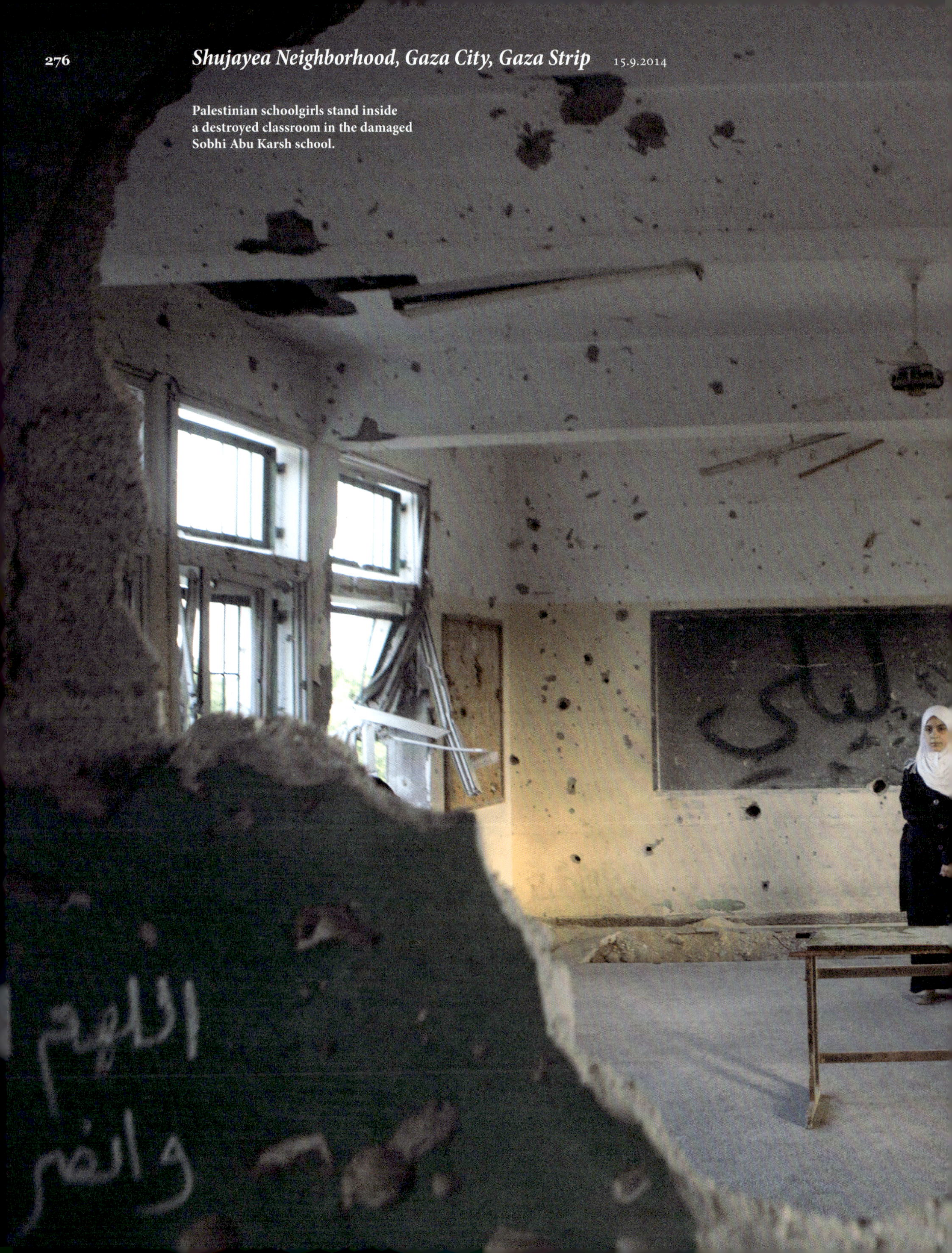

Palestinian schoolgirls stand inside a destroyed classroom in the damaged Sobhi Abu Karsh school.

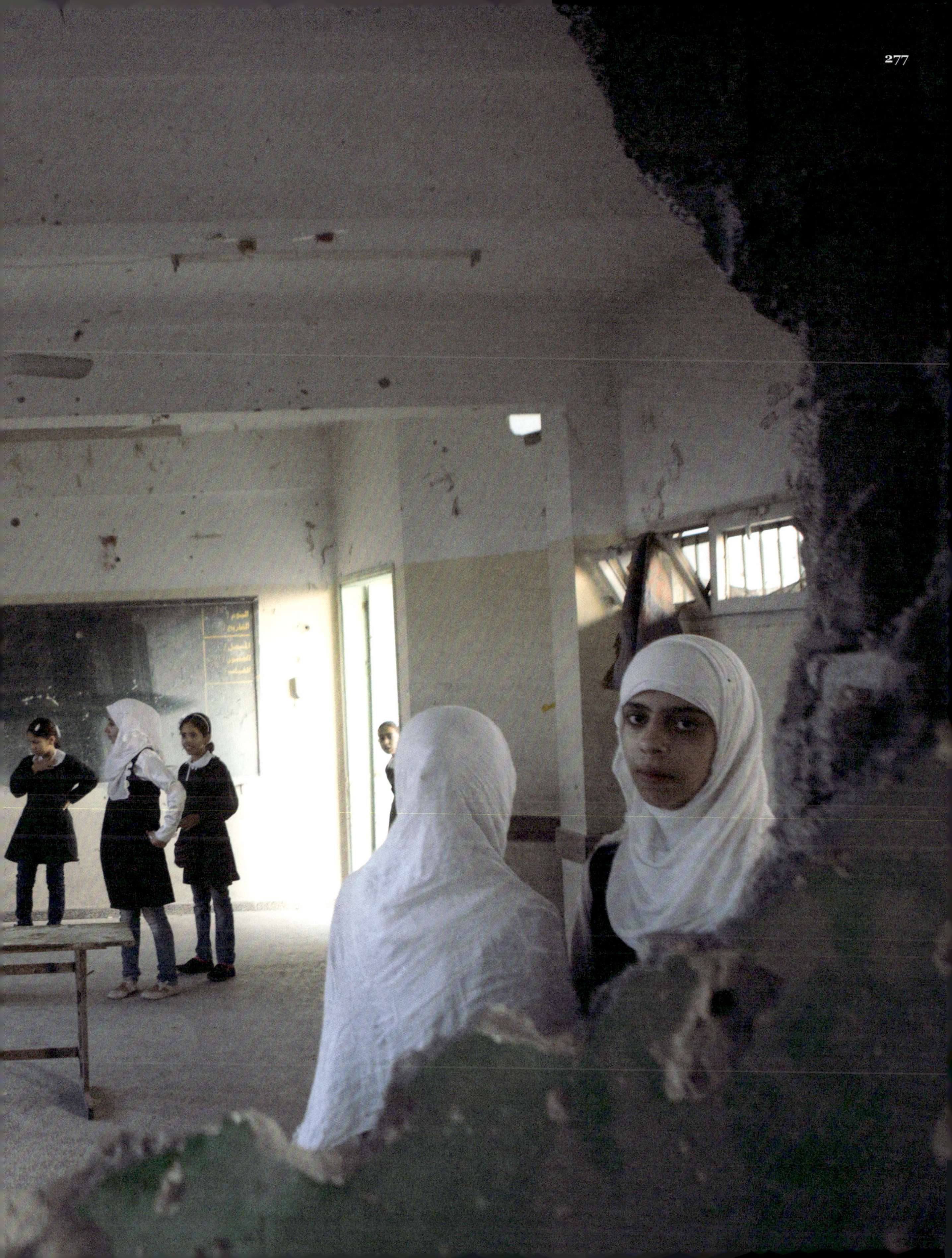

Yotam Ronen

Being on the Other Side of the Frame

The diplomatic-political situation deteriorated rapidly at the start of summer 2014. When it all began, no one imagined how horrible it would become by early fall. Three Jewish teenagers were kidnapped on their way home near the settlement of Alon Shvut in Gush Etzion in the occupied West Bank. The general assumption from the beginning was that they were no longer alive, but the army couldn't find them and imposed a reign of terror over the West Bank—road blocks, raids, and hundreds of arrests—the likes of which had not been seen in years.

After the discovery of the bodies almost three weeks later, there was a huge funeral attended by tens of thousands. For a moment it seemed as if this would be the end of it. But that was not to be. A day after the funeral, the burned body of Mohammed Abu Khdeir, a teenager from East Jerusalem's Shuafat neighborhood, was discovered. It quickly became clear that his killers were right-wing extremists who had kidnapped him near his home and had burned him alive in revenge for the murder of the three youths. Jerusalem exploded. The Israeli Army and the police responded by harshly suppressing the Palestinian protests. At the same time, rockets were periodically fired from the Gaza Strip in the direction of southern Israel. Within days, the decision was made to attack the Gaza Strip, which had not yet recovered from the previous Israeli attack less than two years before.

The border of the Gaza Strip was teaming with tens of thousands of soldiers along with thousands of tanks and artillery. The army began shelling the Gaza Strip, and there were dozens dead on the first day. I made my way down to the border to cover the events. As an Israeli citizen, since 2007 I have been prohibited from entering the Gaza Strip. I found myself in an untenable situation: as a photojournalist I want to be in the center of the events, and as a political person I believe that my duty is to stand alongside the oppressed and suffering. Over the years when I covered the Palestinian struggle in the

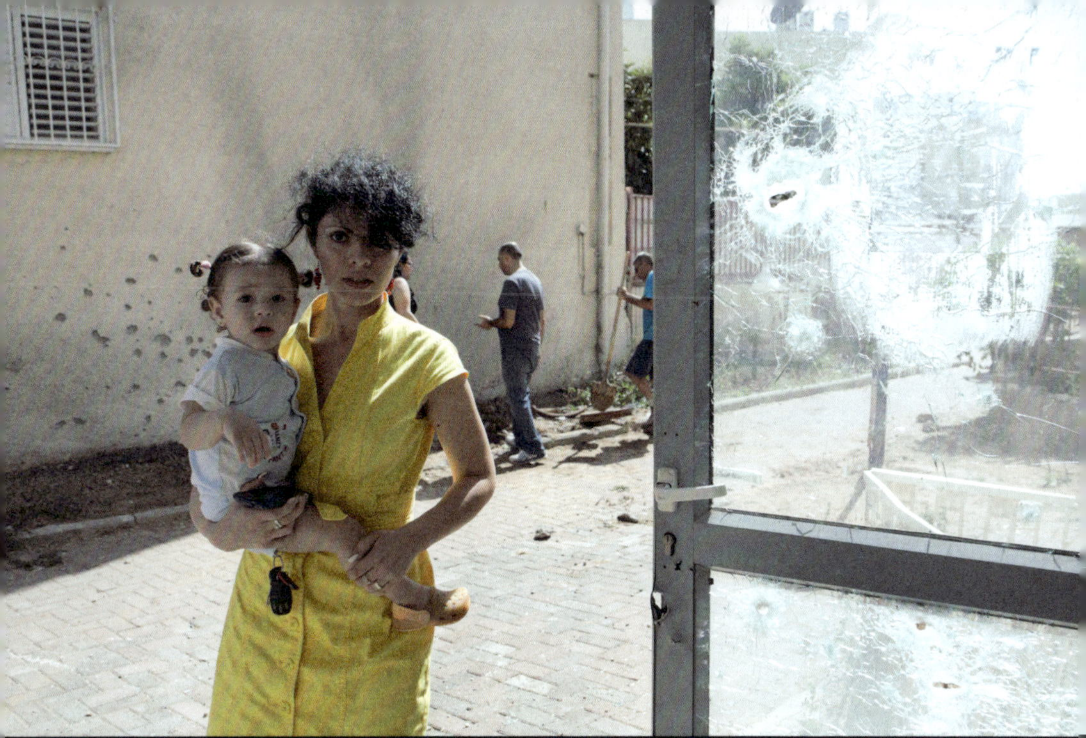

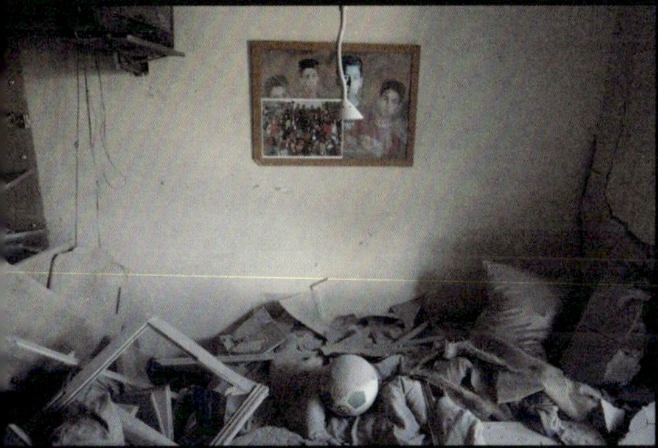

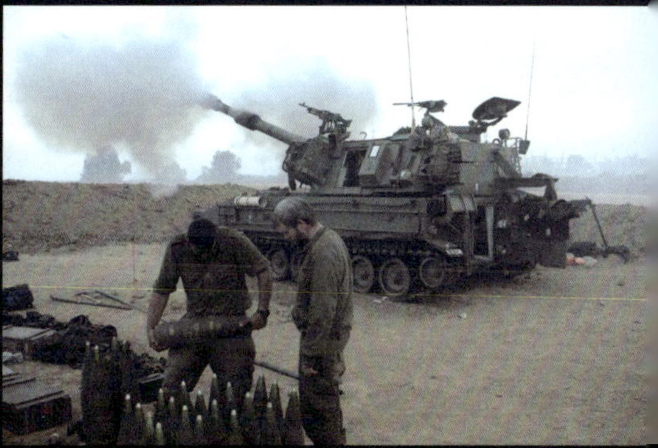

. A woman holding her baby running from an area hit by a missile launched from the Gaza Strip, Sderot, Israel, 5.7.2014 / **2.** Ruins of a room hit by a rocket fired into Israel from the Gaza Strip, Be'er Sheva, Israel, 20.11.2012 / Israeli artillery fires a shell toward the Gaza Strip from its position near the border with Gaza, 24.7.2014

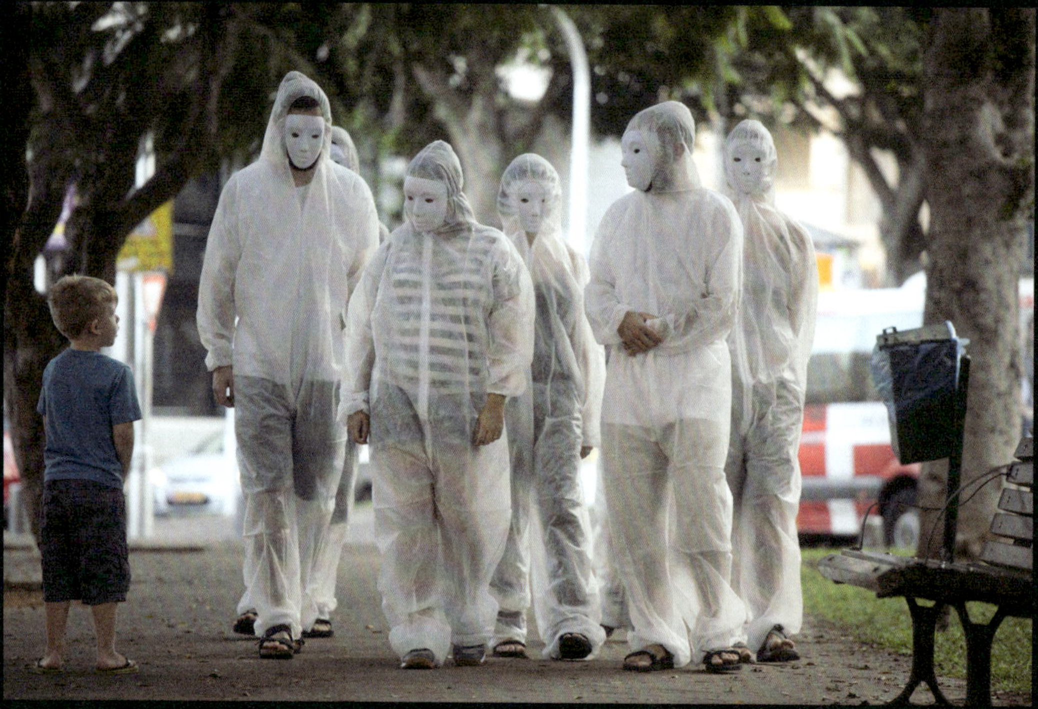

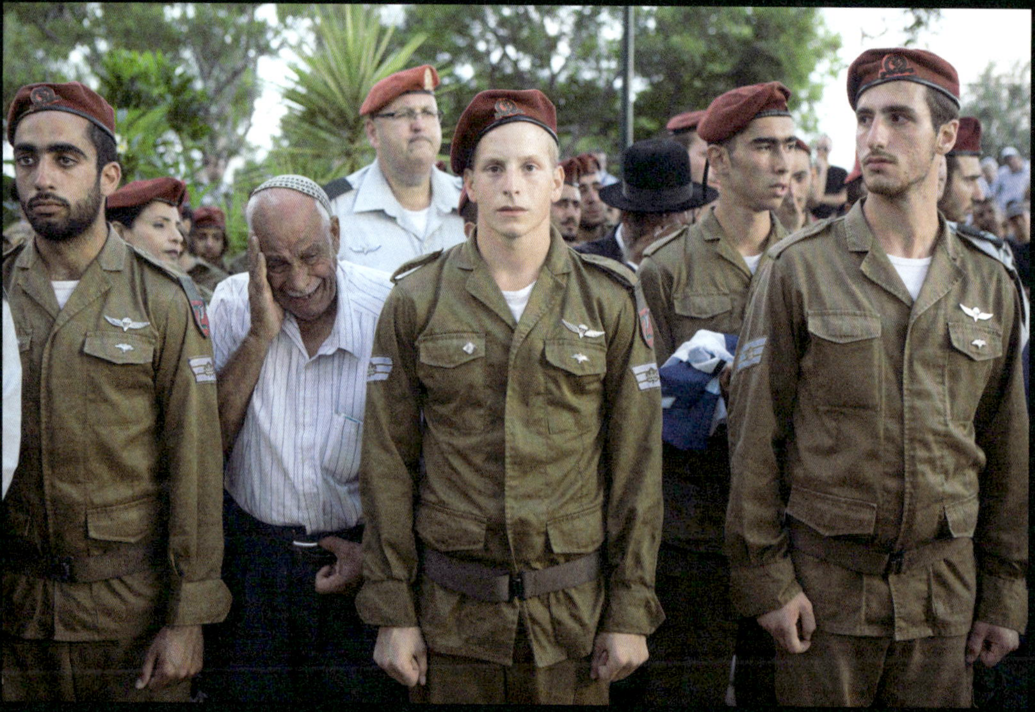

1. Israeli left-wing activists stage an anti-war protest in solidarity with the victims of the Israeli attack on Gaza, Tel Aviv, 12.8.2014
2. Israeli soldiers and relatives mourn at the grave of Sergeant Bnaya Rubel during his funeral, Holon, Israel, 20.7.2014

West Bank, I was able to choose my viewpoint—to march alongside the Palestinians who were fighting against the occupation and to tell their stories as I witnessed them with my own eyes. This possibility was closed to me now. I found myself photographing battalions of soldiers, non-stop artillery fire, and clouds of smoke, the terrible results of which I could see only through foreign media reports. The awful suffering of the people whose stories I wanted to tell remained behind the high fence surrounding Gaza and the smokescreen of the relentless bombing.

Over the years, my work in Activestills has been a combination of several ambitions: to engage in political activity, work as a photojournalist, and create an independent media platform. Ever since I began working in photography in a professional capacity, I have made a living mainly in the established Israeli media outlets, first in sports and then in news. Alongside my first steps in the field, we founded the collective which has been since then, and is still today, my political home. From the start, I discovered that there is an almost irreconcilable conflict between working in media organizations that appeal to the Israeli public and serve as its broker for reality and the aspiration to describe the reality as I see it.

My aspiration as a photographer, as it has developed through my work in Activestills, is to give expression and visibility to the injustice and suffering caused to human beings. I tried to realize this goal in the events I covered, including the rocket attacks on the civilian population in southern Israel. What remained beyond my reach, as an Israeli citizen, was the enormous suffering, many times worse, across the border, inside the Gaza Strip. I found myself on the wrong side of the war, unable to give expression to the suffering of the other side.

This situation was an especially absurd one for me because my childhood home, where my parents still live, was only a few kilometers from the border with Gaza. Every night I returned there to sleep. The area that in normal times was a refuge of serenity and calm for me was turned into a giant military area with the thunder of non-stop explosions in the background, and only a few kilometers away terrible atrocities were taking place. In the midst of the endless traveling in the south, I grappled with the question of how to stay true to myself within a system that is broadcasting a message that for the most part I do not identify with, and on the other hand, how is it possible to reject a position in the media system that shapes public opinion? The platform of the established media, despite the meteoric rise in importance of social networks, is still a significant factor in the construction of the public discourse. As a person who lives in Israel and considers Israeli public opinion one of the factors influencing the future of the region, I see great importance in the attempt to influence it through channels that are accessible to the general public.

I found the missing piece of the story of that summer in the work of my colleagues in the collective, Anne Paq and Bassel Alyazouri. They risked their lives in order to get the images from inside Gaza and distribute them on the collective's website and in various alternative and commercial media publications. The meaning of working in Activestills became sharpened for me in this period: it is the Sisyphean task of opposing the rigid physical and mental separation that the specific power relations of this region impose on everyone living in it. Separation allows for the narrowest of spaces in which to maneuver—for those who choose to challenge it. For me, working in the collective is the constant attempt to widen this space.

Ryan Rodrick Beiler

It Takes a Village

On a frigid January morning in 2013, some 250 local and international activists organized by the Palestinian Popular Struggle Coordination Committee converged on a windy hilltop just east of Jerusalem. Their plan, which until that moment had been kept a closely guarded secret, was simple, as relayed in the organizers' words: "For decades, Israel has established facts on the ground as the international community remained silent in response to these violations. The time has come now to change the rules of the game, for us to establish facts on the ground—our own land."

The busloads of activists quickly erected tents on a hilltop opposite the massive Israeli settlement Ma'ale Adumim. The Israeli government had recently announced plans to build an additional 4,000 housing units in the area not only in violation of international law but in defiance of pressure from the United States and other governments not to build in the so-called "E1" area—a particularly sensitive region where ongoing Israeli colonization functions to surround Jerusalem and cut the West Bank in half, separating north from south.

In contrast to the illegality of Israeli settlements, the tent village built by these activists was constructed on Palestinian land with the permission of local landowners. They named the village Bab al-Shams ("Gateway to the Sun"), after the novel by Lebanese author Elias Khoury about a Palestinian refugee's return to his homeland.

The area was quickly sealed off by Israeli forces who barred journalists from entering. While this made it difficult for mainstream media to cover the event, the activists themselves came armed with cameras and laptops to tell their own story, harnessing the power of social media to bypass mainstream channels.

Activestills members were among them, demonstrating their frequent ability to access events that mainstream media cannot or will not cover—because they choose to ignore the story, are barred by Israeli forces, or because protest leaders only trust fellow activists with their story.

Yet in this case, Bab al-Shams succeeded in making international headlines—including the *New York Times*—which only further illustrated why activists must tell their own stories. The original headline on the *Times'* website: "Palestinians set up camp in Israeli-occupied West Bank territory" was within hours changed to: "Palestinians set up tents where Israel plans homes."

While the *Times* erased the occupation from its headline, and had to rely on telephone interviews with the activists, Activestills reported directly from the ground up until the moment that Israeli forces evicted Bab al-Shams just 48 hours after it was established.

The *Times'* self-censorship illustrates a typical mainstream distortion of the power dynamic present in the Israeli colonization of Palestine. By contrast, Activestills' photos in *+972 Magazine* accompanied the direct testimony of grassroots voices like Irene Nasser, a Palestinian citizen of Israel, who wrote:

> It was not just the level of organization and discipline that set Bab al-Shams apart, nor the media interest that catapulted our story into headlines around the world. What made Bab al-Shams significant was the fact that it asserted that we, as Palestinian activists, would not simply react to injustices the occupation laid at our doorstep, but that we were determined to create our own realities on the ground.

The protest village tactic has been repeated several times in the years since Bab al-Shams. Lasting seven days, the Jordan Valley village of Ein Hijleh was by far the longest standing. Other protest camps included the short-lived Al-Manatir near a settlement outpost overlooking the West Bank village of Burin, and the Ahfad Younis "neighborhood" of Bab al-Shams, timed to protest during the visit to Ramallah of US President Barack Obama. In each case, Activestills photographers were on the scene, from the village's construction to its destruction by Israeli forces.

Bab al-Shams Protest Tent Camp, West Bank 11.1.2013

A night view of the Palestinian tent camp Bab al-Shams (Gateway to the Sun), built by the Popular Struggle Coordination Committee in the area Israel has labeled "E1".

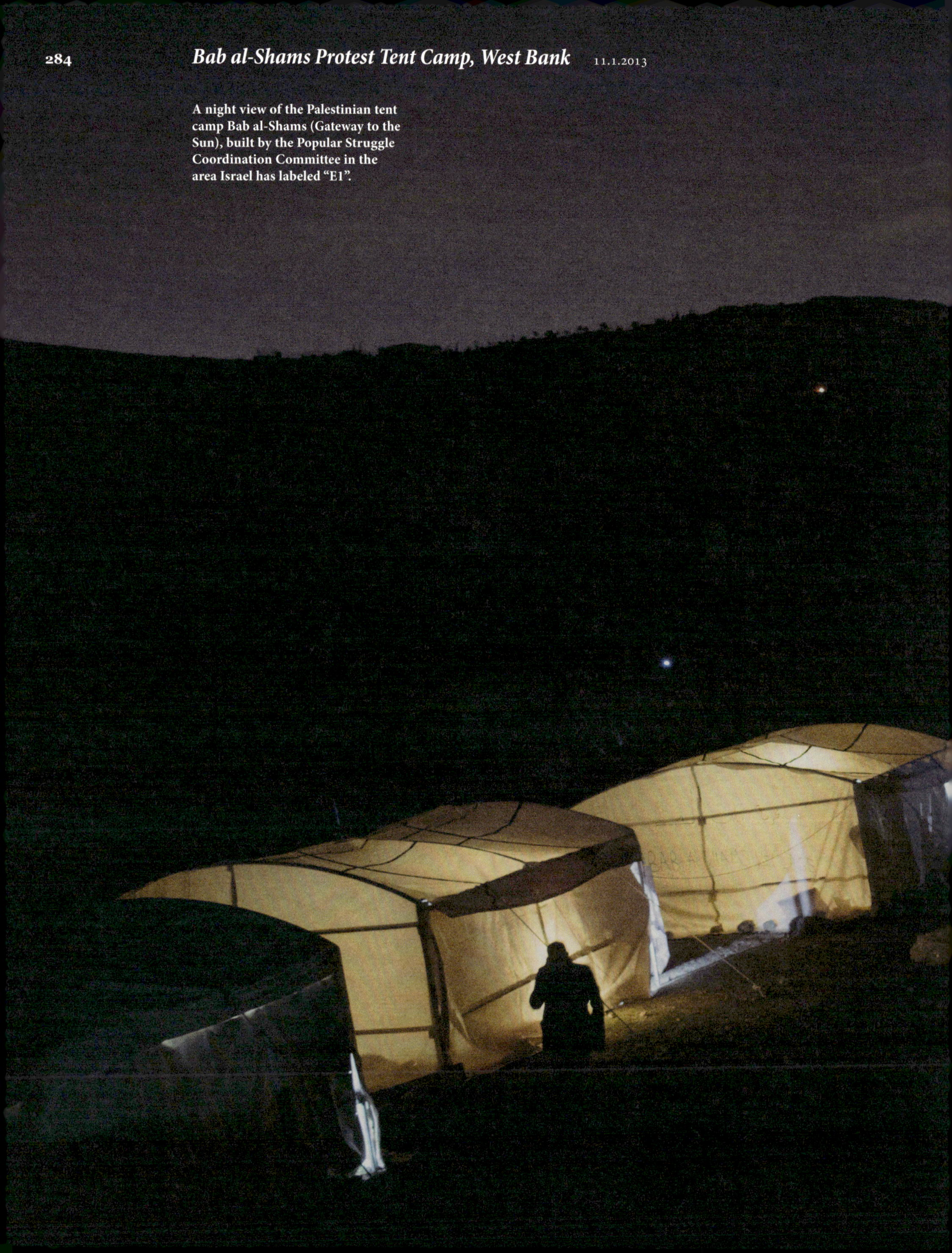

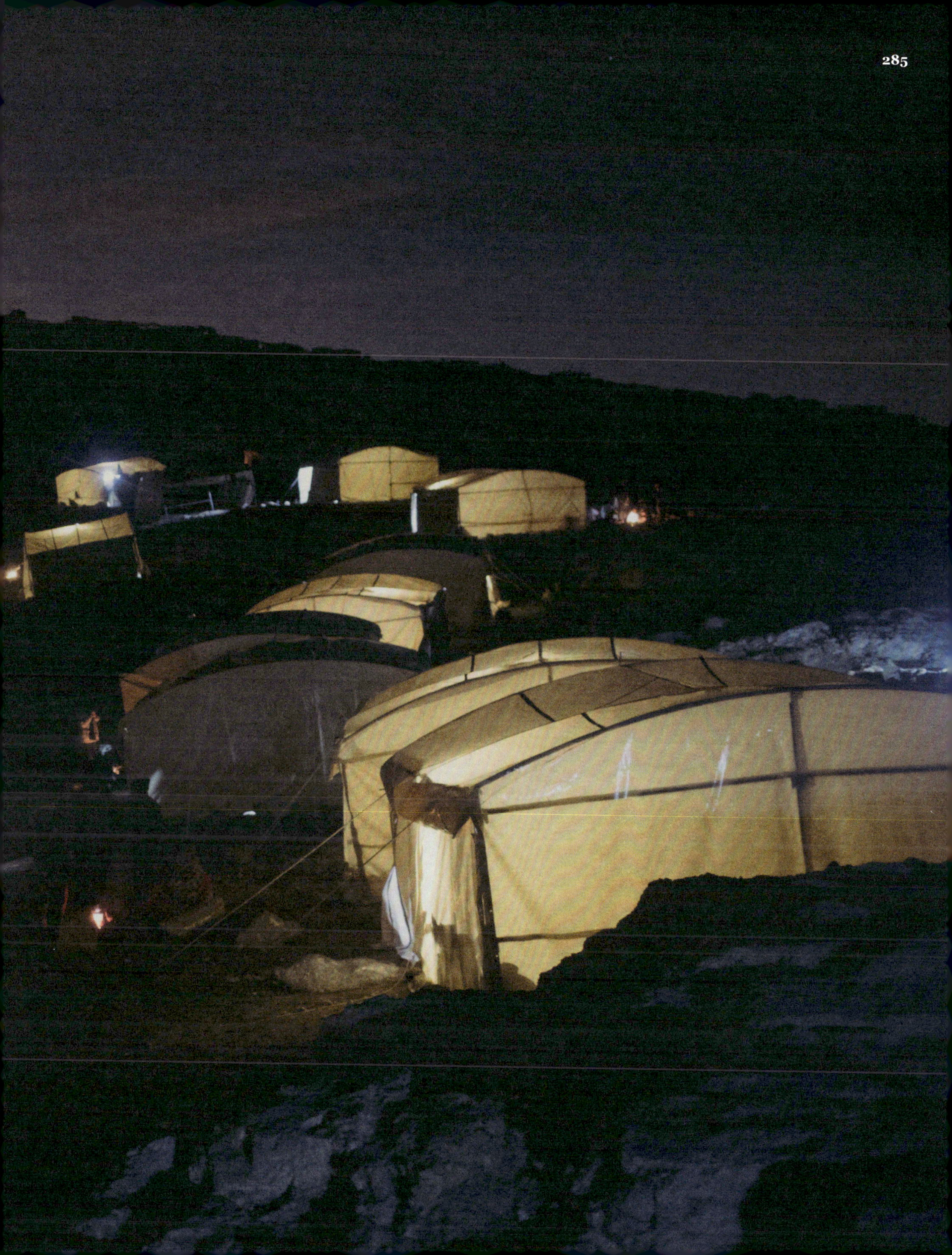

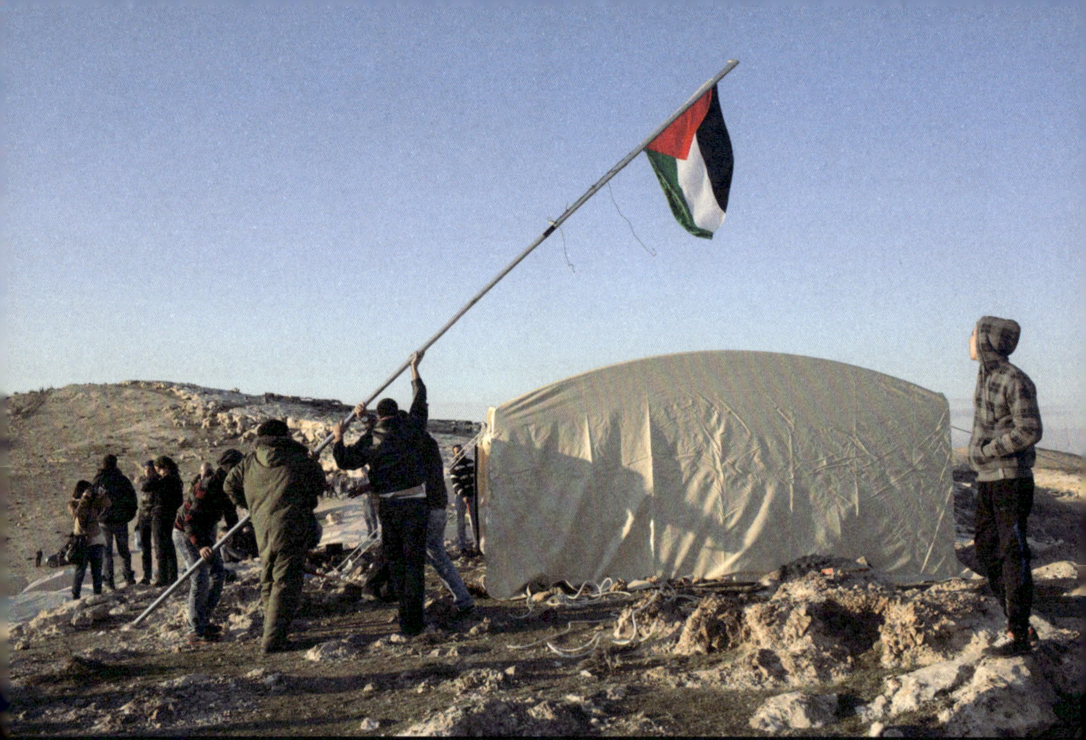

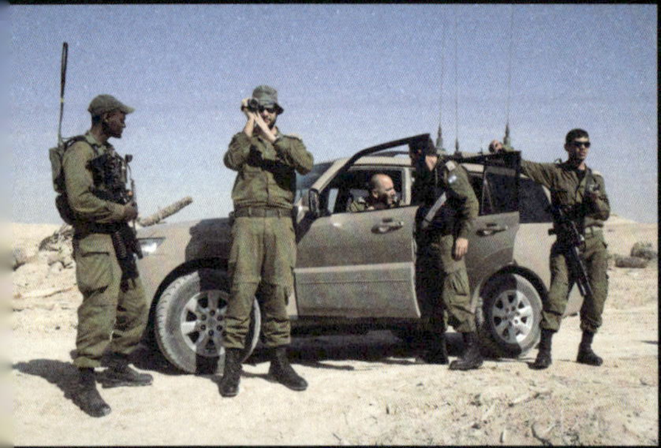

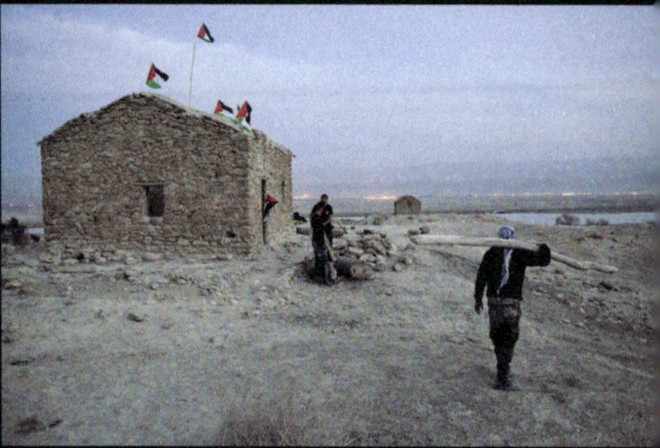

Top left to right}
. Palestinians construct Bab al-Shams camp, 11.1.2013 / . An Israeli soldier films at the entrance to Ein Hijleh camp, Jordan Valley, 1.2.2014 / **3.** Palestinians fix an bandoned building in the Ein Hijleh camp, 31.1.2014 / . Palestinians pray at Bab al-Shams camp, 11.1.2013

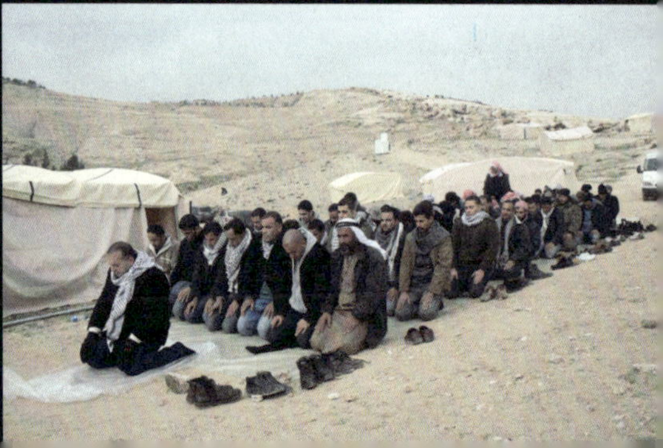

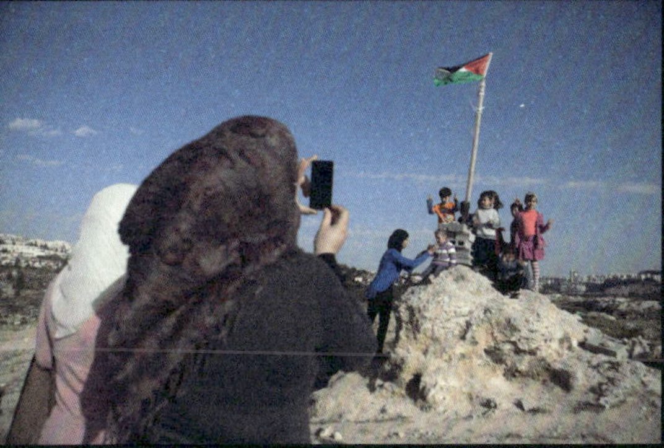
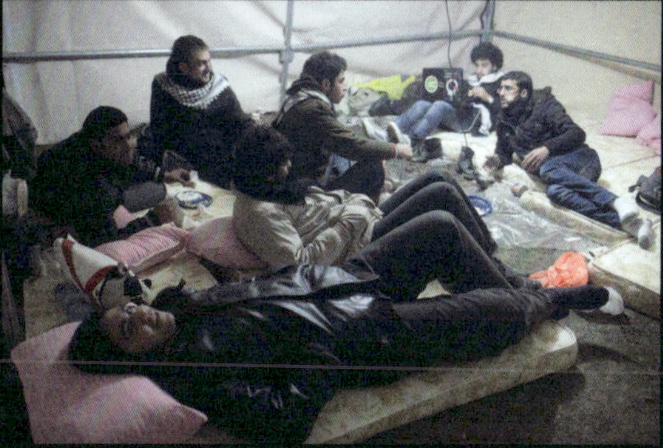
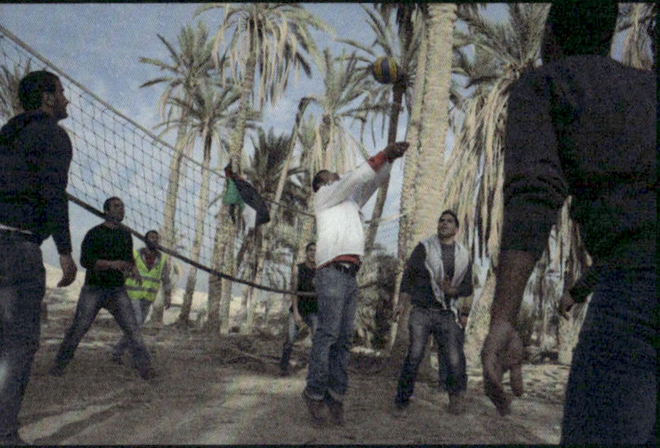
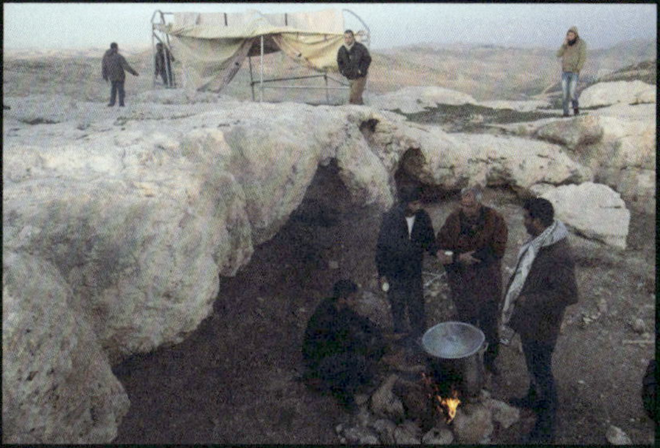
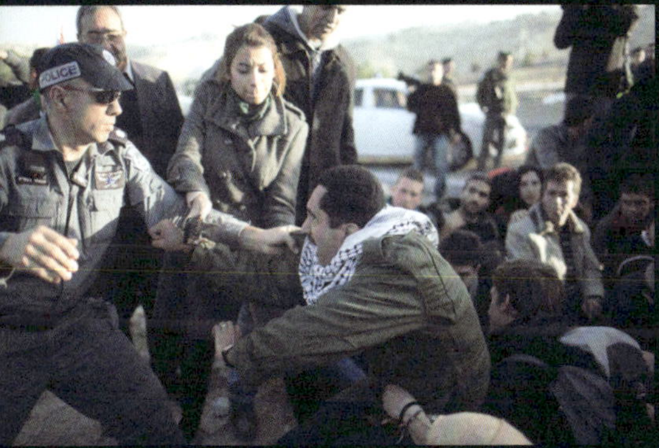

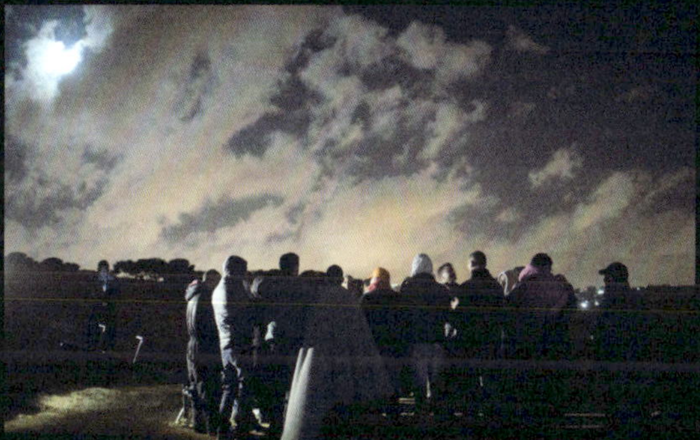
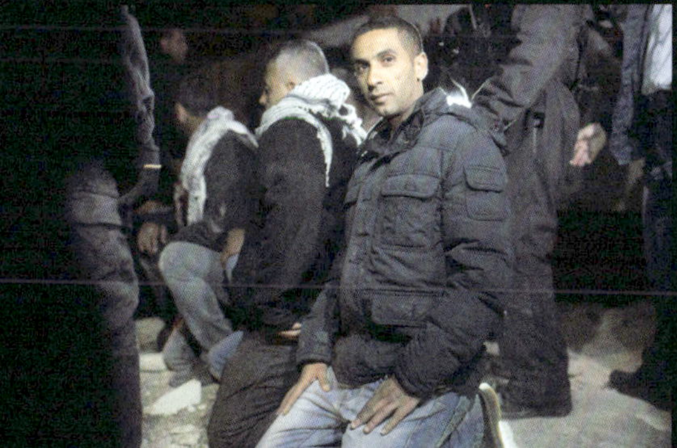

{Top left to right}
1. Palestinians on the lands slated for confiscation in the West bank village of Beit Iksa, following the eviction of Bab al-Karamah camp, 26.1.2013 / **2.** Activists rest in Bab al-Shams camp, 11.1.2013 / **3.** Palestinians play in the Ein Hijleh camp, 31.1.2014 / **4.** Bab al-Shams camp, 12.1.2013 / **5.** Israeli police arrest an activist during an attempt to rebuild Bab al-Shams camp, 15.1.2013 / **6.** Palestinians await eviction from the second Bab al-Shams camp, 24.3.2013 / **7.** Palestinian activists arrested during the eviction of the second Bab al-Shams camp, 24.3.2013

Keren Manor

Taking the Camera in Our Hands

The idea to establish the ActiveVision group came to us a short time after the formation of the Activestills collective. After a few months of participating in the protests in the West Bank village of Bil'in, the idea came to a few of us almost simultaneously, to start a photography course for the youth in the village so that they could tell their stories independently. We established Activestills from a wish to use photography as a tool for political struggles. In a certain sense, ActiveVision, focusing on documentary stills and video storytelling, was for me the collective's new little sister.[1]

Through photography, video, and visual art workshops—which take place in the community—we aim to work with the participants to develop tools to visualize their narratives from their own viewpoints. Our activity stems from the conviction that the community can better turn the lens on itself, as its members have a deeper understanding of the needs and problems they face.

The workshop in Bil'in never got off the ground, but it was a beginning which paved the way for the many workshops that ActiveVision has conducted over the years in various communities. In our first project, "Identity Document" (2006), children of foreign workers, who had grown up and gone to school in Israel, took pictures of the reality of their lives, their desires, and hopes under the threat of being deported back to their home countries. The project came out of a meeting between Activestills' Eduardo Soteras and Romm Lewkowicz from The Hotline for Refugees and Migrants, at the Migrants Day event in Tel Aviv. Around the same time, the order to expel children of foreign workers was announced and the hotline organized youth groups to launch a public relations campaign. We worked for four months with youth who had spent the most formative years of their young lives in Israel and were now, at the most critical period, facing the very real threat

1. ActiveVision was founded in 2006 by Sharon Horodi, Suzanna Lauterbach, Keren Manor, Eduardo Soteras, Keren Shayo, and Cheb Kammerer. Over the years it was joined by Muhamad Ali, Yali Amit, Neomi Lyth, Shachaf Polakow, Timna Peretz and Ben Ronen.

the question: what would you want to say to the Israeli public and government? From their responses, we discovered that they constantly needed to deal with other questions such as: why do I want to stay here? Where do I belong? Why am I different? The results of this project included some forty photographs along with texts in which the participants dismantled and presented the very personal and deep components that comprised their identities and which made up the identity card that the State of Israel was unwilling to give them.

Richard Suarez, one of the children who took part in the course, went to the Ministry of Interior in order to obtain certain permits. This is a very unpleasant experience, especially for a child, and includes a lengthy investigation. And so, in the middle of the day, he took out his camera and started taking pictures. Later he explained to us that the camera helped him in that stressful moment.

> The children of the old man whom my mother takes care of don't have time to give him what my mother gives him. I'm not embarrassed when they come to my mother and ask her, "come take care of our grandfather" or "come clean our bathroom." I'm proud of her. In my eyes, we are the heroes here.

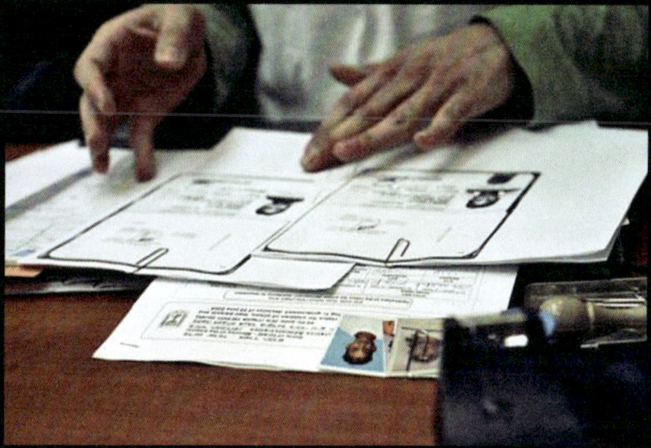

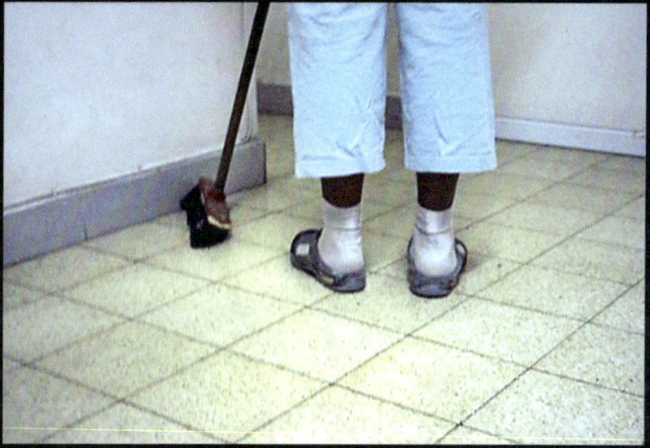

1. Richard Suarez, "Identity Document," stills from video, 2006 /
2. Christian Lazcano, "Mother," stills from video, 2006

The photographs and the texts by the children were shown in an exhibition and received a wide range of publicity as part of the community's struggle against the looming deportation. A short while after, the Israeli government decided in a one-time temporary order to grant citizenship to the children who were born in Israel or had lived in the country for a minimum of six years. As a result of the decision, 900 children and 2,300 family members were granted legal status.

As someone who has been documenting various communities for years, I found myself wondering about my role in documenting those struggles and their subjects; how, in the very act of my documentation, I am preserving existing power relations between documenter and documented. For me, sharing my knowledge and skills is a way to undermine that uneven balance of power.

Toward the end of 2006, hundreds of refugees from Africa began arriving in Israel. Exiled or escaping from their countries, they were fleeing genocide, wars, and dictatorial regimes. After long and arduous journeys, they illegally crossed the border, but once in Israel, where they had hoped to find shelter and an end to their plight, they found that their odyssey was not over. Activestills photographers, including myself, began to document their harsh living conditions and the difficulties the refugee population was facing.

In 2007 we launched the project "Asylum City" (2007–13), in which we worked with refugee youth in various still and video photography courses. This was the beginning of their photographic journey, as individuals and as a group, in dealing with the past they were escaping as well as the future that was filled with uncertainty. A harsh picture emerged from their work, but in the face of the complicated bureaucracy, prejudice, severe living conditions, memories of the long journey, and yearning for family left behind, what also came out was a picture full of humor, love of people, and a strong desire to feel at home.

Alongside technical knowledge, the courses also dealt with the use of the photographic visual medial language as a way of self-expression and as a tool for social engagement. Thus, for example, the participants in the first course produced a newspaper where they decided the nature of the journalistic work. They were responsible for the photography, the interviews, and they also wrote the content, which they then published. They decided what issues they wanted to raise on the public agenda and how they wanted to discuss them. The newspaper was distributed to the Israeli public and the refugee communities, and the products of the photography course were displayed in a street exhibition that was hung in a public shelter in the Shapira neighborhood where most of the refugee communities in Tel Aviv live.

In the second part of the project, we developed a three-month video course for a group of youth aged 13–18, who had come here alone, without families, from various countries in Africa. In one of the short films, Ismail, a 17-year-old boy from Darfur, conducts a street survey in which he interviews Israelis, refugees, and foreign workers in south Tel Aviv about the refugee issue. Through this "role switch," where the refugee is the one interviewing the Israelis, Ismail—taking the microphone in his hand—also takes the power and the control.

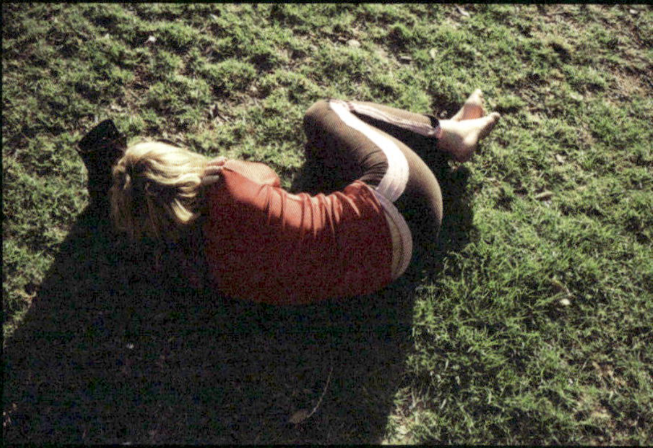

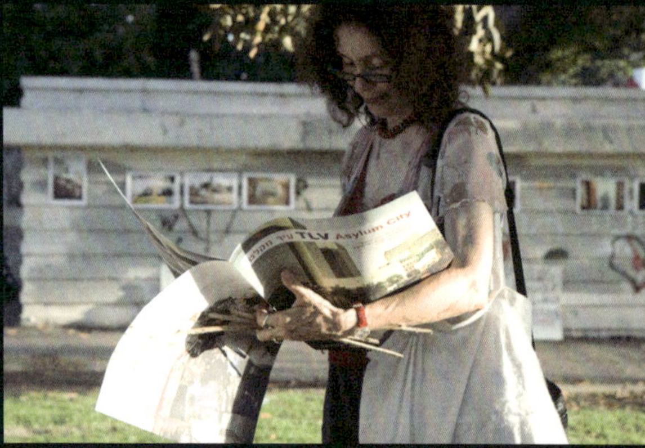

1. Muhammad Zacariya, "Asylum City," 2008 / **2.** "Asylum City," newspaper and street exhibition, Tel Aviv, 20.6.2008

Before going to Bil'in, I was not aware of my privileges and role as an Israeli. Even more, one could say that I was unaware of a significant part of reality. The acknowledgement that I am part of a community that is in a position of power caused me to reflect on my past, my education, army service, and the environment in which I had grown up and that had shaped my consciousness.

Over the years, I found working within my own community also to be very meaningful for me. When we taught the course "Beyond Walls," that focused on documentary activism to Israeli activists, some of the participants chose to turn their cameras on themselves and their own communities. Eden Harel, a 17-year-old high school student, chose to make a film during her final high school year. In her movie entitled *Recruits*, Eden shows the preparation and education for army service in her school through the eyes of her best friend Nina, who is deliberating between criticism of the system and wanting to be part of the Israeli society to which she belongs. Eden's observant eye shows a militaristic society that makes a clear distinction between her and "the other." I wish I had seen this film when I was her age.

For me, Activestills is not just the name of our collective, but also a condensed concept. My activity documenting in Activestills has gone hand in hand with my work as a teacher in the courses initiated by ActiveVision, and has, over the years, blurred the border between the two groups. We struggle together, side by side, taking the camera in hand.

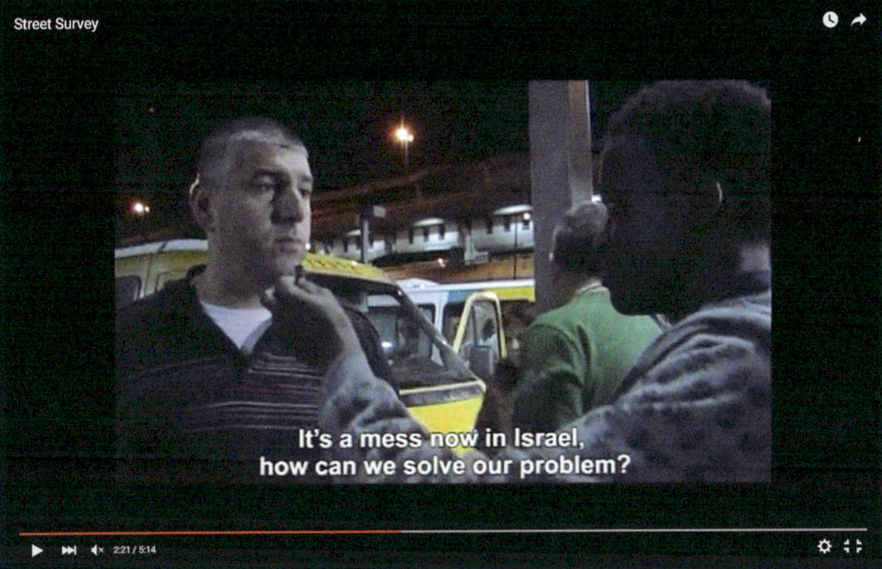

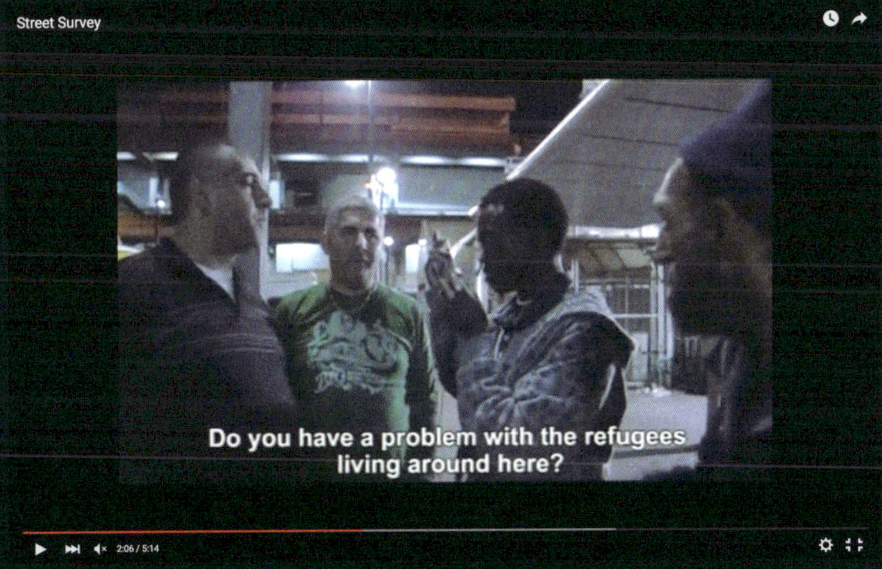

"Street Survey," screenshots from Youtube.

Shachaf Polakow

The Non-Decisive Moment

As a photojournalist and activist, I travel from place to place looking for the next event, the next "decisive moment," in the words of Henri Cartier-Bresson, of violence and oppression. These moments are often chosen to represent the Israeli occupation. However, the more I traveled and witnessed the occupation, the more I came to understand that violence is not only when military forces shoot at protesters, or when families lose their homes, or live through an airstrike. The ongoing occupation is, in itself, violence. While we (Israelis) are able to move freely in and out of the West Bank, our Palestinian photographers and friends are restricted in their movement—this is violence. As Israeli settlements continue to expand and Palestinian lands to contract—this is violence. When our voices are considered valid while Palestinian voices are questioned—this is violence.

These instances of violence, not considered news, take place in between the locations and events of physical confrontations. It is our duty to take pictures of the "non-decisive moments" because we cannot limit our visual documentation only to those decisive and explicit moments that everyone recognizes as acts of resistance or violence.

For me, these two photographs represent such "non-decisive moments" within the occupation. In the spring of 2008, construction of the Israeli separation wall began on the land of the West Bank village of Ni'lin. The village's local popular committee started to organize demonstrations within the broader campaign against the wall's construction. I joined the protests in Ni'lin the first week and immediately felt welcome.

After several years of being involved, I had developed friendships in the village. One weekend, my friend Saeed invited me to stay with his family. After dinner, we went to a wedding that took place on the main street. After it ended, we walked to a hill overlooking the nearby checkpoint. I could see the lights of Tel Aviv on the horizon. The proximity and the contrast of the wedding to the nearby checkpoint made me understand how the occupation is everywhere, always present. This experience in Ni'lin gave me a new point of view, as an Israeli and as a photographer, by introducing me to the importance and challenge of creating more complex images of the occupation and the Palestinian people who struggle against it.

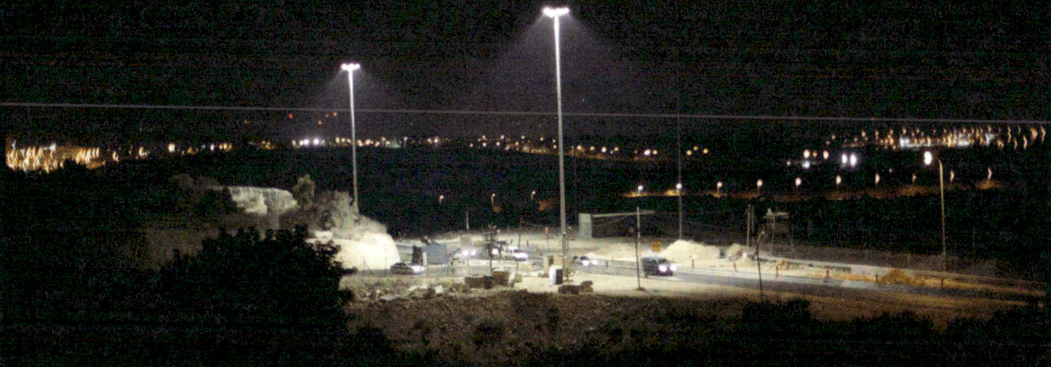

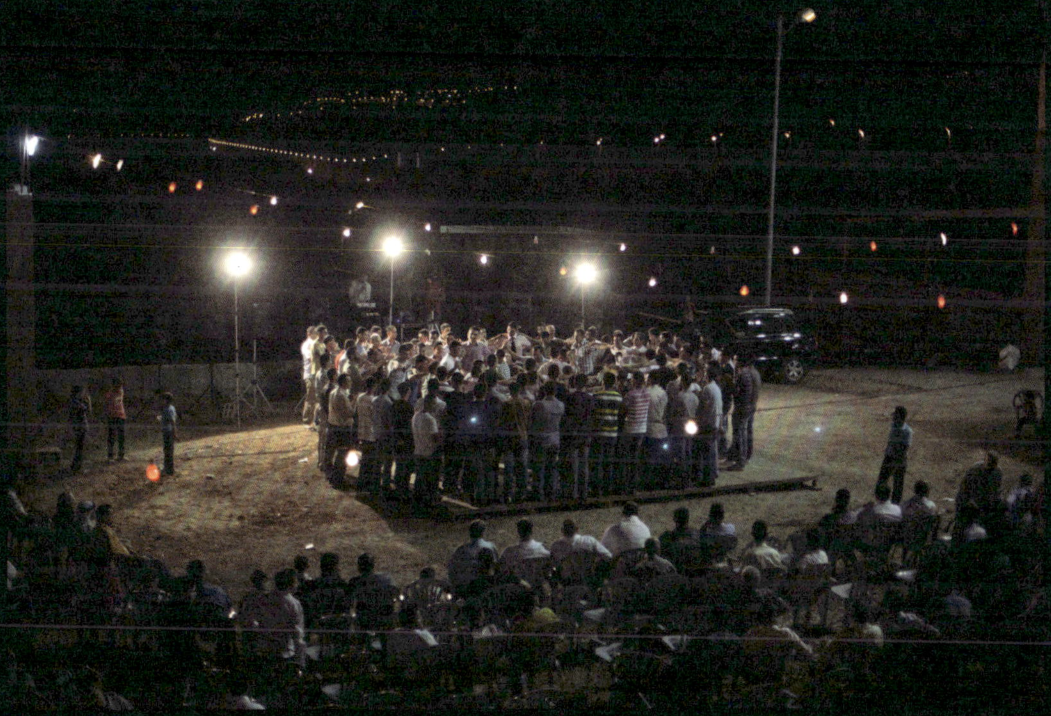

1. The Israeli military checkpoint near Ni'lin village, West Bank, 23.9.2010
2. Residents of Ni'lin celebrate a wedding in the main street of the village, West Bank, 23.9.2010

Jab'a, West Bank 3.11.2007

Palestinian, Israeli, and international activists open an army roadblock near the village of Jab'a.

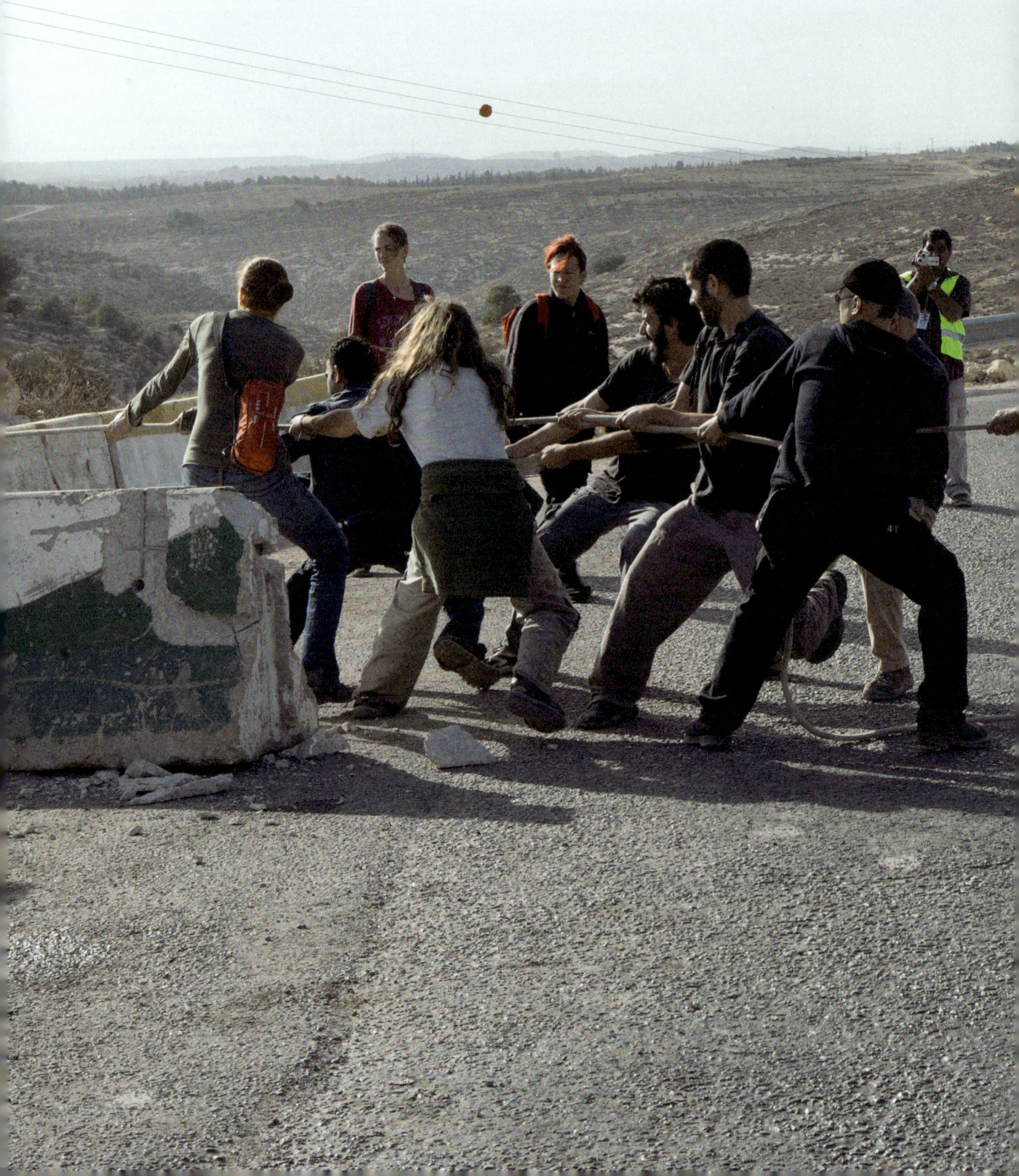

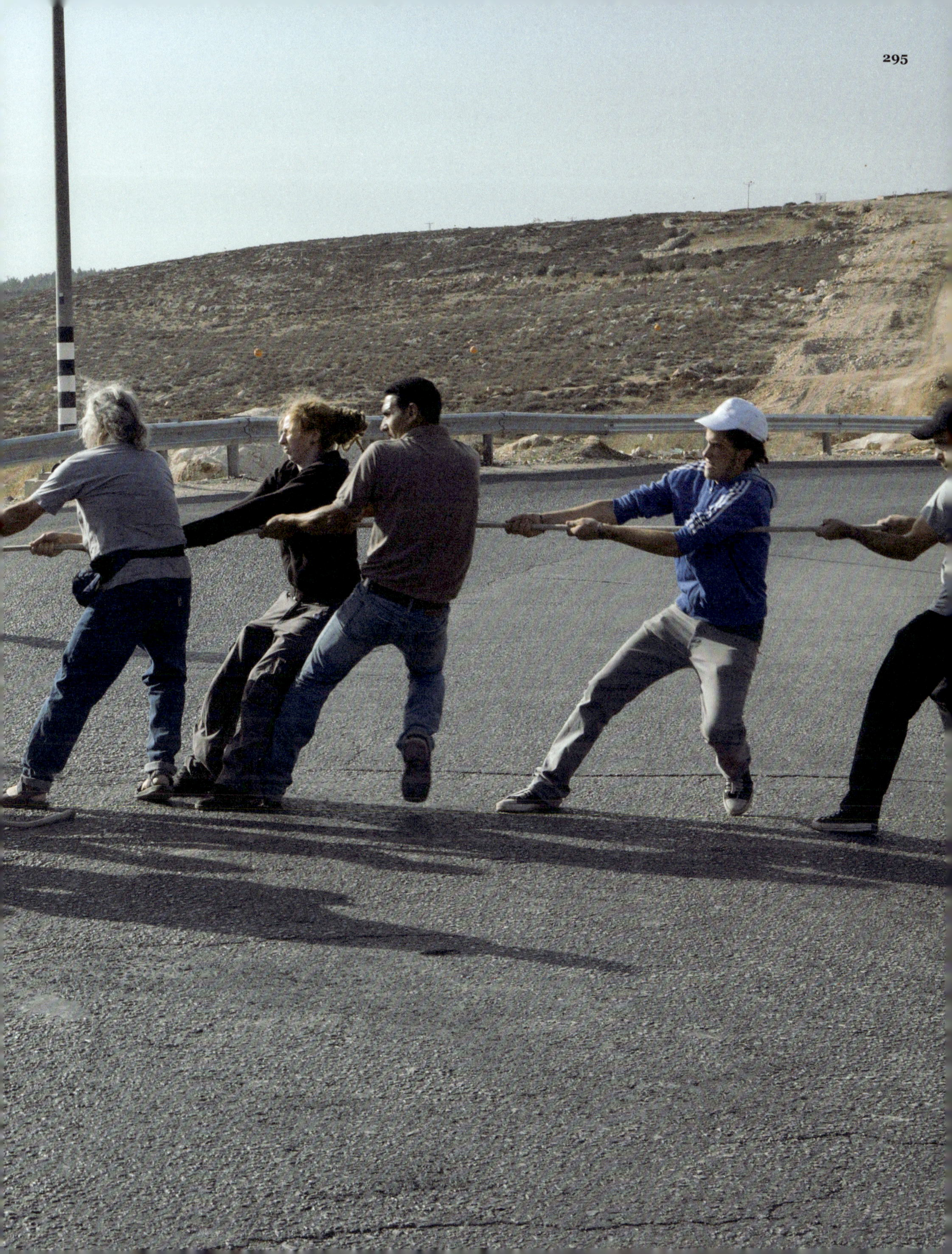

Oren Ziv
Still Active

In 2012, in the midst of the war in Gaza, I went to photograph a funeral in the West Bank. Every time public attention shifts to Gaza and to Israel's south, the army and the police intensify their reaction to demonstrations in the West Bank and the Palestinian villages inside Israel. That same week, army reservists shot and killed Rushdi Tamimi during a protest in the village of Nabi Saleh. While I was on my way there, the photo editor of an agency I freelanced for called me. Sounding annoyed, he asked "Where are you?" He was shocked to find out that I had gone to the funeral of a Palestinian protester. "All this mess down south and you're going on a trip to some village," he hissed, and hung up.

Ever since I started taking pictures at the age of 17, I have tried to decide for myself which topics to concentrate on, not based on what would sell, be published, or photographed well. I was an activist before I became a photographer. I went to demonstrations against the occupation, in support of conscientious objectors and animal rights, refused to be recruited to the army and instead did two years of voluntary national service. I started to take pictures at protests because I wanted to show the struggles that I was taking part in. I hoped that the message of the struggle would be spread to others through the photographs and also felt that it was something practical that I could do besides hold up a sign or shout slogans. It was something that gave additional value for my participation in a demonstration.

In 2005, I would go together with three photographers, Yotam Ronen, Keren Manor, and Eduardo Soteras, to Palestinian actions in various villages in the West Bank joined by the group Anarchists Against the Wall. The Anarchists tried as far as it was possible to form a true solidarity with their Palestinian partners. Even though at the end of the day they would go back to their homes in Tel Aviv, they would position themselves at the frontline with the Palestinians and march toward the soldiers, be arrested, and injured right along with them. The army often put up roadblocks and tried to prevent the Israeli protesters from reaching the villages where the demonstrations were taking place. The activists, risking arrest, would use alternative routes and walk for hours in order to get there.

Joining these protests shaped my political awareness as well as the practical and activist aspects of my work in Activestills. First, this meant being aware that it was not the outcome, in other words it was not the photographs that were the main point, but everything that was going on around that: the political framework, being in the field, and the connection with the people who were photographed. I learned from the Anarchists the importance of returning again and again to the same place.

In those days, the many photojournalists who came to the demonstrations in the occupied Palestinian territories focused on the confrontations with the Israeli Army and the stone-throwing. They would reach the clash point in jeeps provided by the agency they worked for, maybe because they saw no importance in documenting the demonstration itself or in marching with the protesters. As opposed to them, the rest of the members of the collective, myself included, would sleep in the village the night before and stay long after the action was over.

I remember every detail of my first demonstration in the West Bank. As an Israeli, joining the protest from the Palestinian side is nothing short of a reality-changing event. It forced me to get over the fear of just going to a Palestinian village, after years of having been indoctrinated by the Israeli educational system and the media into thinking that all Palestinians wanted was to harm Israelis. It was a solidarity rally with Ahmed Awad, one of the leaders of the local popular committee in the village of Budrus, who was being held in administrative detention. The idea of the action was simple: all the Israeli protesters who chose to be arrested wore signs saying "We are all Ahmed Awad," and marched toward the area where the Israeli separation wall was being constructed. Hundreds of Palestinians took part in the march, including pupils from the local school. When we reached the soldiers, they held up a closed military zone warrant, known as military order no. 101, under which every demonstration in the occupied territories is declared illegal. Soon after, the army started to fire tear gas and stun grenades at the marchers, who tried to reach the construction area of the wall. The soldiers, understanding that everyone was willing to get arrested, detained only a small number of protesters, while the rest were able to reach the Israeli bulldozers. Then the soldiers decided to arrest everyone.

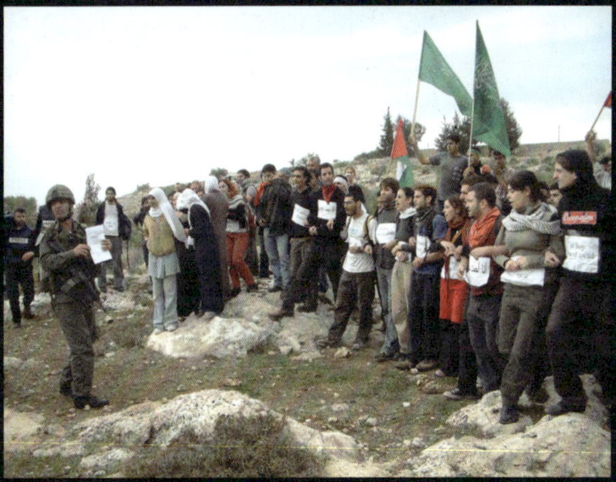

An Israeli solider presents a closed military zone order to Palestinian, Israeli, and international activists protesting against the construction of the Israeli separation wall, Budrus, West Bank, 7.12.2004

At that point, I joined a group of photographers and just before we were about to get arrested we managed to return to the outskirts of the village where young Palestinians were throwing stones at the army. Rather than feeling afraid, as I once did, the strongest emotional reaction was realizing that the only danger was the one posed by the soldiers who were attacking unarmed protesters. It didn't matter how many articles I had read in

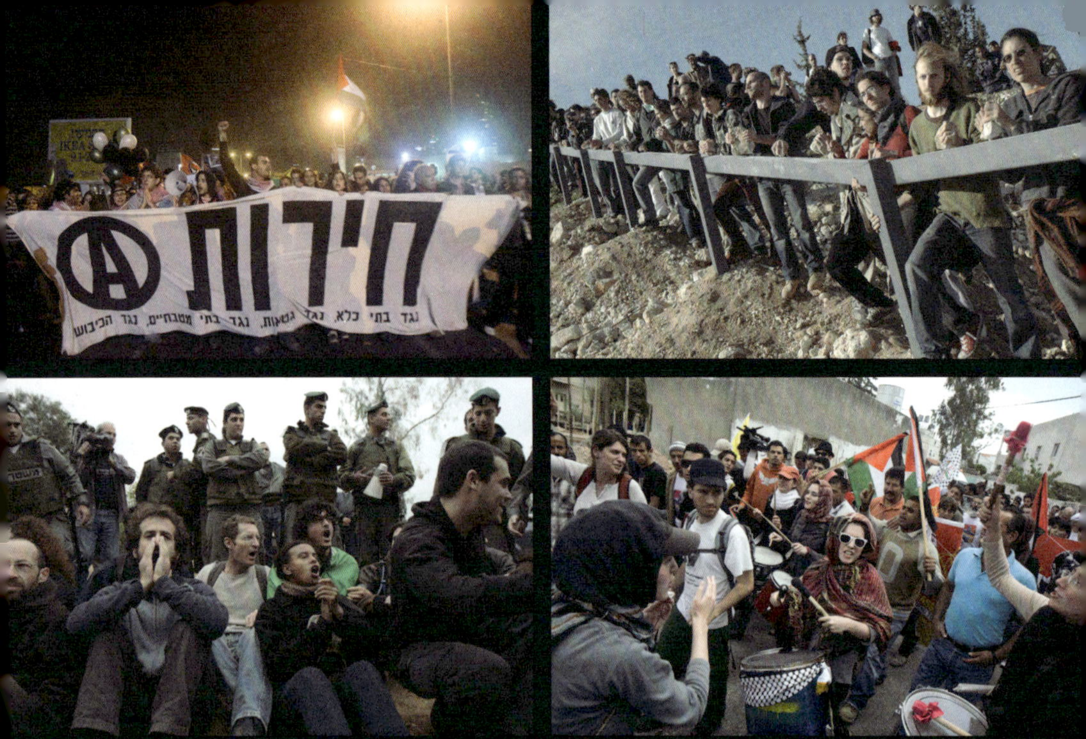

. Palestinian citizens of Israel and AAtW members protest against the Israeli military attacks on the Gaza Strip, Jaffa, Israel, 7.1.2009 / **2.** Protesters bang on a fence at the weekly protest against the Israeli separation wall, Bil'in, West Bank, 20.1.2006 / . AAtW activists and others make a human chain to prevent the eviction of 30 families from their homes in the neighborhood of Kfar Shalem, south Tel Aviv, 25.12.2007 / **4.** Palestinian, Israeli, and foreign activists march in Bil'in, West Bank, 1.5.2009

sraeli or foreign newspapers, being on the Palestinian side, being helped by Palestinian protesters, going into their homes when the army was invading the village, receiving first aid from them, made me experience a reality parallel to the one I knew. The army's attempt to silence every civil act against the occupation is something that cannot be understood from looking at photographs or reading about it in the news. You have to be there.

The violence, the danger of being injured or arrested, and the sameness of the demonstrations often led me to want to stop going or at least consider other photographic projects. The same ritual that unfolded in my first action in Budrus repeated itself in almost every protest that I documented in the West Bank: the demonstrators gather in the village along with a number of Israeli and international activists. After prayer, we march toward the land or the construction site of the Israeli separation wall, and within minutes, soldiers begin firing weapons and using force.

Nevertheless, I didn't stop going. One could say that the camera forced me to not run away and to overcome my fear of injury or arrest. Very quickly, the determination to go week after week became a mission in itself, with the documentation being the main act. What captured my attention, and from then on became the focus of my work were the civilian actions; the marches, the direct and creative acts of the activists. Like the protesters who insisted on continuing, I too tried to show through the camera the continuity and repetitiveness of the demonstrations, as if to shout out, "See, it is still going on." From the Anarchists, I also learned that the linkage between struggles is something that happens in the field. The Israeli activists I had met in Bil'in were the same ones who came in the middle of the night to prevent a home eviction, or who were at a protest in Kfar Shalem in south Tel Aviv.[1]

When we started the online Activestills archive, it was organized chronologically, and this was how our approach to the connection between struggles came about. All the events went up on the website: whether it was a protest in the occupied territories, or an alternative queer event in Tel Aviv. Whoever entered our photo-stream at a specific point was usually exposed to an array of struggles that seemingly had no direct connection. The intent was not to flatten reality and say that the situations in Gaza, the West Bank, or in cities inside the Green Line are identical, but rather to point to the centers of power and oppression and the possible connection between the various struggles. Often it is possible to see that the forms of oppression, the means, the governmental tactics and actions that are implemented in the occupied Palestinian territories are applied in Israel as well—weapons for dispersing protests, arrests, preventing meeting with legal counsel—only with less force. Presenting a number of struggles in parallel was also meant to give the viewers the feeling that not all is lost, that they are not alone, and that there are other places where there is injustice and where people have chosen to rise up.

The importance of being in the field is expressed also in reaching places where there are no demonstrations. For me, an example of this is the village of Al-Araqib, an unrecognized Bedouin village in the Negev, which the authorities have destroyed more than ninety times since 2010—a world record, as far as I know. I went there with Yotam Ronen in 2009 in order to document daily life in the village that was struggling for its land. In 2010, a large force of the civil administration in the Negev arrived and destroyed the entire area of Al-Araqib, including the village's fields, warehouses, olive trees, and roads that the residents had built on their own initiative and with their own funds. The evening before the demolition, a few residents called us and asked us to come. The international media was not interested in this story because it was considered an internal Israeli affair and not related to the wider Palestinian issue. We came late at night and documented the small community trying to save some of its property before the police arrived. At sunrise, over a thousand policemen, accompanied by helicopters, set upon the village, moved the residents out of the way and destroyed the place to its foundations. The following day, the residents built huts which they then lived in. I remained in Al-Araqib for a few weeks, throughout dozens of waves of destruction. I was not there to document Bedouin culture, or because the desert seemed to me like a scenic location; I wanted to be there with the residents. After a while, we printed a booklet with the photographs of the 2010 events which we gave to the residents so that they could show it to visitors, politicians, and international diplomats.

Just like the case of the first demolition in Al-Araqib, in the first years of Activestills' undertakings, if we did not get to a particular event, often the event was not documented. Even if photojournalists did get there, the photographs were not available for viewing, distribution, or use by the organizers. In the last few years, the situation has

1. Kfar Shalem is a neighborhood in south Tel Aviv where many of the low-income residents were being threatened with eviction from their homes. After a big wave of evictions in the 1980s, in 2007 the Israeli police evicted another 20 families from their homes, in order to clear space for a new luxury high-rise building project.

changed and in every action there are independent photographers and the demonstrators themselves either have smartphones or professional cameras. Yet, the long-term work and the repetitiveness have enabled us to keep track of the changes on the ground, and also to analyze the political situation in depth. The cooperative work has taught me the importance of professional photojournalism—that it is able to tell a more complex story than a single news event. The work as a collective did not only constitute a practical solution that enabled us to cover a large number of places. From the start, we founded the collective so as not to have to work alone, and in order to support one another and produce a significant body of work. We decided together, most of the time in consensus, who to photograph and what to work on, and we learned a lot from each other. We all pooled our earnings in a communal fund.

When we put up our first street exhibition in Tel Aviv showing the protests against the Israeli separation wall in Bil'in, we believed that if we could just inform the public, at least some viewers will become interested and want to become involved in the struggle. At that time, we thought that photographs could bridge the gap between the West Bank and Tel Aviv. Every time I would come back from the West Bank, I would be surprised once again at how the routine of daily life of Israelis just goes on; people sit in cafes, in shopping malls, while a tiny distance away the army is violently suppressing unarmed civil demonstrations.

The unwillingness of large segments of the Israeli public to be exposed to, acknowledge, or do something about what is being perpetrated in their name is without doubt the greatest success of the "separation project" initiated by Ehud Barak after the collapse of the Camp David talks and the start of the second intifada. With the exception of the incidences of violence against Israelis, the occupation is kept far away behind the checkpoints and roadblocks, almost completely removed from the public agenda. The same approach is adopted for many other political and social issues. By the same logic, the African asylum seekers are being sent to Holot detention center in the Negev Desert and the poor are pushed to live in the periphery.

These days, I know that the problem is not the lack of information. The main crisis in our work was the sobering of our expectations that photography would bring about some kind of change. Perhaps out of desperation, exhaustion, or cynicism, or simply recognition of the political situation in Palestine/Israel, today, just as ten years ago, I will go to photograph a political event, first of all to be there. But unlike in the past, I have no expectation that the photograph I take will reach a public and convince them of anything. The main power of photography for me is still its ability to express solidarity with the struggle and those who are engaged in it. This is not some theoretical solidarity with an abstract concept of "the oppressed," but one of standing together with those who have chosen to struggle against oppression. The photographs give visibility to the fact that these struggles are still going on, that persevering people continue to oppose the policies of discrimination and racism. It is my hope that by continuing to photograph, I will succeed in memorializing those who persist in contesting the current state of affairs.

{Opposite page}
Palestinian activist Muhammad Bregia (left) and AAtW member Kobi Snitz stand in front of Israeli soldiers during an action against the Israeli separation wall, Al-Ma'asara, West Bank, 10.5.2007

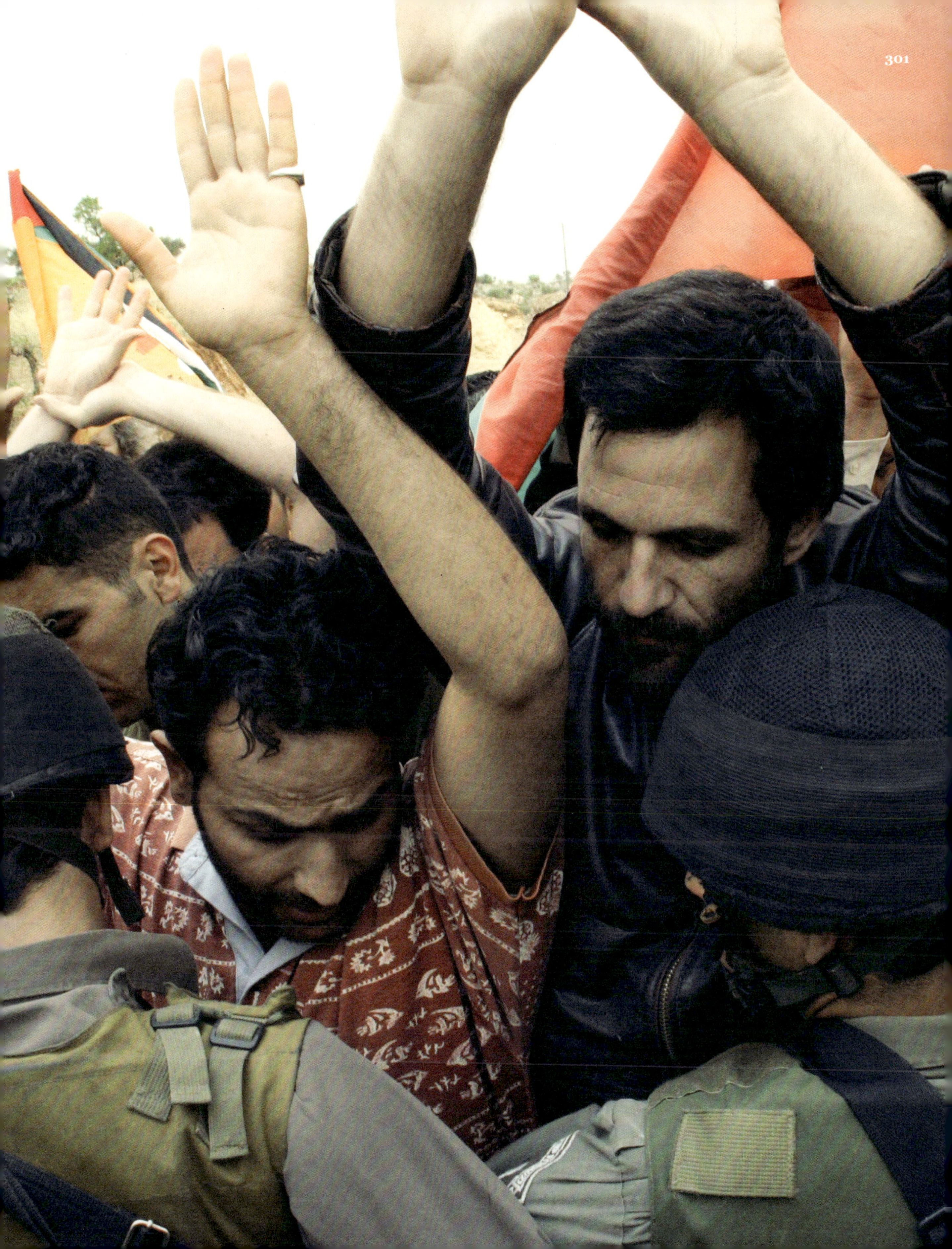

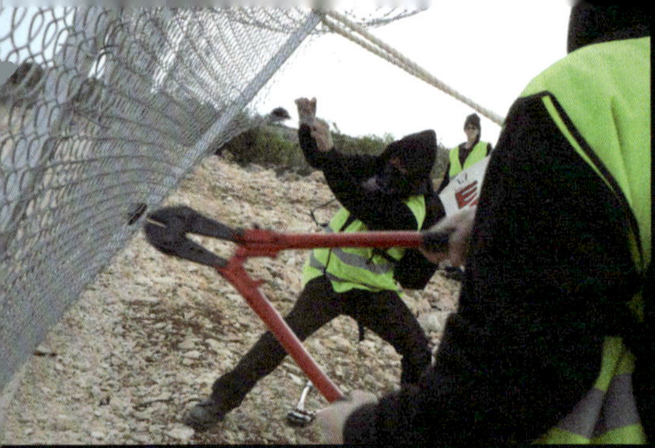

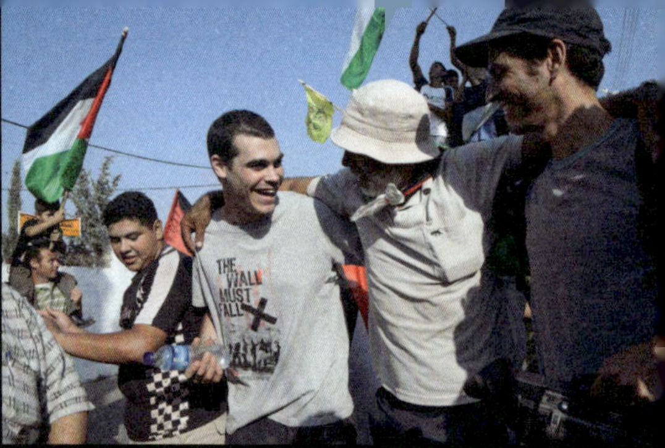

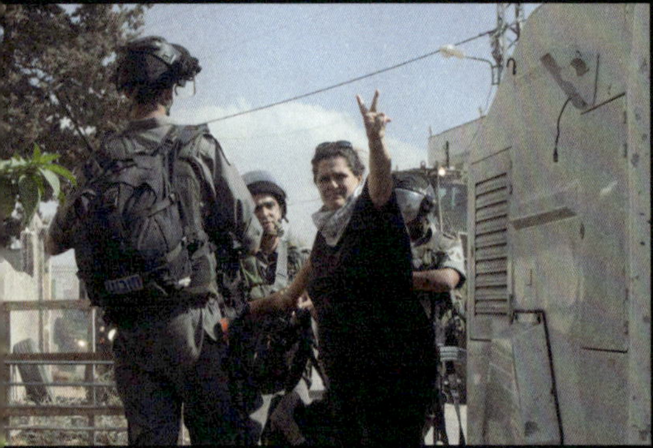

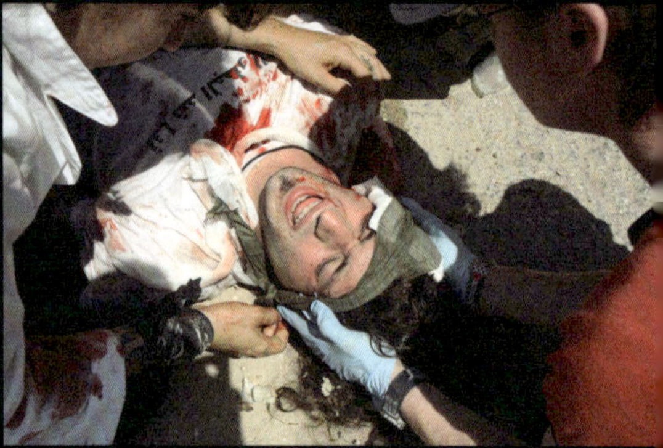

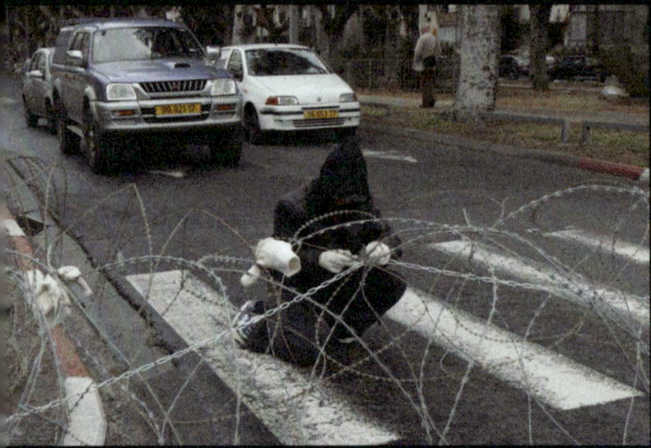

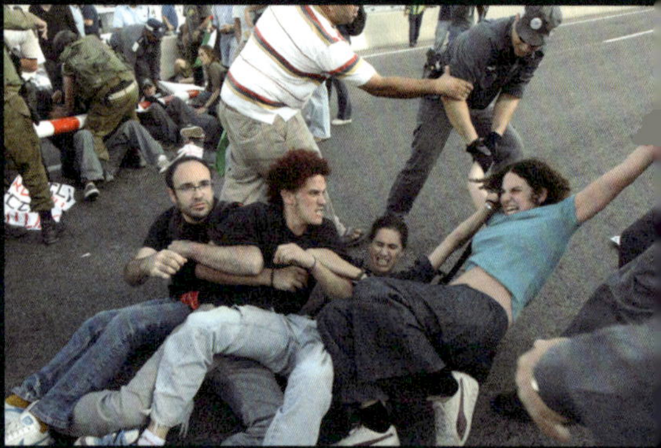

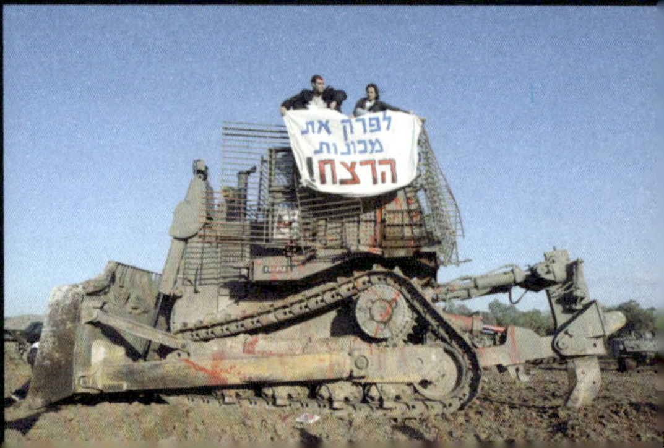

Top left to right}
. Protesters tear down the separation barrier, Beit Jmmar, West Bank, 14.4.2007 / **2.** Protesters celebrate he Israeli High Court ruling to reroute the separation barrier, Bil'in, West Bank, 4.9.2007 / **3.** An Israeli protester arrested, Kafr Qaddum, West Bank, 12.10.2012 / . Injured AAtW protester, Bil'in, West Bank, 11.8.2006 **5.** Activists block a road in Tel Aviv using barbed wire aken from the Israeli separation wall, 3.2.2007 / **6.** Action against movement restrictions for Palestinians on Road 43, West Bank, 25.10.2007 / **7.** An action against the iege on the Gaza Strip, Israel-Gaza border, 18.11.2006

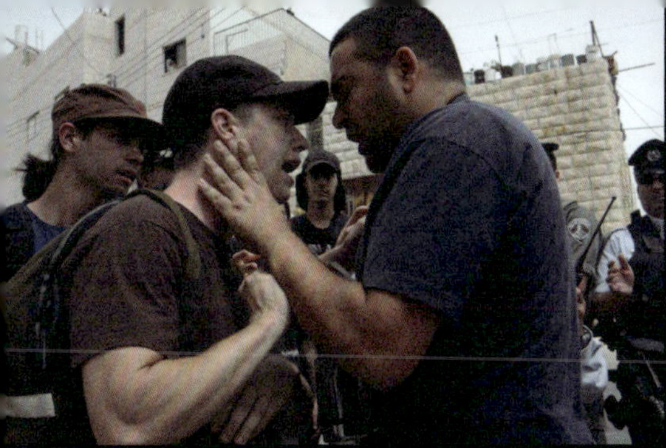

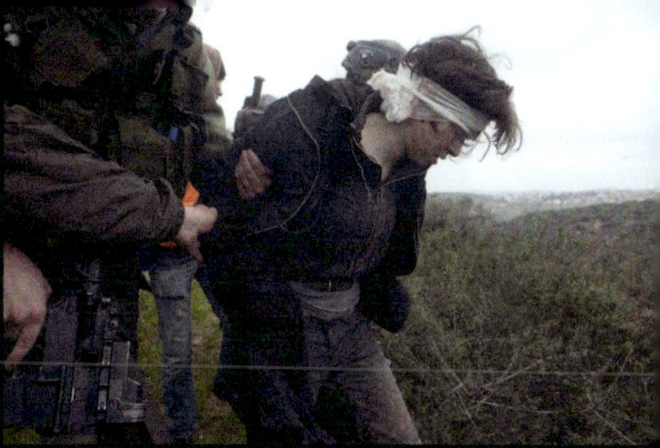

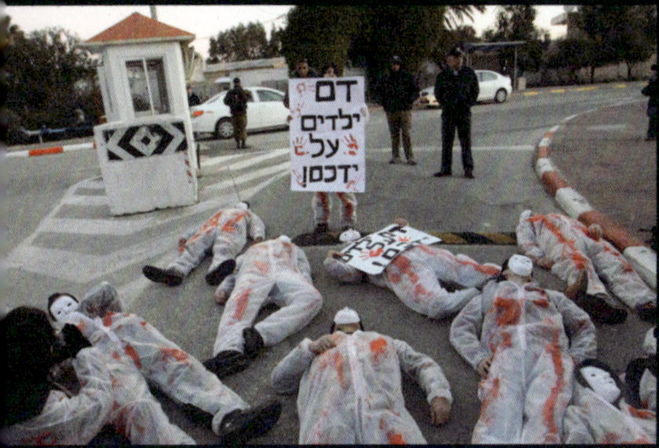

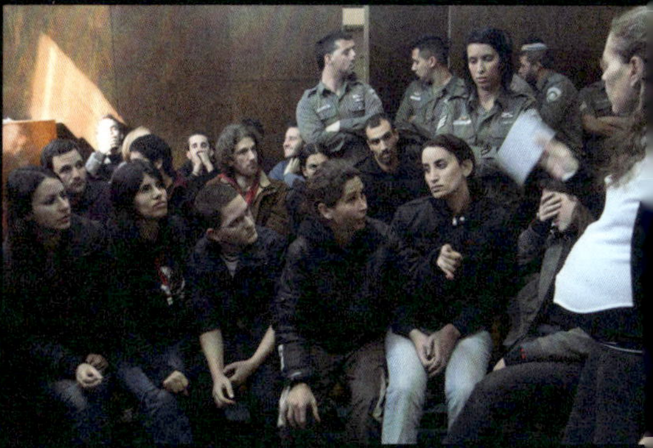

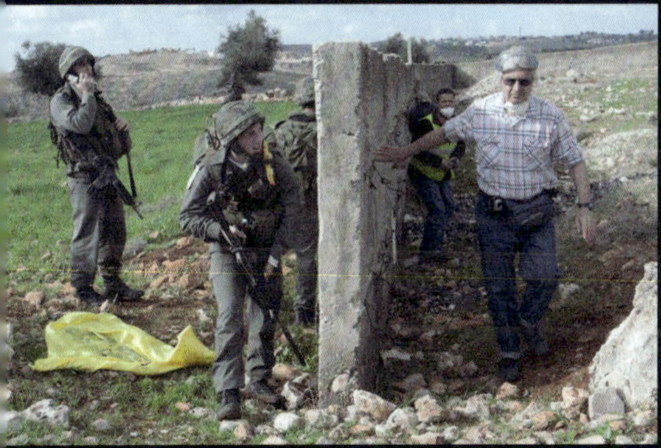

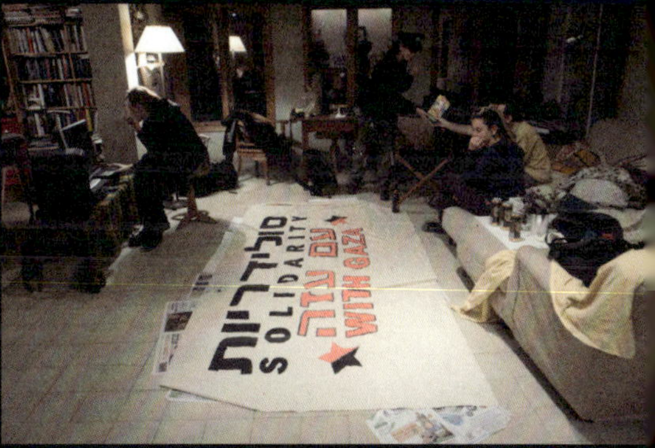

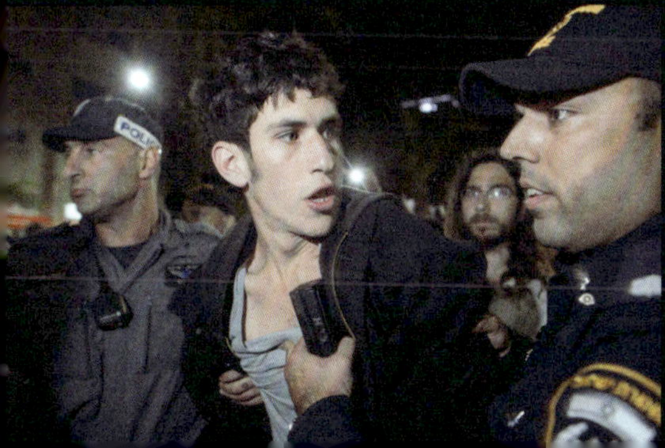

{Top left to right}
1. Israeli protester confronts an Israeli settler, Hebron, West Bank, 25.4.2008 / **2.** Israeli soldiers arrest an injured protester, Nabi Saleh, West Bank, 16.3.2012 / **3.** Activists block the entrance to Sde Dov army base during an action against the Israeli attacks on the Gaza Strip. The sign says: "Children's blood is on your hands," 2.1.2009 / **4.** Activists in court following an anti-war action, Tel Aviv, 4.1.2009 / **5.** Activists opposite Israeli soldiers, Bil'in, West Bank, 21.12.2007 / **6.** Activists prepare a banner, Tel Aviv, 1.1.2009 / **7.** AAtW member arrested at an action commemorating the Palestinian Nakba, Tel Aviv, 26.4.201

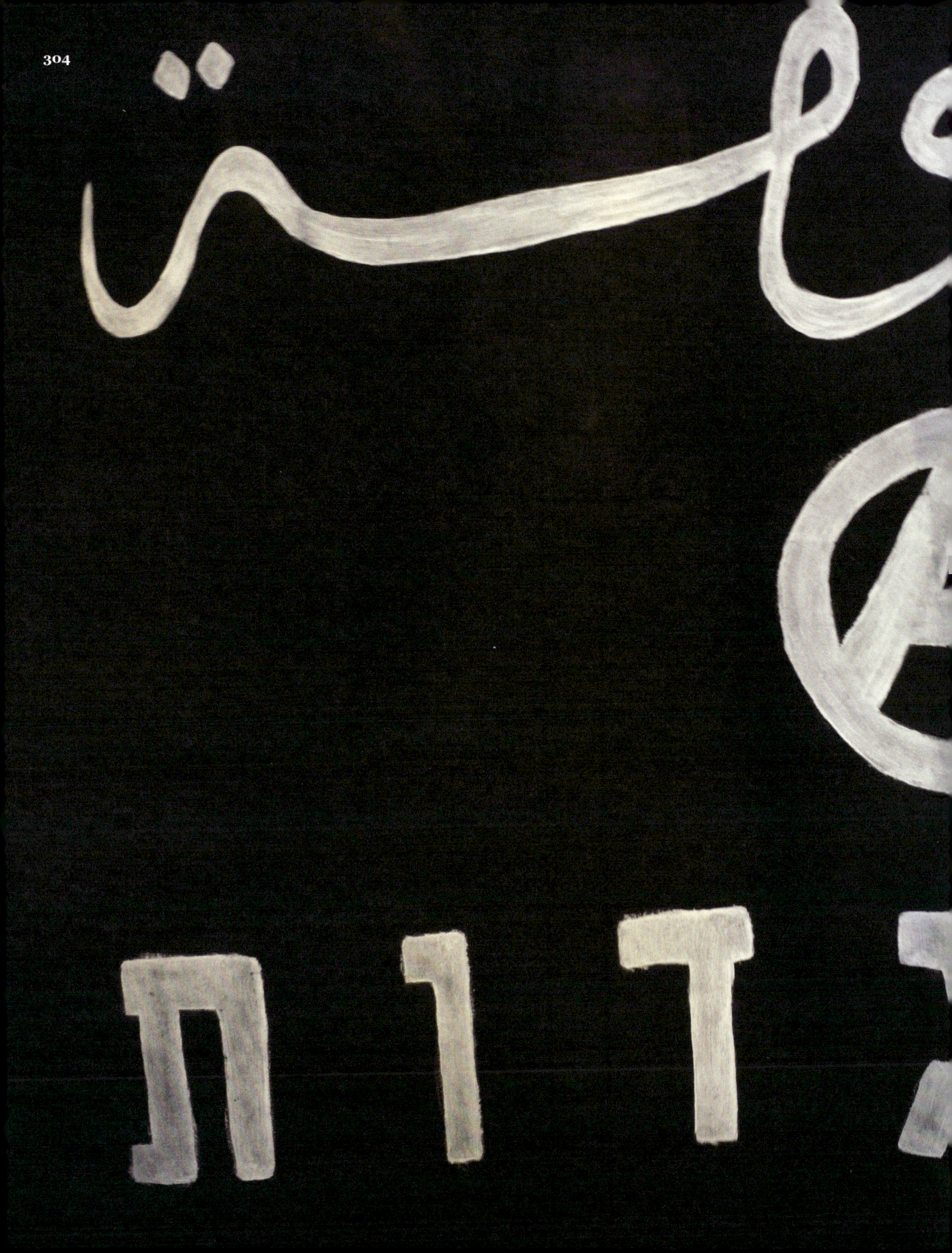

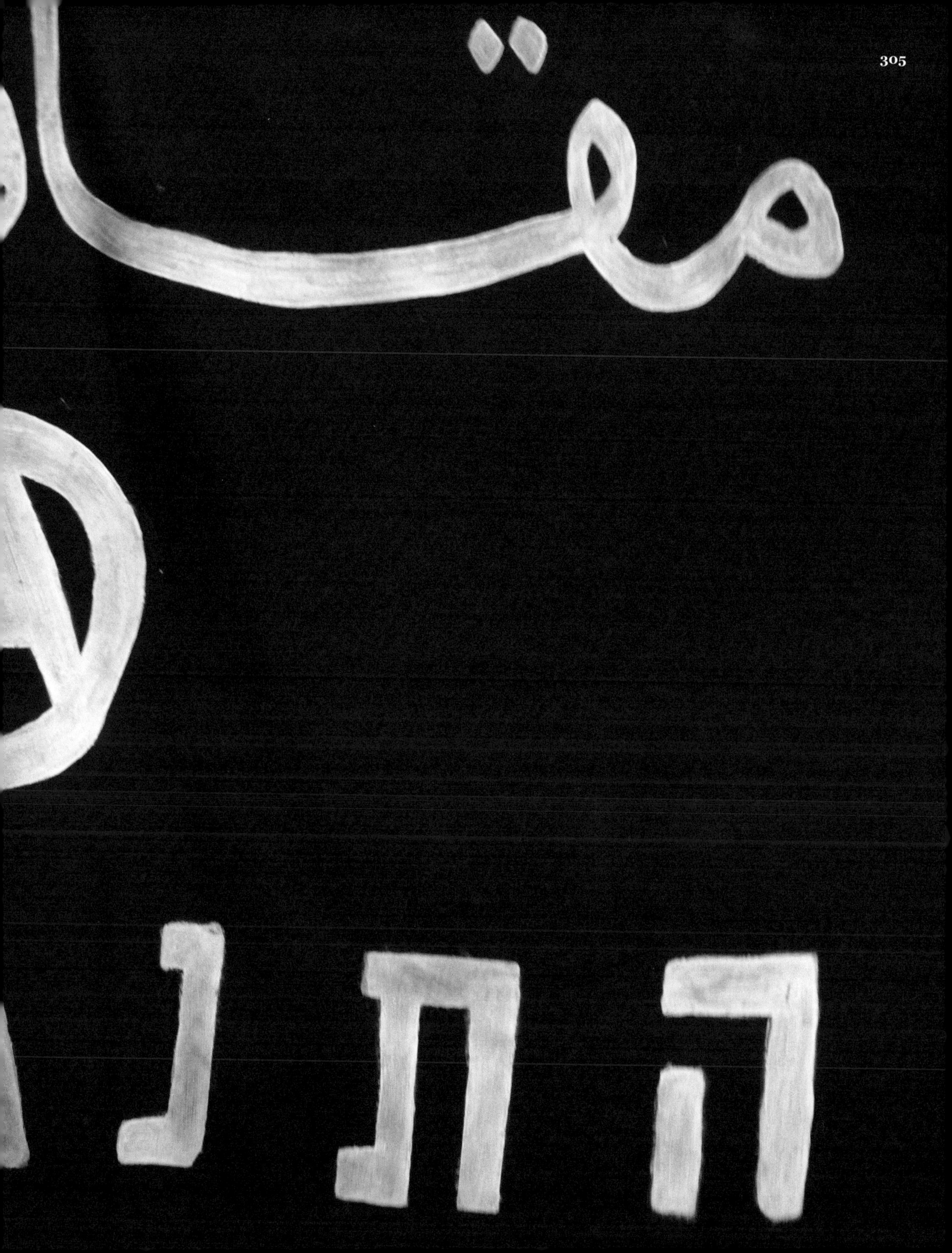

Sarit Michaeli

Sarit Michaeli was the spokesperson of the human rights group B'Tselem between 2005 and 2016. She has been joining protests in West Bank villages since the early 2000s. She uses video documentation to research the Israeli military's misuse of crowd control weapons in its repression of the Palestinian popular struggle. She spent her twenties in London where she ran a queer indie music club.

Our Family Photo Album

In a world of smartphone images instantly shared on social media, it's hard to remember that bygone era, when a clear division of labor existed: activists protested, and photographers—outside observers—documented. The advent of citizen journalism changed this, blurring the distinction, and giving ordinary people the tools to document and create images depicting their own struggles. But even prior to this, Activestills photographers inhabited that liminal space—activists engaged in the struggle, while at the same time professional news photographers documenting it.

As chroniclers of every worthwhile radical cause east of the Mediterranean (and beyond) in the past decade, members of the Activestills collective function as a radical news gathering organization, as supporters of social justice movements big and small, and also as documenters of the beauty and resilience and humanity of those people in our communities who dare to speak truth to power. Activestills members challenge what is newsworthy, and the trust they enjoy among people on the ground enables them to cover remote corners, obscure struggles, inner circles, and they play a key role in defining how we picture this moment in time and our place in it.

But Activestills for me are not merely documenters of a decade of dissident action, but also creators of a radical family photo album of sorts, blending memorable moments from our collective political and personal lives—in some cases, the same image relates to both.

Selecting a single image representative of Activestills' work has been challenging. This is indicative of the great variety of subject matter, all of which is essential to representing our reality. Only on the Activestills feed can one see an anti-war demonstration in Tel Aviv, a border police officer shooting protesters in Bil'in the following day, and a queer rave that same night, attended by many of the same people. The memories associated with these images are far more than just about demonstrations. They represent the very essence of our community and our lives in this troubled place—the schizophrenia, the constant movement between Palestinian and Israeli spaces, the varied identities that emerge as a result.

It's been difficult to select only one image to represent the work of Activestills as I see it, but I know that if there can be a single image that could represent the ideas we commonly share, I'd bet it had been taken by an Activestills photographer.

Previous page: A banner with the word "Resistance" in Arabic and in Hebrew.

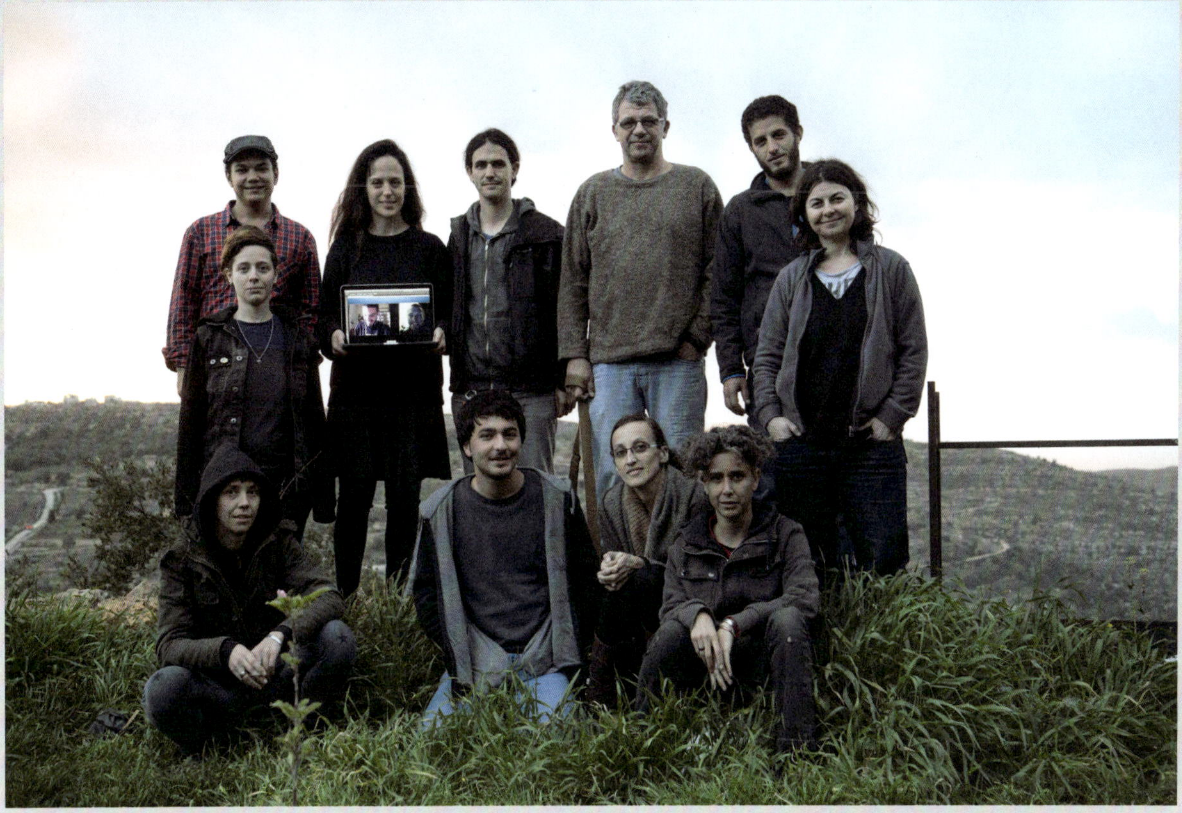

Activestills collective pose for a group photo in Beit Jala, West Bank. *{Top left to right}* Faiz Abu Rmeleh, Shiraz Grinbaum, Oren Ziv, Miki Kratsman, Yotam Ronen, Anne Paq, Anka Mirkin, Mareike Lauken, Ahmad al-Bazz, Mireia Gallardo Avellan (producer), Keren Manor, [on Skype] Ryan Rodrick Beiler and Basel Alyazouri. Missing in the photo: Tess Schaflan, Shachaf Pollakow.

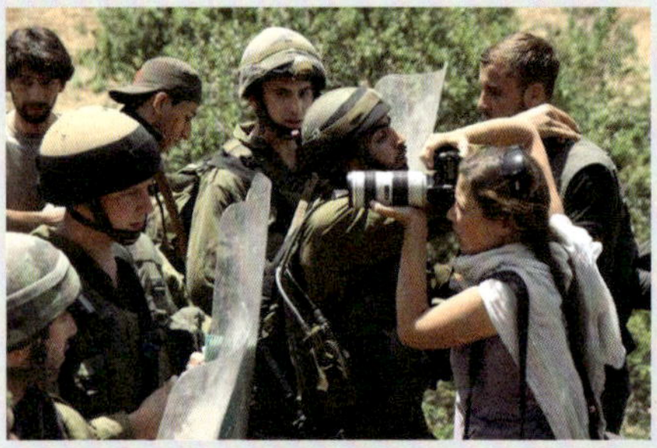
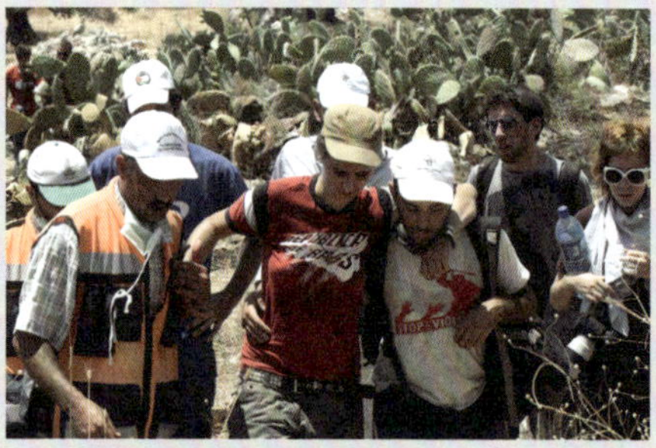
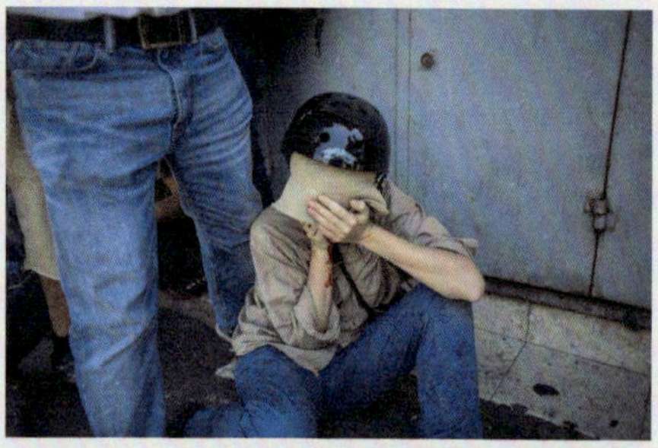
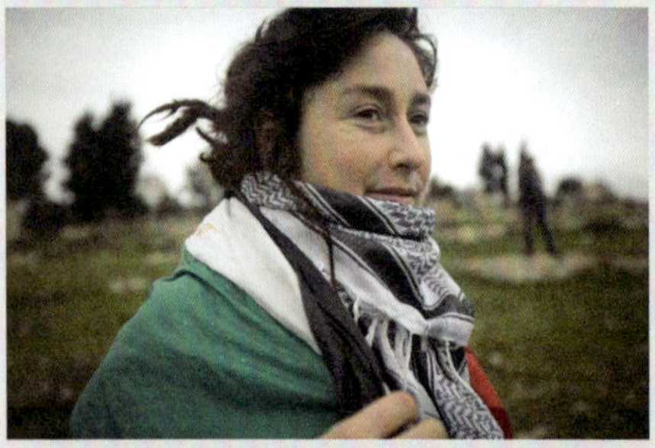
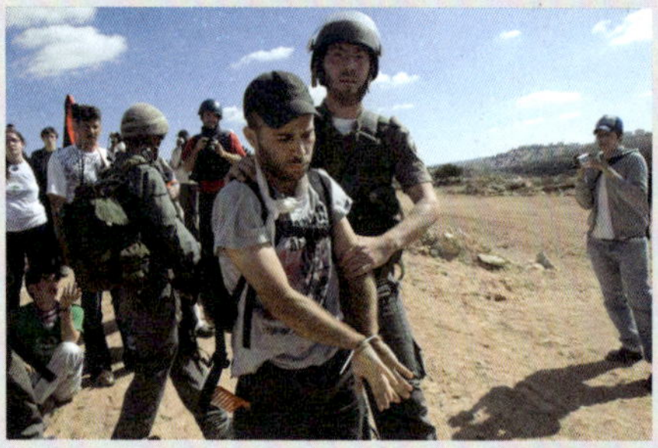
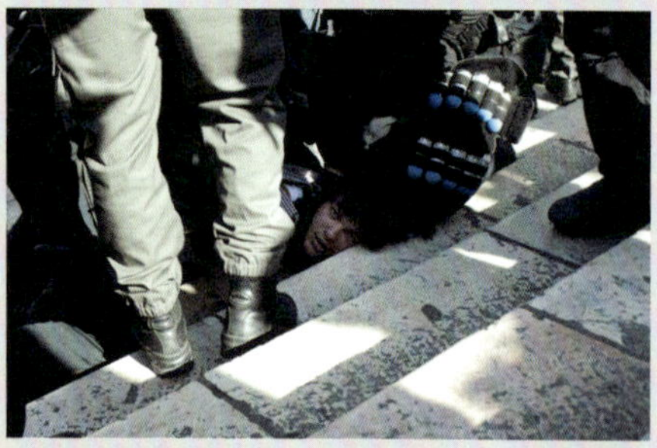
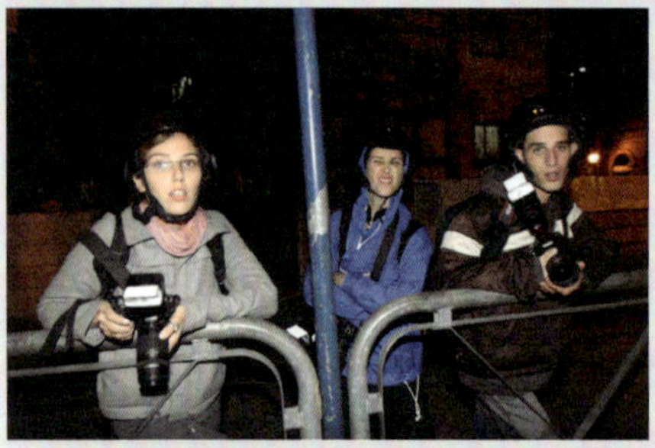
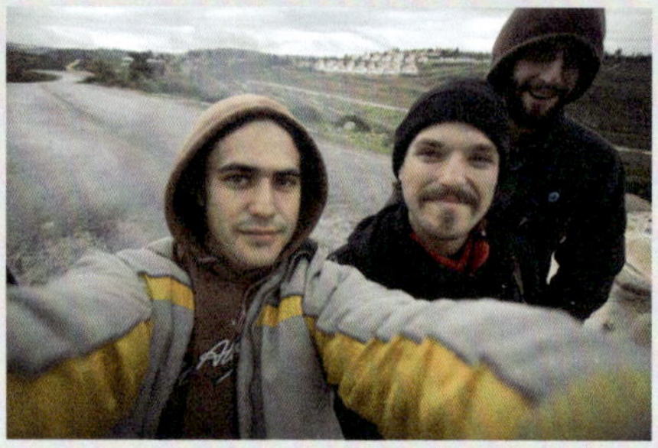
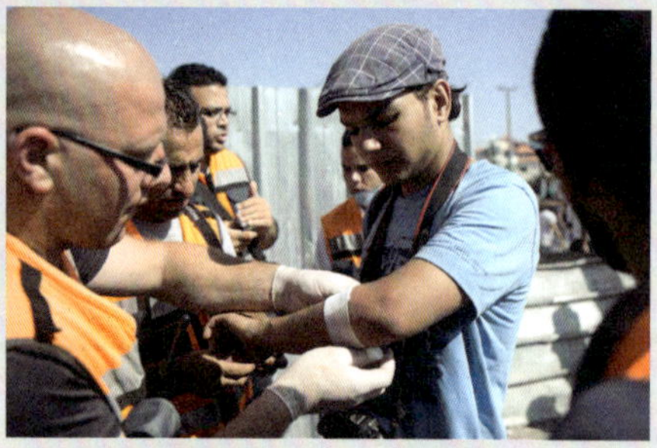
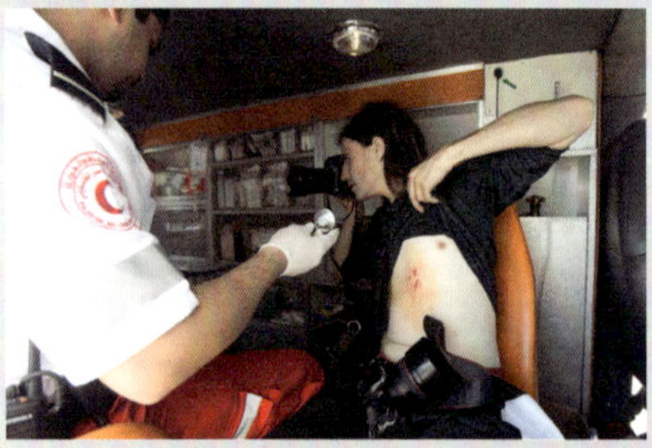
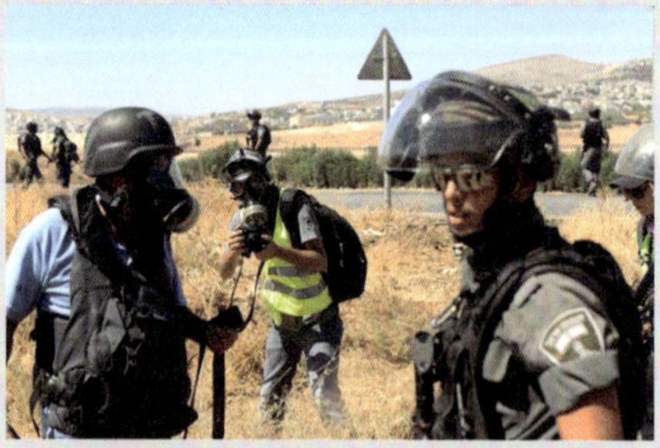
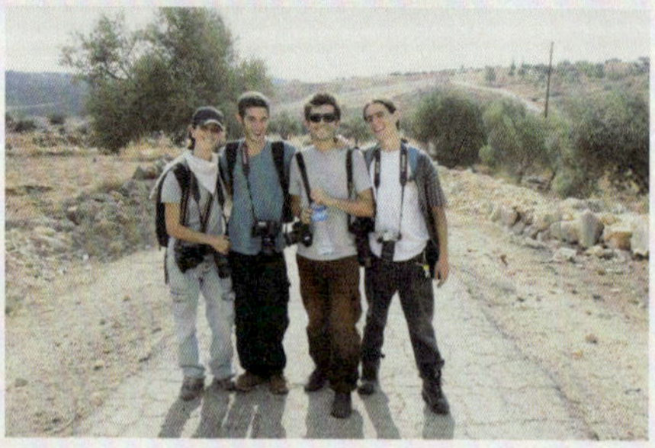
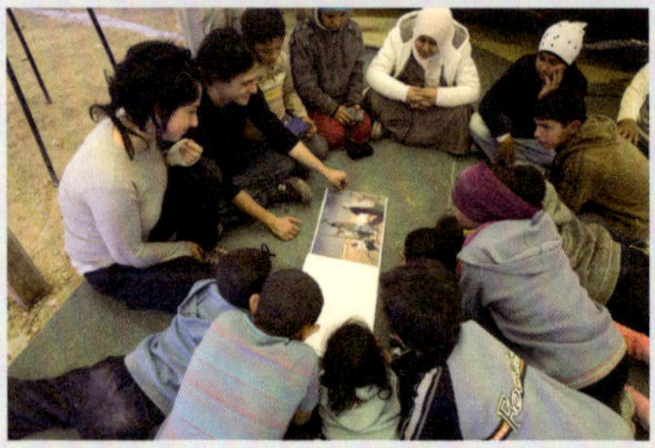
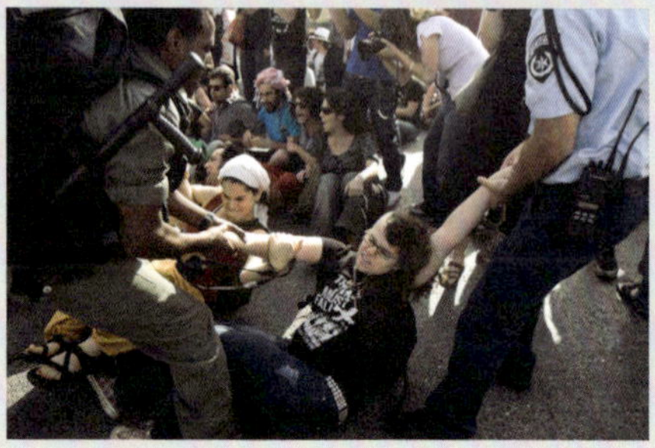
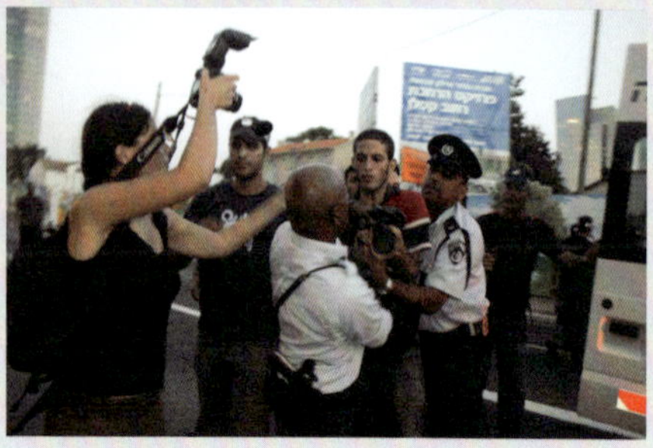

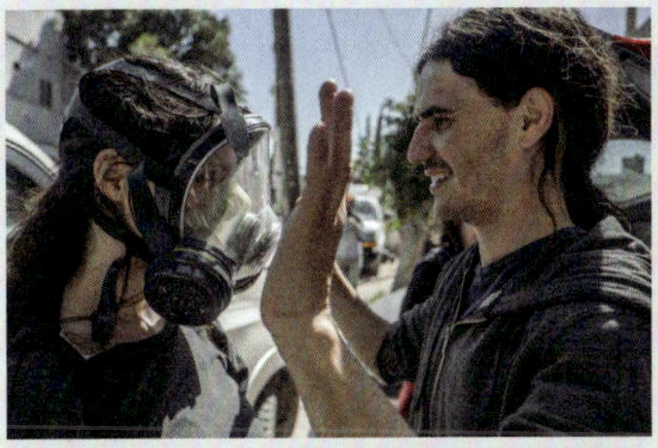
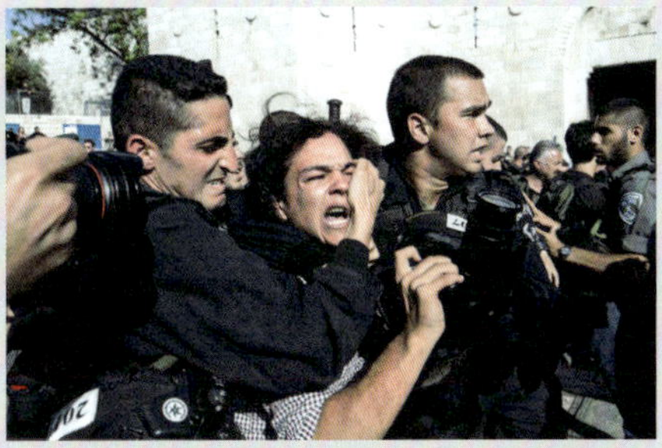
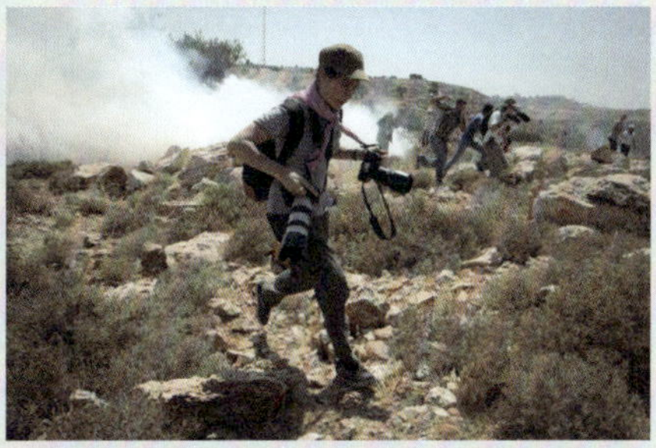
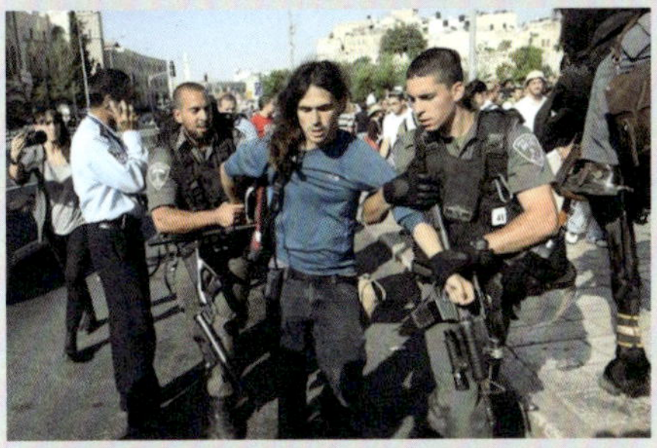
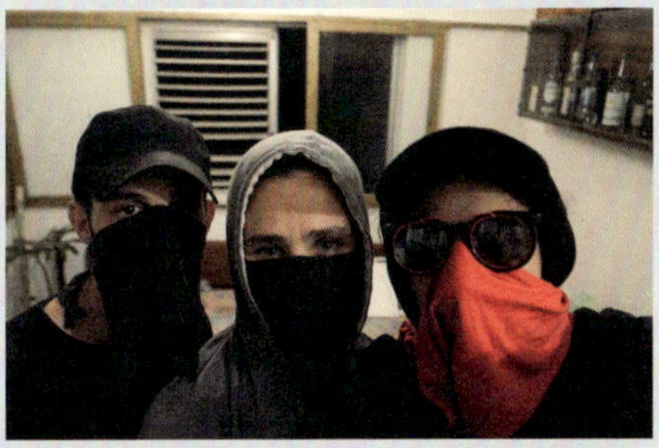
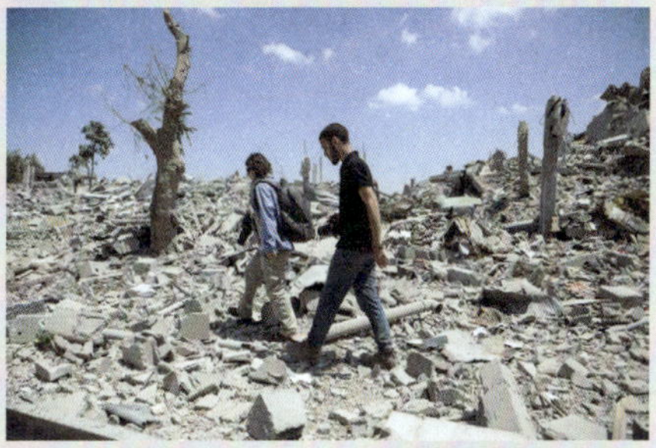
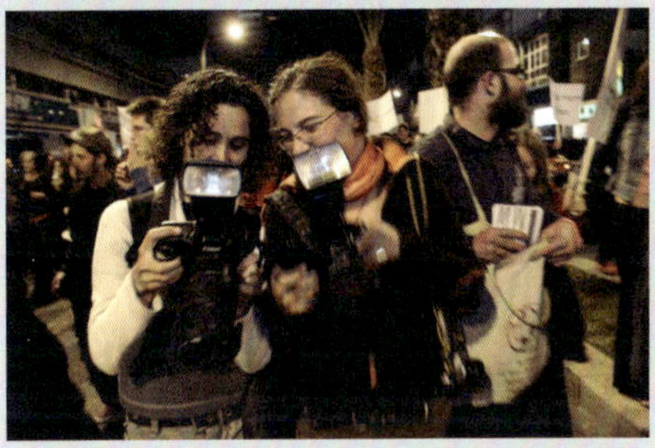
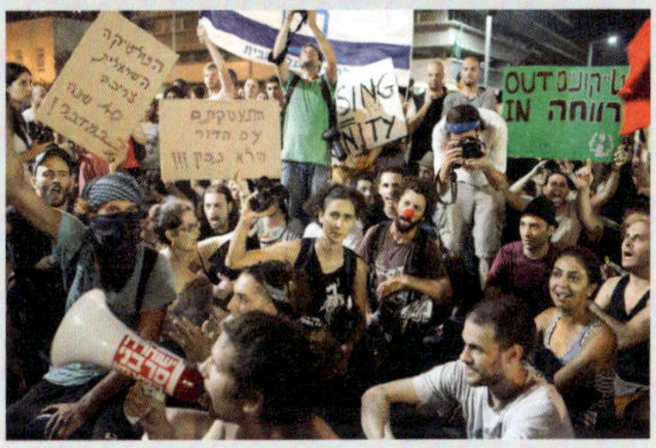
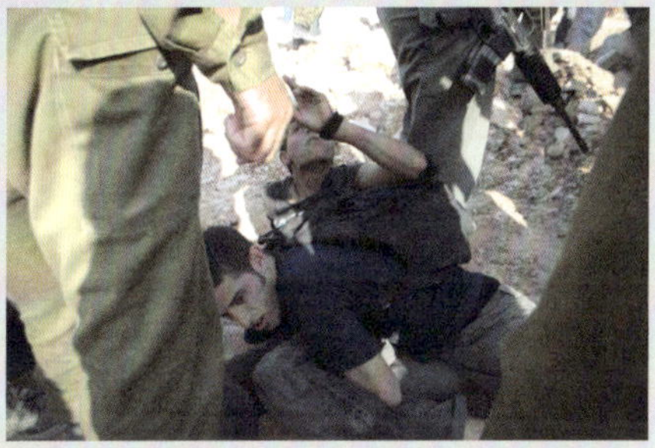
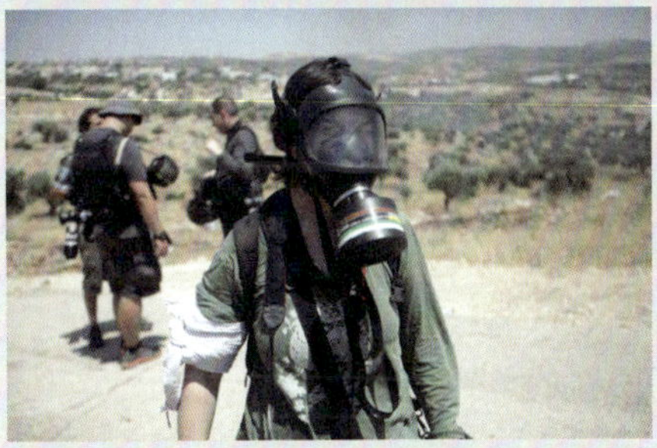
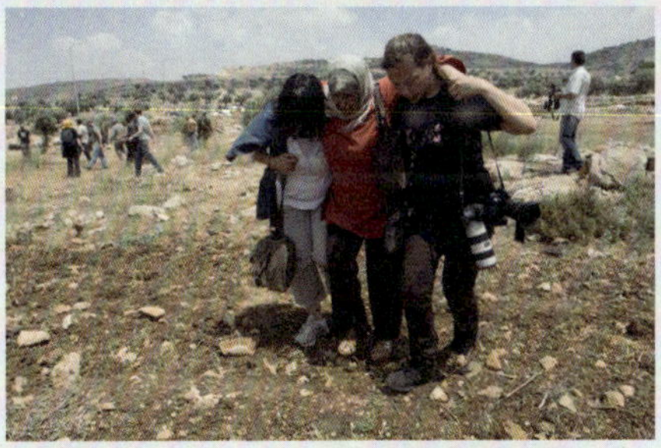
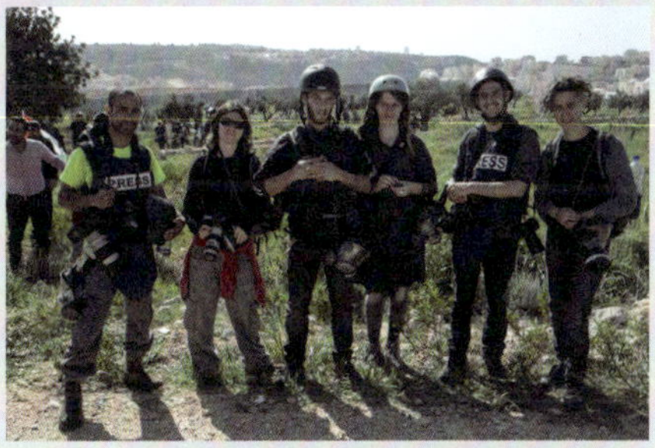
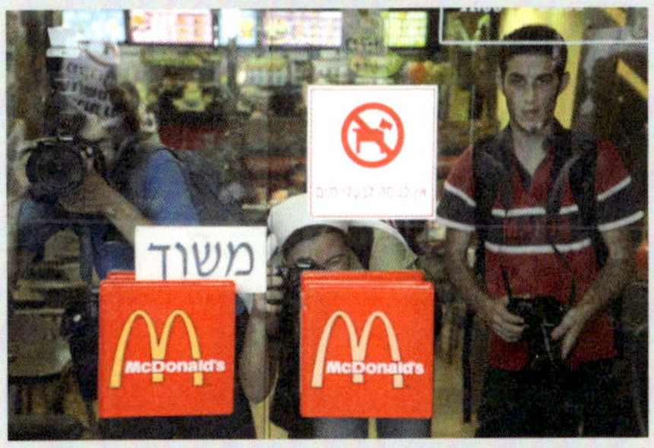
McDonald's
McDonald's
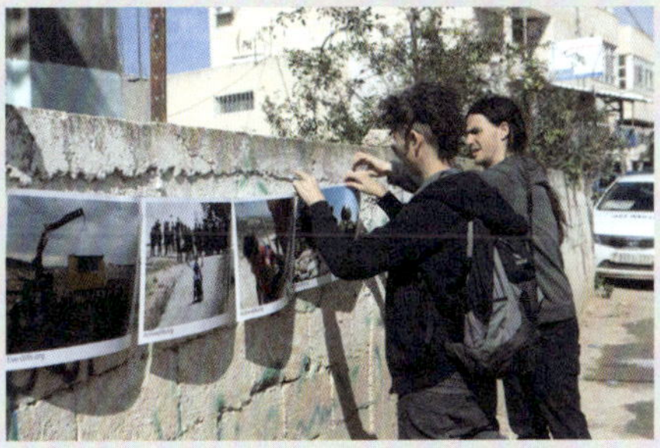
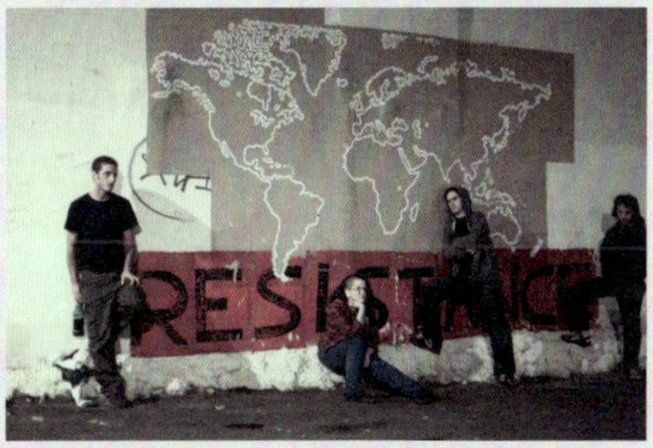

Contributors Bios

Ariella Azoulay is Professor of Modern Culture and Media and Comparative Literature at Brown University, as well as a documentary film director and independent curator of archives and exhibitions. Her books on photography include: *Aïm Deüelle Lüski and Horizontal Photography* (Leuven University Press, 2013), *Civil Imagination: The Political Ontology of Photography* (Verso, 2012), *From Palestine to Israel: A Photographic Record of Destruction and State Formation, 1947–1950* (Pluto Press, 2011), and *The Civil Contract of Photography* (Zone Books, 2008). She was curator of the exhibitions *Potential History* (Stuk/Artefact, Leuven, 2012), *Untaken Photographs* (Igor Zabel Award, The Moderna Galerija, Lubliana, 2010; Zochrot), *Architecture of Destruction* (Zochrot, Tel Aviv, 2008), *Everything Could Be Seen* (Umm El Fahem Gallery of Art, 2004) and was director of *Civil Alliances, Palestine, 47–48* (2012), and *I Also Dwell Among Your Own People: Conversations with Azmi Bishara* (2004).

Ramzy Baroud is an Arab-American journalist, media consultant, and internationally syndicated columnist. He is editor of *Palestine Chronicle* (1999–present), former managing editor of the London-based *Middle East Eye* (2014–15), former editor-in-chief of *The Brunei Times*, and former deputy managing editor of Al Jazeera online. He taught mass communication at Australia's Curtin University of Technology, Malaysia Campus. Baroud also served as head of Aljazeera.net's English Research and Studies department. He is the author of three books and a contributor to many others; his latest volume is *My Father Was a Freedom Fighter: Gaza's Untold Story* (Pluto Press, 2010).

Simon Faulkner is a senior lecturer in the Art History Department at Manchester School of Art. His current research is on the relationships between visual culture and the Israeli–Palestinian conflict. He recently published *Between States* (Black Dog Publishing, 2015), with Israeli artist and activist David Reeb. He is also a co-investigator on "Picturing the Social," an 18-month-long ESRC-funded research project on social media images.

Ruthie Ginsburg researches the visual culture related to human rights, especially from a critical perspective. Her book *And You Will Serve as Eyes for Us: Israeli Human Rights Organizations as Seen through the Camera's Eye* (Resling Press, 2014), examines the practices of local Israeli human rights organizations working in the occupied territories. She is currently leading the Photolexic research group at the Minerva Center for Humanities at Tel Aviv University, which focuses on the political aspects of photographic practice and representation.

Miki Kratsman is a leading documentary photographer in Israel, documenting the Palestinian popular resistance from the 1980s. He was a Schocken Group photojournalist from 1985 to 2012, and head of the Photography Department in the Bezalel Academy of Arts and Design, Jerusalem from 2006 to 2014. His work has been exhibited worldwide.

Vered Maimon is a senior lecturer in the Art History Department at Tel Aviv University. Her essays on the history and theory of photography and contemporary art appeared in *October*, *Oxford Art Journal*, *History of Photography*, *Art History*, *Parallax*, *Third Text*, and *TDR*. She is the author of *Singular Images, Failed Copies: William Henry Fox Talbot and the Early Photograph* (University of Minnesota Press, 2015), and co-editor of *Communities of Sense: Rethinking Aesthetics and Politics* (Duke University Press, 2009).

Haggai Matar is an Israeli journalist and political activist. After writing for *Ha'aretz* and *Ma'ariv*, he is now the co-editor of *Local Call*, a regular contributor to *+972 Magazine*, and board member of the Union of Journalists in Israel. He was awarded the 2012 Anna Lindh Mediterranean Journalist Award for his *+972* series on the Israeli separation wall.

Sharon Sliwinski is an associate professor in the Faculty of Information and Media Studies at Western University in Canada. She is the author of *Human Rights in Camera* (Chicago University Press, 2011), *Mandela's Dark Years: A Political Theory of Dreaming* (Minnesota University Press, 2015), and co-editor of *Photography and the Optical Unconscious* (Duke University Press, 2016).

Meir Wigoder teaches at the School of Communication at Sapir College, Sderot, and the David and Yolanda Katz Faculty of the Arts at Tel Aviv University. A photography theorist and a practicing photographer, he writes on the representation of the Israeli–Palestinian conflict in photography, film, and the media. His writings appeared in *Critical Inquiry*, *Public Culture*, *Third Text*, *Parallax*, *Journal of Architectural Historians*, *History of Photography*, *Psychoanalytic Review*, and *History and Memory*.

Activestills Photographers Bios

Faiz Abu Rmeleh (b. 1989). Abu Rmeleh lives and works in Jerusalem's Old City. He studies photography at the Bezalel Academy of Arts and Design, Jerusalem and joined the Activestills collective in 2014. His work has been published in Al Jazeera English, *Vice*, and *+972 Magazine*.

Ahmad Al-Bazz (b. 1993). Al-Bazz is a Palestinian photographer based in the West Bank city of Nablus. He has been a member of the Activestills collective since 2012. He graduated from the Faculty of Media at An-Najah National University in Nablus in 2014 where he specialized in TV journalism. Al-Bazz's work with the collective focuses on the daily life of the Palestinian population in the villages and cities under Israeli military occupation, especially in the northern West Bank. His work has been shown in local exhibitions in the West Bank and Gaza and various international exhibitions across Europe, the United States, and the Middle East.

Basel Alyazouri (b. 1995). Alyazouri was born in Gaza City and is currently based in New York City. His work has been published in Al Jazeera English, *Electronic Intifada, Middle East Eye, +972 Magazine, Flint*, and *Local Call*. He has been a member of Activestills since 2014. Alyazouri was selected for the Magnum Foundation Photography and Human Rights Fellowship program for 2015. Alyazouri currently studies at Bard College in upstate New York.

Ryan Rodrick Beiler (b. 1975). Beiler graduated from Ithaca College in 1998 with a degree in cinema and photography. He began working with Activestills in 2010. Now based in Oslo, Beiler continues to serve as one of the editors of the Activestills channel on *+972 Magazine*. He also continues to cover Palestine/Israel and other global justice issues for a number of other publications and news outlets, including Al Jazeera, Alternet, *The Christian Century, Forward, Electronic Intifada, Le Figaro, The Guardian*, In These Times, *Middle East Eye, Mondoweiss*, MSNBC, OnFaith, Religion News Service, Sojourners, *Tablet*, Truthout, and *Vice*.

Silan Dallal (b. 1987). Dallal studied photography at the Bezalel Academy of Arts and Design, Jerusalem, and was a photographer with Activestills from 2008 to 2010. Dallal's writing has been published in Israeli magazines such as *Mitaam*, *Maayan*, *A5*, and *Iton 77*. She is a political and human rights activist and is currently a law student in the human rights division of the College of Law and Business in Ramat Gan, Israel.

Shiraz Grinbaum (b. 1979). Grinbaum joined the Activestills collective in 2012. Since then she has worked as the collective's curator and photo editor, and as photo editor with *+972 Magazine*. She has collaborated with dozens of human rights organizations as a photographer, photography editor, content consultant, and social media advisor. Her editorial work has been featured in *Vice*, *LensCulture*, Al Jazeera America, *Le Nouvel Observateur*, CNN, *Forward Magazine* and *Electronic Intifada*, and was exhibited at various photography festivals and events such as Visa Pour L'Image, Perpignan (2013–14), and the International Public Art Award Exhibition (2015).

Eduardo Soteras Jalil (b. 1975). Jalil graduated from Cordoba University, Argentina in 1999 with a degree in economic sciences and in 2007 completed a Master in Photojournalism at the University Autònoma of Barcelona. He is a co-founder of the Activestills collective and was a member until 2009. He was recently awarded "Outstanding Young Man of the Year 2014" by the National Chamber of Commerce of Argentina. His work is represented by Neutral Grey Agency (France). Jalil is currently based in Kinshasa, D.R. Congo, where he is a contributor to Agence France Presse.

Keren Manor (b. 1977). Manor graduated from the Geographic Photography College in Tel Aviv in 2006 and works as a freelance photographer, videographer, and video editor on various projects. She is a member of the Anarchists Against the Wall group. In 2005, she co-founded the Activestills collective, and in 2006 was a founding member of the NGO ActiveVision. Manor's work has been exhibited worldwide and published in various media outlets such as Al Jazeera, *The New Internationalist* and *Electronic Intifada*. In 2009–10, she worked as a coordinator of B'Tselem's video project "Shooting Back", and in 2012-15 as a photo editor with *+972 Magazine*. In 2014, she co-directed the documentary *Moving Perspectives—Discover Football in Brazil*, together with Mareike Lauken.

Anne Paq (b. 1976). Paq, an award-winning French freelance photographer and videographer with a background in international human rights law, has been a member of the Activestills collective since 2006. She is currently working between Europe and the Gaza Strip. Paq's work has been exhibited worldwide and published in various media outlets such as the *New York Times Lens Blog*, *Paris Match*, *Le Nouvel Observateur*, Al Jazeera, *The National*, *Les Inrockuptibles*, *The Huffington Post*, *Dazed and Confused*, *+972 Magazine*, *Electronic Intifada*, and *Stern*. She is regularly commissioned by NGOs, such as UNESCO, and Human Rights Watch. She co-directed the short film *Bethlehem Checkpoint, 4 am* (2007) and co-produced the documentary *Flying Paper* (2013). She is currently working on developing an interactive web documentary called "Obliterated Families," about the families whose lives were shattered in Gaza during summer 2014.

Shachaf Polakow (b. 1979). Polakow studied at the Geographic Photography College in Tel Aviv from 2002 to 2004. In 2006, Polakow began documenting the new wave of Sudanese refugees who were arriving in Israel. He joined the Activestills collective shortly thereafter. He has curated and participated in local and international Activestills exhibitions and books. Since 2011, Shachaf has divided his time between Tucson, Arizona and Cape Town, South Africa, where he works on different social struggles, from the migrant rights in Arizona to informal settlements in Cape Town.

Yotam Ronen (b. 1981). Ronen completed his studies in photography and design at Minshar Art College in 2009. A co-founder of the Activestills collective, he currently works as a main cameraman and photographer at *Walla! News* and covers Israel and the occupied territories as main cameraman for Al Jazeera+. His professional photographic work has been published in various international news organizations and publications including Reuters, AFP and Al Jazeera. Ronen has presented his work with the collective in various exhibitions and festivals such as the Visa Pour L'Image, Perpignan (France) and the Ankgor Photo Festival.

Tess Scheflan (b. 1983). Scheflan worked as a staff photographer for *Ha'aretz* newspaper and as a staffer for various photo agencies and wire services in Israel. A member of the Activestills collective since 2006, she is a founding member of Normal, a documentary photo collective based in Boston, MA. Her work has been commissioned and published by newspapers and magazines worldwide. Scheflan received an associate's degree from the Geographic Photography College in Tel Aviv. She is currently studying for a degree in Middle Eastern studies.

Oren Ziv (b. 1985). Ziv, a co-founder of the Activestills collective, has been documenting social and political issues in Israel and in the Palestinian territories since 2005. Since 2011, he has been working as a staff photographer of *+972 Magazine* and freelance for *Ha'aretz*, AFP, and Getty Images. His work has been published on *New York Times Lens Blog*, Al Jazeera, *Vice*, *Tablet Magazine*, *Electronic Intifada*, among others. Ziv was awarded the Curators' Choice Prize in the Israeli *Local Testimony* exhibition of the Eretz Israel Museum in 2011–14. He was a jury member at the 5th International Activist Award issued by the PhotoPhilanthropy (USA) in 2014.

Activestills contributors: Mohammed Abed, Alejandro Arditi, Hamde Abu Rahmah, Mustafa Bader, Janos Chiala, Mohannad Darabee, Akrm Drawashi, Nayef Hashlamoun, Miki Kratsman, Mareike Lauken, Ariel Levin, Tali Mayer, Wissam Nasser, Omar Sameer, Ezz Zanoun.

Acknowledgments

The Activestills collective would like to thank Chaska Katz, Irene Nasser, and Mireia Gallardo Avellan, our producers, for their endless efforts; Miki Kratsman for his warm encouragement and wise counsel; Anka Mirkin and Mareike Lauken for their time and investment in editing our materials over the years; the teams and editors at *+972 Magazine* and *Local Call*: Noam Sheizaf, Michael Omer-Man, Edo Konrad, Yael Maron, Haggai Matar, and Orly Noy, for a most fruitful collaboration. Warm thanks to Ali Abunimah and Maureen Murphy, from the *Electronic Intifada* team, for featuring our work from its early beginnings. Special thanks to our friends and fellow activists who helped spread our exhibitions in public space, and to the organizations that extended their kind support, especially Physicians for Human Rights, Yesh Din, Coalition of Women for Peace and Who Profits. Our deepest gratitude to Sivmo Amsterdam for making this book possible, and to the Rosa Luxemburg Foundation for facilitating the completion of our online archive.

The editors would like to thank the writers of the book for their engaged contributions. Special thanks to David Shulman from Pluto Press for his continuous and enthusiastic support of this project. We would also like to thank Esther BarEl, Yair Barak, Amir Chajuss, Elisha Baskin, Rona Moran, Shira Wilkof, Yuval Drier Shilo, Ilit Azoulay, and Tal Haran for their significant input; Sharon Assaf for her meticulous editing, and Dana Gez and Nomi Geiger (Studio Gimel2) for their innovative design and endless patience.

Index